Computer Science, Technology and Applications

nova
science publishers
New York

Computer Science, Technology and Applications

Green Computing and Its Applications
Sanjay Kumar, PhD, Rohit Raja, PhD, Alok Kumar Singh Kushwaha, PhD,
Raj Kumar Patra, PhD, Saurabh Kumar, PhD (Editors)
2021. ISBN: 978-1-68507-357-2 (Hardcover)
2021. ISBN: 978-1-68507-363-3 (eBook)

Artificial Intelligence: Work, Machines and Human Interaction
Tonya Randolph (Author)
2021. ISBN: 978-1-68507-313-8 (Hardcover)
2021. ISBN: 978-1-68507-353-4 (eBook)

Advanced Decision Sciences Based on Deep Learning and Ensemble Learning Algorithms: A Practical Approach Using Python
S. Sumathi, PhD, Suresh Rajappa, PhD, L. Ashok Kumar, PhD,
Surekha Paneerselvam, PhD (Authors)
2021. ISBN: 978-1-68507-061-8 (Hardcover)
2021. ISBN: 978-1-68507-207-0 (eBook)

Advances of Machine Learning in Clean Energy and the Transportation Industry
Pandian Vasant, PhD, Valeriy Kharchenko, PhD, Joshua Thomas, PhD,
Gerhard-Wilhelm Weber, PhD, Vladimir Panchenko, PhD (Editors)
2021. ISBN: 978-1-68507-211-7 (Hardcover)
2021. ISBN: 978-1-68507-303-9 (eBook)

Deep Learning and its Applications
Arvind Kumar Tiwari, PhD (Editor)
2021. ISBN: 978-1-68507-185-1 (Hardcover)
2021. ISBN: 978-1-68507-246-9 (eBook)

More information about this series can be found at https://novapublishers.com/product-category/series/computer-science-technology-and-applications/

Shalin Hai-Jew

Common Visual Art in a Social Digital Age

nova
science publishers
New York

https://doi.org/10.52305/BKOT1869

Library of Congress Cataloging-in-Publication Data

ISBN: 978-1-68507-664-1

Published by Nova Science Publishers, Inc. † New York

In the spirit of communal engagement in a time of severe isolation and stress due to the SARS-CoV-2/COVID-19 pandemic, this collection is dedicated to the "common art" artists of the world, especially those who so generously share of their work online. Art is about a celebration of life and hope. Thank you because I have learned so much for you all, even though we have never met in person. Perhaps one day...

Shalin Hai-Jew
December 31, 2021

Contents

Preface

Common Visual Art for the Everyperson

Common Visual Art in a Social Digital Age focuses on a universal and inherent human need for beauty, for aesthetics, for the wonderment that comes from grace, perhaps first learned from the home, then from nature, then from the designed and constructed world, and more formal expressions of art and artfulness. The sensory appreciations may stem from the visual, auditory, tactual, olfaction, and taste, and in various combinations. The appreciation of aesthetics may enhance the lived experience; it may contribute to meaningful living; in times of stress, it can provide a salve.

"Common visual art" is created by regular folks, perhaps without formal training in the creation of art. These works are made for the self but also for others. They are made as crafts for making a living or augmenting other work. In this practice, the general power law might well apply, with a few making it big, and the rest working in the "long tail" in niche spaces. The standards for the work may be local rather than global. In many cases, these are peer-created art generated for other peers. For many who do make common art, some do turn professional, often after years of learning and investment in the skills and visioning.

How this Collection Got Started

The most recent proximate inspiration for *Common Visual Art in a Social Digital Age* has been the SARS-CoV-2/COVID-19 pandemic, which started stateside in January 2020 (but the virus may have been in-country in late 2019). While I have long known of the possibilities of just such a general occurrence, given my instructional design work (including on public health projects), I did not think humanity would allow such crossovers to get out of hand. Needless-to-say, my assumptions were incorrect, and during the past two years, my assumptions of how government would handle these challenges and how various populations would handle these have not been borne out as accurately as I would have liked. I have engaged in mirror-imaging, perhaps, by assuming others would be on top of the facts and that they would act with self-health and other-health in mind. So 2020 was a year of lockdowns and half-hearted reopenings, and then, with the advent of the respective vaccines, 2021 opened with a lot of hope until it became clear that people were not necessarily on board with getting vaccinated. And now, we are in the middle of the Fourth Wave, with the delta variant run amuck and some in the population not even putting up much of any bio-defense.

As with many endeavors, this work then started with the personal. In early 2021, dealing with accumulated fatigue from the pandemic, I became enamored of alcohol inks and synthetic papers based on several videos on YouTube. I was attracted by the brilliant colors. I liked how the ink moved on synthetic paper. And I had a visual idea I wanted to try. And so, I ordered some art supplies via Amazon.com and started experimenting. My "out" would be to scan the various "common art" works and use digital image editing to "salvage" those that went awry. The works would be both analog and digital. This would be one of my ways of distracting myself from the grief and the frustration at the various losses from the pandemic. [These losses include multiple colleagues. It still boggles the mind that we lost over 800,000 Americans and 5.2 million deaths globally and counting.] It may be many years or even generations before we recover from this mass trauma. This book then is a kind of escapism into a loveliness which is only a partial salve. This story is not meant to irretrievably link trauma to common art, but that was my bridge into this in this iteration of artful exploration.

Introduction

"Common art" is about inclusive art, art by and for the everyperson. It is art in the lower case, in the vernacular, in the playing-around sense, in the self-satisfaction space. It is art that is all-inclusive and fully democratic. It is art in the everyday. It is a non-snobbish non-exclusivist approach. It is an art without a threshold. It is art that is "just push play." This is art as concept, not high- or low-. This is art as aesthetics and pleasure. It is the sense of art that is for any lifestyle, for anyone who is entranced by the *practice*s, the *identity* and the *life*. It is about self-definition, into what is personally meaningful. This is about a no-strings approach, and common artists only have to invest as much as they wish and for as long as they wish. Want to emulate a style? There are plenty of reference images online. Want to make a small run at selling common art? The marketplaces exist. Want to find and express your own voice? There are plenty of opportunities. The Web and Internet accommodates, with a variety of art-making communities and gallery spaces and how-to tutorials and reference images for inspiration.

If I were to go back further in time, I would own up to an earlier entrancement with light art-making. While I pursued other interests, ultimately, for a profession, I kept that interest alive with a love of language and other endeavors. There have been artful ways of engaging social network graphs (such as through NodeXL). This is to say that such interests and knowledge accrue over time and based on persistent interests. This work is at once personal (as in related to the person of the editor) and subjective, and it is also somewhat objective. One does not arrive at a text without plenty of preparation. In the intervening years, I have added work in research, instructional design, and other fields, and those influences may be seen in some of the authored works.

A Call for Chapters in April 2021

Art is a product of its time and the person who creates the art; it is culturally informed. The topics that inspire the works are perhaps culturally informed as well: nature, people, built spaces, architecture, fashion, outer space, worlds and creatures of the imagination, and mass media creations (movies, digital games, literature, stories, and others).

In this time, art is created both in physical analog and digital formats, in combined physical-digital. Each type—analog and digital and mixed—has an effect on the work that is possible. Each approach broadens the mark-making potential of the common artist. There are dependencies for every work. Similarly, every book depends on what is possible at the moment. There is no perfect moment to actualize a work, and those who wait will find that the world moves so quickly that every moment passes without an "in," so it makes sense to act in the now. This is a topic with some runway to it.

An initial call for chapters went out in early April, 2021. A call has a pull function. In some ways it is as much for the editor as the target experts. The ask is a tall order, for experts to research, write, and submit their work, to make something real out of their expertise. The request is that strangers (mostly) have to be willing to spend head space, time, resources, and effort on the endeavor, which has opportunity costs. The return is small: little to no remuneration, fleeting and light attention, and maybe a small contribution to the present and future. It helps if contributors are building on to something else, like a career, a rise in professional stature, or perhaps a pay raise. Book endeavors are non-sustainable without good will. In a time of rising prices and inflation, the monetary return on an edited text would not even cover the wireless bill during the period of the work, much less the extensive other inputs: research articles, technologies, expertise, writing, editing, illustration, and all the other work. Every published book is an expression of will and effort against everything else, which militates against the work's completion.

The call serves as a seeding function. Simultaneously, there were multiple outreaches to colleagues. From the various endeavors, only one team stepped forward with a project idea. The work that has finally emerged is more an authored text with a side work. The cost of a dream requires the heavy labor to make it real.

This Collection

This edited collection is set up in five sections:

Part 1: Common Visual Art and the Social Web
Part 2: High Touch and High Technologies and Common Visual Art
Part 3: Common Visual Art for Personal Self-Fulfillment
Part 4: Commercializing Common Visual Art
Part 5: Common Visual Art and Sociality
Part 6: Common Visual Art in the Third and Fourth Dimensions

Bridging to the Respective Works

The respective works are analyzed through both manual and computational means.

Part 1: Common Visual Art and the Social Web

Maureen Ebben and Elizabeth Bull's "Common Art in Troubled Times: Recreating Masterpieces Through Social Media During the COVID-19 Pandemic" (Ch. 1) opens the collection with a timely and thoughtful work about the global Getty Museum Challenge in a time of a global pandemic. In a time of lockdown and mass disruption, the #gettymuseumchallenge resonates with implications about fine art and everyday life, social bonds, and common humanity. "Communal Common Art Spaces on the Social Web and Supports for Artful Novelty" (Ch. 2) asks a basic question about how online social art spaces may promote artful innovation. For this work, two well-known online communities are analyzed, and some surprising findings are shared. Doodling is classically thought of as a distraction from more real work, but more recent work suggests that it may help with thinking and problem solving. "Exploring Digital Doodling on the Social Web" (Ch. 3) involves the exploration of digital doodling in the present hyper-social age.

Part 2: High-Touch and High-Technologies and Common Visual Art

Digital art has been around for generations, and in the various setups, computers and humans have taken on varying roles. In some cases, the humans just let the machines run and generate works, and some of the works are selected out for insights and meaning and artfulness. In others, humans play a highly dominant role, and machines a very small one. In "Humans Back in the Loop: Using Analog and Digital Seed Imagery for Manual Visual Algorithmic Art using Adobe Photoshop 2021 and Adobe Illustrator 2021" (Ch. 4), a particular type of analog-digital blend is described in which the person wields powerful computational capabilities but maintains plenty of control over the artwork. Another form of "common art" involves fan-created artworks based on created cultural contents that attract them and meet particular psychological needs. In "Fanart: A Man, His Gun, His Dog, and His Car" (Ch. 5), the fanart created around a well-known character in a movie trilogy (soon to be a tetralogy) is explored to understand the attraction of this character and context. "Examining "Data Art" for Signs of the 4IR" (Ch. 6) involves a systematic study of social "data art" to understand at mass scale what expectations people may have about data (in a time of big data) and technologies (in a time of the Fourth Industrial Revolution or "4IR"). Contemporary Line Art as "Common Art" on the Social Web (Ch. 7) examines a basic drawing and drafting form for its present state on the WWW and Internet. This work involves manual coding of the 999-social imageset.

Part 3: Common Visual Art for Personal Self-Fulfillment

The SARS-CoV-2/COVID-19 pandemic, which started in late 2019, has been with humanity for several years, and it is being addressed in pockets around the world as more vaccines are being distributed and people vaccinated. The pandemic upended people's lives and livelihoods. It has destabilized governments. It has inflicted massive health effects that may include permanent brain damage. And it is rendered mass death on humanity.

"Engaging in Novel Common Art for Self-Expression and Stress Relief during the COVID-19 Pandemic" (Ch. 8) describes the use of amateur or common art to manage some of the stresses during a pandemic. This work also shows how some knowledge of the human visual system enables the work. "Adult Coloring Books as Emotional Salve/Stress Relief, Tactual-Visual Learning: An Analysis from Mass-Scale Social Imagery" (Ch. 9) continues the concept of going to common art for relief, in this case, involving a social image analysis of visuals around adult coloring books. The analyzed visuals are suggestive of particular foci in the current moment. "'Visual Journaling' Shares and Overshares on the Social Web" (Ch. 10) explores the healthful works of regular journaling using drawing, sketching, painting, and other forms, including text. This work explores how visual journaling manifests on the Social Web across several social platforms.

Part 4: Commercializing Common Visual Art

For many, common art is a personal pastime for individual reasons. Some focus on how to make a living or augment income by earning money for their common art. The online marketplace has enabled many to create works for sale. "Monetizing Common Art: General Practices for Going Commercial Online" (Ch. 11) provides a light analysis of the various channels for earning moneys from such creations, from selling individual works to imprinted products to creating large-scale followings for their videos, among others. The next chapter focuses on "Narrowbanding as a 'Common Art' Artist Self-Branding Strategy Online" (Ch. 12), and this explores whether the online art sharing space corrals common artists into particular recognizable styles, often without sufficient breadth.

Part 5: Common Visual Art and Sociality

The common art on the Social Web involves various forms of sociality and social interactions, even in a time of social distancing and mistrust. "Visual Gists of Common Food Art on the Social Web" (Ch. 13) focuses on "food art" as a particular subcategory of common art. A large set of social imagery of such art is analyzed for social insights. And finally, "'World Creating' in Contemporary Common Visual Art on the Social Web" (Ch. 14) focuses on four social imagesets seeded with related terms to see what the various foci are for the near-term future, based on senses of "metaverse," "alternate universe," "worldmaking," and "fantasy" types of art on the Social Web. These works inform on visions of people for the world they share and will co-create together into the future. "Event-Based Common Art: COVID-19 Visuals" (Ch. 15) explores the expressive range of visuals created about the "pandemic" and "COVID-19" in two social imagesets, to ascertain the efficacy of such visuals in sharing accurate information, and other aspects of massmind in a time of the pandemic. "A Mass-Public Sense of Art from Select Social Media Platforms" (Ch. 16) offers some analytics from a mix of social media platforms to understand a slice-in-time sense of massmind around art on the Social Web.

Part 6: Common Visual Art in the Third Dimension

The next chapter, "Third Dimension in Digital Common Visual Art" (Ch. 17), explores art that involves the z-axis and how these visuals are created and the imaginaries which are sparked. The final chapter, "Mixed Motions: A Pre-Survey of Common Art Animations on the Social Web" (Ch. 18) provides a review of the literature in terms of art animations and then proposes a four-facet approach to exploring and coding "common art" animations for future research. This chapter lays the groundwork for future research.

Conclusion

Onwards

Common art has been a long-time dream for me, since my college days. That is not to say that I had the skills then to achieve the ambitions. If nothing else, I know that skillsets take decades to acquire, to achieve a certain level of satisfaction. Skillsets require constant and iterated attention and feeding to develop.

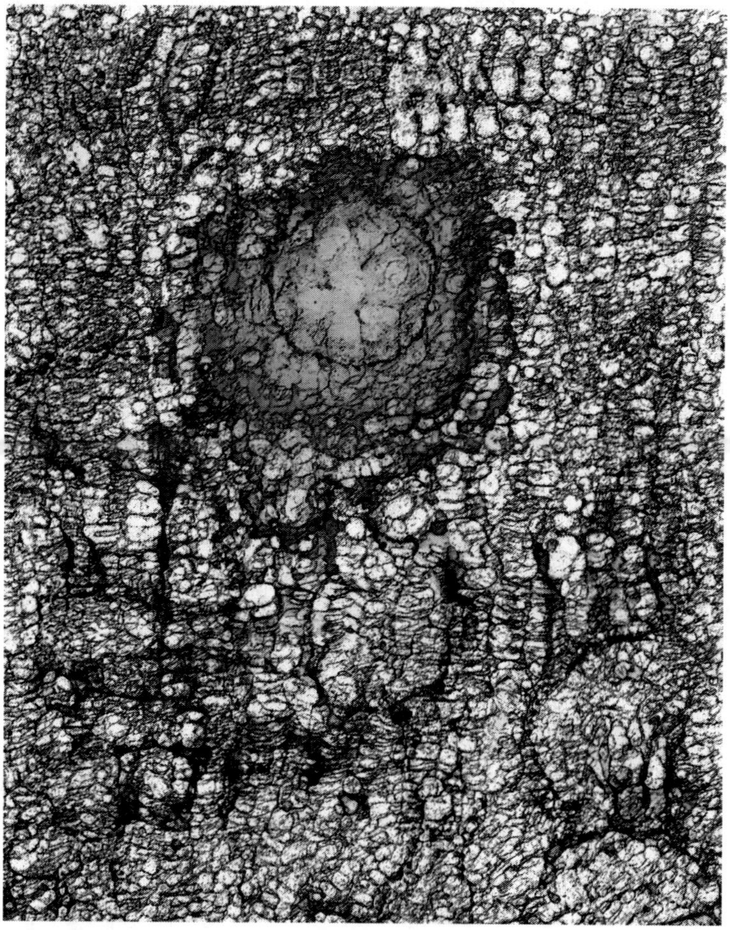

Figure 1. Ancient Sun (alcohol ink on synthetic paper as a digital fresco, by Shalin Hai-Jew).

In the intervening years, I have learned that one can lay the groundwork, piece-by-piece, for a future work, even if one is not at that former moment aware of what that work is or how it will shape out. It is so with research, too, that not all works will be the groundbreaking one. It is only in retrospect that one can start to see what the value is of that work. Something that may have seemed pedestrian in its time may find second life later on based on new future light. Also, for all the ambitions, one cannot know how a work will be actualized until one is actually working on it. I think we're all myopic this way when it comes to trying to create something novel or somewhat novel. All work involves a lot of continuous plodding.

The resources that are available change over time. The thinking also changes. This is why the ambition is always to do the best that one can in the moment and work things from there. We live in a world where all is in flux and motion. Research and writing are attempts to stay the change for a short moment… or at least to see something of a momentary truth… in a highly dynamic moment. For me, books have always been "magical," even as I've learned how they are made and marketed. So, too, art. This project brings those interests together.

Thanks to Dr. Maureen Ebben and Elizabeth Bull for their collaborative work. I know what it takes, to some degree, to achieve quality work, so I am especially grateful.

I am grateful to Nova Science Publishers for signing up this work. We all invest in the shared endeavor. None of this would be possible without readers, so thanks to all the readers of this work as well. Please share what you have to offer! Time is wasting!

This moment is another time of deep peril for the world, with the rise of the omicron variant of the SARS-CoV-2 virus, with the COVID-19 pandemic entering its third year. It does feel like we have sobered up about the biological realities we live within and whose laws affect our lives. By now, we likely have the discipline learned for how to go to ground again and lie low and strive for bio-safety, for ourselves and each other.

Each new year brings with it such promise, and it is no different with 2022 onwards. Let's take care of each other globally, protect each other in this pandemic, and help each other's dreams come true.

In it together for the long haul—

Dr. Shalin Hai-Jew
Kansas State University, Manhattan, KS, USA
December 2021

Part 1: Common Visual Art and the Social Web

Chapter 1

Common Art in Troubled Times: Recreating Masterpieces through Social Media during the COVID-19 Pandemic

Maureen Ebben[1,*] and Elizabeth Bull[2]
[1]Department of Communication and Media Studies, University of Southern Maine, Portland, ME, USA
[2]University Libraries, University of Southern Maine, Portland, ME, USA

Abstract

This chapter uses the phenomenon of the online art challenge, the #gettymuseumchallenge, to explore the meanings and implications of folks' recreations of fine art from the J. Paul Getty Art Museum collection and shared on social media during the SARS-CoV2/COVID-19 pandemic stay-at-home orders and lockdowns. We argue that the recreations of fine art associated with #gettymuseumchallenge function to 1) re-contextualize fine art to the spaces of daily life during pandemic quarantine, 2) foster creativity, express interpersonal connections, and build community, and 3) reimagine and rearticulate persons' relationships with fine art and with the institutions of fine art in ways that give voice to alternative perspectives, thereby potentially shifting relationships of power and control over forms of representation and their meanings. We suggest that all three of these dynamics contribute to the leveling of hierarchical dichotomies of high art and low art as works of fine art become common art when they are recontextualized, engaged with through online communities, and reimagined. This exploration raises questions about the relationships between art creation, interpretation, self-expression, institutions, and community during the SARS-CoV2/COVID-19 pandemic and beyond.

Keywords: art challenge, hashtag, networked publics, #betweenartandquarantine, #gettymuseumchallenge, lockdown art, digital communication, online community, COVID-19, pandemic, fine art, classical art

Introduction

Historically, museums have communicated with their audiences in a unilateral manner through forms of interaction that are primarily defined and controlled by the institution (Kidd, 2020). Social media platforms and channels of communication, however, offer interactive spaces in

* Corresponding Author's Email: maureen.ebben@maine.edu

In: Common Visual Art in a Social Digital Age
Editor: Shalin Hai-Jew
ISBN: 978-1-68507-664-1

which ordinary folks may change the nature and meaning of their relationships with fine art and with the institutions of art. In this chapter, the online art challenge, the #gettymuseumchallenge, is used to explore these shifting relationships between ordinary people and fine art. The "digital revolution" of participatory forms of public engagement have been employed by institutions of art including museums, galleries, and archives largely for the purposes of marketing, public relations, community outreach, and brand identity (Black, 2020; Lukas et al., 2021; Potts, 2020; Samaroudi et al., 2020). Rather than study social media as a strategy of engagement by an art institution, we explore the #gettymuseumchallenge as an art phenomenon with social and communicative dynamics for the ordinary folks who comprise the majority of its participants. The focus is on the ways in which ordinary people recreated works of fine art from the confines of their homes and shared the recreations on social media platforms during the SARS-CoV2/COVID-19 pandemic stay-at-home orders and lockdowns.

We identify three dynamics occurring in ordinary folks' recreations of fine art in the #gettymuseumchallenge. First, the recreations re-contextualize fine art to the particular experiences and spaces of everyday life during the pandemic stay-at-home orders. Second, the recreations foster creativity, express interpersonal connections, and build community. Third, the recreations serve to reimagine and rearticulate persons' relationships with fine art, and with the institutions of fine art, in ways that give voice to alternative perspectives thereby potentially shifting relationships of power and control over forms of representation and their meanings. We suggest that all three of these dynamics contribute to the leveling of hierarchical dichotomies of high art and low art as works of fine art become common art when they are recontextualized, engaged with through online communities, and reimagined. This exploration raises questions about the relationships between art creation, interpretation, self-expression, institutions, and community during the SARS-CoV2/COVID-19 pandemic and beyond.

Getty Museum Challenge Background

The Getty Museum Challenge was born of the unusual and uncertain early days of the first SARS-CoV2/COVID-19 pandemic stay-at-home orders and lockdowns. With a rise in coronavirus cases and the implementation of public health measures, the J. Paul Getty Art Museum in Malibu, California made public its intention to curtail in-person attendance at its two physical museums, the Getty Center and Villa, starting on Saturday, March 14, 2020. Recalling the pivot to online strategies of engagement, Getty museum Director Timothy Potts (2020) stated "like many institutions, once [we] were closed, we focused on increasing our online presence" (p. 218).

On March 25, 2020, the social media strategy #gettymuseumchallenge commenced with an invitation to the general public that encouraged folks to recreate works of art with materials readily available at home. Posted to the Getty Museum's Instagram, Twitter, and Facebook accounts, the call explained that the process was simple and could be accomplished in three easy steps: "1) choose your favorite artwork, 2) find three things lying around your house, and 3) recreate the artwork with those items'' (Getty Museum, 2020). The public was prompted to consult the Getty Museum's online collection of over 100,000 digitized images to gain inspiration for their recreations which could be posted to social media platforms.

It is important to note that the idea of the #gettymuseumchallenge was not unique, nor was the Getty its creator. Anneloes Officier, a 31-year-old communication specialist from

Amsterdam, started the art challenge "as a thing to do with her roommates who had to work from home since March 13, [2020]" with the Instagram account entitled, "Tussen Kunst & Quarantaine" (Adomaite & Tymulis, 2020, n.p.). Translated to English, "Tussen Kunst & Quarantine" means "between art and quarantine." Officier's original art challenge encouraged ordinary folks to recreate works of art from home at the start of the stay-at-home orders precipitated by the COVID-19 pandemic. The Tussen Kunst & Quarantaine social media post was then picked up and shared by the Rijksmuseum Dutch national art and history museum (Harris, 2020, n.p). The Rijksmuseum used hashtags in both Dutch and English to signal the initiative including #tussenkunstenquarantaine and #betweenartandquarantine. Like the Rijksmuseum, the Getty simply copied and posted the art challenge across its social media platforms using the hashtags #gettymuseumchallenge, #gettychallenge, and #betweenartandquarantine.

Online art challenges geared toward the public's recreation of works of fine art flourished during the pandemic as art institutions shifted to digital strategies of involvement after museum closures. In a survey of museums and museum professionals from 107 countries across five continents, the International Council of Museums (ICOM) found that more than half of the institutions increased their social media activity after COVID-19 stay-at-home orders (2020). Worldwide, art institutions and museums "participated in lockdown-themed hashtag campaigns like #MuseumFromHome and #IsolationCreations" (Clerkin & Taylor, 2021, p. 171). In Russia, for example, the Izoizolyacia group on Facebook was "widely popular with users dedicated to making and sharing recreations of iconic artists" (Barnes, 2020, n.p.). The digital art challenges gained global reach and participation enabling international communication and boundary crossing (Dedema & Fichman, 2021).

In addition to the isolation art challenges sponsored by art institutions, quarantine art clubs sprang up to combat the social distancing of the early weeks of COVID-19 quarantines including groups organized around hashtags like #DrawFromADistance, #QuarantineArtClub, and #30DayArtQuarantine, and others. The #gettymuseumchallenge occurred within the social context of myriad art-driven social media initiatives that sought to bring people together to foster interaction, spark creativity, and create community during the pandemic. As one of the most popular pandemic art challenges, the #gettymuseumchallenge garnered more than half a million participants who uploaded images to social media sites (Barnes, 2020, n.p.). Given the widespread appeal and high levels of participation by ordinary folks in the #gettymuseumchallenge, closer examination of its dynamics are warranted.

Limited Prior Research

Although there has been extensive research on art institutions and their strategies of online engagement with the public, there is scant scholarship on the #gettymuseumchallenge. Most research about art institutions and social media have examined its use for marketing, public relations, educational outreach, branding, and social media campaigns (Black, 2020; Lukas et al., 2021; Potts, 2020; Samaroudi, Echavarria, & Perry, 2020). These studies have been conducted primarily from the perspective of the art institutions rather than from the perspective of ordinary participants.

With respect to research on digital art initiatives, literature searches found broad mention of digital art engagement with audiences, but few studies about specific art challenges. For example, Black (2018) mentions art museum-led programs that encourage visitors to take and share selfies alongside their favorite museum pieces. Clerkin and Taylor (2021) cite social media campaigns initiated by art museums that seek to foster digital engagement with their audiences such as sharing themed hashtags related to the art works in their collections. One such effort was the use of the hashtag #caturday to spur the creation and sharing of social media posts that feature cats on Saturdays. However, little sustained scholarship was found that focused specifically on digital art challenges like the #gettymuseumchallenge. No studies were found that examined the #gettymuseumchallenge as a form of common art in which the research inquiry was undertaken from the perspective of the participants.

Thus, while the #gettymuseumchallenge received attention in the popular press (Barajas, 2020; Compton, 2020; Hoffman, 2020), scholarship about the art challenge is an understudied area with just two articles addressing the topic: Kidd (2020) and Dedema and Fichman (2021). Each of these is discussed further for its import in this exploration of the #gettymuseumchallenge.

Kidd (2020) briefly alludes to the #gettymuseumchallenge as an example in their discussion of the ambivalence of art institutions regarding the cultural participation of ordinary folks with "high art"—that is, fine art that has been curated by art experts and held as part of an art institution's collection. In a cursory examination of social media selfies created by folks in the #gettymuseumchallenge, Kidd (2020) uses the social media practice of selfies to raise thorny questions for art institutions, galleries, and archives around "ownership, control, and questions of taste" (p. 53) as institutions engage with their publics. Art institution policies, such as those that ban photography on the premises, may make the practice of creating selfies problematic. Kidd (2020) warns that "the kinds of performance ritualized in the selfie continue to be deemed unwelcome or inappropriate within some [museum] contexts" (p. 53). In other words, while art museums may seek to engage the general public via social media, their institutional policies, such as bans on photography, may be at odds with such efforts. There is a tension between the popular practices that ordinary folks engage in on social media—e.g., taking and sharing selfies—and what art institutions may deem to be acceptable behavior when visitors are physically at a museum site. Perhaps part of the reason for the success of the #gettymuseumchallenge lies in this difference. Participants' creativity and uses of social media in the #gettymuseumchallenge were less circumscribed by art institution policies since the participants' practices occurred outside of the physical institutional spaces.

Writing from the discipline of Information Science, Dedema and Fichman's (2021) exploratory study employed a quantitative approach to measure the relationships among the distribution of posts that used four hashtags associated with the #gettymuseumchallenge on Instagram. The four hashtags studied were: 1) #gettymuseumchallenge, 2) #betweenartandquarantine, 3) #tussenkustenquarantaine and 4) the hashtag written in the Russian language. Results suggest that individuals who posted more often used more hashtags than those who posted less frequently. The use of multiple hashtags enabled boundary crossing with significant overlap across the four hashtags. In addition, no correlation was found between the number of "likes" or "comments" that a post received with the number of hashtags used on the post, even though use of a greater number of hashtags could connect the post to a larger audience (Dedema & Fichman, 2021). The authors do not posit a reason for why the use of more hashtags did not correlate with more likes or comments on a post, nor do the authors explore the recreated images, themselves. Rather, they focus solely on counting the number of times each of the four hashtags was used by participants in the art challenge.

Research about the #gettymuseumchallenge is meager. Moreover, missing from studies about the #gettymuseaumchallenge is a focus on the images, themselves, and how the phenomenon functions socially to generate new interpretations, meanings, and relationships between works of art and the folks who construct the recreations. This analysis addresses the gap in the literature through exploration of some of the dynamics around the recreated images of fine art by ordinary persons in the #gettymuseumchallenge.

Interpretive Approach

In this chapter, an interpretative analytical approach is taken to examine the dynamics associated with the #gettymuseumchallenge as a phenomenon at the nexus of ordinary folks and art in social media. Given the visual nature of the #gettymuseumchallenge, the focus is on its manifestation on social media platforms Instagram, Twitter, and Facebook because these are primarily image-driven media. As Hjorth and Hinton (2019) point out, a key characteristic of social media is "the dominance of the visual ... [that is] amplified through mobile visuality, creating complex digital storytelling narratives" (p. 100). Social media platforms like Instagram, Twitter, and Facebook afford rich forms of synchronous and asynchronous visual communication including photos, images, videos, and slides as well as textual communication (Volo & Irimiás, 2020).

We explore the visual forms created by the general public and posted to social media platforms Twitter, Facebook, and Instagram for the #gettymuseumchallenge. The images examined range from portraits and abstracts, to still life and iconic classics. Also included in the analysis are the writings, captions, comments, and interviews with those who participated in the art challenge. The data set for analysis was comprised of posts from Instagram, Twitter, and Facebook from March 2020 to November 2021. The analysis uses an interpretive lens that draws on the social theories and concepts about hashtags, (Jackson & Foucault Welles, 2015; Leaver & Highfield, 2018) and "networked publics" (Boyd, 2011; Papacharissi, 2011; Papacharissi, 2018) as they relate to community formation and identity expression in social media. In the next section, we explicate key concepts related to hashtags and networked publics that inform the analysis of this exploratory study.

Hashtags

The hashtag #gettymuseumchallenge marks a site of social meaning. Like other hashtags, it offers a way into understanding the significance associated with communication occurring on social media platforms (Highfield & Leaver, 2015; Leaver & Highfield, 2018). Typically, hashtags are understood as a mechanism that organizes content (Jackson & Foucault Welles, 2015), but hashtags also perform wider functions. Hashtags structure interactions, signal and transmit emotions and intentions, and mediate relationships. Participants in social media use hashtags to communicate a variety of purposes: to express amusement, provide inspiration, annotate and summarize content, partake in social bonding, endorse someone or something, spread a message through amplification or "reach," and take part in current trends (Rauschnabel, Sheldon & Herzfeldt, 2019).

Hashtags can be seen as social media affordances that enable ordinary people to play an active role in shaping and organizing digitally created content. "Some [social media] tools allow the general public to take on a role traditionally held by the curator and to freely arrange the museum content and define the mediation components" (Pulh & Mencarelli, 2015, p. 45). Hashtags are a tool by which ordinary people may participate in defining the classification of digital content for various purposes and effects. For example, hashtags can be used to amplify the hashtags of other people, to associate a person's own keywords and phrases with the content of others, to create variations of related hashtags, and to originate new hashtags. Of course there is no guarantee that the intention behind certain uses of hashtags will yield the desired effect, and it is also possible that particular uses of hashtags may result in unintended consequences. But hashtag practices can be regarded as a "folksonomy" (Pulh & Mencarelli, 2015) or a folk-led classification scheme in which everyday users play an active role in indexing digital content, rather than relying exclusively on experts to organize and curate content.

In this way, the hashtags associated with the #gettymuseumchallenge offer space for the creation of a folksonomy of digital content. For example, on Instagram, the most popular hashtags used in the #gettymuseumchallenge articulate places, spaces, and relationships closely connected to the Getty such as #gettymuseum #gettymuseumchallenge #jpaulgettymuseum #gettycenter, #getty. However, other popular hashtags used in the #gettymuseumchallenge express places, spaces, and relationship that do not reference the Getty explicitly and often are well beyond the Getty including #tatemodern #oilpainting #whitneymuseum #artforum #tussenkunstenquarantaine #lacma #painting #moma #museum #betweenartandquarantine #art #rijksmuseum #losangeles #brooklynmuseum #britishmuseum #nationalgallery #guggenheim #museodelprado #thcenturyart #museumart #oil #centrepompidou #paintingart #museums #bhfyp.

The most liked hashtags used with the #gettymuseumchallenge on Instagram denote places, spaces, and relationships that are *not* directly tied to the Getty. These hashtags extend the meanings of the #gettymuseumchallenge through the creation of hashtags that articulate new and different constellations of associations. In this way, the meanings, connections, and relationships communicated through the #gettymuseumchallenge hashtags grow in multiple directions transforming meaning in a virtually infinite manner. Most liked hashtags for the #gettymuseumchallenge include #modernart #baroqueart #artist #baroquepainting #abstractart #museumathome #artbasel #fineartmichaelkilgore #louvre #quarantine #metmuseum #arte #artgallery #california #lacmamuseum #museedorsay #galleriemichaelkilgore #instamuseum #fineartphotography #contemporary #nationalgalleryofart #museothyssen #met #galleriaborghese #artinstitutechicago #sfmoma #yaleartgallery #louvreabudhabi #contemporaryart #gemaldegalerie (*Hashtags for #gettymuseum*, n.d.).

Networked Publics

Hashtags also play a role in the formation of digital communities or "networked publics." Hashtags enable "communities to emerge and form, including ad hoc publics, [that] respond quickly in relation to a particular event or issue. These publics or communities may not persist for long periods, but can be extremely significant" (Highfield & Leaver, 2015, p. 4). Networked publics are "simultaneously 1) the space constructed through networked technologies, and 2) the imagined collective that emerges as a result of the intersection of people, technology, and practice" (boyd, 2011, p. 39). As "both spaces and groups of people who are connected through practice and technology" (Hjorth & Hinton, 2019, p. 19), networked publics enact the confluence of people with technology.

Networked publics arise out of the technological affordances that are built into the design of social media and that influence their use. The four main technological affordances of social media include: 1) persistence (i.e., social media content tends to be permanent and lasting), 2) replicability (i.e., social media content is usually easy to duplicate), 3) scalability (i.e., social media content can be reproduced in large quantities), and 4) searchability (i.e., social media content is often able to be searched) (boyd, 2011). The social and communicative effects of these technological affordances are that 1) people communicate with imagined audiences, 2) social contexts (e.g., work and home) may be collapsed into a unitary context, 3) there is a blurring of public and private, and 4) the notion of authenticity is complicated because it can be difficult to discern what is real. Technological affordances of social media, while not dictating participants' behaviors, configure the social media environment in ways that shape participants' engagement with technology and with each other.

Like the broader notion of publics more generally, networked publics encompass several dimensions. Networked publics can be a digital, imaginary space with no analog corollary (Anderson, 2006). Networked publics are multiple; there is no one, single networked public, but rather a multiplicity of networked publics (Warner, 2002). Networked publics frequently take the form of an audience around a particular text(s), perspective, or performance such as, for example, fandoms (Livingstone, 2005) or, in this instance, the #gettymuseumchallenge. Networked publics often arise at the nexus of the consumption and production of cultural artifacts as people both create and consume cultural forms such as art, music, video, etc. (de Certeau, 2002). Finally, networked publics typically function as spaces in which people carry out social identities with groups devoted to particular affiliations or commitments (Fraser, 1992). Occurring at the intersection of people and technology, networked publics are sites for the expression of multiple dynamics.

Facilitated through the technological affordances of social media, networked publics possess the complexities involved in human social worlds. Marked by the hashtags introduced by the #gettymuseumchallenge, as well as the hashtags created by its participants, webs of human connections are articulated that express relationships between home, art, lockdown life, and the creation of art by the general public. Hashtags like #stayathomechallenge #betweenartandquarantine #museumathome #artselfie give rise to the formation of digital communities—networked publics—that enable the reimagination of relationships between ordinary people and fine art. It is the complexity of these social worlds expressed in the #gettymuseumchallenge that is explored in the next section.

Discussion Preview

Our analysis identified three main dynamics that occurred in the networked publics associated with the hashtag #gettymuseumchallenge. The first dynamic centers around the ways in which the public's recreations of works of fine art function to recontextualize fine art to the everyday spaces and routines of ordinary people's lives during the COVID-19 pandemic. We examine how the recontextualization of classical works of art to everyday life offers insights about the circumstances and lived experiences of ordinary folks in the pandemic. The second dynamic focuses on the networked publics created by the #gettymusuemchallenge, specifically their intimate and affective dynamics. This born-digital networked public community provided an outlet that spurred creativity and relationship-building when in-person social interaction was curtailed during the COVID-19 stay-at-home orders and lockdowns. The third dynamic explores how historically marginalized groups, in particular Black, Asian, Indigenous, and other People of Color (BAIPOC), creatively reimagine and (re)present Western classical artworks. The concept and importance of BAIPOC representation, especially the power of seeing oneself represented in works of fine art held in museum collections, is also brought into the discussion.

Recontextualizing Fine Art to Everyday Life in COVID-19

Writing about mobile art—that is, art created through the use of mobile technologies such as smartphones—Hjorth and Hinton (2019) argue that mobile art can be seen to offer "a mode of practice that provides new canvases, context, and modes of engagement for a range of artists in many different fields" (p. 111). We extend Hjorth and Hinton's assertion to suggest that social media provides new tableaus, spaces, and forms of practice for everyday folks who may not consider themselves to be artists or who may not typically be involved in producing art. The pandemic quarantine offered, for many, additional time and space for the pursuit of novel activities such as the creation of art. Here, the title "artist" is used broadly to include the general public as well as persons who identify as practicing artists.

Whether created by professional artists or the general public, the production of art involves complex practices that are situational and process-driven (Hjorth, 2016). The hashtag #gettymuseumchallenge delineates a context and purpose enabling the coalescence of art creation around the shared vision of the recreation of fine art. Assistant Director of Digital Content Strategy and User Experience Design for the J. Paul Getty Trust, Annelisa Stephan contends that the #gettymuseumchallenge offers a way for the average person to transcend, if only temporarily, their quotidian life in the midst of pandemic restrictions. The #gettymuseumchallenge provides "a simple escape. It really sort of glamorizes our humdrum existence" (Stephan in CBS Evening News, 2020). Recreations of fine art in the #gettymuseumchallenge express the vicissitudes of everyday life under quarantine during the COVID-19 pandemic.

Everyday life becomes the site of creative activity in the recreations of fine art produced by ordinary people for the #gettymuseumchallenge. Captured and expressed in the recreations are senses of lived spaces, mostly spaces of home, where home is not just the interior rooms of a house, but a setting of psychological safety, familial togetherness, and pandemic refuge. The recreations express place as a multiplicity of roles and activities including the workplace and schoolroom, some of which have been altered due to pandemic restrictions that resulted in work-from-home and school-from-home arrangements. Foregrounded are ordinary household items such as chairs, tables, dishes, plants, fruit, pets, and articles of clothing that convey the domestic spaces of quarantine. The recreated images capture the routines of everyday tasks such as cooking, cleaning, and daily rituals of eating, relaxing, and sleeping, reflecting folks' subjectivities and attitudes about pandemic circumstances in mixtures of frustration, humor, and tedium.

In the #gettymuseumchallenge, recreated works of fine art are recontextualized to reflect the circumstances and lived experiences of ordinary persons during COVID-19 pandemic lockdowns. In this context, objects of everyday life are infused with new meanings. Mundane household items like toilet paper rolls, cleaning supplies, disinfecting wipes, and rubber gloves are incorporated into the art recreations signaling their increased salience in everyday pandemic life. The objects speak, in a polyvocal manner, to their newfound roles and significance. Other objects, such as surgical masks and hand sanitizer, having become staples of daily life, are also frequently used in the art recreations. These commonplace items intersect with the realities of pandemic life possessing new-found signifying power that captures and expresses persons' myriad experiences of COVID-19 lockdowns.

The new necessities of everyday pandemic life are prominent in recontextualized works of fine art as gloves, masks, and social distancing are foregrounded. For example, *The Creation of Adam* (ca. 1508-12) by Michelangelo Buonarroti is used to express pandemic domestic life. In the original famous painting, two muscular male figures, representing the Christian God and the first man, Adam, reach toward one another with their arms outstretched, pointer fingers almost touching. The figure of God floats in the sky, surrounded by a group of angels with Eve tucked under God's rib. Across from God, Adam reclines on the barren ground with his upper body propped up by his right elbow. The #gettymuseumchallenge recreation of *The Creation of Adam* depicts a man and a woman in a living room at home, one lying on a sofa and the other reclining on a cushion on the hardwood floor. Both wear surgical face masks with their hands covered by blue, disposable medical gloves. Their arms are outstretched as they reach toward each other with the tips of their index fingers barely touching. Overlaid on the photograph is an annotation of a horizontal red line with the label "1 meter" marking the distance between the two persons, reinforcing the pandemic mantra required for safety in social interactions (Barth, 2020, p. 64).

Basic staples of everyday life, such as food and kitchen items, enabled another type of pandemic recontextualion of museum-quality artworks. Participants in the #gettymuseumchallenge were ingenious in their use of commonplace foodstuffs and household objects as artistic media. For example, one participant recreated Johannes Vermeer's portrait, *A Girl with a Pearl Earring* (ca. 1665) through the skillful arrangement of a sprouting red onion, a blue handled kitchen knife, a yellow dishcloth, and a stark white garlic clove (Tere Sona, 2021). Humble foods like an onion and garlic clove coupled with a cloth and paring knife recontextualize an iconic painting, grounding it in the elements of everyday life while simultaneously imparting a wholly new, abstracted perspective on the work of art. The abstraction distills the painting to its core components—just as the lives of ordinary people were stripped to their essential elements during COVID-19 lockdowns with many persons remaining at home, leaving only for vital tasks. The #gettymuseumchallenge art recreation of *A Girl with a Pearl Earring* renders an abstract quality to a classically painted portrait.

Use of food as a creative medium to express the everyday domestic spaces of quarantine life is also evident in the #gettymuseumchallenge recreations of classical still-life paintings. Where many classical still life paintings emphasize opulence and perfection, the #gettymuseumchallenge recreations portray the imperfect realism of lived experiences during COVID-19 lockdowns. One poignant example is the recontextualization of *Still Life: Tea Set* (ca. 1781–83) by Jean-Étienne Liotard. In the original still life painting, a hand-painted fine-china tea set rimmed in gold sits on an ornate platter accompanied by sterling silverware. Pots of tea, cups and saucers, a full sugar-bowl and milk jug, covered vase, and thick slices of buttered toast convey a sense of lavish abundance. In the digital art recreation, the fine-china is replaced by modern ceramic ware that is haphazardly set on a TV-dinner tray. There are two plates, one is empty and the other contains the remnants of a mostly-eaten peanut butter sandwich. A small bowl holds a couple of broken crackers. A half-eaten apple and two partially-crushed Coca-Cola cans complete the still life scene. While the original still life painting exudes wealth, prestige, and exclusivity, the art recreation, through its use of common elements such as an apple, a peanut butter sandwich, crackers, and cola, all depicted in disarray, expresses life in lockdown, warts and all (Getty Museum, 2020). The #gettymuseumchallenge art recreation recontextualizes the classical still life painting to the realities of everyday quarantine life.

Another aspect of everyday pandemic life that is evident in the #gettymuseumchallenge art recreations is the convergence of home life with work life during the COVID-19 pandemic. For many people, this meant being surrounded by family members throughout the work day and, for some, in charge of their child(ren)'s education. A reworking of *Saint Paul in Athens* (ca. 1844) by Sébastien Norblin speaks to this new reality. In the original, an elderly Saint Paul is situated at the center of the painting. He is robed in orange with his right hand raised, index-finger pointing skyward. He holds a tablet in the crook of his left arm as he preaches in a semi-circular forum, surrounded by a rapt audience of various ages. The art recreation, while repeating these gestures and arrangement, illustrates a different, more domestic scene. A woman, dressed in a pencil-skirt, blouse, and glasses, kneels on the carpeted floor of a living room next to a chalkboard easel. Her right hand is raised, index-finger pointing upward, as she faces her pupils—two toddlers seated on the floor looking back at her with an array of stuffed animals surrounding them (Barth, 2020, p. 9). The recreation's connection to homeschooling is palpable, with the participant going to the length of writing shapes and words on the chalkboard to illustrate the concept.

Art recreations that recontextualize fine art to ordinary life make new meanings possible. Recontextualization of art transports works of fine art into different places and spaces with everyday people and events at the center. These novel recreations produce new interpretations and understandings of art that go beyond the received meanings and associations. The art recreations can be understood to breathe new life into centuries-old works of fine art. Art works that are associated with the context of the particular historical places and times of their creation get recontextualized in the #gettymuseumchallege to encompass aspects of 21st century life, especially everyday life during COVID-19 stay-at-home orders. In this way, the recreations of fine art of the #gettymuseumchallenge operate to produce a more polyvocal set of associations that reflect and acknowledge a wider range of lived experiences.

Affective and Intimate Networked Publics

There is an affective, emotional, dimension to interactions among participants within the #gettymuseumchallenge as "social media platforms can be regarded as technological tools that mediate interpersonal intimacies" (Hjorth & Hinton, 2019, p. 21). Scholars have identified this aspect of social media referring to it as "affective publics" (Papacharissi, 2015) and "intimate publics" (Berlant, 2008). Academic research about interpersonal intimacies in social media seeks to understand how interactions, while mediated through platforms and technologies, are interpersonally meaningful to participants. Hjorth and Hinton (2019) posit that "a sense of community emerges through the performance of personal intimacies" online (p. 21). The strength of relational bonds that are established may be related to the levels and intensities of emotion that are expressed.

We note that technology can be used to mediate emotion and relational intimacy across the whole spectrum of human affect, not just romantic intimacy. In addition, social media are not unique in their ability to foster affective and intimate publics. Various forms of communication technologies have mediated human affect throughout history such as the telegraph, the telephone, written letters, and, more recently and distinct from social media, digital SMS (short message service) text messages. But there may be distinct ways in which social media can facilitate affective and intimate interpersonal connections through networked publics. While the telegraph, telephone, written letters, and SMS technologies are mostly one-to-one forms of communication, there is a community dynamic at work in networked publics.

As persons coalesce around the #gettymuseumchallenge, a community of practice materializes. Communities of practice online "are composed of members that share common interests and interact with each other to discuss topics, exchange ideas, and seek support" (Dedema & Fichman, 2021, p. 697). The emergence of collective interactions related to the #gettymuseumchallenge are especially salient because they occurred during the COVID-19 pandemic when social distancing circumscribed affective and intimate interpersonal connections. As Galani and Kidd (2020) observe "one of the starkest implications of the COVID-19 global health emergency [was] the forced deprioritization of touch and physicality in our encounters with one another" (p. 298). Participation in the #gettymusuemchallenge offered pathways for participants to establish digital communities of practice around their interests, and express affective and intimate connections with others through the shared activity.

Networked publics characterized by affective and intimate communicative expressions are evident in participants' practices in the #gettymuseumchallenge. In recreations of fine art, participants draw upon their own personal lives, choreographing, photographing, and sharing their pets, children, and home spaces. There is an intimacy involved in the self-disclosure of personal relationships and private spaces with others. As participants transform their private spaces to resemble works of art, using personal belongings for props and staging scenes in and around their private domestic spaces, participants acquire a sense of connection to the lives of others.

An excellent example of this can be found in the #gettymuseumchallenge art recreation of a still life painting in which the participant used a *New York Times* crossword puzzle, an apple, a work of floral embroidery on cloth, and a digital thermometer as their own personal spin on the classical still-life painting *Pomegranate, Worm, and Peach* (ca. 1561-62) by Joris Hoefnagel and Georg Bocksay. The original painting depicts a pomegranate flower, a peach, and a worm set below a calligraphic illumination (Barth, 2020, p. 29). Through the participant's thoughtful choices of materials with which to recreate the still life painting, the participant makes significant self-disclosures. In the art recreation, the crossword puzzle and floral embroidery evoke ways of passing the time. The digital thermometer reveals that the participant is not simply passing the time in an idle manner, but that the participant is feeling unwell. In this art recreation, a viewer may learn more about the participant than a conventional selfie may convey, as a selfie often portrays an individual's physical characteristics, but rarely communicates deeper, more intimate information about the person's private life away from social media.

We see another expression of intimacy when children become the focal point of the fine art recreations. While many parents make the active decision not to participate in "sharenting"

(Siibak & Traks, 2019; Steinberg, 2017) and, instead, withhold their child(ren)'s image from social media and the internet, the act of placing one's child(ren) at the center of a digital post imparts private information about personal relationships to others. When children are brought into the recreation of artistic works, the viewer is given a window into the intimate familial life of the participant. The involvement of multiple children along with parents in an art recreation reveals interpersonal familial dynamics through displays of nonverbal communication such as proximity, gaze, and facial expressions. For example, the #gettymuseumchallenge art recreation of the painting *Washington Crossing the Delaware* (ca. 1851) by Emanuel Leutze depicts a family with several young children (Barth, 2020, p. 14). In the original painting, George Washington stands at the helm of a small, shallow boat. A man behind him holds the American flag while a half-dozen other men are rowing and using poles to punt the boat through an ice-covered river.

In the recreation, there is a family of four young children with a mother and father outside on a lawn, likely in their own backyard as a swing set, fire-pit area, fence, and neighboring houses can be seen in the background. The children stand inside a red Radio Flyer pull-wagon holding a broom, spade, and stick to represent the oars and poles of the original painting. One child stands at the front in the pose of George Washington, while the father holds a towel wrapped around a stick to recreate the American flag. The mother is positioned in the front with a pole as if punting through the river ice, which is recreated by clumps and piles of white cloth strategically placed on the green grass. Relational family dynamics are conveyed through the art recreation: the playful levity of the younger children, the serious and purposeful role of George Washington by the oldest child, the mother in front steering the ship, and the father in the center surrounded by the younger children.

Emotional connection as described by the term "affective publics" (Papacharissi, 2015) is also apparent in participants' artistic recreations in the #gettymuseumchallenge. One of the most prevalent emotions shared by participants is humor, particularly in recreations of works of fine art that, in their original forms, are serious and even graphic in nature. For example, humor is at play in the recreations of *Saturn Devouring His Son* (ca. 1820-23) by Francisco de Goya. The original version of *Saturn Devouring His Son* is a dark, brooding, emotive work illustrating the grisly image of a large distorted nude human figure, Saturn, consuming the much smaller, bloodied naked figure of his son. In one humorous recreation of this image, a participant chose a bunch of bananas to stand-in for the blood-stained human figure of Saturn's son. In the recreation, the participant's face is pulled in a grimace. He sports wild wig hair, googly eyes, and wears only a pair of briefs while grasping the bunch of bananas, eating one from the bunch (Barth, 2020, p. 113).

Saturn Devouring His Son was a popular choice for #gettymuseumchallenge participants with multiple recreations of the same image by different persons setting in motion an array of subsequent recreations. Another humorous recreation of this classical artwork shows a toddler sitting on the floor holding a green stuffed animal, with the stuffed creature's arm being chewed vigorously in the child's mouth (Barth, 2020, p. 113). The ubiquity of humor as a feature in the recreations of grotesque classical paintings may be a response to the grave nature of the COVID-19 pandemic, as persons sought ways to bring conviviality into their lives. Through networked sharing of humor in their artistic recreations, a light-hearted sense of camaraderie and community is generated among participants in the #gettymuseumchallenge.

As alluded to in the aforementioned examples, participants in the #gettymuseumchallenge establish networked digital communities of practice around their interests in combination with the shared experiences of living through the COVID-19 pandemic. One impact of COVID-19 lockdowns was the "collapse of local and distant audiences ... show[ing] that online connections, even when not ideal, offer ways to bridge physical distance" (Clerkin & Taylor, 2021, p. 173). Visually-oriented social media platforms provide participants with affective and intimate interactions when many people were unable to see the faces of others due to public health measures like masking and quarantine isolation. Through social media practices of content creation, sharing, tagging, and commenting, the digital art challenge offers opportunities for digital connection. Describing her experience with participating in the #gettymuseumchallenge, one woman stressed the affective and community-building aspects of the experience stating, "I think it makes you feel like you're having a collective experience even though you're all alone" (CBS Evening News, 2020). The affective and intimate networked publics created through the #gettymuseumchallenge fostered interpersonal connections for participants.

The creation of spaces and opportunities that foster participants' experiences of interpersonal connection and relational intimacy in the #gettymuseumchallenge were intentional. Recounting the Getty's approach to the art challenge, Getty Museum Director Timothy Potts (2020) stated "we began by seeing what people were looking for from the Getty at this unusual time. On social media, we emphasized initiatives that were participatory or created 'conversations,' with the goal of ... creating community through art" (p. 218). In a similar vein, Assistant Director of Digital Content Strategy and User Experience Design for the J. Paul Getty Trust, Annelisa Stephan, reflected on the communicative dynamics of the initiative observing "I think it's just this missing sense of community that [the #gettymuseumchallenge] has really tapped into." (in Harris, 2020, n.p.). Likewise, Social Media Lead for the J. Paul Getty Trust, Sarah Waldorf, noted the community-building aspects of the #gettymuseumchallenge that "speaks to the power of art to bond us together. Art invites us into the experience of others and connects us with our shared past. In isolation, a sense of community is sacred" (in Harris, 2020, n.p.).

The success of open-access digital art challenges, such as the #gettymuseumchallenge, suggests the future potential of artistic creation in a digital world. In contemplating the effects of the #gettymusemchallenge as a digital art form, Annelisa Stephan notes that "it [the #gettymuseumchallenge] really has a life of its own. This is something that belongs to the internet, not to us" (in Harris, 2020, n.p.). It is possible that art created in and through social media may change the practices and relationships involved in art production, distribution, and reception as low-barrier, digital avenues may broaden the range of persons involved in these aspects of art.

Reimagining Representations

Institutions of art changed how they communicated with their audiences during the pandemic with profound implications. In the shift to digital forms of engagement, art museums developed "initiatives that envision radically different relationships to their audiences" (Buke, Jorgensen, & Jorgensen, 2020, p. 117). While the shifting relationship between art institutions and their audiences have been well documented from the perspective of art institutions, the changed relationship from the perspective of the public has received less attention. Here we suggest that the ordinary individuals who participated in the #gettymuseumchallenge were able to envision and enact radically different relationships not only with art institutions, but also with works of art, themselves. Changes undertaken during the COVID-19 pandemic did not simply enable art institutions to adapt and expand their digital modes of engagement, but, more significantly, such changes opened spaces for "online audiences [to act] as key agents in the production of digitally-mediated material encounters" (Galani & Kidd, 2020, p. 300). The #gettymuseumchallenge, as a pandemic digital art challenge, created the conditions for ordinary people to reinterpret works of fine art in alternative ways.

The #gettymuseumchallenge enabled the reinterpretations of classical artworks by participants who reflect the diversity of ordinary persons in the general public including persons of color and persons who, historically, have not been centered in Western works of fine art. Portraits and self-portraits of iconic artworks are recreated by participants who place themselves at the center of the paintings. People of color, women, and children are depicted as prominent figures in these recreated portraits, attributing a sense of power and authority to members of historically marginalized groups. In these reinterpretations of classical artworks, ordinary persons, who may occupy relatively subordinate social roles, are (re)presented taking on notable positions in the social hierarchy.

An example that demonstrates how #gettymuseumchallenge participants inserted themselves into iconic portraits can be found in participants' reinterpretations of Johannes Vermeer's *Girl with a Pearl Earring* (ca. 1665). Recreated by women of color and people of all ages, the reinterpretations of Vermeer's painting range from highly detailed to haphazard. Yet each echoes the original by including the key elements of the portrait: hair wrapped up in a cloth, face angled over the left shoulder looking towards the viewer, with the essential pearlescent earring. The prime elements of the portrait are reimagined and (re)presented when a woman of Southeast Asian descent poses using material from a *sari* as the iconic hair wrap, and when a Black woman lets her long braids cascade down, folding over her shoulder (Barth, 2020, pp. 56-57). While preserving the compositional elements of the original, the recreations let the diversity of participants shine, contributing to the reinterpretation and (re)presentation of the ordinary self as icon. Through such recreations, classical artworks are reimagined and (re)presented thereby opening space for new understandings and relationships with works of fine art.

There is power in seeing oneself reflected in a work of fine art. Inserting oneself as the subject into an iconic artwork—indeed, one held in the venerable collection of the Getty Art Museum—may shift understandings of the self, interpersonal and social relationships, and cultural institutions (such as art museums), as ordinary people gain a sense of agency as social actors and art creators. Further, (re)presentation of reified works of fine art may make new forms of cultural capital—i.e., symbolic wealth that comprises "legitimate culture" (Bourdieu, 2018)—available to participants. In the #gettymuseumchallenge, ordinary persons place themselves into positions of historical, mythical, and cultural significance thereby reimagining and (re)presenting artworks. Conventional hierarchies of race, power, and social strata are turned on their head in art recreations that center women, people of color, LGBTQI+ people, disabled people, children, and others. In these ways, participation in the #gettymuseumchallenge may shift self-perceptions as persons come to regard themselves as worthy subjects of art and as creators of art rather than passive viewers of art.

In their study of the racial and ethnic diversity of art museum participants, Olivares and Piatak (2021) assert "museum visitors are not reflective of the diversity present in communities around the nation" (p. 1). The authors cite "historical exclusion and lack of representation as reasons for lower participation of diverse audiences" (Olivares & Piatak, 2021, p. 9) especially by Black and Latinx persons. Given the historic lack of representation of Black, Asian, Indigenous, and People of Color (BAIPOC) in art museum spaces, the cultural and ethnic diversity present in the art recreations of the #gettymusuemchallenge is a remarkable contrast.

While many BAIPOC participants inserted themselves into portraits depicting White subjects as discussed earlier, there is also a dynamic of BAIPOC folks searching the digital Getty collection for works of art that feature sitters (i.e., persons who sit as the subject of a portrait painting) who look like themselves. One such example is a recreation of the painting *Portrait of a Young Woman* (late 18th century) by Jean-Étienne Liotard. In the original, a young Black woman is dressed in an elegant light pink silk gown with ruffles at the neckline. She wears a choker string of white pearls around her neck and small, golden hoop earrings. Her hair is wrapped, turban-style, in fine white cloth that is tied in a neat bow at the crown of her head, as she stands against a sky-blue background gazing over her right shoulder at the viewer.

The #gettymuseumchallenge art recreation of this work is nearly exact: a young Black woman looks at the viewer over her right shoulder. She wears a ruffled, lacey light-colored top, a white pearl choker necklace and small, golden hoop earrings. Her hair is wrapped in a modern, white head wrap that is topped with a silken white bow, as she stands in front of a bright yellow background (Barth, 2020, p. 58). The art recreation works to identify and amplify an instance of BAIPOC presence in Western, classical fine art, moving it into the forefront of public consciousness while, simultaneously, asserting its relevance and relatability for the 21st century. Whether the recreation of *Portrait of a Young Woman* was enabled by the online accessibility of the #gettymuseumchallenge or the ability of participants to browse and select artworks depicting BAIPOC subjects from the Getty's digitized collection, the art challenge was embraced and transformed by communities that have been historically underrepresented in works of fine art in institutional collections.

A compelling example of art recreation as a form of empowerment is Peter Brathwaite's art recreations for the #gettymuseumchallenge. While Brathwaite may have been known to a small subset of people because of his profession as an opera singer, he was mostly unknown to the ordinary persons who participated in the digital art challenge. In his art recreations, Brathwaite focused solely on re-envisioning works of fine art created from the 14th century onward that depict Black people. In each of his social media posts for the #gettymuseumchallenge, Brathwaite summarizes the historical context of the original artwork and then presents his reimagined contemporary version. In his historical summary he introduces the painter, provides a description of the person(s) depicted, and explains the significance of the objects included in the painting.

In essence, Brathwaite decodes and unlocks not only the meanings of the historical works of art, but also, more importantly, uncovers the mostly unexamined role of Black sitters (i.e., persons who pose for a painter or sculptor, an artist's model) in Western art. His recreations "challenge preconceived ideas about Black people's presence in Europe from the medieval period onward, and the multiple and varied roles they have played in Western culture, art and society through the centuries" (Wakeham, 2020, n.p.). Brathwaite's recreations highlight not only Black sitters but also shine a spotlight on largely unacknowledged important Black historical figures like John Blanke who was a skilled musician in the court of England's Henry VIII in the early 16th century. The effects of his art recreations are powerful as Brathwaite attests "It's incredibly inspiring to see that image ... To see that there has been a heritage of Black classical musicians" (in Wakeham, 2020, n.p.). Such rediscoveries of Black historical figures are essential for correcting long-held gaps in history and knowledge with "calls for his project to be turned into a book and included in the curriculum for schools and universities" (Wakeham, 2020, n.p.).

A more specific example of Braithwaite's art recreations is his reinterpretation of *The Paston Treasure* (ca. 1663) by an unknown artist. The original painting is a unique combination of portrait and still life. At the center of the painting is a large table covered with a variety of expensive, rare objects: cups made of nautilus shells with golden stems are artfully placed, bunches of pink and red roses are strewn about, a large, colored globe of the known-world rests on the table, a lute sits on a lush red leather chair in the right-hand corner of the painting, and a heavy, red velvet curtain with thick folds hangs in the background. These are only a sample of the many objects included in the painting, each item expressing a life of opulence. There are also two human figures depicted. One is a small, well-dressed, blonde-haired White girl sitting in a green leather-backed chair by the lute. The other is a young Black man dressed in fine velvet clothes, with an exotic small monkey on his shoulder, who stands at the lower-left corner of the painting holding an empty silver stein in his right hand.

In Brathwaite's recreation, we see a similar, but intentionally different, constellation of objects. A large table is still at the center, but the various items placed upon the table all speak to Brathwaite's personality and lived history. In place of a lute, there is a violin and a ukulele. Instead of nautilus cups lined with gold, we see porcelain and other beloved dishware, and, in lieu of the velvet curtain in the background, there are two handmade patchwork quilts. The young White girl seen in the original painting is replaced by a record album cover with a photograph of the Black, female American opera singer Jessye Norman. Brathwaite, himself, takes the place of the young Black man, wearing an elegant, brightly colored jacket of his own with a stuffed-toy monkey on his shoulder. He holds a vintage, psychedelically-patterned coffee thermos loosely in his right hand (Barth, 2020, p. 15). In his recreation of *The Paston Treasure,* Brathwaite draws on the tropes traditionally used in portraiture and still life paintings to artfully reconfigure them in ways that express his lived experience as a Black, British man in the 21st century.

By means of this and other recreations, Brathwaite reclaims the ways in which Black histories and Black identities have been portrayed over the centuries. As a whole, Brathwaite's recreations can be seen as a powerful contribution to decolonizing works of art that, while depicting Black people, were rendered through the White gaze of White artists. His recreations suggest new ways of seeing Black subjectivity and agency. For example, his inaugural recreation in the challenge was a reimagined version of a painting of a Black servant from the 18th century. Brathwaite tags his posts not only with the #gettymuseumchallenge hashtag, but he also includes additional hashtags that extend the conversation and meanings of the recreated work. For example, he often uses the hashtag rediscovering #blackportraiture to assert that his recreations offer "re-imaginings, disruptions, and a re-empowering" of Black (re)presentations (Burke, Jorgensen, & Jorgensen, 2020, p. 121). In their re-centering of Black people and experiences, Brathwaite's recreations carry further significance connecting to the disparities in health outcomes of Black and marginalized people during the COVID-19 pandemic. Given also that many of Brathwaite's art recreations were produced, circulated, and received in the height of the #BlackLivesMatter social justice movements of summer 2020, the representations articulate further signifying power.

Produced by groups of persons who have been historically marginalized in Western classical art, digital art recreations such as those in the #gettymuseumchallenge hold the potential to break down barriers between art institutions and their audiences. The art challenge also holds the potential to bring to light the lesserknown artistic works that feature BAIPOC sitters and artists. Finally, the art recreations possess transformative potential for the participants, themselves. As Brathwaite maintains "once you've put yourself in a painting, you view it very differently" (Migdol, 2020, n.p.). The increased engagement of BAIPOC as audience, but also as active subjects of art and as agents of art creation, may open spaces for further participation in the arts in ways that fruitfully expand the expression of a diversity of experiences through new forms of representation.

Future Research Directions

Through exploration of some of the dynamics of the #gettymuseumchallenge, this chapter highlights ways in which the relationships between ordinary people, fine art, and institutions of art are changing. Interpretations and reinterpretations of works of fine art in the #gettymuseumchallenge by the general public can be understood as a recontextualization of fine art through the interactive, community-building, and self-expressive dynamics afforded by social media during the COVID-19 pandemic. This study is just a start. There are other aspects of the #gettymuseumchallenge to be explored in further depth and detail. For example, future research could investigate digital art challenges like the #gettymuseumchallenge as well as other art challenges, to make meaningful contributions to understandings about how art challenges shape museum-audience interactions and forms of engagement. Are art challenges effective? How so? For whom? Under what circumstances? The #gettymuseumchallenge emerged during the unique time of the COVID-19 pandemic which likely impacted its trajectory and effects. What about art challenges that may occur in the midst of other distinctive cultural and historical circumstances?

Another direction that warrants further research is inquiry into the relationships between visual social media, digital art-making and sharing, and traditional modes of art production, dissemination, and reception. As social media, increasingly, become sites of creative practice, these relationships evolve in nuanced and complicated ways. How does digital art creation, distribution, and reception impact each of these aspects of art? Finally, scholarly attention to hegemonic representations of race and expressions of colonial histories in Western art, especially portraiture, continues to be imperative. These are but a few of the possibilities for future research to explore around the rich and complex nexus of digital art and digital social life.

Conclusion

This exploratory analysis explicates three dynamics related to how ordinary folks recreate works of fine art and share them on social media in the #gettymuseumchallenge, initiated at the start of the global SARS-CoV2/COVID-19 pandemic. The first dynamic focuses on the ways in which folks' recreations recontextualize fine art to the lived experiences of ordinary people during the pandemic. The second dynamic centers on the ways in which the networked publics, created through the #gettymuseumchallenge, enable and express affective and intimate relational connections. The third dynamic explores the ways in which common artists, particularly those from historically marginalized groups, use the #gettymuseumchallenge to reimagine and reclaim their own (re)presentions through digital art recreation. Such dynamics raise further questions about the changing relationships between art creation by the general public, the practices of art institutions, and the role of social media that will likely persist well beyond the pandemic.

Conflict of Interest

The authors have no conflicts of interests to disclose.

References

Adomaite, L., & Denis, T. (2020). *People are recreating paintings in this Dutch Instagram Account and Here are 30 of the best ones*. Bored Panda.

Anderson, B. (2006). *Imagined communities: Reflections on the origin and spread of nationalism* (2nd ed.). Verso Books.

Barajas, J. (2020, April 15). *Famous paintings come to life in these quarantine works of art*. PBS Newshour.

Barnes, S. (2020, April 21). *Widely Popular Russian Facebook Group Has People Recreating Famous Paintings While in Isolation*. My Modern Met.

Barth, R. (Ed.). (2020). *Off the walls: Inspired re-creations of iconic artworks*. Getty Publications.

Berlant, L. (2008). *The female complaint*. Duke University Press.

Black, G. (2018). Meeting the audience challenge in the 'Age of Participation.' *Museum Management and Curatorship*, 33(4), 302-319. doi:10.1080/09647775.2018.1469097.

Black, G. (Ed.). (2020). *Museums and the challenge of change: Old Institutions in a new world* (1st ed.). Routledge.

Bourdieu, P. (2018). Cultural reproduction and social reproduction. In R. Brown (Ed.), *Knowledge, education, and cultural change* (pp. 71-112). Routledge.

Boyd, D. (2011). Social network sites as networked publics: Affordances, dynamics, and implications. In Z. Papacharissi, *A networked self: Identity, community, and culture on social network sites* (pp. 47-66). Routledge.

Burke, V., Jørgensen, D., & Jørgensen, F. A. (2020). Museums at home: Digital Initiatives in Response to COVID-19. *Norsk museumstidsskrift*, 6(02), 117-123. DOI:10.18261/issn.2464-2525-2020-02-05.

CBS Evening News. (2020, April 30). *People recreate famous paintings with household items in viral challenge*. [Video]. Youtube. https://youtu.be/p79uvP8oL7c.

Clerkin, C. C., & Taylor, B. L. (2021). Online Encounters with Museum Antiquities. *American Journal of Archeology*, 125(1), 165-175. doi:10.3764/aja.125.1.0165.

Compton, N. B. (April 3, 2020). *People are re-creating famous artworks with their pets and whatever else is lying around.* The Washington Post.

de Certeau, M. (2002). *The practice of everyday life* (2nd ed.). University of California Press.

Dedema, M., & Fichman, P. (2021). Boundary Crossing in Online Community of Practice: "Between Art and Quarantine." *Proceedings of the Association for Information Science and Technology*, 58(1), 697-699. doi:10.1002/pra2.533.

Fraser, N. (1992). Rethinking the public sphere: A contribution to the critique of actually existing democracy. In C. Calhoun (Ed.), *Habermas and the public sphere* (pp. 109–142). MIT Press.

Galani, A., & Kidd, J. (2020). Hybrid material encounters—expanding the continuum of museum materialities in the wake of a pandemic. *Museum & Society*, 18(3), 298–301. doi:10.29311/ mas.v18i3.3565.

Getty Museum [@gettymuseum]. (March 25, 2020). We challenge you to recreate a work of art with materials at home. *It's easy: - Choose your favorite artwork - Find* [Photograph Slideshow]. Instagram. https://www.instagram.com/p/B-Kcv77HdTA/.

Harris, G. (2020, July 28). "*New Getty Publication Brings Together Life-affirming DIY masterpieces made During Lockdown*." The Art Newspaper.

Hashtags for #gettymuseum. (n.d.). *Best-hashtags.com.* Accessed Nov. 15, 2021 from http://best-hashtags.com/hashtag/gettymuseum/.

Highfield, T., & Leaver, T. (2015). A methodology for mapping Instagram hashtags. Fi*rst Monday*, 20(1), 1-11. doi:10.5210/fm.v20i1.5563.

Hjorth, L. (2016). Mobile art: Rethinking intersections between art, user created content (UCC), and the quotidian. *Mobile media & communication*, 4(2), 169-185. doi:10.1177/2050157915619210.

Hjorth, L., & Hinton, S. (2019). *Understanding social media* (2nd ed.). Sage.

Hoffman, A. (2020, March 30). *Put These Artistic Masterpieces Re-created With Household Items in a Museum*. Time.

International Council of Museums. (2020). *Report: Museums, Museum Professionals and COVID-19.*

Jackson, S. J., & Foucault Welles, B. (2015). Hijacking# myNYPD: Social media dissent and networked counterpublics. *Journal of communication*, 65(6), 932-952. doi:10.1111/ jcom.12185.

Kidd, J. (2020). Social Media and Participation: The selfie as a curious cultural artefact. In G. Black (Ed.), *Museums and the Challenge of Change: Old Institutions in a New World* (pp. 53-59). Routledge.

Leaver, T., & Highfield, T. (2018). Visualising the ends of identity: pre-birth and post-death on Instagram. *Information, Communication & Society*, 21(1), 30-45. doi:10.1080/1369118X. 2016.1259343.

Livingstone, S. (2005). *Audiences and Publics: When Cultural Engagement Matters for the Public Sphere* (Vol. 2). Intellect Books.

Lukas, N., Gilmore, A., Jay, C., & Yo, Y. (2021). The impact of COVID-19 on digital data practices in museums and art galleries in the UK and the US. *Humanities & Social Sciences Communications*, 8(1). doi:10.1057/s41599-021-00921-8

Migdol, E. (2020, May 27). *Rediscovering Black Portraiture through the Getty Museum Challenge*. Getty.

Olivares, A., & Piatak, J. (2021). Exhibiting inclusion: An examination of race, ethnicity, and museum participation. *VOLUNTAS: International Journal of Voluntary and Nonprofit Organizations.* doi:10.1007/s11266-021-00322-0.

Papacharissi, Z. (2011). Conclusion: A networked self. In Z. Papacharissi (Ed.), *A networked self: Identity, community, and culture on social network sites* (pp. 304-318). Routledge.

Papacharissi, Z. (2015). *We have always been social. Social Media + Society*, 1(1). doi:10.1177/2056305115581185

Papacharissi, Z. (Ed.). (2018). *A networked self and platforms, stories, connections*. Routledge.

Pulh, M., & Mencarelli, R. (2015). Web 2.0: Is the museum-visitor relationship being redefined?. *International Journal of Arts Management*, 18(1), 43-51.

Rauschnabel, P. A., Sheldon, P., & Herzfeldt, E. (2019). What motivates users to hashtag on social media?. *Psychology & Marketing*, 36(5), 473-488. doi:10.1002/mar.21191.

Samaroudi, M., Echavarria, K. R., & Perry, L. (2020). Heritage in lockdown: Digital provision of memory institutions in the UK and US of America during the COVID-19 pandemic. *Museum Management and Curatorship*, 35(4), 337-361. doi:10.1080/09647775.2020.1810483.

Siibak, A., & Traks, K. (2019). The dark sides of sharenting. *Catalan Journal of Communication & Cultural Studies*, 11(1), 115–121. doi:10.1386/cjcs.11.1.115_1.

Steinberg, S. (2017). Sharenting: Children's Privacy in the Age of Social Media. *Emory Law Journal*, 66(839), 839-884.

Tere Sona [@tere.sona] (Nov. 22, 2021). "Because cutting garlic and onion is an art … I'll do mine too!." "*Girl with a Pearl Earring*," Johannes Vermeer (1665). Instagram. https://www. instagram.com/p/CWlkhSALWRg/.

Volo, S. & Irimiás, A. (2020). Instagram: Visual methods in tourism research. *Annals of Tourism Research*, 103098. DOI:10.1016/j.annals.2020.103098

Wakeham, A. (2020, Sept. 15). *Meet the Opera Singer Reframing Black Portraiture*. Country and Town House.

Warner, M. (2021). *Publics and counterpublics* (eBook ed.). Zone Books.

Chapter 2

Communal "Common Art" Spaces on the Social Web and Supports for Artful Novelty

Shalin Hai-Jew*

Kansas State University, Manhattan, KS, USA

Abstract

In the Fourth Industrial Revolution (4IR), people go online to meet various professional and personal needs. For artists, both amateur and professional, they go online to acquire new skills, find inspirations, create a professional identity, showcase their style and capabilities, market and sell their work and services, make and maintain collegial and friendly relationships, find and engage in collaborative projects, acquire employment, conduct research, and other instrumental and art-based objectives. One of the most critical factors for an artist is the maintenance of continuing creativity, particularly in the high and difficult range of creating novel artworks that express something of the artist's own sensibilities and person. Novel art requires various elements to coalesce: seeing differently, thinking differently, executing on those visions, harnessing serendipity and chance, mastering various materials and technologies, and other aspects. This work explores two highly popular spaces on the Social Web for artists, DeviantArt and Behance, to identify what aspects of those environments apparently contribute to novel art. This work includes a review of the literature, content analysis on both social sites, and in-depth analysis.

Keywords: common art, online communal art spaces, Social Web, Web 2.0, novel art, DeviantArt, Behance, 4IR, Fourth Industrial Revolution

Introduction

In a phase of human history when people go online to engage in every facet of life, common artists also go online to meet various needs: learn new skills, inspire themselves, express their professional and personal selves, showcase their work, sell their work and labor, socialize, collaborate with others, find work, conduct research, and others. A critical element for working (and non-working) artists is to maintain their creativity and to enable the building of a unique vision and artist hand. The gold standard is to create work that is distinctive and novel. For many, there are not just the general social platforms for blogging, vlogging, social networking,

* Corresponding Author's Email: haijes@gmail.com

In: Common Visual Art in a Social Digital Age
Editor: Shalin Hai-Jew
ISBN: 978-1-68507-664-1

image-sharing, video-sharing, news-sharing, and others, but there are dedicated sites for art of various genres, to enable "creatives" to form online communities of practice, which can sustain each in their ambitions.

Work in the creative industries "is often unstable" and results in creative workers having to engage in various side hustles to survive (Tan & Yuen, 2018, p. 66), making portfolios and dedicated artist websites/pages critical. Different art-based social media platforms attract different sub-populations and showcase different works based on different appeals of the respective spaces (Tan & Yuen, 2018, p. 63). There is "considerable opportunity for social media researchers to engage in qualitative approach to studying people interactions and creative discourses" in the various evolving platforms (Tan & Yuen, 2018, p. 67). One question of interest involves how social media platforms "support art related skills acquisition and communicate creativity among the art community" (Tan & Yuen, 2018, p. 63).

In this current social moment, social media applications are relevant in each artful phase: research, creation, presentation, and dissemination (Christodoulou & Styliaras, 2008, pp. 159-163), with different use cases. They have relevance in creating digital vector images and animations, digital paintings, digital photos, 3D models, digital videos, algorithmic or generative art, digital literature, and art installations (Christodoulou & Styliaras, 2008, pp. 158-159). The works may be designed by individual artists or involve larger works by collaborative ones.

In this work, two popular spaces for artists, common and uncommon, are studied: DeviantArt and Behance. DeviantArt was founded in August 2000. DeviantArt has over 61 million users and 350 million pieces of art on the site as of mid-July 2021. DeviantArt has a tagline as "the largest online art gallery and community." One work highlights its numbers in 2012: "With its 19 million members, 100 million images and 45 million monthly visitors (all as of May 2012), surpassing any real or virtual museum" (Salah, Salah, Buter, Dijkshoorn, Modolo, Nguyen, van Noort, & van de Poel, 2012, p. 486). DeviantArt is "one of the largest online social networks for art" (Huckle, Garcia, & Nakashima, 2020, p. 128). Behance was founded in November 2005. It has some 12 million users as of mid-July 2021.

Both spaces enable broadscale access to their data to computer scientists for training algorithms and for researchers in various fields. Other sites mentioned in the literature have not stood the test of time, with many rebranded for other purposes and some gone without a trace online. Others are mainline sites without focuses on art per se.

Limitations: Both DeviantArt and Behance have social media accounts on other spaces, like microblogging sites, social networking sites, pinning sites, social image sharing sites, video sharing sites, and others. These are beyond the purview of this work.

Review of the Literature

People have engaged "artistic practices using the computer as a production method precede the existence of the internet, dating back to the 1970s" (Blume, 2017, p. 97), and other sources pointing to the 1940s and 1950s. Computer art has been part of a long tradition over multiple generations. One researcher suggests that now is the age of "post-internet art" (Blume, 2017, p. 102), where cyber influences have become central to the creation of art. One definition of "post internet" is as "a state of mind characterized by the ubiquity of internet culture" (Storfner,

2014, as cited in Blume, 2017, p. 102). Artmaking today often involves "the participatory Web and social media" and engagement in various art collectives (Blume, 2017, p. 104).

The rise of the "amateur media producer" on DeviantArt and other spaces used to be conceptualized in a two-dimensional model separating "personal media and mass media according to an interactional axis and an institutional/professional axis; personal media are de-institutionalized/de-professionalized and facilitate mediated interaction" (Lüders, 2008, p. 683, p. 694). That model seems somewhat dated out, with the integration of the personal and professional in how many use the Social Web 2.0 for artful expression and commerce.

Two Online Art Community Spaces

These two popular online art communities share quite a few differences even as some core focuses seem shared.

DeviantArt

DeviantArt, whose users are known as "deviants" once they're registered on the site (Tan & Yuen, 2018, p. 64), involve something of inherency in the idea of deviating from a norm and perhaps exploring novelty, unusual spaces. The name of this online network of artists has a rebel or divergent vibe. "Normal" is a contested term, and it is often seen as derogatory in many contexts. There is valuing of difference and celebrating it. DeviantArt functions as a site for portfolios and "less as (a) discussion forum" (Lamerichs, 2018, p. 56). As a site, DeviantArt offers meaningful and substantive interactivity and engagement, not just up and down votes (Ables, Apr. 19, 2019). In July 2021, the filters were for the following: Digital Art, Fan Art, Cosplay, Drawings and Paintings, 3D, Anime and Manga, and Traditional Art. The available types of art were the following categories: 3D, Adoptables, Anime and Manga, Anthro, Artisan Crafts, Comics, Cosplay, Customization, Digital Art, Drawings and Paintings, Emoji and Emoticon, Fan Art, Fan Fiction, Fantasy, Fractal, Game Art, Horror, Kinky, Literature, Nude Art, Photo Manipulation, Photography Pixel Art, Poetry, Resources, Science Fiction, Sculpture, Stock Images, Street Art, Street Photography, Traditional Art, Tutorials, and Wallpaper. Its uses are myriad, including some going to DeviantArt for unverified health data (Bowler, Mattern, Jeng, Oh, & He, 2013, p. 6).

One powerful study found an association between a person's personality (based on the Five Factor Model) and their choices of websites. More specifically, they found "psychologically meaningful links between users' personalities, their website preferences and Facebook profile features" (Kosinski, Bachrach, Kohli, Stillwell, & Graepel, 2014, p. 357). The five factors, generally defined, include openness to experience (curiosity), conscientiousness (preference for an "organized approach to life" vs. spontaneity), extroversion (seeking stimulation in the world, socializing with others), agreeableness (keeping positive social relations), and neuroticism (proneness to mood swings) (Kosinski, Bachrach, Kohli, Stillwell, & Graepel, 2014, p. 359). For DeviantArt, users tend to rank higher on openness, lower in conscientiousness, lower in extroversion, lower in agreeableness, and higher in neuroticism (Kosinski, Bachrach, Kohli, Stillwell, & Graepel, 2014, p. 363). DeviantArt…

> attracts an audience that tends to be liberal and artistic rather than conservative and traditional (i.e., with high Openness), spontaneous and flexible rather than well organized (i.e., low Conscientiousness), shy and reserved rather than outgoing and active (i.e., with low Extroversion), and emotional rather than calm and relaxed (i.e., with high Neuroticism) (Kosinski, Bachrach, Kohli, Stillwell, & Graepel, 2014, p. 363).

DeviantArt as a site that attracts "alternative art enthusiasts and artists" (Kosinski, Bachrach, Kohli, Stillwell, & Graepel, 2014, p. 363). Thinking about the user base of an art website may be helpful in understand which demographic slices of a sub-population are being reached. The dynamic of homophily (preferring those who are similar to the self) has also been observed on social media platforms through social network analysis.

Behance

"Behance" focuses on the "enhancement" of artwork and having creatives "be" themselves (Belsky, March 2014). Behance, a service of Adobe, Inc., hosts a number of livestreams for Creatives. This space involves the posting of works-in-progress as well as finished ones. For this online artspace, too, there is inherency in the idea of making something new (Tan & Yuen, 2018, p. 65), through tools, through collaborations, through inspirations, and others. Adobe Behance is "a portfolio website for professional and commercial artists" (Fiorucci, et al., 2020, p. 103). Behance is a "social network" (Halstead, Serrano, & Proctor, 2015, p. 2426). Behance is "a creative content discovery platform" (Modani, Jain, Soni, Gupta, & Agarwal, 2017, p. 145). Said another way: Behance is "a social network specializing in portfolios for design professionals" (Cochrane & Antonczak, 2013, p. 434) and enabling the development of design learning via mobile devices (p. 430). Behance is a space for those engaged in "typography, street art, industrial design, and fashion" (Rudolph, Hoffman, & Hertzmann, 2016, p. 581). In a July 2021 visit to the Behance site, the filters included Projects, Images, Prototypes, People, Moodboards, and others.

A study conducted several years ago captured some information about the interactions among the membership of Behance:

> In summary, being male suggests more followers and appreciations, most users focus on a few topics, and grayscale colors mean fewer appreciations" as some extracted patterns found on the Behance online community of creative professionals. (Kim, 2017, p. 1)

Some other social patterns include the following: "Having more project appreciations leads to more followers. Residing in the United States also suggests more followers, while from India, Brazil, and Egypt indicates fewer followers... We also observed specializing in graphic design, which occupies the highest proportion of users, results in fewer followers...; not that users can specialize in more than one topic. Other top topics, not included in the table, that have positive effects include typography, fashion, illustration, and digital arts. Male users attract more followers" (Kim, 2017, p. 6). Both male and female members "produce a similar number of projects" according to this (Kim, 2017, p. 6).

In this study conducted in Behance, color in the artwork has an effect on appreciation. White has the "highest effect on appreciation" (Kim, 2017, p. 8). "Gray color, saturation, and colorfulness"... having a negative effect on appreciation (Kim, 2017, p. 8). Value (brightness) has a positive effect on appreciation (Kim, 2017, p. 8). These findings may reflect something of the evolving aesthetics for the particular time.

Another work proposed a different algorithm to include more "fairness" in the recommender system inside Behance, touching on how content is ranked based on particular text searches (Modani, Jain, Soni, Gupta, & Agarwal, 2017). A different work proposes profiling the "viewing behavior and social network of users on Behance" in order to enrich the "cold start" of new users to the site and to enable the system to more effectively suggest persons to follow on the site (Rudolph, Hoffman, & Hertzmann, 2016, p. 583).

The exposure to a wide variety of work styles, attitudes, cultures, aesthetics, and skills, may benefit those creating art. These may trigger ideas that would not otherwise be formed. Such art sites are not only for art career instrumentalities. These may be spaces for fanart. They may be political spaces, for various types of political expression.

Finally, one note is in order: Internet art communities do rise and fall. One researcher explains: "As the internet moved toward homogeneity and passivity, once-vibrant art communities became casualties in social media's rapid, obliterative rise" (Ables, Apr. 19, 2019). Some communities are more elite and require a review of works to be accepted in. (This may be a way to control for lurkers.)

This work involves a content analysis of these two spaces to identify practices and technologies that support the development of novel works by the respective members of these online art communities.

Online Communities and Strategies to Benefit Individual and Collaborative Art Making

Collaborative projects on the Social Web are known to have high failure rates. The general trajectory is high enthusiasm early on, some limits to skills, and then dwindling interest over time. One work describes specially designed tools to lessen the work burdens on "leaders of online creative projects" and other forms of "distributed leadership" (Luther, Fiesler, & Bruckman, 2013, p. 1007) to try to ensure that such projects are more successful than they have been historically. Sociotechnical systems benefit from features such as project planning tools, task assignments, task instructions, and others. There are other considerations, too, for creatives.

Sharing Works-in-Progress

If many social spaces focus on final artworks only, others are starting to encourage the sharing of works-in-progress, so there is more focus on process and method. Works in intermediate stages may lessen the difficulty in acquiring thoughtful feedback on the respective works (Kim, Agrawala, & Bernstein, 2017, p. 246). The thinking is that there can be beneficial insights and supports for artists at any step of the creative process. The *status quo* may make it so that "sharing in-progress work can be technically and socially challenging in environments designed for sharing completed pieces" (Kim, Agrawala, & Bernstein, 2017, p. 246). By the time an artwork is fully refined and finished, any feedback may be too late to inform its development. This study found various categories of comments posted to works-in-progress:

"describing actions, justifying action, intent, struggle, assessment, idea, ask(ing) for help, goals for growth" (Kim, Agrawala, & Bernstein, 2017, p. 253). In terms of feedback by others, they included "specific like, thanks (creator), answer (creator, encouragement, suggestion/critique, intent (creator), commiseration, technique, communication, response action, question, other" (Kim, Agrawala, & Bernstein, 2017, p. 253). Teaching and learning occurs through engaging works-in-progress, even if "showcasing failure is uncomfortable" (Kim, Agrawala, & Bernstein, 2017, p. 254).

A focus on process vs. outcome, initial vision vs. the evolving one, the struggles vs. the triumph, may be more beneficial to the development of artists, as individuals and as groups. Perhaps seeing works in their rough draft stages can make the work more approachable. Seeing process can help those new to the field understand that the end state of an artwork is not arrived at that easily. It can help them be more understanding as they face challenges and face problems that need solving. However, there have been expressed concerns of the theft of intellectual property even with the in-between phases of the work, even with works that are not display-ready (Kim, Agrawala, & Bernstein, 2017, p. 255). The art community online may have an expanded sense of what useful artifacts are. Finally, the design of the socio-technical space is relevant for the effective work of the creative community.

Open-source communal projects often do not tend to "make" over time, as people lose interest and drift away. This dynamic also applies to user-generated contents and collaborative projects, resulting in partial works shared online. One research team suggests that user-contributed contents are still valuable, even if incomplete (Alluvatti, Capiluppi, De Ruvo, & Molfetta, 2011, p. 81). The pieces and parts can still be used for learning.

Since so much learning in creative spaces comes from failures, those engaging in creative work may benefit from engaging in "practice failure" (Kim, Bagla, & Bernstein, 2015, p. 158).

> While experts have developed strategies for engaging in risky experiments and learning from mistakes, novices lack the experience and mindset needed to use failures as opportunities for growth. Current tools intimidate the unsure novice, as they are designed around showcasing success or critiquing finished work, rather than providing safe spaces for experimentation. (Kim, Bagla, & Bernstein, 2015, p. 157)

Being persistent in the learning is also important. One study suggests that sharing a work iteratively as it evolves and eliciting constructive feedback may lead to powerful outcomes. The willingness to iterate is important. They write:

> Our results showed that more and longer comments, comments with less positive tone and comments with more thought-provoking statements correlated with iteration. Our analysis also showed that two or more iterations were shared for only 21% of the projects. The survey results explained that the rate of iteration was due in part to designers sharing their projects with the community near the end of their design process. (Crain & Bailey, 2017, p. 80)

In this study, some identified categories for the critique discourses included the following: "brainstorming, comparison, direct recommendation, free association, identity-invoking, interpretation, investigation, judgment, process-oriented, (and) support" (Crain & Bailey, 2017, p. 85). Online communities benefit those in design when community feedback is encouraged so creatives can respond with iterative design and optimally create stronger designs.

Sometimes, computational affordances may provide designers with appropriate feedback. One work describes the enriching of "mood board" designs with automated semantic labels. "Mood boards" are composite visuals that convey design inspirations and concepts. Designers may think visually first, but the application of semantics may introduce more precision to support the creative work (Koch, Taffin, Lucero, & Mackay, 2020).

Intellectual Property

One of constant challenges in online creative communities is the practice of intellectual property laws and practices, both for the protection of the creators and of the consumers of those contents. One study found that many feel that they have a right to download visual media shared on social sharing sites (Marshall & Shipman, 2011), and their expectations likely inform behaviors. In another study, remixers were found to be working engaging online with social norms that that did "not always track to what the law actually says," but was guided by their self-defined ethics (Fiesler & Bruckman, 2014, p. 1023). There were some identified legal misconceptions, that "noncommerciality" is "a sole deciding factor of fair use"; that there is a "blanket exception for educational use," that the "addition of attribution" is an "explicit fair use factor" and a tendency to find justifications for remix, such as the idea that there should be "more consideration for the 'little guy' with respect to market harm" and even suggesting a potential for 'market good' in remix (Fiesler & Bruckman, 2014, p. 1029).

The "terms of service" for various content sharing and social computing sites often do not include intellectual property rights, which is "often invisible" (Fiesler, Lampe, & Bruckman, 2016, p. 1450). There is variance in licensing terms. Some are written in "legalese" that may be convoluted (Fiesler, Lampe, & Bruckman, 2016, p. 1454). Some users of these sites maintain a naïve assumption that the social content sharing sites are set up to protect user interests (Fiesler, Lampe, & Bruckman, 2016, p. 1459). Only a minority of site users read the fine print.

Researchers have found the need for more clarity around intellectual property in sites that share user-generated contents (UGC) based on pervasive confusions about "reuse and remix" and "legal or policy rules" (Fiesler, Feuston, & Bruckman, 2015, p. 116). Often, there is high variance in how the respective laws are understood, resulting in complex norms of behavior (Fiesler, Feuston, & Bruckman, 2015, p. 117). Misconceptions of copyright and intellectual property are widespread in terms of remixed prior works of various types (Fiesler, Feuston, & Bruckman, 2015, p. 118). Another challenge is that "contacting copyright owners rarely has a positive result" (Fiesler, Feuston, & Bruckman, 2015, p. 121), meaning that many works that would have otherwise been created would not be or at least not be shared or published on the Social Web. At the other extreme, plagiarism and appropriation are seen as common problems, with many artists striving to display their works digitally, albeit without being copied (Fiesler, Feuston, & Bruckman, 2015, p. 122). Online art communities show "strong evidence of social norms against plagiarism" (Fiesler, Feuston, & Bruckman, 2015, p. 123). The challenges of protecting IP may be partially handled with built-in content identification systems, based on artificial intelligence and automation in some social sharing systems, such as the video sharing site YouTube (run by Google).

Where understandings of the complex formalisms of IP do not exist, that gap tends to be filled with informalisms: "Where legal knowledge is imperfect, ethical intuitions and community norms fill in the gaps in online environments of creative sharing" observes one researcher, citing work on his dissertation (Fiesler, 2014, p. 49).

The social norms around copyright may help enforce cooperative behavior, for a healthy and vibrant online community. Implicit norms arise based on how people interact. In terms of IP, people stay in line in many cases because of concerns of various "social consequences" such as public shaming (Fiesler & Bruckman, 2019, pp. 15-16). Communities enforce regulations among themselves in many ways. Given the power of social norms in a social group, based on social identity and the need for belonging, one research team proposes the benefit of creating formal rules organically based on the community's existing and evolving social norms (Fiesler & Bruckman, 2019, p. 1). This is a bottom-up sort of policy making proposed.

Going Online for Design Studio Learning Experiences

Web 2.0 platforms offer various tools for the modern art student: tagging, social image sharing, blogging, podcasting, wiki-sharing (Buffington, 2008, p. 303). These enable learners to find their own voice and engage an audience. Learners can collaborate around art, to explore the larger world of art, and to be able to engage "a broader audience" through publishing their work online (Buffington, 2008, p. 306).

Various social media are used to create a design studio learning experience. One work found that the "ease of communication, unlimited exposure to peer progress, and archiving and backtracking capabilities attained through social media use had positive effects on student success" (Güler, 2015, p. 192). This researcher also found that "peer plagiarism and pedagogical lurking did not negatively affect students' performances" (Güler, 2015, p. 192) although these were concerns. The centrality of constructive critiques in design studios helped learners improve their work. These setups involved participation between the learners and also with the presence of supportive experts.

Some online sites have similar features to design studios such as those "supporting interaction, active learning, and social engagement" (Fleischmann, 2014, p. 39). The tools can enrich studio culture (Fleischmann, 2014, p. 39), and these enable long-distance collaborations with other learners (p. 42).

A more recent work found significant learning gains for learners of design engaging in cross-organizational communities of practice online (Mavri, Ioannou, & Loizides, Cross-organisational…, 2021). Design students benefit from engaging with industry players and developing an awareness of "the broader geography of professional practice" to help adjust their goals to align better with realities (Mavri, Ioannou, & Loizides, 2020, p. 1). Their study found that "feedback came mostly in the form of 'direct recommendations' (process-oriented), rather than plain 'judgements' (task-oriented)" (Mavri, Ioannou, & Loizides, 2020, p. 10), in this community of practice on Behance. The online community of practice interactions enabled "a strong *immediate learning* value" for students in higher education (Mavri, Ioannou, & Loizides, Value creation…, 2021, p. 2); further, they found "extensive and challenging forms of feedback" (Mavri, Ioannou, & Loizides, Value creation…, 2021, p. 27), resulting in changes to learners' senses of ambition.

DeviantArts and other similar sites enable learners to create electronic portfolios to showcase their work and stand to benefit student learning (Christopher, 2011). The uses of electronic portfolios would require pedagogical design if it is to replace analog portfolios for students of design (McDermott-Dalton, 2021, p. 1). Various factors may need work: the rules of the portfolio, the different versions of technologies, the target subject matter, and others. There may be some "primary contradictions in the design portfolio activity system" (McDermott-Dalton, 2021, p. 11) that require resolution.

Researchers have studied some constraints to using Behance for a small group of students in higher education over a 14-week period in a formal course. Some of the challenges identified were technical ones, such as the graphical user interface, the limitations on file formats, and platform tool functionality. This research studied also found non-technical reasons: "(a) social factors, (b) conflict of learning styles, (c) time to learn and use, (d) use of languages, (e) lack of resources, and (f) security and privacy" (Tan & Yuen, 2018, p. 335).

Another work explains how to enable community-enhanced web-based tutorials to enable enriched teaching and learning online (Lafreniere, Grossman, & Fitzmaurice, Apr. 2013, p. 1779). There are benefits to designing learning contents based on some wisdom from crowds.

Others have noted the affordances for learning in online informal learning communities, too, such as on news sharing sites and communities (Hudgins, Lynch, Schmal, Sikka, Swenson, & Joyner, 2020, p. 91). This study involved classifying various members of the online space based on how they participate, whether they engage broadly or selectively (exclusively) or initiate discussion threads broadly or exclusively, among others (Hudgins, Lynch, Schmal, Sikka, Swenson, & Joyner, 2020, p. 96). People learn by creating in skill-building communities, by consuming others' works, and socializing in the online communities, with differing experiences in different spaces (Hudgins, Lynch, Schmal, Sikka, Swenson, & Joyner, 2020, p. 97); they learn by engaging through asking and answering questions and moderating discussions (p. 98); critiquing, reading, and writing (p. 99), posting and sharing (p. 110), tagging, and other activities.

Many agree that there are benefits for arts educators to "further consider digital platforms when designing formal learning experiences and create curriculum that harnesses the informal learning mechanisms supported by affinity spaces" (Wu, 2016, p. 22), so that popular culture can inform arts education. One favorite is DeviantArt, an "online affinity space" that cultivates "prosumers" (Wu, 2016, p. 24), people who both produce and consume online materials (in this case, art). The site may be used to acclimate art-making novices into the work (Wu, 2016, p. 24). The learning here tends towards social learning and less individual learning (Wu, 2016, p. 25). This research focuses on works derived from the "narrative or visuals of Minecraft, with various artifacts such as "drawings, paintings, media, and objects" (Wu, 2016, p. 30). The researcher observes: "In essence, prosumers are practicing with each other the reciprocal relationship between art making and art appreciation; they are learning to how to give criticism as well as how to incorporate criticisms into revising their production practices" (Wu, 2016, p. 33).

Engagement on DeviantArt is thought to benefit art skills, New Literacy learning, new conceptualizations of art, and professional dispositions, among others. The learning on this space may stand in for more formal learning in many cases. Participants may upload "visual cultural products" (Jones, 2015, p. 342). In this context, teaching involves "participatory sharing" (Jones, 2015, p. 351). It includes collective problem solving.

Teacher roles do change with the integration of social media in the teaching and learning (Castro, 2012). While some online "third spaces" are harnessed for helping teenagers engage visual culture and "playful pedagogy," as part of formal learning, such spaces are rooted in "a discourse of dissent and conflict" with various implications for art education (Olson, 2016, p. 8). The "conflicting ideas or values" result in tensions (Olson, 2016, p. 13), and there may be contested senses of appropriate pedagogy (p. 18). Teachers who use the Social Web's affordances for their teaching may have to enable adjustments for their teaching and their students' learning.

There has been the long practice of using available tools for educational purposes and the improvement of creative outcomes, including for students of art and design (Al Hashimi, Zaki, Al Muwali, & Mahdi, 2019). It helps to learn where learners are actually going for particular artful purposes, in real life. The coauthors write:

> When asked to brainstorm at the beginning of the experiment, most respondents (94%), n = 30) indicated that they used Pinterest to draw inspiration. Instagram (41%, n = 13) and Google Images (41%, n = 13) were used by some, followed by Tumblr (31%, n = 10). Only (a) few students used Google + (16%, n = 5), Mind Map (13%, n = 4), YouTube (9%, n = 3), WhatsApp (6%, n = 2), Behance (3%, n = 1), and Facebook (3%, n = 1) respectively. (Al Hashimi, Zaki, Al Muwali, & Mahdi, 2019, p. 324)

Certainly, this is a highly dynamic space, with a lot of changes even in short time spans. There is wide variance, also, among different learner groups. The creative economy requires "digital literacy" for creatives (whether digital natives or immigrants) to engage in the use of digital technology (Nikou, Cavalheiro, & Widén, 2020, p. 343). To invest the time to learn such technologies, they have to see the practical value in such engagement, such as through "perceived usefulness" and "ease of use and related "social norms" (Nikou, Cavalheiro, & Widén, 2020, p. 343).

For university courses in the creative disciplines, creative online collaboration using Social Web technologies has to be designed effectively. One work presents a framework for how to enable creative online collaboration. The research team offers some practical directions:

1. Encourage coaching and peer-driven learning
2. Nourish a culture of open feedback and reflection
3. Encourage your staff and students to experiment with the latest online collaboration tools
4. Create authentic contexts for creative projects, e.g., by approaching industry partners
5. Evaluate and research creative online collaboration within its own context (and not from the perspective of a physical collaboration. (Stockleben, et al., 2017, p. 595)

The learning benefits from pedagogical design, not just setting learners loose in technologies per se.

Social Image Datasets, Art Collaborative Data for Computational Innovations

Given the "deluge" of social imagery, including art, the only real effective way of analyzing such bounty requires computational means, to "analyze large sets of user-created art related imagers using image features describing color, texture, composition and orientation" to classify works into different groups with different "feature vectors and clustering parameters" (Ushizima, Manovich, Margolis, & Douglas, 2012, p. 30). Digitized large-scale visual arts collections are used for various computational deep learning (Castellano & Vessio, 2021, p. 487), to benefit cultural learning.

Various image datasets from both sites have been used to inform computer science research. One involves using computational means to extract affect or emotion from abstract paintings, based on human-informed software programming (Sartori, 2014). The foci are on color and texture. Humans will read the titles of the visual artworks for meaning making (Sartori, 2014, p. 387), so having quality metadata is important. The DeviantArt dataset with "220 million individual pieces of art" (Sartori, Yanulevskaya, Salah, Uijlings, Bruni, & Sebe, 2015, p. 8:25) was used to study human emotions encoded in artworks and how well algorithmic processes could be applied to understand these emotions. If humans can experience the emotions that artists imbue in their work, is it possible also to design computer programs to enable the same capability albeit with machine perception? Is it possible to code art theory knowledge into machines to enable the application of these ideas to analyze both professional and amateur art for emotions? Indeed, a team has created such a program that can be empirically shown to perform emotion extraction (recognize emotions) from visual artworks (Sartori, Yanulevskaya, Salah, Uijlings, Bruni, & Sebe, 2015). Another later work involved the creation of labeled image datasets with emotion polarities identified (Alarcao & Fonseca, 2018, p. 47), to enable research based on that data. Another study based on affective computing is based on "large-scale heterogeneous multimedia data," such as imagery, video, sound, and other multimedia contents (Zhao, Wang, Soleymani, Joshi, & Ji, 2019, p. 1).

Computational means have been applied to making photos more memorable to viewers by applying various style filters from a seeding style image (Siarohin, Zen, Majtanovic, Alameda-Pineda, Ricci, & Sebe, 2017), with empirically supported results. People tend to remember visuals that are surprising in some dimension or dimensions.

Another work has used socially shared visuals (from the wild) to train a computer program to clean up rough manual sketches (of various kinds) to vector graphics. The cleanup enables smoother handling of real-world ambiguity; it may help express something of the sketcher's intentionality (Yan, Vanderhaeghe, & Gingold, 2020).

Another work applied computational art analysis to a mixed art set with social graph network data on social connections and found that there was "no connection between a visual style on the one hand and social proximity, gender, and nationality on the other" (Huckle, Garcia, & Nakashima, 2020, pp. 126 and 139).

Machine vision and various algorithms (like classifiers) benefit from training on people's artwork, which is "not constrained to mimic the physical world," and so is more challenging for machine vision and computers to parse. Putting together an artistic dataset from Behance helps to improve the performance of algorithmic classifiers (Wilber, Fang, Jin, Hertzmann, Collomosse, & Belongie, 2017, p. 1202). This way, researchers can test their new algorithms against a set of labeled or tagged visuals.

Another study explored the language used around creative inspiration by users of user-generated contents. One study examined how people use language to show their "level of motivation" and to inferentially predict future work (Tomlinson, Bracewell, Krug, & Hinote, 2014, p. 176), based on prospect theory.

Another study used data from a site for artists and designers (Dribbble) to study whether viral events occurred on such a site. The researchers took a user-experience perspective for their work based on interview data. On this particular site at the time of the research, users could share URLs but not directly do "a share or retweet" (Hemsley & Tanupabrungsun, 2018, p. 29) from the platform. They found that many of the users went to the site to keep up with art trends (Hemsley & Tanupabrungsun, 2018, p. 32). They found virality does exist on the platform but suggest that this phenomenon of fast popularity may differ on different social media platforms.

Evolution of Social Networks

One study focused on how social networks evolve on online platforms, with initial predictions about who will become popular based on initial link formation (Brandt & Leskovec, 2014, p. 229). Another finding in this work was that the "mutual-friend motif" was uncommon in DeviantArt as a social space. The researchers found that network structure is indicative of future user behavior (Brandt & Leskovec, 2014, p. 230). People do interact in different ways on different social media sites. For DeviantArt, "while degree features successfully identify a few popular nodes, especially at high values of k, motif features allow the algorithm to distinguish many more" popular nodes (Brandt & Leskovec, 2014, p. 230). Small group connections can be revelatory.

Open creative production occurring on portals built around design culture involve inherent tensions. One study identified tensions "between production and consumption, professional and amateur practices, work and play and expression/exploration and service" (Turner-Rahman, 2008, p. 371). Creative knowledge spaces online offer opportunities for "reinterpretation and remixing," sharing of resources, discussions of techniques, and other activities (Turner-Rahman, 2008, p. 373). A critical aspect of such spaces includes the offering of "inspirational work" (Turner-Rahman, 2008, p. 377). However, there has been a long-standing challenge with corporations usurping the works of many unpaid creatives, even as they make work "that breaks down long-standing paradigms and advances not only some fabled visual style or technical methodology but also the designer's own reputation" (Turner-Rahman, 2008, p. 378). Still, it is important to note that the creative sector is critical for the "economies of all advanced capitalist countries" (Freedman, 2010, p. 9). Artful express involves both "reproduction as well as production" (Freedman, 2010, p. 13), drawing on prior knowledge. The artful creator is not often creating work that is wholly original but is somewhat derived from the past and prior practice.

A lesser-known threat is also present in the social content-sharing sites. "Repurposing attacks" involves injecting malware into content—such as those of shared artworks online—to create vulnerabilities in computer systems in order to steal data or funds or other compromises. This is a type of attack that "specifically targets sites that host user uploaded content on Web 2.0 sites" (Sundareswaran & Squicciarini, 2019, p. 199). Various technologies are arrayed against this type of cybercrime, given the evolving cyber threat environment, including the

DeCore system (Detecting Content Repurposing) (Sundareswaran & Squicciarini, 2019, p. 200).

Another work focuses on the migrating of an online fandom art community from one social platform to another. Fan communities move for reasons such as the platform and various technological affordances and community interactions and dynamics (Fiesler & Dym, 2020, p. 42:8). Perhaps a newer site offers different affordances (p. 42:9). There may be problems of trust of the platform and those who run it (p. 42:11) because users of the platforms need to feel aligned with the values and design of the technology and trust in the protection of their contents. A move is not without costs, with the losses of art contents (Fiesler & Dym, 2020, p. 42:13), some members staying behind, and other challenges. Some fandom groups disappear, with members heading off to different platforms, and losing their sense of being an entity. In some cases, there may be no other platform in the social ecological space for a group to go to with the desirable features (Fiesler & Dym, 2020, p. 42:17). Moves may progress at different paces, and it helps to preserve both members and content in a move.

Does virality exist on art communities? If so, how does it manifest on niche sites? One study found that such viral-like events do exist. The dynamics of such virality is similar to those found on other more generalist social media sites (Hemsley & Tanupabrungsun, 2018, p. 91).

Various special interest communities are meaningful to many. These affinity spaces bring together those with shared interests on particular topics. One work looks at how people interact in rich ways around miniatures used to depict wargaming and how these artifacts may be datafied in a time of the Internet of Things (IoT) (Darzentas, Brown, Flintham, & Benford, 2015, p. 2427). This community engages on art-space communities and are an example of community based around specific interests. The activities involve both a physical analog and the digital, the social, and the historical. The coauthors write: "The complexity of miniatures' lives is reflected in the richness of their data footprints. A striking feature of our study was the time and attention given over to documenting their lives in various forms, from notebooks and files to databases and blogs, and for diverse audiences including owners, players, opponents, crafters, traders and collectors" (Darzentas, Brown, Flintham, & Benford, 2015, p. 2434).

Fan focuses arise based on various interests, particular cultural facets and practices. Various events in the art space may have long-term effects on art practices and cultures (Lam, 2010). Fan focuses may be on the renowned dark poet and writer, Edgar Allan Poe, memorialized with various artworks on DeviantArt (Zimmerman, 2014). Fan communities are places where teaching and learning occur. One work points to the benefits of informal "distributed mentoring" on social fanfiction communities online in helping fans evolve their creations (Evans, Davis, Evans, Campbell, Randall, Yin, & Aragon, 2017, p. 259). Some affinity spaces are built around particular modalities of creative contents, such as animated illustrations and narratives (Shi, Li, Xu, & Cao, 2021, p. 1).

In terms of artful expressions, some suggest that they may be adopted in more ubiquitous ways for people to socialize and interact. One research team suggests that sketching "as a social medium has been largely left behind" (Cowan, Weibel, Pina, Hollan, & Griswold, 2011, p. 395). They propose some technology that may be integrated on social media to enable "sketching's unique affordances for visual communication" and to enable the conveying of "visuo-spatial ideas directly" through "minimal detail" and with "the peculiarities of handwriting" (Cowan, Weibel, Pina, Hollan, & Griswold, 2011, p. 395). They suggest that "ubiquitous sketching creates a synergy with the practice of posting context-dependent information, and ... it broadens and deepens social interactions" (Cowan, Weibel, Pina, Hollan, & Griswold, 2011, p. 395).

Acquiring Critiques and Feedback Online

An important aspect towards developing as an artist and a designer involves receiving design critique and working constructively with that information. Many crowd-source design critiques, but the quality of the feedback may vary, with some comments perhaps off-topic. Some respondents may have "limited skills, motivation, or time" (Xu & Bailey, 2011, p. 1183). One way to enhance the value of such feedback is to break down the critique into subtasks (Xu & Bailey, 2011, p. 1184). One setup for crowdsourcing online critique involves a few basic steps: describing the work, identifying its strengths and weaknesses, and summarizing the feedback (Xu & Bailey, 2011, p. 1185).

Another research work involves comparing various crowd platform types and the feedback acquired from each in terms of "quantity, quality, and content of the feedback received" (Yen, Dow, Gerber, & Bailey, 2016, p. 773). Here, crowds are "driven by social status, enjoyment, and financial gain," as some main motivators (p. 773). The co-researchers summarize: "Our results show, for example, that task markets yield more suggestions, online forums provide more process feedback, and social networks give the most suggestions without payment" (p. 773). From this work, there are strategies for eliciting feedback from more appropriate crowds. There are suggestions for how to enhance feedback services. They write:

> If a designer fears criticism, which can affect self-efficacy and receptivity to the feedback, it is best to solicit feedback from a financial crowd. Our results showed that this type of crowd produced the most positive-valenced feedback and was not sensitive to the design iteration. The other two crowds were equally critical. (Yen, Dow, Gerber, & Bailey, 2016, p. 781)

What if there is interest in acquiring content feedback? "From the content analysis, if a designer wants to receive insight or observations about the process for creating the design, she should solicit feedback from enjoyment crowds. If it is an initial design, the designer could also choose to get feedback from their social network" (Yen, Dow, Gerber, & Bailey, 2016, p. 781).

In terms of recommendations for improvement, the "financial crowd" should be accessed "regardless of the iteration"; if the designer needs to watch funds, "the next best choice is to use his or her social network" (Yen, Dow, Gerber, & Bailey, 2016, p. 781). The financial crowd is also suggested for those who want their designs "to be assessed holistically" and if they want the most "elaborative feedback" (Yen, Dow, Gerber, & Bailey, 2016, p. 782). Interestingly, the quality of feedback is similar in quality "from any of the crowd genres tested" (Yen, Dow, Gerber, & Bailey, 2016, p. 782).

Designers have a "demand for authentic, timely, and affordable feedback" (Foong, Dow, Bailey, & Gerber, 2017, p. 4454). According to this research team, online spaces that enable feedback and critique are complex. They describe a need for social systems to "address broader socio-psychological factors, such as how intent should be communicated online, how dialogue can support the interpretation of feedback, and how to balance the tradeoffs of anonymizing feedback providers" (Foong, Dow, Bailey, & Gerber, 2017, p. 4454), given complex human intersubjectivities. They explore various mechanisms of online feedback exchange (OFE) systems, including the definition of "crowd genre," "rewards for giving feedback," ways to connect with designers, anonymization options for feedback providers, and other contents (Foong, Dow, Bailey, & Gerber, 2017, p. 4457). This work also advocates for structuring the feedback process to be more beneficial to designers.

The phrasing of language—particularly its affect—affects whether a critique is received or not. The mechanisms are explained this way: "...critiques with positive affective language increased positive emotions and reduced participants' annoyance and frustration, which led to an increase in work quality" as contrasted with those without positive language (Nguyen, Gancarz, Ng, Dabbash, & Dow, 2017, p. 1024). They write: "Feedback *without* positive affective language led to more edits, but not better work outcomes" (Nguyen, Gancarz, Ng, Dabbash, & Dow, 2017, p. 1024). Feedback from "an anonymous source than from a peer or an authority" (Nguyen, Gancarz, Ng, Dabbash, & Dow, 2017, p. 1024) was better received. Online platforms on which people collaborate can be designed to encourage more "fruitful feedback" (Nguyen, Gancarz, Ng, Dabbash, & Dow, 2017, p. 1024). Other research has focused on how to improve crowdwork quality especially for complex tasks. Research teams have found that it is beneficial to educate crowd workers of the target task and then structure the work to elicit quality insights (Greenberg, Easterday, & Gerber, 2015, p. 237). Offering scaffolds for the feedback, and offering scaffolds with examples both resulted in longer critiques and in "a higher quantity of idea units coded as High Quality units" (Greenberg, Easterday, & Gerber, 2015, p. 240). However, both scaffolded conditions "produced a higher quantity of Low Quality idea units as well" (Greenberg, Easterday, & Gerber, 2015, p. 241). Crowd-based reviewers also provided more examples when the elicitations for their reviews involved scaffolding with examples (Greenberg, Easterday, & Gerber, 2015, p. 241). Structuring and modeling responses enhances the quality of the responses.

Those working hard problems may benefit from crowd-provided novice-based formative feedback.

> The project found that to provide formative feedback on ill-defined problems, crowdcritique (sic) systems should provide a combination of technical features, including: quick invite tools; formative framing; a public, near-synchronous social media interface; critique scaffolds; 'like' system community hashtags; analysis tools and 'to do' lists; along with social practices including prep/write-first/write-last script and critique training. (Easterday, Lewis, & Gerber, 2017, p. 623)

This group integrates the social dynamics of groups and understandings of human psychology to the work. The research resulted in the identification of the main challenges of crowdcritique systems: "understanding quality early, sharing work, over scaffolding, evaluation apprehension, (and) reviewing/synthesizing" (Easterday, Lewis, & Gerber, 2017, p. 645), which they address with possible socio-technical solutions, summarized as "scaffolding with social-media conventions" (p. 647).

Another method to improve crowd-sourced design feedback involves "a novel semi-automated method to support feedback providers by analyzing feedback language" (Krause, Garncarz, Song, Gerber, Bailey, & Dow, 2017, p. 4627), to raise the awareness of what is being shared by the reviewer. The analysis of the language may predict "perceived helpfulness" of the feedback (Krause, Garncarz, Song, Gerber, Bailey, & Dow, 2017, p. 4633), and it may inform the style of critiques so that the feedback may be more readily accepted.

Feedback may be delivered in different ways. On one system, feedback is delivered as "annotations" of the creative work (Chakraborty, 2015, p. 209). This system also enables the creator of the work to explain the context and goals to help inform the crowd critique.

Livestreaming around Art Practice

Many artists of varying levels of expertise livestream their art-making online. One platform enables an artist to co-draw with others in a live whiteboard-like workspace. As they work, they share their thought processes. They may engage in text chats, voice interactions, and other communications modalities. This platform features various tools enabling enrichment of interactions, including graphic symbols, interactive overlays with various functionalities, additional collaborative interaction spaces (Lu, Kazi, Wei, Dontcheva, & Karahalios, 2021, p. 58:6), user-generated live tagging (p. 58:9), commenting on videos (p. 58:10), and others. These researchers suggest the importance of building tools for the needs of the livestreaming presenter as well as those of the audience.

Researchers have explored why artists engage in livestreaming. For some, it provides them with an external sense of "accountability" for their "solitary creative work" (Fraser, Dontcheva, Kim, & Klemmer, 2019, p. 48). Conducting live online events enables some with a sufficient number of viewers to acquire funds for their work. For others, they may acquire new clients. There are challenges to dealing with the "split attention" of creating while also engaging with a live audience (Fraser, Dontcheva, Kim, & Klemmer, 2019, p. 49). Certainly, live streamers are *in situ* physically but also virtually, and focusing on their own minds and that of the live audience. The competition for attention on the Social Web is also harsh.

Researchers have explored the various types of creative livestreams. They found four common types: "teaching, making, socializing, and performing" (Fraser, Kim, Thornsberry, Klemmer, & Dontcheva, 2019, p. 144). Many watch creative livestreams to be inspired and to learn (Fraser, Kim, Thornsberry, Klemmer, & Dontcheva, 2019, p. 145) but also to have a sense of community (p. 152). They benefit from observing the challenges that the artist (or art team) faces and the mistakes made along the way.

There are proposals to enrich the communications of participants engaging in a livestream. One is to enable participant screenshotting a part or a whole screen of a livestream event and comment on that and share in the chat window (Yang, Lee, Shin, & Kim, 2020, p. 1). This extends the modality of communications into the visual space, for higher dimensionality.

For all the value of creative livestreams, many are too natively long for full viewing (some running several hours). Researchers have created a tool for "automatic temporal segmentation of creative live stream videos" based on audio transcript and log data of software use (Fraser, Kim, Shin, Brandt, & Dontcheva, 2020, p. 1). This enables chunking of the various segments, so viewers may experience archives of livestreaming broadcasts in more meaningful ways. The value of the livestream archives may be extended.

High Technology Innovations for Creating Visuals

There have been various innovations to extend people's capabilities to paint. One program enables the drawing of digital textures and malleable digital objects (Lukáč, Fišer, Bazin,

Jamriška, Sorkine-Hornung, & Sýkora, 2013, p. 1). In some cases, the technologies take on various roles. A separate work shares just how much designers are going to the cloud to work, and how much cloud-based design has different effects on workflows and productivity (Naskova, 2017, p. 540).

Enabling Job Hunts

Various aspects of online social art communities enable job seeking for job seekers and employee finding for those hiring. One research work describes a program to scrape curriculum vitae (CV) data from online social networks and to create an XML CV that may be used with other technologies (Dias, Gancarski, & Henriques, 2015, p. 258).

Another work explored the seeking of top user experience (UX)/user interface (UI) talent on Behance, given the many artistic disciplines of those using the site. In this work, the researchers created a UX/UI designer social network subgraph by identifying intensity clusters. They described their method in their abstract:

> We…developed a metric to assess the influence and importance of a specific member of the community based on structural properties of the subgraph and additional measures of prestige. For that purpose, we identified appreciations as a useful measure to include in a weighted PageRank algorithm, as it adds a notion of perceived quality of the work in the artist's portfolio to the ranking, which is not contained in the structural information of the graph. (Halstead, Serrano, & Proctor, 2015, p. 2426)

The information was used to identify geographical locales with "a high density of influential UX/UI designers" (Halstead, Serrano, & Proctor, 2015, p. 2426).

Another approach uses social network structures to "rank designs and users in online design communities" (Deka, et al., 2015, p. 1887). Such information may be used to inform on work and hiring on projects.

At-Home Manufacturing

Technologies play an important part in present-day common art-making. Home entrepreneurs or "homepreneurs" use at-home manufacturing and personal fabrication for moneymaking online and offline (Annett, 2020, p. 99:1) even as each strives to find a place in "saturated markets" (p. 99:26). On the Social Web are many do-it-yourself (DIY) communities, where "expert amateur" individuals go to work and create and share (Kuznetsov & Paulos, 2010). Some e-commerce sites' administrators select particularly creative leaders who embody the values of the online community, such as top sellers of creative works on Etsy (Pace, O'Donnell, DeWitt, Bardzell, & Bardzell, Feb. 2013, p. 1023). In this work, many of the "featured sellers" have professional training in their respective art and craft fields (Pace, O'Donnell, DeWitt, Bardzell, & Bardzell, Feb. 2013, p. 1027), so these are not typical "amateurs" by any stretch.

Self-Branding Online

Many creatives create identities online as part of a personal brand, to vie for attention, name recognition, and paid work. One study found that while creatives are supposed to create a consistent personal brand, they engage in a continuous negotiation of self-presentation in different ways on different social media platforms. They build identities based on the "imagined affordances" of the particular platform, their sense of audience, and "the producer's self-concept" (Duffy, Pruchniewska, & Scolere, 2017, p. 1). Freelancers do "face acute challenges securing work" (Foong, 2020, p. 26), and they benefit from various design elements on online platforms that help them manage their impressions with potential clients. Those who would create job opportunities for themselves online often have to self-brand in a competitive social media ecology.

Finally, a small research team has conducted some early research on the flow of innovation in DeviantArt. They explore how ideas and practices can travel through such sites and become shared by others on sites that host user-generated artworks. They write:

> Each artwork is by definition something new, in the sense that it shows skill and imagination and has novelty beyond what exists up to its creation. In reality, artists are always influenced by other artists, artworks and ideas when creating new works, and it is sometimes possible to trace these influences. (Salah & Salah, 2013, p. 140)

They make an art-historical observation: "Even though it's common to have multiple artists apply and develop similar techniques, usually only one artist (or at most a few) will be associated with it" (Salah & Salah, 2013, p. 140). Novelty can be identified using "visual inspection" to identify transfer of visual materials, even by non-experts (Salah & Salah, 2013, p. 143) even though in more formal art spaces, "historical information and close scrutiny of technique, composition and content are required to establish influences between artworks." (Salah & Salah, 2013, p. 147). Computational means may be used for identifying visual novelty based on "comparing an image with prior images in terms of these derived features" ("content and structure defined using an Inception neural network" and "capturing visual aesthetics using classical compositional features" (Wachs, Daróczy, Hannák, Páll, & Riedl, 2018, p. 163). In this study, the co-researchers found the following:

> We find that on this professional platform, users with dense local networks tend to produce more novel but generally less successful images, with important exceptions. Namely, users making novel images while embedded in cohesive local networks are more successful. (Wachs, Daróczy, Hannák, Páll, & Riedl, 2018, p. 163)

One insight from the above is that there are other dimensions besides novelty that inform on the success of a visual design. The individuals at the center of particular denser collectives also did not seem to create the most novelty (p. 171), perhaps because their social roles are too constrained.

Research Methods

This research work will focus on both DeviantArt and Behance to see what aspects of the online social networks contribute to visual art novelty.

Results

This section begins with a light "overview" of both sites based on some indirection, in this case, how both are seen indirectly based on a third-party social image sharing site and related tags surrounding both entities: DeviantArt and Behance.

DeviantArt and Behance on Flickr

Flickr is among the "five most popular photo-sharing websites" (Lu, Wu, & Sang, 2017, p. 55), and analyzing related tags network data from this site may be insightful of mass-scale thinking around the topic of "DeviantArt" and "Behance" (with names which are disambiguated and unique). To acclimate to the visual space, a related tags network was conducted for both terms.

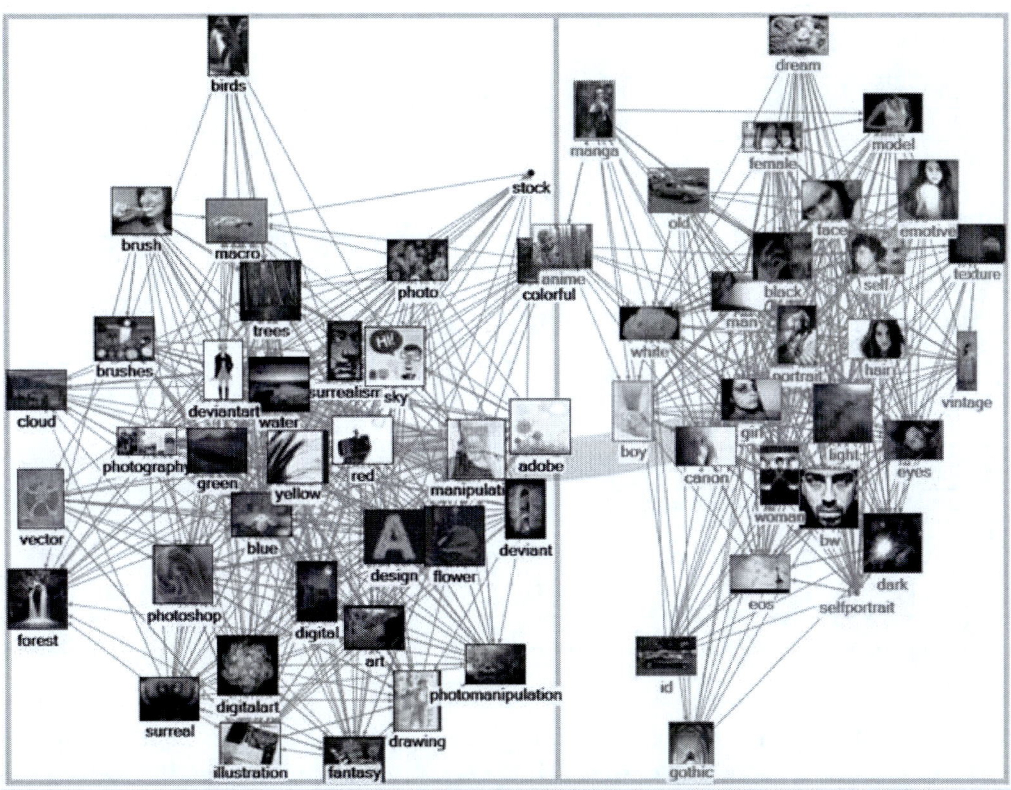

Figure 1. "DeviantArt" related tags network on Flickr social image sharing site (1.5 Deg.).

Table 1. Graph metrics table for "DeviantArt" related tags network on Flickr social image sharing site (1.5 Deg.)

Graph Metric	Value
Graph Type	Directed
Vertices	62
Unique Edges	1335
Edges With Duplicates	0
Total Edges	1335
Self-Loops	0
Reciprocated Vertex Pair Ratio	0.198384201
Reciprocated Edge Ratio	0.331086142
Connected Components	1
Single-Vertex Connected Components	0
Maximum Vertices in a Connected Component	62
Maximum Edges in a Connected Component	1335
Maximum Geodesic Distance (Diameter)	2
Average Geodesic Distance	1.388137
Graph Density	0.352987837
Modularity	Not Applicable
NodeXL Version	1.0.1.336

Table 2. Graphic metrics table for "Behance" related tags network on Flickr social image sharing site (1.5 Deg.)

Graph Metric	Value
Graph Type	Directed
Vertices	5
Unique Edges	15
Edges With Duplicates	0
Total Edges	15
Self-Loops	0
Reciprocated Vertex Pair Ratio	0.5
Reciprocated Edge Ratio	0.666666667
Connected Components	1
Single-Vertex Connected Components	0
Maximum Vertices in a Connected Component	5
Maximum Edges in a Connected Component	15
Maximum Geodesic Distance (Diameter)	1
Average Geodesic Distance	0.8
Graph Density	0.75
Modularity	Not Applicable
NodeXL Version	1.0.1.336

The DeviantArt related tags network on Flickr shows two groups (based on clustering of the extracted data using the Clauset-Newman-Moore clustering algorithm). The first group on the left focused more on art and design, and the second group on the right focused more on photography. The tags evoke various types of visuals: macro photography such as of insects and smaller objects; tools such as "brush" and "brushes"; subjects of imagery such birds, trees, clouds, forest, flowers, and others; styles like gothic, fantasy; self-portrait, black/white, vintage, manga; modeling as a practice; modalities of digital image types, like vector, stock imagery; common software for digital image editing, like "Adobe" and "Photoshop"; artful practices, like art, digital art, illustration, design, and others. The connections show the co-appearance of folk tags applied to works uploaded to Flickr. The graph may be seen in Figure 1, and the underlying network graph data may be seen in Table 1.

The "Behance" related tags network on Flickr resulted in only one group. There are extracted tags like "poster" and "illustration" and "design" and "art." The tags are less diverse (Figure 2 and Table 2).

The visualized tags from Flickr are those determined by the site for the term. These are not very dynamic visuals; rather, they stay the same over time. Finally, it is likely that some members are active on both sites. DeviantArt and Behance offer different affordances.

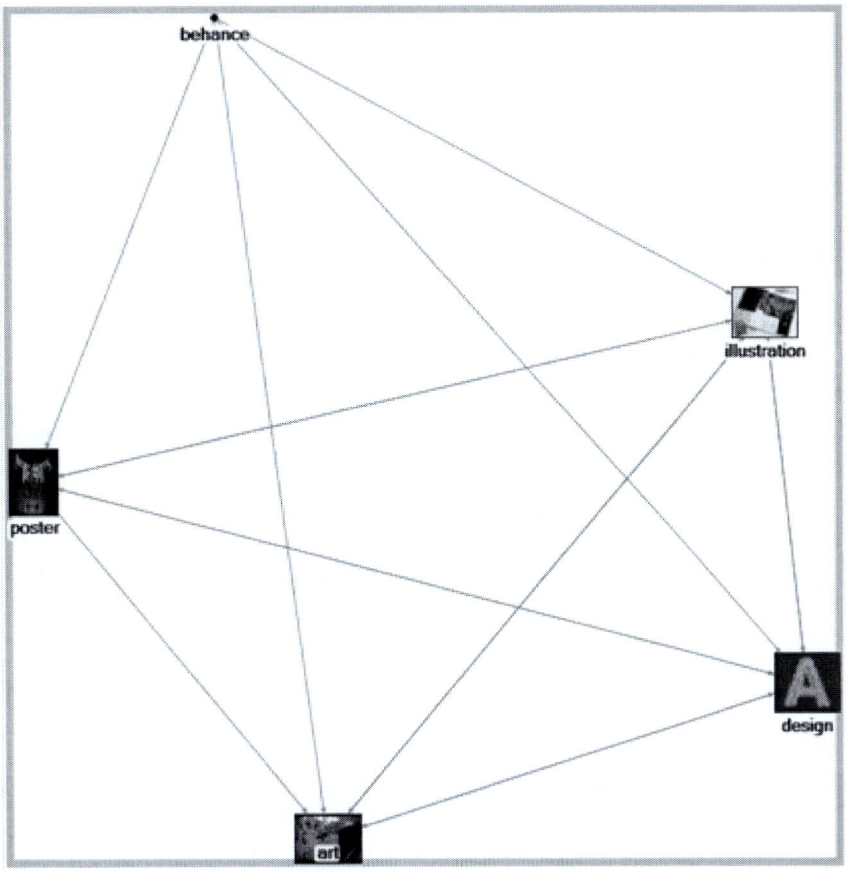

Figure 2. "Behance" related tags network on Flickr social image sharing site (1.5 Deg.).

Innovation Everywhere

Initially, the idea was to find ways to identify novelty…and then to see how the artist described arriving at the work…and then seeing if there were references to the respective platforms and other indicators (like callouts to other artists on the platform). The idea was to systematize the research even though this would be a qualitative manual research process. Then, when I finally had time to more fully immerse in both DeviantArt and Behance, I realized that the works are all individually quite novel on the platform even if they may not have been directly so within the genre. There are so many influences possible: culture and cultural references, intention, material, art style, art modalities, textualities, narratives, symbols, aesthetics, colors, numbers…that the high dimensionality alone would result in novelty. Then, it becomes an issue of what is novel to the viewer, and that depends on subjectivities and prior experience and taste.

Discussion

The presentational features of the respective sites, the built-in recommender systems, the search capabilities, the navigational affordances, the social membership affordances, and other factors all enable the sharing and the discovery of novelty. The personhood of individuals enables collaborations for those who so choose to connect and co-create something together.

Future Research

Future research may include ways to get closer to what innovation looks like, particularly in a focused sub-part of the common art space…to get closer to answer the questions proposed in this work. Also, as online communality evolves and as various art practices evolve, the research may evolve to adapt to the various circumstances. Similar research may be achieved on different art-based social platforms for creatives.

There are private online communities for art sharing, too, and what is learned about novel art making may differ than in public online spaces. Perhaps the members are by invitation only. These private communities may be an interesting topic for research.

At the broader level, doe2s sharing socially result in early lock-in to particular statements and practices? After all, one informal artist made a video explaining why he liked to sketch with a mechanical pencil on a paper sketchbook because it limited him from making too many edits (since the paper only can take so much). At one point, he mentioned that the sketchbook was just for the individual artist, and no one else needed to see what was drafted. Yet, there he was showing his sketchbook to over a million views (and perhaps hundreds of thousands of viewers) in his b-roll. He said he did not like to paint on paper because of the mess of setting up the space to paint, in part because he has done so much of his art learning on digital devices. So are there risks to over-commitment to a stance or practice based on public statements? Does an artist—common or otherwise—lose flexibility with a false sense of need for commitment?

Conclusion

This work does offer some unique insights on how researchers and instructors harness the affordances of two well-known collaborative art spaces. Both read as fairly global in approach. The variety enabled by the high dimensionality of inputs into visual and other artworks make the shared contents vibrant and highly novel. The constant churn of art on both sites and the large number of members of both sites results in a deep dynamism. In one sense, the foundational goal of this work—exploring how novel artfulness may be enhanced with online communications—has been addressed albeit not in the way initially considered.

Acknowledgments

This is for the many common artists on DeviantArt and Behance for their unique sensibilities and unique hands in creating aesthetically pleasing works.

References

Ables, K. (2019, Apr. 19). *The rise and fall of Internet art communities*. Artsy.net.

Al Hashimi, S., Zaki, Y., Al Muwali, A., & Mahdi, N. (2019). Infusing creativity and technology through repurposing existing digital tools and social media apps for educational purposes. In *Interactivity, Game Creation, Design, Learning, and Innovation* (pp. 319-330). Springer, Cham.

Alarcao, S. M., & Fonseca, M. J. (2018). Enriching image datasets with unrestrained emotional data: A study with users. *J. Vis. Lang. Sentient Syst.*, *4*, 47-55.

Alluvatti, G. M., Capiluppi, A., De Ruvo, G., & Molfetta, M. (2011, September). User generated (web) content: trash or treasure. In *Proceedings of the 12th International Workshop on Principles of Software Evolution and the 7th annual ERCIM Workshop on Software Evolution* (pp. 81-90).

Annett, M. (2020). Understanding the Homepreneurship Opportunities Afforded by Social Networking and Personal Fabrication Technologies. *Proceedings of the ACM on Human-Computer Interaction*, *4*(CSCW2), 1-48.

Belsky, S. (2014, Mar.) Scott Belsky – The meaning of the word Behance. Creative Chair. Retrieved from https://creativechair.org/scott-belsky-the-meaning-of-the-word-behance/.

Blume, J. (2017). Exploring the potentials and challenges of virtual distribution of contemporary art. In *Digital Environments* (pp. 97-116). transcript-Verlag.

Bowler, L., Mattern, E., Jeng, W., Oh, J.S., & He, D. (2013). 'I know what you are going through': Answers to informational questions about eating disorders in *Yahoo! Answers:* A qualitative study. In the *proceedings of ASIST* 2013. Nov. 1 – 6, 2013. Montreal, Quebec, Canada, 1 – 9.

Brandt, C., & Leskovec, J. (2014, April). Status and friendship: Mechanisms of social network evolution. In *Proceedings of the 23rd International Conference on World Wide Web* (pp. 229-230).

Buffington, M. L. (2008). Creating and consuming Web 2.0 in art education. *Computers in the Schools*, *25*(3-4), 303-313.

Castellano, G., & Vessio, G. (2020). A brief overview of deep learning approaches to pattern extraction and recognition in paintings and drawings. In *ICPR Workshops (3)* (pp. 487-501).

Castro, J. C. (2012). Learning and teaching art through social media. *Studies in Art Education*, *53*(2), 152-169.

Chakraborty, A. (2015, June). Scranvas: Gamified forum for amateur designers to share creative work and generate constructive feedback. In *Proceedings of the 2015 ACM SIGCHI Conference on Creativity and Cognition* (pp. 209-212).

Christodoulou, S. P., & Styliaras, G. D. (2008, September). Digital Art 2.0: Art meets Web 2.0 trend. In *Proceedings of the 3rd international conference on Digital Interactive Media in Entertainment and Arts* (pp. 158-165).

Christopher, T. E. C. (2011, July). Encouraging student learning through online e-portfolio development. In *International Conference on ICT in Teaching and Learning* (pp. 8-21). Springer, Berlin, Heidelberg.

Cochrane, T., & Antonczak, L. (2013, September). A mobile learning community of practice: Facilitating conceptual shifts in pedagogy. In *European Conference on Technology Enhanced Learning* (pp. 430-435). Springer, Berlin, Heidelberg.

Cowan, L. G., Weibel, N., Pina, L. R., Hollan, J. D., & Griswold, W. G. (2011, August). Ubiquitous sketching for social media. In *Proceedings of the 13th International Conference on Human Computer Interaction with Mobile Devices and Services* (pp. 395-404).

Crain, P. A., & Bailey, B. P. (2017, June). Share once or share often? Exploring how designers approach iteration in a large online community. In *Proceedings of the 2017 ACM SIGCHI Conference on Creativity and Cognition* (pp. 80-92).

Darzentas, D. P., Brown, M. A., Flintham, M., & Benford, S. (2015, April). The data driven lives of wargaming miniatures. In *Proceedings of the 33rd Annual ACM Conference on Human Factors in Computing Systems* (pp. 2427-2436).

Deka, B., Yu, H., Ho, D., Huang, Z., Talton, J. O., & Kumar, R. (2015, April). Ranking designs and users in online social networks. In *Proceedings of the 33rd Annual ACM Conference Extended Abstracts on Human Factors in Computing Systems* (pp. 1887-1892).

Dias, S. M., Gancarski, A. L., & Henriques, P. R. (2015, June). Automatic generation of CVs from online social networks. In *International Symposium on Languages, Applications and Technologies* (pp. 258-263). Springer, Cham.

Duffy, B. E., Pruchniewska, U., & Scolere, L. (2017, July). Platform-specific self-branding: Imagined affordances of the social media ecology. In *Proceedings of the 8th international conference on social media & society* (pp. 1-9).

Easterday, M. W., Lewis, D. R., & Gerber, E. M. (2017). Designing crowdcritique systems for formative feedback. *International Journal of Artificial Intelligence in Education*, *27*(3), 623-663.

Evans, S., Davis, K., Evans, A., Campbell, J. A., Randall, D. P., Yin, K., & Aragon, C. (2017, February). More than peer production: Fanfiction communities as sites of distributed mentoring. In *Proceedings of the 2017 ACM Conference on Computer Supported Cooperative Work and Social Computing* (pp. 259-272).

Fiesler, C. (2014, February). Copyright and social norms in communities of content creation. In *Proceedings of the companion publication of the 17th ACM conference on Computer supported cooperative work & social computing* (pp. 49-52).

Fiesler, C., & Bruckman, A. S. (2019). Creativity, copyright, and close-knit communities: A case study of social norm formation and enforcement. *Proceedings of the ACM on Human-Computer Interaction*, *3*(GROUP), 1-24.

Fiesler, C., & Bruckman, A. S. (2014, February). Remixers' understandings of fair use online. In *Proceedings of the 17th ACM conference on Computer supported cooperative work & social computing* (pp. 1023-1032).

Fiesler, C., & Dym, B. (2020). Moving across lands: Online platform migration in fandom communities. *Proceedings of the ACM on Human-Computer Interaction*, *4*(CSCW1), 1-25.

Fiesler, C., Feuston, J. L., & Bruckman, A. S. (2015, February). Understanding copyright law in online creative communities. In *Proceedings of the 18th ACM conference on computer supported cooperative work & social computing* (pp. 116-129).

Fiesler, C., Lampe, C., & Bruckman, A. S. (2016, February). Reality and perception of copyright terms of service for online content creation. In *Proceedings of the 19th ACM conference on computer-supported cooperative work & social computing* (pp. 1450-1461).

Fiorucci, M., Khoroshiltseva, M., Pontil, M., Traviglia, A., Del Bue, A., & James, S. (2020). Machine learning for cultural heritage: A survey. *Pattern Recognition Letters*, *133*, 102-108.

Fleischmann, K. (2014). Collaboration through Flickr & Skype: Can web 2.0 technology substitute the traditional design studio in higher design education?. *Contemporary Educational Technology*, *5*(1), 39-52.

Foong, E. (2020, January). Understanding and designing sociotechnical systems to support the impression management practices of online freelance workers. In *Companion of the 2020 ACM International Conference on Supporting Group Work* (pp. 25-33).

Foong, E., Dow, S. P., Bailey, B. P., & Gerber, E. M. (2017, May). Online feedback exchange: A framework for understanding the socio-psychological factors. In *Proceedings of the 2017 CHI Conference on Human Factors in Computing Systems* (pp. 4454-4467).

Fraser, C. A., Dontcheva, M., Kim, J. O., & Klemmer, S. (2019). How live streaming does (and doesn't) change creative practices. *Interactions*, *27*(1), 46-51.

Fraser, C. A., Kim, J. O., Shin, H. V., Brandt, J., & Dontcheva, M. (2020, April). Temporal segmentation of creative live streams. In *Proceedings of the 2020 CHI Conference on Human Factors in Computing Systems* (pp. 1-12).

Fraser, C. A., Kim, J. O., Thornsberry, A., Klemmer, S., & Dontcheva, M. (2019). Sharing the studio: How creative livestreaming can inspire, educate, and engage. In *Proceedings of the 2019 on Creativity and Cognition* (pp. 144-155).

Freedman, K. (2010). Rethinking creativity: A definition to support contemporary practice. *Art Education, 63*(2), 8-15.

Greenberg, M. D., Easterday, M. W., & Gerber, E. M. (2015, June). Critiki: A scaffolded approach to gathering design feedback from paid crowdworkers. In *Proceedings of the 2015 ACM SIGCHI Conference on Creativity and Cognition* (pp. 235-244).

Güler, K. (2015). Social media-based learning in the design studio: A comparative study. *Computers & Education, 87*, 192-203.

Halstead, S., Serrano, H. D., & Proctor, S. (2015). Finding top UI/UX design talent on Adobe Behance. *Procedia Computer Science, 51*, 2426-2434.

Hemsley, J., & Tanupabrungsun, S. (2018, March). Dribbble: Exploring the concept of viral events on an art world social network site. In *International Conference on Information* (pp. 27-36). Springer, Cham.

Hemsley, J., & Tanupabrungsun, S. (2018, July). Viral design: User concepts of virality on the niche social media site, Dribbble. In *Proceedings of the 9th International Conference on Social Media and Society* (pp. 91-101).

Huckle, N., Garcia, N., & Nakashima, Y. (2020, August). Demographic influences on contemporary art with unsupervised style embeddings. In *European Conference on Computer Vision* (pp. 126-142). Springer, Cham.

Hudgins, W., Lynch, M., Schmal, A., Sikka, H., Swenson, M., & Joyner, D. A. (2020, August). Informal learning communities: The other Massive Open Online 'C'. In *Proceedings of the Seventh ACM Conference on Learning@ Scale* (pp. 91-101).

Jones, B. L. (2015). Collective learning resources: Connecting social-learning practices in deviantART to art education. *Studies in Art Education, 56*(4), 341-354.

Kim, J., Bagla, A., & Bernstein, M. S. (2015, June). Designing creativity support tools for failure. In *Proceedings of the 2015 ACM SIGCHI Conference on Creativity and Cognition* (pp. 157-160).

Kim, J., Agrawala, M., & Bernstein, M. S. (2017, February). Mosaic: designing online creative communities for sharing works-in-progress. In *Proceedings of the 2017 ACM Conference on Computer Supported Cooperative Work and Social Computing* (pp. 246-258).

Kim, N. W. (2017). Creative community demystified: a statistical overview of Behance. *arXiv preprint arXiv:1703.00800*. 1 – 10.

Koch, J., Taffin, N., Lucero, A., & Mackay, W. E. (2020, July). SemanticCollage: Enriching digital mood board design with semantic labels. In *Proceedings of the 2020 ACM Designing Interactive Systems Conference* (pp. 407-418).

Kosinski, M., Bachrach, Y., Kohli, P., Stillwell, D., & Graepel, T. (2014). Manifestations of user personality in website choice and behaviour on online social networks. *Machine learning, 95*(3), 357-380.

Krause, M., Garncarz, T., Song, J., Gerber, E. M., Bailey, B. P., & Dow, S. P. (2017, May). Critique style guide: Improving crowdsourced design feedback with a natural language model. In *Proceedings of the 2017 CHI Conference on Human Factors in Computing Systems* (pp. 4627-4639).

Kuznetsov, S., & Paulos, E. (2010, October). Rise of the expert amateur: DIY projects, communities, and cultures. In *Proceedings of the 6th Nordic conference on human-computer interaction: extending boundaries* (pp. 295-304).

Lafreniere, B., Grossman, T., & Fitzmaurice, G. (2013, April). Community enhanced tutorials: improving tutorials with multiple demonstrations. In *Proceedings of the SIGCHI Conference on Human Factors in Computing Systems* (pp. 1779-1788).

Lam, F. Y. (2010). Comic market: How the world's biggest amateur comic fair shaped Japanese *dōjinshi* culture. *Mechademia, 5*(1), 232-248.

Lamerichs, N. (2018). 2. Fan Membership: Traditional and Digital Fieldwork. In *Productive Fandom* (pp. 47-66). Amsterdam University Press.

Lu, D., Wu, R., & Sang, J. (2017). Overlapped user-based comparative study on photo-sharing websites. *Information Sciences*, *376*, 54-70.

Lu, Z., Kazi, R. H., Wei, L. Y., Dontcheva, M., & Karahalios, K. (2021). StreamSketch: Exploring multi-modal interactions in creative live streams. *Proceedings of the ACM on Human-Computer Interaction*, *5*(CSCW1), 1-26.

Lüders, M. (2008). Conceptualizing personal media. *New media & society*, *10*(5), 683-702.

Lukáč, M., Fišer, J., Bazin, J. C., Jamriška, O., Sorkine-Hornung, A., & Sýkora, D. (2013). Painting by feature: Texture boundaries for example-based image creation. *ACM Transactions on Graphics (TOG)*, *32*(4), 1-8.

Luther, K., Fiesler, C., & Bruckman, A. (2013, February). Redistributing leadership in online creative collaboration. In *Proceedings of the 2013 conference on Computer supported cooperative work* (pp. 1007-1022).

Marshall, C. C., & Shipman, F. M. (2011, June). The ownership and reuse of visual media. In *Proceedings of the 11th annual international ACM/IEEE joint conference on Digital libraries* (pp. 157-166).

Mavri, A., Ioannou, A., & Loizides, F. (2020). Design students meet industry players: Feedback and creativity in communities of practice. *Thinking Skills and Creativity*, *37*, 100684.

Mavri, A., Ioannou, A., & Loizides, F. (2021). Cross-organisational Communities of Practice: enhancing creativity and epistemic cognition in higher education. *The Internet and Higher Education*, 49, 100792, 1 - 13.

Mavri, A., Ioannou, A., & Loizides, F. (2021). Value creation and identity in cross-organizational communities of practice: A learner's perspective. *The Internet and Higher Education*, 100822.

McDermott-Dalton, G. (2021). Putting the 'e' in portfolio design: an intervention research project investigating how design students and faculty might jointly reimagine the design portfolio activity. *International Journal of Technology and Design Education*, 1-19.

Modani, N., Jain, D., Soni, U., Gupta, G. K., & Agarwal, P. (2017, May). Fairness aware recommendations on Behance. In *Pacific-Asia Conference on Knowledge Discovery and Data Mining* (pp. 144-155). Springer, Cham.

Naskova, J. (2017, June). Designers' experience on the cloud. In *Proceedings of the 2017 ACM SIGCHI Conference on Creativity and Cognition* (pp. 539-543).

Nguyen, T. T. D. T., Garncarz, T., Ng, F., Dabbish, L. A., & Dow, S. P. (2017, February). Fruitful feedback: Positive affective language and source anonymity improve critique reception and work outcomes. In *Proceedings of the 2017 ACM conference on computer supported cooperative work and social computing* (pp. 1024-1034).

Nikou, S., Cavalheiro, S., & Widén, G. (2020, March). Digital natives and digital immigrants in the creative economy: How these groups adopt and continually use digital technologies. In International Conference on Information (pp. 343-362). Springer, Cham.

Olson, B. (2016). Tensions in the third space: Examining the digital visual culture of teenagers. *Visual Arts Research*, *42*(1), 8-21.

Pace, T., O'Donnell, K., DeWitt, N., Bardzell, S., & Bardzell, J. (2013, February). From organizational to community creativity: Paragon leadership & creativity stories at Etsy. In *Proceedings of the 2013 conference on computer supported cooperative work* (pp. 1023-1034).

Rudolph, M. R., Hoffman, M., & Hertzmann, A. (2016, April). A joint model for who-to-follow and what-to-view recommendations on Behance. In *Proceedings of the 25th International Conference Companion on World Wide Web* (pp. 581-584).

Salah, A. A. A., & Salah, A. A. (2013). Flow of innovation in deviantArt: following artists on an online social network site. *Mind & Society*, *12*(1), 137-149.

Salah, A. A., Salah, A. A., Buter, B., Dijkshoorn, N., Modolo, D., Nguyen, Q., van Noort, S., & van de Poel, B. (2012). DeviantArt in spotlight: A network of artists. *Leonardo*, *45*(5), 486-487.

Sartori, A. (2014, November). Affective analysis of abstract paintings using statistical analysis and art theory. In *Proceedings of the 16th International Conference on Multimodal Interaction* (pp. 384-388).

Sartori, A., Yanulevskaya, V., Salah, A. A., Uijlings, J., Bruni, E., & Sebe, N. (2015). Affective analysis of professional and amateur abstract paintings using statistical analysis and art theory. *ACM Transactions on Interactive Intelligent Systems (TiiS)*, *5*(2), 1-27.

Shi, Y., Li, Z., Xu, L., & Cao, N. (2021, May). Understanding the design space for animated narratives applied to illustrations. In *Extended Abstracts of the 2021 CHI Conference on Human Factors in Computing Systems* (pp. 1-6).

Siarohin, A., Zen, G., Majtanovic, C., Alameda-Pineda, X., Ricci, E., & Sebe, N. (2017, June). How to make an image more memorable? A deep style transfer approach. In *Proceedings of the 2017 ACM on International Conference on Multimedia Retrieval* (pp. 322-329).

Stockleben, B., Thayne, M., Jäminki, S., Haukijärvi, I., Mavengere, N. B., Demirbilek, M., & Ruohonen, M. (2017). Towards a framework for creative online collaboration: A research on challenges and context. *Education and Information Technologies*, *22*(2), 575-597.

Sundareswaran, S., & Squicciarini, A. C. (2010, September). Decore: Detecting content repurposing attacks on clients' systems. In *International Conference on Security and Privacy in Communication Systems* (pp. 199-216). Springer, Berlin, Heidelberg.

Tan, Y. Y., & Yuen, A. H. (2018, November). Learning process of designers: Qualitative content analysis of online platforms for art community. In *Proceedings of the 2018 2nd International Conference on Education and E-Learning* (pp. 63-67).

Tan, Y. Y., & Yuen, A. H. (2018, October). Understanding the constraints to using social media platform as a tool for design learning in higher education from students' perspectives. In *Proceedings of the 10th International Conference on Education Technology and Computers* (pp. 335-340).

Tomlinson, M. T., Bracewell, D. B., Krug, W., & Hinote, D. (2014, April). # impressme: The Language of Motivation in User Generated Content. In *International Conference on Intelligent Text Processing and Computational Linguistics* (pp. 176-187). Springer, Berlin, Heidelberg.

Turner-Rahman, G. (2008). Parallel practices and the dialectics of open creative production. *Journal of Design History*, *21*(4), 371-386.

Ushizima, D., Manovich, L., Margolis, T., & Douglas, J. (2012, May). Cultural analytics of large datasets from Flickr. In *Proceedings of the International AAAI Conference on Web and Social Media* (Vol. 6, No. 1), 30 - 34.

Wachs, J., Daróczy, B., Hannák, A., Páll, K., & Riedl, C. (2018, May). And now for something completely different: Visual novelty in an online network of designers. In *Proceedings of the 10th ACM Conference on Web Science* (pp. 163-172).

Wilber, M. J., Fang, C., Jin, H., Hertzmann, A., Collomosse, J., & Belongie, S. (2017). Bam! The Behance artistic media dataset for recognition beyond photography. In *Proceedings of the IEEE international conference on computer vision* (pp. 1202-1211).

Wu, H. A. (2016). Video game prosumers: Case study of a Minecraft affinity space. *Visual Arts Research*, *42*(1), 22-37.

Xu, A., & Bailey, B. P. (2011). A crowdsourcing model for receiving design critique. In *CHI'11 Extended Abstracts on Human Factors in Computing Systems* (pp. 1183-1188).

Yan, C., Vanderhaeghe, D., & Gingold, Y. (2020). A benchmark for rough sketch cleanup. *ACM Transactions on Graphics (TOG)*, *39*(6), 1-14.

Yang, S., Lee, C., Shin, H. V., & Kim, J. (2020, April). Snapstream: Snapshot-based interaction in live streaming for visual art. In *Proceedings of the 2020 CHI Conference on Human Factors in Computing Systems* (pp. 1-12).

Yen, Y. C., Dow, S. P., Gerber, E., & Bailey, B. P. (2016, June). Social network, web forum, or task market? Comparing different crowd genres for design feedback exchange. In *Proceedings of the 2016 ACM Conference on Designing Interactive Systems* (pp. 773-784).

Zhao, S., Wang, S., Soleymani, M., Joshi, D., & Ji, Q. (2019). Affective computing for large-scale heterogeneous multimedia data: A survey. *ACM Transactions on Multimedia Computing, Communications, and Applications (TOMM)*, *15*(3s), 1-32.

Zimmerman, B. (2014). Poe on the deviantART Website. *The Edgar Allan Poe Review*, *15*(2), 241-246.

Chapter 3

Exploring Digital Doodling on the Social Web

Shalin Hai-Jew*
Kansas State University, Manhattan, KS, USA

Abstract

"Doodling" is a simple form of drawing that people often engage in as a distraction and sometimes as a way to focus or brainstorm. The "common art" of doodling has changed in the digital age. Doodling is now conceptualized as instrumentation; it is about creativity and art. This work explores what "doodling" and "digital doodling" look like in the present moment, based on multiple explorations on the Social Web: a related tags network from a large social image sharing site, video transcripts from a social video sharing site, scraped social imagery from a mass-scale search engine, and a #doodle hashtag network on a microblogging site.

Keywords: doodling, digital doodling, visual thinking, instrumentation, interactivity, common art

Introduction

The cost of entry to doodling is low. It merely requires some writing/drawing instrument and paper. In an informal sense, a doodle is a simple drawing done often created as a distraction while a person's main attention is elsewhere. Often, a "doodle" is described as occurring during a workplace meeting when an employee is somewhat bored and wants to split attention from the meeting. Or perhaps a doodle is made while a person is waiting, for a bus, for a meeting, for a doctor's appointment, or something else. The doodle is not the main event, but it helps redirect attention.

Doodling, as a visual form of fidgeting, helps dispel nervous surplus energy even as it is a non-goal-directed action (Perrykkad and Hohwy, 2020, p. 2). Other fidgeting behaviors occur across various modalities: vestibular, tactile, auditory, taste, and proprioception (internal awareness of body position); they include "touching own face," "clicking a pen," "humming," "chewing gum," and "bouncing one's leg" (Perrykkad and Hohwy, 2020, p. 2). Doodling is sometimes a sign of boredom or insufficient arousal (Anderson, 1996, p. 117, as cited in Taberham, 2018, p. 61). In this sense, this activity is mindless (non-intentional, incidental, even

* Corresponding Author's Email: haijes@gmail.com

In: Common Visual Art in a Social Digital Age
Editor: Shalin Hai-Jew
ISBN: 978-1-68507-664-1

subconscious) and not particularly instrumental (or practically applied to direct work). In this telling, the doodle takes attention away from the actual work. In general, a doodle is generally thought of as formless, shapeless, and even meaningless. It is drawn on the back of a napkin or on scrap paper. It is not retained or archived except in the few cases of notable artists and leaders. For many, doodling is non-goal directed actions.

A doodle has been linked to "free sketching" or "freeform drawing," unbounded by any obvious rules. A doodle can be a one-off, an end-in-itself, with nothing to follow. In the present day, a doodle is "an idiosyncratic form of visual expression" (Eatman, 2020, p. 8). The drawing quality itself may be primitive and amateurish. Doodles may be temporary, like chalk drawings on a sidewalk. "Doodle quality," in a visual sense, often means simple and quickly made and even "unfinished". The interpretation of a doodle may be limited if based on the drawing(s) alone and may require interpretation by the person creating the visual. Manual signatures, as line drawings, are used for biometric verification; sometimes, these are referred to as doodles (in the scribble sense). [There are many senses of what "doodle" may refer to. As a side note, the word "doodle" appears in reference to various digital games, a programming language, and other references. This researcher could not find any formal ontology for visual or digital doodles.]

Doodles, as an important form of "common art," have been reimagined. They manifest on the Social Web in various ways. There are the famous doodles by CEOs and world leaders that have made it into journalistic articles and through those into the mapped social imagery online. There are the stylized doodles on various art forums; these are often reminiscent of coloring book pages with different patterns in each closed shape. There is a school of "psychotic doodles" that include those by actual people identified as psychotic and then emulative pieces that evoke dark human psyches. There are doodles created with computational machines (Hamburger, 2002). There are Google's interactive Doodles based on various versions of their brand logo, with clever visual wit and interactivity in some cases. This work explores the state of "digital doodles" in this present moment.

Review of the Literature

Some doodles may be more intentional and more advanced. Doodles can be an aide de memoire; after all, prior research has found "cognitive benefits of doodling, which may at times actually aid concentration and recall" (Andrade, 2010, as cited in Krueger, 2011, p. 647). The humble doodle can also be instrumental in enabling new thoughts and problem solving. The abstract informal art may serve as a warm-up to more ideas, and perhaps, more directly applicable knowledge visualizations and ideas. They may help identify various forms of "intellectual intuition." For example, one experimental study found that artists experienced higher brain activation than non-artists while doodling (Kaimal, et al., 2017, p. 90), suggesting that some experience with visual expression may inform brain activation or sparked thinking. Another research team has found some biological basis for drawing skills based on genetics in identical and non-identical twins studies (Podobnik, Peternel, and Selan, 2021).

The act of doodling enables people to come across "a novel combination accidentally" (Anderson and Helstrup, 1993, p. 241) and originate something wholly new. This activity can help the person doodling get into a creative mental space. It may help them surface whatever is in the subconscious or unconscious, or externalize the internal, express or articulate the unspoken. The external artifacts may enable more social evaluation of ideas and designs. Doodling is sometimes related to other methods of thinking like sketching and journaling. Given the inherent ambiguity of visuals, instrumental doodles may benefit from augmenting information. The simple off-the-cuff drawing can be the beginning of something more serious. In a practical sense, doodling itself "is a free-form method for drawing sketches, including discarding, changing, or combining to find solutions" (Jack, 2021, p. 121).

Doodles in Human Research

Doodles have been used in human subjects therapies and research. Doodles are used to elicit insights in a research context. For example, one study asked students of a clinical instructor to create doodles about their teacher to identify "collective interpretation of the essence of health professions" (de Guzman, et al., 2008, p. 48). "Doodles have roles in the structuring, understanding, extending and articulating of individual experience" (Robertson, 2003, as cited in de Guzman, et al., 2008, p. 49).

Doodles created by experiment participants have been used in studies about creativity in visual-spatial abilities and image-based performance (Anderson and Helstrup, 1993, p. 233). The researchers observe: "One benefit of having subjects draw while working out patterns is that the actual doodles can be used to examine the independence of composition and interpretation" (Anderson and Helstrup, 1993, p. 245).

Organizational Strategy and Doodles

Another applied use of doodles involves having employees draw individuated visuals of strategy (dubbed "stratography" or "strategic graphing" apparently), or as their own interpretation of organizational strategy (Cummings and Angwin, 2011, p. 435), informed by the power of managerial "idea-doodling" as part of their strategic thought (Cummings and Angwin, 2011, p. 436). The doodles here help with personal sense-making and inform work.

Doodling for Quick Storyboarding and Design Ideas

For some types of informational contents, like slideshows, applications, games, videos, and other contents, storyboards are used to offer a visual and textual walk-through of the experience. Doodling is often a fast method to jot down ideas for storyboarding.

Technological Enablements for Digital Doodling

The advent of various forms of digital ink, through "digital pens, tablet PCs, and laptop PCs," has brought digital doodling to the fore for children (Read, 2006, p. 1) and adults. There are various portable devices, such as "doodle pads," "think pads," sketch diaries, visual planners, "drawing pads," sketchbooks, and sourcebooks that enable digital doodling. Doodling is a common part of media art practice for many.

There are even more dedicated technologies. A "doodle-book" helps develop children's drawing creativity and creative thinking (Dziedziewicz, Oledzka, and Karwowski, 2013, p. 85); these include "sets of artistic tasks aimed at stimulating imagination and creative thinking" for "preschool and early elementary school children" (p. 87).

The open-endedness of the tasks is seen as promoting of a wide range of free-thinking and imagination-broadening.

Google, Inc. started changing its logo on its search engine site in 1999 to remember important events and peoples. Theirs was a "mutating logo" and an innovation on brand expression (de Carvalho, Soares, das Neves, and Medeiros, 2013, p. 510). While the changes were static initially, over time, Doodles "evolved to increasingly complex interactions, and has resulted in games based on the configurations of its logo" (de Carvalho, Soares, das Neves, and Medeiros, 2013, p. 508). The visual playfulness, the changing styles, and the interactivity, all have added modernist understandings of doodles. Their interactive doodles have been studied for playability and the delivery of fun to the user (de Carvalho, Soares, das Neves, and Medeiros, 2013). Another has observed: "The Google doodles are an interesting use of series: from a branding perspective they break the usual convention of consistency, but the variations add interest, invention and surprise in true rhetorical style (Carruthers, 1998) and are a way of humanizing the Google home page (Hogenboom, 2012, as cited in Davison, 2014, p. 28).

Research Methods

This work begins with a basic review of the literature, which is fairly sparse. Then, extractions were taken from various social media platforms, including a related tags network from Flickr (1), video transcripts from YouTube (2), and social imagery from Google Images search (3), a #doodle hashtag network on the Twitter microblogging site (4), and other information that may inform on a contemporaneous sense of doodles.

Results

As a massive social image sharing site, Flickr's available data can inform on what a mass-scale public sense of "doodle" means based on a related tags network. Such a network identifies commonly recurring folk tags applied to social images shared on this platform that are also tagged with "doodle".

Flickr Social Image Sharing Site (1)

Flickr originated in February 10, 2004, in Vancouver, British Columbia, in Canada. It was later sold to Yahoo in 2005, and is now currently owned by SmugMug, Inc. (since 2018). Figure 1 shows that "doodle" does have co-occurring relationships at a macro level. This may be seen in the group of tags to the left, with ties to practices (design, scribble, sketch, illustration, painting, and others) and materials [journal, paint, pen, sketchbook, marker, ink, moleskine (brand), book, notebook, sharpie, and others]. The group of tags to the right consist of various color and other adjectives and art terms.

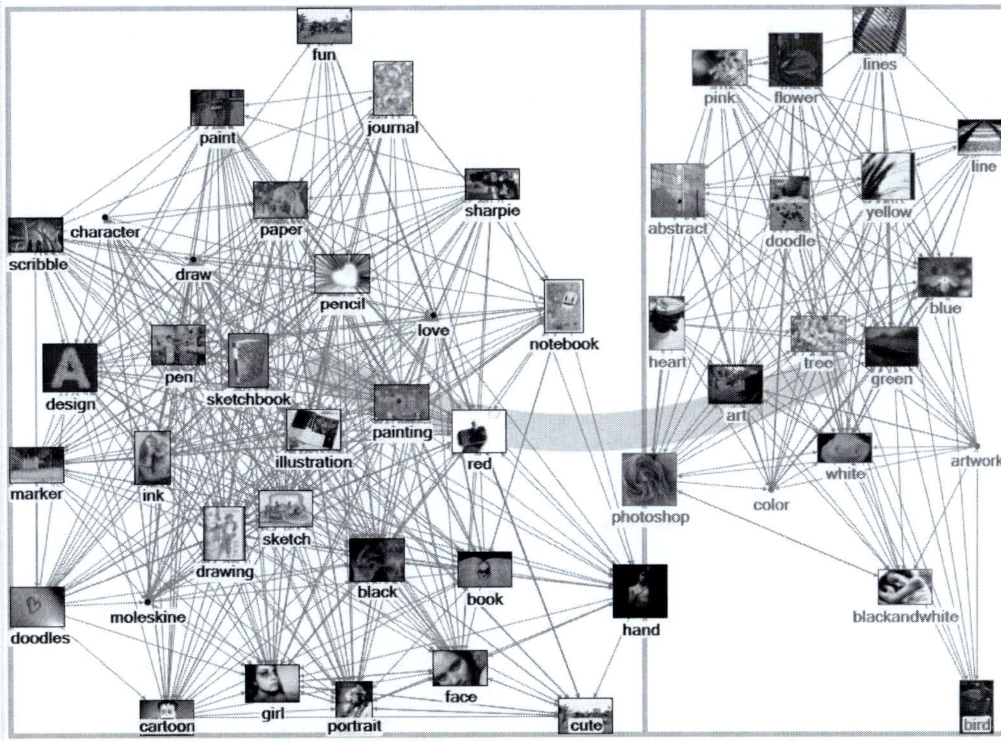

Figure 1. "Doodle" related tags network on Flickr social image sharing site.

Youtube Social Video Sharing Site (2)

On the social video sharing site, various videos are shared around "doodles." Many are "how-to" ones. One is about getting started: he advises drawing lines on a page with one's eyes closed and then riffing off those lines. Another shows doodling characters. Yet another is about doodling abstract shapes.

One doodle begins with a circle that is filled with smaller circles and expands from there with thick-lined whirls and cones and spirals extending outwards radially. Some are in color, some in b/w, some in grayscale. Many of the tutorials are about getting over artist block. Many are improvisational and "go with the flow." This is a judgment-free zone, and doodles are about warming up the hands and freeing up the mind.

In terms of using various drawing tablets, doodling programs, and particular methods. Some of these are product reviews, with the doodling as a vehicle for assessing the stylus or pen-and-tablet setup or software. In one, a child shows how to use a doodling app on a smart phone. Some are regular livestreams with artist interactions with a live audience on YouTube. Some videos have no voice over but only show the artist working through various drawings. There are speed draws. There is a time lapse of a digital doodle. There are some binaural ASMR doodles, without talking, so the only sounds are of the art making. The videos in general do not have many views when they are closed and personal.

For this study, a number of YouTube videos was viewed, and 17 transcripts were downloaded from the site from "doodle" videos from 2016 – 2021). Videos that only had music or minimal talking and those without closed captioning enabled were not directly included in the transcript set. Figure 2 shows a word cloud from a word frequency count of the collected "doodle" transcripts from YouTube. Nothing was added to the stopwords list. The word cloud is notable in the amount of encouraging words, but also in the non-inclusion of particular semantic terms about doodling. Perhaps this is a form without necessary core meaning or target contents.

In NVivo, various auto-extracted topics and subtopics were identified using an unsupervised machine learning approach. Here, three main topics were identified: yeah, things, and epic. Under each category were the subtopics: "general yeah" and "22 yeah things"; "little things" and "22 yeah things," and "pretty epic" and "epic music" respectively. These also do not show much in the way of semantic contexts in terms of doodling (Figures 3 and 4).

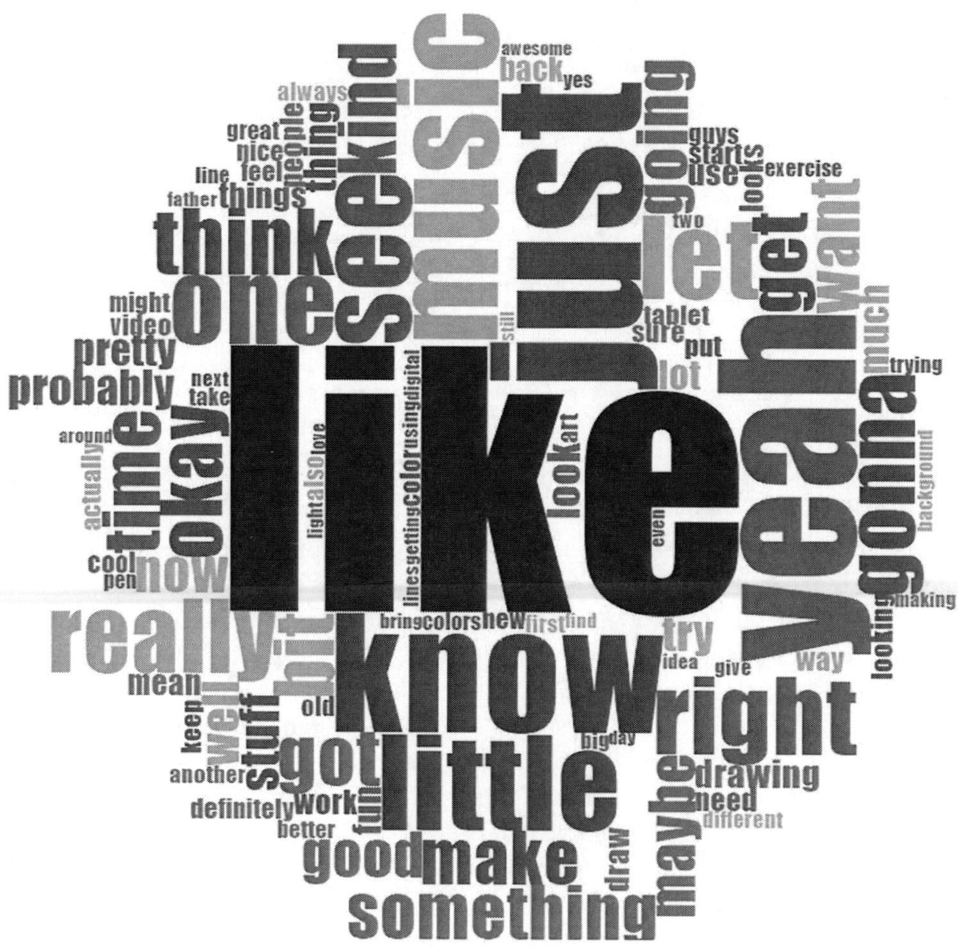

Figure 2. Word cloud from a word frequency count of "Doodle" video transcripts from YouTube.

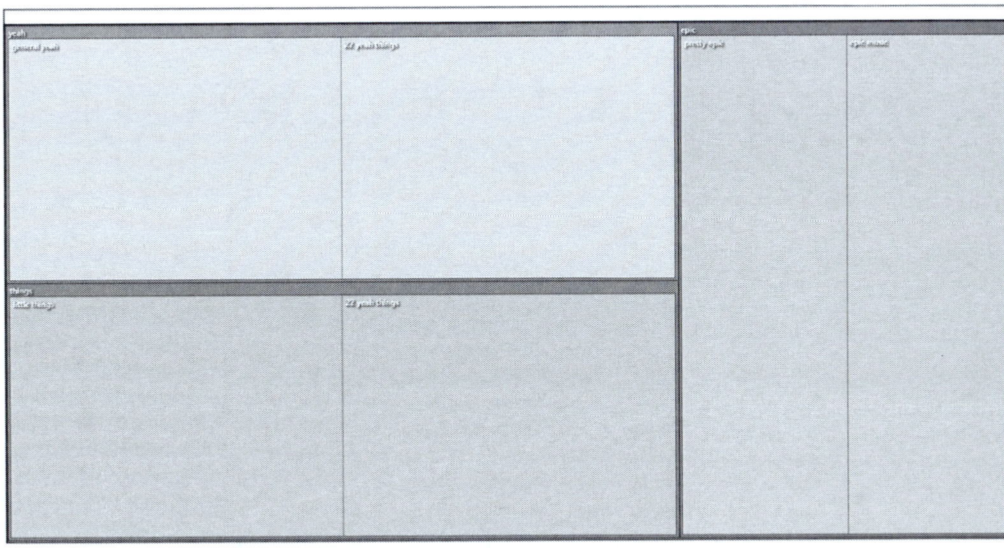

Figure 3. Auto-extracted topics and subtopics from the "Doodle" video transcripts from YouTube.

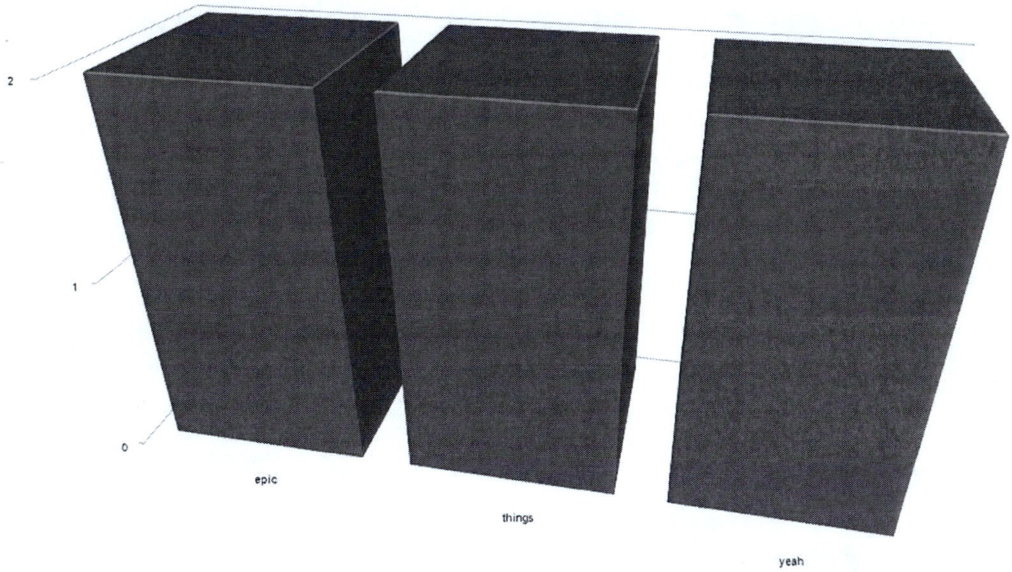

Figure 4. Auto-extracted top-level topics from the "Doodle" video transcripts from YouTube (3D bar chart).

An automated sentiment overview of the language in the transcripts shows a large amount as neutral text, and the sentiment-laden text is mixed (not purely negative, not purely positive) (Figure 5). This may be seen in the treemap diagram, which is an area chart.

Figure 5. Auto-extracted sentiment overview from the "Doodle" video transcripts from YouTube.

In a more fine-tuned sense, the transcripts show a fairly unusual distribution in terms of the four categories: very negative, moderately negative, moderately positive, and very positive. Here, the terms are seen as fairly extreme, on the polar ends of very negative and very positive. This suggests, perhaps, a tendency towards hyperbole, the breathless exaggeration that is a hallmark of some types of videos. The sentiment analysis was conducted at the sentence level of granularity (vs. the paragraph) (Figure 6).

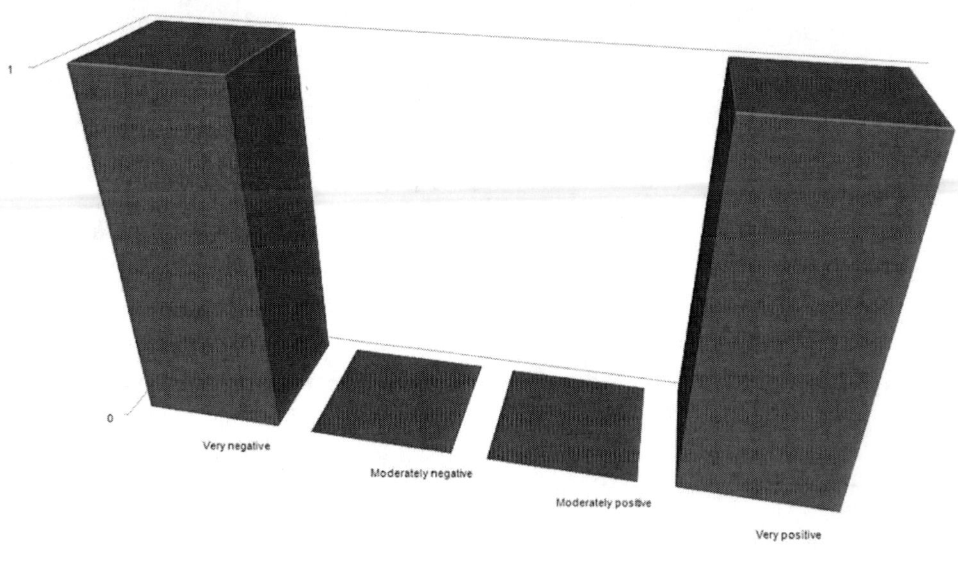

Figure 6. Auto-extracted sentiment classification from the "Doodle" video transcripts from YouTube.

Google Image Search Images (3)

A Google Image search was conducted with the seeding term of "digital doodle." The tag-based filters were as follows: "digital art, anime, illustration, cute, transparent, drawings, colorful, simple, marketing, digital marketing, ink drawing, png, cartoon, jon burgerman, clipart, wacom, sunni brown, camera, hand drawn, sketch, vector, doodler, digital age." Jon Burgerman is a leading "doodle artist" and media personality. Sunni Brown is a speaker who advocates the use of doodling for learning and cognitive outcomes. From this, 1,107 images were collected using a third-party image downloader on the Chrome web browser.

An analysis of this imageset found only 6% (62) of the social images were about doodling for ideas and information, technology, innovation, design, business practice, and such, in a practical sense. One showed doodle notes for chemistry. Some were informational graphics. Two were covers of slideshows. There were several book covers. The other "doodle" visuals showed drawing drills, doodling patterns, web pages, travel doodles, side-by-side visuals (with one a reference image and the doodle next to it), and some algorithmic art (vector graphics drawn with light programming).

Twitter #Doodle Hashtag Network (4)

A data scrape involved the capture of a recent 9,494 records from Twitter (Figure 7).

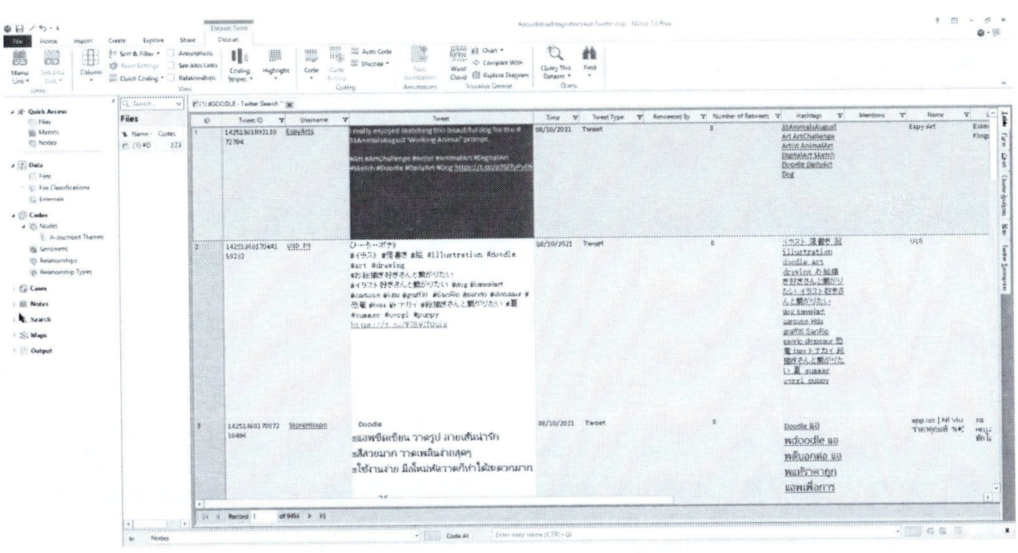

Figure 7. Dataset from #doodle hashtag network on Twitter microblogging site.

It is possible to auto-extract and map the locations of the various participants of the hashtag network (Figure 8).

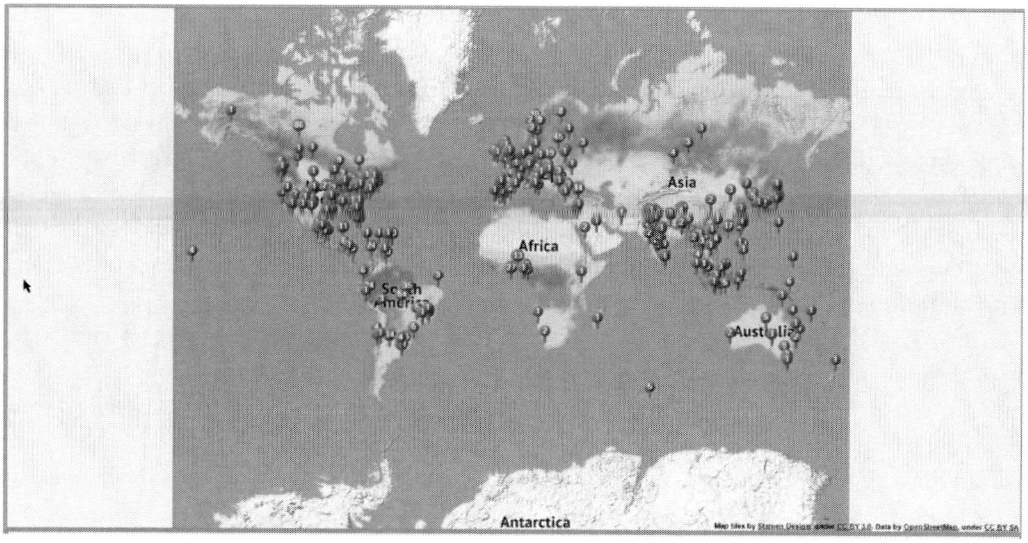

Figure 8. Global map of participants from #doodle hashtag network on Twitter microblogging site.

The various interrelationships among the members based on their communications behaviors may be mapped and shown (Figure 9).

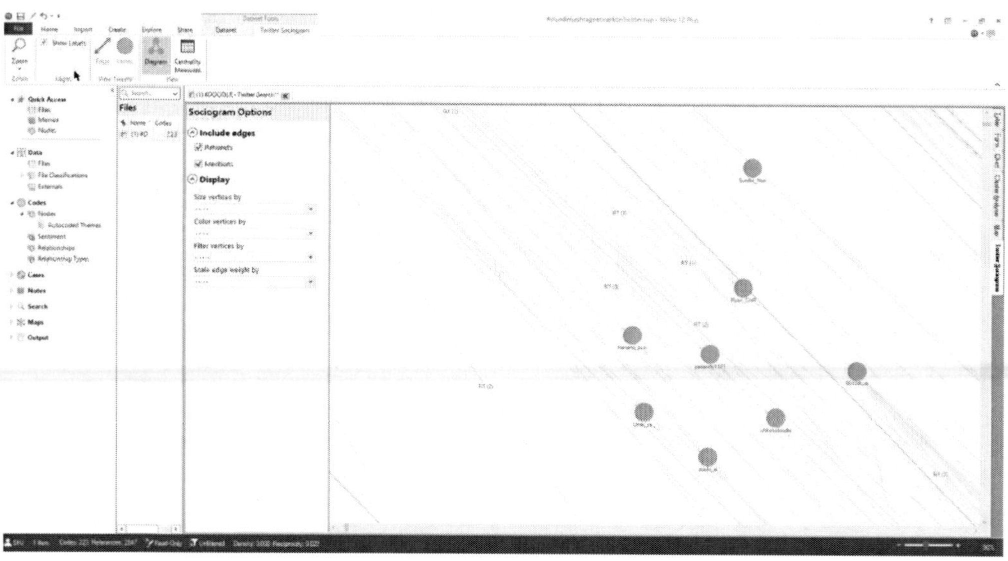

Figure 9. Mapped social networks of participants from #doodle hashtag network on Twitter microblogging site.

A perusal of the word cloud from the #doodle hashtag network messaging shows an international level of engagement with many of the world's languages represented.

There are other hashtag networks within, involving #illustrator, #drawings, #conceptart, #furry, #myart, #design, #furryart, #doodleart, #sketchbook, #manga, and others (Figure 10).

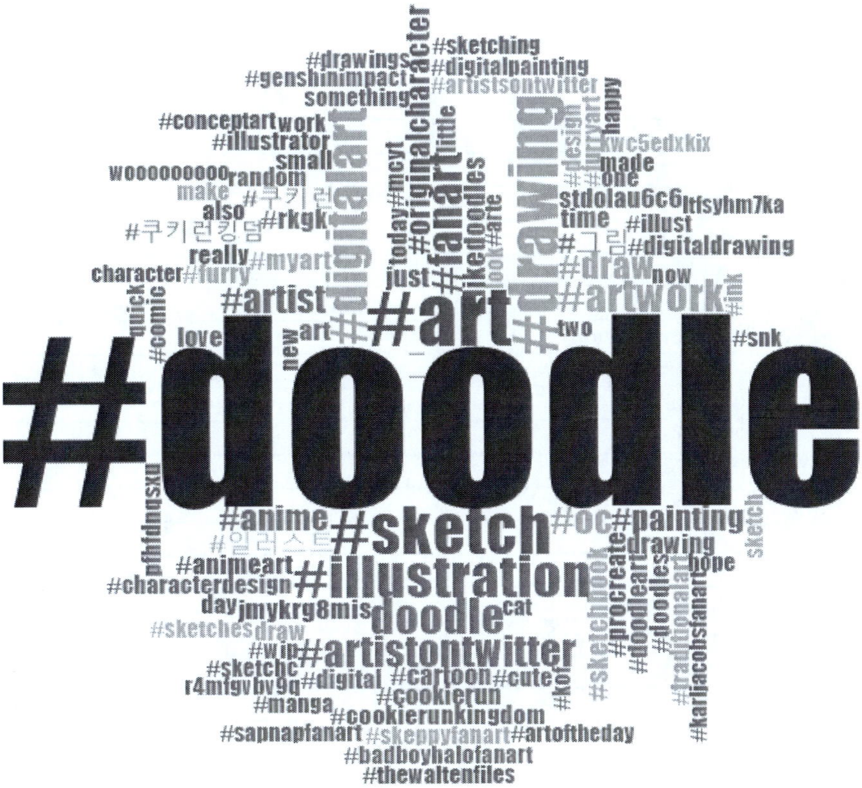

Figure 10. Word cloud from word frequency count from #doodle hashtag network on Twitter microblogging site.

The autocoded topics and subtopics may be seen in full detail in Table 1. This way, the occluded subtopics in the treemap in Figure 11 may be fully explicated.

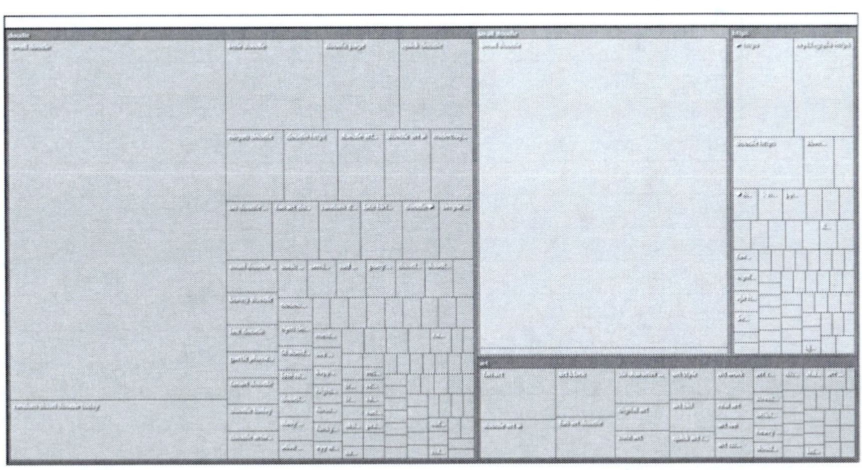

Figure 11. Autocoded topics and subtopics from #doodle hashtag network on Twitter microblogging site (a treemap diagram).

Table 1. Autocoded topics and subtopics from #doodle hashtag network on Twitter microblogging site

art	
	art account
	art bid
	art block
	art block sketches
	art challenge
	art commission
	art gods
	art haha
	art ive
	art post
	art request
	art style
	art work
	chat request art stream
	consistent art style
	cute art
	digital art
	distinctive art
	doodle art
	doodle art ด
	fan art
	fan art doodle
	heavy gear art
	last art post
	little art dump
	mandala art
	official art
	oneshot art
	pixel art remaster lol
	practice art
	quick art raffles
	real art
	recent art style
	ship art
	six character fan arts
	small anthro art dump
	stress art
	summer art homework
	tiny art
	traditional art
	un art trade
	unfinished art
	wilbur art

doodle	
	6th doodle
	anthy doodle
	blue doodle
	bunny boi doodle
	bunny doodle
	carnage doodle
	colour doodle
	concept doodle
	cute doodle
	daily doodle
	doodle art
	doodle art ด
	doodle artwork
	doodle artwork drop
	doodle break
	doodle comm
	doodle dump
	doodle honors
	doodle https
	doodle idk
	doodle lads
	doodle lol
	doodle maker
	doodle page
	doodle prize
	doodle srry
	doodle stuff
	doodle therapy
	doodle tier
	doodle time
	doodle today
	doodle versions
	doodle yayayayuayay
	doodle❤
	doodle✨ character
	doodled lines
	doodles void
	doodling class
	doodling doppio
	early doodles
	eye doodle
	eyy warmup doodle
	fan art doodle
	fanart doodle
	fast doodle
	frustrated doodles

Table 1. (Continued)

doodle	
	fun doodles
	funky doodles
	funny doodles
	fursona doodles
	gartic phone doodles
	grayscale doodle
	highschool doodle
	kappa doodle
	kyoshin doodle
	last doodle
	late birthday gift doodle
	late night doodle
	light doodle
	lil doodle
	litte leave doodle
	little doodle
	live doodling
	messy doodle
	midnight phone doodle
	midotsuyu doodle gif
	minute doodles
	morning doodle
	next morning doodle
	nieyao doodle
	notebook doodle
	nym doodle
	oooold doodles
	pauling doodle
	perspective doodle
	phone doodle
	pony day doodle
	power outage doodle
	practice doodle
	quick doodle
	quick doodle yesterday night
	random ass doodle
	random doodle dump
	random doodles
	random notebook doodle
	random shiori doodle today
	recent doodles
	resura doodle
	rough pencil brush version doodle
	sad doodle gif
	saeran doodles

doodle	
	semishira doodle
	simple doodle
	skiing doodles
	small doodle
	small doodle gift
	smudger doodles
	snail doodle design
	sonic doodle
	stupid doodle time
	taiyoukei disco doodle
	toilet break doodle
	trash doodle
	trench lurker doodle
	un doodle rápido por
	vlive doodle
	watercolour doodling
	wee leetle doodle
	weird doodle
	yoimiya doodle
https	
	▸ https
	☀ https
	☆ https
	☺ https
	♀ https
	♥ https
	3bvehh4scq https
	5lkouzzu6o https
	5vwki7jbb3 https
	6twrvhthay https
	7wi3udfjnj https
	a7fwmxevy2 https
	aja https
	atmuw2fywf https
	bjjqcclvyu https
	blue https
	clg7rew30o https
	dk8xogjq0s https
	doodle https
	eqnf3sslp7 https
	favourite character ❤ https
	g5ooiblzvz https
	hat https
	hexkj5xh3y https
	iagtpft3ey https
	inuoka https
	iq1jskigf2 https

Table 1. (Continued)

https	
	jouifhw0ra https
	jream https
	junglecruisemovie https
	king https
	link https
	little guy https
	lunch break https
	model sheet https
	nryk2egq8a https
	o7ohtnmhin https
	oversubscribed https
	parenting https
	ppyd2tifpu https
	qy1ihrv1oo https
	rain https
	reminder https
	rlhrzttbfh https
	sexy amiin https
	shinobu https
	skwy40ueae https
	sorry https
	sp0yo1j9ws https
	su independencia https
	sunset cafe https
	t7ldgc5hnd https
	tatsujin https
	uds19jdbkv https
	unfinit https
	variant https
	venisse tolto https
	xq8rxung99 https
	yldjjfottc https
	yzjj1fyfcy https
	zeagjb2bau https
	擬人化 https
small doodle	
	small doodle
	small doodle gift

Discussion

As to the state of digital doodles in the present moment, what is on the Social Web shows some usages for stress relief, entertainment, manual warm-up and mental limbering up, character creation and design, and other uses. The approaches show both distraction and concentration in the work. Certainly, drawing using digital image editing tools requires some attending since the software programs require some level of sophistication. In terms of eye-popping visuals or very unusual techniques, these were lacking. Perhaps the need to protect copyright and intellectual property means that highly original works are deployed through other channels than the Social Web. Perhaps at the macro level, this particular slice-in-time was fairly limited.

Future Research

This work may be extended with explorations of doodles on art forums. Many of the "doodles" there stretch the definition of the term and offer drawings that are much more developed than could be done in a short time span. Some seem to use the term "doodle" as a way of lowering expectations for their work, so they can surprise viewers with quite developed works that may have taken days to design and execute.

As technologies and techniques evolve, the state of doodles will change into the future. It will be helpful to see if doodles evolve with those tools. If the Google Doodles are any indication, perhaps motion and interactivity may come more to the fore. As always, however, in unfunded work, those who contribute are those willing to develop the skillsets and then invest their free time to create and share (so a small minority of people). The numbers of views are "thin gruel."

The doodle sensibility is not unapparent in formal art, whether graffiti or sculpture or other forms. Perhaps a study of formal art may begin with the seeding of doodle sensibilities.

Conclusion

This work explored the phenomenon of "digital doodles" as a subset of common art. Here, a social image sharing site, a social video sharing site, and the scrapings of a search engine were used to capture metadata, textual, and visual senses of "digital doodles." The general findings were that only a small amount of the doodles were informational. The other visuals were for warming up, for personal and other entertainment, and other applications. The sampling in this time frame, even though drawing from three macro-scale sources, show limits to the social sharing of doodles and the state of public doodle art.

Acknowledgment

Thanks to the social doodling artists online, whose spirit of lightness and fun enable so much creativity.

References

Davison J. (2014). Visual rhetoric and the case of intellectual capital. *Accounting, Organizations, and Society,* 39, 20-37.

de Carvalho BJA, Soares MM, das Neves AMM and Medeiros RP. (2013, July). Interactive doodles: A comparative analysis of the usability and playability of Google trademark games between 2010 and 2012. In *International Conference of Design, User Experience, and Usability,* (pp. 508-517). Springer, Berlin, Heidelberg.

Helstrup REAT. (1993). Multiple perspectives on discovery and creativity in mind and on paper. *Imagery, Creativity, and Discovery: A Cognitive Perspective,* 223-253.

Cummings S and Angwin D. (2011). Stratography: The art of conceptualizing and communicating strategy. *Business Horizons*, 54(5), 435-446.

de Guzman A, Pablo LA, Prieto RJ, Purificacion VN, Que JJ and Quia P. (2008). Understanding the persona of clinical instructors: The use of students' doodles in nursing research. *Nurse Education Today*, 28(1), 48-54.

Dziedziewicz D, Oledzka D and Karwowski M. (2013). Developing 4- to 6-year-old children's figural creativity using a doodle-book program. *Thinking Skills and Creativity,* 9(2013), 85-95.

Eatman ME. (2020). Unsettling vision: Seeing and feeling with machines. *Computers and Composition,* 57, 102580, 1-15.

Hamburger P. (2002). Doodles and doilies, non-simple symmetric Venn diagrams. *Discrete Mathematics*, 257(2-3), 423-439.

Jack H. (2021). Concepts and technical specifications. Ch. 4. In H. Jack's *Engineering Design, Planning, and Management,* 2nd ed. Amsterdam: Elsevier. 109-147.

Kaimal G, Ayaz H, Herres J, Dieterich-Hartwell R, Makwana B, Kaiser DH and Nasser JA. (2017). Functional near-infrared spectroscopy assessment of reward perception based on visual self-expression: Coloring, doodling, and free drawing. *The Arts in Psychotherapy*, 55, 85-92.

Krueger J. (2011). Extended cognition and the space of social interaction. *Consciousness and Cognition*, 20(3), 643-657.

Perrykkad K and Hohwy J. (2020). Fidgeting as self-evidencing: A predictive processing account of non-goal-directed action. *New Ideas in Psychology*, 56, 100750, 1-8.

Podobnik U, Peternel V and Selan J. (2021). Drawing development of identical and non-identical twins: A case study of triplets. *Heliyon,* 7, e06431, 1-14.

Read JC. (2006). The usability of digital ink technologies for children and teenagers. In *People and Computers XIX—The Bigger Picture*, (pp. 19-35). Springer, London.

Taberham P. (2018). *Lessons in Perception: The Avant-Garde Filmmaker as Practical Psychologist*. Berghahn Books. 25-66.

Part 2: High-Touch and High-Technologies and Common Visual Art

Chapter 4

Humans Back in the Loop: Using Analog and Digital Seed Imagery for Manual Visual Algorithmic Art Using Adobe Photoshop 2021 and Adobe Illustrator 2021

Shalin Hai-Jew*

Kansas State University, Manhattan, KS, USA

Abstract

From time immemorial, the creation of art by people has been both individual and social. Algorithmic art, created for human enjoyment (and to both human and machine aesthetics), is originated and evolved in various ways, with various amounts of contributions by people and by computing machines. These works also may be processed through various sequences. The core feature is that there is some interaction between humans and machines, and the outcome of the art is human-perceivable, created to various human art standards, and human-meaningful. This work describes a type of algorithmic art that involves using seeding images (both analog and digital) to create common artwork using a contemporary digital image editing tool (with filters, neural filters, and other capabilities).

Keywords: Adobe Photoshop 2021, Adobe Illustrator 2021, analog seed imagery, born-digital seed imagery, algorithmic art, aesthetics, human-computer art, common art

Introduction

Contemporaneous algorithmic art comes in various flavors, with inputs from humans and computers in various ways. Figure 1 shows various work sequences in which art may be made, with the influence of computers. Some works are nearly wholly generated by computing machines, and others have some degree of human inputs. The sequences here do not show some of the finer nuances of more complex sequences, but these are to be understood as including them.

The respective roles of people (individuals and groups) and technologies vary based on the particular traditions of the art-making methods. This work describes a particular case of modern algorithmic art using analog and digital seeding of original visual works and then the application of high-level digital image editing for hybrid works.

* Corresponding Author's Email: haijes@gmail.com

In: Common Visual Art in a Social Digital Age
Editor: Shalin Hai-Jew
ISBN: 978-1-68507-664-1

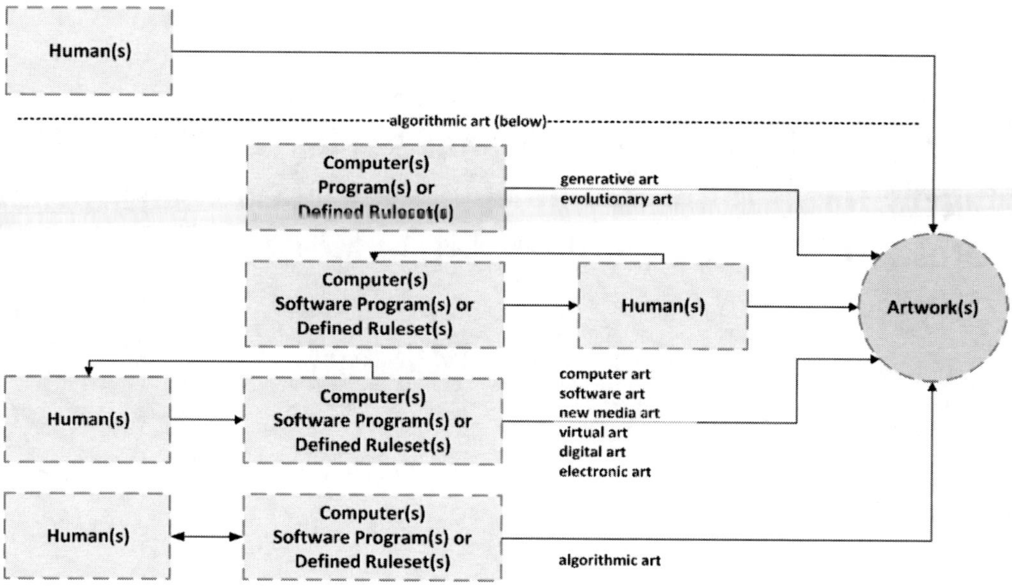

Figure 1. Some common "Algorithmic Art" creation and evolution sequences.

Review of the Literature

"Art" is defined as whatever a society and its members decide is artful at a particular point-in-time. Algorithmic art, informed by custom or off-the-shelf algorithms, with some level of human inputs (or sometimes none at all), has been referred to in various ways: computer art, digital art, virtual art, media art, techno-art, chameleon art, and others. There are sub-focuses, such as on robotic art, bio-art (biological art), and other types. Computer art is traced back to 1960s (Verdicchio, 2016, p. 287), and some even point to the 1950s. In early days, there were even nonconventional studio computers made for the creation of sculptures (Oberquelle & Beckmann, 2008, p. 20). Another program dealt with a modern style called "circlism," thought to be "a fusion of *pop art* and *pointillism*," in which circles were packed into particular discrete shapes and spaces in the two-dimensional plane (De & Bhowmick, July 2013, p. 69). In the history of computer art, people conducted experiments using mainframes in the 1950s and 1960s to create art (Dreher, 2014). In the ensuing decades, there were various technologies and practices that advanced computer art: 1970s visual culture, 1980s animation, 1990s with 3D animations and gaming, and so on (Dreher, 2014).

Visual art has long moved beyond the canvas "since the beginning of the twentieth century," and computers and computer art have been prevalent since (Ahmed, Camerano, Fortuna, Frasca, & Jaccheri, 2009, p. 567). Computers are "used in nearly each art form in such an omnipresent way" (Guliciuc, 2007, p. 333). Information Technology (IT)-based art draws in people with various roles: "cyber-artists, designers, software engineers, researchers, electronic and robotic engineers, theorists and critics, engineers" and others (Ahmed, Camerano, Fortuna, Frasca, & Jaccheri, 2009, p. 569), often with overlapping roles. For decades, people have been considering the possibilities of "robot" and "cyborg" art (Smith & Leymarie, 2017). Robots have been harnessed for the creating of analog artworks, such as acrylic painting on canvas informed by a seeding electronic image (Aguilar & Lipson, 2008, p. 372).

Understanding the algorithmic art possibilities have been part of the new literacy, for K-12 through higher education and beyond. Some software programs like Logo and Scratch have been used to create generative art that is also educative about "biological, social" and other aspects of life (Tempel, 2017, p. 1). Evolutionary art includes coded genetic information, adaptivity, and a competitive evolutionary process to which the artist "cedes control" (Galanter, 2008, p. 317), so the science is built into these processes.

For decades now, people have asked what an *indigenous* computer art form may look like (Clauser, 1988, p. 120). A similar question asks how artists engage the "truth to materials" in the work, so what is truth in code and algorithms in an art sense? (Galanter, 2010, p. 327)

There have also been discussions around computer aesthetics. In describing a particular work, one research team described a "computational sublime: the instilling of simultaneous feelings of pleasure and fear in the viewer of a process created in a computer whose complexity operates at the edges of human comprehension" (McCormack & Dorin, 2001, as cited in McCormack, 2017, p. 216). Some early works were comprised of "pictures composed of binary elements on a square grid" (Thompson, 1977). Information elements—such as ASCII text—has been used for artful expressions. Another work shows Fortran-coded art and some range of outputs, in terms of textures, patterns, glyphs and icons, 3D cubes, and 3D structures (Knowlton, 1972). There are computational methods to create digital "doodles" and round "doilies" (Hamburger, 2002). Pixel arts have been created from "limited resolution and limited colors" for simple images (Han, Wen, He, Zhu, Tan, Han, & Wong, 2018, p. 243:2). In early days, computers were used to create line art (Dehlinger, 2007). The programs were derived from human practice. There were emulations of known art practices, such as programs that emulated the woodcut look. There was early thinking that machine art lines should show their machine nature (Dehlinger, 2007). This is contrasted to the present where machine art is adversarially tested for detectability of the machine "hand" in the work; the idea is to emulate the original human-created work as closely as possible so as to be discernible. Other programs based on GANs (generative adversarial networks) involve judgment of novelty, given that "novelty, surprise, complexity, ambiguity, and eccentricity tend to be the most powerful stimuli in works of art" (Berlyne, as cited in Elgammal, 2019); the goal is to create something recognizably unique.

Early computer art was informed by "information aesthetics" (Nake, 2005, p. 60). Some other works involved the making of mosaics and collages by combining visuals and symbology in a kind of digital scrapbooking to artmaking. Many works combined physical or analog materials into the digital. One researcher captures some of the ways earlier computer art produced digital visuals:

> The design elements that contribute to the aesthetics of computer art have developed as computer technology expanded and responded to visual needs. There are eight readily recognizable design elements that relate to how computers function to produce images that make up the computer aesthetic. They are 1. Repetition of forms. 2. Randomness. 3. Variable viewpoints. 4. Modeling of the real world. 5. Texture mapping. 6. Color changes. 7. Interactivity. 8. The program as a design element. (Prince, 1987, p. 13)

The above ideas may be used as a light baseline against which to understand contemporaneous harnessing of computers for art production. Some artworks evoke data. Many are patterned, such as fractal art, often created with genetic algorithms based on cell structure and genetics, iterating to improved and more fit models over time. For example, interactive genetic algorithms enable users to "explore…the solution space" of the creation of fractal and algorithmic images (Mengesha & James-Reynolds, Dec. 2016, p. 377). Algorithms are used to create various types of visual patterns (via cellular automata) may be used as experiments and be revelatory of dynamics in biological complexity, physics insights, and other aspects (Wolfram, 2002), so there are research and hypothesizing applications. One researcher writes:

> Complexism is the application of a scientific understanding of complex systems to the subject matter of the arts and humanities. We will see that the significance of evolutionary art is that it takes complexism as both its method and content. Evolutionary art is a new kind of dynamic iconography: The iconography of complexism. And complexism offers nothing less than the reconciliation of the sciences and the humanities through a higher synthesis of the modern and the postmodern. (Galanter, 2008, p. 311)

Generative art can reveal various non-linearities. It can highly irreducible emergent complexity, even if originating rules of the generative algorithms may be simple. (Such findings have been used to argue that complexity can spring from simplicity, and a complex present world may have originated from simple rules vs. the hand of a Creator or Maker.)

They are used practically in various industries. One prototype program generates decorative art to inspire design tasks (Singh, Rajcic, Colton, & McCormack, 2019, p. 51), based on a seeding image from a smartphone's camera (p. 53). The resulting imagery has low visual similarities with the seed images but can provide inspiration to the designer.

In another case, a program is used to generate new patterns for possible usage in the textiles industry. Here, art patterns are computer generated using various approaches: fractals, shape grammars, layouts, knowledge, and such, to offer different patterns beyond human imagination and manual creation (Geng, 2010, p. 91). The computational methods also enable various layout methods (evenly distributed, complex, continuous, overlapping, bidirectional continuities, four-directional continuities, among others) for the textile patterns (Geng, 2010, p. 93). Various color patterning may be applied as well. There is also "art by computers" (Joo, Oct. 2006, p. 1), with a series of mathematical transformations over particular "time-evolution" (p. 4). So-called "mathematical art" is a subset of algorithmic art (Chappell, 2016, p. 449). There is agent-based modeling with various elements on a 2D space interacting with elements around it, based on particular thresholds and parameters. Another program enables the algorithmic creation of layouts (Lin & Eades, Oct. 1994). Yet another harnesses algorithmic design in architecture (Caetano, Santos, & Leitão, 2020), often to illuminate the potential "solution space" of possible designs. Another generative program enabled portrait sketching of faces in photos with a stylized portrait mimicking the drawing style of one of the developers of the tool; the algorithm involved "image segmentation, filtering, shape selection and depiction, filling and shading" (Tresset & Leymarie, Oct. 2005, p. 739). The codification of the portrait artist's style enables the "immortalization" of the portrait drawing style.

Fractal art, which can look kaleidoscopic, is another type generated using algorithms. Fractal art often involves interdisciplinarity and is used in post-modern art practice to create abstract, pseudo-figurative, and other-worldly forms (Garousi & Kowsari, 2011, p. 215). Such work may shed light on the world, as per Wolfram's work. One insight is that much of the world is self-similar. Researchers observe: "The world must now be seen as largely fractal. It is hard to impress the importance of this insight, but in the last decade, fractal geometry has found its way into many sciences and arts" (Garousi & Kowsari, 2011, p. 221). The artworks reveal "a simultaneous chaotic-ordered world" (Garousi & Kowsari, 2011, p. 227), given the self-repeating forms at various levels of scale and zoom. One offshoot involves polynomiography, or the uses of polynomials to create a new art form (Kalantari, 2004). Various algorithmic art practices may result in a certain set of particular patterns, telltale looks and feels, even "a certain cast or sameness" (Galanter, 2010, p. 324), leading to critiques that there are not sufficient innovations occurring. There is a "generic" or "repetitive" character of some algorithms (McCormack, Gifford, & Hutchings, 2019, p. 10).

Those who used computer programs to draw had to work the problem of deterministic code. For many, the solution was to introduce randomness. "Almost all early experimenters in visual computer art made use of random numbers" (Nake, 2005, p. 56), in some ways to infuse dynamism and unpredictability and serendipity. Algorists (algorithm creators or writers) introduced pseudo-randomness/randomness to get past the deterministic aspects of algorithms (Verdicchio, 2016, pp. 292 - 293). The "algorithmic principle is the principle of computability" (Nake, 2010, p. 55). The quality of the digital also meant theoretical endless reproducibility. Software as "algorithmic programming code") "is inevitably at work in all art that is digitally produced and reproduced" (Cramer & Gabriel, 2001, p. 1). An older work describes the use of Adaptive Resonance Theory (ART) to enable "a serial machine" inspired by "recurrent brain structures" to create "fuzzy art"; in this system, there is a function which tests the fitness of the potential artworks using a recursive algorithm (Burwick & Joublin, 1998, p. 37).

One researcher has woven a theory that aligns human pursuits and those of computers, in a way that explains what is artful:

> I postulate that human or other intelligent agents function or should function as follows. They store all sensory observations as they come—the data is 'holy.' At any time, given some agent's current coding capabilities, part of the data is compressible by a short and hopefully fast program/description/explanation/world model. In the agent's subjective eyes, such data is more regular and more *beautiful* than other data. It is well-known that knowledge of regularity and repeatability may improve the agent's ability to plan actions leading to external rewards. In absence of such rewards, however, *known* beauty is boring. Then *interestingness* becomes the *first derivative* of subjective beauty: as the learning agent improves its compression algorithm, formerly apparently random data parts become subjectively more regular and beautiful. Such programs in data compression is measured and maximized by the *curiosity* drive: create action sequences that extend the observation history and yield previously unknown/unpredictable but quickly learnable algorithmic regularity. (Schmidhuber, Oct. 2007, p. 26)

As described, a computer can implement the above. Machine learners may be programmed to pursue data and to sense-make of that data in beautiful ways.

The "machine control code" (Cramer & Gabriel, 2001, p. 2) is often overlooked and not credited. Algorithms are defined as "logic interpretations" or "the translations in computer language of geometric matrices" for algorithmic art (Colabella, 2014, p. 114). Those who create such programs have worked to focus on the art-making process along with the artwork.

Some aesthetics involve combinations of digital modalities. One approach called "troiage" in the digital age "uses a style of computational apparency which articulates the edges of our current representational forms and processes as the semantic elements of culture" (Brown, 2010, p. 199). Troiage is comprised of the methods of collage, montage, and assemblage, applied to visual art, film, and sculpture, respectively (Brown, 2010, p. 199). The author explains "*troiage aesthetics* as a way to describe…inquiry into the operation of cultural conditions that come from the continuing development of computing" (Brown, 2010, p. 200) and connotes "a synthesis of multiple domains of visuality—collage, montage and assemblage—and their application to the domains of the still-image, the image in time, and the object" (p. 200).

Some Forbears of Algorithmic Art

In the research literature, there is recognition of some historical computer artists whose works are evoked. Three of the earliest individuals to use algorithms to create art—independently of each other—were George Nees (Siemens), A. Michael Noll (Bell Labs), and Nake (University of Stuttgart) in the 1960s (Verdicchio, 2016, p. 289).

In the High Art Realm

Of historical interest (and with a philosophical basis), humanity has wrangled over time with what they consider aesthetically pleasing and meaningful about art. Art itself is defined in various ways:

If one takes an analytic rather than continental view of philosophical aesthetics, there are many theories of what art is. In approximate historical order these include:

- art as representation;
- art as expression;
- art as form;
- art as experience;
- art as open concept and family resemblance (neo-Wittgensteinianism);
- art as institution;
- art as historical definition. (Galanter, 2016, p. 147)

Art then serves various social purposes. Artists and populations reflect on society through art (Zheqian, 2021, p. 372; Ahmed, Camerano, Fortuna, Frasca, & Jaccheri, 2009, p. 572). The art can spark societal-level discussions. For some, art may be an engine of social change (Hertz, 2009, p. 59). One of the more well-known generative art works involves the growing of computer-synthesized plant forms through artificial evolution and generative grammars, seeded with the visual logos of global petrochemical industry companies (McCormack, 2013, p. 71). The works are visually evocative and other-worldly, and the political messaging is forefronted.

Another major thinker in this space describes the social aspects of art, which is a social construct. It does not have an existence outside of people's estimation and valuation:

> People generate objects and they design processes. They do not generate art. Art, in my view, is a product of society—a judgement. Without appearing in public and thus without being

> confronted with a critique of historic and systematic origin, a work remains a work, for good or bad, but it cannot be said to have been included in the broad historic stream of art… It is only in the public domain that art can emerge (as a value judgement!). Individuals and institutions in mutual interdependence are part of the processes that may merge to the judgement that a work is assessed and accepted as a work of 'art'—often enough, as we all know, sparking even more controversy. (Nake, 2012, p. 74)

The societal establishment around fine art, including "museums, galleries, art historians, critics, and mainstream art publications," has been accused of neglecting computer art (Hertz, 2009, p. 60). One reason for this has been posited as an insufficient record of computer art to reference. He writes: "In a broad sense, the critical themes of art produced through computation are simply the critical themes of all art: the investigation of form and meaning, the realization of objects that communicate as art, cultural mediation of the interpretation of art, and the social context of art production" (Hertz, 2009, p. 65), and the prior may inform approaches to computer art.

Even though computational evolutionary art has been practiced since the 1990s, it has not achieved its due recognition perhaps due to insufficient "art theory around evolutionary and generative art" (Galanter, 2010, p. 321). He writes: "Art is more than a series of sensory experiences. It is also a stream of ideas that bind art production, art criticism, and art meaning to the larger culture" (Galanter, 2010, p. 326). Another researcher concurs:

> If it is certain that computer art must be exposed to the same critiques that shaped contemporary art, it is also clear that it has its own body of theory and sheaf of formal strategies to contribute. Early computer art borrowed its formal lexicon from science. Pioneering artists decoupled the forms of science and mathematics from their contexts and opened them to processes where they could be mapped onto new meanings. They borrowed concepts from contemporary art and recast them in code. (Hertz, 2009, p. 75)

The idea is that computer art has its own history and tradition and needs to capitalize on that to establish its own space. (Hertz, 2009, p. 75) Another element may involve the need for creating a proper lexical set of references for discussing art, the interrelationships between various art objects, the various types of art, in order to optimally apply computational means (Pflüger, 2021, p. 1). While an artist creates a work, it is interpreted and shared in a community and transmutes in that process into art; the definition of art is based in part on "developments in society and art worlds" (Pflüger, 2021, p. 2). Art is social, and language is part of the social glue that enables people to engage the art. As a side note, one study found a speed-accuracy tradeoff in terms of human aesthetic sensibility. The finding was that "good taste" in assessing art was better expressed when the human viewer took a little more time and used more "extensive processing strategies" (Myszkowski, 2019, p. 188). The researcher found that "a differentiating factor between individuals with high good taste use more demanding processing strategies when facing such tests" of visual aesthetic sensitivity (Myszkowski, 2019, p. 192).

Such computer-enabled art is still informed by human aesthetics. It may be possible to formalize and define human aesthetics and codify that into computers (McCormack, Bown, Dorin, McCabe, Monro, & Whitelaw, 2014, pp. 136 - 137). Technically, it is a challenge to "write a logical fitness function that has an aesthetic sense" for evolutionary computation that generates artworks (DiPaola & Gabora, 2009, p. 2451).

Computer-generated art started in the low-brow space. Machine-produced artworks like prints are considered artwork but less so high art, which tends towards established rarity and provenance. There has been resistance because of "technophobia" (Mazzone & Elgammal, 2019, p. 6). There may also be resistance due to prior cultural practice:

> Many artists and art historians resist seeing work created with AI as art because their definition of art is based on the modern artist figure as the sole locus of art creation and creativity. Therefore, the figure of the artist is necessary to their definition of art. But understanding art as a vehicle for the personal expression of the individual artist is a relatively recent and culturally-specific conception. For many centuries, across many cultures and belief systems, art has been made for a variety of reasons under a wide range of conditions. More often created by groups of people rather than an individual artist (think medieval cathedrals or guild workshops), art is often made to the specifications of patrons and donors large and small, made to order, funded by a variety of groups, civic organizations, or religious institutions, and made to function in an extraordinary range of situations. (Mazzone & Elgammal, 2019, p. 7)

There is other resistance to the acceptance of computer artwork into mainstream media art. One author has taken exception with the "positivist approach to capture neural correlations of aesthetic feelings (which) endangers the classical understanding of art, and evokes a host of illuminating reactions from art historians" (Salah, 2008, p. xi). Software is "not a neutral tool, but a semantically and ideologically charged set of instruments which have to be purposefully shaped and designed" (Broeckmann, 2006, p. 158). Software is a "cultural technique" with various implications and so should be handled with care (Broeckmann, 2006, p. 159). What people may find aesthetically pleasing, such as "surprise" "in both the production and reception of artwork" is politically freighted, in that this pursuit of surprise "mirrors neoliberal capitalism, training us to seek surprise and to find pleasure in its repeated production" (Soderman & Howe, 2019, p. 3).

Others suggest that "…the shifts in aesthetic theory brought about by the introduction of computer art are more complex than a clear-cut subsumption to mathematics, information theory or cybernetics" (Kane, 2010, p. 73), the turning of societies into technoverses. Rather, at least one work suggests the possibility of "the reglorification of the role of the artist, and new digital color" (Kane, 2010, p. 73). Computers may extend the human artist's capabilities by offering "the computer artist new tools for expression and even a new visual language" (King, 1995, p. 3). Another suggests that using computers for drawing is not "tightly bound by convention but enable fresh insights about the drawing process itself for art and design (Whale, 2002, p. 65) for people. But this turning to computers to make art is not without risk: that "the computer replaces and obfuscates the true, original and the real, with fetishized technical re-representation" (Kane, 2010, p. 89). Perhaps there are Fordist implications, too, with machines able to create production lines of art, by many orders of magnitude than can be done over a human lifespan. Unique objects of generative art can be mass produced (Galanter, 2016, pp. 168-169). Algorithms can continue creating long after the demise of the creator of the algorithms as well, so the natural limiting factors of an artist lifespan can theoretically and practically vanish. One researcher makes a potent observation in a post hoc "manifesto" of sorts:

> Algorithmic art… denies the concept of a masterpiece. This is to say that in algorithmic art, there cannot be a masterpiece any more in the traditional sense of the word. Each and every

> individual piece of algorithmic art is no more than only one instance of the potentially infinitely many from the class of works defined by the algorithm. (Nake, 2010, pp. 56-57)

He adds further: "Computer art is almost entirely happening in the semiotic domain" (Nake, 2010, p. 56). Said another way, computer art is often conceptual, based on "operational descriptions" (Nake, 2010, p. 57).

For many investors to purchase high and fine art, they require clear stories of the artists (dramatic human biographies), the artworks, their places in history, and other established narratives. Artworks are often made salient when related to a particular artist personality and persona (Belke, Leder, Harsanyi, & Carbon, 2010). Multiple experiments suggest that art is recognized as such "at the subordinate level of the producing artist" (Belke, Leder, Harsanyi, & Carbon, 2010, p. 191).

There are benefits to understanding works in known "schools." These practices do not include algorithmic and artificial intelligence (AI)-created works. [AI "is a set of algorithms designed to function as parallel to human intelligence actions such as decision-making, image recognition, language translation/comprehension, or creativity" (Mazzone & Elgammal, 2019, p. 8).] What artistic aesthetics may be applied? What values? What stories may be told of algorists who may have lives in companies and institutions of higher education (and perhaps preferences for privacy)? Should such algorithmic artworks be evaluated by humans or machines or both? How can provenance be established? How can an artist's original "hand" and "personality" be seen (whether the artist is human or machine or full-cyborgian? How can fakes be defined and identified?

Over time, though, computer art did not just remain in the purview of algorithm writers and technologists. "Serious computer art started to appear in galleries, publications, and soon also in museums, as far back as in 1965" (Nake, 2007, p. 305). Some of the works appeared also in coffee table art books. Famously, an artwork wholly generated by computer with the support of an art collective named Obvious, *Edward Bellamy*, was sold to an undisclosed buyer for six figures at Christie's in 2018 (Elgammal, 2019). This is not to say that there have not been flameouts: "It is fair to say that the art world quickly grew tired of evolutionary and A-life art only a few years after it began and has had little or no interest since" (McCormack, 2013, p. 3). Other recent purchases of digital art have been linked to blockchain technologies and embedded "smart contracts" that are self-enforcing, and perhaps the promotion of non-fungible tokens (NFTs) (as a technology, as a new "business model"). One researcher describes this effort at creating artificial digital scarcity of digital art by using blockchain technologies to affirm that particular digital artworks are proprietary and may be financialized because of the enforced rarity:

> In a global economic landscape of hyper-commodification and financialization, efforts to assimilate digital art into the high-stakes commercial art market have so far been rather unsuccessful, presumably because digital artworks cannot easily assume the status of precious object worthy of collection. (Zeilinger, 2018, p. 15)

Even if copies can be made digitally of the work, given the endless theoretical and practical forge-ability of digital works (and the potential muddying of origins and authorship), the affirmed one (version) becomes a first among equals. It is notationally identifiable as such. If there are multiple authentic versions of an artwork, if the works are "allographic" duplicates per Nelson Goodman's differentiating terms (1978), each can be affirmed with NFTs. Digital images can be interpreted as either "allographic" or "autographic" in the Goodman sense, or natively non-forgeable or natively forgeable, depending on various contextual and technological issues (D'Cruz & Magnus, 2014).

This researcher suggests that such an approach is not particularly benefitting or empowering artists but rather "serve to financialize digital creative practices as a whole, curtailing the critical potential of the digital as an inherently dynamic and potentially uncommodifiable mode of production and artistic expression" (Zeilinger, 2018, p. 15). The digital is often conflated with the immaterial and considered less worthy than something material and directly perceivable in multisensory ways. There is the sense, too, that such blockchain technologies may lead to societal effects that are not "open, free, and egalitarian" but will lead "towards a society that is more strictly surveilled and controlled and that affords us less creative and critical freedom… and not result in "a self-governing utopia of digital art" (Zeilinger, 2018, p. 37). There is a disalignment between the ideals of art and the technological-dominant world that blockchain technologies may portend.

Algorithmic art creation has played a role in modern art movements: Fluxus, Conceptual Art or Happening" (Daudrich, 2016b, p. 75). Some aspects of modern art movements do inform algorithmic art (Daudrich, 2016a, p. 37). Computer art, as a cultural phenomenon, has arrived and now exists in some instances in rarefied air. Most commonly, various forms of computer arts have infused into the culture: "There are no images now with no traces of digital art. Digital Art exists as computer art, algorithmic art, net art, web art, software art, interactive art, computational art, generative art, and more" (Nake, 2010, p. 55). Another observes that the fact that "computer art intrigues the masses" may make such works of less interest to the formal art world (Prince, 1987, p. 13). Indeed, creators of algorithmic art are turning to the Social Web/Web 2.0 to engage every aspect of their work from finding inspiration to creating art to finding an audience to performing, by using wikis, blogs, web sites, social network services, and social media (Christodoulou & Styliaras, 2008, p. 160). The prior work does suggest a democracy, an egalitarianism, in terms of the low points of entry into the making of art. Evolutionary art is part of cyberculture (Hertz, 2009, p. 74). If "selfies" are a "thing" in the present moment, AI has also enabled "deep technical self-portraits" (Poltronieri & Hänska, 2019, p. 6), which speak somewhat to something of the creator "ego."

Fourth Industrial Revolution (4IR) and the 21st century. There has been work over several decades to enable computers to create art in various semi-autonomous and autonomous ways. The various programs have been informed by artists, artworks, nature, and other approaches. Much effort has been put into the design of the so-called "creative kernel" of software programs for art creation. Now, in the time of the Fourth Industrial Revolution (4IR), more modern algorithms have come to the fore. In the art space, they are used for style analysis (based on machine vision), art classification, artist identification, visual style transfer, forensics, and many other applications. Algorithmic art may be understood as existing along a continuum in terms of inputs by humans vs. machines (Figure 2). This concept of input does not involve only quantity of contribution to the final artwork but also quality, thus the "determinative" designation. In some cases, there are "humans in the loop" and in other cases, none.

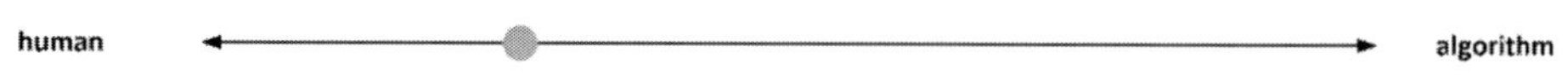

Figure 2. A slider of (determinative) inputs to the algorithmic art.

There are more esoteric approaches. One algorithmic art creation method was inspired by the "collective feeding behavior of sand-bubbler crabs" on tropical beaches (Richter, 2018, p. 1) and another by the ancient cultural counting practices of the Inca (Osio, 2019). Dedicated software programs and computer programming languages like Processing are used to generate visuals (Reas & Fry, 2014; Bohnacker, Groβ, & Laub, 2012). An add-on to Excel enables the capture of social media data (through third-party data exporters) and then the computation of social networks from that data (with related metrics) and then the drawing of various social network graphs [using Network Overview, Discovery, and Exploration for Excel (NodeXL)] (Hai-Jew, 2017). There are quantum algorithms used to create various quantum artworks: 3D meshes, and images with qubit representations (Caraiman & Manta, 2009). Generative art systems include "dynamic systems, agents, or expert systems" (Hertz, 2009, p. 69). Generative neural networks have been used for artful representation (Vianna, 2020). In a self-assembly approach, simple rules are encoded into particular objects, and these objects self-assemble particular visuals as they interact with the environment (and sometimes other elements). Self-assembly is "a process of construction through specific, localized interactions among component parts that result in organized structures" (John & Bar, 2005, as cited in Deaton, 2010, p. 1). The micro-level interactions result in emergent macro-level visuals.

Another approach to algorithmic art draws on so-called artificial life (a-life). Here, various entities are designed and let loose to interact with the immersive environment and themselves and other elements. The interactions here can result in visual art. The encoded entities are forms of artificial "life" that exist in their virtual ecosystems which simulate "organism and environmental interactions within a real ecosystem" (Dorin, 2008, p. 296). Virtual ecosystems can autonomously create generative electronic art that is "rich, complex and interesting aesthetically" (Dorin, 2008, p. 289), both static visuals and dynamic and changing ones. In terms of aesthetic ideals for such art, "coherence" and "unity" are some desirable features (Dorin, 2008, p. 298). Such a-life approaches have been compared to nature, which generates "an apparently open-ended variety of designs" (Dorin, 2008, p. 303). One off-shoot of a-life algorithms for art generation involves algorithms inspired by ants and ant-colonies (Greenfield & Machado, 2015, p. 293) and "flocking, herding, schooling" behaviors like swarm art (p. 297). There are pheromone algorithms and neural nets (Greenfield & Machado, 2015, p. 298) and "foraging behavior" algorithms (Greenfield & Machado, 2015, p. 302).

A-life has also been used as the base structure for a display in a science museum. One work describes a "fully interactive stereoscopic" virtual reality environment that depicts disease spreading through a population, to enable a better understanding of epidemics (Dorin, Mar. 2005, p. 448).

Virtual ecosystems can be used to generate electronic art because of four foundational reasons: "It demonstrates complex dynamics over fine and coarse timescales; its (sic) may explore large search spaces independently of human input; it has the potential for user-events to influence its behaviour; it has the potential to allow artist-laid constraints on the search spaces" (Dorin, 2004, p. 467), as compared to cellular automata. Indeed, there are various strengths and weaknesses of various systems to computationally generate or (co)create art. By contrast, cellular automata though could create "dynamic complexity and novelty" more effectively as compared to those of the digital ecosystem in this work (Dorin, 2004, p. 474).

Generative art "long preceded the computer" and may well be "technology-agnostic" in some practices (Galanter, 2016, p. 174). Generative art as a practice predates the uses of computers for art generation:

> Generative art refers to any art practice where the artist uses a system, such as a set of natural language rules, a computer program, a machine, or other procedural invention, which is set into motion with some degree of autonomy contributing to or resulting in a completed work of art (Galanter, 2003, as cited in Galanter, 2016, p. 151; Galanter, 2016, as cited in Chappell, 2016, p. 449)

Generative art is about defined process and rules. The creative work of the algorithmic artist involves making "executable schemas" (Nake, 2009, p. 102). It is about using an "autonomous system or process" (Galanter, 2016, p. 146). Generative art as art created when "the artist gives up some degree of control to an automated system" such as "a mechanical drawing machine or a digital computer" or "prescribed rules that the artist (or someone else) follows in producing the work" (Chappell, 2016, p. 449). Generative art methods may not be simple linear steps; they may involve an ensemble of methods. In generative art, there may be a lack of clear separation between abstraction and representation.

> Generative art and mathematical art are remarkably effective at blurring the boundaries between abstraction and representation. Any mathematical object is inherently abstract. However, a detailed rendering of a mathematical object that is made to faithfully reproduce its properties might also be classified as being representational (it represents the form of the abstract, mathematical object). (Chappell, 2016, p. 450)

An essential element of generative art is the focus on the *process* of making the artwork. For computer generated art, the "degree of autonomy and independence assigned to the computer varies significantly" (McCormack, Bown, Dorin, McCabe, Monro, & Whitelaw, 2014, p. 135). In terms of art goals, the idea is to pursue works that are "new, meaningful, surprising and of value" (McCormack, Bown, Dorin, McCabe, Monro, & Whitelaw, 2014, p. 135), including those that are co-created between human and machine (p. 136).

The use of computational approaches for "generative art" may be understood as a subset of GA practice. Computers may be powerful because "they can simulate any other machine or process, past or future" (Galanter, 2016, p. 175). There have been some formal efforts to categorize various types of electronic generative art (Boden & Edmonds, 2009, p. 21), with focuses on electronics, technology usage, interactivity with an audience, random variations, virtual immersiveness, and other aspects (in contrast to mechanical and analog types of art).

Generative art is not agnostic, not independent of history and ideology (Soderman & Howe, 2019, p. 3). There are embedded assumptions and values in the modern practice of generative art:

> Generative art and the computational sublime also mirror capitalism's religion of innovation and reinforce our impulse to be surprised by the appearance of the new (Soderman & Howe, 2019, p. 9)

Many modern programs are trained using information from the world. Machine learning algorithms that are used to generate art are sometimes trained using copyrighted images. Artworks created by those algorithms are then partially informed from learning from copyrighted imagery as a derived work of sorts. One study involves the application of European Union laws on the rightsholders of various artworks, given that there are temporary acts of reproduction of their works (authorized in some cases, not in others) sometimes during this process (Chiou, 2012, p. 406). Is the use of such copyrighted artworks for machine learning an exception to copyright law to create new knowledge [similar to text and data mining (TDM) (with the output data captured often as shadow datasets]? (Chiou, 2012, p. 407) The researcher observes:

> Firstly, in the era of the 4th industrial revolution and Web 4.0, works will not (be) perceived merely as digital content but rather as (big) data that are used as 'training material' in order to 'teach' machines how to make 'intelligent decisions', including the production of algorithmic creations. In addition, works *are also turned into (meta)-data*, especially through their analytical processing, which allows the recognition and extraction of patters, styles and other features to be read and understood by machines. (Chiou, 2012, p. 410)

While generative art approaches may enable the creation of novel art styles (Srinivasan & Uchino, 2021, p. 41), these techniques are often influenced by human art history. The uses of various training visuals for the algorithms and AI result in some programs showing racial bias, such as in the handling of skin tones (Srinivasan & Uchino, 2021, p. 41). Various "latent biases in generative art" have been observed (Srinivasan & Uchino, 2021, p. 42). Human artists may not have any ill intent, but they may have "limited understanding" of algorithms that might "stereotype artists' style and not reflect their true cognitive abilities" and muddy their intent and emotions (Srinivasan & Uchino, 2021, p. 42). Generative algorithms that are used to create art may have embedded "racial bias, gender bias, and other types of discrimination" (Srinivasan & Uchino, 2021, p. 42). Artworks may be complex and multidimensional and may be interpreted in different ways. If algorithms are to be used to create art, they should be used with due care. There are human-generated algorithms and machine-generated ones, and what is fed into a program to train a program...can lead to unintended effects.

Evolutionary algorithmic art refers to the process of generating visuals over different time phases, with some combination of human creativity and computability. A core feature is the ability to refine the various forms over evolutions or iterations or generations (Greenfield, 2010, p. 291), to enable outcomes closer to what is desired in terms of features. Well-designed evolutionary art algorithms iteratively improve solution spaces ("function sets, value ranges"), but there are difficult challenges in terms of defining that solution space with precision (Lewis, 2008, p. 21).

One contemporary method, the so-called generative adversarial networks (GANS), involves feeding curated images (a training dataset) into a generative model (algorithm, program) that then creates AI-generated artworks which are then adversarially tested for similarity to the feeder images. (Mazzone & Elgammal, 2019, p. 2) There is the artist hand in the curation of images and the tweaking of the parameters in the software. Thereafter, the program handles the output fairly autonomously. One often-mentioned program is Harold Cohen's AARON, known as a Good Old Fashioned Artificial Intelligence (GOFAI), for AI art (Poltronieri & Hänska, 2019, p. 1). GANs have been called "an almost autonomous artist," which creates novelty through "stylistic ambiguity" as one method. The machine either follows the observed or learned aesthetics of the art or departs from the particular method (so there are multiple forces at work) (Mazzone & Elgammal, 2019, p. 3).

This create-critique-correct dynamic, or generator-critic one, is built into another program using adversarial coevolution:

> We create artworks using adversarial coevolution between a genetic program (HERCL) generator and a deep convolutional neural network (LeNet) critic. The resulting artificially intelligent artist, whimsically named Hercule LeNet, aims to produce images of low algorithmic complexity which nevertheless resemble a set of real photographs well enough to fool an adversarially trained deep learning critic modeled on the human visual system. Although it is not exposed to any pre-existing art, or asked to mimic the style of any human artist, nevertheless it discovers for itself many of the stylistic features associated with influential art movements of the 19th and 20th Century. (Blair, Apr. 2019, p. 18)

There is not a trained system that intakes visual images to learn an approach. Rather, this program engages a "hybrid evolution and deep learning system." The system is presented with real images and is designed "to produce synthetic images which have low algorithmic complexity…but which nevertheless resemble the real images well enough to fool an adversarially trained (LeNet) critic with an architecture modeled on the human visual system" (Blair, Apr. 2019, p. 19). This system is designed to be as efficient as possible given pressures from other art-generation programs of the type.

Interactivity in algorithmic art. In modern algorithmic art, there may be a requirement for viewer responses for interactivity. One researcher projects out to "generative art sculptures that are in constant flux" and may interact with viewers of the art (Galanter, 2016, p. 175). Another such approach uses brain-computer interfaces. This way, the person's mental state may become material in an artistic piece "as a complementary part of the artwork" (Rincon, Rodriguez, & Vera, 2019, p. 1). A BCI device enables the brain "to communicate with external mechanical devices" and enables the "voluntary control of electroencephalographic signals, synchronization of brain rhythms and the measurement, interpretation and classification of neuronal activity" (Rincon, Rodriguez, & Vera, 2019, p. 2). The heart of the dynamic is an algorithm that "takes as input the values of the brainwaves provided by the user who interact(s) with the device, in order to produce art through brain activity" (Rincon, Rodriguez, & Vera, 2019, p. 6). Some such works are both "high tech" and "high touch," with human inputs to the algorithm, to the art experience design, and to the actual interactivity in the artwork. Several works describe the use of Kinect for interactive doodling. Interactivity with an audience is often suggestive of engagement with the artwork or the art experience.

One experimental study examined how live human participants categorized artworks, those made by humans vs. those by machines. Did people rank human-created art higher than those created by computers? It turns out that the study participants did not rank human-created art as higher than those created by computers (Ornes, Mar. 12, 2019), and in many cases, they could not discern the difference. The author suggests that computers can be seen as "assistants" to artists (Ornes, Mar. 12, 2019), as a tool more than in the sense of subservience.

Another study examined the visual realism of computer-generated facial images and studied the human ability to differentiate between a photograph or a computer-generated image:

> Our findings indicate that both holistic and piecemeal processing are involved in visual realism perception of faces, with holistic processing becoming more dominant when resolution is lower. Our results also suggest that shading information is more important than color for holistic processing, and that inversion makes visual realism judgments harder for realistic images but not for unrealistic images. Furthermore, we found that eyes are the most influential face part for visual realism, and face context is critical for evaluating realism of face parts. (Fan, Wang, Ng, Tan, Herberg, & Koenig, 2014, p. 1)

In early days, computer-generated imagery tended towards two polar opposites: photorealism and non-photorealism (Kasao & Miyata, 2006, p. 14), the first involving accurate representation of the world, and the latter not. Not all programs deal with "ground truth," which require representational accuracy (Gil-Fournier & Parikka, 2020, p. 8). Certainly, some computer programs are used to generate non-photorealistic rendering (NPR) of "drawing primitives, such as dots, lines, and textured strokes" (Spicker, Götz-Hahn, Lindemeier, Saupe, & Deussen, 2019, p. 1). Some may be designed for diagram effects, cartoon effects, and others. Other algorithms are designed to "depict real scenes, but on closer examination, defy coherent spatial interpretation" (Hertzmann, 2020, p. 424); they are designed to create so-called "visual indeterminacy," a feature (or a bug) of GAN models that feature "a powerful-but-imperfect image synthesis model that must combine general classes of objects, scenes and textures" (p. 424). Fortuitously, such visual indeterminacy is a characteristic of "much modern representational art" (Hertzmann, 2020, p. 424).

Various works describe experimental art-generation programs. One uses voice volume (loudness) to create visual art with computer mediation (a voice-art system) (Perera, Eales, & Blashki, 2008, p. 211). Another approach involves an alterable physical input interface to enhance generative art, some involving visuals, and others visuals and accompanying music and sound (Jin & Liu, 2015, p. 292). Augmented reality (AR) is a "processual entity" vs a "discrete form or technical medium" (Wright, 2019, p. 263), which can be engaged dynamically through various interfaces for 3D and 4D art.

One charming and innovative study used the Interactive Evolutionary Algorithm (IEA) method to organize human artists to collaborate with each other based on evolutionary procedures to co-create a collective artwork. In other words, people learned from computer methods and took that into analog space for art creation (de Vega, Cruz, Navarro, Hernández, Gallego, & Espada, 2014, p. 379), in an "unplugged" approach. The algorithm sequence for the artists to co-execute were as follows: Main Goal, Initialization, Materials, Fitness Evaluation, Genetic Operators, Stopping Criteria, Results, and Art Exhibits (de Vega, Cruz, Navarro, Hernández, Gallego, & Espada, 2014, p. 385).

Prior have been examples of semi-autonomous to fully autonomous artworks. Some suggest that computers are necessary for computer art, but they are not sufficient to create "a *really generative* art expression" (Colabella, 2014, p. 114). For this, given the social and emotional requirements of artwork, the human artist is necessary. One writes: "A generative artist performs an artificium as expression of his own impressions following an emotional tonality" (Colabella, 2014, p. 115).

The use of artificial intelligence in art-making is "blurring the definition of artist" (Elgammal, 2019). High creativity now is no longer in the purview of just humanity. There are scenarios "where the computer acts as a generator of variation, heavily mediated by its user" (Bown, 2012, p. 361). Computers may engage both "generative creativity" ["a system creating new patterns or behaviours to the benefit of that system" (as "an explanation for the creative outcome, but not a reason")] (Bown, 2012, p. 364) and "adaptive creativity" ["an instance of a system creating new patterns or behaviours to the benefit of that system" so as to satisfy a function] (p. 364). Both types are necessary for effective art creation: "Human-like adaptive creativity is the more traditional goal of arts-based computationally creative systems, but faces the challenge that the embodiment and situatedness of the artificial system is a poor reproduction of that of the human" (Bown, 2012, p. 374). Novelty requires a higher level of creativity.

Another work suggests that "creative novelty" is required. This is defined as "the statistical capacity of a system to generate previously unseen patterns" and requires that the system is "computationally tractable" (Kowaliw, Dorin, & McCormack, Dec. 2009, p. 1). They describe a software system that engages interactive evolutionary art to generate biomorphs in iterative generations that evolve from earlier versions…albeit with improvements…towards novelty. The system is able to identify "creativity-indicating regions" of the biomorphs (Kowaliw, Dorin, & McCormack, Dec. 2009, p. 3). In their work, they have found computational genomes that "generate regions of space which are highly unlikely through random generation" with some that are "human-recognizably distinct" with the idea that their system "can detect human-recognizably novel generators" (Kowaliw, Dorin, & McCormack, Dec. 2009, p. 10).

"Is the art in the object, the system, the code, or something else entirely?" asks one of the foremost thinkers of computational generative art (Galanter, 2016, p. 171). This is a prescient question or ask. Some do center the algorithm in the heart of the generation of algorithmic art. They ask whether algorithms themselves should be credited as the creating artists. They ask whether creators of algorithms should be given authorship credit, along with the programs and algorithms they created and loosed (Verdicchio, 2016). Others who understand the various equations and formulas and code laud algorithms as artful and elegant as much as the resulting artworks. In digital art, the "code" is the "clay" (Edmonds, 2017, p. 74). Said another way:

> If creativity is the process of surmounting the resistance of some material, it is the algorithm that takes on the role of the material in algorithmic art. Thus, creativity has become relative to semiotic situations and processes more than to material situations and processes. (Nake, 2012, p. 61)

Certainly, various algorithms are constantly pitted against each other for outputs and efficiencies. One work involved the study of generative art algorithms:

> Highly ordered or disordered generative art artifacts are generated from efficient algorithms that are simpler than those used to generate artifacts classified as lying between the order and disorder extremes. Control is embedded in the programs and it expresses the intention and strategy of the creative process. (Phon-Amnuaisuk, & Panjapornpon, 2012, p. 43).

In this space, there are subpopulations like demoscene-creators in the digital age creating art as an expression of group identity, such as hackers in some cases (Hansen & Halskov, n.d., p. 2). Software is used as an art "material" (Hansen & Halskov, n.d., p. 4).

Still for others, algorithms and software programs are just another tool, another paintbrush (nothing to anthropomorphize). In a sense, the question of authorship in electronic art involves where agency resides. How much power does the "programmer/artist" have over how the software or program deals with abstract inputs? (Dorin, 2001, p. 1) An open approach suggests that generative algorithmic art may be considered as a collaborative work:

> Ascribing authorship of a creative work is only meaningful in a particular cultural and legal context. In a contemporary Western context, authorship of AI generated art will be shared between the artist, the developer of the underlying algorithms, and possibly any number of contributors to the training data whose style is being abstracted. (McCormack, Gifford, & Hutchings, 2019, p. 10)

Here is an inclusive approach. Who gets to benefit financially from such artworks may well be decided in wholly different ways. The issue of authorship is not an actual settled question in terms of ideas or of practice.

Some have posited that artworks created by "social agents," so "computers cannot be credited with authorship of art in our current understanding" although such approaches to art crediting can change (Hertzmann, 2018, p. 1). To anthropomorphize artificial intelligence (AI) would be an error since algorithms are mere tools (Hertzmann, 2018, pp. 11-12). The argument goes that there are other non-human authors of artworks, such as natural processes, animals, and other authors, who are not directly credited (Hertzmann, 2018, p. 17). Others set conditions for crediting AI as artists: such as when the AI has "human level intelligence and consciousness," or becomes "social" (Hertzmann, 2018, pp. 20-21). Machine artworks fit into art-based discourse, and they exist in relationship with "their human artists and the wider context of history, institutions, styles, and approaches and with audiences and artworlds" (Ch'ng, 2019, p. 1), asserts another. Machines are sufficiently viable to serve as artists, such as of collective artworks based on "the input of multiple agents, human or machine" (Ch'ng, 2019, p. 13). As yet, there are no laws of copyright or intellectual property (IP) in the U.S. to protect the interests of art-making machines (Ch'ng, 2019, p. 14); however, it is not fair to expect machines to come to some level of human-based consciousness to be able to be credited since humanity has evolved over much longer time spans (Ch'ng, 2019).

Societies have defined and re-defined what art is over time, especially in light of advances in new technologies. Art itself is a social and human experience: "Art is a human enterprise, defined by experience, of both artist and audience" (McCormack, Gifford, & Hutchings, 2019, p. 4). Art "is also a progression of ideas with a history and a correspondence to the larger culture" (Galanter, 2008, p. 311), so art is culturally situated and also speaks into its culture and occasionally also into the future. Art is not an unmoored activity, and the inspirations for various works do not usually exist *ex nihilo*.

Algorithmic art in a generative sense, to simplify, is comprised of art-making processes and the visual outputs. The artist makes a process and then creates the art with some degree of autonomy. Or artists may work on cross-functional teams to actualize the work (Figure 3).

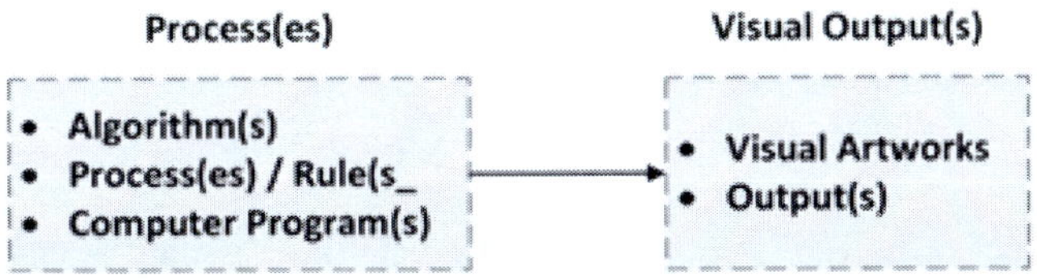

Figure 3. Algorithmic art as both process and visual output.

Where some may focus on algorithms—the combinations of sequences, conditionals, various processes—others suggest algorithms are mostly hidden source codes. Artists have to work the various software programs to desired outcomes based on their understandings of artful aesthetics. Their human vision, hand, and history then inform the actual art. Others see moral hazard risks in algorithms for limiting creativity as all programs offer both affordances and constraints. The new reality for artists that use high technology is that they need to develop much more complex fusion skillsets. Artists often develop their knowledge, skills, and abilities

(KSAs) over a lifetime. For knowledge, they must know something of their culture, art history, people, and how the human visual system works. They need to have knowledge and skills to use the requisite art materials and technologies. They need the ability to create and co-create in the world, with a mix of passion and technique. If computers themselves are too mechanized for art creation, perhaps the artists have to bring more of the human soul and sensibility for the outputs to be considered art (Guliciuc, 2007, p. 333). Algorithmic art has been criticized as just offering a "new cult of nature" (Crano, 2018, p. 345) instead of something transcendent and socially transformative. There is a desire for art that "can challenge our vision, redistribute the sensible…and shake up our image of the world and of what remains possible therein" (Crano, 2018, p. 352). Others defend the authenticity of computer art against charges that computer art is "inauthentic, even strictly impossible, because it lacks certain essential features of genuine art" (Boden, 2007, p. 1).

There is an even more nuanced sense to the question given how much technologies enabling "manual" digital illustration, digital painting, digital compositing, and other tools are supported by technologies that may support the suggestion of reference images (Holinaty, Jacobson, & Chevalier, 2021) and process steps (Williford, Doke, Pahud, Hinckley, & Hammond, 2019; Dixon, Prasad, & Hammond, Apr. 2010). Advances in artificial intelligence mean more tools for "co-creative" drawing workflows between human artists and machines (Jansen & Sklar, 2021, p. 1). These technological augmentations stand to change the artwork and so have a hand in the outcomes and final works. The augmentary "assistive" technologies, if you will, may further degrade manual drawing skills (Fava, 2020). In the computational space, there are a number of non-photorealistic techniques that enable works that are more emulative of interpretive works by human hands than photorealistic ones by cameras. The difficulty of identifying provenance of such works has forced leading digital image editing software companies to create methods to try to establish a verifiable provenance of a work.

The nature of creativity may have been shifted with algorithmic art. Perhaps different varieties of creativity (such as "trivial, personal, and historic creativity") are at work with algorithmic art (Nake, 2009, p. 97), with perhaps only the historic level of creativity as transcendent. Perhaps only historic-level creativity can result in artwork accepted by larger society as being meaningful and impactful. Algorithmic artists conceptualize or "think… their images" and bring them into being computationally (Nake, 2009, p. 101). He uses the idea of polygons (a figure with at least three straight lines and various angles on a two-dimensional plane) to explain the criticality of conceptualization and the ephemeral nature of art:

> In mathematics, a *polygon* is a sequence of points (in the simplest case, in the plane). Polygons also exist in spaces of higher dimensions. As a sequence of points, the polygon is a purely mental construct. In particular and against common belief, you cannot *see* the polygon. As a polygon, it is invisible. It shares this fate with all of geometry. This is so because the objects of geometry—points, lines, planes—are pure. You describe them in formulae, and you prove theorems about them. (Nake, 2012, p. 64)

In the same that geometric entities are "purely mental" but are actualized in graphics, graphics are "the human's consolation for geometry" (Nake, 2012, p. 65). Graphics help people see or perceive the elusive theoretical. Analogically, art is ideas, and artworks are a consolation for art.

The "human-algorithm collaborations" (Yamshchikov & Tikhonov, 2018, p. 1) still feel "personal" to the human artist "as long as the state space…is big enough and the means to navigate such state space are provided to the human" (p. 2). To engage in contemporary algorithmic art, people need to cobble digital and analog elements, various dimensions, and various technologies:

> Within this context, artistic practices remind us their relationship with crafts and skills. Artists not only produce images and confront us with ideas about our society and the world, but they also invent materials, discover surfaces, combine techniques and define workflows. (Reyes-Garcia, 2013, p. 1)

Technological art that uses artificial intelligence (AI) "requires some degree of technical competency" (Zylinska, 2020, p. 14). Still, while artificial intelligence is high-tech at present, it is traced back to "Aristotle's work on formal logic" and "the syllogism, i.e., A form of deductive reasoning that allows one to reach a conclusion derived from a number of statements with an assumed truth value"; computational research into AI is dated to the 1950s (Zylinska, 2020, p. 23). This time is defined as "the Age of Machinic Creation" (Zylinska, 2020, p. 65).

The bringing into being something that has not existed before, if balanced properly between poetics and thought, ends up in a space for "free play" ultimately over the constraints of rule-based processes for the artist, even of algorithmic art (Asaf, 2014, p. 30). In other words, there is a freedom to create once particular understandings and skills are acquired. If they engage the 4th dimension (changes over time), they also need to be able to conceptualize various "motion structures" and "the shape of movement" (Reyes-Garcia, 2013, p. 3). In every art practice, there is subtlety and nuance. Computers offer "liberation and restriction on creative practice" in art-making (McCormack, 2017, p. 213).

Research Methods

This work describes a human-intensive type of algorithmic art that still benefits from the many features of machine learning, artificial intelligence, neural filtering, and other capabilities built into the foremost digital image editing tool of the time, Adobe Photoshop 2021, and one for creating and editing scalable vector art, Adobe Illustrator 2021.

Adobe Photoshop was created by Adobe, Inc. and debuted on Feb. 19, 1990, over three decades ago. Adobe Illustrator was released by the same company earlier in January 1987. For both, the graphical user interface (GUI) is intuitive, and many have just picked up the tools by watching social videos and talking to friends (without knowing anything about the decades of development and cutting-edge computer science work in the product or high-end computation occurring underneath the GUI). There are various features like virtual embossing can be done (also built into digital image editing tools) (Sourin, 2001, p. 77); digital halftones (while circumventing the "grey pattern problem") (Misevičius, Guogis, & Stanevičienė, Oct. 2013, p. 285), and other capabilities. (The cited works may or may not have had direct impact on the cited software, but the hard problem challenges of dealing with visual image editing, both still and motion, apply.)

Adobe Photoshop is "a great piece of software…(with) a huge collection of marvelous functions in the guise of tools" (Nake, 2010, p. 59). Coauthors of a research work made the observation that "a tool like Photoshop is theoretically capable of creating any style or kind of image" (McCormack, Gifford, & Hutchings, 2019, p. 11). The software enables many capabilities: changing of hue/saturation, texture-based filters, artificial lighting, deformations, digital painting, masking, layer edits, and others. It is possible to turn a 2D image into a 3D one or even a panoramic display, and vice versa. It is beyond the purview of this chapter to summarize the various capabilities. This tool is often used with tablet drawing devices to enable even more control in the application of digital paints (but this was not used here). In the academic literature, there are various "how-to" books on how to use both Adobe Photoshop and Adobe Illustrator.

The general sequence involves starting with the analog space and creating variant seeding images. In this case, alcohol ink and synthetic papers were used. Then, the artworks were scanned or photographed (digitized) and edited in Photoshop and sometimes additional augmentary software programs (Figure 4). This process is described in an informal Business Process Model and Notation (BPMN) diagram.

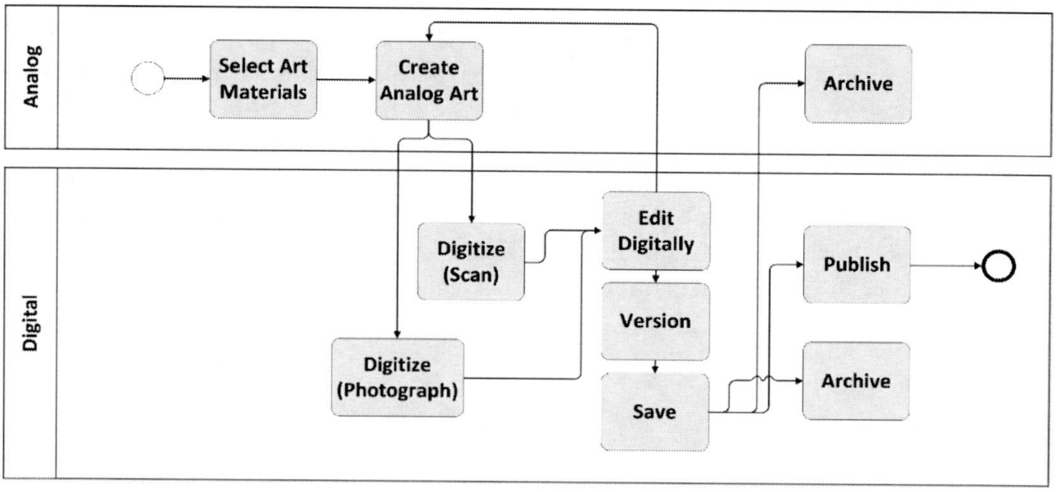

Figure 4. A Human-intensive algorithmic art creation sequence (in an Informal BPMN).

While many artworks originate based initially on some conceptualizations or ideas, algorithmic art may not have an original seeding inspiration but evolves from a process of "discovery, a kind of experiment" that links the "mind, code and matter" (Edmonds, 2017, p. 78). "Contemporary digital art" tends to be both "non-material and borderless" (Zheqian, 2021, p. 376). Perhaps algorithmic artists are working in the so-called "post-internet art" phase (Blume, 2017, p. 102), where cyber influences have become central to the creation of art. These works' observations apply to this sequence.

The BPMN diagram does not depict a potential transcoding of the digital back into the analog. However, some research works do show that potential phase of an artful sequence. One example involves generative art that may be defined with a "specified printing-direction" and other complexities for the making of a 3D printed objet d'art (Kanada, 2016, p. 636).

The seeding images were mostly born analog and digitized, but it is wholly possible to use born-digital visuals (from data, digital photos, diagrams, data visualizations, and other types).

It is possible to create digital visuals within Photoshop 2021 (such as their fire effects) and evolve creative artworks from that.

The evolution of the seeding visual depends on decisions made at ever iteration due to the sensitivity of the steps of the sequences. The order of the applied visual processes have major effects on what follows and the available decisions that may be taken.

Results

If there is an algorithmic art continuum with high human inputs on one end and high computational inputs on the other, this approach would tick both polar ends, and perhaps the continuum would be better represented as a circle. How algorithmic art instantiates depends so much on artist vision and capabilities, intentions, inputs, and other tendencies. In many cases, the original seeding visual can benefit the work by being novel itself, so that the two-dimensional plane is already seeded with something different.

Discussion

This work opened with a broad-ranging summary of the research literature on algorithmic art, with many of the works focused on cutting-edge algorithms and automations. Even quantum computing has been brought into the digital art space (Lioret, 2016).

This work, by contrast, brings in both retro methods (painting on canvas) with cutting edge materials (alcohol inks and synthetic papers) and the foremost digital image editing tool in history. The author brings in six months of direct experience with the work sequence described in the BPMN diagram. This work highlights a high focus on both high-touch (human artistry) and high-tech (the digital image editing using sophisticated means and applied in a sophisticated way).

Future Research

Different forms of algorithmic art may be developed through various technological innovations. There is space for innovating at the creative level, too, in terms of harnessing available technologies for different artful outcomes.

Conclusion

It is said that humanity needs to make and consume art for their existence. This may be especially so in a time of a major global challenge, such as the SARS-CoV-2/COVID-19 pandemic. Creating high-touch high-manual art using the foremost digital image editing tool on the planet, with its powerful algorithms, is perhaps a powerful way of exploring different visual possibilities.

References

Aguilar, C., & Lipson, H. (2008, December). A robotic system for interpreting images into painted artwork. In *International conference on generative art* (Vol. 11), 372 - 387.

Ahmed, S. U., Camerano, C., Fortuna, L., Frasca, M., & Jaccheri, L. (2009). Information technology and art: Concepts and state of the practice. In *Handbook of Multimedia for Digital Entertainment and Arts* (pp. 567-592). Springer, Boston, MA.

Asaf, I. (2014). The Poetic and the Thoughtful: The Creative Poiesis of Algorithmic Art and Design. *Electronic Visualisation and the Arts (EVA 2014)*, 30-35.

Belke, B., Leder, H., Harsanyi, G., & Carbon, C. C. (2010). When a Picasso is a "Picasso": The entry point in the identification of visual art. *Acta Psychologica,* 133 (2010), 191 – 202.

Blair, A. (2019, April). Adversarial evolution and deep learning–how does an artist play with our visual system?. In *International Conference on Computational Intelligence in Music, Sound, Art and Design (Part of EvoStar)* (pp. 18-34). Springer, Cham.

Blume, J. (2017). Exploring the potentials and challenges of virtual distribution of contemporary art. In *Digital Environments* (pp. 97-116). Transcript-Verlag.

Boden, M. A., & Edmonds, E. A. (2009). What is generative art?. *Digital Creativity, 20*(1-2), 21-46.

Bown, O. (2012). Generative and adaptive creativity: A unified approach to creativity in nature, humans and machines. In *Computers and creativity* (pp. 361-381). Springer, Berlin, Heidelberg.

Broeckmann, A. (2006). Software Art Aesthetics. *Monodisperso.* Special issue, edited by Fernando José Pereira and Miguel Leal. Mono, 1, 158-67.

Brown, S. (2010). Troiage aesthetics. In *The Structure of Style* (pp. 199-218). Springer, Berlin, Heidelberg.

Burwick, T., & Joublin, F. (1998). Optimal algorithmic complexity of fuzzy art. *Neural Processing Letters, 7*(1), 37-41.

Boden, M. A. (2007). Authenticity and computer art. *Digital Creativity, 18*(1), 1 - 25.

Bohnacker, H., Groβ, B., & Laub, J. (2012). *Generative Design: Visualize, Program, and Create with Processing.* New York: Princeton Architectural Press.

Caetano, I., Santos, L., & Leitão, A. (2020). Computational design in architecture: Defining parametric, generative, and algorithmic design. *Frontiers of Architectural Research.* 9, 287 - 300.

Caraiman, S., & Manta, V. I. (2009, May). New applications of quantum algorithms to computer graphics: the quantum random sample consensus algorithm. In *Proceedings of the 6th ACM conference on Computing frontiers* (pp. 81-88).

Ch'ng, E. (Ed.). (2019). Art by Computing Machinery: Is Machine Art Acceptable in the Artworld?. *ACM Transactions on Multimedia Computing, Communications, and Applications (TOMM), 15*(2s), 1-17.

Chappell, D. (2016). Thoughts on Generative Art. In *Proceedings of Bridges 2016: Mathematics, Music, Art, Architecture, Education, Culture* (pp. 449-452). Tessellations Publishing.

Chiou, T. (2019). Copyright Lessons on Machine Learning: What Impact on Algorithmic Art. *J. Intell. Prop. Info. Tech. & Elec. Com. L., 10*, 398 – 411.

Christodoulou, S. P., & Styliaras, G. D. (2008, September). Digital Art 2.0: Art meets Web 2.0 trend. In *Proceedings of the 3rd international conference on Digital Interactive Media in Entertainment and Arts* (pp. 158-165).

Colabella, E. (2014). *Generative Artist behind machine.* GA2014. 109 – 119.

Cramer, F., & Gabriel, U. (2001). Software Art. *American Book Review, issue "Codeworks"*(Alan Sondheim, ed.).

Crano, R. D. (2018). A context for complexism: Between neoliberal social thought and algorithmic art. *Open Cultural Studies,* 2, 341 – 352.

Daudrich, A. (2016a). Algorithmic art and its art-historical relationships. *CITAR Journal, 8(1),* 37 – 44.

Daudrich, A. (2016b). *Human vs. Machine: Algorithmic Methods in the Realm of Artistic Production.* xCoAx.org. 75 - 84.

D'Cruz, J., & Magnus, P. D. (2014). Are digital images allographic?. *The Journal of Aesthetics and Art Criticism, 72*(4), 417-427.

de Vega, F. F., Cruz, C., Navarro, L., Hernández, P., Gallego, T., & Espada, L. (2014). Unplugging evolutionary algorithms: an experiment on human-algorithmic creativity. *Genetic Programming and Evolvable Machines*, *15*(4), 379-402.

De, S., & Bhowmick, P. (2013, July). Digital Circlism as Algorithmic Art. In *International Symposium on Visual Computing* (pp. 69-78). Springer, Berlin, Heidelberg.

Deaton, R. (2010). Self-assembled art. In *ACM SIGGRAPH 2010 Posters* (pp. 1-1).

Dehlinger, H. (2007). On fine art and generative line drawings. *Journal of Mathematics and the Arts*, *1*(2), 97-111.

DiPaola, S., & Gabora, L. (2009). Incorporating characteristics of human creativity into an evolutionary art algorithm. *Genetic Programming and Evolvable Machines*, *10*(2), 2450 - 2456.

Dixon, D., Prasad, M., & Hammond, T. (2010, April). icandraw: Using sketch recognition and corrective feedback to assist a user in drawing human faces. In *Proceedings of the SIGCHI Conference on Human Factors in Computing Systems* (pp. 897-906).

Dorin, A. (2005, March). Artificial life, death and epidemics in evolutionary, generative electronic art. In *Workshops on Applications of Evolutionary Computation* (pp. 448-457). Springer, Berlin, Heidelberg.

Dorin, A. (2001). Generative processes and the electronic arts. *Cambridge Core.* 1 – 3.

Dorin, A. (2008). A survey of virtual ecosystems in generative electronic art. In *The Art of Artificial Evolution* (pp. 289-309). Springer, Berlin, Heidelberg.

Dorin, A. (2004, April). The virtual ecosystem as generative electronic art. In *Workshops on Applications of Evolutionary Computation* (pp. 467-476). Springer, Berlin, Heidelberg.

Dorin, A., McCabe, J., McCormack, J., Monro, G, & Whitelaw, M. (2012). A framework for understanding generative art. *Digital Creativity,* 23 (3-4), 239 – 259.

Dreher, T. (2014). *History of Computer Art.* 1 - 403.

Edmonds, E. (2018, March). Algorithmic art machines. In *Arts* (Vol. 7, No. 1, p. 3). Multidisciplinary Digital Publishing Institute.

Edmonds, E. A. (2017). Generative Art: A Semiotic Exchange. In *Conversations Around Semiotic Engineering* (pp. 71-79). Springer, Cham.

Elgammal, A. (2019, Jan. – Feb.) AI is blurring the definition of artist: Advanced algorithms are using machine learning to create art autonomously. *American Scientist,* 107(1).

Fan, S., Wang, R., Ng, T. T., Tan, C. Y. C., Herberg, J. S., & Koenig, B. L. (2014). Human perception of visual realism for photo and computer-generated face images. *ACM Transactions on Applied Perception (TAP)*, *11*(2), 1-21.

Fava, M. (2020). A decline in drawing ability? *International Journal of Art & Design Education*, *39*(2), 319-332.

Galanter, P. (2008). Complexism and the role of evolutionary art. In *The Art of Artificial Evolution* (pp. 311-332). Springer, Berlin, Heidelberg.

Galanter, P. (2016). Generative art theory. *A Companion to Digital Art*, 146-180.

Galanter, P. (2010, April). The problem with evolutionary art is... In *European Conference on the Applications of Evolutionary Computation* (pp. 321-330). Springer, Berlin, Heidelberg.

Garousi, M., & Kowsari, M. (2011). Fractal art and postmodern society. *Journal of Visual Art Practice,* 10(3), 225 – 229.

Geng, W. (2010). Computer-aided design of art patterns. In *The Algorithms and Principles of Non-photorealistic Graphics* (pp. 91-112). Springer, Berlin, Heidelberg.

Gil-Fournier, A., & Parikka, J. (2020). Ground truth to fake geographies: machine vision and learning in visual practices. *AI & SOCIETY*, 1-10.

Goodman, N. (1978). *Ways of worldmaking* (Vol. 51). Hackett Publishing.

Greenfield, G. (2010, April). Generative art and evolutionary refinement. In *European Conference on the Applications of Evolutionary Computation* (pp. 291-300). Springer, Berlin, Heidelberg.

Greenfield, G., & Machado, P. (2015). Ant-and ant-colony-inspired alife visual art. *Artificial life*, *21*(3), 293-306.

Guliciuc, V. (2007). The wondering angels of the fractal art. In *Model-Based Reasoning in Science, Technology, and Medicine* (pp. 333-345). Springer, Berlin, Heidelberg.

Hai-Jew, S. (2017). Creating "(Social) Network Art" with NodeXL. In *Social Media Data Extraction and Content Analysis* (pp. 342-393). Hershey, Pennsylvania: IGI Global.

Hamburger, P. (2002). Doodles and doilies, non-simple symmetric Venn diagrams. *Discrete mathematics, 257*(2-3), 423-439.

Han, C., Wen, Q., He, S., Zhu, Q., Tan, Y., Han, G., & Wong, T. T. (2018). Deep unsupervised pixelization. *ACM Transactions on Graphics (TOG), 37*(6), 1-11.

Hansen, N. B., & Halskov, K. *Generative design materials in DIY digital art creation.* 1 - 7.

Hertz, P. (2009). Art, code, and the engine of change. *Art Journal, 68*(1), 58-75.

Hertzmann, A. (2018). Can computers create art? *Arts,* 1 – 25.

Holinaty, J., Jacobson, A., & Chevalier, F. (2021). *Supporting reference imagery for digital drawing. In the proceedings of ICCV workshop.* 2434 - 2442.

Jansen, C., & Sklar, E. (2021). Exploring co-creative drawing workflows. *Frontiers in Robotics and AI.* 1 – 26.

Jin, Y., & Liu, Z. (2015, August). StringWeaver: Research on a Framework with an Alterable Physical Interface for Generative Art. In *International Conference on Human-Computer Interaction* (pp. 292-304). Springer, Cham.

Joo, J. M. (2006, Oct.) The breathtaking algorithmic art. *The VirtualDynamics Intelligencer.* 1 – 6.

Kalantari, B. (2004). A new visual art medium: polynomiography. *ACM SIGGRAPH Computer Graphics, 38*(3), 21-23.

Kanada, Y. (2016). 3D printing of generative art using the assembly and deformation of direction-specified parts. *Rapid Prototyping Journal.* 636 - 644.

Kane, C. L. (2010). 'Programming the Beautiful' Informatic Color and Aesthetic Transformations in Early Computer Art. *Theory, Culture & Society, 27*(1), 73-93.

Kasao, A., & Miyata, K. (2006). Algorithmic Painter: a NPR method to generate various styles of painting. *The Visual Computer, 22*(1), 14-27.

King, M. (1995). Manipulating Parameters for Algorithmic Image Generation. *Digital Creativity,* University of Brighton. 1 - 6.

Knowlton, K. (1972, October). A report on the use of FORTRAN-coded EXPLOR for the teaching of computer graphics and computer art. In *Proceedings of the symposium on Two-dimensional man-machine communication* (pp. 103-112).

Kowaliw, T., Dorin, A., & McCormack, J. (2009, December). An empirical exploration of a definition of creative novelty for generative art. In *Australian Conference on Artificial Life* (pp. 1-10). Springer, Berlin, Heidelberg.

Lewis, M. (2008). Evolutionary visual art and design. In *The art of artificial evolution* (pp. 3-37). Springer, Berlin, Heidelberg.

Lin, T., & Eades, P. (1994, October). Integration of declarative and algorithmic approaches for layout creation. In *International Symposium on Graph Drawing* (pp. 376-387). Springer, Berlin, Heidelberg.

Lioret, A. (2016, May). Quantum art. In *Proceedings of the Joint Symposium on Computational Aesthetics and Sketch Based Interfaces and Modeling and Non-Photorealistic Animation and Rendering* (pp. 135-139).

Liu, H., & Liu, X. (2007). Generative Art Images by Complex Functions Based Genetic Algorithm. *Trends in Computer Aided Innovation*, 125-134.

Mazzone, M., & Elgammal, A. (2019). Art, creativity, and the potential of artificial intelligence. *Arts,* 8(26), 1 -9.

McCormack, J. (2013). Aesthetics, art, evolution. In P. Machado, J. McDermott, A. Carballal's *EvoMUSART.* 1 – 12.

McCormack, J. (2013). *Representation and Mimesis in Generative Art: Creating Fifty Sisters. Proceedings of xCoax* 2013. 71 - 79.

McCormack, J. (2017). Working with generative systems: an artistic perspective. *Electronic Visualisation and the Arts (EVA 2017)*, 213-218.

McCormack, J., Bown, O., Dorin, A., McCabe, J., Monro, G., & Whitelaw, M. (2014). Ten questions concerning generative computer art. *Leonardo, 47*(2), 135-141.

McCormack, J., Gifford, T., & Hutchings, P. (2019, April). Autonomy, authenticity, authorship and intention in computer generated art. In International Conference on Computational Intelligence in Music, Sound, Art and Design (Part of EvoStar) (pp. 35-50). Springer, Cham. Preprint.

Mengesha, L. H., & James-Reynolds, C. J. (2016, December). Interactive evolutionary generative art. In *International Conference on Innovative Techniques and Applications of Artificial Intelligence* (pp. 377-382). Springer, Cham.

Misevičius, A., Guogis, E., & Stanevičienė, E. (2013, October). Computational algorithmic generation of high-quality colour patterns. In *International Conference on Information and Software Technologies* (pp. 285-296). Springer, Berlin, Heidelberg.

Myszkowski, N. (2019). The first glance is the weakest: "Tasteful" individuals are slower to judge visual art. *Personality and Individual Differences*, *141*, 188-195.

Nake, F. (2007, June). Computer art: Creativity and computability. In *Proceedings of the 6th ACM SIGCHI conference on Creativity & cognition* (pp. 305-306).

Nake, F. (2005, April). Computer art: A personal recollection. In *Proceedings of the 5th Conference on Creativity & Cognition* (pp. 54-62).

Nake, F. (2012). Construction and intuition: Creativity in early computer art. In *Computers and creativity* (pp. 61-94). Springer, Berlin, Heidelberg.

Nake, F. (2009, October). Creativity in algorithmic art. In *Proceedings of the seventh ACM conference on Creativity and cognition* (pp. 97-106).

Nake, F. (2010). Paragraphs on computer art, past and present. *CAT 2010: Ideas before their time: Connecting the past and present in computer art*, 55-63.

Oberquelle, H., & Beckmann, O. (2008). Beckmann's Studio Computers Specified for Early Computer Art. *IEEE Annals of the History of Computing*, *30*(3), 20-31.

Ornes, S. (2019, Mar. 12). *Science and culture: Computers take art in new directions, challenging the meaning of 'creativity.'* PNAS.

Osio, U. R. (2019). Using the Inka's calculator for generative art. In *the proceedings of the XXII Generative Art Conference*. 1 – 10.

Perera, D., Eales, R. J., & Blashki, K. (2008, December). Voice art: a novel mode for creating visual art. In *Proceedings of the 20th Australasian Conference on Computer-Human Interaction: Designing for Habitus and Habitat* (pp. 211-218).

Pflüger, H. (2021). A language to analyze, describe, and explore collections of visual art. *Visual Computing for Industry, Biomedicine, and Art*, *4*(1), 1-21.

Phon-Amnuaisuk, S., & Panjapornpon, J. (2012). Controlling Generative Processes of Generative Art Somnuk Phon. *Procedia Computer Science*, *13*, 43-52.

Poltronieri, F. A., & Hänska, M. (2019, October). Technical Images and Visual Art in the Era of Artificial Intelligence: From GOFAI to GANs. In *Proceedings of the 9th International Conference on Digital and Interactive Arts* (pp. 1-8).

Prince, P. D. (1987). Computer aesthetics: new art experience, or the seduction of the masses. *ACM SIGGRAPH Computer Graphics*, *21*(1), 13-13.

Reas, C., & Fry, B. (2014). *Processing: A Programming Handbook for Visual Designers and Artists.* 2nd Ed. Cambridge, Massachusetts: The MIT Press.

Reyes-Garcia, E. (2013, March). On visual features and artistic digital images. In *Proceedings of the Virtual Reality International Conference: Laval Virtual* (pp. 1-5).

Richter, H. (2018, April). Visual art inspired by the collective feeding behavior of sand-bubbler crabs. In *International Conference on Computational Intelligence in Music, Sound, Art and Design* (pp. 1-17). Springer, Cham.

Rincon, R. A. D., Rodriguez, P. J., & Vera, J. M. R. (2019) An approach to Generative Art from Brain Computer Interfaces. In the proceedings of the XXII Generative Art Conference - GA2019. 1 - 12.

Salah, A. A. A. (2008). *Discontents of computer art: A discourse analysis on the intersection of arts, sciences and technology.* University of California, Los Angeles. 1 – 178.

Schmidhuber, J. (2008, June). Driven by compression progress: A simple principle explains essential aspects of subjective beauty, novelty, surprise, interestingness, attention, curiosity, creativity, art, science, music, jokes. In *Workshop on anticipatory behavior in adaptive learning systems* (pp. 48-76). Springer, Berlin, Heidelberg.

Schmidhuber, J. (2007, October). Simple algorithmic principles of discovery, subjective beauty, selective attention, curiosity & creativity. In *International Conference on Discovery Science* (pp. 26-38). Springer, Berlin, Heidelberg.

Singh, D., Rajcic, N., Colton, S., & McCormack, J. (2019). Camera obscurer: Generative art for design inspiration. In A. Ekart et al.'s *EvoMUSART* 2019. 51 – 68.

Smith, G. W. & Leymarie, F. F. (2017). The machine as artist: An introduction. *Arts, 6(2),* 1 – 19.

Soderman, B., & Howe, D. C. (2019). A Critique of Surprise in Generative Art. *Leonardo Electronic Almanac*, *24*(1), 1 - 22.

Sourin, A. (2001, March). Functionally based virtual computer art. In *Proceedings of the 2001 symposium on Interactive 3D graphics* (pp. 77-84).

Spicker, M., Götz-Hahn, F., Lindemeier, T., Saupe, D., & Deussen, O. (2019). Quantifying visual abstraction quality for computer-generated illustrations. *ACM Transactions on Applied Perception (TAP)*, *16*(1), 1-20.

Srinivasan, R., & Uchino, K. (2021, March). Biases in Generative Art: A Causal Look from the Lens of Art History. In *Proceedings of the 2021 ACM Conference on Fairness, Accountability, and Transparency* (pp. 41-51).

Tempel, M. (2017). Generative art for all. *Journal of Innovation and Entrepreneurship*, *6*(1), 1-14.

Thompson, M. (1977). Computer Art: Pictures Composed of Binary Elements on a Square Grid. *Leonardo*, 271-276.

Tresset, P., & Leymarie, F. F. (2005, October). Generative portrait sketching. In *Proceedings of VSMM* (Vol. 5, pp. 739-748).

Verdicchio, M. (2015, October). The Role of Computers in Visual Art. In *International Conference on the History and Philosophy of Computing* (pp. 287-299). Springer, Cham.

Vianna, B. C. (2020). Generative Art: Between the Nodes of Neuron Networks. *Artnodes*, (26), 1-9.

Whale, G. (2002, October). Why use computers to make drawings?. In *Proceedings of the 4th conference on creativity & cognition* (pp. 65-71).

Williford, B., Doke, A., Pahud, M., Hinckley, K., & Hammond, T. (2019). DrawMyPhoto: assisting novices in drawing from photographs. In *Proceedings of the 2019 on Creativity and Cognition* (pp. 198-209).

Wolfram, S. (2002). *A New Kind of Science.* Champaign, Illinois: Wolfram Media, Inc.

Wright, R. (2019). Defacing the 'Balloon Dog': Art, Algorithmic Culture and Augmented Reality. In *Augmented Reality Games II* (pp. 263-274). Springer, Cham.

Yamshchikov, I. P., & Tikhonov, A. (2018). I Feel You: What makes algorithmic experience personal?. *Politics of the Machines-Art and After 7*, 1-6.

Zeilinger, M. (2018). Digital art as 'monetised graphics': Enforcing intellectual property on the blockchain. *Philosophy & Technology*, *31*(1), 15-41.

Zheqian, D. L. (2021, January). The Visual Performance of Technology and Philosophy in" Contemporary Art". In *Proceedings of the 2021 International Conference on Bioinformatics and Intelligent Computing* (pp. 372-378).

Zylinska, J. (2020). *AI Art: Machine Visions and Warped Dreams* (p. 181). Open Humanities Press.

Chapter 5

Fanart: A Man, His Gun, His Dog, and His Car

Shalin Hai-Jew*
Kansas State University, Manhattan, KS, USA

Abstract

Enthusiasts of various created media works may express their personal connection, interests, and obsessions, with various artworks. Depending on the fanartist's vision and skills, some of these may be fairly derivative, and others may be quite original. Many such works may be seen on the Social Web on art-sharing sites, personal websites, social media accounts, image-sharing sites, and other locales. This work explores a thin slice of contemporary fanart in the exploration of a fictional character featured in a movie trilogy (soon to be a tetralogy), with films released in 2014, 2017, and 2019.

Keywords: fanart, common art, enthusiast amateur art, derivative works

Introduction

One popular form of "common art" is "fanart," artworks created by amateurs who are passionate about particular cultural materials, like movies, television shows, games, literary works, artworks, art styles, comics, and other individual or combined works. The fanart creators are enthusiasts who can relate to particular worlds, characters, times, lifestyles, storylines, messaging, symbolism, or other aspects, that draw them to the artifacts. The "fan labor" is often provided by the amateur artist, who is often not paid for their efforts. Their works may be wholly original, or they may be derivative of particular cultural content ("Fan art," Aug. 9, 2021), given remix and re-interpretation. The concept is that media are not to be consumed passively but actively, in which the audience participates and breaks down the so-called fourth wall (dramaturgy term); they jump into Huizinga's magic circle. Fanart, which generates surplus value, is produced as part of prosumer (producer + consumer) culture. Some re-portrayals are for amusement; others are for political statements, offering the voices of the disempowered, the fan activists. (One example is the re-portrayal of superheroes as those of different races and genders. Some visuals refer to "BIPOC" or "Black, Indigenous, and people of color" solidarities. Some works advocate for various forms of civil rights). When fans riff on cultural contents and messaging, they are engaging in "what-if"-to show a desirable or

* Corresponding Author's Email: haijes@gmail.com

In: Common Visual Art in a Social Digital Age
Editor: Shalin Hai-Jew
ISBN: 978-1-68507-664-1

undesirable state of the world, and to provoke thoughts and discussions and even actions. For example, one video game elicits a range of works. "…the fandom of Animal Crossing reinterprets the ideologies of the game producing a critique of struggles present in society against sexism and consumerism" but other fanart related to Animal Crossing "aligned with the neoliberal and sexist ideas that emanate from the canonical text" (Moreno, 2020, p. 212). Fanworks are polysemous. They may center or de-center the original inspiring work. The work may be treated with primacy or not.

Textual fanart may be created for "homage, collaboration, or intervention" (Seymour, Nov. 2018, p. 98), so intentionality of the fanartist may also differ. The "homage" case involves the sharing of "love of the original text: the book, graphic novel, movie, TV show, etc." (Seymour, Nov. 2018, p. 102). The "collaboration" case occurs when multiple artists work to create a new work based on the original, perhaps through "remix," to reach a new audience (Seymour, Nov. 2018, p. 104). "Intervention" refers to contrasting the artist vision with the portrayal of the original work to make a comment, such as by gender-bending the various characters or depicting a relationship that may not have existed in the original (Seymour, Nov. 2018, pp. 108-111). Fan artifacts are a product of "social negotiation of meanings and the subcultural production of fantasies, but they are also intended as provocations for further elaboration" (Jenkins, 2018, p. 19).

For many, their works show appreciation for the original. For others, they prefer to tell alternative narratives based on the other work. They may show characters that are more inclusive, such as racial-alternate gender-alternate forms of recognizable characters. For some, these are opportunities to help them develop art skills (through self-apprenticeships) and to gain publicity for their work. Many bring aspects of their own lives and lived experiences to the works. For many, they are expressing a social affiliation and affinity to other fans who have similar interests, by sharing their work.

The range of skills required to engage in fanart varies from those wholly new to certain art practices to those that require high-level skills. Some works are fast sketches and notebook drawings; others may be whole comic books, complex digital drawings, short videos, sculptures, and other artworks. Some fanart may include the practices of "hacking and modding" and involve "the reverse-engineering of media, such as video games, and the reinsertion of their fanart into the hacked media" (Aloisio-Shearer, 2019, p. 7). The Internet (1983) and Web (1989), social media (1997), the Social Web/Web 2.0 (1999), and mobile computing are important technologies that enable fanart to be broadly shared. Various "technology and media" are part of daily life for "Neomillennials" (Králová, 2019, p. 12). These works have come about in a time of transmedia storytelling, in a context of participatory culture.

Review of the Literature

The world of fandom (fans + kingdom) refers to a community of particular fans dedicated to a particular practice or practices. Fandom is "a subcultural community that exists to express a shared enthusiasm for a topic" including those that are "extremely abstruse, rarified, and sophisticated, and in others being broad, open, and easily apprehensible" (Piña, 2020, p. 534). Such communities usually form around particular media works or a particular canon of works.

The fans opt-in to the role, perhaps based on self-identification with a particular fictional world or storyline or character or aesthetic, or some combination of factors.

Historically, fandoms are thought to have existed "for as long as stories have been told" (Lantagne, 2014, p. 263), and "fanworks are as old as creativity itself" (p. 267). Precursors to modern-day fandoms "include oral and mythic traditions of collective interpretation" (Kalinowski, 2013, p. 659). Prior versions of fandoms show them as having "lurked in the shadows, outside the spotlight of the dominant culture" (Lantagne, 2014, p. 266). Fandom was "a marginalized collective" in prior years (Moreno, 2020, p. 216).

Fandom is comprised of "all fan interactions, forums, fanart, and fan fiction on the Internet" (Kalinowski, 2013, p. 658), in online affinity spaces. Fandom today is "a noisy, enthusiastic, and boisterous world" (Lantagne, 2014, p. 266). Fan communities are said to have evolved terms of their own, in part, to differentiate between insiders and outsiders. The various in-groups have their own subcultural milieus and in-group language and understood values. In some cases, there is the sense that fan fiction is for expression in "private" vs. "public" spaces (Lam, 2014, p. 75). The types or modalities of fan production includes the following:

- fanart or fan art (still imagery in analog or digital formats),
- fan comics,
- fanfiction (spinoff retellings of other narratives in text form),
- fanzines (magazines, often themed),
- fanvids (videos),
- fanfilms (films),
- machinima (machine + cinema, in reference to videos created in virtual worlds),
- podific (podcasts, broadcast audio),
- songs,
- music,
- vidding (music videos from multiple media sources),
- cosplay (costuming, performing in character costumes),
- mods or modifications (of computer games, of software, of simulations, of films),
- walk-throughs of videogames (cribsheets for game play, identification of Easter Eggs in games)
- fandubbing (a re-recording of live-action, animation, machinima, or other, with "fundubbing" focused on humorous re-recording),
- multimedia (varied and all combinations)
- and others.

The respective fanartists can respond along particular pre-defined templates (memes, humor, various art styles, and so on), or they may reimagine a wholly different path forward.

They may choose to affirm the original canon, or offer challenges to it. While the works are not *ex nihilo* (and even formal art often is not wholly "out of nothing" or "from nothing"), fanart can range from "blind copying" to "independent art" (Perova, 2018, p. 31). Even a simple inspiration, like the Disney mermaid Ariel, can result in highly different visual interpretations and styles, with different "compositional dynamics" as shown in one research work (Perova, 2018, p. 33). Fans are inspired in different ways, and they see and illustrate and express differently. One researcher writes:

> Fan comics, then, are not merely artworks read and written by the wider fan community. They are also reflected by and reflections of the personal lives of the artists. They can be personal pieces whose context takes meaning from the everyday, or exploratory narratives that explain the gaps in a fandom by referring to the artist's everyday experience. (Price, Jan. 9, 2014).

The creations may also be analog ones, not just digital. Fanart is considered as an "art form" (Manifold, 2007, p. 2). The creations are mimetic and derivative in a sense, but the execution of the respective works can be highly original. Still, the work involves "appropriation of characters and storylines of popular narratives (i.e., novels, comics, graphic stories, films and television stories)" (Manifold, 2007, p. 1), and this harnessing of pop culture triggers concerns by copyright holders.

There is no known comprehensive archival of the diverse production of fanartists. One researcher writes: "Due to the extraordinary diversity in fandoms, it is unlikely that a complete, exhaustive accounting of the creativity of all fandoms can ever be given" (Piña, 2020, p. 537). In many cases, such works are private and never see the light of public day, and many online shared works are transiently shared, without archival.

In one study, the researcher observes a tie between early youth and fandoms. She writes: "Entrance into fandom communities typically began (69%) when the respondents were between the ages of 12-14, although a significant number of respondents (nearly 25%) became fans as older adolescents or adults" (Manifold, 2007, p. 3). The youth were drawn by "complex stories people by characters with intricate psychologies in complicated relationships" (Manifold, 2007, p. 3). Many engaged in fanart to better understand characters' internal lives and motivations and more about themselves: "The purpose of fanart and cosplay was not to lose one's sense of self in the pop-culture story or character, but to *find oneself.* The character that was drawn repeatedly or imitated in cosplay presented an *instructive* archetype" (Manifold, 2007, p. 6). This point is also made in a more recent work. For some, the play in fanart enables people to explore new identities and ways of being and can really change people's lives. One example is described in a research work in which a fanartist renegotiated self-identity through fan art design and experienced "an increase in self- and linguistic confidence and social inclusion" (Sauro, 2017, p. 135). Another work suggests the crafting of "fanart illustrations as images of self" by youth (Manifold, 2009, p. 7).

Over time, however, as more skills are gained, perhaps the artist has moved beyond seeing the character as self: "By the time a fanartist has developed basic skills and some confidence in her abilities to create competent fanart images, she is less likely to see the characters she illustrates as extension of her own persona" (Manifold, 2009, p. 13). The interest transfers, perhaps, to drawing skills or other facets in the space. The personal art journey (Hunt, Apr. 2015), extending from fan art, may mean a more mature sense of the artist-self, ultimately.

Youth engage in fanart to better understand the larger world (Manifold, 2007, p. 3), including diverse other cultures. Some of the relatively older fanartists acquired self-taught skills (Manifold, 2007), in both analog and digital formats.

At the high end, a fanartist is skilled and insightful: "The consummate fanartist is an excellent craftsperson whose unique aesthetic approaches to framing significant metaphoric elements of others' stories distinguish his or her works as original reproductions" (Manifold, 2012, p. 37). They can auteurs at framing an issue; they are able to see differently. Once a fanartist masters the ability to "exactly copy a subject," he or she then progresses to experimenting with variations (Manifold, 2012, p. 44). They advance to learning more complex aspects of artmaking like "shading, foreshortening, use of texture, or process related to particular media" (Manifold, 2012, p. 44). They may try for attention from experts in the space.

Fan art is harnessed for less formal (informal, nonformal) learning paths to art (Karpati, Freedman, Castro, Kallio-Tavin, & Heijnen, 2017); however, some may develop a deeper sense of interest in art skills. Educators see promise in online fan practices leading to interest in formal art learning (Manifold, 2007), so fanart can be a pipeline into formal and accredited art learning. This is not to say that there are not tensions arising between teen learners and teachers as they negotiate the digital visual culture outside the classroom (Olson, 2016, p. 8), according to one study of Visual Culture Learning Communities (VCLC) online. Youth online engage in "gaming, fanart, video, graffiti, and other 'off-limits' art" (Olson, 2016, p. 10), which may be too "subversive" for the formal classroom. An earlier work studying visual culture learning communities highlights the power of "learning through production" (Freedman, Heijnen, Kallio-Tavin, Kárpáti, & Papp, 2013, p. 112), given the augmentary power of such learning to complement classroom curricular and instruction (Freedman, Heijnen, Kallio-Tavin, Kárpáti, & Papp, 2013, p. 113); further, there are benefits to immersing in "art and art context knowledge" (p. 114). Tensions between a fanartist learner and an art teacher can result in the learner dropping out (Manifold, Nov. 2013, p. 12). Fandoms "represent a kind of intense learning environment-minus the 'grown-ups'" (Gutiérrez, Jan. 2011, p. 230). There are differences between in-school and "outside-of-school literacies" (Gutiérrez, Jan. 2011, p. 226) for those in K12.

Fanart is seen as leading learners to language and literacy learning (Sauro, 2017). The initial interest, if maintained, may expand from a focus on an artifact or character to cultural interest and then foreign language acquisition (Sauro, 2017, p. 134). The researcher writes:

> Fansubbing and scanlation encompass cooperative fan practices that merge technology, popular media, and second language learning and use. Fansubbing is the amateur subtitling of television shows, movies, and especially *anime*... while scanlation, a portmanteau of scan and translation, is the translation and distribution of comics and graphic novels, in particular *manga*... (Sauro, 2017, p. 138).

In some ways, the cultural production of a society may be used as soft power, given the power to attract globally.

Where some teachers see students coming from fanart, librarians also describe the benefits of harnessing fan fiction enthusiasms to reach out to their shyer patrons (Ford & Deja, 2016, p. 34). Some librarians are even starting fan fiction groups. Others observe how the enthusiasms of fans may show the co-harnessing of entertainment and education cultures (Králová, 2019). There are beneficial effects of fandom culture on learning for the so-called neo-millennials

(Králová, 2019). Fanart may be the start of professional competence given the power of social affinity for long-term enduring interests and persistence (Bergin, 2016).

Online fan spaces are described as follows:

> In online spaces, fans, defined as individuals 'with a relatively deep positive emotional conviction about someone or something famous' (Duffet, 2013, p. 18) make use of digital tools and communication technologies to discuss, share, create, or otherwise respond to a public performance or figure including, for example, music and musicians, literature, sports and athletes, theater television, and film and performers (Sauro, 2017, p. 132).

In healthy online fan spaces, fans share information, camaraderie, enthusiasms, and inspirations; they offer each other mutual support and respect. They have not just been herded into an online space to be turned into money-spending consumers.

In creative-focused online fan spaces, the organizers and members offer challenges, competitions, and events to encourage particular focuses. Digital networked society practices with the hyper connectivity of ICT enables the sociality of fandoms, in which practitioners may be attracted by "a book, movie, or performer" (Sauro, 2017, p. 133). The interrelationships among the fans themselves and between fans and their favorite celebrities may evolve into parasocial relationships, one-way connections in which the followers may imagine that there is a two-way mutual connection. The imagined parasocial relationship by fans of their focal celebrities tend to "weaken the mental and psychological boundaries between fans and celebrity" (Hung, 2014, p. 159). In some cases, the fans experience strong emotional connections with the characters, with whom they relate or empathize. The characters may sometimes be proxies for themselves. There may be aspirational motivations, with fans wanting to emulate the celebrity (Hung, 2014). The fans may be engaging in "wishful identification" or wanting to be like the character (Giles, 2002, p. 12, as cited in Moyer-Gusé, 2008, p. 410).

Some fandoms involve the creation of x-rated adult materials by non-professionals, mostly used to arouse users (Anisimowicz & O'Sullivan, 2017). In a review of the literature (not listed here), the co-authors find that "predictors of sexually explicit fandom use" include "lower religiosity...higher sexual esteem...more permissive sexual attitudes...greater numbers of sexual or romantic partners...being single...and more permissive attitudes toward SEM" (Anisimowicz & O'Sullivan, 2017, pp. 824-825). The usages of the various materials, the types of contents, and the message preferences differed between genders based on the research.

The various online communities are studied, for "fanthropology" (fan + anthropology) and other areas of study (Granshaw, Mar. 19, 2014). Fanart is generally studied within the discipline of cultural studies (Moreno, 2020, p. 213), and there are benefits to engaging in the "microanalysis of fandom pieces" (p. 233).

Commercialization

On the commercial front, various media companies encourage fandom because it drives consumption of their mediated contents and related paraphernalia (t-shirts, mugs, posters, books, and the like), which become collector items. Some fan clubs may include financial charges, for special access, for behind-the-scenes insights. Fan enthusiasms may be monetized through fan events and conferences. The fan experience may be, for some, all-encompassing in a 24/7 way. Some fans extend their commitments into years and even decades.

Hot enthusiasms also drive social media chatter and other echoes. Various self-appointed analysts have set up a cottage industry of "analysis" around particular works, often enriching the consumption. For fans whose imaginations are sparked, they may engage with the particular works at more than surface level; they may bring meta perspectives in terms of symbolism, iconography, themes, and other aspects. Beyond the initial hype with releases of various contents, there may be an extended hype cycle, to extend fan interest.

IP and Fandom

There have been challenges with a sense that fanworks are infringing on intellectual property rights of the creators of the original works. Several though see fanworks as contributory to "a profitable value" (Moreno, 2020, p. 216). Another argues that fanworks can "actually enable further creativity by the copyright-holder and increase the value of the original work rather than detract from it" (Lantagne, 2014, p. 263), under fair use doctrines. The argument goes as follows: "active fandoms producing a large amount of fanworks tend to aid the goals of copyright" with positive effects on the market (Lantagne, 2014, p. 263). Their works may draw attention to the works and rally mass enthusiasms, in participatory culture. Modern fans are not lulled into a commercial relationship with a company to express their enthusiasms monetarily only but choose to engage more on their own terms and in active ways (Gutiérrez, Jan. 2011, p. 227).

Research Methods

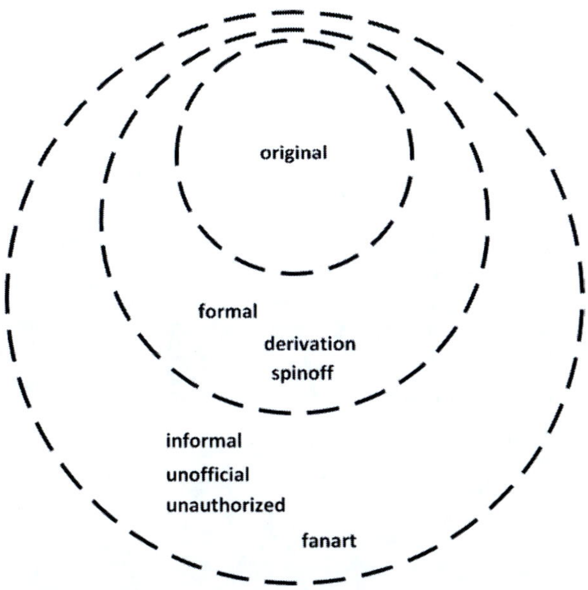

Figure 1. Fanart in the third circle from the original center.

To summarize, fanworks exist in the outer circle (or ring) of concentric circles. At the heart are the original works which inspire the fanworks. In the second circle are formal derivations and spinoffs. The two inner circles are original cultural contents. In the third circle are informal, unofficial, and unauthorized (for the most part) works by the fanartists. [In a few rare cases, fanartists are recruited by brand owners to promote the cultural products]. The fanworks are more diluted and vary in their connection to the original (Figure 1).

Selecting "John Wick"

To explore fanart, the researcher had to select a topic that could seed a set of social imagery. The researcher had to have sufficient background in the original work to assess the fanart. There had to be sufficient visual resources for meaningful analysis. Ideally, the works would be created in various visual traditions. Finally, the author chose "John Wick," even though she had only seen *John Wick Chapter 3: Parabellum* (2019) and only had a vague impression of the general multi-movie storyline. This film is the most recent in the franchise, and it garnered many accolades for both the central star and the director. Perhaps a pseudo-naïve approach may surface different insights, in the same way that blurring the eyes temporally can highlight some aspects of a scene and not others. In the movie, John Wick is trying to escape death with various bands of assassins chasing him since a bounty was placed on his life by the High Table. As an ex-commando, he has various effective fighting skills, and he leaves stacks of bodies behind in various confrontations. The fighting is visceral and cinematic. The actor behind the John Wick character is Keanu Reeves, who has a reputation as a "nice guy" in Hollywood, a dedicated and hard-working actor who does most of his own stunts (with an impressive IMDB profile), and an artist in his own right besides. A Google Search under "Keanu Reeves" results in 19 million hits on the Web and Internet.

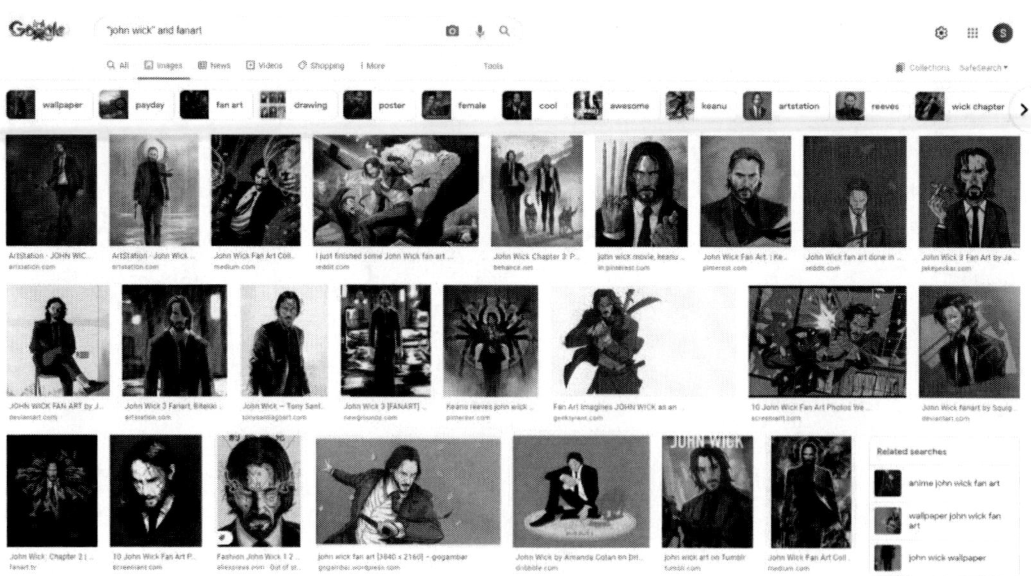

Figure 2. Results from the "'John Wick' and fanart" social imagery search on Google Images.

To capture a social image set, the seeding terms "'john wick' and fanart" were used. This resulted in a collection of 473-images across the Web from the Google Image Search. The tags for filtering were the following: "wallpaper, payday, fan art, drawing, poster, female, cool, awesome, Keanu, artstation, reeves, wick chapter, movie, twitter, Keanu reeves, artist, artstation john, illustrator" (Figure 2).

An early set of questions were drafted to aid in the image coding. The first block deals with the original work. The second block deals with the fanart.

Original work (in this case, a film):

- What is the original work or series?
- What is the created world? What are the rules of this created world, and why?
- What is attractive of a particular personality? Charisma? Character? Physicality? Clothing? Body art? Decorations?
- What themes are prevalent in the original work?
- What phenomena are being depicted and shown?
- What sorts of critiques are made in formal reviews?
- What is the culture from which the work has emerged?

Derived fanart (in this case, depictions in social imagery):

- What is conveyed about context?
- Of the created fanart, what is apparently derived? (inauthentic)
- Of the created fanart, what is apparent not derived? (authentic)
- What variations are there to the created world?
- What sorts of social commentary are apparently made?
  - What other messages are being conveyed?

- What is conveyed about tools?
- What are the cultures from which the work has emerged?
- What sorts of obsessions are being communicated?
- What psychological needs of the fanartists are being met?

Results

A majority of the social imagery linked to the "'john wick' and fanart" pay homage to a beloved character, a man who has lost his wife to illness, and then is victimized by petty thugs who kill his dog, Daisy, his dying wife's last gift to him. He is provoked into defending his territory and responds with effective violence against his enemies. On-screen, John Wick is stylishly dressed… to kill. He has a tattoo on his back, which reads "fortune favors the brave" in Latin (or *fortis fortuna adiuvat*). In *Parabellum*, he lives in a dangerous world where those who approach him are out for his blood, including those who were former allies.

The 473 visuals focus almost singularly on John Wick, with a few depictions of other characters, like "Winston" and "Sofia" and a few on the Belgian Malinois dogs from *Chapter*

3. Several of the visuals draw on the dark color palette and atmospherics of a city at night, with the neon and other lights reflecting off the wet pavement. A number of works show John Wick in familiar iconography: a man walking in a suit with a gun in hand. There are depictions of a man, his gun, and his loyal dog. Then, there is a man, his gun, his dog, and his car. Several works show a John Wick discharging large automatic weaponry. One visual shows a shooting target on John Wick's midriff. One work shows John Wick with a bruised and cut face. One visual shows the character John Wick surrounded by hands pointing guns; in another, he is approached by attackers carrying pencils, with the sharp ends pointed at him. A number of visuals show a man alone, beset upon by the world, but pushing back. [This theme appears in many movies and novels for an American audience. There is a cultural allure of a highly skilled man vs. the world]. John Wick is also civilized, as indicated by his taste in high-end suits and high-end weaponry. He lives by an internal code of vengeance, paying back in kind, two-fold or three-fold. In many senses, these elements are parts of Americana. In another sense, these are universals.

Several works show him as something of a poet-warrior, with one work reconceptualizing John Wick as Auguste Rodin's *Thinker.* On apparent fanartwork is memorable. It is a watercolor of John Wick, with his eyes closed. It is a closeup depiction. His signature dark hair is white. He looks contemplative, maybe pained in his recollections. A professionally rendered cartoon shows John Wick taking on multiple men in a fight simultaneously and discharging a weapon in the fight. It is all kinetics and fit men fighting with brains, brawn, training (Japanese jiujitsu, Brazilian jiujitsu, and judo), and weaponry (knives and guns, mostly guns). When the world encroaches, a cinematic response involves massive violence. Several of the visuals show a John Wick character with pencils. In one, three fingers of his right hand are made up of long sharpened pencils. In another, a cartoon rendering of John Wick shows him with a dog and a pencil. Apparently, in one of the earlier movies, Wick used pencils to dispatch a number of those attacking him (in some memorably gross scenes). [The movie uses the build-up of tension and then the release of it through fight scenes and humor as a repeating motif].

One work shows John Wick holding a bleeding finger that has been separated from someone else's body. Another work shows a t-shirt with a John Wick character wearing a shirt labeled "boyfriend." In another photo, there is a "don't mess with my dog!" shirt. In yet another t-shirt, John Wick's face is imprinted on a black t-shirt worn by a man with a beard. One shows a suit without a wearer.

In terms of quality, there were some professional drawings, some professional movie filters, and others. There were some lightly digitally edited screengrabs from the films, applied with light image filters (color overlays) and light editing. Other pieces in this collection include screengrabs (as thumbnails), logos, icons, and other desiderata.

Several visuals show John Wick with eye sockets without irises. In some they are yellow. The depiction may represent something of fierceness. Perhaps they represent something of a soullessness. Or perhaps this is a signifier of being "badass" (considered a positive).

One visual looks like a 3D animation, in which a John Wick character is shooting guns with both hands and has his dog nearby. Another similar one shows a man on the run, shooting cross-wise from each hand, albeit with a dog riding on his shoulders; this one is a line drawing. These works seem mostly derivative without much in the way of dilution. The essential dynamics and drama are depicted. This imageset did not result in any obvious predominant work or two, except those of the highly reproduced movie posters. Most seemed to be re-enactments and figurative visuals.

Discussion

With each new film release, former fans and new ones are activated and perhaps inspired to create celebratory artworks. The works in the social image data scrape show references to understandings from the very first movie onwards, and only some referred to the most recent one. While Keanu Reeves and his character John Wick are both highly appealing to many, perhaps creating art is not the most common way that people show their devotion. Over time, as the movie franchise around John Wick ends, perhaps the fan club fervor will slowly dissipate, and only a few diehard fans will remain (as with every other fanart community). The creation of art is effortful, and this is not a typical direction to go with the showing of enthusiasm for a movie character, except a few.

Future Research

The John Wick franchise is characterized by quality bravura filmmaking, and it features a highly charismatic and talented star, Keanu Reeves. A sampling of 473 social images related to "fanart" around John Wick did not show narratives that challenged the storytelling of the film series per se. Perhaps future research may expand to other forms of fan art, like fanfiction, that may show higher dimensionality than paying homage to a Hollywood star and a fictional world of highly stylized violence.

[As a side note, there are more professional artworks based on "'John Wick' and 'celebrity art'" social image sources. This set includes film posters, paintings, poster prints, canvas prints, printed blankets, handmade wall decors, pixel art, string art, concept art, portraits, mixed media sculptures, mixed media sketches, word art ("You got my car"), paraphernalia from film scenes (coinage, guns, suits), and sendups (photos of a regular man posing as John Wick, cartoon-inspired drawings)].

Conclusion

The cost of entry to fanart, as a common art, is a low one. Participation in this space is open to any who may be interested. Depending on the collected works and modalities, these may touch on something of the massmind around a particular topic or character or plotline. The fanart around John Wick suggests foci on American loves: a handsome hero, cinematic violence, love of a faithful pet dog, adoration for cars, a sense of justice, and other simple cares. It turns out that celebrities do not own or monopolize their likeness in terms of others' portrayals, and they do not own what goes on in the imaginations of the wider public audiences who adore them.

References

"Fan art." (2021, Aug. 9). *Wikipedia.* Retrieved from https://en.wikipedia.org/wiki/Fan_art.

Aloisio-Shearer, N. (2019). Fragile Fantasy: Photography and Critical Responses to 3D Video Game Images. *Master's thesis.* UNSW Art and Design.

Anisimowicz, Y., & O'Sullivan, L. F. (2017). Men's and women's use and creation of online sexually explicit materials including fandom-related works. *Archives of sexual behavior*, 46(3), 823-833.

Bergin, D. A. (2016). Social influences on interest. *Educational Psychologist*, 51(1), 7-22.

Ford, A., & Deja, T. (2016). Fellowship of the fans. *American Libraries*, 47(11-12), 34-39.

Freedman, K., Heijnen, E., Kallio-Tavin, M., Kárpáti, A., & Papp, L. (2013). Visual culture learning communities: How and what students come to know in informal art groups. *Studies in Art Education*, 54(2), 103-115.

Granshaw, L. (2014, Mar. 19). *When academia and Tumblr combine: The fascinating new field of fanthropology.*

Gutiérrez, P. (2011, Jan.) Focus on policy: The right to be a fan. *Language Arts,* 88(3), 226-231.

Hung, K. (2014). Why celebrity sells: A dual entertainment path model of brand endorsement. *Journal of advertising*, *43*(2), 155-166.

Hunt, K. (2015). *Internet Culture, Nature, and Fanart: A Year of Exploration in Technique and Inspiration.*

Jenkins, H. (2018). Fandom, negotiation, and participatory culture. In P. Booth's (ed.) *A companion to media fandom and fan studies,* 13-26. Hoboken, New Jersey: Wiley Blackwell.

Kalinowski, P. (2013). The fairest of them all: The creative interests of female fan fiction writers and the fair use doctrine. *Wm. & Mary J. Women & L.*, 20, 655.

Karpati, A., Freedman, K., Castro, J. C., Kallio-Tavin, M., & Heijnen, E. (2017). Collaboration in visual culture learning communities: Towards a synergy of individual and collective creative practice. *International Journal of Art & Design Education*, 36(2), 164-175.

Králová, J. (2019). *The Influence of Fandom Culture On Individual Learning and Acquiring the English Language in Relation to Krashen's Hypotheses* (Doctoral dissertation, Masaryk University, Faculty of Arts).

Lam, C. (2014). Breaking the fourth wall: dynamics of fan fiction production. In *Living in the Limelight: Dynamics of the Celebrity Experience* (pp. 75-85). Brill.

Lantagne, S. M. (2014). Sherlock Holmes and the case of the lucrative fandom: recognizing the economic power of fanworks and reimagining fair use in copyright. *Mich. Telecomm. & Tech. L. Rev.*, 21, 263.

Manifold, M. C. (2007). Culture convergence or divergence? Spontaneous art-making and participatory expression in the private and collective lives of youth. *Art Education as Critical Cultural Inquiry*, 262-275. Preprint.

Manifold, M. C. (2009). Fanart as craft and the creation of culture. *International Journal of Education through Art*, *5*(1), 7-21.

Manifold, M. C. (2012). From amateur to framauteur: Art development of adolescents and young adults within an interest-based community. *Studies in Art Education*, 54(1), 37-53.

Manifold, M. C. (2013). Enchanting tales and imagic stories: The educational benefits of fanart making. *Art Education*, *66*(6), 12-19.

Moreno, J. A. (2020). Game rules vs. fandom. How Nintendo's Animal Crossing fan-made content negotiates the videogame meanings. *Ámbitos. Revista Internacional de Comunicación*, (47), 212-237.

Moyer-Gusé, E. (2008). Toward a theory of entertainment persuasion: Explaining the persuasive effects of entertainment-education messages. *Communication Theory,* 407-425.

Olson, B. (2016). Tensions in the third space: Examining the digital visual culture of teenagers. *Visual Arts Research*, 42(1), 8-21.

Perova, O. (2018). Fan-Art: Independent Art or Blind Copying? *Young Scientist USA*, 14, 31-36.

Piña, J. (2020). Geeks. Encyclopedia of Creativity: 3rd ed., Vol. 1. 534-538. Elsevier.

Price, L. (2014, Jan. 9). *Fan comics: Comics as fan sense-making in the everyday.* www.hcommons.org.

Sauro, S. (2017). Online fan practices and CALL. *Calico Journal*, 34(2), 131-146.

Seymour, J. (2018). Homage, Collaboration, or Intervention: How framing fanart affects its interpretation. *Participations*, 15(2), 98-114.

Chapter 6

Examining "Data Art" for Signs of the 4IR

Shalin Hai-Jew*

Kansas State University, Manhattan, KS, USA

Abstract

In the current datafied moment, as a subset of algorithmic art, "data art" which uses data as the medium or one of the mediums is a common visual in online spaces. Visualize glowing node-link diagrams floating in black space like promising galaxies, comets of data streaking across expanding space, cubes of data floating across people's faces, and mountains made up of lines or bars. This work applies content analysis to examine "data art" (with "data" as an adjective and "art" as a noun) from the Social Web for signs of the Fourth Industrial Revolution (4IR). If this is a seminal moment in human history, with major shifts to human work based on a mesh of technological advancements (affecting the physical, digital, and biological) and advancing artificial intelligence (AI), automation, and robotics in workplaces, then how much of this mass-scale awareness has seeped into data art, writ large, and assumed generally to be prescient ahead of general knowledge?

Keywords: data art, Fourth Industrial Revolution, 4IR

Introduction

The widespread access to laptops, mobile devices, and desktop machines, and related office software programs and digital image editing programs, have enabled the broad public to engage in the creation of "data art." These are works that are aesthetically created from available data, both real and faux. The real data may come from various sources. The data may be static, dynamic (real-time and changing), or a mix. In an Einstein relativity sense, the data may be situated in space (geospatial), situated in time (time-based data), situated in motion (changes in space over time). They may be based on people's open-ended textual responses to survey questions. The data may be based on networks of various kinds: social, tag, disease, and others. Data, even in simple datasets, tend towards multi-dimensionality. The data may come from sensor arrays, for environmental and other purposes, as well as from the Internet of Things (IoT). The data may be "big" or "small." Data may be used to generate other data. The data may be the classically structured data or unstructured. People live in a time where there is a

* Corresponding Author's Email: haijes@gmail.com

In: Common Visual Art in a Social Digital Age
Editor: Shalin Hai-Jew
ISBN: 978-1-68507-664-1

constant and "invisible flow" of data, an "endless murmur" (Waelder, 2010), separate from physical location. Data is "at the heart of digital culture," and with ubiquitous digital technologies, digital data and materials are "a legitimate material through which to reflect our lives" (Freeman, Wiggins, Starks, & Sandler, 2018, p. 75). As part of scientific practice, data is often made openly available to enhance research and discovery (Pasquetto, Randles, & Borgman, 2017). In democratic systems, open data is a common value, with hundreds of thousands of datasets available on the data.gov data portal of the U. S.

The shape of data has varied instantiations in a particular contemporaneous-historical moment. The Fourth Industrial Revolution (4IR) is said to be upon humanity. The adoption of technologies for various efficiencies will "alter the way we live, work, and relate to one another" and will be "unlike anything humankind has experienced before" (Schwab, Jan. 14, 2016) [The First Industrial Revolution was based on the uses of steam power to "mechanize" production; the Second around electronic power to enable mass production; the Third around "electronics and information technology to automate production"; the Fourth based on "a fusion of technologies that is blurring the lines between the physical, digital, and biological spheres" (Schwab, Jan. 14, 2016)]. The SARS-CoV-2/COVID-19 pandemic, started in late 2019, has been seen as an accelerant into the advances of technologies, given the human need to socially distant to protect each other from the air-transmissible pathogenic virus. How humanity engages post-pandemic, with themselves, with each other, with technologies, and with the world, is as-yet unclear.

If art is a way for humanity to engage mass discussions about social issues, then perhaps, data art may reveal something about people's relationships to data and technologies in a 4IR moment. "Data art" is "a full-fledged and maturing artistic practice" (Singer, 2016, p. 1). It is taught in art education programs. There are mentions of data art in graduate theses and dissertations. In the academic research literature, there are mentions of data art in tangibles, wearables, jewelry, fiber art, museum installations, sculptures, public projections on large-scale structures, LED sculptures and arrays, event-based shows (using UAVs), and other manifestations. They are multi-sensory: visual, auditory, and tactual, and in various combinations. Some are built into the environment as forms of "ambient displays" to be viewed at the periphery of human attention, in some cases (Moere, 2007, p. 80).

Perhaps a data scrape of "data art" social imagery may enable insights into how people transcode data into visuals in analog (physical), digital, and mixed forms. If professional artists and common folk who make art are sentient carriers of culture, perhaps the artworks themselves may show something of human metamorphosis into data-consuming creatures, who are both forward and backward facing simultaneously.

This work explores some aspects of "data art" as acquired as social imagery. The research questions are the following, based on bottom-up coding and top-down coding (in terms of the focus on the 4IR).

1. Underlying data: What apparent data are used in "data art"? Is it possible to re-identify data from the various data art?
2. Techniques: What are the apparent methods for the creation of the common data art? The related design concepts? What methods were used to transcode the underlying data or mixed data into a visual representation? Is there a direct indexing or mapping from the data to the visual? Or what other variated approaches are there to arrive at the still visuals?

3. Data art manifestations: How are the data art pieces used virtually, in hybrid space, in physical space? How do they manifest? What are the most common apparent types of manifestations based on the social imagery?
4. Aesthetic pleasures: What is meant by aesthetic pleasure in relation to data art? How much of the aesthetic pleasure is "universal" vs. "subjective"? (On what basis can this assertion be made, if possible?)
5. 4IR: What does "data art" show about the Fourth Industrial Revolution (4IR)? Technologies? Humans in relation to fusions of cutting- and bleeding-edge technologies?
6. Messaging. What sort of messaging was embedded in the "data art" social imagery? What are some of the political statements made by the artists using data as the material for their artworks and pieces?

Review of the Literature

In the modern information age, "data art" is thought to have originated in the late 1990s. One researcher describes data art this way:

> Data art, put most simply, is an artistic practice that uses data as its medium. Artists are both using data from external sources and collecting or creating data as part of their work. The art works cut across many mediums (e.g., digital, sculpture, photography) and genres. This makes the category nebulous. Data art can be conceptual or abstract. Data art is sometimes overtly political, but not always. It can be straightforward and functional or intentionally obscure… Despite this vagueness, the category of data art is undeniable. (Singer, 2016, p. 1)

Artists are "recombining bits to build something new out of the commonplace" (Singer, 2016, p. 1). Others affirm the sense that data art is still evolving: "Data art, as a practice, is still defining itself, more precisely because of the lack of conceptualization of data as an art material" (Freeman et al., 2018, as cited in Paquin, 2019, p. 37).

The ambitions of data art go beyond aesthetics. Some "data art" works involve novel creations to help people engage with the world differently. One project involves the creation of two devices - a hydrogen cubed (or H^3) tool and a Solar Radiation Dowsing Rod (as "crossmodal data-driven artefacts" with tangible interfaces) to enable access to information usually only accessed by experts (Hogan & Hornecker, Feb. 2013, p. 275). People can better see the otherwise invisible. Other works are educative, too, and enhance science communication (Pelto, Dec. 2018) and promote environmentalism (Singer, 2016, p. 1). Data art may provide insights into "hidden, inaccessible worlds" or enable new understandings beyond the surface meanings of data (Singer, 2016, p. 2). Network data art can show interconnections and perhaps inform improved ethical decision making (Pilcher, 2012) based on a more intuitive understanding of systems and power. The data art may enable knowledge transfer that leads to behavior change.

In the education context, learners may familiarize themselves with methods for effective visual representations of data (Klein, 2014). There are efforts at articulating standards to evaluate artful data visualizations (Taylor, 2017). Data art may have effects on art education.

For example, it is possible to mine big data for more hidden insights. (Tian, Nov. 2016, p. 1433) Data visualization is used for "teaching creative design principles" (Moere, 2007, p. 71).

Conventional Informational Visualization Standards vs. Artful Communications Approaches

On the more traditional end, data art may be based on defined standards (from statistical modeling and informational visualization), which may be in tension with artful communications standards. There may be concerns about "the discrepancy between the visual appeal of these displays and their divergence from the usual principles of statistical graphics" (Gelman & Unwin, Mar. 2013, p. 3). Data has been visualized for thousands of years, such as through the work of mapmakers and designers (Freeman, Wiggins, Starks, & Sandler, 2018, p. 75). Data art fulfills multiple goals simultaneously, with the various standards held in tension.

At the other extreme, the data art transmutes to something beyond the original data. One definition for "data artification" makes this case:

> Data ratification is not concerned with making data aesthetically appealing, hence it should not be confused with the notion of aestheticization… data artification is intellectually dissident in more radical ways than academia. It is critically meta-artistic and meta-scientific since it deconstructs empty data fetishes and produces new meanings or knowledge-making forms in interstitial and intersemiotic ways. (Civiliene, 2020, n. p.)

From the data comes something original and novel and provocative.

Some data artworks are not encapsulated inside the four walls of museums and art galleries. One work describes massive digital projections on structures (like a river-spanning bridge) and data sculptures. The researcher writes: "Data art has evolved quickly in the last decade. The practice that was mainly based on a diffusion on a screen now also materializes itself in the public space under different formats and shapes" (Paquin, 2019, p. 32). Such works inform the digital placemaking of a city or location (as a global destination). These works augment and enrich the physical spaces:

> Digital art, in this context, can provide new relationships to a place or provoke new sensory experiences in a way that can also be dynamic and renewable. Interactivity allows people to engage with the artwork, which, accordingly, mediates the space. Digital placemaking involves a redefinition of the notion of space, from the physical to an augmented one; it is a 'process of using digital media or shaping experiences that are citizen-centric, in modes of 'augmenting' and positively reinforcing urban space' (Tomitsch, 2016, p. 340, as cited in Paquin, 2019, p. 35)

Plays on Materiality

Some of the research works describe interactions between data and materiality. One work describes the design of a silver-plated 3D teapot with an original design informed by an actual teapot (Starrett, Reiser, & Pacio, 2018, p. 381). This work shows the dynamics of so-called "data materialization" based on data informed designs, from analog to digital to analog.

Another clever work focuses on human exchanges based on valuations of commodities used historically as forms of exchange (rice, sugar, and salt) interacting in an updated way with valuations of a cryptocurrency, which affect electronic lighting interwoven through a kilogram of the raw food products. How do people value non-digital and digital commodities, and how do they engage the data of valuations? This work touches on the weight of "physical, edible commodities - rice, sugar and salt" (Kim, 2018, p. 1) and a contrastive ephemera of the value of cryptocurrencies simultaneously. Underlying this work is "an algorithm that calculates the value of single cryptocurrency into the weight of each commodity value" (Kim, 2018, p. 1), with the data updating every two minutes.

Multimodal Manifestations

Some data art is created in interactive and live contexts, with multi-sensory signals. One performative data art piece involves using dynamic real-time data sources to create sonic outputs, allowing a performer to "alter the scale, granularity, timbre, hierarchy of elements, spatialization, spectral filtering, key/modality, rhythmic distribution and register 'on-the-fly' to both perform data-generated music, and investigate data in a live exploratory, interactive manner" (Beilharz, & Ferguson, 2009, p. 35).

Several of the research works describe the uses of personal data for data art. One builds on the "quantified self" concept. In one work, the researcher suggests the importance of individuals applying some artful creativity to their personal self-tracking sensor data to be more meaningfully expressive. In this conceptualization, the quantified self is "determined more by creative skills and less by the tools used" (O'Neill, 2019, p. 163). The digital doppelgänger should be informed by individual agency:

> The tools of self-tracking are about constructing digital versions of ourselves that allow us to reflect to ourselves and others, who we are and how we change over time. Lack of agency and control over the tools we use to make these versions of ourselves, restricts our ability to manifest who we really want to be. (O'Neill, 2019, p. 170)

Individual biometrics may be harnessed for data art. One such art installation enables the turning of people's unique biometric iris data into musical sounds and 3D animated imagery and some sculptures (Han & Surve, May 2019, p. 1). The iris offers a unique biometric signature, as data, to drive the performative art.

> In this installation, audience members can capture their iris images with a customized USB web camera… They can observe personalized audiovisual outcome based on their captured and manipulated iris data. A three-dimensional converted image is projected on a wall, and it starts playing sound once the image is animated. Extracted visual features of the iris data determine the timbre and melody of the sound. The audience can also observe 3D printed sculptures… next to the interactive art installation. Selected distinct iris data is selected and printed in 3D form, and it includes projected images over the sculptures that loop iris image along with audio based on the iris image data. (Han & Surve, May 2019, p. 2)

Another work captures the mood of a crowd based on their tagging of social imagery to create unique LED light sculptures, based on a collaboration between "artists and information scientists" (Kim, Gay, Reynolds, & Hong, Apr. 2015, p. 347). Group moods are transient, and communal emotional statuses may help people understand those around them. There are creative uses of data "in alternative modalities" to enable tangible embodied experiences of data (Hogan, Jan. 2015, p. 425).

Interactivity

Some data art take as inputs some direct feedback from the general public. One is "an interactive web application to explore neural style transfer using models trained on data visualizations" (Dubey, Otto, & Forbes, 2019, p. 1). This program enables people to interact with the program through a mode in which "casual creators" can contribute to the creation of original artworks (Dubey, Otto, & Forbes, 2019, p. 1).

Political Communications

One researcher focuses on "outliers" in data as a basis for data art. The researcher writes: "Minorities in data are often left out from or under-represented in the collection and contextual processing of data due to being anomalies" (Kim, 2020, p. ii). The artwork then builds on this concept of minorities by using data outliers for artful exploration.

Research Methods

This work involves the application of content analysis to social media images scraped from across the Web based on the seeding term "data art" in Google Images Search. This resulted in the collection of 1,002 images. For this imageset, the autogenerated filtering tags on Google Images included the following: installation, visualization, climate change, science, graphic, artistic, digital, abstract, beautiful, generative, interactive, statistical, design, music, infographic, star trek, immersive, computer, poster, illustration, creative, drawing, wall, lieutenant commander, global warming, cool, nature, vector, information, transparent (Figure 1). On the whole, the social images were topical, with only a few outlier works [Side note: Another attempt to capture "data art" and "4IR" resulted in only 20 visuals, many of them book covers].

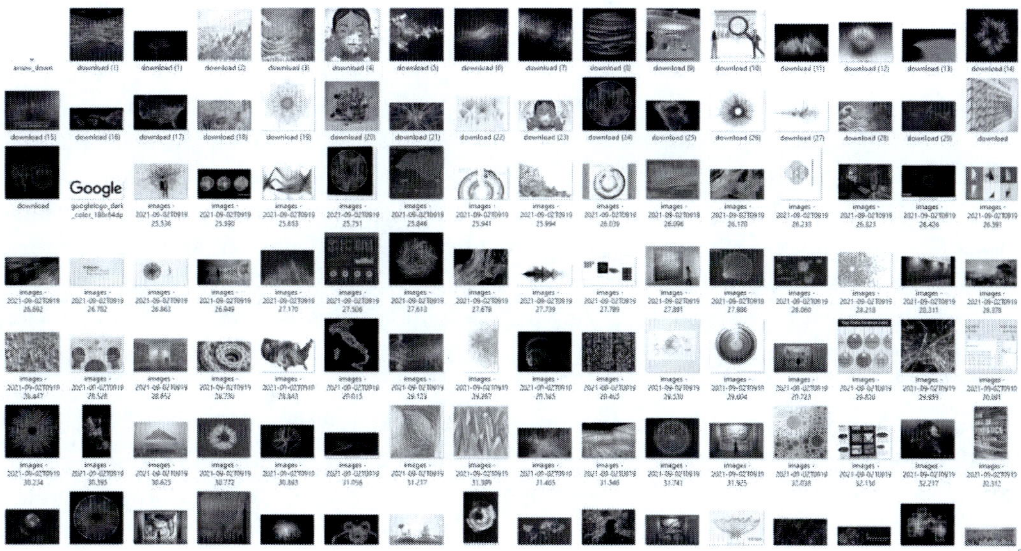

Figure 1. A sampling of "Data Art" from the Social Web (from Google Images Search).

The social imagery was coded in a bottom-up way, through multiple iterations. Six general angles were used, based on the following questions:

1. Underlying data: What apparent data are used in "data art"? Is it possible to re-identify data from the various data art?
2. Techniques: What are the apparent methods for the creation of the common data art? The related design concepts? What methods were used to transcode the underlying data or mixed data into a visual representation? Is there a direct indexing or mapping from the data to the visual? Or what other variated approaches are there to arrive at the still visuals?
3. Data art manifestations: How are the data art pieces used virtually, in hybrid space, in physical space? How do they manifest? What are the most common apparent types of manifestations based on the social imagery?
4. Aesthetic pleasures: What is meant by aesthetic pleasure in relation to data art? How much of the aesthetic pleasure is "universal" vs. "subjective"? (On what basis can this assertion be made, if possible?)
5. 4IR: What does "data art" show about the Fourth Industrial Revolution (4IR)? Technologies? Humans in relation to fusions of cutting- and bleeding-edge technologies?
6. Messaging. What sort of messaging was embedded in the "data art" social imagery? What are some of the political statements made by the artists using data as the material for their artworks and pieces?

The social images are de-contextualized. On a few occasions, the works may be recontextualized with citations in academic articles. The researcher did not purposefully try to reidentify the locations of the works with reverse image searches but focused on available observations with the works as stand-alone ones.

Results

The "data art" social imageset from Google Images is dominated by data as various objects in space: nodes and links exploding out like fireworks against a black sky, a planetary shape with various undulating lines, a wide comet tail of colors speeding off into space, a sphere created from patterned lines radiating outwards in angles, constellations of brightly colored dots against a black sky, and others. One shows a Rubrik's cube floating in space. With floating cubes all around. Another work showed glowing cubes (purple and blue) levitating from a box.

There are Earth-based visuals: a global map with clusters of blue bubbles of different intensities in different regions, a glowing node-link network placed on the U. S. against a black backdrop (for contrast), flowing hills and valleys of lines against a black backdrop, a representation of Italy, and other spatially mapped data. One frequency curve is depicted as a jagged mountain range. Another shows a frequency curve on top of a roller coaster's scaffolding. One work evoked a 3d topographical map, expressed as artful lines. One aerial photo showed landscape art being formed with sheep (who move to the location based on feed placement in the field).

Then, there are some visuals without a physical location equivalent: yellow spheres held in suspension, crisscrossing straight lines of light (or glowing digital lines) across a black background, a b/w hairball with a background gradient, tiered concentric circles, and similar works.

Some visuals show humans in relation to the data art. Several show a silhouetted person in front of a lit ceiling-to-floor art installation of various abstract forms. Others show various data representations (vertical bars, area chart shapes) on people's faces, both male and female. Several works used the image of fingerprints to suggest something of human identity and uniqueness. Several works show mesh-based representations of people: one shows a person walking down a walkway with server racks on both sides; another shows a man's face in mesh, with glowing eyes. One work shows a man in seated lotus position and floating on light above a world that is backlit, evoking a version of Buddhism. One visual shows a human brain depicted in a digital illustration.

Some works look to be programmatically generated, with fractal shapes, others geometric shapes.

Some of the social imagery showed book covers. One showed an open book with digital depictions shown in 3D above (a sailing ship, a man on an island). Several of the social images show academic articles. One work shows a mix of various colorful electrical wires and parts in what looks like a 3D sculpture.

Some of the works build on shapes found in nature, such as trees and flowers. In one data artwork, vertical lines are topped by spanning colorful brushes. One work shows a white fern leaf against a black background, evoking fractal art.

Some of the works look to be classic data visualizations and data plots, with labeled x-, y-, and z-axes. There are several ring lattice (circle) graphs with connecting straight lines inside. There are bubble charts against a quadrant. Some social network graphs are in the set. Some show hub-and-spoke node-link diagrams. One visual shows a glowing grid. Some visuals show treemap diagrams, with high dimensional sub-maps. Several showed streamgraph visualizations, albeit with dots instead of solid fills. One work showed swirling black lines expanding out from the left and moving right, which evokes time-series data.

One work emulates a classic image of Japanese waves transitioning into a mesh image from left to right, with the Great Wave off Kanagawa by Katsushika Hokusai to the left and mesh to the right. Another work showed a watercolor painting that was digitized, so moving from analog to the digital. There was one diptych.

Some are photos of various physical art installations. One shows stacked blocks comprising a frequency curve on a table, and some blocks on the floor below. Some shows involve hanging panels of 2D visuals that people can walk around and view from different angles. Sometimes, there are humans in the photos to evoke scale. Another photo shows an analog area chart, with white blocks representing some of the data. Another photo shows a four-panel foldout screen with bamboo illustrations.

Another showed a book cover with Vincent van Gogh's eyes at the top and abstract shapes below. One referred to his Starry Night, another to his Wheatfield series. Some classic artworks were given the digitization treatment, with various blurring. Several works use the common visual of a stylized motherboard and other circuitry. One work used the common representation for genetic data. One node-link diagram showed Bokeh lights in the background. One visual showed an R2D2 head on a round device used for bathymetry. There was one word cloud. One visual looked to be a screenshot from a virtual immersive world, of a building curve inward (with a sense of virtual physics and not human-world gravity). One showed two wolves cavorting on ice, with floes in the background. Several visuals showed screenshots of web pages. One photo showed an artist drawing with a stylus on a large digital tablet. One photo showed a digital screen on a wall with apparently randomly sequenced natural whole numbers. Another showed a hexagonal hive stack. Another showed falling digital dominos.

Discussion

So what did the 1,002 social images show about the six questions?

1. Underlying data: What apparent data are used in "data art"? Is it possible to re-identify data from the various data art?

Based on visual conventions around data, the data were from frequency data, time series data, social networks, geographical data, and genetic data. In most cases, the data could have been faux data because re-identifying data would not be possible. Certainly, some of the visuals were simple graphic designs. Others were digital image-edited visuals. Others were computer-generated art, with programs written with Processing, and others like fractal art programs.

2. Techniques: What are the apparent methods for the creation of the common data art? The related design concepts? What methods were used to transcode the underlying data or mixed data into a visual representation? Is there a direct indexing or mapping from the data to the visual? Or what other variated approaches are there to arrive at the still visuals?

The social visuals did not show visuals that apparently required much customization. Any number of publicly available programs.

3. Data art manifestations: How are the data art pieces used virtually, in hybrid space, in physical space? How do they manifest? What are the most common apparent types of manifestations based on the social imagery?

In most cases, the visuals showed virtual aspects of the data art, and only a few in physical space (art installations). While the academic literature showed some hybrid manifestations of data art, those were not apparent in the social imagery collection.

4. Aesthetic pleasures: What is meant by aesthetic pleasure in relation to data art? How much of the aesthetic pleasure is "universal" vs. "subjective"? (On what basis can this assertion be made, if possible?)

The aesthetics of the 1,002 social images in the "data art" imageset were simple, with various forms of symmetries, asymmetries, layout, lines for eye movements, and contrasts between glowing lines and black backdrops. There was little in the way of complexity in the visuals themselves, perhaps requiring backstories and context for their power.

5. 4IR: What does "data art" show about the Fourth Industrial Revolution (4IR)? Technologies? Humans in relation to fusions of cutting- and bleeding-edge technologies?

Based on research into the phase of the 4IR and the present moment, perhaps there would be illustrations of health-giving vaccines. There might be visuals of robots, from the micro (nano-scale) to the macro scales, from the humanoid to the non-humanoid, and others. There might be depictions of industrial robotics set up to process human food, human medicines, human cars, and so on. Perhaps there would be depictions of artificial intelligence (AI) and the various types of datasets and data visualizations possible.

6. Messaging. What sort of messaging was embedded in the "data art" social imagery? What are some of the political statements made by the artists using data as the material for their artworks and pieces?

In terms of the 4IR, the "data art" social imagery showed an excitement around technologies, and perhaps an intergalactic hope based on the data and what humanity might do with that data. However, there was nothing to show AI directly, robotics, or much of the biologics suggested by the academic literature around 4IR.

There was generic messaging venerating data, paying homage, perhaps, to its potentials. Very few of the visuals were original; most were visual clichés (data and network graphs floating in space).

Future Research

Data art manifests in a variety of ways based on a review of the academic literature. The social imagery shows a small subset of the data art in the world, perhaps due to the issues of intellectual property. As defined early on, the idea behind "data art" in this work is with "data" as an adjective and "art" as a noun, with art forefronted. Another approach can focus perhaps on "data art" with "data" forefronted and "art" as an accent. The works in this set really did not enable re-capture of the original data, however.

Perhaps the "data art" available on particular art platforms may offer different insights. Or the works of particular art shows (with the art show catalogs) may provide other angles to the six questions.

Certainly, there can be other topics explored, with particular foci around aspects of the Fourth Industrial Revolution, such as biologics in a time of the SARS-CoV-2/COVID-19 pandemic.

Conclusion

Data represents intimate connections to human lives. With the advent of wearable sensors and the IoTs, researchers suggest that users may be sharing raw sensor data without full understanding of how derived knowledge may be extracted from that data and compromise their privacy and result in exploitation (Schneegass, Poguntke, & Machulla, May 2019). Even as the captured social imagery around "data art" shows projections into outer space and other worlds, powerful escape velocity to other planets, the data really is closer to home. The data is us.

Acknowledgments

I adore data in all its forms. I am thankful to the many researchers and data analysts I've worked with over the years, who have strengthened my work.

References

Beilharz, K., & Ferguson, S. (2009). An interface and framework design for interactive aesthetic sonification. *Georgia Institute of Technology*. 35-36.

Civiliene, G. S. (2020, November). Data Artification. In: *International Conference on Design and Digital Communication* (pp. 234-243). Springer, Cham.

Dubey, M., Otto, J., & Forbes, A. G. (2019). *Data Brushes: Interactive style transfer for data art* (pp. 1-9). IEEE.

Freeman, J., Wiggins, G., Starks, G., & Sandler, M. (2018). A concise taxonomy for describing data as an art material. *Leonardo*, 51(1), 75-79.

Gelman, A., & Unwin, A. (2013). Infovis and statistical graphics: different goals, different looks. *Journal of Computational and Graphical Statistics*, 22(1), 2-28.

Han, Y. C., & Surve, P. (2019, May). Eyes: Iris Sonification and Interactive Biometric Art. In: *Extended Abstracts of the 2019 CHI Conference on Human Factors in Computing Systems* (pp. 1-4).

Hogan, T. (2015, January). Tangible Data, a Phenomenology of Human-Data Relations. In: *Proceedings of the Ninth International Conference on Tangible, Embedded, and Embodied Interaction* (pp. 425-428).

Hogan, T., & Hornecker, E. (2013, February). In touch with space: embodying live data for tangible interaction. In: *Proceedings of the 7th international conference on tangible, embedded and embodied interaction* (pp. 275-278).

Kim, Y. (2020). Seeking for outliers: Artistic exploration of data through creative practice (Doctoral dissertation, Queensland University of Technology). 1-157.

Kim, Y. (2018). SIGCHI extended abstracts weight of data. In: *the proceedings of CHI 2018.* Apr. 21-26, 2018. Montreal, Quebec City, Canada. 1-6.

Kim, Y., Gay, G., Reynolds, L., & Hong, H. (2015, April). mood. cloud: Data as Art. In: *Proceedings of the 33rd annual ACM conference extended abstracts on human factors in computing systems* (pp. 347-350).

Klein, S. R. (2014). Making sense of data in the changing landscape of visual art education. *Visual Arts Research*, 40(2), 25-33.

Moere, A. V. (2007). Aesthetic data visualization as a resource for educating creative design. In: *Computer-Aided Architectural Design Futures (CAADFutures) 2007* (pp. 71-84). Springer, Dordrecht.

O'Neill, S. J. (2019). The Artist as Model User: Reflections on Creating with a Quantified Self. In: *Proceedings of the 2019 on Creativity and Cognition* (pp. 163-172).

Paquin, A. G. (2019). Public data art's potential for digital placemaking. *Tourism and Heritage Journal*, 1, 32-48.

Pasquetto, I. V., Randles, B. M., & Borgman, C. L. (2017). On the reuse of scientific data. *Data Science Journal*, 16, 8, 1-9.

Pelto, J. (2018, December). Art as a Platform for Science Communication. In: *AGU Fall Meeting 2018.* AGU.

Pilcher, J. (2012). Network Art Unbound?. *Leonardo*, 45(5), 470-471.

Schneegass, S., Poguntke, R., & Machulla, T. (2019, May). Understanding the impact of information representation on willingness to share information. In: *Proceedings of the 2019 CHI Conference on Human Factors in Computing Systems* (pp. 1-6).

Schwab, K. (2016, Jan. 14). The Fourth Industrial Revolution: Wat it means, how to respond. *World Economic Forum.*

Singer, B. (2016). A chronology of tactics: Art tackles Big Data and the environment. *Big Data & Society*, 3(2), 2053951716665869.

Starrett, C., Reiser, S., & Pacio, T. (2018). Data materialization: a hybrid process of crafting a teapot. In: *ACM SIGGRAPH 2018 Art Gallery* (pp. 381-385).

Taylor, P. G. (2017). Artistic data visualization and assessment in art education. *Visual Arts Research*, 43(1), 59-75.

Tian, L. (2016, November). The Development of Art Education and the Innovation of Talent Cultivation Mode under the Background of Big Data. In: *4th International Conference on Management Science, Education Technology, Arts, Social Science and Economics 2016* (pp. 1430-1433). Atlantis Press.

Waelder, P. (2010). The Constant Murmur of Data. *M/C Journal*, 13(2).

Chapter 7

Contemporary Line Art as "Common Art" on the Social Web

Shalin Hai-Jew*

Kansas State University, Manhattan, KS, USA

Abstract

"Line art" is minimalist, with simple strokes and shapes (and sometimes fills and patterns) on a limited two-dimensional space. These drawings evoke visual ideas, from simple to complex, on people's visual systems. Line art may be created using pen and paper, stylus and tablet, or some combination of the analog and the digital. This work involves the capture of some 999 social images based on "line art common art" as the seeding terms for the visuals from Google Images… and the analysis of these visuals, to understand the current state of line art by amateurs on the Social Web.

Keywords: line art, linework, sketch, draft, common art, Social Web, minimalism

Introduction

The making of visual art "is one of the defining characteristics of the human species" (Morriss-Kay, 2010, p. 158). Drawing is a fundamental practice in the making of visual art of various types. As such, this practice is elemental and ancient.

Line art is probably one of the easiest and earliest types of drawing that a child engages in. It only requires a drawing instrument (crayon, chalk, pen, pencil, or marker) and some sort of drawing surface (sidewalk, white board, chalk board, cardboard, or paper). For adults, line art may be part of a quick sketch, a conceptual rendering, or an early draft. It may be part of fast notetaking. For artists in training, many would use a reference image and thin tracing paper to practice lines, shapes, forms, and textures. Or line art may be something more refined and finished. Then, there are computational ways to draw with stylus and tablet. There are digital image editing programs that enable the extraction of lines from a photograph or digitized (scanned) drawing or painting. In terms of common art online, line art is not uncommon.

On the Social Web, with profligate sharing, artists view others' works and reflect on their own in order to inspire new work and learning. Art viewing inspires creativity by evoking a

* Corresponding Author's Email: haijes@gmail.com

In: Common Visual Art in a Social Digital Age
Editor: Shalin Hai-Jew
ISBN: 978-1-68507-664-1

dual process of both "evaluating the artworks of others and reflecting on one's own art making" for inspiration (Ishiguro & Okada, 2021, p. 489). The idea is to be inspired without being obviously derivative. Innovations should be done in the artist's own style.

This work aims to explore what "line art" as a form of "common art" looks like on the Social Web. A baseline understanding was set based on a review of the literature. The social imagery used for this analysis is captured from Google Images with the seeding search phrase "line art common art." First, there was a conducting of bottom-up image coding to understand the imageset of 999 images, and then, the more precise analyses to address the questions below were conducted.

To understand the state of "line art" on the Social Web, a number of interrelated exploratory research questions are asked:

- What are the common topical subjects of "line art" as "common art" on the Social Web?
- How sophisticated is the "line art" on the Social Web?
  - What technologies and methods are apparently used for the "line art" on the Social Web?

- Who are the apparent creators of the "line art" works on the Social Web?
  - What are the apparent purposes of such "line art" on the Social Web for the creators?

- Who are the apparent users of the "line art" works on the Social Web?
  - What are the apparent purposes of such "line art" on the Social Web for the viewers?
  - Does the line art serve mostly hedonic (pleasure-seeking) or eudaimonic (self-actualization) purposes? Pleasure-seeking or more practical and instrumental purposes?

- What does "line art" tell us about "common art" on the Social Web?
  - Are there rich cognitive challenges to line art that add value to the cognitive interpretation?

This work offers some fresh insights about line art as a contemporary common art form online.

Delimitations

The image scraped was not an N=all but included everything that could be captured with the data scrape. The visuals are cross-cutting across the WWW and Internet, so these were not works collected from a dedicated art site, which would likely result in different findings. The images were coded by the author, singly, who does not have art expertise beyond some basic courses and years of working with visuals in publishing and then in multimedia teaching and then instructional design. In terms of reproducibility, the coding was done as systematically as possible, but this is not with the rigor of computer vision or trained team coding.

Review of the Literature

"Art" is a contested term. There have been attempts at universalist definitions but also discipline specific definitions. How art is defined is based in part on what aspects are focused on:

> One distinctively modern, conventionalist, sort of definition focuses on art's institutional features, emphasizing the way art changes over time, modern works that appear to break radically with all traditional art, the relational properties of artworks that depend on works' relations to art history, art genres, etc.—more broadly, on the undeniable heterogeneity of the class of artworks. The more traditional, less conventionalist sort of definition defended in contemporary philosophy makes use of a broader, more traditional concept of aesthetic properties that includes more than art-relational ones, and puts more emphasis on art's pan-cultural and trans-historical characteristics—in sum, on commonalities across the class of artworks. Hybrid definitions aim to do justice to both the traditional aesthetic dimension as well as to the institutional and art-historical dimensions of art, while privileging neither. ("The Definition of Art," Oct. 23, 2007, Aug. 14, 2018)

From long practice, a work has to be called art based on the "conferring (of) arthood" by "qualified members of society" (Young, Oct. 1995, n.p.). At the individual level, one research study found complex individual factors ("personality variables, tastes, and decision strategies") informed how research participants assessed various images as "art" or "not art" (Pelowski, Gerger, Chetouani, Markey, & Leder, 2017, p. 1). The research participants often conflated personal "liking" with "art" (Pelowski, Gerger, Chetouani, Markey, & Leder, 2017, p. 1).

The Recognition and Appreciation of Art

There are cogent arguments against treating art as something separate from "real things" (Grigoriev, 2005, n.p.) and artworks are "mere real things." There is the risk of "the danger of convincing ourselves that the primary function of art is to advance aesthetic theory rather than to provide meaningful experiences of enjoyment and appreciation" (Grigoriev, 2005, n.p.). ["Aesthetics" and "art theory" are sometimes used interchangeably.] There have been questions of whether humans can universally recognize art as a biological capability. Human biology underpins human vision, but the human brain processes the visual data and interprets it. The debate is how much of one or the other affects the perception and appreciation and critique of art.

One experimental research work suggests that there is "a strong bottom-up and objective aspect to perception of emotion in abstract artworks that may tap into basic visual mechanisms" (Melcher & Bacci, 2013, p. 191), based on perceptual features of the artworks. Art viewers may also capture a fast gist of the abstract artwork, on which future senses of the work may be based. One research study found that 50 milli-seconds to about 3 seconds of time was sufficient for capturing image composition of abstract artworks, with fast senses of human visual systems, and to inform a "consistent aesthetic evaluation" even with little cognitive processing

(Schwabe, Menzel, Mullin, Wagemans, & Redies, 2018). Other works show that there are different aesthetic preferences among people in different age groups, so there may be a developmental element.

In the art history space, there have been discussions of conceptual art, where the art is the idea (Cray, 2014, p. 235) and less any material rendering. Given the current focus on studying human mental responses to art, one researcher has suggested that the study of neuroaesthetics would benefit from a way of understanding how conceptual art triggers human neuro-systems (Minissale, 2012). The researcher wrote:

> At the risk of simplifying, conceptual art brings together non-art objects ('readymades') and concepts that appear to have no author, purpose or artistic process by which to distinguish them. Its themes challenge traditional notions of beauty and formal design, artistic dexterity, aesthetic composition and technique. In short, conceptual artists devalue the qualities that neuroaesthetics find so important. (Minissale, 2012, p. 43)

Artworks are seen to contain moral angles, and moral, immoral, and amoral angles. One theorist has argued that "the moral value of a narrative work depends on some of the artistic properties of that artwork" (Harold, Spring 2006, p. 259), so intertwining the aesthetic with moral value. The moral aspects may come from circumstances of the work; it may come from direct features of the work (Harold, Spring 2006, p. 260).

Future research in this space may involve ways to capture and study conceptual art. The research approach here meant that there had to be a digital artifact for the analysis, perhaps leaving out line art that might be more conceptual than material-digital. Future work may include a purposeful effort at including conceptual art. A similar challenge exists with "non-perceptual art" that does not communicate aesthetically to a person through the five senses, if such an art exists (Shelley, Oct. 2003, p. 363).

The present thinking is that there is not universality emanating from similar responses to aesthetic features of visual art (like lines, colors, shapes, and so on). One rigorous study applying empirical testing of universality in responses to art resulted in the finding of "significantly lower agreement than expected": "For the whole artworks, participants agreed on the effects of warm-cold, heavy-light, and happy-sad, but not on 11 other dimensions" (Specker, et al., 2020, p. 1). There was more agreement "on the whole artwork than on single elements" (Specker, et al., 2020, p. 1). In this study, the level of art expertise "did not play a significant role and agreement was especially low on dimensions usually of interest in empirical aesthetics (e.g., like-dislike)" (Specker, et al., 2020, p. 1). A more typical understanding is that culture and experience play roles in the interpretation of art. What is seen as artful changes in human populations over time and periods.

One model describes a more complex embodied engagement with artwork that goes beyond empathy. This research describes "the perception-action and motion-emotion loops" as complementary processes (Brinck, 2018, p. 201), requiring the whole body to respond to art in a fully present way. This researcher writes: "I argue that aesthetic experience emerges by participatory sense-making and revolves around movement as a means for creating meaning. While entrainment merely plays a preparatory part in this, aesthetic engagement constitutes the phenomenological side of coupling to an artwork and provides the context for exploration, and eventually for moving, seeing, and feeling with art" (Brinck, 2018, p. 201). Another model of aesthetic experience posits that there are five stages: "perception, explicit classification, implicit classification, cognitive mastering and evaluation" (Leder, Belke, Oeberst, & Augustin, 2004, p. 489). The output in this model is twofold: aesthetic emotion and aesthetic judgment (Leder, Belke, Oeberst, & Augustin, 2004, p. 489). Aesthetic experiences involve both cognition and emotion.

About Line Art

In a general sense, "line art" is often considered part of "minimalism," as a practice, often without color and with as few lines (strokes) as possible. Minimalism refers to art in which the "subject is reduced to its necessary elements" ("Minimalism," Aug. 31, 2021). Minimalism is "an art movement that began in post-World War II Western art" ("Minimalism," Aug. 31, 2021), and it was applied to paintings and sculpture of the 1950s. Minimalist works are often sparse, with no excess.

The research literature shows that expert analysts of artworks tend to respond with more sophistication. Experts, those with formal training in the arts, were found to rate abstract artworks as more "*Interesting, Beautiful, Informative* and *Sophisticated*" and distinguished them "less markedly from Representational artworks" than non-experts (Bimler, Snellock, & Paramei, 2019, p. 11). Experts are informed by their training and less by personal feelings than non-experts. Art has to make original statements and be interpretable in "an artworld context" (Danto, as cited in Lind, 1992, p. 17). Art has to do more than raise an initial perceptual interest but has to spark "a second sort of interest, a meta interest" (Lind, 1992, p. 121), enabling the viewer to "decipher" the work towards meaning making (p. 124). The appreciation of art is enhanced when the art's complexity is aligned with the viewer's amount of working memory (Sherman, Grabowecky, & Suzuki, 2015). Another thinker suggests that part of the pleasure of art is that "it puts reality at a distance" (Danto, 1974, p. 145). The art context helps frame the art experience and enables sufficient emotional distancing, to enable the viewer to "judge negative stimuli aesthetically more positively—thus suppressing the immediacy of emotional stimulus content" (Gerger, Leder, & Kremer, 2014, p. 174), even as art may evoke strong emotions. The art frame enables more objective appraisal.

Still, the works here are common art, often made for other common folk, without the ambitions or the pretentions of the making of high art or serious aesthetic objects. Line art (or linework) is often thought of as a preliminary study to set shapes, sizing, and interrelationships; it is not a finalized sort of artwork itself, except for established masters who have already established their artfulness. (After the lines are set, the next steps are to add shading, textures, and then details.) In many cases, the line works are without complex dimensionality, and often without artist back stories, and without work-based contexts.

Research Methods

To understand what sorts of "line art" are present in a "common art" set on the Social Web, the terms "line art common art" were used to seed a set of social images from Google images. In mid-October 2021, some 999 images were collected this way. The auto-generated tags included the following: dandelion, objects, ostrich, starfish, sunflower, desert rose, kestrel, loon, fish, common loon, daisy, flower, birds, pablo picasso, examples, and sunflower clipart (Figure 1).

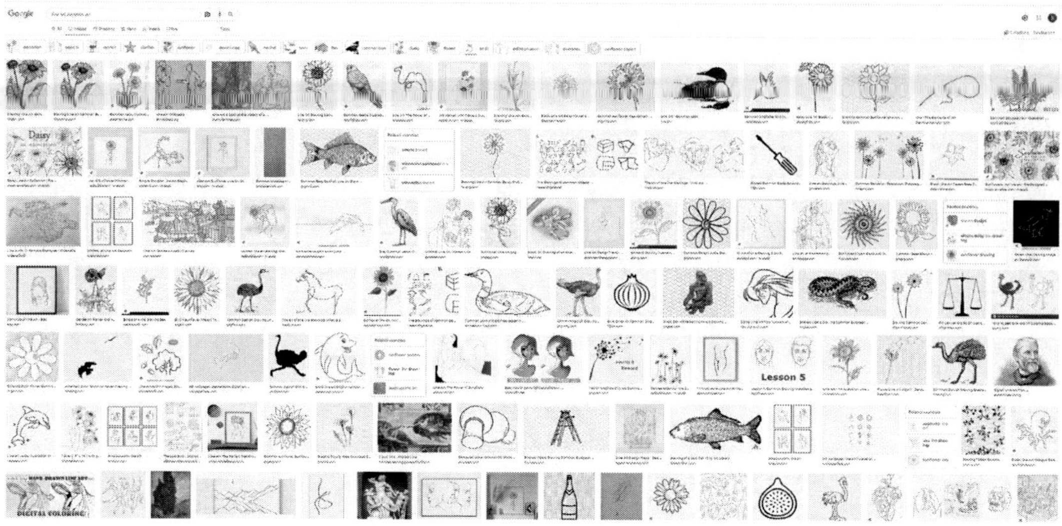

Figure 1. "Line art common art" social imageset from Google Images.

Results

To introduce the social imageset, it helps to offer some bottom-up coding on some basic elements.

Bottom-Up Coding of the "Line Art Common Art" Social Imageset along Various Dimensions

In the coding, most works were identified to one category only, not multiple ones, even if the work was a composite of several works (such as diptychs, quadtychs, collages, and others). Where there were words and images, the images were focused on first. For example, how abstract or figurative are the works? (Figure 2) What about the proportion of the depiction of humans vs. animals vs. both humans and animals together? (Figure 3) What about the proportion of those focal elements that are animate vs. inanimate? (Figure 4) What about the uses of color, such as the proportion of line art that is black and white or grayscale vs. in color? (Figure 5) Then, beyond the descriptive aspects, what about the proportion of works with high levels of finish and refinement vs. those that are not? (Figure 6) What about works that are "original" vs. "derivative"? (Figure 7) The sequence here begins with descriptions of the works and evolves to light analytics.

Abstract, Figurative, or Abstract Representational Forms

The first data visualization here shows a comparison between abstract vs. figurative (representational of forms derived from life) works. On the whole, most of the social imagery in this "line art common art" set tends towards the representation. (Figure 2) The "abstract" works included various filled doodles and swirls and scribbles. The "figurative" ones included ladders, perfume bottles, bacteria, furniture, buildings, and others; these also include humans and animals. The "abstract representational" category include works that are abstract but have representational meaning within their own symbolic and shape systems; these include letters, calligraphy, alphabets, words; maps; mathematical symbols; signatures; abstract data representations (data dashboards), book covers, textual articles, technology graphical user interfaces (GUIs), and various other abstract-type signifiers. One work read: "Common sense is genius dressed in its working clothes." Interestingly, even with the human tendency towards apophenia (seeing patterns where there may just be random information), the line art works were fairly well defined, even though the visuals were often low-resolution thumbnails.

As an aside, one research team "found that the private taste proportion was much higher in abstract artworks, accounting for 75% of taste compared to 40% in the face condition. Abstract artworks were also less affected than faces by the instruction to rate according to others' taste and therefore less susceptible to incorporation of external beauty standards" (Leder, Goller, Rigotti, & Forster, 2016, p. 1). The non-figurative qualities of abstract works may enable the viewer to input more of their own private taste in interpreting the works and enables the "crystalizing" of private taste, perhaps even at the expense of socially shared taste (from the broader culture).

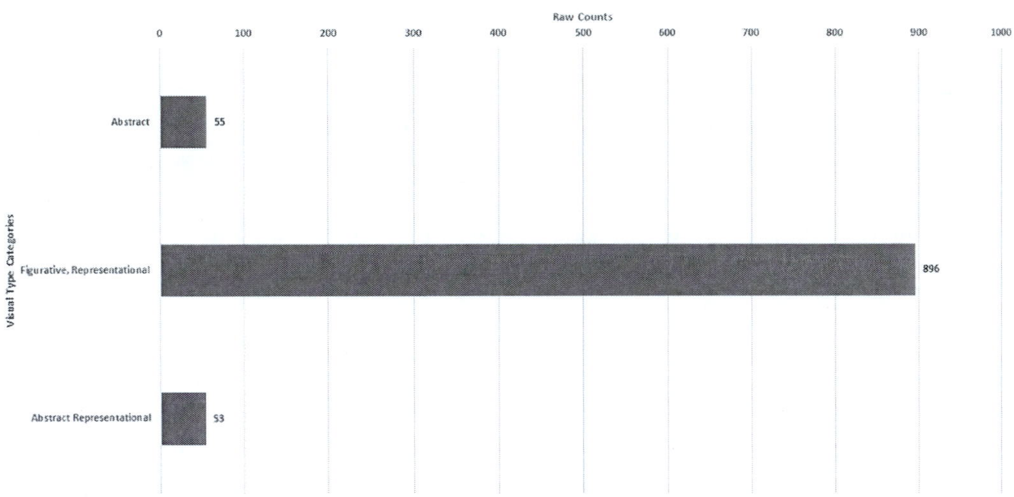

Figure 2. Abstract vs. Figurative, Representational vs. Abstract Representational in Frame of "Line Art Common Art" social imageset.

Humans, Animals, and Combinations in Frame

For the figurative works, many involved depictions of various living beings. These were separated out into the following three categories: human(s), animal(s), and both human(s) and animal(s) together in frame. (Figure 3) The numbers of humans vs. animals in the social images were about equal. There was a small group of visuals showing humans and animals together: mermaids, people riding horses, a girl holding a stork, a woman holding a finch-like bird, and others. Visual synecdoche was applied to the coding. A pair of human hands was counted as a person; likewise, a face, a back, a pair of feet, and so on. A pair of shark fins indicated sharks.

Some of the animals are imaginary: a pig with wings, a monster, a dragon, mermaids, and others.

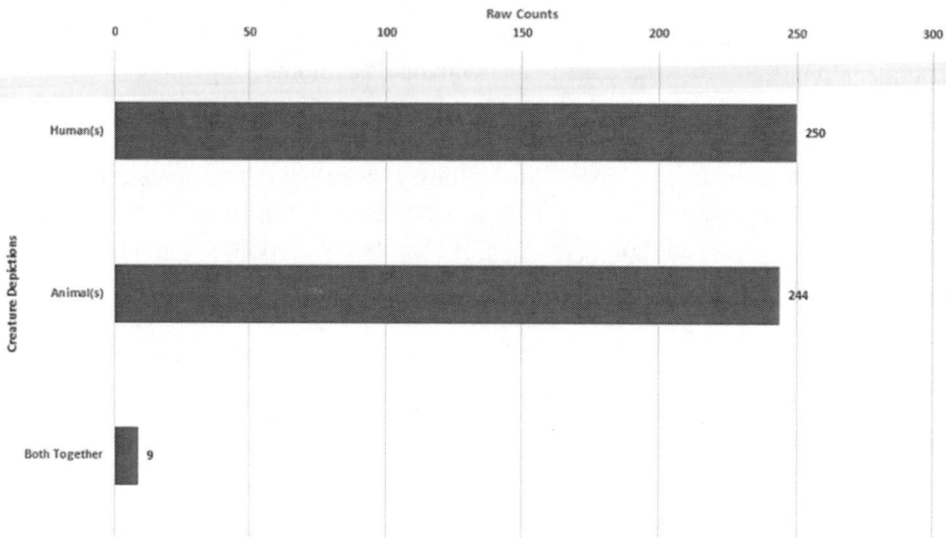

Figure 3. Human(s), animal(s), and both together in frame of "Line Art Common Art" social imageset.

Animate vs. Inanimate Focuses

Then, there was another iteration of manual coding across the social imageset for animate and sentient focal points of the visuals vs. inanimate. There was a little more of the animate and sentient (humans, animals) vs. the inanimate (plants, trees, flowers, plates, vases, houses, and the like). (Figure 4) [Some may argue sentience for plants, but the author went with generalized understandings].

B/W or Grayscale vs. Color

Next, the author coded the visuals by color: either black and white (b/w) or grayscale or color (including tinting, shading, and such with hues and various saturations). Midtones existed in some works, but in most that used b/w, clearly, there was just high contrast between the two colors and little in the way of textuality or shading (Figure 5). The line art social imageset was dominated more by b/w and grayscale as opposed to some define hue and saturation. The going to B/W and grayscale over color was initially surprising, given the challenges of minimalism: lines and fills (sometimes) and patterns (sometimes) on a limited two-dimensional plane. For the color palettes that go beyond b/w and grayscale, there are single-hue visuals and some single-hue overlays. There are a few that are typified by bright colors. In general, though, the color palette is fairly muted in this social imageset.

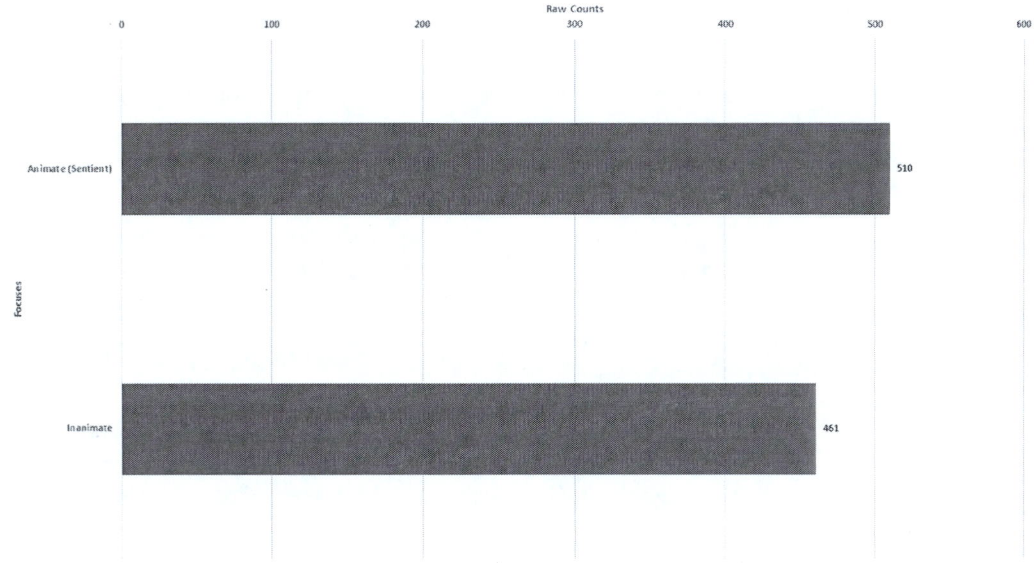

Figure 4. Animate (and sentient) vs. inanimate focuses in frame of "Line Art Common Art" social imageset.

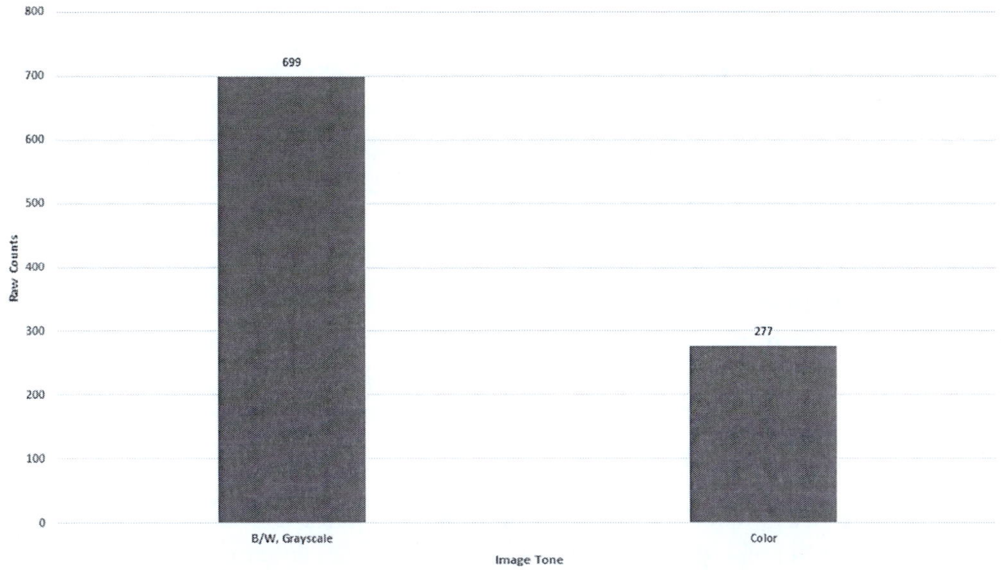

Figure 5. Black and white/grayscale vs. color visuals in the "Line Art Common Art" social imageset.

Finished (Refined) or Partially Finished/Unfinished (Unrefined)

Another dimension involved the level of "finish" or "unfinish" to the various visual works. (Figure 6) The finished works looked ready to deploy, to publish. These may not have been fully artful or necessarily aesthetically pleasing, but they seemed to be in a ready state for usage. The visual balance was already present in the work. The level of granularity of detail was also fairly regular and developed. As for the unrefined, these were works that seemed interrupted. There was a curved line without context. There were various basic geometric shapes. One work showed a flat hand holding a flat sword, without shape. There were some doodles. One sketched nude of a man's back showed many light and short strokes, without commitment yet to line. Indeed, some of the unrefined works may have been examples for various types of drawing, such as creating a contour, shading an object, using space effectively, and others. Line art often tends to be suggestive in broad strokes, but not defined in granular ones. (Line art is not used for hyperrealism)

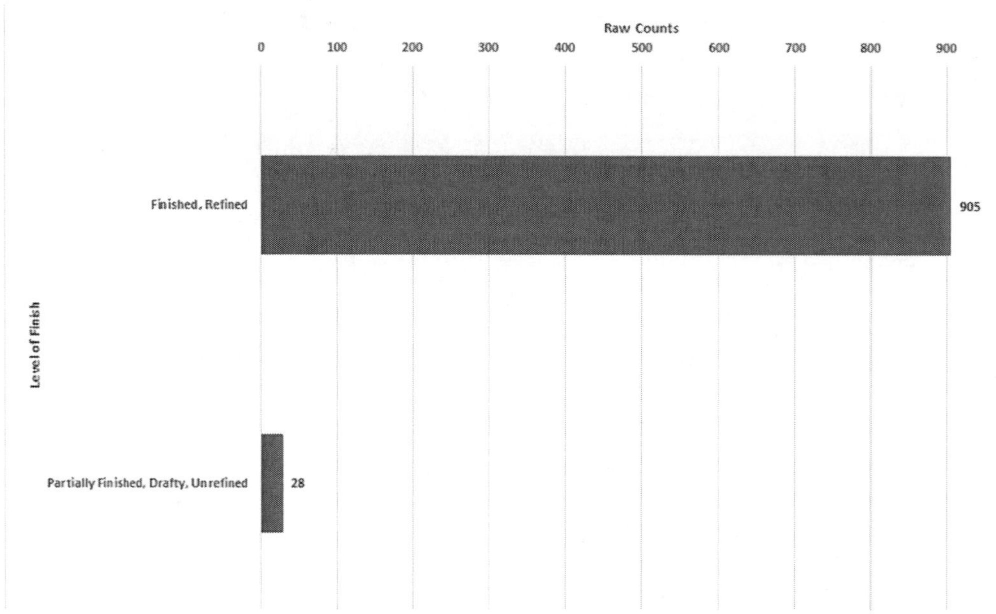

Figure 6. Level of finish in frame of "Line Art Common Art" social imageset.

Originality vs. Unoriginality

The most complex part of the initial manual coding to represent the contents of the social imageset is probably the category of uniqueness. Here, only 15% of the works were found to be fairly original. These included portraits of people (some known, some not), with various aspects of character and personality shown. There were pleasing drawings, such as of a wine bottle and glasses. A withering weed was rendered memorably and dramatically. There were scenes of cityscapes, a farmhouse, mountains, and other locations. The originality was not about effortfulness alone but also the depicted concept, the mood. The unoriginal works included various vague flowers, butterflies, starfish, small animals, and common topics, without unique approaches or execution. Many of these did not show an original artist hand (Figure 7).

A core tenet of "common art" is that profundity can emerge from anywhere, even though such achievement is rare and difficult, however. The collected social imageset did not directly offer a work that might support this assertion though.

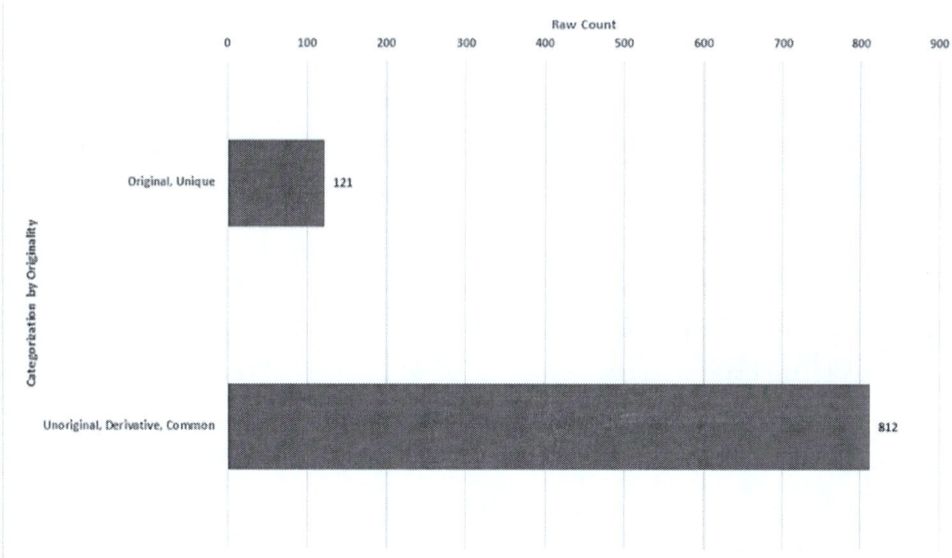

Figure 7. Level of originality in frame of "Line Art Common Art" social imageset.

One empirical study about art found that research participants enjoyed subjectively experienced higher degrees of ambiguity within an artwork and found it "more interesting and affecting" aesthetically (Muth, Hesslinger, & Carbon, 2015, p. 1). Whether the participants could "solve" the artwork or not was not so important for their satisfaction; rather, they enjoyed the creation of insights in their own minds from the art viewing experience (Muth, Hesslinger, & Carbon, 2015, p. 1). They write: "The estimated solvability of the experienced ambiguity…was not relevant for liking and even negatively linked to interest and affect" (Muth, Hesslinger, & Carbon, 2015, p. 1). If this sense of mystery is positive for artworks, perhaps more such complexity would benefit line art, especially that created by artists interested in art aspiration than mere marketing.

Discussion

The research questions then follow, first as the group of interconnected questions and then separated out for address.

- What are the common topical subjects of "line art" as "common art" on the Social Web?
- How sophisticated is the "line art" on the Social Web?
  - What technologies and methods are apparently used for the "line art" on the Social Web?

- Who are the apparent creators of the "line art" works on the Social Web?
  - What are the apparent purposes of such "line art" on the Social Web for the creators?

- Who are the apparent users of the "line art" works on the Social Web?
  - What are the apparent purposes of such "line art" on the Social Web for the viewers?
  - Does the line art serve mostly hedonic (pleasure-seeking) or eudaimonic (self-actualization) purposes? Pleasure-seeking or more practical and instrumental purposes?

- What does "line art" tell us about "common art" on the Social Web?
  - Are there rich cognitive challenges to line art that add value to the cognitive interpretation?

- What are the common topical subjects of "line art" as "common art" on the Social Web?

The common topics were generally of sentient beings (humans and animals, about equally) and then non-sentient common objects and landscapes. These were mostly rendered in black-and-white and grayscale vs. color.

- How sophisticated is the "line art" on the Social Web?
  - What technologies and methods are apparently used for the "line art" on the Social Web?

The line art showed various types of skill. Some of the line art were created all in one line, with a clear start point and a clear end point, and the drawing object never directly leaving the page or paper. There were some examples of visual wit and optical illusions, showing an image that could be interpreted multiple ways (like Rubin's vase). One sequence on a sheet shows a clock morphing into an owl, in four drawings. Some of the art seemed merely decorative, evoking nudes (male and female, and various mixes of couples). Many depicted flora and fauna (plants and animals) and various landscapes.

The "technologies" were both analog (paper and drawing implements) and digital (including some that looked to be digitally edited albeit non-generatively created). Actual manual drawing skills are thought to be in decline given the turn to digitization of visuals (Fava, 2020).

- Who are the apparent creators of the "line art" works on the Social Web?
  - What are the apparent purposes of such "line art" on the Social Web for the creators?

The creators of the line art do seem to range from the amateurs to the professionals.

The line art works were created for the following applications: advertising products and events, enabling coloring, teaching and learning, the study of insect morphology, and other apparent applications.

Art has historically served to "serve extrinsic functions, such as the propitiation of the gods, the enrichment of ritual, the communication of religious and other lore, the illustration of virtue and vice, the glorification of its owners, and so on" historically prior to the 19th century in the West where art could exist for its own sake (Davies, 2006, p. 224).

- Who are the apparent users of the "line art" works on the Social Web?
  - What are the apparent purposes of such "line art" on the Social Web for the viewers?
  - Does the line art serve mostly hedonic (pleasure-seeking) or eudaimonic (self-actualization) purposes? Pleasure-seeking or more practical and instrumental purposes?

The users of the line art seem to be the general public, or perhaps parts of the general public. Some of the art is clearly designed for decorative pleasure, such as a dramatic perfume bottle with curls of fragrance; a stark bird standing on bare tree branches; and others. Some are detailed drawings of plants and insects and animals, apparently for study.

As for whether the line art is mostly for hedonic pleasure-seeking or eudaimonic self-actualization purposes, by the users, many of the works by engaging nature seem to be conveying something of both meaning and respect for the world's beauty and aesthetic pleasure. It is not possible to break apart to visual to a binary code of "hedonic" (pleasure-seeking) or eudaimonic (self-actualization through meaning and purpose). The more stylized, the more abstract, the more "hedonic" the images seem. The more figurative, the more visually detailed, the more realistic, the more "eudaimonic" the images seem. Also, the more externally referential the visual, the more "eudaimonic." [A few of the drawings refer to historical artists. Some seem to refer to a story].

- What does "line art" tell us about "common art" on the Social Web?
  - Are there rich cognitive challenges to line art that add value to the cognitive interpretation?

Based on abductive logic (reasoning through the visuals found on the Social Web) and manual coding, much of the available line art seems to have been created digitally. Where a few of the works seem to have been rendered using pencil or pen on common paper, a majority looked to be digital creations.

The "line art" as "common art" on the Social Web show instrumental depictions for events, advertisements, branding, and other applications. The works seem to be created to draw the eyes, to elicit a laugh. Most of the works are not so original. Even the visuals that profess to show animals in their habitats seem to go with a fantasy or romanticized version. There are whales frolicking in the waves. A wheat plant has perfectly aligned wheat grains. Gourds in a colorful still life are perfectly rendered. A couple embrace in soft focus. A crab, a salamander, a snake, a bird, and others, are rendered in swirly shapes.

So-called "minimalist enthusiasts" enjoy bold line art depictions in a fictionalized world, as creators and creatives. What the mass public or segments of the public enjoys may differ.

Future Research

Computational capabilities have come to the fore in the art space. Various algorithms and software programs can generate algorithmic art. A software program has been created to generate "hypnotic line art" based on seeding images (Yeh, Liu, Lin, Zhang, & Lee, 2020, p. 1), to lessen human artist workload. Some have created new forms, like non photorealistic rendering (NPR) of artworks in the Optical Art (Op Art) space (Inglis, 2012, p. 1). Another tool involves the computational creating of silhouettes in the non-photorealistic rendering space (Zakaria & Seidel, June 2004), with 2D and 3D objects. An older technology enabled line art renderings of 3D as well (Rössl & Kobbelt, Oct. 2000). Another approach rendered line art using "coverage of isoparametric curves" of the 2D and 3D objects (Elber, 1995, p. 231). Even back in the late 1990s, there have been computer programs that enabled the drawing of freeform shapes as line art using computation (Elber, Jan. – Mar. 1998).

Some programs help clean off digital artifacts and glitches from machine-generated Op Art for smoother visuals (Inglis & Kaplan, Aug. 2011). Another program can take a static image and recreate a plausible drawing order, for usage in a narrated video sequence and other applications (Fu, Zhou, Liu, & Mitra, Dec. 2011, p. 1), obviating the need for a human artist to manually walk through such a demonstration. Another set of algorithms creates line-art illustrations for "conveying shapes and shading of complex objects" including specular surfaces (both reflective and refractive ones), which suggests ability to handle how light interacts with the particular material surface (Kim, Yu, Yu, & Lee, 2008, p. 1). Many of the capabilities described in the research literature have been integrated into high performing software programs for digital image editing, video editing, modeling, animation, and other software tools.

Computers are also used in managing, evaluating, categorizing, and archiving art. Both the human visual system and art information can benefit from technological affordances. Various systems have been created in helping identify visual similarities between artworks and organizing them in series (Monroy, Furuta, & Mallen, 2003). Computer scientists have created programs to differentiate between different styles of manga drawings (Chu & Chao, 2014). Other technology tools have measured self-similarity in artworks. Others have brought back hidden images under layers of paint by masters (Nakano, Tabe, Shimoyama, & Tsuji, 2016).

This work was created to analyze the "line art common art" on the Social Web, and the dimensionality of the various manual coding was based on bottom-up coding after various iterative walks through the social imagery. As machine vision improves and more custom programming may be applied to extract insights, this work will be less laborious. Still, the human approach for manual coding is fairly necessary to achieve image coding saturation. That said, as imagesets get larger, at some point, only machine coding will become feasible.

Endogenous Factors That May Affect the Experience and Evaluation of Artworks

The absence of context for the line art in this approach may mean a less enriched evaluation, given that information provided with artwork can influence how the artwork is interpreted and the valuation placed on it (Abe & Fukushima, 2020). A basic hypothesis was that positive information would positively affect the viewer's sense of art value and art preference towards the artwork, and that negative information would do the opposite; however, the actual research did find that for some artworks, "negative information such as artists' scandal may not influence the evaluation of artworks" (Abe & Fukushima, 2020, p. 3092). It was also found that by withholding information about artworks, they could enable research participants to engage in more creative and wider interpretations of artworks (Abe & Fukushima, 2020, p. 3092).

People can be sensitive to other outside factors beyond the art when assessing art. Another work suggests that if people are asked to verbalize their appreciation for art, they tend to focus on representative or figurative art vs. abstract works. Articulating liking or disliking abstract art was more difficult. The researchers suggest that the tendencies from verbalization may lead to biased assessments of art assessment, leading to a work of art being "both undeservedly loved and unjustly maligned" (Yamada, 2009, p. 1140).

Adding Dimensionality

Future research may benefit from line art that is more than two dimensions, but include a third dimension (x-axis) and even the fourth (changes over time).

Art Making as Research?

One published work argues against art making as a form of research and art works as knowledge objects. The author expressed leeriness at the creation of art in the service of other learning, by using art creation as research. Perhaps such an approach demystifies artmaking and art. He argues: Visual art objects can communicate knowledge but knowledge "typically of a superficial nature" and not the "deep insights that art is usually thought to endow into emotions, human nature and relationships, and our place in the World…" (Scrivener, 2002, p. 1). There is a move towards preserving the vaunted place of art in human societies. This work does raise the question of the informational value of the line art. Perhaps it evokes the kind of learning that is going on in the creation of line art.

Art Making as Political Change

"Phenomenally strong artworks" enable the capture of people's perceptions (Fielding, 2015, p. 280) and may lead to consciousness-raising and political change.

Conclusion

Art is considered to have value based on human visual systems that value some aspects more than others, such as a built-in appreciation for symmetry, as universals. Then, there is the cultural training about what is artful, for learned appreciations. Line art does seem to exist all around the world, albeit informed by different aesthetics. This line art set did show some works from different traditions, but mostly from the West, from Europe, and Japan (one manga character).

Many of the works seem descriptive vs. impressionistic; they are wooden and literal. The "feat" in some is the use of only one continuous line or maybe only under 10 shapes to make complex forms. In some, there is implied motion and directionality. The works show objects in idealized state, except for some evocative drooping and desiccated weeds (which have more character). [This is not to say that skill is not required to achieve such effects. The idea is that the artworks that are valued are interpretive, not merely descriptive].

Overall, the visuals here seem tied to various endeavors: commercial and educational. The visuals also seem to have been rendered mostly using computers…but perhaps more practices involving both manual drawing and computational finish would benefit the space. After all, many professions in various fields have noted the loss of the skill of drawing manually given the turn to the exactitude and affordances of computation.

Line art as common art practice on the Social Web seems like it could benefit from less refined works and higher originality if it is truly to be of the people. The irony is that computer-aided drawing lends to a perfectionistic sheen.

Acknowledgments

This is for the many common artists online, who are an inspiration, every one of them. Each voice has its own resonance.

References

Abe, A., & Fukushima, K. (2020). How will the information change the sense of values during art appreciation?. *Procedia Computer Science*, *176*, 3083-3092.

Bimler, D. L., Snellock, M., & Paramei, G. V. (2019). Art expertise in construing meaning of representational and abstract artworks. *Acta psychologica*, *192*, 11-22.

Brinck, I. (2018). Empathy, engagement, entrainment: the interaction dynamics of aesthetic experience. *Cognitive processing*, *19*(2), 201-213.

Chu, W. T., & Chao, Y. C. (2014, November). Line-based drawing style description for manga classification. In *Proceedings of the 22Nd ACM international conference on multimedia* (pp. 781-784).

Cray, W. D. (2014). Conceptual art, ideas, and ontology. *The Journal of Aesthetics and Art Criticism*, *72*(3), 235-245.

Danto, A. C. (1974). The transfiguration of the commonplace. *The Journal of Aesthetics and Art Criticism*, *33*(2), 139-148.

Davies, S. (2006). Aesthetic judgements, artworks and functional beauty. *The Philosophical Quarterly*, *56*(223), 224-241.

"The Definition of Art." (2018, Aug. 14; 2007, Oct. 23). Stanford *Encyclopedia of Philosophy*. Retrieved Oct. 25, 2021, from https://plato.stanford.edu/entries/art-definition/.

Elber, G. (1998). Line art illustrations of parametric and implicit forms. *IEEE Transactions on visualization and computer graphics*, *4*(1), 71-81.

Elber, G. (1995). Line art rendering via a coverage of isoparametric curves. *IEEE Transactions on Visualization and Computer Graphics*, *1*(3), 231-239.

Fava, M. (2020). A decline in drawing ability? *International Journal of Art & Design Education*, *39*(2), 319-332.

Fielding, H. A. (2015). Cultivating Perception: Phenomenological Encounters with Artworks. *Signs: Journal of Women in Culture and Society*, *40*(2), 280-289.

Fu, H., Zhou, S., Liu, L., & Mitra, N. J. (2011, December). Animated construction of line drawings. In *Proceedings of the 2011 SIGGRAPH Asia Conference* (pp. 1-10).

Gerger, G., Leder, H., & Kremer, A. (2014). Context effects on emotional and aesthetic evaluations of artworks and IAPS pictures. *Acta psychologica*, *151*, 174-183.

Grigoriev, S. (2005). Living Art, Defining Value: Artworks and Mere Real Things. *Contemporary Aesthetics (Journal Archive)*, *3*(1), 4.

Harold, J. (2006). On judging the moral value of narrative artworks. *The Journal of aesthetics and art criticism*, *64*(2), 259-270.

Inglis, T. C. (2012). *Op art rendering with lines and curves*. 1 – 6. Preprint.

Inglis, T. C., & Kaplan, C. S. (2011, August). Generating op art lines. In *Proceedings of the International Symposium on Computational Aesthetics in Graphics, Visualization, and Imaging* (pp. 25-32).

Ishiguro, C., & Okada, T. (2021). How Does Art Viewing Inspires Creativity?. *The Journal of Creative Behavior*, *55*(2), 489-500.

Kim, Y., Yu, J., Yu, X., & Lee, S. (2008). Line-art illustration of dynamic and specular surfaces. *ACM Transactions on Graphics (TOG)*, *27*(5), 1-10.

Leder, H., Belke, B., Oeberst, A., & Augustin, D. (2004). A model of aesthetic appreciation and aesthetic judgments. *British Journal of Psychology*, *95*(4), 489-508.

Leder, H., Goller, J., Rigotti, T., & Forster, M. (2016). Private and shared taste in art and face appreciation. *Frontiers in Human Neuroscience*, *10*, 155, 1 - 7.

Lind, R. (1992). The aesthetic essence of art. *The Journal of Aesthetics and Art Criticism*, *50*(2), 117-129.

Melcher, D., & Bacci, F. (2013). Perception of emotion in abstract artworks: a multidisciplinary approach. *Progress in brain research*, *204*, 191-216.

"Minimalism." (2021, Aug. 31). *Wikipedia*. Retrieved Oct. 22, 2021, from https://en.wikipedia.org/wiki/Minimalism.

Minissale, G. (2012). Conceptual art: A blind spot for neuroaesthetics?. *Leonardo*, *45*(1), 43-48.

Monroy, C., Furuta, R., & Mallen, E. (2003). Creating, Visualizing, Analyzing, and Comparing Series of Artworks. In the proceedings of JCDL '03. May 27 - 31, 2003. Houston, TX. 1 - 6.

Morriss-Kay, G. M. (2010). The evolution of human artistic creativity. *Journal of Anatomy,* 216, 158 – 176.

Muth, C., Hesslinger, V. M., & Carbon, C. C. (2015). The appeal of challenge in the perception of art: How ambiguity, solvability of ambiguity, and the opportunity for insight affect appreciation. *Psychology of Aesthetics, Creativity, and the Arts*, *9*(3), 206.

Nakano, K., Tabe, A., Shimoyama, S., & Tsuji, K. (2016). Visualizing a black cat drawing hidden inside the painting by confocal micro-XRF analysis. *Microchemical Journal*, *126*, 496-500.

Pelowski, M., Gerger, G., Chetouani, Y., Markey, P. S., & Leder, H. (2017). But is it really art? The classification of images as "Art"/"Not Art" and correlation with appraisal and viewer interpersonal differences. *Frontiers in psychology*, *8*, 1729, 1 – 21.

Rössl, C., & Kobbelt, L. (2000, October). Line-art rendering of 3d-models. In *Proceedings the Eighth Pacific Conference on Computer Graphics and Applications* (pp. 87-96). IEEE.

Schwabe, K., Menzel, C., Mullin, C., Wagemans, J., & Redies, C. (2018). Gist perception of image composition in abstract artworks. *i-Perception*, *9*(3), 2041669518780797.

Scrivener, S. (2002). The art object does not embody a form of knowledge. Working paper. *Working Papers in Art & Design - Volume 2*. University of the Arts London. 1 - 14.

Shelley, J. (2003). The problem of non-perceptual art. *The British Journal of Aesthetics*, *43*(4), 363-378.

Sherman, A., Grabowecky, M., & Suzuki, S. (2015). In the working memory of the beholder: Art appreciation is enhanced when visual complexity is compatible with working memory. *Journal of Experimental Psychology: Human Perception and Performance*, *41*(4), 898, 1 – 14.

Specker, E., Forster, M., Brinkmann, H., Boddy, J., Immelmann, B., Goller, J., ... & Leder, H. (2020). Warm, lively, rough? Assessing agreement on aesthetic effects of artworks. *Plos one*, *15*(5), e0232083.

Yamada, A. (2009). Appreciating art verbally: Verbalization can make a work of art be both undeservedly loved and unjustly maligned. *Journal of Experimental Social Psychology*, *45*(5), 1140-1143.

Yeh, C. K., Liu, Z., Lin, I. H., Zhang, E., & Lee, T. Y. (2020). WYSIWYG Design of Hypnotic Line Art. *IEEE Transactions on Visualization and Computer Graphics*. 1 – 14.

Young, J. O. (1995). Artworks and artworlds. *The British Journal of Aesthetics*, *35*(4), 330-338.

Zakaria, N., & Seidel, H. P. (2004, June). Interactive stylized silhouette for point-sampled geometry. In *Proceedings of the 2nd international conference on Computer graphics and interactive techniques in Australasia and South East Asia* (pp. 242-249).

Part 3: Common Visual Art for Personal Self-Fulfillment

Chapter 8

Engaging in Novel Common Art for Self-Expression and Stress Relief during the COVID-19 Pandemic

Shalin Hai-Jew*
Kansas State University, Manhattan, KS, USA

Abstract

During the SARS-CoV-2/COVID-19 pandemic (Jan. 2020 – present), personal artfulness may provide some emotional salve in a difficult time. Some people, including the author, started creating amateur or "common art" during the pandemic, and they shared their experiences on the Social Web. This work is comprised of a review of the literature. Then, a light insider auto-ethnography follows, based on practice-led research. Then, an environmental scan of some amateur artists and their works follows based on the following social media platforms: (1) social video, (2) slideshow sharing, (3) dedicated art platforms, and (4) social news sharing channels. Altogether, this work explores some common art by amateurs shared on the Social Web in the craw of a devastating pandemic.

Keywords: common art, amateur art, Social Web, SARS-CoV-2, COVID-19, pandemic, isolate art

Introduction

Making art is a good way to spend time under social lockdown, it would seem. During the SARS-CoV-2/COVID-19 pandemic (January 2020 – present), humanity itself is under threat from the novel air-transmissible pathogenic virus and experiencing unprecedented stresses and mutual traumas. People's lives have been upended. The social distancing, the masking, and other measures are porous, at best. Amateur "common art," free-choice non-remunerative work, may be a way to cope in this time. For some, given the massive job losses during the pandemic, common art is a way to create a small income stream. Indeed, many people have gone online to share their personal art on the Social Web. Digital culture is a participatory one, and nonprofessionals (common folk) engage in creating media "texts" in various modalities. The various roles of online participants suggest that studying "art, artists, and arts audiences" in various art venues may benefit the psychology of creativity (Lindauer, 2011, p. 63).

* Corresponding Author's Email: haijes@gmail.com

In: Common Visual Art in a Social Digital Age
Editor: Shalin Hai-Jew
ISBN: 978-1-68507-664-1

Review of the Literature

Amateur art has long existed, likely predating formal art. These involve the uses of various materials and skills. These may be performative (as in theatre, musical performances, magic, and others), or they may be exhibitions (as in art displays, museums, galleries, digital shows, and others). These may be created for various reasons: personal exploration, creative expression, social aesthetic work, self-development, political statement, and others.

Within the context of amateur art, there are varying levels of seriousness, based on intention, but also investments of the artist and the art type (doodles are less serious than oil paintings, modality-wise). The artists themselves may invest dedicated effort in taste-building, time, money, learning, and skill development. They may work hard at freeing their minds from prior habits and seeing the world differently. There are different tracks of development and different market reactions to various works. Since art is fungible, it may be seen as having different value in different locales: art museums, art galleries, personal collections, corporate displays, farmer's markets, county fairs, and so on.

The human world is a constructed space, with numerous design elements. People can find inspiration from others' works, from nature, from concepts, and other sources.

For example, crafts are considered generally informal, even if the artist may be a long-term practitioner. Jewelry-making may be both low- and high-art, depending on the artist name, the uniqueness of the works, the market valuation of the works, and other factors. "Felting" is considered hobbyist but requires aesthetic eyes and skill.

For some, there is a negative connotation to amateur art, the sense that amateurs appropriate others' professionalism and are carpet bagging and emulating.

Amateur Art in History

Historically, amateur art has existed for generations. A cited cultural historian, Jacques Barzun observed that "the most salient fact in the artistic culture of this country since 1930 is the rise of the amateur" (1956, as cited in Bryan-Wilson & Piekut, 2020, p. 1). Some cognates of "amateur" in the past century include the following: "dabbler, enthusiast, hobbyist, dilettante" (Bryan-Wilson & Piekut, 2020, p. 12). There have been some derogatory senses to the idea of "amateur," such as "unskilled." A more neutral sense is that amateur artists are "self-taught" and "uncredentialed" (Bryan-Wilson & Piekut, 2020, p. 15); they work outside the formal regimes of art production. If there is the idea of the formally trained as those at the center of a profession, amateurs are on the periphery. They are the subaltern. In part, the rise of amateurs may be part of the broadscale movement away from expertise (Nichols, 2017).

The move to amateur-based creations has been enabled by various technological innovations (Bryan-Wilson & Piekut, 2020, p. 1) and manageable costs. There have long been do-it-yourself (DIY) movements for various skills, most recently buoyed by how-to videos on social video sharing sites. Online, followers of particular public figures engage in fan art and enact derivations; their reframings are valued both for their devotion but also their originalist reframing of others' work. There is the influence of democratization and egalitarianism which enables opportunities for people to pursue their interests. The Social Web supports participatory culture, where people can all play a role, as consumers, as producers, and as prosumers (a portmanteau word for those who both consume others' creative production and also create and share their own). Many who contribute do not have direct ties to capitalist culture and are expressing for self-fulfillment. Others create art in the service of political action, not by diktat from the top, but against the existing societal and political powers. The role of "amateur" manifests in different ways:

> …'the amateur' is an unstable, mutable figure across various geographic contexts, context that have shaped an extraordinary range of activity, from non-remunerated, self-organised, unofficial, anti-ruling class insurgent artistic efforts, to programmatic state efforts to marshal 'folk' production into national narratives of 'authentic' belonging. (Bryan-Wilson & Piekut, 2020, p. 8)

In the community of practice, amateurs may come at the work with a range of different backgrounds and levels of learning. In the literature, some older women take up art-making in later life after retirement to enrich their mental life, enhance their sensations of color, and enable "new challenges…playful experimentation…and fresh ambitions" (Reynolds, 2010, p. 135). Theirs is a leisure activity. The participants in this study involve 32 participants in the 60 – 86 years age range. Of this group, two of them turned professional. Their art gave them social connections to others "outside the home and immediate family" (p. 135). Some expressed feeling validated by others (p. 141). Others expressed a sense of reward with a creative identity (p. 141).

Amateurs have differential practice. Some may have no background at all and are learning by doing. Others may have piecemeal formal learning. Their works may show various levels of knowledge, skills, and abilities (KSAs). Much of this work may be amateurish and derived. Other amateur artists take on the role of "defiantly unprofessional" (Bryan-Wilson & Piekut, 2020, p. 9) and "outsider" persona who create "outsider art" (p. 15); their work may be understood as a statement against the formal system. For some, an amateurism phase may be a gateway to future practice as a professional. In the prior case, there are no hard lines between an amateur and a professional. The thinking is that if there is sufficient talent and will, an amateur can become professional. An individual does not require formal education or affiliation to art schools or art societies. If the individual can find a voice and a style and a market for the art, then they can define their own paths and go through various transition states that result in their emerging as a recognized professional.

Amateur Artists in Academic Research

Historically, amateur artists have not been a serious subject in art-historical research. Their contributions were not seen as having artistic value. This reality shifted in the early 21st century:

> Monographs dedicated entirely or largely to amateur artists appeared from the beginning of the twenty-first century, although some countries, including the United Kingdom, France, and, to a lesser extent, the United States, were forerunners. The interest in amateur artists was a direct consequence of the change in the approach to art history—from the monographic progressive approach of the first half of the twentieth century to the 'new art history,' which included cultural, societal, economic, and political context, to the production of art from the 1980s onward. (Wiertz, 2020, p. 120)

For non-professional artists, their "lack of a name, the low expected quality of the nonunique work, and the negative perception" were no longer sufficient barriers to art historian evaluation (p. 122). Amateur artists may have been seen as less of a potential threat to the professionalism "on which academia and academic research, associated institutional validation and state support" relied (Wiertz, 2020, p. 125).

The advent of amateurs on social media may disintermediate potential arts agents. They may contribute to a de-professionalization of some types of art, given technological means to create various professional looks-and-feels.

Harnessing the Informal for Formal Research

Work by amateurs may benefit the professionals, in the same way that citizen scientists' observations and simple experiments benefit scientists. Amateurs have been found to provide solutions to various societal-level problems, with their innovations, such as during wartime (Ingalls, 1943).

The advent of the Social Web has also led to the creation of "amateur online museums, archives, and collections" (Terras, 2010, p. 425). Here, non-professionals may self-curate various contents and information. They may digitize analog objects, with historical value. The informal photographing of "digital curiosities" outside the purview of formal institutions can provide rich source materials for professionals who work at "memory institutions" that maintain collective memories (Terras, 2010, p. 427).

Flickr, a social image sharing site, enables the amateur sharing of cultural and heritage content. It serves as "a forum for hosting, discussing, and collecting vintage ephemera" (Terras, 2011, p. 686), with photographers digitizing analog items into digital for mass sharing. The online space has various groups based on topics of shared interest, and it also has digital means to collate various similar or related objects.

In another case, a user-generated arts space online has informed formal education. People gather at deviantArt.com in order to acquire art-related skills based on New Literacy practices. deviantArt (dA), a global space, is described as embodying "youth visual culture" (Jones, Summer 2015, p. 342). The shared works are in varying levels of finish and refinement. Part of the culture of collective learning is "asserting a New Literacy right to mimic, remediate, and appropriate the authority of professional artifacts (Deuze, 2006; Duncum, 2013; Grusin & Bolter, 2000; Lessig, 2008, as cited in Jones, Summer 2015, p. 350). There is both direct and indirect learning from others, with "teaching as (a) participatory sharing norm" (Jones, Summer 2015, p. 351) and highly motivated participants already practiced in autonomous learning.

Historically, there have been social barriers to being an artist. Social elites consumed the fine arts, and the arts were not seen as something for the masses. A study of journalistic coverage of the arts over two time periods (the 1950s and then the 2000 – 2009 period) found continuance of such practices using "fungibility, social hierarchies, and disinterested language" to uphold the traditional sense of fine arts' tie to upper-class status and education (Ten Eyck & Christensen, 2012, p. 330). The researchers write: "According to Kimmelman (2005), anyone can create art. We agree, but to be involved in the art scene one must have access to social spheres characterized by limited and highly guarded access" (Ten Eyck & Christensen, 2012, p. 337). A research team has observed "modern art's large number of individualized styles, innovativeness and conceptuality" for positive aesthetic experiences (Leder, Belke, Oeberst, & Augustin, 2004, p. 489), so there is a sense of a "big tent" to aesthetics.

Art for Socio-Political Action

Some approach the making of art as something essential to living even as "it is not easy to pay bills or afford life as an artist, art critic, or art historian" (Diaz, 2020, p. 137). There are responses to art beyond sensory pleasure or hedonic enjoyment. The artful creation of posters for political protest offers opportunities for encapsulating "sociopolitical dreams" to fight "political disenfranchisement and sustained oppression" (p. 152.)

Art may mobilize people to particular awareness and actions where the work may serve as reinforcement; however, sometimes, "the power of symbolic expression may themselves produce quiescence" (Lee & Lingo, 2011, p. 316). There are complex entities in the performing arts space, including artists, scholars and academics, donors, consultants, policy centers, lobbying groups, local government, national government, and others (Lee & Lingo, 2011, p. 328). Advocacy here may be fairly dynamic. These coresearchers write:

> The role and value of art in collective action is far more ambiguous and contested than sociologists asserting the importance of the arts to collective action have typically claimed. Researchers studying the role of the arts in mobilization might productively examine how cultural assumptions about the value and power of art in society—particularly with respect to the central role of arts institutions in producing and reinforcing normative assumptions about relevant actors and audiences (who) and about instrumentality (why)—shape their use in movements. (Lee & Lingo, 2011, p. 332)

Social and cultural beliefs and norms might limit social movement activity instead of expanding it.

Another work looks at the role of art in identity politics, in the socio-political space. Disability art, both performances and exhibitions, stems from the disability rights movement. The works include both disability and non-disability topics (Solvang, 2012, p. 178), and these include the mainstream to enhance understandings of different points of views among those in this identity.

Yet another showcases participatory arts to advocate sustainability and environmentalism, by encouraging the making of heirloom-quality objects that can be used for a long time and be repaired as needed, for a more sustainable world (Holmer, DiSalvo, Sengers, & Lodato, 2015, p. 119). Amateur art can speak to social practice.

Amateur Art Enabled by Technologies

Several works describe the harnessing of digital means to create interactive art experiences, through various forms of human-computer interaction (HCI). Early manifestations of art linked to technologies involve "aesthetic computing" in the early 2000s.

Information and communication technologies (ICT) stand to change up the fundamentals. One author writes:

> The character of authorship, evaluation and production of artworks is being altered with new communication technologies. Online amateur and participatory work challenge the existing symbolic and economic structure of artistic fields. (van Dijk, 2014, p. 86)

Art-based online digital communities work as social networks. Online artful interactive productions may exist in their own right. The "'genres' no longer need an institutional base in the offline world" and "exist without bookstores, libraries or the press" (van Dijk, 2014, p. 98). For many, the measure of the artful output as "pleasure and creativity rather than economics" (van Dijk, 2014, p. 86). In the present day, information technologies showcase the promise of "immersive environment, robotic art, and machine intelligence in art" (Jeon, Fiebrink, Edmonds, & Herath, 2019, p. 108).

How People Engage (and Consume) Art

An artwork is generally seen as the material manifestation of the internal imagination of the artist. In some perspectives, emotions are a central focus in terms of how people engage art. Here, artworks are a conduit of the creator's emotions and affect those of the viewers/consumers. Recent research evaluates whether amateur abstract paintings' emotions may be discerned by using computer vision and machine learning to learn what elements of abstract paintings convey positive and negative emotions (Sartori, Yanulevskaya, Salah, Uijlings, Bruni, & Sebe, 2015, p. 1). This study involved both a professional artist dataset and one of amateur artists. One finding: dark colors seen as negative and light ones as more positive (Sartori, Yanulevskaya, Salah, Uijlings, Bruni, & Sebe, 2015, p. 24).

Other research has found "correspondence between the emotional characteristics of artworks and viewers' emotional responses" (Tinio & Gartus, 2018, p. 319). The various aesthetic encounters between people and art may be mapped emotionally in empirical research through the drawing of "emotional heat maps." The researchers explain: "The study focused not on the usual measures of preference, liking, or pleasure—the focus of the majority of previous empirical studies in aesthetics—but instead took into account complex aesthetic reactions involving self-related processing and emotions" (Tinio & Gartus, 2018, p. 322). They also found some consensus among consumers of art as to their emotional responses. Prior exposures to art, which affect aesthetic fluency, also were found to affect their emotional responses, whether the exposure was formal or informal (p. 325). The researchers found evidence of "self-related processing" (p. 331), from those less exposed to art information.

If art is created a particular way based on the background of the artist, how contemporary visual art is perceived and enjoyed by particular consumers is "influenced by their cultural capital, habitus and class—which in turn, are affected by their life course experiences" (Newman, Goulding, & Whitehead, 2013, p. 456). Many without formal training in the arts respond based on self-interpretations and personal meanings. The artworks are not considered in the context of the relevant art genres, artists, and other information.

Various Art Markets

In formal spaces, the primary market for art involves so-called "art dealerships" (galleries, art houses) and independent agents. The secondary market for art is comprised of auction houses. If there are central art markets, with name recognition and various types of in-house expertise, there are also peripheral markets (alternative galleries, and others). Artists that can command high fees for their exclusive and novel works may go the formal route. (Many practicing formal artists themselves cannot afford representation.) Some may go with third-party content providers who can make prints and reach a wide potential consumer audience. Amateur artists, however, have to go with other venues to reach a market: mass media coverage, publications, social media platforms, and others. Some may teach online while funded by online patrons. Others go to social fundraising sites to fund particular works. Many pursue small government grants. (These moneys do not suggest that the art has to be official art. They are usually generally strings-free moneys for the creation of art by the artist based on his/her own vision.) Many sell directly to the public: sculptures, jewelry, paintings, ceramics, glassware, and others. The valuation of such low- and middle-brow art depends on what sellers are willing to pay and what artists ask.

In early pragmatic economic thought, art was considered "luxury, waste and dissipation" (Goodwin, 2006, p. 26). How to value art has long been a subject of consideration.

> Attention to art and culture goes far back in the history of economic thought. In the seventeenth century those activities were viewed suspiciously as likely to be either wasteful extravagances of the aristocracy, or dangerous distractions for the working classes. Eighteenth century economic thinkers offered more positive and thoughtful speculations. Mandeville and Galiani observed that the prices of art works were determined almost entirely on the demand side of the market, often by fashion and the search for distinction. The Enlightenment economic thinkers were intrigued by various aspects of art markets. Hume and Turgot perceived positive social benefits emerging from the arts, and they attempted to understand of what these consisted. (Goodwin, 2006, p. 26)

There are other-than-economic ways of valuing art. Modern aesthetics inform, in part, how art is valued. In contemporary thinking, beauty is not inherent to the object but trained into the eye of the beholder. Said another way: Aesthetic judgments are "always particular and cannot be rule governed" (Kant, 1790/1986, as cited in Hutter & Shusterman, 2006, p. 181). There is the sense that "aesthetic theory in the twentieth century displays considerable diversity, including some skepticism with respect to the possibility of universal theories of aesthetics because of the worry that 'art' named a historically constructed concept of rather ambiguous, contested, and shifting boundaries rather than signifying a natural kind with a common essence." (Hutter & Shusterman, 2006, p. 189)

What aspects of art are valued? One work suggests that the following are relevant: their sense of "moral or religious vision," its "deep expressiveness," its "communicative power" (p. 197), its "social and political value," its "cognitive value," its "experiential value" (Hutter & Shusterman, 2006, p. 198), and its aesthetic power ("unity, harmony, complexity, balance, intensity, dramatic tension, etc." as formal values) (p. 198), "art-technical value" or technique or innovation, "art-historical" value (p. 199), and others. The economic value may increase when there are "several varieties of artistic value…combined in a single work" (p. 200) and the "highest prices…for rare works…by most highly ranked masters that combine emotional impact with status and entertainment value" (p. 200). Art often has its own space as contrasted against "ordinary consumption goods" (p. 200).

Online sites may capture a sense of artist value based on their numbers of followers and the amount of attention they receive in the online attention economy (electronic word-of-mouth). Many artists may be known for particular styles or works. They may be experts in particular aspects of the art space. Perhaps they have particular single works or series of relevance. There has been some research work in designing online spaces to help develop amateur artists (Cho, 2019). In general, the Web has enabled wider information of artists to be disseminated and also enabled a sense of a global market. Digitization has "had a profound impact on the art market and its institutions" (Arora & Vermeylen, 2013, p. 1).

About "Making" and "Crafting"

Several academic works address "crafting" as a kind of common art. Amateur craftswomen who engage in various types of making—of toys, clothing, jewelry, quilts, hand-knitted goods, cushions, and other goods—apparently "experienced subtle pressures, both internal and external, to subdue their passion for craftmaking" (Grace & Gandolfo, 2014, p. 56) and had to take the position of "critique, resistance and subversion" and not buying into dominant narratives that would have them doing other things (p. 56).

A study of amateur crafting of creative goods submitted to county fairs found that the works that won prizes were those that adhered to established norms for the particular objects, not those works that were novel. The reward structure focused on "mastery of established techniques in a relatively narrow range of applications" (Paulsen & Staggs, 2005, p. 134) and conservative reproduction of traditional forms.

Government Interest in Public Art

Finally, in liberal democracies, there are taxpayer dollars set aside to fund public art. One recent study focused on particular social dimensions in such funding by establishing a tie between "confirmative art and bonding cohesive behavior on the one hand and challenging art and bridging cohesive behavior on the other" (Otte, 2019, p. 1). In other words, art can help bring homogenous people together, and art that challenges common ideas may help bridge heterogeneous groups by challenging perceptions and enhancing empathy and understandings of others' points of view. Social cohesion is defined by a "'we'-feeling" (Otte, 2019, p. 2) or a sense of closeness and shared social identity. This researcher observes: "Cultural policies with the aim of fostering social cohesion tend not to support expressions of modern art, but rather those of amateur art and folk cultures" (Otte, 2019, p. 4), a finding that is supported by the research on county fairs. Challenging art is about a new sense of the world as seen from a different perspective (Otte, 2019, p. 5). [Perhaps government funds for public art could have been used in a time of high-stress and high-threat and mass-scale lockdowns to enable more of a sense of collectivism and togetherness instead of political strife and othering.]

Research Methods

The primary research here involves two parts. The first involves a light insider auto-ethnography over a six-plus month period beginning a year into the pandemic. By January 2021, the author had been in lockdown since about March 2020 and had been telecommuting from home. She had lost several colleagues to the virus. She had family and friends who had taken on undue risks, when there was as-yet no actual bio-defense (except common sense, masks, hand hygiene, social distancing, and so on). In the year of going-to-ground, while still keeping some in-person commitments, the stress had taken a toll: graying hair, some weight gain, and fatigue. She took on "common art" after seeing a social video about alcohol inks on YouTube and was entranced by the interaction behaviors of those inks with synthetic papers (made with plastic). The materials involved some cost, but it all totaled to a low cost of entry. Even so, she still needed the ability to "salvage" the paintings through digital image editing before she could get past her frugal nature and to take on the risk. There is "forgiveness" in digital image editing because mistakes can often be undone, and works may be taken part to prior states based on the memory in the tool. She also engaged in reuse of some of the paintings by painting over them. She actually physically recycled some of the plastics (Type 5) in the local recycling center. Ultimately, she went on to create hundreds of such works—both born analog (the alcohol ink-based works) and digital (digital images seeded with the alcohol ink paintings)…shared on a slideshow sharing site…and continues through the present. [In some ways, creating a fast alcohol ink piece is faster than even drawing up something with a digital painting. Perhaps this is a matter of common artist preference and experience level. Perhaps this is only a matter of what is most available at-hand.]

The second part of this work involves an environmental scan of other amateur artists' works based on social shares from the following platform types: a social video sharing site, a slideshow sharing site, some dedicated art platforms, and some social news sharing channels. The scan is not a comprehensive one but is more to capture some insights and perhaps suggest some research angles.

The combined approach, involving both emic and etic approaches, provides something of an internal view by an amateur artist who socially shared…and an outside-in approach in exploring some of the shares by others.

Results

Taking on the role of an amateur can be experienced in different ways. In one sense, it can be highly freeing to enable one to dabble and experiment. In others, some may feel a need to emulate formal artists and formal works and methods.

During a segment of the SARS-CoV-2/COVID-19 pandemic (January 2021 – present), the author engaged in "common art" for self-expression and stress relief as a way of coping. She released these works in open-source slideshows on a social slide sharing social media platform. Her works were created using alcohol ink and synthetic paper (very thin plastic materials), and many of these works were digitized and further digital image editing and filtering effects were applied for different visual effects. The works are shared as unedited scans and then also as digitally edited reconfigured visuals in both two and three dimensions. The works are both analog and digital. The interactions between the analog materiality and digital immateriality varied over the respective works.

In terms of commenting, there are multi-pronged motivations and personal intentions mentioned: stress relief, distraction, self-soothing, therapeutics, sensemaking, learning digital image editing, exploring alcohol inks and synthetic papers, and self-amusement. Given the complexity of the human mind, it could be various mixes of the prior motivations or none, and perhaps there are other unmentioned motivations. Perhaps the pandemic itself is a kind of pretense, given how "late" into the pandemic the works started (January 2021, or over a year into the pandemic, and with early signs of potential reprieve through the vaccines).

There is the sense that the works are a visual diary, with the slideshows enabling commenting directly on the pandemic but also the learning progress related to the art materials and digital image editing. The works serve as a kind of digital sketchbook, with experimental practices and self-assigned work.

The works are named, which somewhat limits the interpretive range but which also gives forms to some of the more amorphous works. The works show off mental flits from one visual idea to another. There can be seen some development over time, as the author became somewhat more versed in the materials and in visual expression.

The whole sequence of slideshow displays are as follows in chronological order (all released to the public on SlideShare, a slideshow sharing site now owned by Scribd):

1. "Salvaging Inartful Mixed Media on Paper through Digital Means." (2021, Jan.)
2. "Alcohol Ink 'Drip Playing.'" (2021, Jan.)
3. "Liquid Incursions." (2021, Jan.)
4. "Fluidity." (2021, Jan.)
5. "Dilution and Concentration." (2021, Feb.)
6. "Molten." (2021, Feb.)
7. "Splash." (2021, Feb.)
8. "Illiquid." (2021, Feb.)
9. "Water Cycle." (2021, Feb.)
10. "Rain." (2021, Mar.)
11. "Flow." (2021, Mar.)
12. "Dry Spell." (2021, Mar.)
13. "Wet Season." (2021, Mar.)
14. "Spatter." (2021, Mar.)
15. "Hidden Water." (2021, Apr.)
16. "Flood." (2021, Apr.)
17. "Sleet." (2020, Apr.)
18. "Trickle." (2021, May)
19. "Evaporation." (2021, May)
20. "Steeping and Blooming." (2021, May) *
21. "Meanders." (2021, May)
22. "Slosh." (2021, June)
23. "Froth." (2021, June)
24. "Emulsion." (2021, June)
25. "False Light." (2021, June)
26. "Xeros." (2021, June)

27. "Torrential." (2021, July)
28. "Waves." (2021, July)
29. "Sluice." (2021, July)
30. "Pool." (2021, July)
31. "Rinse." (2021, August)
32. "Deluge." (2021, August)
33. "Soak." (2021, August)
34. "Surge." (2021, August)
35. "Freeze." (2021, September)
36. "Swell." (2021, September)
37. "Overflow." (2021, October)
38. "Turbid." (2021, October)
39. "Live Sea." (2021, November)
40. "Rivulet." (2021, November)
41. "Mist." (2021, November)
42. "Immersion." (2021, December)
43. "Light Rain." (2021, December)
44. "Stain." (2021, December)
45. "Aqua." (2022, January)

* The computational text analytics include the first 20 slideshows only. The works continued beyond the writing of this chapter. The works are included in the list should anyone be interested in seeing the entire series as hosted on SlideShare. [It is assumed at some point that the site may be discontinued, but until then, the works will be available online.]

The inspirations seem to come from both nature and concepts. The digital renditions range from recognizable [from the seeded image (such as straight single-plane extrusions)] to highly unrecognizable ones such as sequences of distortions and blurs and other filters. These latter ones look as if they might well have been born digital. While the alcohol ink works are original and built from scratch, the digital versions are variations on a range of possibilities based on various sequences of processing. On the one hand, there are infinite potential variations possible; on the other, there are constraints to the inks and the synthetic papers on a Cartesian plane and so, too, in digital image with x and y axes…and x, y, and z axes (2D and 3D respectively). Similarly, even if there are a range of potential topics that may be addressed, there are built-in limits based on the person's sensibility and personality and limited beginner's skills. These works may be analyzed later to understand the common artist's state of mind during the respective phases of art creation.

While the work seems to have only started in January 2021, the learning of the digital image editing software started several decades ago. The technologies—a flatbed scanner, the image editing software—had long been in use albeit for other purposes. The only newly acquired elements included alcohol inks, synthetic papers, watercolors, and so on. The basic sequence involved applying the inks and watercolors and then scanning the dried paintings. Then, those were given names. Some of the scans were used as "seeds" and re-versioned using the digital image editing software, and those works were also re-named and included in the slideshows.

The alcohol inks move in atypical ways on synthetic (plastic) paper, and for a newbie, there is a sense of little control. Editing on Adobe Photoshop 2021 does enable a fair amount of control and power given the strength of the software, but that also requires a lot of front-end learning and continuing acquisition of knowledge, skills, and abilities (KSAs) with this software tool.

There is some value in exploring what inspiration feels like to create alcohol ink art. There may be a fleeting visual concept, occurring live or at an inconvenient time; however, the concept is so compelling, it is noted or recalled, and it is expressed. Perhaps there is a moment of quiet after a long day. Sometimes, the inspiration may be a concept based on a certain turn of phrase, radio news story, written article, novel, or some other source. Perhaps there is an alluring reference photo. Perhaps there is a sunset viewed through tree branches. Perhaps there is some visual wit that is appealing.

Computational Text Analysis

One way to approach these works is through the computational analysis of the writing. Two software programs were used for this work: Linguistic Inquiry and Word Count (or LIWC2015, pronounced "luke 2015") and NVivo. The first is a linguistic analysis tool based on big data natural language datasets and counts of occurring words based on an in-depth dictionary. (Pennebaker, Boyd, Jordan, & Blackburn, 2015) The latter is the foremost qualitative data analytics tool on the market today. Both cover different dimensions although there is a slight overlap. The outcomes are reproducible given the technological methods.

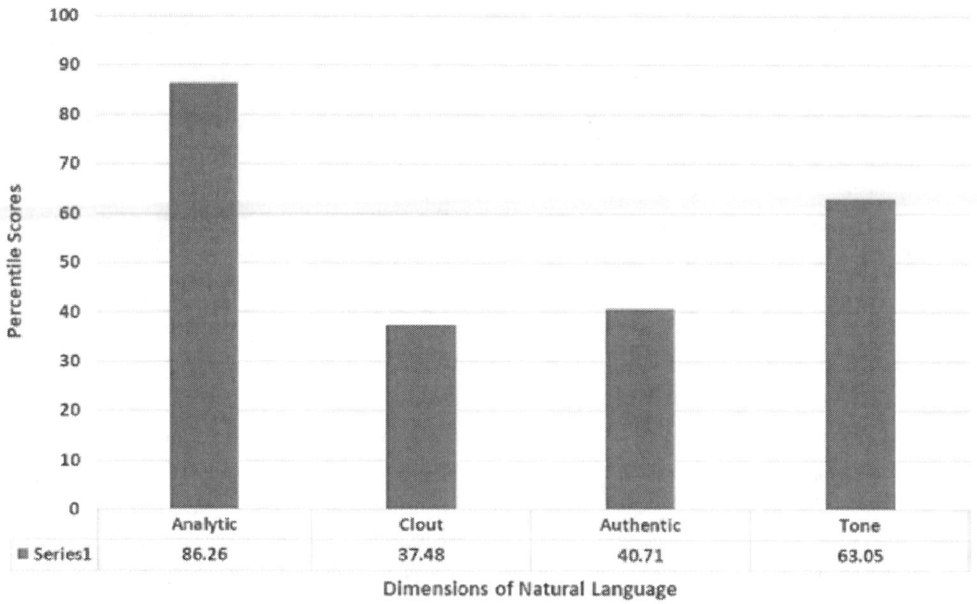

Figure 1. Language dimensions in the combined slideshows set.

The respective slideshows 1 - 20 were collated into one .pdf file. (The additional slideshows were created after the computational text analysis had already commenced.) The percentile ranks of the summary variables may be seen in Figure 1. Compared to other natural language, the language in the slideshows show a high Analytic tendency (86th percentile). There is less of a focus on Clout or power dimensions 38th percentile). In terms of "Authentic," a term which points to connecting language indicating social warmth, the slideshows ranked low (41st percentile). Then, the Tone (which is "sentiment" in other contexts) was seen as positive (with anything over 50 considered positive and any below 50 as negative) (Pennebaker, Boyd, Jordan, & Blackburn, 2015, p. 6). The Tone came in at the 63rd percentile (Figure 1).

In NVivo, automated theme-coding was applied to both the cumulative slideshow set and to the individual slideshows as a collection. The cumulative set results may be seen in Figure 2 and Table 1. And then separate slideshow set results may be seen in Figure 3 and Table 2.

Both analytics approaches show variations of focuses given nuanced differences in how the algorithms in NVivo handle the information—as either one file or 20.

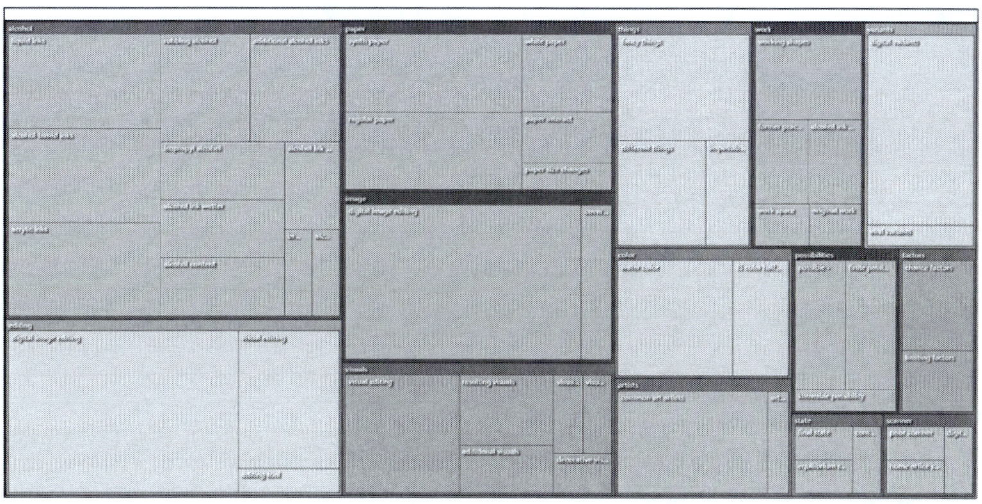

Figure 2. Autocoded themes and subthemes from cumulative slideshows in collection in a treemap diagram.

Table 1. Autocoded themes and subthemes from cumulative slideshows in collection

alcohol	
	acrylic inks
	additional alcohol inks
	alcohol content
	alcohol ink wetter
	alcohol ink work
	alcohol markers
	alcohol-based inks
	brown alcohol inks
	isopropyl alcohol
	liquid inks
	rubbing alcohol
artists	
	artist friend
	common art artists

Table 1. (Continued)

color	
	15 color halftone shape
	water color
editing	
	digital image editing
	editing tool
	visual editing
factors	
	chance factors
	limiting factors
image	
	cover image
	digital image editing
paper	
	paper interact
	paper size changes
	regular paper
	synth paper
	white paper
possibilities	
	finite possibilities
	knowable possibility
	possible •
scanner	
	digital scans
	home office scanner
	poor scanner
	constant state
	equilibrium state
	final state
things	
	different things
	fancy things
	impossible thing
variants	
	digital variants
	viral variants
visuals	
	additional visuals
	decorative visuals
	resulting visuals
	visual editing
	visual rendering
	visually coherent
work	
	alcohol ink work
	former practice works
	original work
	work space
	working shapes

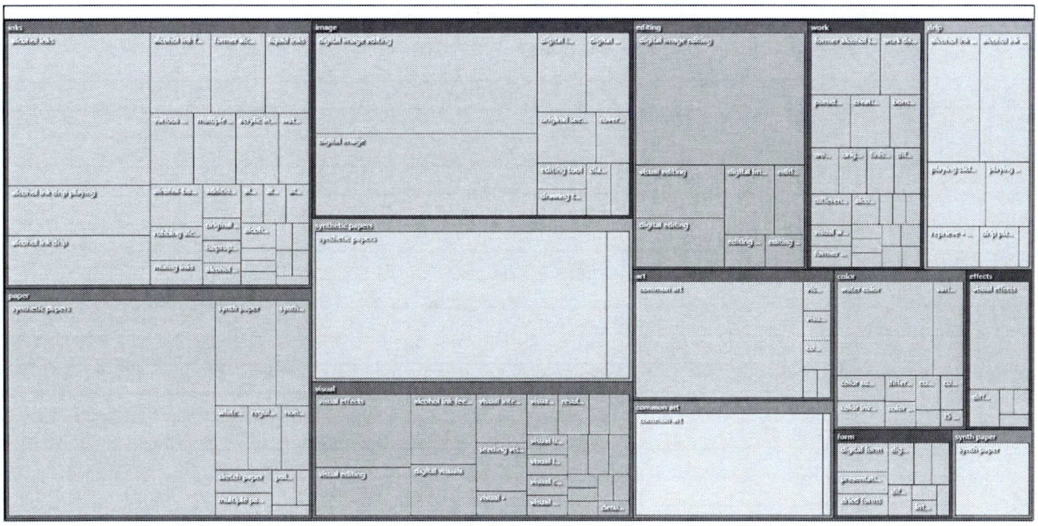

Figure 3. Autocoded themes and subthemes from separate slideshows in collection in a treemap diagram.

Table 2. Autocoded themes and subthemes from slideshows

art	
	art supplies
	art world
	common art
	common art artists
	visual art space
	visual arts
color	
	15 color halftone shape
	color combinations
	color inversion
	color substitution
	color theory
	color values
	different color palettes
	subtle colors
	various alcohol ink colors recombine
	water color
common art	
	common art
	common art artists
drip	
	alcohol ink drip
	alcohol ink drip playing
	drip playing
	drip playing experiences
	playing collection
	playing slideshows
	reprieve • dripping

Table 2. (Continued)

editing	
	digital editing
	digital image editing
	digital image editing tool
	editing filters
	editing software
	editing tool
	visual editing
effects	
	different filter effects
	layer effects
	special effects
	visual effects
	water effects
Form	
	desirable form
	different forms
	digital form
	digitized forms
	dried forms
	dry form
	intelligible form
	mercurial form
	presentational forms
	right form
image	
	cover image
	diagramming tools
	digital image
	digital image editing
	digital image editing tool
	digital image space
	drawing tools
	editing tool
	original seeding image
	visual image
inks	
	acrylic inks
	additional alcohol inks
	additional inks
	alcohol content
	alcohol dilutions
	alcohol ink drip
	alcohol ink drip playing
	alcohol ink drip-art
	alcohol ink feedstock visuals
	alcohol ink placement
	alcohol ink space
	alcohol ink work
	alcohol ink-play
	alcohol inks
	alcohol markers
	alcohol pool
	alcohol-based inks
	brown alcohol inks

inks	
	former alcohol ink works
	inks move
	isopropyl alcohol
	liquid inks
	mixing inks
	multiple alcohol inks
	original seeding alcohol inks
	rubbing alcohol
	various alcohol ink colors recombine
	varying inks
	water-based ink
paper	
	multiple papers
	non-synthetic paper
	paper interact
	paper size changes
	pulp-based papers
	regular paper
	sketch paper
synthetic papers	synthetic paper •
	white paper
	synth paper
	synth paper
	synthetic papers
	synthetic paper •
	synthetic papers
visual	
	additional visuals
	alcohol ink feedstock visuals
	combining visuals
	decorative visuals
	digital visuals
	resulting visuals
	seeding visuals
	various visuals
	visual
	visual art space
	visual arts
	visual concept
	visual cutouts
	visual editing
	visual effects
	visual ideas
	visual image
	visual interest
	visual language
	visual outputs
	visual rendering
	visual revelation
	visual works
	visually coherent
work	
	alcohol ink work
	born-digital works
	bornphysical works
	creating works

Table 2. (Continued)

work	
	decorative work
	different work
	different work contexts
	digital work
	finished work
	focused work
	former alcohol ink works
	former practice works
	initial work
	original analog work
	original work
	pseudo-artful works
	various work
	visual works
	work days
	work decades
	work space
	working shapes
	working time

The tables are included given the occlusion of some of the subthemes in the treemap diagrams.

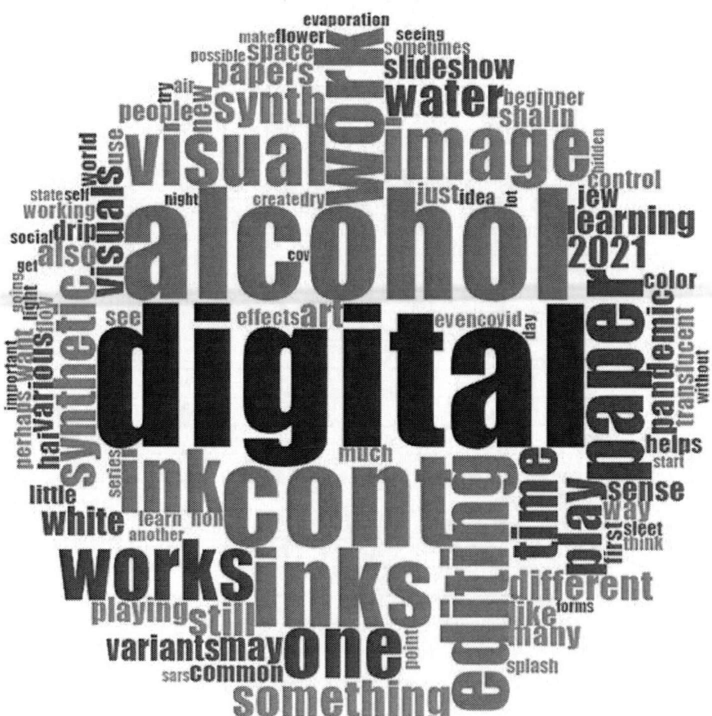

Figure 4. Word frequency word cloud from collected separate slideshows.

Another way to approach the slideshows is to run word frequency counts to see which terms appear most frequently. A light sense is that the more mentions there are, the more interest on the terms. NVivo generally treats word counts as one-grams and does not create bigrams, three-grams, four-grams, and so on. A word frequency word cloud follows in Figure 4 and a derived cluster diagram in Figure 5. The cluster diagram shows words that co-occur in physical proximity.

An autocoded sentiment analysis was run across the separate slideshows, and these do show variance (Figure 6). The applied coding was at the sentence level of granularity (vs. paragraph or cell).

In terms of a cumulative set, a majority of the text showed mixed sentiment (the rectangle to the left in the treemap diagram) in Figure 7. In less-mixed sentiment, much of it is negative. Then there is a part that is "neutral". At the far right is the sliver of positive sentiment. Given a focus on the SARS-CoV-2/COVID-19 pandemic and the related struggles, the respective sentiment foci are not surprising.

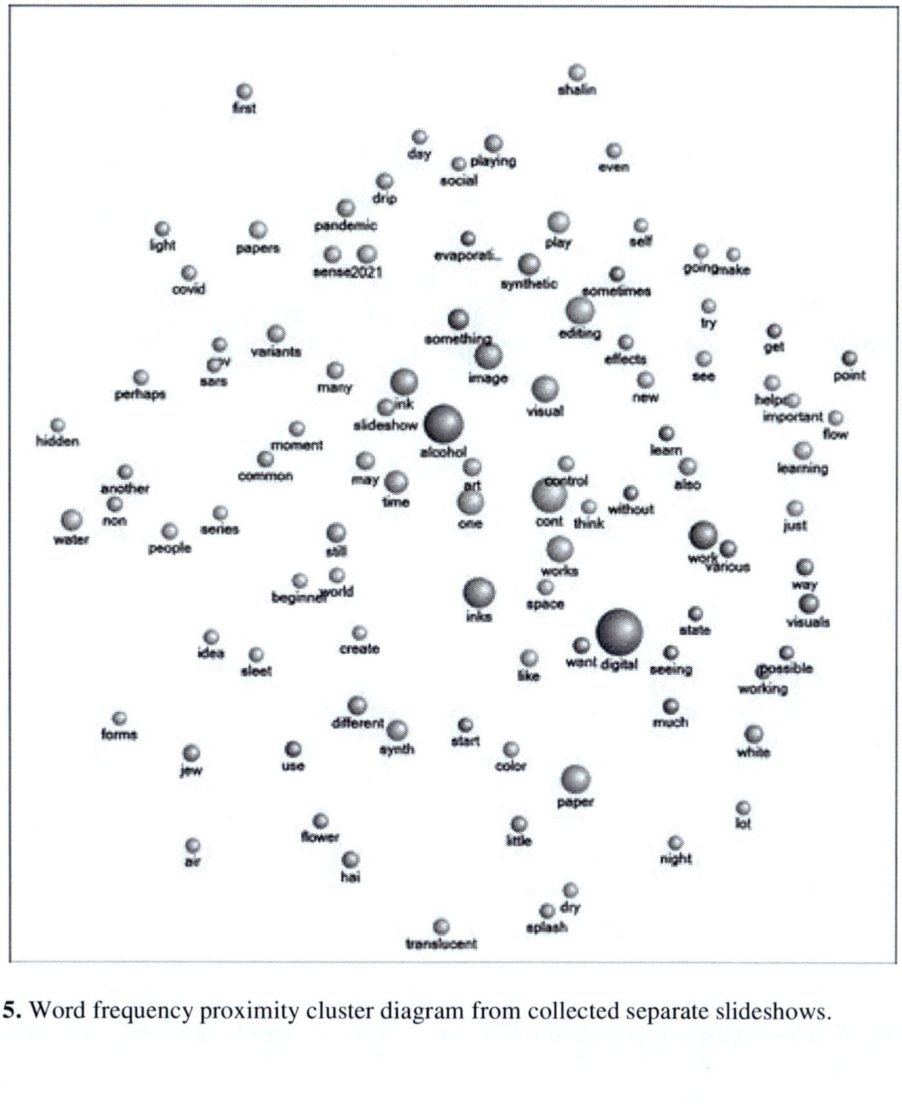

Figure 5. Word frequency proximity cluster diagram from collected separate slideshows.

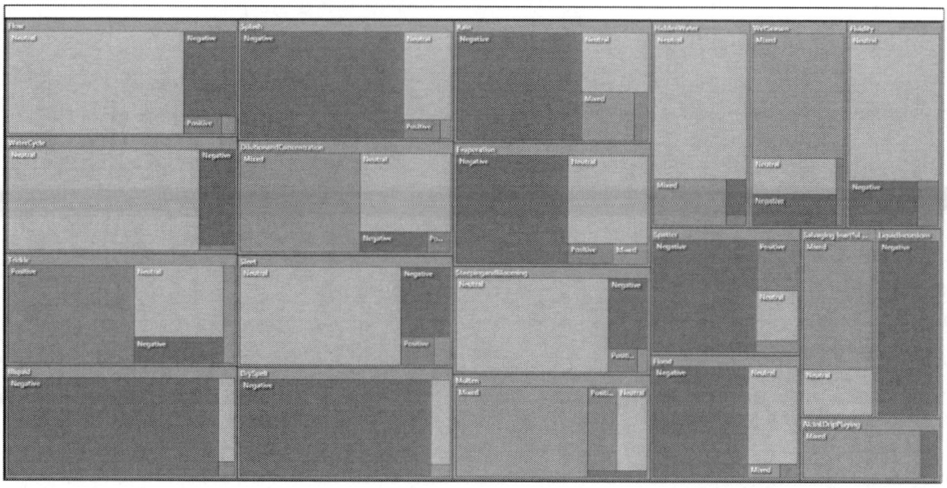

Figure 6. Autocoded sentiment mixes from separate slideshows in a treemap diagram.

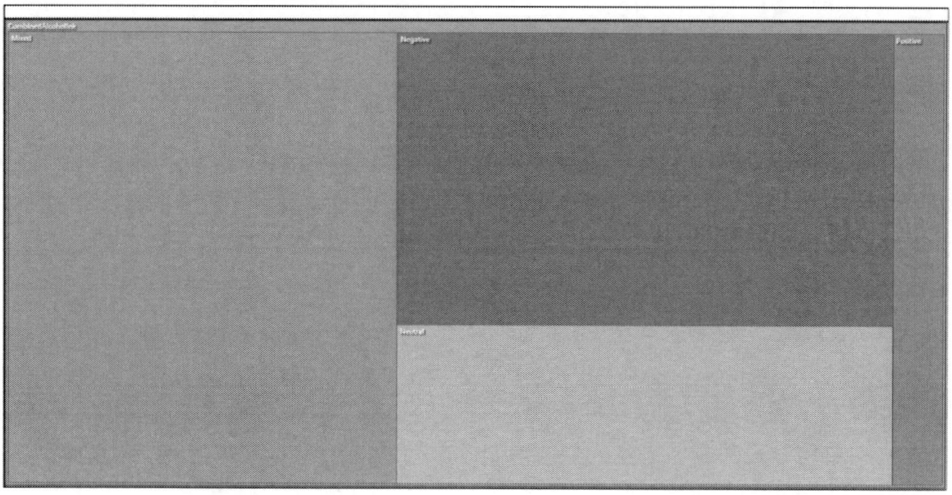

Figure 7. Autocoded sentiment analysis of combined slideshow collection.

Figure 8 shows a 3D bar chart of the sentiment split into four categories: very negative, somewhat negative, moderately negatively, moderately positive, and very positive. The text sets in each category show what was coded there. For the "very positive" set, for example, there were a range of titles. (If there is a shape that is "recognizable," the titles were then more about labeling. If the work was more abstract, the titles then seemed to trend more abstract. This is only a pseudo-pattern of practice, however, and did not apply in every case.) And there were sentences, including: "Many of the paintings start out looking more gloriously and peculiarly lurid than what happens after the inks and paints dry…and then are scanned." Several observations alluded to the fact that alcohol inks move, interact with each other and the synthetic paper, and they evolve. Their colors change if hot air is applied to hasten the drying. There are other changes as well when the work is digitized and transcoded (and then further digitally edited in some cases).

In LIWC2015, the cumulative slideshow set was seen as more positive than negative (Table 3). Indeed, different software programs may analyze a particular set in different ways.

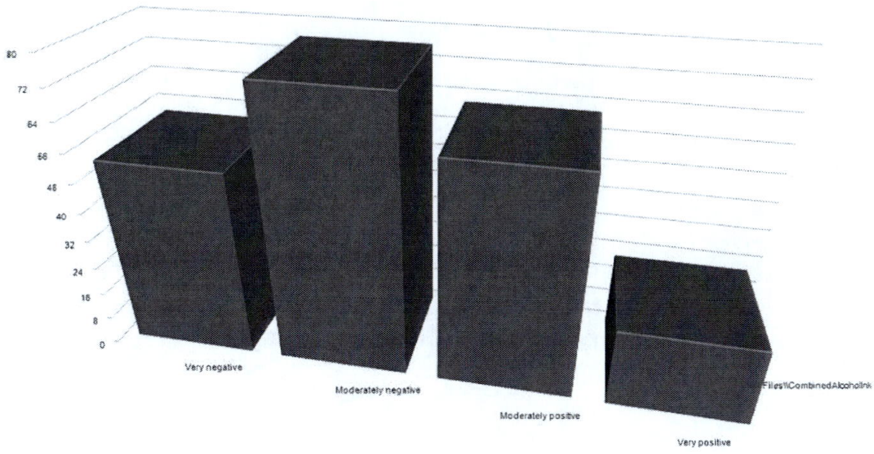

Figure 8. Autocoded sentiment analysis of combined slideshow collection in a 3D bar chart.

Table 3. Positive vs. negative emotion in the combined slideshow set

posemo	negemo
2.89	0.92

The language in the slideshows, according to LIWC2015, involved various types of cognitive processing, involving insight, causation, discrepancy, tentativeness, certainty, and differentiation. The prior variables indicate nuanced cognitive writing (Figure 9).

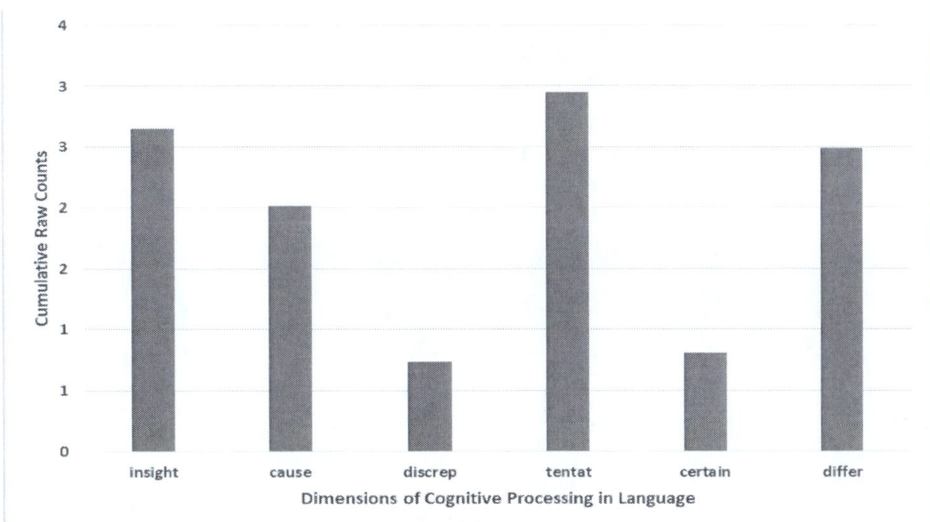

Figure 9. Types of cognitive processing in combined slideshow sets.

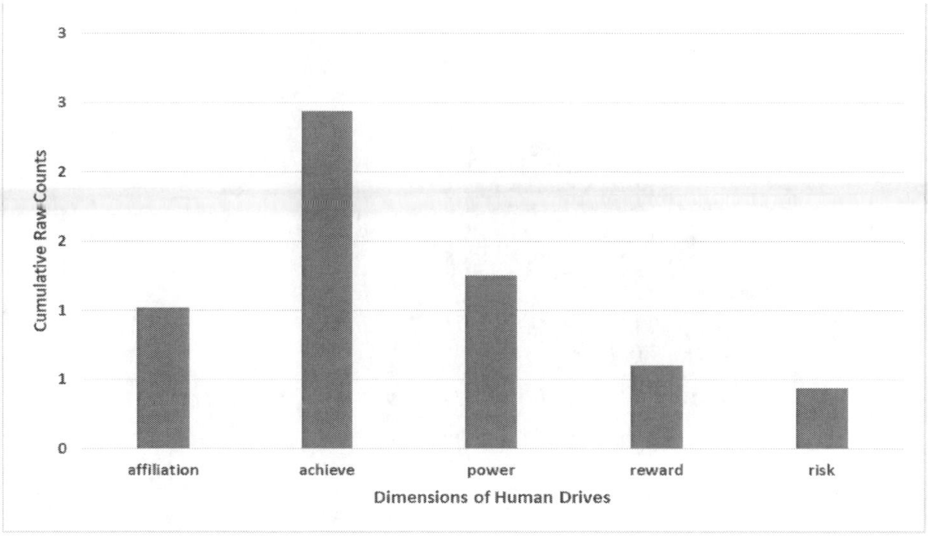

Figure 10. Types of human drives in combined slideshows set.

LIWC2015 also enables the capture of psychometrics. What of human drives indicated in the language in the slideshows? Figure 10 shows a high focus on "achievement" language, then "power," "affiliation," "reward," and then "risk," in descending order.

The analysis in LIWC2015 also found very much a focus on the present (8.96) and then on the past (1.57) and the least on the future (1.02) (Figure 11).

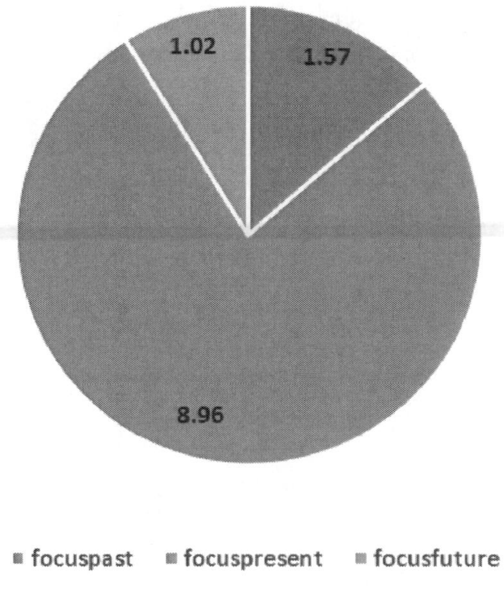

Figure 11. Time focuses in the combined slideshows set.

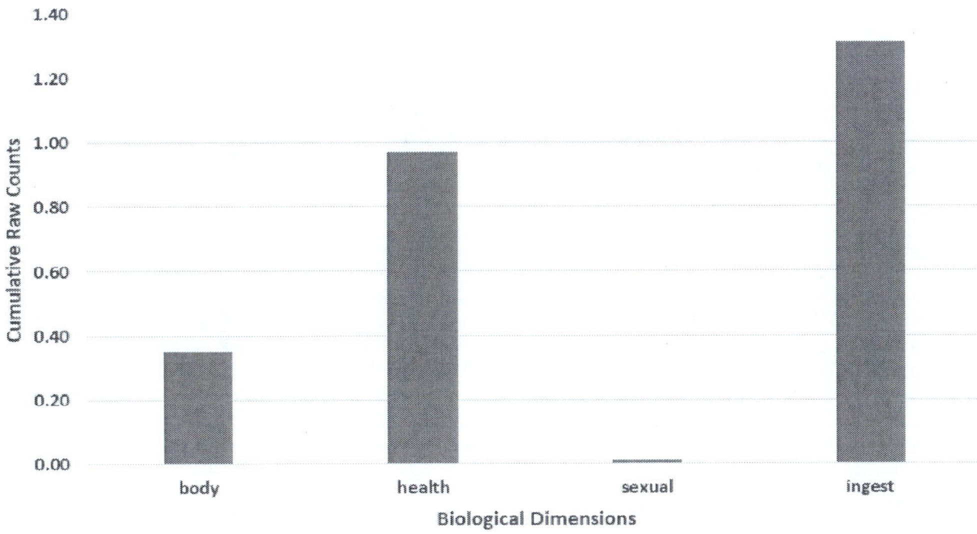

Figure 12. Biological functions in the combined slideshows set.

The language was also revelatory about biological functions, with language about ingestion, health, the body, and sexual foci (in descending order) (Figure 12). The titles of various works were food-related in some cases. In terms of the narrative sentences, those focused mostly on health in relation to the pandemic and art in relation to the work.

In the time of a pandemic, perceptually, time both speeds up ("it's been a month already") and slows down ("another day in lockdown"). As there are opportunity costs in life, there is also a sense that real life is suppressed. Even as life is intensified and foreshortened and ending for many, it also feels diffuse and dilute. The visuals are a way of putting the topsy-turvy and upended world right. The works are diversionary and pleasurable, hedonic. The making of artworks evoke a sense of child's play and enable a way to process the traumatic moments. The works enable a change of scenery, into a tumultuous other space. In a time of hypervigilance and invisible pathogenic threat, the work enables explorations from a kitchen table in a controlled home space.

Certainly, it is possible to go to amateur art for private creations and private usage. In this case, the art was shared publicly given a long history of publishing and sharing.

Common Art on the Social Web in a Time of COVID-19

To capture a social sense of "art" on the Social Web, related tags network data was extracted from Flickr, a social image sharing site. These two groups show something of the various types of artworks shared and their visual features. There are lived human aspects in the tagging as well. (Figure 13 and Table 4) This information was captured using NodeXL. The Clauset-Newman-Moore algorithm was used for the clustering. The thumbnail visuals related to the particular tags are those assigned by Flickr and tend to be recurring images for each tag.

Table 4. Graph metrics for "Art" related tags network on Flickr social image sharing site

Graph Metric	Value
Graph Type	Directed
Vertices	62
Unique Edges	1487
Edges With Duplicates	0
Total Edges	1487
Self-Loops	0
Reciprocated Vertex Pair Ratio	0.331244405
Reciprocated Edge Ratio	0.497646268
Connected Components	1
Single-Vertex Connected Components	0
Maximum Vertices in a Connected Component	62
Maximum Edges in a Connected Component	1487
Maximum Geodesic Distance (Diameter)	2
Average Geodesic Distance	1.386576
Graph Density	0.393178213
Modularity	Not Applicable
NodeXL Version	1.0.1.336

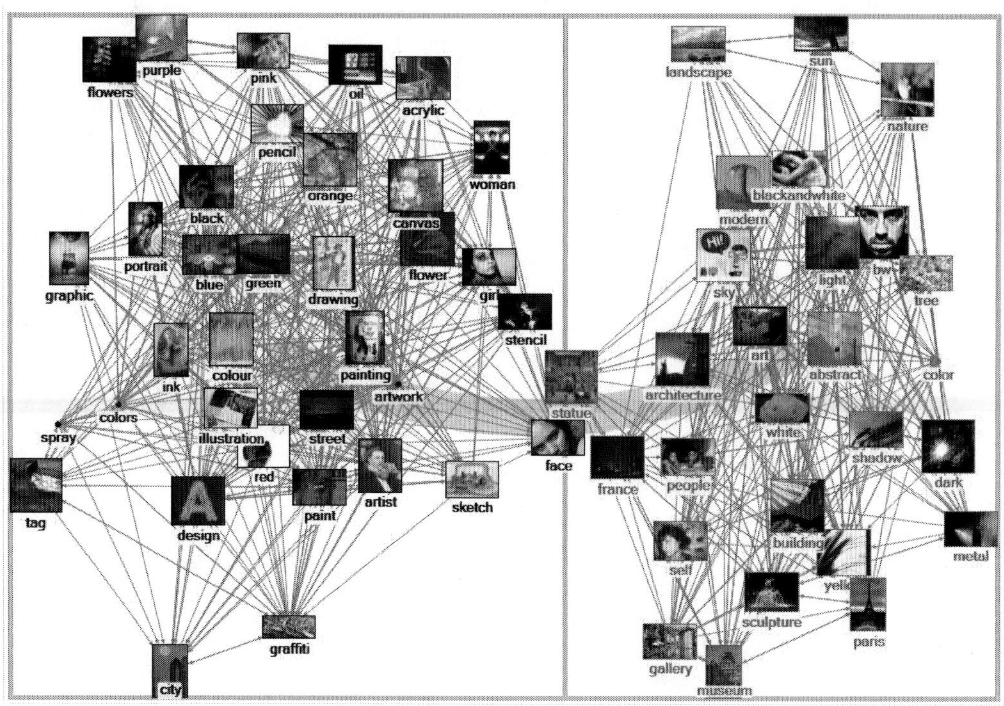

Figure 13. "Art" related tags network on Flickr social image sharing site.

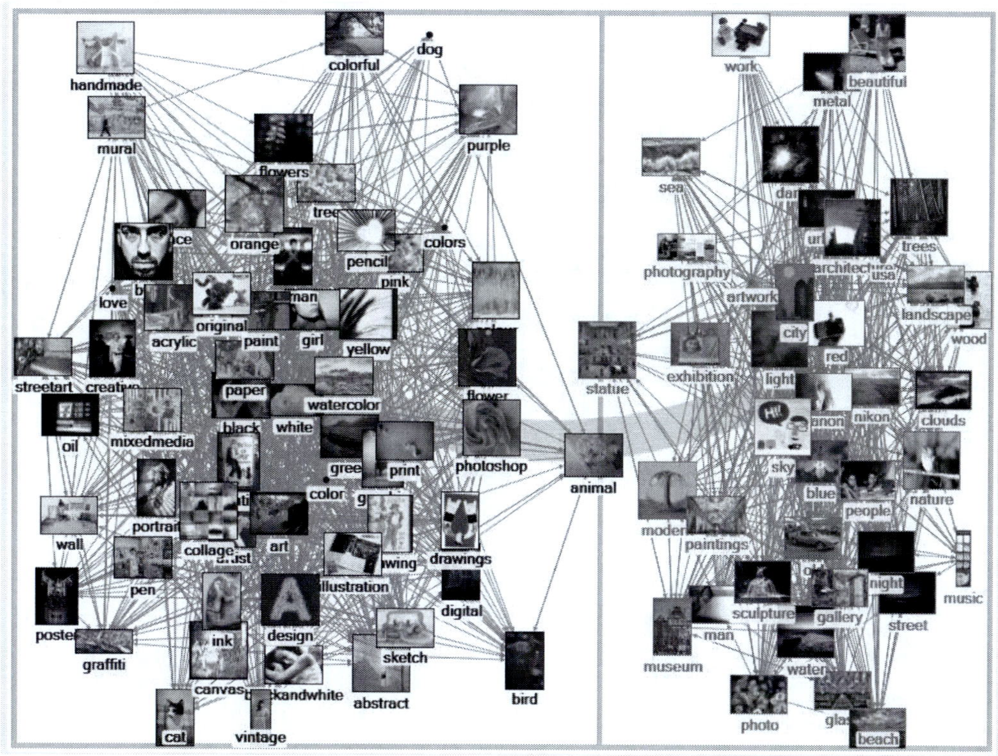

Figure 14. "Artwork" related tags network on Flickr social image sharing site.

Table 5. Graph metrics for "Artwork" related tags network on Flickr social image sharing site

Graph Metric	Value
Graph Type	Directed
Vertices	97
Unique Edges	3001
Edges With Duplicates	0
Total Edges	3001
Self-Loops	0
Reciprocated Vertex Pair Ratio	0.256174131
Reciprocated Edge Ratio	0.407864045
Connected Components	1
Single-Vertex Connected Components	0
Maximum Vertices in a Connected Component	97
Maximum Edges in a Connected Component	3001
Maximum Geodesic Distance (Diameter)	2
Average Geodesic Distance	1.47157
Graph Density	0.322272337
Modularity	Not Applicable
NodeXL Version	1.0.1.336

Another variation involves using "artwork" as the seeding tag in the social images in Flickr (Figure 14 and Table 5).

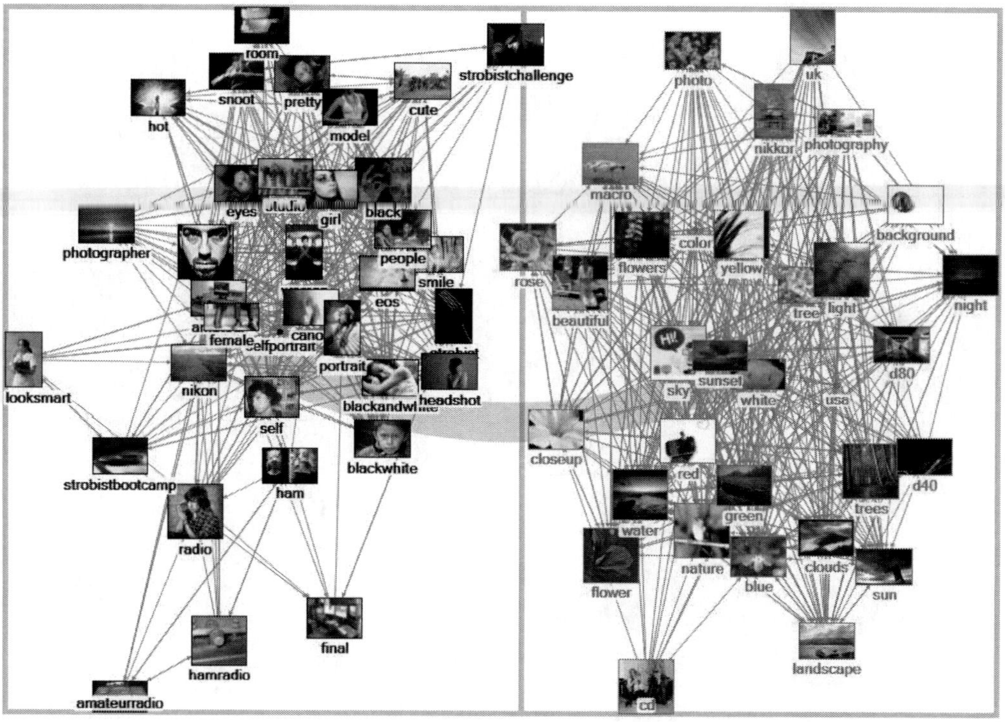

Figure 15. "Amateur" related tags network on Flickr social image sharing site.

Table 6. Graph metrics for "Amateur" related tags network on Flickr social image sharing site

Graph Metric	Value
Graph Type	Directed
Vertices	67
Unique Edges	1506
Edges With Duplicates	0
Total Edges	1506
Self-Loops	0
Reciprocated Vertex Pair Ratio	0.303896104
Reciprocated Edge Ratio	0.466135458
Connected Components	1
Single-Vertex Connected Components	0
Maximum Vertices in a Connected Component	67
Maximum Edges in a Connected Component	1506
Maximum Geodesic Distance (Diameter)	2
Average Geodesic Distance	1.455558
Graph Density	0.340569878
Modularity	Not Applicable
NodeXL Version	1.0.1.336

Finally, the "amateur" tag was used to seed a network on Flickr. These show a range of neutral related terms related to shared social imagery. Amateur practice is not uncommon on the Social Web (Figure 15 and Table 6).

Beyond the "inartful" and "artful" visual works of the researcher, the researcher also conducted a light environmental scan of the amateur art shared during the SARS-CoV-2/COVID-19 pandemic (January 2020 – present). This review is based on several social platform types. Given the lack of comprehensive analysis of the bodies of works by the respective amateur artists, the artist names are not specifically mentioned in a personally identifiable way.

Social Video

The author has followed several artists for several years on a social video sharing site.

One was the focus of a chapter (Hai-Jew, 2020). Both observed artists earn money on the Social Web by cultivating followers for their instructional videos. One using a patron site (with more exclusive videos for subscribers) as well as a public social video sharing site. Neither have an online marketplace for selling their works even as they have presences on social image sharing sites. Both have mentioned the pandemic as asides. One is in the U.S., and the other is in Canada. The American draws using various pencils and markers. She creates evocative fan art. The Canadian amateur artist uses watercolors and various ink pens for doodling. Both have distinctive art styles.

Slideshow Sharing

A search for slideshows showing amateur art on the slideshow sharing site did not result in much, not even the work of the author. Perhaps the search function on the slideshow sharing site is not sufficiently nuanced.

Dedicated Art Platforms

Seventeen collections were identified on one dedicated art platform. These were mostly comic-style drawings of humanity fighting a global menace.

On another platform, various artists showcase their ability to use the Adobe Creative Cloud suite of tools. The pandemic is mentioned as affecting the work, but the focus is not directly on the pathogenic virus.

Social News Sharing Channels

On a well-known social news sharing site with channels, there were channels for COVID-19 but nothing that focused on amateur art simultaneously. The lists were r/CLOVID19, r/Coronavirus, r/LockdownSkepticism, r/COVID, r/COVID19positive, r/conspiracy, r/China_Flu, and then channels linked to various locations and mentions of the pandemic.

Discussion

The SARS-CoV-2/COVID-19 pandemic is the most recent pandemic in modern history. It has led to mass human suffering, losses, and deaths, on a scale unprecedented in contemporary times. To cope, humanity has gone to various endeavors to address survive the present multi-year challenge. Amateur art is one approach.

Future Research

The creating of common art can be highly soothing in a time of pervasive pressures, such as during a pandemic. Other types of art practices may be explored to contribute to this research topic. Perhaps there are other combinations of analog and digital "common art"-making as well. Perhaps there is a category of "isolate art" from artists in lockdown, during the 2020 – 2021 - 2022 time period. Exploring such works for relevant themes would be intriguing to study.

Conclusion

Living through a pandemic involves high uncertainty in the context of health and mortal risk, often without any credible bio-defense except face masks, hygiene, and social distancing. This present historical moment has resulted in a particular set of circumstances. The pandemic manifested in different ways among different populations with their respective leadership, resources, values, and other factors.

Interesting, on social media, people can make all sorts of assertions about themselves, and only sometimes will people call them out. Being an amateur artist online is a little like being an "Instagram model," where people can use filters and digital image editors to create a look-and-feel that is pretty far from reality and can make claims about their professionalism even if they are amateurs with less developed skills (in many cases). In general, other amateur artists do not call out each other, and people give each other space for their own self-explorations and visual ideas and visual expressions. Indeed, some of common art is for people to work through personal issues. In a time of mass-scale pressures, perhaps people are more understanding of each other's needs to explore and express visual and other ideas through personal art.

This is an early work related to amateur art tied to the pandemic. It is likely much more will flow online as time progresses. And in the present moment, a majority of humanity is still at very high risk. For the author, the substantial aspects of art are digital, not material per se. While this work is focused on alcohol ink and synthetic papers, a wide variety of materialia may be brought into play for common art as salve. Perhaps it is because that it is by digital means that the works have an audience at all, in a time where people's lives are at heightened risk in each other's proxemic presences.

Acknowledgments

Thanks to all the amateur artists online who generously share of their work and provide so much inspiration. I am appreciative of YouTube, SlideShare, deviantArt, Behance, Reddit, Instagram, Flickr, and other sites. The technologies used for data capture and analysis in this chapter include NodeXL, LIWC2015, NVivo, and others.

References

Arora, P., & Vermeylen, F. (2013). Art markets. In R. Towse and C. Hanke (eds)'s *Handbook on the digital creative economy*. Edward Elgar Publishing. 1 - 12.

Bryan-Wilson, J., & Piekut, B. (2020). Amateurism. *Third Text,* 34(1), 1 – 21.

Cho, E. J. (2019). Design for mutual development of amateur artists: Planning of online communication platform for amateur artists. 1 - 95. Master's thesis. Graduate School of Creative Design Engineering, UNIST>

Diaz, E. M. (2020). Poster dreams: The art of protest and social change. In Christine Henseler's *Extraordinary Partnerships: How the Arts and Humanities are Transforming America,* 137 - 157. Lever Press.

Goodwin, C. (2006). Art and culture in the history of economic thought. In V. A. Ginsburgh and D. Throsby's. *Handbook of the Economics of Art and Culture*, 1, 25-68. Elsevier.

Grace, M., & Gandolfo, E. (2014). Narrating complex identities: Contemporary women and craft. *Women's Studies International Forum,* 47, 56 – 62.

Hai-Jew, S. (2020). Abstracting transnational celebrity (and sell) on a social video sharing platform: One 'neutral' exemplar. Chapter 8. In Hai-Jew's *Maintaining Social Well-Being and Meaningful Work in a Highly Automated Job Market.* Hershey, Pennsylvania: IGI Global. 202 – 243.

Holmer, H. B., DiSalvo, C., Sengers, P., & Lodato, T. (2015). Constructing and constraining participation in participatory arts and HCI. *International Journal of Human-Computer Studies,* 74, 107 – 123.

Hutter, M., & Shusterman, R. (2006). Value and the valuation of art in economic and aesthetic theory. *Handbook of the Economics of Art and Culture*, *1*, 169-208.

Ingalls, A. G. (1943). A hobby goes to war. *Scientific American*, *168*(5), 202-205.

Jeon, M., Fiebrink, R., Edmonds, E. A., & Herath, D. (2019). From rituals to magic: Interactive art and HCI of the past, present, and future. *International Journal of Human-Computer Studies*, *131*, 108-119.

Jones, B. L. (2015). Collective learning resources: Connecting social-learning practices in deviantART to art education. Studies in Art Education, 56(4), 341-354.

Leder, H., Belke, B., Oeberst, A., & Augustin, D. (2004). A model of aesthetic appreciation and aesthetic judgments. *British Journal of Psychology*, *95*(4), 489-508.

Lee, C. W., & Lingo, E. L. (2011). The 'got art?' paradox: Questioning the value of art in collective action. *Poetics,* 39, 316 – 335.

Lindauer, M. S. (2011). Art, artists, and arts audiences: Their implications for the psychology of creativity. Elsevier.

Newman, A., Goulding, A., & Whitehead, C. (2013). How cultural capital, habitus and class influence the responses of older adults to the field of contemporary visual art. *Poetics,* 41, 456 – 480.

Nichols, T. (2017). The death of expertise: The campaign against established knowledge and why it matters. New York: Oxford University Press.

Otte, H. (2019). Bonding or bridging? On art participation and social cohesion in a rural region of the Netherlands. *Poetics,* 76 (101355), 1 - 14.

Paulsen, K. E., & Staggs, K. (2005). Constraint and reproduction in an amateur craft institution: The conservative logic of the county fair. *Poetics,* 33, 134 – 155.

Pennebaker, J. W., Boyd, R. L., Jordan, K., & Blackburn, K. (2015). *The development and psychometric properties of LIWC2015.* Austin, TX: University of Texas at Austin. doi: 10.15781/T29G6Z.

Reynolds, F. (2010). 'Colour and communion': Exploring the influences of visual art-making as a leisure activity on older women's subjective well-being. *Journal of Aging Studies,* 24, 135 – 143.

Sartori, A., Yanulevskaya, V., Salah, A. A., Uijlings, J., Bruni, E., & Sebe, N. (2015). Affective analysis of professional and amateur abstract paintings using statistical analysis and art theory. *ACM Transactions on Interactive Intelligent Systems (TiiS)*, *5*(2), 1-27.

Solvang, P. K. (2012). From identity politics to dismodernism? Changes in the social meaning of disability art. *ALTER, European Journal of Disability Research,* 6, 178 – 187.

Ten Eyck, T. A., & Christensen, E. (2012). Speaking of art: Class code or historical residual?. *The Social Science Journal*, *49*(3), 330-338.

Terras, M. (2010). Digital curiosities: resource creation via amateur digitization. *Literary and linguistic computing*, *25*(4), 425-442.

Terras, M. (2011). The digital wunderkammer: Flickr as a platform for amateur cultural and heritage content. *Library trends*, *59*(4), 686-706.

Tinio, P. P., & Gartus, A. (2018). Characterizing the emotional response to art beyond pleasure: Correspondence between the emotional characteristics of artworks and viewers' emotional responses. *Progress in brain research*, *237*, 319-342.

Van Dijk, Y. (2014). Amateurs online: Creativity in a community. *Poetics,* 43, 86 – 101.

Wiertz, W. (2020). A lack of a name, of artistic value, and of a positive perception: Overlooking amateur artists in scholarly research. *History of Humanities*, *5*(1), 111-129.

Chapter 9

Adult Coloring Books as Emotional Salve/Stress Relief, Tactual-Visual Learning: An Analysis from Mass-Scale Social Imagery

Shalin Hai-Jew*
Kansas State University, Manhattan, KS, USA

Abstract

As a "common art" form, adult coloring books have been in use for decades, since the 1960s, for educational uses, initially about art education and then later, about health, anatomy, nature, and other learning. In the present day, in the time of a pandemic, adult coloring books have come to the fore again, as emotional salve/stress relief and as tactual-visual learning. This work explores the visual gist of adult coloring books on social media at mass scale, through a data extraction of thumbnail images on the Social Web, based on the seeding term "adult coloring book" on Google Images (875 thumbnails). In a Social Digital Age, adult coloring books exist beyond paper: in downloadables (like .pdfs), e-books, digital apps, games, augmented reality, virtual immersive spaces, and others. There are automated coloring book generators online that may create colorable-visuals based on photos, hand drawings, and others.

Keywords: adult coloring books, aesthetics, common art, social media imagery, stress relief, emotional salve, visual learning, tactual

Introduction

One highly recognizable form of "common art" is the coloring book, defined as "a type of book containing line art to which people are intended to add color using crayons, colored pencils, marker pens, paint or other artistic media" ("Coloring book," July 21, 2021). Coloring books may be more than line art: "Coloring books may also incorporate other activities such as connect the dots, mazes and other puzzles. Some also incorporate the use of stickers" ("Coloring book," July 21, 2021). Some coloring books have words on the pages (Fitzpatrick & McPherson, 2010, p. 131). Adult coloring books are a subgroup of coloring books, and their

* Corresponding Author's Email: haijes@gmail.com

In: Common Visual Art in a Social Digital Age
Editor: Shalin Hai-Jew
ISBN: 978-1-68507-664-1

subject matters and messaging are based on topics that adults may relate to: fairytales, myth, humor, nature, sweets, and other fare.

Review of the Literature

The original coloring book was credited to the McLoughlin brothers who started with *The Little Folks' Painting Book* in the 1880s ("Coloring book," July 21, 2021). For children, coloring books are often educational. Art-sensory materials enable users to engage in hands-on exploration of art materials and the development of motor skills (Schwarz & Luckenbill, 2012, p. 27). There are benefits of open-ended exploratory activities (Schwarz & Luckenbill, 2012, p. 28). In another example, an augmented reality coloring book is used to help children with autism spectrum disorders "focus on specific nonverbal social cues to promote their social skills" (Lee, 2019, p. 256). For children, they are used also for art therapy, counseling, and health education. One child-friendly work, *My Asthma Coloring Book*, was created to teach rural children about asthma, the main chronic disease among children in the U.S., and how to control it in their daily lives (Naumann, Huss, Calabrese, & Smith, 2004). Another similar type includes oncology coloring books. A digital coloring book has been used for the purposes of "occupational therapy" and "cognitive rehabilitation" (Skinner & Trachtman, 1985, p. 470). Coloring books have been used for trauma reduction (such as in the aftermath of accidents). Coloring books are sometimes included as parts of kits to keep children distracted during disaster scenarios (Severin & Jacobson, 2020, p. 97). Copied pages (aka "coloring placemats") are often used in restaurants to distract children before the food arrives.

Through the years, coloring books have been researched in the academic literature, although some have found only a "dearth of literature on coloring books" (Fitzpatrick & McPherson, 2010, p. 135).

Given that coloring books have digital forms, there have been studies of unstructured and spontaneous interactions of children with screens while engaging with drawing and coloring applications (Lanna & Oro, 2019, p. 1), in children under three. Touch and haptics, gestural interactions, and other approaches have effects on design. In this study, only a third of the sample "actually colored part of the outlined figure" although a majority did initiate "at least one interaction with the app for coloring" (Lanna & Oro, 2019, p. 8). The researchers did find some age effects in terms of how children used the respective coloring applications.

Controversies around Coloring Books for Children

While such coloring books have been fairly ubiquitous, these have not always seen as uncontroversial. The structure of coloring books in having lines already drawn and children just filling in color in the lines is seen as potentially suppressive of natural childhood curiosity and perhaps pushing children to work within too much constraining structure. One of the main proponents of this idea was Viktor Lowenfeld, who suggested "that coloring books are detrimental to the creative expression of children" (King, 1991, p. 36). This assertion was of especial interest given that it was by "the father of art education in this country" (King, 1991, p. 36). Lowenfeld asserted, in particular, that coloring books "limit a child's freedom to create";

"make a child inflexible"; "block emotional relief"; "do not promote skills and discipline"; and may dissuade children from drawing "on their own" (Lowenfeld, 1957, as cited in King, 1991, p. 40). Contrary to finding the so-called Lowenfeld's Proof, however, one researcher suggests that coloring books may lead children to "a deeper understanding and appreciation of art" (King, 1991, p. 36), in a direct challenge to Lowenfeld's proposition.

Another critique of coloring books is that limiting stereotypes of gender roles may be present in coloring books. One experimental study studied "the impact of gender and gender-related color stereotypes" among Israeli preschoolers and third graders (Karniol, 2011, p. 119). This researcher found the following: "Color was ignored in booklet choice. More colors were used for figures stereotypically associated with one's own gender. Boys' use of female-stereotyped colors did not vary across figures and differed significantly from chance. Boys avoided coloring the female-stereotyped figure and using pink. Girls sued fewer female-stereotyped colors for the male-stereotyped figure but used both types of color equally for the other figures" (Karniol, 2011, p. 119). Coloring itself has traditionally been a gendered activity, and researchers have found that coloring books are "geared specifically for one gender, as found in a recent analysis of randomly selected coloring books in the United States" (Fitzpatrick & McPherson, 2010, as cited in Karniol, 2011, p. 121). Coloring book topics for girls tend to be "fairies, princesses, and various fashion dolls whereas coloring books for boys feature vehicles, weapons, and action figures" (Fitzpatrick & McPherson, 2010, as cited in Karniol, 2011, p. 122). There were more nuanced findings:

> ...children's gender-linked color preferences are overruled by the illustrations on the cover of coloring books. Boys overwhelmingly selected a pink coloring booklet with Batman on its cover. In a complementary fashion, girls overwhelmingly elected a blue coloring booklet with a Bratz doll on the cover. Hence, although color may dominate children's choices when items are in their own-gender, stereotypical color or in other-gender stereotypical color..., color is a less important cue for children when it conflicts with other gender-linked cues. (Karniol, 2011, pp. 126 - 127)

Some findings align with other research that suggests that color choice "is an expression of one's gender identity" (Karniol, 2011, p. 128).

Another work observes that coloring books from the 1980s and 1990s depict Barbie dolls in various scenes, including as Western Barbie and Barbie in cowgirl gear (Thomas, 2000, p. 78). Some Barbie coloring book covers show her "with horses" (Summers 1996, p. 199, as cited in Thomas, 2000, p. 79).

A central study involved a stratified random sample of contemporaneous coloring books and a study of 889 depicted characters, with a focus on their gender roles. Males were "depicted more often than were females" (Fitzpatrick & McPherson, 2010, p. 133). The researchers found the following:

> As hypothesized, males were more active; gender stereotypes were common. Gender neutral behaviors were more likely to be done by males. Females were more likely to be depicted as children and humans, whereas males were mostly depicted as animals, adults, and superheroes. (Fitzpatrick & McPherson, 2010, p. 127)

Gender stereotypes "were common, especially stereotypes in coloring books aimed at girls" (Fitzpatrick & McPherson, 2010, p. 134); in the "superhero category, 90% were males"

(p. 135). There are concerns that such depictions in coloring books may be built into children's schemas of the world and affect their attitudes and behaviors and decision making. ("Stereotype threat," when activated, may affect actual mental and other performance).

In the early 1900s, coloring books were used to advertise various goods...to adults ("Coloring book," July 21, 2021), based in part on their familiarity as a common art form. Coloring books are used as an analogy to explain algorithmic tiling (Goodman-Strauss & Sloane, 2019), historical socio-political realities (Kopper, 2012, p. 277), strategy, and other applications. They are used to promote learning about artificial intelligence (AI) architectures for problem solving, limited thinking in politics, and others. As a metaphor, the lines of a coloring book are the "pregiven contours within which the picture is to evolve" (Kopper, 2012, p. 278), and coloring within lines is seen as unthinkingly provincial and limited.

Adult Coloring Books for Adult Interests

Adults have "co-opted" this coloring books for their own purposes. Adults started using coloring books in the early 1960s as part of the "democratization of art"; then, coloring books were used as a form of "adult therapy" in the 2010s ("Coloring book," July 21, 2021). More sophisticated art for adult coloring books was created by a commercial illustrator of wine bottle labeling (Basford, 2011, as cited in Raphel, July 12, 2015). This initial work sold in the multiple millions of copies. The practice of "Art-thérapie: 100 coloriages anti-stress" (2012) sold more than three and a half million copies worldwide (Raphel, July 12, 2015). Social media has fueled some of the FOMO, which has resulted in mass-scale sales, with colorists showing off their "elaborate creations on Facebook and Pinterest" (Raphel, July 12, 2015) as well as other spaces. Another motivation has been a mass trend of adults moving towards "childhood objects and experiences," termed the Peter Pan market (Raphel, July 12, 2015). This market includes adults wanting summer camps and preschool classes (Raphel, July 12, 2015). Coloring books are part of "infantilizing activities like 'adult summer camps' and 'adult preschool' (Rowe, May 31, 2018). Such activities may be a flight to comfort, a kind of adult self-soothing through "common art." Where some may see constructive coping, others may suggest that adult regression to adult coloring books may be escapist and non-constructive and not help them focus on actual in-world challenges.

Adults have used coloring books for entertainment, titillation; skill-building in coloring and drawing, in spatial assessment; education and learning (across a range of topics); emotional salve/stress reduction, and other applications.

Coloring books have been used assess knowledge. For example, adult teachers have used coloring books to assess the stage of child learning of language by having them fill in a digital coloring page based on sentence stimuli. By their coloring, teachers may ascertain their "interpretation of grammatical constructions and lexical items" (Pinto & Zuckerman, 2019, p. 2609). Teachers can also assess vocabulary knowledge. The new task "decreases external task-related effects and offers a more reliable measurement of children's linguistic knowledge" (Pinto & Zuckerman, 2019, p. 2609), both online and offline (p. 2610). There are various types of mobile coloring book games with different interfaces and different affordances and constraints (Lee & Jung, 2019, p. 109). Another work describes an augmented reality coloring book "with a transitional user interface" (Cho, Kim, & Lee, 2016, p. 1). There are different painting experiences in "real, augmented and virtual worlds" (Cho, Kim, & Lee, 2016, p. 3).

Social Communal Coloring

Another use is the application of the coloring book structure or concept for building software. One work describes an algorithm to color or shade in the shapes in a coloring book (and other two-dimensional space) with colors or textures or patterns (Lieberman, 1978, p. 111).

Some use coloring books for community "coloring book clubs" to attract everyone from tweens to the elderly, with people socializing and talking as they color (Marcotte, Nov./Dec. 2015, p. 18). These activities serve as a creative outlet for people (Marcotte, Nov./Dec. 2015, p. 18) and are important in library programming (p. 19).

Stress Relief

Some coloring books are used to help nursing professionals decompress and head off work burnout (Jones, 2020, p. 122). Here, visual self-expression in various forms "helps with attention and improves health and well-being" (Kaimal, Ayaz, Herres, Dieterich-Hartwell, Makwana, Kaiser, & Nasser, 2017, p. 85). The human brain is activated based on "coloring, doodling, and free drawing" (Kaimal, Ayaz, Herres, Dieterich-Hartwell, Makwana, Kaiser, & Nasser, 2017, p. 85), with artists. All three tasks resulted in "significant activation of the medial prefrontal cortex compared to the rest conditions" (as baseline) (Kaimal, Ayaz, Herres, Dieterich-Hartwell, Makwana, Kaiser, & Nasser, 2017, p. 85). They write of their pilot study, further:

> Emergent differences were seen between artists and non-artists for coloring and doodling. All three visual self-expression tasks activated the medial prefrontal cortex, indicating potential clinical applications of reward perception through art making. (Kaimal, Ayaz, Herres, Dieterich-Hartwell, Makwana, Kaiser, & Nasser, 2017, p. 85)

Human physiology is wired to respond to hues for a color experience as the neuronal level. One study describes the finding that "the posterior inferior temporal cortex" of the brain is where "the tuning of chromatic sensitivities of neurons cluster around the unique hues" (Stoughton & Conway, 2008, as cited in Neitz & Neitz, 2008, p. R700).

There have been other studies on how the human visual system works. One used ambiguous artworks by Picasso, who combined "multiple viewpoints" in some of his works to better understand how research participants interpreted the drawings. In this study, researchers found a confluence in visual interpretations of the pictorial reliefs (Koenderink, van Doorn, & Wagemans, 2012, p. 394). They found "observers also use the sparse depth cues provided by the artist to evoke volumetric impressions" (Koenderink, van Doorn, & Wagemans, 2012, p. 394).

Education and Learning

Adult coloring books include a variety of topics for learning: microbiology, human vision, ocular anatomy, sexually transmitted diseases, visual illusions, religious studies, veterinary anatomy, and other topics. They are used in medical studies (Pinion, Sept. 30, 2017, p. 1578).

There are titles of adult coloring books around anatomy, physiology, the human brain, math, and other topics.

Political Messaging

One research work described the harnessing of coloring books for promoting radical politics (Marsh, Dec. 28, 2015).

The Coloring Book Market

In terms of the publishing industry, coloring books were considered "the dark horse of the publishing industry, as a surprising surge in sales boosted major players' revenues" in 2015…until 2017 when "the trend is officially dead" (Rowe, May 31, 2018). According to Nielsen Bookscan, some 12 million adult coloring books were sold in 2015 (Rowe, May 31, 2018). Some "60% of crafts/hobbies/games books in 2016 were being sold by non-traditional publishers (indie self-publishers as well as Amazon imprints)" (Rowe, May 31, 2018), so the smaller presses were seen as taking market share away from the mainline large-scale publishers. Adult coloring was helping address "symptoms of depression and anxiety" (Rowe, May 31, 2018).

Coloring books today come in much more than paper formats: downloadables, electronic (e)-books, digital apps, games, augmented reality, virtual reality, and others. Indeed, there are web-facing "coloring book" generators online that use machine-generated line-art for coloring from photos and manual line art, among others.

Technology-Based Coloring Books

With technological advances, books benefit not only with "visually stimulating content but also means for students to interact, create, and express themselves" (Clark & Dünser, 2012, p. 7), such as through mixed-reality (MR) book experiences. Some MR books build on a pop-up book metaphor (Clark & Dünser, 2012, p. 7), such as an educational coloring book with augmented reality. Book technologies have broadened. Digital enables showing 3D data, time-varying changes, animations, and other augmentations to physical books (Craig, 2013). Various magic books can enable digital coloring of books:

> This type of application can encourage kids in their endeavor to read and also in content creation. The fact that the child actually colored the picture provides a personal tie to the AR content. As the application developers point out, usually when a child finishes coloring a coloring book page the activity is over, but with the ColAR application the fun has just begun. (Craig, 2013, p. 250)

Children create the augmented reality (AR) content. Still, "AR is only really important when it is applied to some problem or goal" (Craig, 2013, p. 253).

Research Methods

Above is a brief review of the academic literature around coloring books for both children and adults. As noted earlier, this research involves a scrape of social media imagery for "adult coloring book" (seeding phrase) on Google Images and resulted in the acquisition of 875 thumbnail images for light bottom-up coding per grounded theory. The idea was to see what is being shared and what themes may emerge about how adults are using coloring books today. Interestingly, the images mostly showed print coloring books and not digital applications or augmented reality/virtual reality/mixed reality (AR/VR/MR) versions.

In general, whether the initial inspiration is the real or the fully imaginary, the drawings are works of the imagination. There are simple animal forms and maybe some eyes and the rest are curlicues, spirals, swirls, circles, and other elements to create a cohesive scene. Virtually everything in it except the lines are colorable. Some have implied color-by-numbers directions, and others are wholly freeform. Some are hand-drawn, and others are computationally created. While various disparate topics of interest are shown, a through-line goes through the works...which is the coloring book structure. The respective topics do inform the aesthetics. Some celebrate adulthood, in all its strangeness... Others celebrate nature and the Earth. Others, still, are apparent "fan works" celebrating cities and culture and cultural practices and mass media film. The coding occurred once-through but was revalidated in a few cases where notes were insufficiently detailed.

Results

The manual coding of the social imageset resulted in the extraction of some themes from the adult coloring books. This section includes the most common to the least common clusters.

Managing Stress

A large number of the social images dealt with issues of stress relief, with terms like "anti-stress coloring," "an anti-stress coloring book," "mindfulness," "calm your t*ts and color," "for relaxation," "color me happy" (mood control), "adult coloring books stress relieving patterns," "creative therapy," "color to relax and create," a coloring book "for anxious people," "creative therapy," "color me stress free," "anti-stress," "color me calm," various self-care books, "the calm coloring book," "beautiful relaxation," "just breathe," "doodles inspired by Zen," and others. Perhaps a subtext is relaxation in other coloring books that do not mention these specifically. Some provide advice such as to "only dwell on the positive." Another professes love to the colorist: "I love you." Another approach to stress relief involves the use of humor through irreverence. Quite a set deal with inner frustrations and even hostilities. Cursing can be a relief, a catharsis (vs reinforcement): "swear word coloring book," "maybe swearing will help?" "f*k yeah!," "F*k F*ckity F*k F*k," "sassy and snarky and saucy swears," "sweary (sic) coloring books," "how teachers swear coloring book for adults" ("oh shish kabob" and other inert forms); "calm the f*ck down," "F*ck that shit," and other variations. This language is not directly at people in the near-space but more to the general universe. Another approach in using language to cope is to go #snarky, and there were several coloring book visuals about going snarky about #marriedlife and being a #housewife, and other topics. Another exclamatory work suggests that "Work sucks!" One is focused on "censored" speech. [Perhaps some of the adult coloring books are for those who experience high reactance when they feel they are being told to do something that they do not want to. And coloring books help them express some of their frustrations, albeit indirectly.]

For all the colorful language above, those approaches are supposed to trigger surprise and laughter. Humor comes to the fore in various social images about adult coloring books. One image reads: "I'm the first person you see after you say 'hold my beer and watch this shit.'" The quote evokes a relationship and some foolishness. Another is a suggestive cartoon that shows two women talking to each other about a lifeguard spanking an adult female swimmer (apparently enjoyably for both): "He's great! The girls hardly ever misbehave at this pool!" Another visual shows something about "dog shaming" with jokes to follow. Mood shifting is about changing up the emotions.

Lauding Nature

Another group involves a celebration of nature, in multiple ways. Nature scenes include mountain scenes (including one highly stylized one), secret gardens, enchanted forests, magic jungles, beach scenes, seascapes, underwater scenes, and other combinations of land-sea-air. Some seasons are celebrated, particularly summer and winter. For summer, there are ice cream cones, sandals, flowers, and sunshine. Another uses sunglasses, watermelon, beach balls, sandals, and pineapples to evoke summer. For the winter, there is a snowman and cozy cottage scenes.

Flora and Fauna

Then, there is various flora and fauna. The flora includes giant flowers, a "world of flowers," and various plants. Some are growing in the wild, and others are potted or vase-d. The fauna or animals include wild animals from particular regions and ranges; insects (like butterflies, dragonflies); sloths and mother-and-baby sloths; a fox made of plants; owls, squirrels, sea horses, lions, hummingbirds, whales, dolphins, octopus, puppy, cat, horses, foxes, pandas, rooster, frogs, toads, birds, crabs, fish, turtles (on land and sea), koala bear, capybara, piglet, goldfish, lizards, iguanas, owls, peacocks, leopard, bear, moose, panther, sword fish, snake, deer, squirrel, chipmunk, giraffes, rabbits, rams, chimpanzees, bats, mountain goats, and a piglet, a whale, sheep, and various birds. One shows predators, like lions and panthers. Fungi include plenty of mushrooms.

Celebrating Human Civilization

Another cluster shows a celebration of human civilization. There are coloring books featuring locales around the world, various global cities, colorful celebrations, world "wonders," and even a drawing of Earth from outer space. Another shows the planets and the stars.

Closer to people's lived levels, there are depictions of various architectural wonders: castles, Russian onion-dome (*lúkovichnaya glavá*) buildings, and other sites. There are featured locations: towns, neighborhoods, walking paths between houses, a city block of buildings, building facades, neighborhoods, storefronts, and other buildings. There are various farmhouses and light houses. There are modern cottages and houses. There are various cars on roads, some with scenic mountains in the background.

Various national cultures are celebrated: Indian, Japanese, Native Americans, contemporary Americans, Celts, and others. Various known holidays are featured: Easter, Christmas, Dia de los Muertos, cherry blossom festival, and others. Another form of human civilization involves various aspects of culture and cultural practice. There are various kinds of religious foci: Christianity, Hinduism, and Zen Buddhism (with related artifacts of crosses and scripture, religious figures like Ganesha, and references to Buddhist beliefs).

Some of the coloring books focus on published books. One includes Grimm's fairytales, with various scenes and moments and characters. Aesop's fables is another. The works of Beatrix Potter, creator of Peter Rabbit, is also appealing. There are inspirations from the "small screen": Dr. Who, Breaking Bald (after *Breaking Bad*), and Game of Thrones. Several focus on music: one shows a guitar with music notes floating around it; another illustrated message reads: "nothing is real strawberry fields forever." Another focuses on video games, in this case, the Super Mario Brothers.

Some of the coloring books laud horror, both in the pure form, and in various combinations: "beauty horror," "Disney horror" (Mickey and Minnie Mouse and horror), and "horror and abnormality." There are fantasy worlds: imaginary creatures, mermaids, monsters, vampires, giants, cartoon characters, unicorns, dragons, elves, garden fairies, and others. Some adult coloring books have references to various Disney artifacts: movies (*Frozen, Moana*, etc.); villains; animals; characters (Mickey Mouse); princesses, and others. Another work shows Marvel superheroes. There is an adult coloring book about graffiti. There is another about manga. Some are built around bird feathers. One work focuses on tropical birds: parrots, toucans, and other tropical birds. Several focus on tattoos. Another one focuses on Steampunk. Several show decorative skulls.

For the technologically minded, there are coloring pages about robots and machines (mechanical objects). There is one about nanotechnology.

Comfort Foods and Drinks

Food is another topical category for adult coloring books. One drawing showed pizza slices, cake slices, cupcakes, candies, and ice cream. Another showed a fruit medley. One coloring book contains drawings for various tater tot casseroles, which may be a comfort good for some. Several coloring books include sweets: "delightful desserts sweet treats," a small piglet in front of various desserts and cookies like macarons, and others. One sub-category here involves alcoholic beverages ["when life gets complicated, I wine" (and coloring around wine and other alcoholic beverages)] and coffee (with steam coming out of decorative cups of java).

Light Erotica

More than human food appetites are described. A number of the adult coloring books involve various scenarios (several gentleman's clubs, a "dirty" housewife (with depictions of handcuffs, a heart-shaped pillow, a face mask, a suggestive duster, and other fetish-type objects), references to body parts (a book of c*cks, one of "big c*cks," "cock and balls," "b*obs," and so on. One focuses on various fetishes. Other adult coloring books focus on "curse words and naughty sayings." Some are both "naughty and nice." Indeed, these works do show an appeal of the "inappropriate," and there is a high emphasis on the "adult" in adult coloring books, in some cases.

Idealized People

Another cluster involves idealized depictions of people. There are young women with flowing hair and thick braids, "beautiful women," "goddesses," and people depicted in a pristine state. Several of the social images refer to female innocence: pin-up girls in "vintage & retro styles," "girls and flowers," and so on.

Another form of idealized persons involves public personalities: political leaders, scientists, entertainers, and other recognized people. Portraits of common people—male and female models—is also popular. Then, too, there are particular focal parts: hair styles (chignons and up-do's) and closeups of eyes (perhaps for makeup).

Artmaking

Some of the visuals in the adult coloring books show tools for artmaking, like cameras ("smile") and paintbrushes.

Alphanumeric Features

There are designs with letters or numbers or both. There are focuses on various font types.

Politics, Social Commentary, and Advocacy

Several of the visuals show coloring books used for advocacy. One related to trans pride. Another was an Audubon bird coloring book for fund-raising. Some works are about endangered species of animals. There are certainly political leaders, who stand in for particular policy stances and who stand in for segments of the voting public. The "people of Walmart" coloring book messages on multiple dimensions. One work focuses on feminism.

Escapism and Composites

If stress relief involves some level of escapism, there are drawings of hot air balloons filling the sky. Several of the social images show hearts, love, intertwined swans, "love quotes," and other contents. There are fanciful composites: pens and pencils, candies, and forks, in a bouquet; a wagon wheel with birds and flowers; overlapping circles with various designs; a young child with butterfly wings; two snails sitting on a mushroom; a "lion city"; animals with human characteristics holding various alcoholic drinks, and others. One is a cornucopia of objects, perhaps suggesting plenty. There are other common objects to structure the coloring: twisting vines, umbrellas, wreaths, stuffed animals, pumpkins and gourds, and others. Patterns are also popular: paisley, mandalas, general abstractions, "glorious shapes," "intricate" patterns, various in-world scenes in a "bottle," and other basic premises.

Light Inspirations

Some of the coloring books show inspiring sayings: "small acts change the world"; "live, laugh, love"; Biblical verses (Psalms, Colossians); "Love is like a pineapple sweet and undefinable," and others. In a sense, these seem designed to be light pick-me-ups.

About the Pandemic

If there is an elephant in the room, it is the pandemic, which has wrought destruction and upended lives. One social image about "adult coloring book" shows "quarantine chill." That said, perhaps a subtext of many of the coloring books involves the pandemic…but does not directly address that.

Others

Some of the visuals show "inexpensive" as a selling point of the particular works. Several are "calendared," with "30 days of free coloring pages" and "beginner watercolor painting with painterly days." These provide entertainment and comfort for months at a time. One shows something that looks gamified, with hidden objects in pictures. One work shows a colorable cartoon suggesting bestiality, a farmer with a sheep. One adult coloring book is designed for a "stoner" audience. Another features tree houses, which suggest something playful and fanciful. While some coloring books show an interest in cars, others show an interest in trucks. One coloring book referred to "grayscale coloring," which refers to the uses of the shades of gray in the image to know where to place various colors. Several coloring books refer to coloring outside lines. One was about witch hats. Another showed a range of watches of various kinds. Several show dinosaurs. Others focus on couture, such as ball gowns and dresses. One coloring book is for executives. One is based on remakes of classic artworks. One focuses on Cowboys of the Old West. Another focuses on ancient Mexico. Another focuses on a medieval castle and village. One is based on ancient Egypt and various engineering marvels of the times. One is focused on democracy and has images of the Statue of Liberty and Ellis Island, among others.

These themes show some of what people are willing to mull when they purchase adult coloring books. Many of the works directly addressed various types of "art therapy" and "cheer the f*ck up" approaches to mood regulation; others were less direct about this approach. Here, colorists are asked to get a grip and handle their own business. The natural world is the object of celebration and fascination: natural settings, animals, plants, and other wonders. Some coloring books are focused on aesthetic pleasure from shapes and patterns, whether figurative or abstract. Some suggest the allure of transgression, going against social norms, exercising one's own agency, and engaging in "inappropriate" things (albeit in a way that seems harmless, in the spirit of cheap thrills). Some feature fan art from other movies, television shows, video games, and so on. Only one of the social images focused on the pandemic: "quarantine chill."

One photo showed social coloring, with four young women sitting around a table and each coloring a section of a coloring book. Another showed a cardboard display of coloring books common in some grocery stores. These works, no matter the message, still convey something of calm, of a patterned world, as a predictable place. Most are fully empty; some are partially colored in. Some of the works have clear authorship of the named artist or illustrator. In other cases, there are no named illustrators on the cover; that, combined with the regularity of the visuals suggest that some come from computational creations.

Adult Coloring Books Listed from a Major Bookseller

Finally, to offer a comparative baseline to the social imagery, there was a light review of available "adult coloring books" on a popular online sales site. Indeed, many were about stress relief: positive vibes, "relaxing flowers," psychedelic "stoner" coloring books, and the like. There were messages of encouragement: "you f*cking got this" and "fearless in the pursuit of what sets your soul on fire" and "badass." Another book cover had the exhortation: "never give up." One humorous work focused on "boredom busters" and a humorously sarcastic tone. One "mature" coloring book was advertised as a gag gift, to embarrass the receiver. One showed "island life," and another focused on "camping," both potential escapist fare. Several drew inspiration from the Bible.

Several offered stained glass patterning. There were books of botanicals. There were coloring books of baby animals. Another book covered bragged on visuals that were "f*cking adorable." There was a meld of "country" (landscape) and "summer." Several books featured cute dogs.

Another mixed approach involved "pastel goth." Another advocated environmental awareness given a "fragile" world. Several books featured drag queens. One book featured magic, as embodied in witches and wizards. One focused on bird houses. Another focused on pixel art (art comprised of large "picture elements" as boxes).

One coloring book was built off the works of Renoir, another of Norman Rockwell. One book featured the famous television painter, Bob Ross. There was one book about spring scenes. Floral cows figured in another work. One coloring book was about classic pickup trucks. Another was about "slowrider" cars. Another showed Japanese gardens, in their glory. Another showed "autumn scenes." Some blooms were shown at midnight (against a dark background). One mixed set showed "cat mandalas. Another was focused around Valentine's Day. Others showcased geometric patterns.

Adult Coloring Online

On social video sharing sites, colorists share their coloring in various ways. Some narrate their color decisions and rationales for different approaches. Some take ASMR (autonomous sensory meridian response) approaches and whisper to their audiences, with the assumption that the whispering is less potentially rough to the ears (and maybe even more relaxing and pleasurable) for those who are sensitive.

Discussion

As a form of "common art," adult coloring books have a built-in interactive component that draws out some aesthetics and creativity for colorists. Given the relatively small size of this genre, it was beneficial to analyze the various topics and themes that may be seen in the respective social imagery related to "adult coloring book" thumbnails on the Web and Internet.

Future Research

In this work, a sampling of the adult coloring book space was achieved through social imagery scraped at mass scale. These capture many of the commercially available works advertised on book sites as well as lesser-known works. From this scraping, various themes were extracted, from which various uses may be understood. In a sense, this is a fairly remote approach, and closer-in analyses within whole books may provide different insights that would not be obvious otherwise.

A review of the literature did not result in any metric for how coloring books are reviewed although there are likely editing standards by commercial publishers. Some light approaches may include whether the visuals are recognizable and whether there is potential for learning and coloring pleasure. Perhaps the main commercial standard is whether the coloring books sell. Or the works have to be recognizable and visually consistent for the built purpose.

What do these themes suggest about American adulthood? Pressures of modern life and healthy coping? Present-day mainstream culture?

Conclusion

Adult coloring books are valid subjects of studies. They can be revelatory of something of adult thinking and activities and needs.

Acknowledgments

Thanks to the generous social sharers who describe their experiences on pre-recorded videos and livestreams and so share parts of their lives.

References

Cho, K., Kim, H., & Lee, Y. (2016). Augmented reality coloring book with transitional user interface. *Indian Journal of Science and Technology*, *9*(20), 1-5.

Clark, A., & Dünser, A. (2012, March). An interactive augmented reality coloring book. In *2012 IEEE symposium on 3D user interfaces (3DUI)* (pp. 7-10). IEEE.

"Coloring book." (2021, July 21). *Wikipedia*. Retrieved from https://en.wikipedia.org/wiki/ Coloring_book.

Craig, A. B. (2013). Augmented Reality Applications. (Ch. 8). In A. B. Craig's *Understanding Augmented Reality*. 1st Ed. Morgan Kaufmann, Elsevier. 221 – 254.

Fitzpatrick, M. J., & McPherson, B. J. (2010). Coloring within the lines: Gender stereotypes in contemporary coloring books. *Sex roles*, *62*(1-2), 127-137.

Goodman-Strauss, C., & Sloane, N. J. A. (2019). A coloring-book approach to finding coordination sequences. *Acta Crystallographica Section A: Foundations and Advances*, *75*(1), 121-134.

Jones, B. (2020). Fifteen minutes may decrease nursing burnout: A discussion paper. *International journal of nursing sciences*, *7*(1), 121-123.

Kaimal, G., Ayaz, H., Herres, J., Dieterich-Hartwell, R., Makwana, B., Kaiser, D. H., & Nasser, J. A. (2017). Functional near-infrared spectroscopy assessment of reward perception based on visual self-expression: Coloring, doodling, and free drawing. *The Arts in Psychotherapy*, *55*, 85-92.

Karniol, R. (2011). The color of children's gender stereotypes. *Sex roles*, *65*(1), 119-132.

King, I. L. (1991). In search of Lowenfeld's proof that coloring books are harmful to children. *Studies in Art Education*, *33*(1), 36-42.

Koenderink, J., van Doorn, A., & Wagemans, J. (2012). Picasso in the mind's eye of the beholder: Three-dimensional filling-in of ambiguous line drawings. *Cognition*, *125*(3), 394-412.

Kopper, Á. (2012). The imaginary of borders: From a coloring book to Cezanne's Paintings. *International Political Sociology*, *6*(3), 277-293.

Lanna, L. C., & Oro, M. G. (2019). Touch gesture performed by children under 3 years old when drawing and coloring on a tablet. *International Journal of Human-Computer Studies*, *124*, 1-12.

Lee, I. J. (2019). Augmented reality coloring book: An interactive strategy for teaching children with autism to focus on specific nonverbal social cues to promote their social skills. *Interaction Studies*, *20*(2), 256-274.

Lee, J. H., & Jung, H. W. (2019). A Study on The Improvement of Mobile Coloring Book Game Interface. *Journal of Korea Game Society*, *19*(4), 109-118.

Lieberman, H. (1978, August). How to color in a coloring book. In *Proceedings of the 5th annual conference on Computer graphics and interactive techniques* (pp. 111-116).

Marcotte, A. (2015). Coloring book clubs cross the line into libraries. *American Libraries*, *46*(11/12), 18-19.

Marsh, L. (2015, Dec. 28). The radical history of 1960s adult coloring books. *The New Republic*.

Naumann, P. L., Huss, K., Calabrese, B., & Smith, T. (2004). A+ Asthma rural partnership coloring for health: An innovative rural asthma teaching strategy. *Pediatric nursing*, *30*(6), 490 - 494.

Neitz, J., & Neitz, M. (2008). Colour vision: the wonder of hue. *Current Biology*, *18*(16), R700-R702.

Pinion, S. (2017). Design for life. *The Lancet*, *390*(10102), 1578.

Pinto, M., & Zuckerman, S. (2019). Coloring Book: A new method for testing language comprehension. *Behavior research methods*, *51*(6), 2609-2628.

Raphel, A. (2015, July 12). Why adults are buying coloring books (for themselves). *The New Yorker*.

Rowe, A. (2018, May 31). If the adult coloring book craze is dead, it needs a postmortem. *Forbes Magazine*.

Schwarz, T., & Luckenbill, J. (2012). Let's get messy! Exploring sensory and art activities with infants and toddlers. *YC Young Children*, *67*(4), 26-30.

Severin, P. N., & Jacobson, P. A. (2020). Types of Disasters. *Nursing Management of Pediatric Disaster*, 85.

Skinner, A. D., & Trachtman, L. H. (1985). Use of a computer program (PC Coloring Book) in cognitive rehabilitation. *American Journal of Occupational Therapy*, *39*(7), 470-472.

Thomas, J. B. (2000). Ride 'em, Barbie girl: Commodifying folklore, place, and the exotic. *Worldviews and the American West: The life of the place itself*, 65-86.

Chapter 10

"Visual Journaling" Shares and Overshares on the Social Web

Shalin Hai-Jew*

Kansas State University, Manhattan, KS, USA

Abstract

Visual journaling has applied uses in higher education, therapy and counseling, professional development, and innovation. In many cases, the visual journaling works are privately held or used in narrow applications. On the other hand, in an age of blogging and social image sharing, many visual journals are publicly consumed on the Social Web. These works include everyday topics for visual study and quick sketches. There are daily urban sketching blogs, plein air works, fast sketches of people on subways, and other topics. There are rich insights about the work of artmaking and the various art supplies used. This work involves an analysis of visual journaling practices on the Social Web, on social image-sharing sites, on social video-sharing sites, on blogging sites, and other locales, with shares and overshares (such as "too much information" or "TMI").

Keywords: visual journaling, common art, urban sketching, plein air sketching, too much information (TMI)

Introduction

Visual journaling (and visual diary-ing) involves using self-created visuals of everyday life to maintain a record for learning, therapeutic purposes, professional development, creativity, and various forms of personal growth, among others. Many such journals are multi-modal, inclusive of text, visuals, audio, and video. Some of these are made for personal consumption and usage only, while others are shared broadly on the Social Web on various platforms: social image-sharing sites, social video-sharing sites, web logging or blogging sites, and others. Visual journaling is so present online that there are podcasts and other social media creations that refer to such works.

This chapter explores the phenomenon of "visual journaling" as a form of "common art," as publicly present on the Social Web. This work will involve mixed methods research, with both manual coding and computational coding to understand this practice of curating

* Corresponding Author's Emails: haijes@gmail.com

In: Common Visual Art in a Social Digital Age
Editor: Shalin Hai-Jew
ISBN: 978-1-68507-664-1

experiences and illustrating lives from various angles. The research focus is on five research questions:

- RQ1: How do visual journals manifest on the Social Web? What are some typical contents—informationally and visually? Technologically?
- RQ2: Who are those who are creating visual journals? How do they self-present?
- RQ3: What are the levels of sophistication of the shared visuals in the visual journals?
- RQ4: What do the visual journaling show about "common art" on the Social Web?
- RQ5: Do visual journals merely "share" publicly valuable information, or do they lapse into "oversharing" and spillage of excessive personal information?

The above questions will enable some top-down coding although bottom-up coding will be included as well.

Review of the Literature

In the academic research literature, there are various applied uses of visual journaling. Various works describe the uses of visual journaling to enable healing from trauma, such as for particular groups like military veterans (Mims, 2015), those dealing with childhood trauma (Warner, 2021), those in the helping professions who experience vicarious traumas (Gibson, Nov. 2016), those who work in Christian care who need to de-stress and care for the self (through "visual prayer journaling" (Woolley, 2017), and others. Art journaling may help people deal with indirect trauma (Roberts, 2017), based on mass media messages. Art interventions for health may align with "a native concept of wellness focusing on the complex interaction between mind, body, spirit, and context" (Warson, 2012, p. S47).

Students can lead stressful lives, and visual journaling may help them deal with such life stresses (Pastore, 2020), such as for medical students (Mercer, Warson, & Zhao, 2010).

Visual journaling has been used as school assignments (Nolan, 2013, p. 237). Students in preservice learning as arts educators also benefit from keeping visual journals (Hofsess, Summer 2015). Visual journals used in education themselves have been the object of sophisticated analyses (Sinner, Spring 2011). For pre-service teachers in an undergraduate program, visual (or art) journaling serves as a "contemplative-pedagogical strategy" (Ankori & Hammer, 2018 – 2019, p. 66). Such work enables learners to achieve a metalevel of considering "the mind while engaging in the creative process" (Ankori & Hammer, 2018 – 2019, p. 69). Such journaling may encourage learners to read the assigned readings more thoroughly and analytically (Ankori & Hammer, 2018 – 2019, p. 76).

Visual journaling may help graduate students develop constructive relationships among their peers and with their faculty, given the importance of relationships for the successful learning and graduation. An arts-informed pedagogy, which includes the use of a "visual/verbal journal," has been found to benefit graduate student self-care and social relationships (Jesup, Lucas, Nelms, Woodruff, & Shields, 2017, p. 1). Visual journals benefit the creation of knowledge "through linking sensing, feeling, thinking and doing, and how, when used purposefully" to enhance the work of researchers during doctoral studies (Messenger, 2016, p. 129). In other research contexts, researchers have used visual journaling as an open-ended elicitation for information (Camfield, Crivello, & Woodhead, 2009, p. 19). Certainly, researchers conducting fieldwork in various locales may maintain work journals—in either or both analog and digital formats—to process and record observations and ideas. While historically visual journals have been analog and created with paper, there is the harnessing of high technology for art therapy and visual journaling (AlSadoun, Alwahaibi, & Altwayan, July 2020).

A sub-category of visual journaling may be bullet journals, analog and digital, through which people organize themselves and their own lives through "crafting" data (Tholander & Normark, Apr. 2020, p. 1), visually and in other ways. A bullet journal has been described as a combination of "calendar, journal and planner" (Tholander & Normark, Apr. 2020, p. 1). Bullet journals are used for self-tracking but also "reflecting on everyday life" (Ayobi, Sonne, Marshall, & Cox, Apr. 2018, p. 1). Based on studies of how people use bullet journals, a team has been working on creating digital versions of bullet journals to enhance the self-tracking (Ayobi, Sonne, Marshall, & Cox, Apr. 2018, p. 1) and the mood recording (p. 5). When people engage their personal information, they engage in "processes of self-creation and reflection on personal life trajectories (Tholander & Normark, Apr. 2020, p. 1), and they may come to terms with an "appreciation of ourselves" and a recognition of "the world around us as imperfect" (Tholander & Normark, Apr. 2020, p. 1) and using various aesthetics to engage personal data (p. 6). The work of maintaining a bullet journal "balances the lines between doodling and decoration, and curation of personal data in the creation of various individually designed information structures" (Tholander & Normark, Apr. 2020, p. 8).

The various research works show that visual journaling has been applied to a range of objectives. They show lessons about art, nature, research, social justice, self-awareness, and personal health, among others. One work described the uses of such a journal for necessary behavior change for healthfulness. Some works describe journalistic or mass media applications. In the present-day form, visual journals are often digital and expressed through mixed and multimodal media.

Research Methods

A search for "visual journaling" on the Google Search engine found 178,000 results. The research contents will be from social image-sharing sites, on social video-sharing sites, on blogging sites, and other locales. The ambition here is not to offer a comprehensive analysis of the phenomenon of "visual journaling" on the Social Web but to capture a limited time slice of this creative production as a "social practice."

To map the space, the guiding research questions include the following:

- RQ1: How do visual journals manifest on the Social Web? What are some typical contents—informationally and visually? Technologically?
- RQ2: Who are those who are creating visual journals? How do they self-present?
- RQ3: What are the levels of sophistication of the shared visuals in the visual journals?
- RQ4: What do the visual journaling show about "common art" on the Social Web?
- RQ5: Do visual journals merely "share" publicly valuable information, or do they lapse into "oversharing" and spillage of excessive personal information?

Results

Two social image-sharing sites were accessed for this work: Flickr and Google Image Search.

On a Social Image-Sharing Site

Flickr is a still-popular space for many to share social imagery. A "journal" related tags network shows ties between (visual) journaling and crafting, bookbinding, diaries, collage, art, and various mixed media (Group 1, to the left) along with other artful endeavors like painting, drawing, water-coloring, sketching, and illustrating (Group 2) (Figure 1). The grouping was based on the Clauset-Newman-Moore clustering algorithm. The NodeXL tool was used to extract the related tags network at 1.5 degrees.

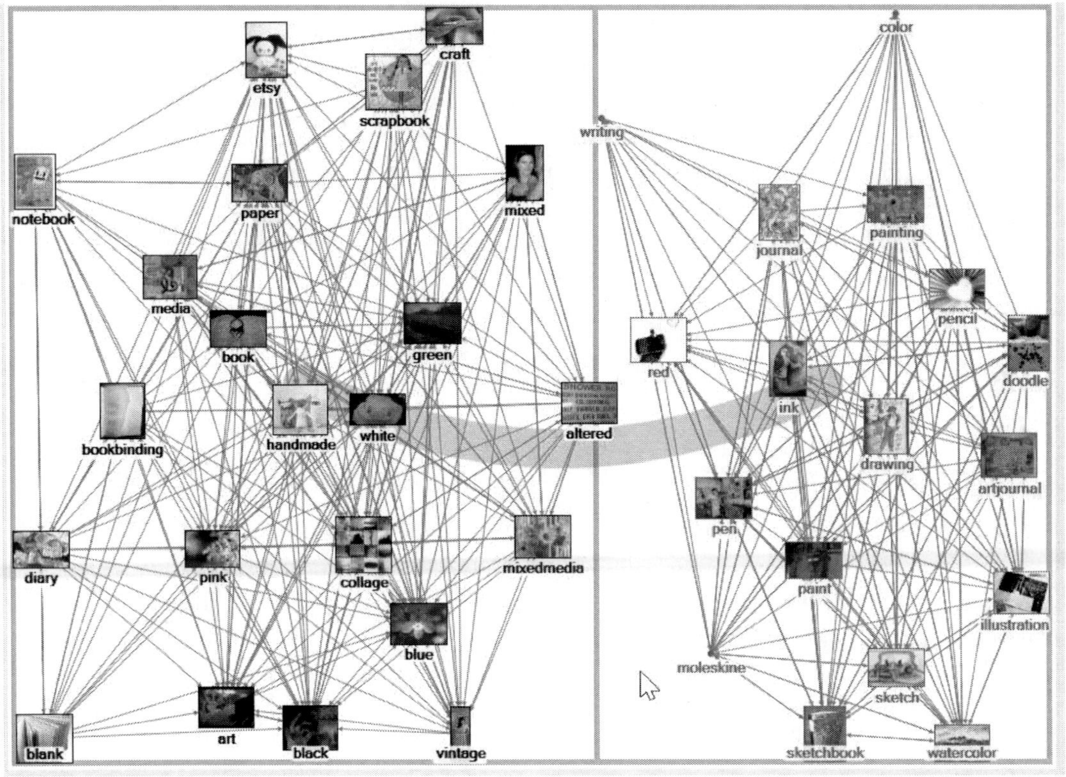

Figure 1. A "Journal" related tags network on Flickr (1.5 deg).

Then, "visual journal" was used to seed a search on Google Images Search, which resulted in 743 visuals. The auto-created tags for this imageset included the following : "art, collage, inspiration, gratitude, middle school, pages, watercolor, sketchbook, doodle, colourful, design, anxiety, depression, book, happy, therapeutic, calligraphy, journals, class, girl, pinterest, music, travel, family, nature, science, easy, yellow, meal, writing." These were written in the lower case as per the convention for tags.

A manual analysis of these visuals showed a predominance of academic uses of visual journaling, apparently from the K12 space. There are photos of groups of children and adults working on visual journals. There are articles about the uses of visual journals for creativity, for stress relief, and for coping. There are affirmations: "You do not need anyone's approval. Believe in you!" Several offered the advice: "Be kind, for everyone you meet is fighting a hard battle."

Several of the visuals have quotes from Michael Bell that describe the learning value of the approach : "Visual journaling allows us to access our inner language of imagery and express it both verbally and visually, while exploring the connection between image and word." Another quote attributed to Bell reads: "Exploring the thought process through visual journaling is essential in a world that is in continuous change." [One journal's cover reads: "A revisionary journal."] An unattributed quote reads: "Art is a constant agent of transformation and is indeed the soul's drive to health."

The adult visual journaling focuses on brainstorms around particular topics, such as a "dream job" and explorations of the self.

One work evoked Leonardo da Vinci's own journals used for engaging ideas and including both notes and image, which each inform the other. This visual read as the act of discovery based on direct observations and theorizing.

In general, though, the visuals are the work of non-professionals as people engage the assignments. One shows a girl who is crying tears from her eyes but also from her heart. There are nature scenes. Several visuals seem to be coloring books, one of mandalas. Quite a few works show collages overlaid with acrylic or watercolor paint. Some works are comprised of both ink and watercolor. One painting shows a man's face lit up with a single light source in ambient light. One work is a brainstorm of reality "because of Covid-19." One work showed some creative digital art effects. One read as retro, with pressed flowers. Some stencils evoke the pressed flowers motif. Some involve scribbles. Some are doodles. Some works are consciously artful. One is a "letter" to Henri Matisse, beginning, "Dear Henri." Some visuals are swatch pages, with the common artist trying out colors. There is a pointillist side view of a mustachioed man. Several photos show the binding of the visual journals. Some word art uses letters cut from magazines. There was one Euler diagram. Some of the visuals show labels, perhaps for websites. One indicated "multi-genre writing."

On a Social Video-Sharing Site

A search for "visual journal" on YouTube (Google) resulted in autocomplete terms such as the following: visual journal, visual journal flip through, visual journal ideas, visual journaling techniques, visual journaling cageless birds, visual journaling drawing your feelings, visual journal tour, visual journal strathmore, visual journal mixed media, visual journal watercolor, visual journals in the classroom, suraj visual journal, visual arts journal, (and) strathmore visual journal bristol smooth." These show some notable personalities and brand names in the space. These also show that there are how-to videos about how to create a visual journal. And there are narrative walk-throughs of various visual journals. To disambiguate further, "visual journal personal" was used to seed the search, and some 34 transcripts from these videos were collected. One had only music. A half-dozen or more of the other videos had no transcripting (the owners of the videos did not enable the closed captioning on the YouTube site). The autocoding of the topics may be seen in Figure 2 and Table 1 (more detailed). As the analysis shows, there are various types of visual journals, with some quite idiosyncratic and subjective. [These analyses were achieved using NVivo.]

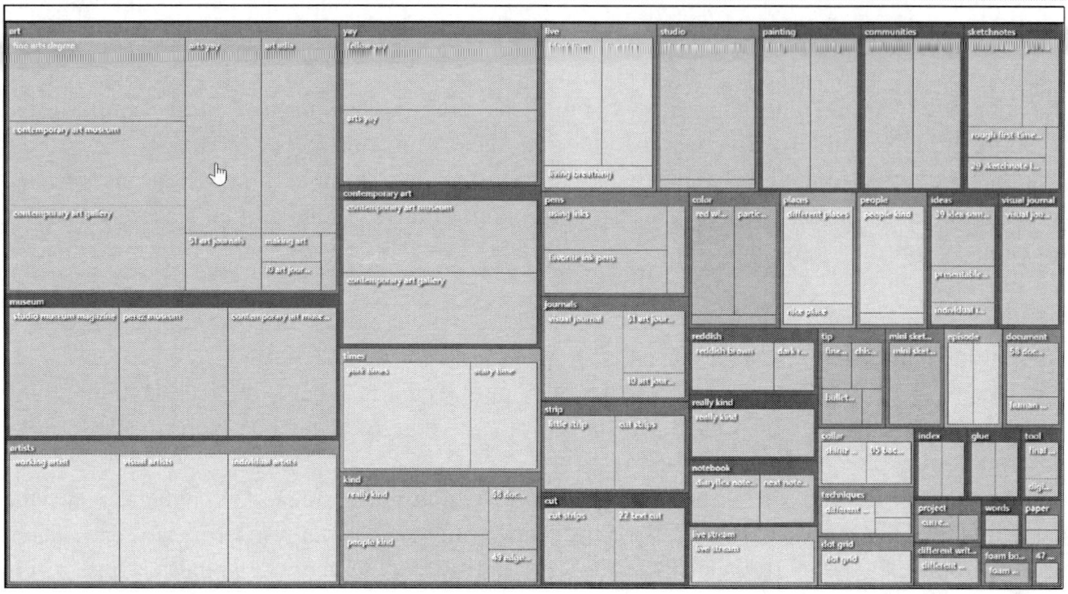

Figure 2. Autocoded theme extraction from "Visual Journaling" transcripts from YouTube videos (treemap diagram).

Table 1. Autocoded theme and subtheme extraction from "Visual Journaling" transcripts from YouTube videos

47 watercolor pencils	
	47 watercolor pencils
art	
	10 art journals
	51 art journals
	art adia
	arts yay
	contemporary art gallery
	contemporary art museum
	creating art
	fine arts degree
	making art
artists	
	individual artists
	visual artists
	working artist
collar	
	05 background collar
	shiraz collar

color	
	different color
	particular color
	red wine color
communities	
	black community
	different communities
contemporary art	
	contemporary art gallery
	contemporary art museum
cut	
	22 text cut
	cut strips
different writing techniques	
	different writing techniques
document	
	58 document kind
	human document
dot grid	
	dot grid
episode	
	episode number
	podcast episode
foam boards	
	foam boards
glue	
	favorite glue
	hate glue stick
ideas	
	39 idea something
	individual ideas
	presentable ideas
index	
	using index cards
	white index
journals	
	10 art journals
	51 art journals
	visual journal
kind	
	49 edges kind
	58 document kind
	people kind
	really kind
live	
	black lives
	live stream
	living breathing
live stream	
	live stream

Table 1. (Continued)

mini sketchnote	
	mini sketchnote
museum	
	contemporary art museum
	perez museum
	studio museum magazine
notebook	
	diaryflex notebook
	next notebook
painting	
	exact painting
	last painting
paper	
	blank copy paper
	glossy paper
pens	
	black pen
	favorite ink pens
	using inks
people	
	people kind
	sometimes people
places	
	different places
	nice place
project	
	big projects
	current project
really kind	
	really kind
reddish	
	dark reddish
	reddish brown
sketchnotes	
	29 sketchnote illustrations
	mini sketchnote
	personal sketchnotes
	public sketchnotes
	rough first-time sketchnotes
strip	
	cut strips
	little strip
studio	
	garage studio
	studio museum magazine
techniques	
	common technique
	different writing techniques
	simple technique

times	
	scary time
	york times
tip	
	13 brush tip
	bullet tip
	chisel tip
	fine tip
tool	
	digital sketching tool
	final tool
	visual journal
	visual journal
words	
	certain words
	finding words
yay	
	arts yay
	fellow yay

There are some references to techniques and materials; there are references to some political expression.

An autocoded sentiment analysis does not show a lot of sentiment in the transcripts though. A majority of the text is neutral in terms of sentiment (Figure 3). Of the language which has sentiment, it tends to run mixed.

Figure 3. Autocoded sentiment breakdown of "Visual Journaling" transcripts from YouTube videos.

To further elaborate, of the subset of sentiment-laden language in the work, most of that runs "moderately positive" (Figure 4).

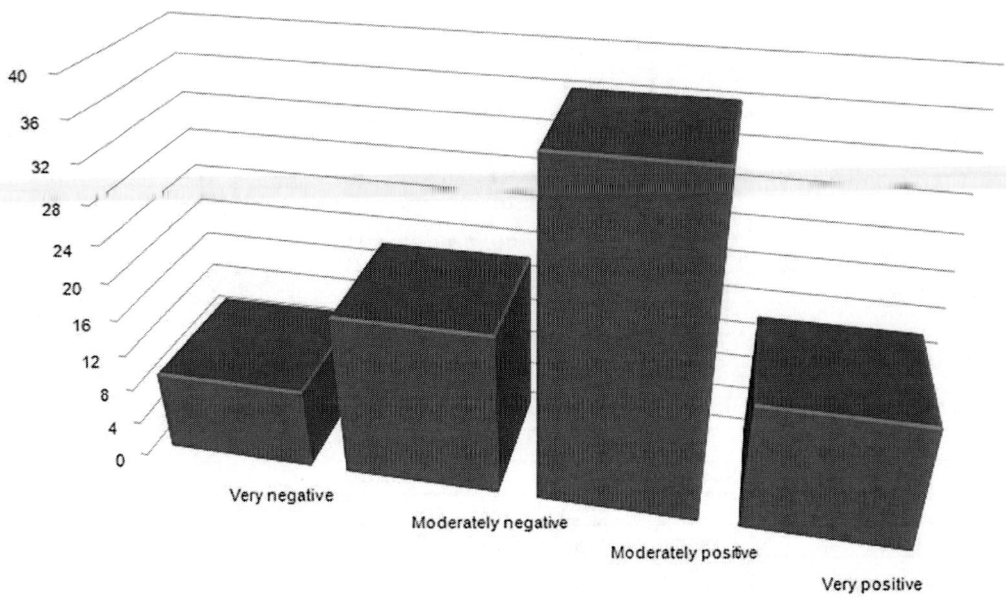

Figure 4. Autocoded sentiment analysis of "Visual Journaling" transcripts from YouTube videos.

Visual journaling includes not only the sharing of completed works but some performative videos, where individuals share processes.

On a Blogging (Web Logging) Site

For this work, the author went to a blog by her first editor who published her first poem. This former editor has a blog with a distinct Pacific Northwest vibe. She said in a recent podcast that she started engaging in urban sketching as a low-pressure way to get into regular drawing, which she had wanted to for decades, but which she'd put off because of her professional work as a writer and perhaps a high-pressure perfectionism. When she discovered visual journaling, she realized that she could engage in daily drawing and painting without undue pressure. When she retired, she invested much more time into this effort. Interspersed among her personal observations are insights about various analog drawing and painting materials, even though her product placement is un-compensated. [She was invited onto the podcast which was about art materials. During the show, she described purchasing an expensive $160 sketchbook as a forcing function to encourage her to draw daily to develop the skill.]

Her drawings and watercolors are narrated with accompanying text. She has quick sketches of people painting, a roller skater taking a break on a bench, a person stretching in various poses, people exercising in a park, a couple sitting together on a pier lakeside, buskers performing streetside, and others. She has drawings of a bird eating. Another shows flocks of foraging birds at a local park. She has sketches of homes, cars parked on streets, earthmovers of various types, a tree cutter in a bucket, an electrical lineman, and others. Several drawings show a fascination with electrical lines; one shows an electrical substation. She has depicted abandoned furniture, especially sofas, left curbside. Her works show local foliage in different seasons. Several show tomatoes, another tomatoes and plums, some of a misshapen peach.

Some drawings show bridges and roads. Several show alleyways. Parks are a favorite—including playgrounds, including stretches of green, including sculptures. In one series, she has drawings of her own hands, in various positions, a drawing challenge for many. During the pandemic of 2020 and 2021, there are various musings about the time and the challenges. One sketch shows a man in loose clothing face masked and pushing a shopping cart, just as the city was starting to reopen. One drawing includes the Space Needle. Several works show a burned-out car, a pile of rubbish by the side of the road. Several drawings show dancers and drummers taking part in a Bon Odori ceremony. Her watercolors are especially powerful, showing street scenes and people. In between the drawings, there are photos of various art supplies, close-ups of color swatches. Her blog includes some selfies with her urban sketching group. In her ten years of drawing and painting, apparently daily, she has a sharp mastery of perspective and scaling and shape. She is working more on motion and color and textures. Her works in plein air show a masterful hand. She does not only have presence on her own blog but also on a social image sharing site, with followers cross-fertilized across these platforms. During a recent podcast interview, she said she kept the urban sketching blog for her own sense of multi-sensory memory based on her time working on various pieces, often in the company of her urban sketching friends.

Her digital work seems to be limited to scanning or photographing various works to share digitally. The works themselves do not seem to have undergone much in the way of digital editing, except perhaps with auto color balancing.

The creative production around visual journaling varies. Each visual journal has its own vibe and unique style depending on the common artist. Others are less textual. Some are just images with light captioning, such as many on other image-based social sharing platforms.

Discussion

So what was found about the five-plus research questions? Again, these include the following:

- RQ1: How do visual journals manifest on the Social Web? What are some typical contents—informationally and visually? Technologically?
- RQ2: Who are those who are creating visual journals? How do they self-present?
- RQ3: What are the levels of sophistication of the shared visuals in the visual journals?
- RQ4: What do the visual journaling show about "common art" on the Social Web?
- RQ5: Do visual journals merely "share" publicly valuable information, or do they lapse into "oversharing" and spillage of excessive personal information?

The insights are described question-by-question below.

- RQ1: How do visual journals manifest on the Social Web? What are some typical contents—informationally and visually? Technologically?

The visual journals are a subset of the common art on the Social Web. The contents include some simplistic works (collages, amateur drawings) related to academic studies, where the focus is more on the thinking content than the artfulness or aesthetics of the respective works. Then, there are those who are more practiced who share memorable drawings with a sense of style and originality.

- RQ2: Who are those who are creating visual journals? How do they self-present?

A majority of the visual journaling individuals are self-identified amateurs and non-pros. Some have found a common schtick and stick with their approaches. Others are retired and are interested in enjoying their post-work lives.

- RQ3: What are the levels of sophistication of the shared visuals in the visual journals?

A majority of the works shared in still images and videos seem fairly basic. A few were by an identified professional artist. In one video, she did a walk-through of her works, which were powerfully rendered oil and acrylic paintings. Another had spent decades as a graphic artist, and her professionalism also showed in the quality of her drawings, prints, photographs, and other works.

- RQ4: What do the visual journaling show about "common art" on the Social Web?

Visual journaling suggests the low cost of entry into regular common art. Here, the regularity of postings by common artists suggests that there are many who can approach this work in a disciplined and even longitudinal way (the artist featured in the blog had been engaging in urban sketching for ten years already).

- RQ5: Do visual journals merely "share" publicly valuable information, or do they lapse into "oversharing" and spillage of excessive personal information?

In terms of visual journals, while these are personal for many, those who shared online had a public-facing focus for the most part. When tips were shared, there was a sense of others perhaps benefitting from the knowledge. When stories were told on the blog, they were told in a public facing sense, to amuse and inform others. When pain was expressed, the details were left unshared. One example is of an artist who created a video of her multimedia paintings (watercolor, colored pencils, and metallic overlays); while she shared about personal heartache, she did not offer details, and she was careful to leave in place bright lines not to cross in terms of a personal life.

In general, then, there were not "overshares" but some disciplined focus on the art-making at hand. Too much information (TMI) seemed to be more of a rarity in this space.

Future Research

To build on this research, there are many ways to broaden the amount of source material, by capturing more visual journaling blogs from various platforms, by scraping more social imagery, and so on. Given the visual aspects of the videos, it would help to engage in more visual descriptions, too.

Within the visual journaling community, there are professional subgroups, and those may be explored in future works. As noted in the review of the literature, there may be professional applications in education, therapy, professional development, innovation, and others.

Also, while there was computational analysis in this work, these were only of textual contents. Computational analysis of the visuals captured as part of "visual journaling" should include machine vision and machine learning in future iterations.

Conclusion

Visual journaling on the Social Web involves both academic and personal ones. On the whole, the practice is depicted in a positive way for people to become more self-aware, to surface creativity, to learn and process ideas, to make visual observations, to express personal and collective emotions, and to heal and remain in mental health. As a form of common art, visual journaling offers benefits for many. There are commercial angles to visual journaling, with a range of supplies from the low-cost to the fairly spendy.

Acknowledgments

Thanks to the many researchers I've worked with and for over the years. I have learned from every project and every interaction.

References

AlSadoun, W., Alwahaibi, N., & Altwayan, L. (2020, July). Towards Intelligent Technology in Art Therapy Contexts. In *International Conference on Human-Computer Interaction* (pp. 397-405). Springer, Cham.

Ankori, G., & Hammer, R. (2018-2019). From Constructivism to Contemplative Art Journaling: A Case Study of a Course Evolution. *Multi Colors: An International Journal of Educational Research and Theory,* 1(1), 66 - 78.

Ayobi, A., Sonne, T., Marshall, P., & Cox, A. L. (2018, April). Flexible and mindful self-tracking: Design implications from paper bullet journals. In *Proceedings of the 2018 CHI conference on human factors in computing systems* (pp. 1-14).

Camfield, L., Crivello, G., & Woodhead, M. (2009). Wellbeing research in developing countries: Reviewing the role of qualitative methods. *Social Indicators Research*, *90*(1), 5-31.

Gibson, D. (2018). A visual conversation with trauma: Visual journaling in art therapy to combat vicarious trauma. *Art Therapy*, *35*(2), 99-103.

Hofsess, B. A. (2015). The map of true places: Moving onward in artist-teacher preparation. *Visual Arts Research*, *41*(1), 1-15.

Jesup, C., Lucas, I., Nelms, R., Woodruff, A., & Shields, S. S. (2017). 'We've shared a lifetime with one another': using reflective visual/verbal journals to develop graduate student relationships. *Reflective Practice*, *18*(2), 161-182.

Mercer, A., Warson, E., & Zhao, J. (2010). Visual journaling: An intervention to influence stress, anxiety and affect levels in medical students. *The Arts in Psychotherapy*, *37*(2), 143-148.

Messenger, H. (2016). Drawing out ideas: Visual journaling as a knowledge creating medium during doctoral research. *Creative Approaches to Research*, *9*(1), 129.

Mims, R. (2015). Military veteran use of visual journaling during recovery. *Journal of Poetry Therapy*, *28*(2), 99-111.

Nolan, D. (2013). Visual Communication. *Counterpoints*, *391*, 233-242.

Pastore, C. (2020). Stress management in college students: why journaling is the most effective technique for this demographic.

Roberts, D. (2017). *Processing indirect trauma associated with the 9/11 terrorist attacks using visual journaling* (Doctoral dissertation).

Sinner, A. (2011). The visual journal as an image sphere: Interpreting artworks with an anamorphic perspective. *Studies in Art Education*, *52*(3), 183-195.

Tholander, J., & Normark, M. (2020, April). Crafting Personal Information-Resistance, Imperfection, and Self-Creation in Bullet Journaling. In *Proceedings of the 2020 CHI Conference on Human Factors in Computing Systems* (pp. 1-13).

Warner, M. (2021). *Visual journaling in treating childhood trauma* (Doctoral dissertation).

Warson, E. (2012). Healing pathways: art therapy for American Indian cancer survivors. *Journal of cancer education*, *27*(1), 47-56.

Woolley, S. (2017). *Visual Prayer Journaling for Christian Care Professionals: A New Self-Care Intervention Model* (Doctoral dissertation).

Part 4: Commercializing Common Visual Art

Chapter 11

Monetizing Common Art: General Practices for Going Commercial Online

Shalin Hai-Jew*

Kansas State University, Manhattan, Kansas, USA

Abstract

Amateur artists may engage the work of art production for any number of reasons. For many, the work itself offers personal learning and pleasure. Some, however, create "common art" to make a living (very few), and others to augment their incomes. If the art market exists as a power law, amateur artists are usually practitioners in the "long tail," with very few who can make it into the elite group that can command high fees for their works. This work is about how amateur artists trade their work and artworks for moneys in various ways at this current time, often through online representation and public personalities honed on the Social Web and e-commerce.

Keywords: common art, marketplace, monetizing, commercial, online art markets

Introduction

A person or group creating common art may do so in private their entire lives and never go public with any of their work, if they so choose. Some may choose to go public with some limited work and share broadly in public space, in a narrowcast way or to wider audiences in a broadcast way. Some may share their works in unlimited ways online and not strive for direct compensation; rather, open source meets their needs. And still others may choose to go public and to sell their artworks and related talents (teaching, demonstrations, and so on) to a private audience and/or a public audience. The risk of sharing broadly online is that unique visions, their core inspirations or styles, may be usurped for commercial purposes without compensation (Sung, Jan. 4, 2022). For many creatives, it is incumbent on them to pursue both credit and compensation. The channels to sell common art may be formal ones and informal ones. There are primary markets (where the artworks are sold for the first time) and secondary ones (where the common artworks are sold after the first sale). Some common art artists may be financed even prior to the creation of a work through a patron. Some are supported by the attentional

* Corresponding Author's Email: haijes@gmail.com

In: Common Visual Art in a Social Digital Age
Editor: Shalin Hai-Jew
ISBN: 978-1-68507-664-1

views of followers on social video sharing platforms (from which the social influencers may acquire funds for their ability to drive traffic). This work explores how common art and artistic talent are monetized in a time of e-commerce and the Social Web.

The basic research question is the following:

RQ1: What are general practices for contemporary "common artists" to sell their artworks online?

Review of the Literature

Those who create collectible and venerated fine art, by historical accounts and narrations, are rare individuals. Their lives inform unique personalities and result in original ways of engaging the larger world and fellow citizens. Said another way: "The artist's unique style, concepts, technique, point of view, and emotional attitude are an integral part of the experience of the work, *built into* the piece, and not just background information" (Lind, 1992, p. 127). Art buyers "intuitively evaluate artwork as a physical extension of its creator—the extended-self hypothesis" where the "artist's mental state and the degree of physical connection to the work" are relevant (Newman & Smith, 2018, p. 103). Studies of the amounts that practicing artists can command show a high Gini coefficient, with a few artists capturing the concentrated wealth and a vast majority earning very little. There are high disparities in terms of funding for respective artists. There is evidence of "a cubic law of art prices that hints to a general pattern for the distribution of artistic talent" that maps to the power law, and such a pattern has persisted historically over centuries and across "heterogeneous markets" (Etro & Stepanova, 2018, p. 217). The pattern has persisted so much that some have wondered at the natural limits of artistic talent distribution and mused if humanity is seeing a universal law. A few artists achieve high recognition and rewards, and the vast majority achieve little renown (if any) and little recompense (if any). (Figure 1) Many with formal trainings in creating art do not spend their lives as full-time artists. The career opportunities are few, and the skillsets are difficult. There are opportunity costs to maintaining that life. Actual talent may be rare. To succeed, artists often need high concepts, a surrounding social narrative about them and their work; they require named shows, installations, catalogs, books, and media attention and social fanfare; they require various accoutrement to bolster the sense of talent. The standards are elusive. It would seem that artist have to develop themselves and their sensibilities to a new vision that captures the imagination of others and brings them along to a larger narrative of their relevance and talent. The sense of artful standards is elusive and perhaps non-formulaic and non-predictable. The elite performance of such artists is not guaranteed for a lifetime even if they have had moments of high production. Others are only discovered posthumously.

If this power law applies to fine art artists, it could also apply to "common art" artists, with such "outsiders" only occasionally achieving success, with only some named artists and the others unknown. In each space, perhaps, particular works are lauded, and others retreat into the woodwork.

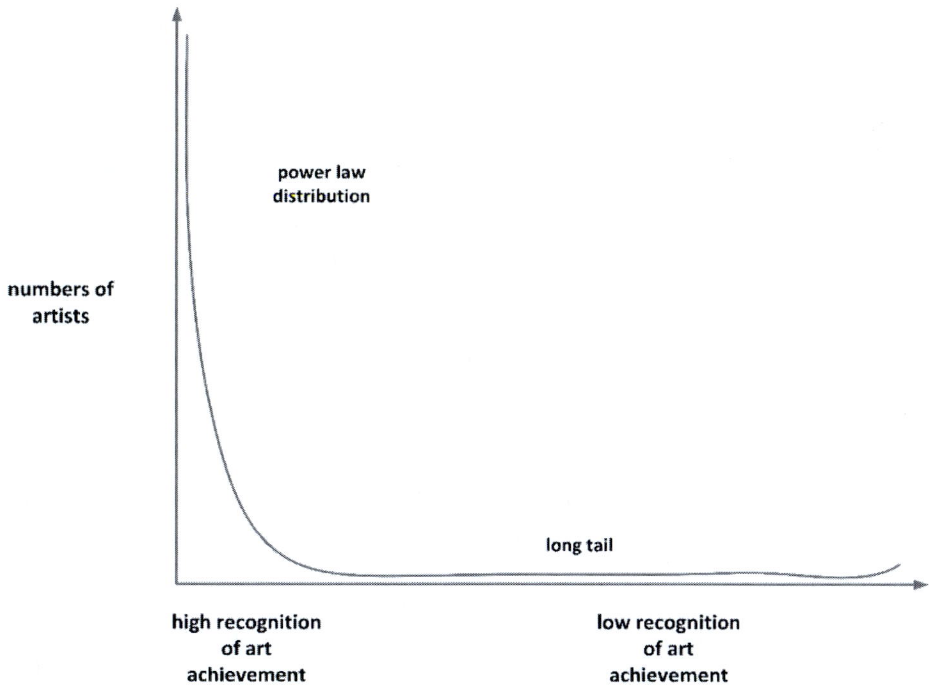

Figure 1. Frequency distribution of artist population (by achievement).

Arts labor may be viewed in other ways, too. One writes:

> Style is labor and the trace of labor (what labor leaves behind), an imposition of the will on the world, and in a manner that has not been prescribed. It is thus unlike other forms of labor in which the outcome is predicted and predictable. (Rhodes, Spring 2012, p. 59)

Novelty is part and parcel of this type of work. One older study analyzed arts labor from three perspectives: the human capital, the household production, and the evolutionary approaches. "When the first two approaches are followed, the supply of labour results from the maximization of utility over the entire life span of the individual. Within an evolutionary approach, individuals are supposed to search for local maxima" (Caserta & Cuccia, 2001, p. 185) given their particular "capabilities and decision rules that are used to maximise the objective function" so working more towards pursuing objectives and maximizing these objectives (Caserta & Cuccia, 2001, p. 194).

Artists with higher human capital can command higher wages. Art has a skill can be difficult to transmit: "Once the art skill is acquired, the problem is how to transmit it and make it survive. Skills in the arts have a(n) important tacit component. This means that the skill cannot be transmitted independently of the individual who possesses it" (Caserta & Cuccia, 2001, p. 196). The artists who have high fit for survival depends on how tuned they are with the institutional system of which they are a part. The institution is comprised of "the complex of socially learned and shared values, norms, beliefs, meanings, symbols, customs, and standards that delineate the range of expected and accepted behaviour in a particular context" (Nelson, 1995, p. 80, as cited in Caserta & Cuccia, 2001, p. 197). This attunement to the institution is also seen in another work:

> One of the sectors in which creative competition is fiercest is the contemporary visual arts. It is a sector that by definition produces culture. In an international market that is substantially private, with a significant volume of sales off the books, there are thousands of painters and sculptors seeking success. The prime condition for producing culture is obtaining market share, which means excelling in quality and the ability to sell symbolic and aesthetic values. (Santagata, 2010, p. 85)

Artworks are often "valued for their communication potential" (Hutter, Knebel, Pietzner, & Schäfer, 2007, p. 248) and their ability to reach a wider audience. Perhaps there is an alluring narrative related to the artwork, and it evokes social excitement. Further, it may spark positive market sentiment, maybe an irrational exuberance about the investment, the sparking of animal spirits. What artworks speak to their societies matters and so can have powerful value beyond the cost of the artwork. For example, an artwork may encourage social comity. It may encourage or inspire learning in the sciences or humanities. There are different ways in which artists "come up" in the world, based on both their efforts and those of others. The conventions of so-called "contemporary art" are informal and "not written down or promulgated by a legal authority" (Santagata, 2010, p. 88).

More recent researchers suggest that art emerges from an endosystem and society (Tschacher & Tröndle, 2017, p. 72). Humanity has had different epochs of art: antiquity, early middle ages, middle ages, Romanesque, Gothic, Renaissance, Baroque, Classic, Romantic, Modernity, to Postmodernity (Tschacher & Tröndle, 2017, p. 73). Art emerges when particular social conditions enable the art:

> As said before, unless an endosystem has arrived at a stage of self-referential overheating, it will produce complexity reduction as well as diversification, both at the same time. There are indications of both dynamics in our system of interest, art. Moreover, both dynamics attach to art its two prominent features, pattern formation together with continuing diversification, i.e., from the point of view of recipients, familiarity together with novelty. (Tschacher & Tröndle, 2017, p. 74)

An even more recent work suggests that creative production is forged and honed by intense competition. These coauthors write of social motivations for artists: "Incentive structures and the intensity of competition play a key role in shaping the quality and direction of creative work" (Balietti & Riedl, 2021, p. 1). High level art is created by involving various stakeholders: "The top tier maintains high quality standards by attracting many submissions and then filtering its output, operating as an effective sorting device for budget-constrained consumers. However, reward stratification leads to higher levels of inequality and market exit among producers who fall behind in earnings, despite producing high-quality work" (Balietti & Riedl, 2021, p. 1). This suggests the importance of monetizing their fine art creations to survive. While people survive by creating art on the one hand and crafts on the other, it helps to understand that "painting, sculpture, and printmaking" evoke art, and "ceramics, weaving, and wood- and metalwork" evoke craft (Markowitz, 1994, p. 55), so there is a materiality aspect to the type of aesthetic creation made and its value in the marketplace.

Trading Art for Money

Art objects have apparently been sold and traded since the time of the Roman empire (27 BC onwards). The sale of art has been part of ancient practice and into the present. Art markets have manifested in various forms over the centuries. In the history of art markets, there is "payment for invention" (De Marchi & Van Miegroet, 2006, p. 69), starting first with the upper classes and then expanding to the "less wealthy" but with "latent demand" for art over time, and then across the social spectrum, with a "mass demand for paintings" (De Marchi & Van Miegroet, 2006, p. 70). The general art sales sequence goes as follows: "commission nexus, cost-reduction and novel sorts of paintings, mass retail, then resale markets" (De Marchi & Van Miegroet, 2006, p. 70), with the broadscale popularization of art. Social class identity informs the approach to various forms of culture. These informing factors include "the aesthetic disposition of the upper class, the cultural goodwill of the middle class, and the taste for necessity of the working class" (Bourdieu, as cited in Ollivier, 2008, p. 129). Still, there is often high-minded rhetoric used in relation to art as defined by the upper classes, the cultural elite [as compared to "pop art" which may first attract the attention and affection of the masses or "art that is most enjoyed by most people in today's diverse societies" ((Shusterman, 2003, p. 289)]. If art exists on various strata by cost, at the top would be the fine arts, some types of pop art, and perhaps "common art" at the least expensive.

Broadly, the "creation and reception of works of art" are seen as uniquely powerful indicators of humanity (Tschacher & Tröndle, 2017, p. 67). The ability to appreciate art is seen as an aspect of human refinement and linked for many years with the upper classes. And yet, where art is sacred, money is often seen as profane. Where art is priceless, money is eminently priced. There is, too, the challenge of trying to objectively measure the "quality of visual arts" (Bonus & Ronte, 1997, p. 103), with a general consensus that there are not universal objective measures. Art is dubbed a "mysterious commodity," and their characteristics affecting pricing (Rubião, Summer 2018, p. 5). Art is also known as "experience goods" (with the value based on the experiential consumption) and "confidence goods" (with product "quality appraised individually" and/or by experts) (Rubião, Summer 2018, p. 6). Even though art may be generally either performative (theatre, concert, shows, and other events) or presentational (physical objects), or both, this work focuses mostly on visual art, in physical/analog format and in digital.

Sometimes, there are tradeoffs when artwork is commercialized. Street art is one example. Street art—graffiti, murals, tagging, and other practices—often involve the defacement of property and is countercultural. There are unique artist styles and signages. These communicate something of urban coolness and rebellion. Street art is used in "fashion design, city branding, guerrilla marketing campaigns, … (and as) attraction in alternative city tours" and other uses (Molnár, 2018, p. 43), but it retains its gritty cool because it is "incompletely commodified" (Molnár, 2018, p. 43). There are also digital versions of street art (Molnár, 2018, p. 44). Still, many artists find that they have an uncomfortable relationship with mainstream publishers and other consumers of their art, who do not compensate the original artists for uses of their work in publication (Molnár, 2018, p. 52), even as royalties are often extremely low in most cases.

Street art murals are "non-permanent heritage elements" and require restoration and maintenance, to preserve the artistry and social statements and other aspects of culture (La Nasa, et al., 2021, p. 129). There are different ways that these artworks get funded. So, too, with other place-based art, such as land art.

Art plays major roles in marketing and advertising, in the commercialization of art. Art is used in physical retail spaces. Art is commercialized through art-infused products and other cross-pollination with retail (Kim, Deng, & Unnava, 2020, p. 302). This may be a mix of the sacred and the profane concept.

Art Markets

From an external perspective, the art market is "a sector of economic activity that is highly entrepreneurial and comprised of many small businesses and individuals" (Taylor, Cardenas, & Edwards, Summer 2019, p. 5). In many senses, the work of artists may be hidden from the public, given that the "primary actors have no requirements for public disclosure" (Taylor, Cardenas, & Edwards, Summer 2019, p. 5). Art production is often achieved in micro-enterprises and as subsectors. Art markets are not homogeneous but fairly localized and differentiated in many aspects. Art markets are not comparable to "the public securities markets—that is, a broad-based, consistent trading market" (Horvitz, 2009, p. 87). The size of the global art market at about $40 - $70 billion or "larger than the revenues of all but the top 40 or even top 25 of publicly traded U.S. corporations" (Horvitz, 2009, p. 89). There are boom and bust cycles in art markets.

The formal art market is generally divided into primary and secondary markets. The primary ones refer to the places where the first sales of new artworks occur: galleries, art dealerships, art agents, and others. The secondary (resale) markets are where sales of artworks *after* the first sale occur, often in terms of auction houses, art agents, and others. In general, the various entities require some funding to create catalogs, run the respective events, design show spaces, market artworks, frame or otherwise present physical artworks, and other overhead costs related to presenting the works. There may be costs to host artists to talk about their works. There have to be security systems to protect the works. There has to be insurance to cover potential damage, forgeries, vandalism, and other risks. Expertise in the respective artworks can also be expensive. There are always private sales which may not involve the primary or secondary art markets. Trust relationships are critical for this work. The primary market is known for high transaction costs ranging from the 20 – 40% range based on various publications. Major buyers include museums, corporations, private families, and individuals.

How much do investors use "information regarding the activity of four major auction houses" and how much is that information reflected in the stock prices? One research team studied how efficient auction houses are at signaling art market robustness. They found: "While some stocks exhibit market efficiency, other(s) present a slow assimilation of information in the stock price and hence past information can be used to make predictions" (Munteanu & Pece, 2015, p. 82).

Another work studied whether art markets are rational.

> Museums optimize choices among art (that is) historically significant authentic paintings distributed as stochastic rare events in the tertiary market for art. Such paintings have few, if any, art historically equivalent substitutes, causing the demand for such works of art to be extremely inelastic. Museums tend to buy at the top of the information curve; paying prices which exceed market averages for similar art. As a result, society pays the cost of institutional risk aversion. In contrast, collectors often purchase art before all art historical information is

> complete, and often earn a reward for assuming a risk due to incomplete information… (Singer & Lynch, 1997, p. 197)

The dimension of "art historical significance" is the "product of an interaction between one or more artists and social consciousness in a particular historical period" (Singer & Lynch, 1997, p. 198). The condition of a painting also affects its price; excessive touchup may result in the painting to be deemed "not by the artist's hand. Overall, this empirical research found that art markets are rational and use "all relevant information on art historical significance in determining prices as well as all relevant information on authenticity" (Singer & Lynch, 1997, p. 214). Further, there is the finding that high art can function "as a quasi-substitute for financial instruments. The stochastic process of money flows in the top auction houses and the stock markets tends to be statistically significantly related by transfer functions Money tend to flow into the art market after a lag of several periods, when the market for financial instruments is less attractive and vice-versa. Such a relationship could not be found for the middle or lower end of the art spectrum" (Singer & Lynch, 1997, p. 214). High art can hold stored value and appreciate in value over time, so making it an option for financial portfolios.

Art Market Dynamics

Buyers and sellers both have to exercise due diligence to find the true value of an artwork in a marketplace, which is an essential function of a functioning art market. One challenge to proper pricing involves informational asymmetry in which one side may have more information than the other. Studies of art markets have found "market inefficiency in almost all sectors" which they attribute to "asymmetrical information, influential galleries (sic) power, and differentiated pieces and talents in the art markets" (Assaf, Kristoufek, Demir, & Mitra, 2021, p. 1).

One way to mitigate such imbalances involves using "guarantees, insurance, branding, stock market valuations, and audit" in markets (Dolgin, 2009, p. 145). The "lack of transparency" is "a major functional deficiency of art markets" (Bianchi, 2015, p. 133), with "unequal access to verifiable information" (p. 133). As such, art goods are "trust-intensive goods" (Bianchi, 2015, p. 138); they are "highly differentiated" with "novelty appeal" (Bianchi, 2015, p. 138). With heightened transparency, there should be increased trust and perhaps a greater willingness to take on the risks of buying art. However, each such "…relational trust can be and has been used as one form of privileged access and to gain positions of power" (Bianchi, 2015, p. 149). Those outside privileged social circles would not have access to privy information. Another barrier to entry involves costs, with many works in the five, six, and seven figures. This targeting to very small audiences may be seen in another work where "auctions are an effective way to achieve transactions in markets where there may be as few as a dozen potential customers worldwide" (Hutter, Knebel, Pietzner, & Schäfer, 2007, p. 249).

Another approach to minimizing informational asymmetries is to collect additional semantic information to enrich current data and enable more rational decision making. One such approach uses DBpedia data source to augment various art indices for data enrichment (Filipiak & Filipowska, June 2015, p. 322).

Knowledge of local art market information may also be important since there is variant pricing in different locales. There is "no universal standard" to value the art (Komarova, 2017, p. 325).

The sense that those who invest in art are not only pursuing financial gain or profit but are swayed by "some emotional attachment to the art objects" (Assaf, Kristoufek, Demir, & Mitra, 2021, p. 13). The provision of information to accompany art may inform the heightened appreciation of the art or even change the direction of the art interpretation (Abe & Fukushima, 2020, p. 3083). The framing of an artwork is important. Experientially, the "role of emotions in economic decision making" (De Silva, Pownall, & Wolk, 2012, p. 167) can also affect pricing, based on a dataset of auction prices for art from 1990 – 2007 overlaid with weather data. The researchers write: "We find that mood affects the lower end of the price distribution. We use the existence of a cartel between the auction houses to proxy the variation in the common value component. Our evidence shows that it is only the upper end of the price distribution that is affected by the cartel" (De Silva, Pownall, & Wolk, 2012, p. 176). More recent studies have affirmed the emotional value of artworks (Bernales, Reus, & Valdenegro, 2020, p. 6). Some people evaluate the value of art inappropriately, conflating value "with material production, with auction sales, cult of celebrity, and endless gossip" (Claassen, 2012, p. 278).

Statistical methods are used to model out consumer preferences in an art market, such as those from the Renaissance (Grigoroudis, Noel, Galariotis, & Zopounidis, 2021, p. 718). There are ways to understand consumer preferences at scale (in the aggregate) from available data.

Ironically, however, sometimes more information used for pricing an artwork can result in suboptimal pricing and have "complex outcomes" (Coslor, 2016, p. 13). There are "advantages and predictable problems from increased price data in markets that contain substantial qualitative and non-numerical data" given "evaluative frictions" (p. 13). Non-price factors about an art product may be relevant to a price in invisible or less visible ways (p.13). There is need for particular expertise to use particular types of available information, particular historical data which requires sufficient contextualization (Coslor, 2016, p. 19).

The fine arts markets have other unique characteristics:

> The art markets are heterogeneous markets in which the average work changes hands very rarely and different than financial markets with high transaction costs. They have their own characteristics and evolve differently in response to common and idiosyncratic shocks. The artworks are also considered to be not very liquid and are not divisible and have values that are determined by subjective beliefs on present and futures prices with tastes and fashion effects. (Assaf, 2018, p. 346)

In primary art markets dealing in fine art, "prices positively correlate with an artist's reputation and negatively correlate with a gallery's reputation" (Schönfeld & Reinstaller, 2007, p. 143). The artist needs to have public credibility in order to command particular high values. Part of this credibility comes from expert evaluations: "Since the public cannot in general ascertain the quality of an artist's oeuvre directly, experts must themselves be credible to the public in order to lend credibility to a given oeuvre" (Bonus & Ronte, 1997, p. 103), based on the application of cultural knowledge.

A common secondary market is the auction house. The auction house is the entity through which some 50% of the art trade moves (Charlin & Cifuentes, 2020, p. 1). The auction house sets the reserve price for the various works being sold. This is the lowest acceptable price of the seller for an item sold at auction, and it can have an anchoring value in terms of understood price. If a work is overpriced and fails to sell at auction, there are typical future devaluations of the artwork.

A critical difference between the primary markets (dealers) and the secondary ones (auctions) involves pricing. One empirical study found a steady price increase for living artists practicing in the contemporary art space when represented by international dealers (but not when works sold by auction) (Hutter, Knebel, Pietzner, & Schäfer, 2007, p. 250). Dealer prices tend to be about at least twice as high as those of auction prices, and as artists age, up to some four times as high as the auction price (Hutter, Knebel, Pietzner, & Schäfer, 2007, p. 254).

One study suggests that the secondary art market is "not efficient" because "price formation is opaque to outsiders who lack information on unsold artworks" (David, Oosterlinck, & Szafarz, 2013, p. 23). This is a finding based on auction-based index data that "returns on artworks exhibit high positive auto-correlation" (David, Oosterlinck, & Szafarz, 2013, p. 23), which the authors attribute to "price truncation resulting from unobservable reserve prices in auctions" (p. 23). The minimum set prices for a sale as the reserve price

> Put differently, we argue that it is structurally impossible for auction prices to be efficient. Sellers set a minimum transaction price on the artworks for which they have a monopoly. Since hammer prices are determined solely by bidding, there is no upper limit. As a consequence, relying on realized prices is insufficient to build unbiased predictions of future prices. Market inefficiency is thus rooted in the design of the trading system currently used in the art market. In fact, the auction mechanism itself does not distort prices. Rather, the distortion comes from unreported missing sales and undisclosed reserve prices, which give informational superiority to market insiders, typically auction firm managers. (David, Oosterlinck, & Szafarz, 2013, p. 24)

In a functioning market, equilibrium prices could float and be arrived at more naturally with market mechanisms. They write:

> Equilibrium prices reflect the true value of the good. In contrast, art auctions currently function in a way that drags the market into a vicious circle of inefficiency. Reserve prices arise from sellers' awareness that they cannot trust the market. In turn, reserve prices create market inefficiency. (David, Oosterlinck, & Szafarz, 2013, p. 25)

Art markets involve varieties of risks. The discovery of art fakes can harm the larger art market and suppress prices. A study of the impacts of art fakes found the following: "Prices only react negatively with a lag, suggesting that sellers try to postpone their sales as long as possible" after the revelation of fakes but then have to sell at some point and so put their works onto market and face lower prices (Bocart & Oosterlinck, 2011, p. 124). This study was based on a database of mentions of discoveries of fakes as ways to ensure memory for expensive artworks. The researchers observe: "The first negative coefficient appears for a window starting 136 days after the discovery" of the fake (Bocart & Oosterlinck, 2011, p. 126). Then: "Eventually, close to a year after fakes have been made public, prices increase indicating that buyers view the market as purged" (Bocart & Oosterlinck, 2011, p. 126).

An empirical study found that the "art price index is a smooth function of time and has a variability that is comparable to the volatility of stock indices" (Bocart & Hafner, 2012, p. 3091). So, the value of art tends to rise over time but also is responsive to stock volatility.

In cases when artists pass away, effectively ending the ability for the artist to create new works, does the value of their art go up, from the viewpoint of a "durable goods monopolist"? asks a research team. (Ekelund, Ressler, & Watson, 2000, p. 283) Based on an empirical analysis of U.S. auction data, the threat to art supply from this artist does result in a higher valuation of works after artist death. [Prior to the artist's death, their work generally tends to appreciate in price and rise as they age (Hutter, Knebel, Pietzner, & Schäfer, 2007, p. 247)].

What about the risks of speculative buying in the arts markets and resulting bubbles (and investment risk)? One researcher examined a period explosive growth in the art markets from 1998 – 2015 to assess whether or not there were bubbles. With some statistical methods, the researcher did not find evidence of bubbles, but he was able to detect "more than one bubble with most of the bubbles happening in the period 2002 – 2005" when using the right-tailed ADF method; he also made the same discoveries using bootstrap test methods. (Assaf, 2018, p. 340) Art markets are seen as becoming "more sensitive to economic and geopolitical events, with the artworks demonstrating a level of maturity similar to other alternative investment classes" post the 2008 global economic crisis. (Assaf, 2018, p. 340) There has been "double digit growth rate in the past 20 years, caused by a mix of investment logic, speculation and collection passion" (Assaf, 2018, p. 354).

Another work studying bubbles in art markets focused on the period of 1970 – 2014 given "an explosive movement in today's 'Impressionist and Modern,' 'Post-war and Contemporary', 'American', and 'Old Masters' fine rt market segments" (Kräussl, Lehnert, & Martelin, 2016, p. 99). Two historical speculative bubbles were found.

There are various risks in art market. The speculative risk comes from various sources: "artist death *(asset supply constraints),* collectors' wealth *(background risk)* and forgery risk *(risk of investment fraud),* under short-sale constraints and risk aversion" (Bernales, Reus, & Valdenegro, 2020, p. 1). Background risk involves the background risk of collector wealth, which may skew what the buyer is willing to pay for an artwork. An older source expressed the risk: "The subjective nature of aesthetic valuation would suggest that the only constraint limiting the price of a work of art is the wealth of the collectors who desire it" (Goetzmann, Dec. 1993, p. 1375). On the other hand, the personalized pricing of goods based on the perception of the buyer's ability to pay in online markets and the potential for abusive practices (Botta & Wiedemann, 2020, p. 381) is a known risk.

Regulatory Regimes for Art Markets

Some of the research works explore some of the regulatory regimes in different spaces. The European Union has rules guiding the sales of visual arts ("paintings, drawings, engravings, prints, sculptures") in primary and secondary markets (Bises, 1997, p. 311). There is valuing of works that embody "cultural heritage" (p. 315). There is interest in preserving both private and collective benefits (p. 315). Given the supranational stature of the EU, and the valuing of free trade overall, the overarching rules do not supersede those of member states with their own laws and interests regarding protection their own "national treasures" (p. 319).

In practice, however, such as the presence of frauds and fakes in the aboriginal art market, there are limits of legal systems to deal with such transgressions (Alder, Chappell, & Polk, 2011, p. 189). In part, the legal enforcement requires expertise that may not be available.

Various legal doctrines that affect the visual arts including "copyright and trademark issues; moral rights which cover the right of an artist to prevent the mutilation and destruction of his work; resale royalties; rules governing ownership disputes between innocent parties such as a good faith purchaser and an earlier owner of the work of art; disputes over the authenticity of a work of art which cause material changes in the market value of the work; and the valuation of art-rich estates" (Landes & Levine, 2006, 212). Various laws affect the copying of visual works (Landes & Levine, 2006, 219). Only some digital copies or versions are seen as "second originals," such as in contexts when the first is lost to history, and the next rendition is the next best thing. And there are other complexities.

In the SARS-CoV-2/COVID-19 Pandemic

Art markets lost ground in COVID-19 crisis from 2020 – present. "The decline of face-to-face interaction, previously essential to art market transactions, has placed strain" on the art market (Buchholz, Fine, & Wohl, 2020, p. 462). Many buyers preferred experiencing physical co-presence with the artworks and "art world actors" (p. 462), so that they could evaluate the artworks in-person. There was a lack of "collective effervescence" without co-presence (p. 462), resulting in lost opportunities for sales. This work would suggest that atmospherics matter as well as in-person trust-based interactions.

High Art as Financial Instruments

Those who have read about the Tulipmania of 1636 – 1637 may be forgiven for expressing concern about continuing focus on the role of flowers and the Dutch economy, and on art and the economy. National economies represent a nation's markets but also include "many cultural and social trends, such as Holland's interest in flower(s)…and botany" which culminated in Tulipmania in 1636 – 1637 (Ji, 2020, p. 231). Said another way, there are very human and cultural components to an economy.

The art market is inherently uncertain and requiring "strategic sensemaking" (Samdanis & Lee, 2019, p. 476). It helps to understand the strategic configuration of the art space based on knowledge, legitimacy, and artistic innovation (Samdanis & Lee, 2019, p. 479). The market returns on art can be uncertain and hard to capture (Charlin & Cifuentes, 2017, p. 186). Some view art to inspire their own works (Ishiguro & Okada, 2021), so the value may be outside of the object itself.

Artworks are seen as one method to diversify financial portfolios. "Investible art" has characteristics that enable it to be "transacted"; said another way, such art is "readily identifiable to the buyers and sellers for whom it is a relevant transaction and have characteristics that can be valued by reference to basic characteristics" (Horvitz, 2009, p. 92). As a "luxury good," an artwork "confers status and provides pleasure in sheer ownership" (Horvitz, 2009, p. 95). As a luxury good, the prices of artwork may be affected by aggregate levels of wealth among investors (Kräussl & Logher, 2010, p. 314), such as when wealth rises, and there is extra to spend on status. There have been long ties between the luxury and art markets (Lagier & Godey, 2007).

Investible art has to be highly recognizable and created by a named artist; it should have a provenance or documented history of ownership (Horvitz, 2009, p. 96). It should be a work listed as a known work by the artist in publication or *catalogue raisonée* (Horvitz, 2009, p. 98). The provenance of the work should be clear. Stylistic analysis has long been applied along with other means to ascertain the authorship and authenticity of a work (Prown, 1980, p. 209). High technology plays a role in authenticating artworks by their material features to deter fraud and counterfeiting.

A more recent hedonic price analysis of the South African fine art auction scene involved data from 2009 – 2014. They write:

> Results validate full scale hedonic pricing. Identities of artists, medium and genre, dating characteristics, and physical characteristics of artwork are significant. External validity of hedonic pricing is supported by out-of-sample price prediction for 40 individual artists. Auction house catalogue presentation of art work also provides correlated with realized auction prices. (Fedderke & Li, 2020, p. 88)

Art prices were found to be countercyclical to GDP and domestic equity markets but were pro-cyclical with off-shore equity markets (Fedderke & Li, 2020, p. 88) and so has a diversification role to play to balance investments in more traditional financial instruments. There have been findings of some feedback effects between art markets and some other markets; this finding is suggestive of the benefits of "diversification for practitioners, investors and collectors" who deal in the art market (Le Fur, 2020, p. 167).

One study mapped ties in the fields of art and economic capital (Vigerland & Borg, 2018, p. 182). Works with cultural capital may overlap with economic variables. Another study found "a stationary long-run relationship and significant short and long run causal linkages between the various painting market and between the equity market and painting markets" (in the period from 1976 – 2001) in terms of "Contemporary Masters, Surrealists, 20th Century English and Modern US" paintings (Worthington & Higgs, 2003, p. 649). However, this team also found that "returns on paintings are much lower and the risks much higher than in conventional financial markets" (Worthington & Higgs, 2003, p. 649). Artworks are "not very liquid assets, almost never divisible, transaction costs are high, and there are lengthy delays between the decision to sell and actual sell" (Worthington & Higgs, 2003, p. 651). Direct investing in art requires sophisticated knowledge. This is a market with "pervasive" risk of "fire and theft and the possibility of reattribution to a different artist" (Worthington & Higgs, 2003, p. 651). Depending on the type of artwork collected, there may be a high cost of entry.

In theory, art may be held as a hedge against price volatility in other financial assets. That said, art is often not seen as a safe investment for "a risk-averse agent" (Goetzmann, Dec. 1993, p. 1370). One study of 271 years of painting prices resulted in the finding of "a basic connection between art and money" (Goetzmann, Dec. 1993, p. 1375). Also, it was found that aesthetic values globalized since WWII and resulted in a heightened demand for art (p. 1375).

In times of mass financial duress, many turn to art as an option, as a counter-cyclical investment. One researcher argues for the strengths of buying art as an alternative financial investment given the "comparatively poor performance of traditional asset classes in recent years" (in the time of the Great Recession and bear market in 2008) (Campbell, 2008, p. 119). To make this argument, the researcher created indexes based on a mix of works by artists to ascertain the performance of the art market. Also, this work offers a "hypothetical fund that holds a composition of 30% Old Masters, 15% European Impressionists, 15% Modern, and 40% Contemporary, the average return using data from the various sectors is 7.05%...for the 20-year period from 1985 (Campbell, 2008, p. 129). Still, there are high transaction costs for art at some 37.5% (or 1.5% per year for 25 years) (Campbell, 2008, p. 143).

Still, the purchasing of fine art is often linked to macro-economic trends and art pricing (Spaenjers, Goetzmann, & Mamonova, 2015, p. 90). This suggests that there are massmind trends in terms of investment in art.

A study of a price index for art market auctions found that "art prices are unrelated to financial assets prices" but there was "a positive correlation with real estate prices" in the Italian art market space (Candela & Scorcu, 1997, p. 175). The topline observation in this older work is that art prices are not "driven by persistent fads" but have some relation to the prices of other assets based on some underpinning of economic fundamentals (Candela & Scorcu, 1997, p. 176). Interestingly, collector tastes are observed to change slowly (p. 177), so purchased artworks need to be allowed to ripen over time to avoid capital loss. There are not fast turnarounds on art resales for this reason. A more recent horizon analysis of art investments involved the modeling out of short, medium, and long horizon artwork for various financial returns. Generally, "short-horizon art investors focus on arbitrage" (buying and selling) while "long-horizon art investors focus on value" and tend to "favor masterpieces" and "ancient artworks" (Park, Ju, Liang, & Tu, 2017, p. 17).

Certainly, there are indirect ways to invest in and own art through various art-based financial instruments. There are investment instruments that may involve art (as an asset class) purchased by experts and managed professionally. Some methods involve the pooling of resources for indirect investing in the art market (Campbell, 2008, p. 145).

In cultural economics, investing in art may involve a "psychic return" which is outside of or in addition to the financial considerations. One research team has set up a way to calculate this variable in equations (Candela, Castellani, & Pattitoni, 2013, p. 351). Perhaps this is a way to show the effect of emotion and some non-rationality in art investments.

Similarly, buyers of art experience a private-value sense of the art. Researchers observe:

> An artwork is essentially a claim on the pleasure and pride experienced as its owner. As the 'consumption' of art is discretionary, the marginal utility of—and therefore the willingness to pay for—its non-pecuniary payoffs can be expected to vary with wealth shocks... (Spaenjers, Goetzmann, & Mamonova, 2015, p. 82)

There is a subjective ego-based element to art ownership. The pleasure from the art investment goes beyond the aesthetics. There is also the pride of ownership of that artwork (with the "endowment effect") and the pleasure from displaying their wealth from the art acquisition: "The durability of art makes it not only a consumption good, but also a store and display of wealth" and "social status" (Spaenjers, Goetzmann, & Mamonova, 2015, p. 84). Others have noted that the art market is "a status market" (Aspers, 2009, as cited in Komarova, 2017, p. 325). There is value in having others see what one owns and how much it is worth, particularly, perhaps, for the *nouveau riche*.

Various other works found mixed results in terms of returns on art investments. One work found the following: "Returns to art investments are positively correlated in the short run...but may reverse in the longer run" (Pénasse, Renneboog, & Spaenjers, 2014, p. 432). Sentiment is found to predict "short-term returns" on art prices (Pénasse, Renneboog, & Spaenjers, 2014, p. 432). There was also an observed "slow-moving fad component in art prices" (Pénasse, Renneboog, & Spaenjers, 2014, p. 432).

One study focused on return on investment (ROI) on an annualized basis of particular works from particular countries, like Poland (Lucińska, 2015, p. 67). Art purchased as a financial investment has to perform, by holding and/or gaining value against inflation.

Emerging art markets for Russia, China, and India found "a significant long-term relation with other financial market instruments, but short-term relations are largely absent" (Kräussl & Logher, 2010, p. 301). This may suggest that a nimble art investment strategy may be effective although the complexities are enormous.

Bolstering of Formal Fine Art Prices

Overarching market narratives about art markets justify market norms, such as pricing. These stories manifest in different ways in different locations and serve different purposes (Komarova, 2017).

Various professional practices also help bolster art prices. The maintaining of institutional memory of validated artworks and provenance is one example. Then, too, there are academic and popular narratives of artists and their art, the interactions between the artist and the larger society, and other details, which communicate the sense of artists breathing rarefied air. Various museums will collect draft works (sketches, notes, diaries, letters, and others) of artists whose works are worthy of curation, collection, study, preservation, and generational attention. These works show the investments that go into artful works. Some works require years of inputs to actualize.

Another research work explored what is top of mind for editors in the literary arts. Many editors focus on "aesthetic values" more so than market logics (Pareschi & Lusiani, 2020, p. 1). Those who engage in the arts spaces have to deal with complex dimensionality.

Another research work, the Turner Prize, dubbed "today's most prestigious art award," selects a young British artist annually for recognition and status. One study found that conferral of this honor results in "fast market ascension and *hastened,* rather than 'deferred,' commercial success" based on the prize's "three innovative valuation mechanisms: *brokerage, deliberation, and institutional labeling"* (Pénet & Lee, 2014, p. 149). The prize comes with a year of build-up and then broadscale mass media coverage, including television. Price setting in the art market is "a social process that occurs between the qualities of an artwork and the assessments of buyers and sellers" but "no objective (production or labor cost) or moral standards by which value can be produced, stabilized, and diffused" (Pénet & Lee, 2014, p. 152). A prize can offer leverage in this competitive space. The imprimatur of the prize disrupts "the typical pace of art valuation" by speeding success for British contemporary artists (Pénet & Lee, 2014, p. 166).

As a side note, some art markets (such as the Canadian one) are supported by buyers of the same nationality as the artists, perhaps as an indication of the relative maturity of the artists and respective artworks (Hodgson & Seçkin, 2012, p. 867). It can take long effort for artists to achieve international renown, beyond the local.

Price determinants may vary in different local markets. In the Korean art market, the modality of the artwork has an effect on price (such as oil paintings bringing the highest prices, "followed by mixed media pieces and acrylic paintings" but the finding that gouache and watercolor paintings were not priced significantly differently from those of other media pieces in the Korean art market in one study (Nahm, 2010, p. 287). There were also genre effects based on topics. The works of late artists are often much higher than for living ones, by 20x in one study (Nahm, 2010, p. 293), based on art auction data.

International buyers of artworks from emerging markets may have particular preferences. One research study identified certain collector preferences of "abstract artworks..." over figurative and landscape paintings" from Venezuela in the international market from 1969 – 2014 (Garay, 2021, p. 413).

Formal Fine Art (Center) Emergent from the Periphery

Many of the newer works that set the art world on fire emerge from the peripheries and the margins (Zolberg, 2010). Low art in one generation can be the high art of subsequent generations given evolving cultural aesthetics and values (Shusterman, 2003, p. 292). New ideas and practices do not necessarily come from those with educated or formally trained senses. There is a popular sense that those who have gone through formal higher educational training tend to inculcate too much in what has already been to create wholly new works. They have steeped too much into conventions to truly innovate. There is constant surveillance for what is new and exciting, so that what is novel can be adopted (and some would say appropriated) for other uses.

This occurs in a process in which "outsider" art is legitimized in the formal art space. The legitimizing processes in art is seen as "always ongoing and never final," and that contestation "can persist even in legitimated fields" (Alexander & Bowler, 2021, p. 1). The contestation in aesthetic fields is a constant. Certainly, the work of even established artists is constantly evaluated and assessed and commented on. One definition of "outsider art" involves work by artists "who produce outside established art worlds and who come from disadvantaged social worlds" (Alexander & Bowler, 2021, p. 1).

The legitimizing of art, no matter where it originated, has been analogized to successful social movements which require "political opportunity structures, resource mobilization, and framing processes" (Baumann, 2007, p. 47). Art legitimization is a social construct that can be influenced by various social mechanisms. Art legitimacy is not a binary but can be present in "varying amounts and among various constituencies" (p. 49). Ideas can be critical to frame the value of art (Baumann, 2007, p. 57), with art bolstered by "an extensive corps of critics and theorists to speak for it" (Markowitz, 1994, p. 63). Indeed, various thinking about art and artfulness changes over time as well.

Some view outsiders, who have learned art on their own, as people who belong to their own social and artist category.

> Although the domain of self-taught art is ostensibly defined by the fact the artists have not been formally trained, in practice self-taught art is known through the social position of the creators, and, thus, I label it as *Identity Art.* (Fine, 2003, p. 155)

Such artists who work outside "the standards of professional practice" may experience "alternative models of esteem" (Fine, 2003, p. 159). Such artists need to embody the art through "biography and reputation" (Fine, 2003, p. 171), especially since "stories affect sales" (p. 172)

The role of art in underserved communities can be salutary and socially beneficial. Here, "art and culture entrepreneurs engage in a continuous process of adaptation, learning, and innovation and seek opportunities to serve their business goals" (Wang, Ogilvie, & Richardson, 2021, p. 1) to advance the community. Their efforts can support the sense of "artistic placemaking" (p. 1) through the development of creative industries for ethnic and racial minority entrepreneurship.

Insider Perspectives of the Art World

An "emic" approach focuses on the perspective of artists and other stakeholders in the art space. One researcher studied China's art market actors and their perceptions of their roles in a globalized space using a metaphor research approach (Kharchenkova, 2018, p. 71). This researcher observes some bias in the "othering" of these artists, who are sometimes seen as collaborating too closely with auction houses, in ways that are not considered appropriate abroad. On the other hand, those who participated in the research sometimes held (unwarranted) idealization of foreign markets (Kharchenkova, 2018, p. 74). These participants in the contemporary Chinese art market see it as an "organism" embedded in a larger international environment, with various systemic dimensions that are important to understand in order to survive: socio-political, economic, cultural, legal, and others.

Another study explored a supply side of the art market and the persons who work to supply art to the world. This team found a series of network interactions in the process. They write: "Results indicate that the art product and the art production process is reliant on a range of mutually beneficial and reciprocal interactions that serve as bases for value creation in the art market" (Lehman, Wickham, & Fillis, 2018, p. 57). In a sense, then, artworks stem from social processes as well as individual ones.

Another work shows the importance of collective memory in art markets. In this study of the art market in Mumbai, this shared memory mediates changes in the art market (Sooudi, 2018, p. 83). Such knowledge can be used strategically to help steer the community forward.

Pricing for various artworks may depend on a variety of factors. If a work is commissioned as part of public arts funding, then the amount paid depends on the set funding of the grant. If a work is commissioned by a private organization, then the funder decides the funding. Those that would compete for such grant funding accept the terms, or they will not generally apply. Some companies will commission fan art to raise enthusiasm about their respective products. And then, private individuals may commission artworks. They may negotiate different prices for different works with various artists and arts cooperatives and agent representatives.

Local art markets have a range of pricing styles even as the value of contemporary artworks has been described as "highly uncertain" (O'Neil, 2008, p. 94). From the artist perspective, when they set pricing, they consider the following most common factors (in descending order): "size, expenses, status, market factors, and the artist's own perception of value" (O'Neil, 2008, pp. 94 and 100). The artists do show some strategy, such as raising prices "when demand is strong" (in both fine arts and crafting) (O'Neil, 2008, p. 110). In general, there does not seem to be convergence on one method of pricing (O'Neil, 2008).

Art centers may not just be national contexts. Much research often focuses on metropolitan centers than nations in terms of the international art market (Fletcher & Helmreich, 2019, p. 328). Art markets have different specializations and focuses on different goods (Fletcher & Helmreich, 2019, p. 332). This work closes with the question of what it would look like to model the international art market? What about the global online art market? Is such information even collected?

Pre-sale catalogues were influential in price anchoring and were found to be "statistically significantly associated with realized auction price" (Fedderke & Li, 2020, p. 101). Other anchoring effects in the art markets were found based on "past auction prices" in the Chinese art market especially if "time intervals between two auctions of the same paintings are relatively short" (Bian, Huang, Zhe, & Zhang, 2021, p. 1).

The Informal Art Market

The informal art market may be comprised of sales in various contexts: local community art shows, local galleries, farmer's markets, county fairs, garage sales, and other venues. The "common art" creator may achieve personal satisfaction from such work and social satisfaction and other pleasures and "utils." When selling their work, they have to consider their inputs and then if they attain a profit or a loss when they sell. How they do this back-of-the-napkin math may differ, and those that actually consider their full learning and other inputs over many hours and days and months and years may have to set their prices much higher in order to achieve their return on investment (ROI). For those with other sources of income and livelihood, perhaps they do not have to make the numbers even out or to gain an actual real profit from their "gig work" in common art. Few work full-time as "common art" artists. The works of such artists do not garner respect per se in the formal art world, perhaps for various ecological reasons: a lack of respect for the mediums (seen as non-professional), a lack of training to formally evaluate the various types of common art, a lack of representation by galleries and agents, and other factors.

Others have noted that artworks cannot be measured by their selling price alone. Something with cultural value is valued differently than normal other goods. Such artworks may help societies relax in their presence. Perhaps artworks drive travel to particular locations. Perhaps they help inform the culture of particular global cities. Perhaps such artworks help society hold mass-scale social discussions about history, about values, about social identities, about aesthetics, or some combination of issues. Perhaps they help with the branding of locations. There are various public externalities, positive and negative, available from widely public artworks. Artworks may enable cultural capital and "consumer surplus."

The Online Art Market Today for "Common Art" Artists

The wide access of the Internet and WWW can convey a sense of anything displayed online as excessively common and not particularly valuable. If someone can be seen with so many eyes, what can it be worth? Some myths around "Internet art" include the ideas that "Internet art is impossible to collect" and that it "will never be important because you can't sell a Web site" (Ippolito, 2002, p. 487).

On the Social Web, many amateur (and professional) artists sell their works through various digital storefronts or their own sites. [One study suggests that some 57% of elite "featured sellers" are professional and hold "a formal degree in craft or art disciplines and a significant minority (22.4%) claiming professional training in other fields" (Pace, O'Donnell, DeWitt, Bardzell, & Bardzell, Feb. 2013, p. 1027)].

A perusal of e-commerce spaces hosting artworks show collections of decorative and even pedestrian works. Some are mirrors and decorative wall hangings with simple messages of encouragement and inspiration. [One is a smiling whale with the advice to "just keep swimming."] There are photos of sunsets. Sometimes, poetry snippets are overlaid over photos. There are decorative glass tiles that may be used as coasters. There are some simple messages expressing political values. There are garden gnomes and garden chickens. A line-art print shows a woman in a sun hat. Some messages are romantic, others snarky. Some political messages are about committing to a cleaner environment. Another is about racial and ethnic pride. One work is a large flaming copper heart that can be used as a wall hanging. This and others seem sized for over-the-sofa sorts of works. There is plenty of hand-crafted jewelry. There are postcards. These is a religious tree of life triptych as metal wall art. There are miniatures, such as a small fairy house. The general min-max range of costs is $10 to about $200. One 3D-printed dress was labeled as going for $4,000. In some ways it was hard to find a unique hand in the works. Even when works were original, many seemed derivative, emulative. The various expressed styles seem emulate-able and yet still requiring of talent and skill. Many of the goods had a feeling of transience, as if maybe only one or two were made or available. Or perhaps that impression was created to raise the cost of the respective works. None of the artist names were given high attention. On the e-commerce site, the works were shown in final form, without any of the leadup work, the drafts, and other inputs. There is no record-keeping of the works except perhaps in the hands of the respective "common art" artists.

On other sites, there are single-artist pages that showcase their works as a type of gallery show and portfolio. In a sense, their sites serve as their calling card. They also serve as a digital portfolio of the artist hand. There is a fine balance between flooding the market with their works (and diluting value from rarity) and showing a diversity of skills. The trade in reproducible art is thought to be governed by the same economic rules as between other differentiated products (vs. a one-of-a-kind work). It is not hard to imagine that "common art" artists might change their styles or produce more of a kind of a thing that is popular in the market.

Many "common art" artists find their niches in various online communities that can help them acquire new skills and find a supportive audience that can help them incubate their talent and their new businesses.

Social media, in the context of the World Wide Web (WWW) and Internet, also enables other channels for gig work for artists. Visual artists and others may engage in creative live streaming by demonstrating their work processes to audiences. Those who are able to draw a sufficient audience may earn moneys from various platforms. These presentations may provide "advertisement for the artist's work" and "lead to new clients and commissions" and help the artist sell merchandise (Fraser, Dontcheva, Kim, & Klemmer, 2019, p. 49). Those artists who use the online space often have to create multiple accounts across multiple platforms to have a sufficient presence.

For years now, people have observed that digital art has not made headway in the formal art space. One author writes:

> Digital art is inherently medium-specific, yet the market has not been able to accommodate this change, and continues to depend on object-hood, scarcity and conferring value by authority figures. As long as these values remain untouched, there will be little appeal to commercial galleries and institutions in fully integrating Digital art into existing structures of physical art exhibition. (Blume, 2017, pp. 111-112)

Digital art itself is not often archived (Guzman-Serrano, Oct. 2019). Foundational changes in how people think of art may be necessary for change to occur.

Digital Art and (En)forced Rarity

Digital artworks have not found more than a limited market. Some suggest that others do not see digital objects as worthy of collection.

> In a global economic landscape of hyper-commodification and financialisation, efforts to assimilate digital art into the high-stakes commercial art market have so far been rather unsuccessful, presumably because digital artworks cannot easily assume the status of precious object worthy of collection. (Zeilinger, 2018, p. 15)

Some think that the use of blockchain technologies to "create proprietary digital art markets in which uncommodifiable digital artworks are financialized as artificially scarce commodities" may be the solution (Zeilinger, 2018, p. 15). Perhaps non-fungible tokens (NFTs) may enable an enforcement regime against the profligate copying of digital art and contents, as a follow-on technology to other digital rights management tools. In unconstrained ways, digital goods may be non-rivalrous; they are not used up and consumed with each new user given the negligible cost of making the object usable by others.

One author offered a prediction: "…the combination of blockchain-based protocols with established ambitions of intellectual property policy yields hybrid conceptual-computational financial technologies (such as self-enforcing smart contracts attached to digital artefacts) that are unlikely to empower artists but which serve to financialise digital creative practices as a whole, curtailing the critical potential of the digital as an inherently dynamic and potentially uncommodifiable mode of production and artistic expression" (Zeilinger, 2018, p. 15). Certainly, earlier efforts have been made at trying to limit the copying of others' copyrighted goods online, with mixes of legal, technological, and other approaches. The "copyability of intellectual property assets has been described as an existential problem for artists for decades, if not centuries" (Zeilinger, 2018, p. 29).

A new recent twist has been the selling of "non-fungible tokens" (NFTs) tied to digital artworks and memes. NFT is "a one-of-a-kind asset that lives online and is managed in a digital ledger" (McCarthy, May 16, 2021), creating a verifiable scarcity of digital objects which come with a unique identifier. The idea is that unique verifiable assets, validated as such through blockchain technologies, may confer a pride of ownership and limit reproduction of such objects. Such NFTs may be purchased through third-party online marketplaces or NFT exchanges. Some recent pricey purchases (in the six and seven figures) of digital arts to use with NFTs have brought attention to this new method of using blockchain to validate digital artworks. Perhaps some are calculating that the attention for the purchases justify the expenditures, and if these purchases can spark others' to onboard NFTs, the ROI can be achieved. One artwork sold as an NFT at Christie's Auction House for almost $70 million in March 2021 (Kaczynski & Kominers, Nov. 10, 2021). There is broadened thinking now, too, given the ability to program NFTs, which enable holders of particular NFTs to be an investor, a member of a club, a brand shareholder, and a participant in a loyalty program all at once" (Kaczynski & Kominers, Nov. 10, 2021). NFTs may bring together social communities of users, who engage in "NFT ecosystems," in the real and the virtual (Kaczynski & Kominers, Nov. 10, 2021). Indeed, there are numerous efforts as creating markets around NFTs. Within this art practice, there have been reports of rampant piracy and fraud, including through the deployment of automated agents or 'bots (Collier, Jan. 10, 2022).

Selling limited licensure to digital objects is another way to monetize "common art." Various social image sharing sites offer some free visuals alongside those that come with licensing costs in order to attract traffic. Limited rights may be purchased for single or time-limited uses on various digital visuals. Many of these are photos and clipart and diagrams.

Another approach involves jobs for hire by so-called patrons, who sponsor artists to create exclusive works or series of works. The various contracts under which artists work may vary, with different standards for artwork acceptance, rights of first refusal, exclusive access, and/or other clauses. There is an online site that enables "followers" of particular people (with talents) online to subscribe to a particular artist. A percentage of those funds are used pay the artist for live presentational sessions, exclusive videos, and other perks at higher levels of exclusive access. They may offer sketchbook tours, as an analysis of their own artwork, and perhaps as a type of sentimental review. Some art talents will create downloadable "coloring pages" for their patrons.

Some do not directly go the patron route but share their learning and work via social video as a way of teaching other artists Hai-Jew (2020). Some may receive free art packages if they are willing to mention the company. (Companies create subscriber-based art boxes to regularly send art supplies out to individuals, so people can broaden their knowledge of art supplies and their skillset, and so the companies can move art product. Social influencers who advocate the uses of various products can have an effect on the purchases.) Others may benefit from followers who subscribe to the particular social video viewing channels. The payments seem to be fairly small, however, and not particularly useful for a full income stream at least in the West. Video production does require various technologies which are not low-cost.

If skill-building takes some 10,000 hours and finding a unique voice and sensibility takes untold hours, the small compensation for "common art" works is wholly insufficient. And yet, the general market narrative is that these works are at the level of crafting and maybe apprenticeship, not of masters.

On unique artist pages, they may sell various types of goods imprinted with their work: clothing (sweatshirts, t-shirts); bedding (comforters, blankets); shower curtains; dishes (plates, mugs, cups, coasters, and others), and others. These are not generally mass produced, but many are created as needed, given the capabilities of newer technologies.

Crediting Art to Artificial Intelligence (AI)?

With the advent of artificial intelligence (AI), technologies have come to the fore when it comes to considering how to credit artwork. Should AI be given partial or full credit for art requiring computational creativity? There continues to be debate about how artificial intelligence-generated artworks should be credited. A research team suggests that how AI is referred to, whether as a "tool" or an "agent" affects how AI is created for artwork (Epstein, Levine, Rand, & Rahwan, 2020, p. 1). They note that some AI-generated works have sold in the six figures. If credit is given to the AI, what of the responsibility of those humans behind the AI? They write:

> No AI acts alone, completely divorced from the influence of humans... When an AI system achieves something great or causes a serious problem, how is responsibility attributed to the humans surrounding it?...Instead of reducing perceived responsibility of all human actors, we

> instead find that anthropomorphizing the AI system serves to increase responsibility to some actors and decrease responsibility to others. In particular, anthropomorphizing the AI system mitigates the responsibility to the artist, while bolstering the responsibility of the technologist. (Epstein, Levine, Rand, & Rahwan, 2020, p. 7)

Their observation suggests that there is some need to consider the issue of crediting and apportioning responsibility between people engaged in various roles and the actions of particular technologies.

Online Art Auctions

There are various art auctions online as well. There are "tens of thousands of works of art" on sale daily on eBay auctions (Canals-Cerdá, 2012, p. 67). One study found that negative reputation has an effect such as "a significant reduction in the number of bidders and a reduction in the probability of sale" (p. 67), so artists would do well to maintain a good reputation with those who buy art on the space. A negative reputation for artists was also found to be associated with "a significant reduction in sale price" (p. 67). Artists need to be mindful that they are public figures in a sense and that others' word-of-mouth or electronic word-of-mouth (WOM or EWOM) can have huge effects on their livelihood.

Even for the performing arts, social media are important destinations to market the performing arts (Hausmann & Poellmann, 2013, p. 143). There have been studies on the effects of corporations on the arts (in this case, live theatre) (Thomas, 2019, p. 1) to better understand the market. This work also found that there may be a "carrying capacity" limit in terms of how many corporations can be active in the theatre space without limiting possible success.

In summary, then, the literature review suggests that the fine arts are mostly sold first in primary markets and then after the first sale in secondary markets. Informal sales may also occur with direct artist to buyer/patron, in-person or online. There may be heavy mediation in the formal art markets and much lighter or no intermediation in the informal art markets. (Table 1).

Table 1. Formal and informal art markets (in both primary and secondary usages)

	Primary Markets	Secondary Markets
Formal Art Markets	Art galleries Art dealers and agents Salons, studios Exhibitions, shows NFT (non-fungible token) dealers	Auction houses Art dealers and agents NFT (non-fungible token) dealers Online auction sites E-commerce sites/digital storefronts
Informal Art Markets	Direct artist-to-buyer/patron: In person (salons, studios) Websites E-commerce sites/digital storefronts Online marketplaces	Direct owner-to-buyer: In person (various locales) Websites E-commerce sites/digital storefronts Online marketplaces

For "common art" artists, they may occasionally sell via formal art markets like their salons and studios but usually only if they have earned some renown. Their typical ways to reach buyers are online (especially during a pandemic), and theirs are informal art markets for both primary and secondary sales. There is no current catalog of such sales, and the artworks are of the more practical use vein than high art. More on this follows.

Research Methods

The research question used for this work is the following:

> RQ1: What are general practices for contemporary "common artists" to sell their artworks online?

After an initial review of the literature about fine art pricing, an environmental scan was conducted of online storefronts, social image sharing sites, video sharing sites, and other spaces where artists of "common art" congregate to market and sell their artworks. These storefronts are both local and global, given computational affordances, and the only limits have to do with the amount of attraction to the respective works.

Social Media and Art

On the Social Web, there are limited senses of what products art entails. A search of "artmarket" in a related tags network search on the Flickr social image sharing site (using NodeXL and a third-party data exporter) found a sparse network of related tags, including performative art ("music") and presentational art ("painting," "drawing"). There were two groups of sparse tags as clustered using the Clauset-Newman-Moore clustering algorithm (Figure 2 and Table 2).

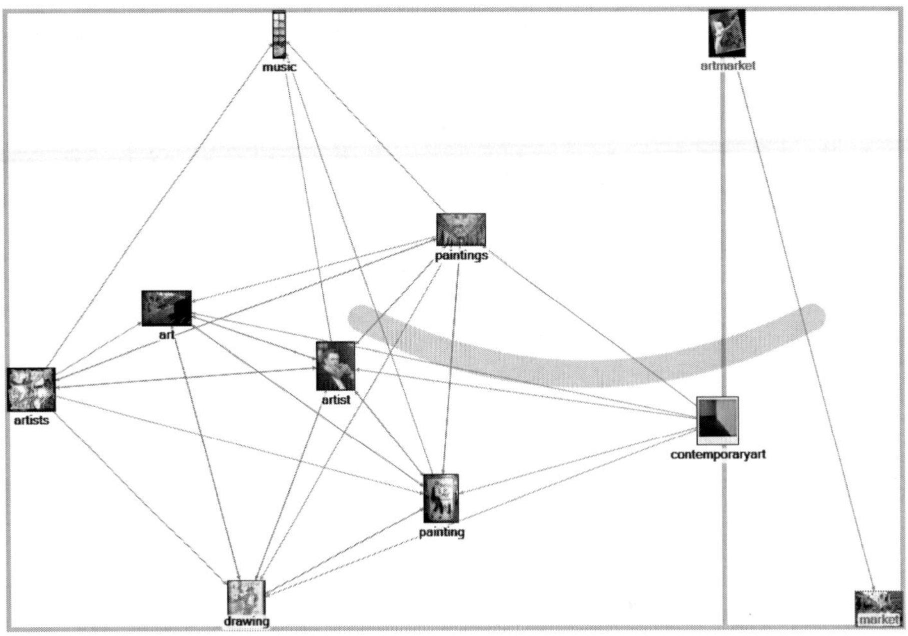

Figure 2. "ArtMarket" related tags network on Flickr social image sharing site.

Table 2. Graph metrics for "ArtMarket" related tags network on Flickr social image sharing site

Graph Metric	Value
Graph Type	Directed
Vertices	10
Unique Edges	43
Edges With Duplicates	0
Total Edges	43
Self-Loops	0
Reciprocated Vertex Pair Ratio	0.303030303
Reciprocated Edge Ratio	0.465116279
Connected Components	1
Single-Vertex Connected Components	0
Maximum Vertices in a Connected Component	10
Maximum Edges in a Connected Component	43
Maximum Geodesic Distance (Diameter)	2
Average Geodesic Distance	1.14
Graph Density	0.477777778
Modularity	Not Applicable
NodeXL Version	1.0.1.336

Results

The artists who share videos of their work involve affable personalities. One says that if people do not want to hear her narrate her work, they can just mute her and use the video to relax. While some may imagine that painting for the camera and the audience behind it is all that easy, it is clear that there is some anxiety for the artists in sharing…and that they have people who may be trolls in their audience. Some host live events and interact with their audiences and even take advice as they draw and paint. The camera is highly zoomed in, so the respective artists sometimes have highly manicured hands. Those who purchase items from these common art artists may do so in part due to the emotional connection with the artist persona and perhaps to support their lifestyles.

A marketplace for art has to meet the needs of various stakeholders. Those who create art need to be able to find buyers for their works, who will buy at a fair price. Those who want to buy art need to find artists with original and authenticated works. All benefit from having fair pricing, so that no one is shorted. Those who would invest in part as financial vehicles need to have artworks which retain their value. The various go-betweens who handle art works have to ensure recourse if buyers or sellers are dissatisfied. All ideally would be law-abiding and pay taxes as needed and adhere to relevant laws in the space. If there are questions about a work's originality, if that is possible to be established, then that should also be addressed. Insurers have to be able to validate the artwork and apply a value to it. People's reputations and privacy should be protected.

There are multiple points-of-entry for people to learn about and start to participate in "common art" or "amateur art" or even "low art." For many, they invest time and effort to learn the craft, and they often purchase the requisite equipment and material to achieve the work. They self-subsidize their own art production. The labor of art creation involves the effort to conceptualize and create the artworks. Their capital outlay may never be recompensed in the larger market, especially if the labor itself is considered immaterial. There is high competition for people's funds, and many will not invest in art unless it somehow resonates with their sense of acquired taste. For many, "common art" is seen as "junk art," "illegitimate art," and even "sub-artistic" in terms of quality. This is not to say that there are not "expert amateurs" in the do-it-yourself (DIY) space (Kuznetsov & Paulos, 2010). However, in general, the alternative art market is not seen as justifying high costs.

Those who want to sell their work may have to work on marketing and other related tasks to find buyers for their work. Many have to deal with mailing artworks back and forth and handling payments and non-payments, whatever the case may be. There are no real economies of scale unless they are making copies and prints, or digital copies. They also have to protect their own copyright. They have to protect their own creative reputation. If they have a trademark, they have to register that. Also, if they have bought their own URL domain, they have to register that and keep that registration updated.

In general, the strategy is to create fast and sell fast. If they can do so with the least friction, they can perhaps earn a little money. Their inputs produce value, even if the general public defines their work as that of artisans, artistes, technicians, and maybe crafters in their market segment. There is a sense that these works are low-brow and targeted to the middle class, with increasing disposable incomes. The pleasures here are to the decorative, for those who want just a little more than "mass produced" imprints that are available off-the-shelf. Perhaps they want the appearance of custom work. These works may offer something a little more unique for self- and other- gifting. Still, in an online space where there are debates around whether user-generated contents are "trash or treasure" (Alluvatti, Capiluppi, De Ruvo, & Molfetta, 2011), the value proposition may be elusive. Not only may the work not justify the initial asked-for price, in some cases, but the asserted value may dissipate in short order, unless there is a user base of individuals who see value in the work and are willing to back up their valuation with purchase (and competition to purchase).

It is unclear how long people conceptualize the lifespan of digital art to be. The longer a work is seen to hold value, the easier it may be to justify a heftier investment. If a work is seen as temporal, that may be understood as potentially less valuable.

For many, their artwork provides a partial side income, and they have to find other ways to make an actual living. A few may be able to make a full living from art, but these are few and far between. Others may be represented by agents, who handle the marketing, the selling, artist representation, the legalities, and other aspects of the work.

Discussion

A democratized approach to art making enriches people's lives broadly, even if most will not have the single-mindedness or the fire or the commitment to develop the related skills to an extreme level or further perhaps the unique vision and artist hand to create various works that resonate with a broad audience. They impetus is not necessarily to express and to have voice, which may be core motivations for many serious artists. Common artists can engage the artful play for personal enjoyment, self-expression, memory, therapeutics, and other reasons. They may engage to entertain their friends. They may engage to earn some money or to engage in barter or trade, both local and online.

Still, this work does raise various questions:

- Are there other methods beyond the offering of videotaped trainings (to patrons, to the general public) and the selling of various artful goods to provide funding streams for common art artists?
- What are some ways to elevate common art to fine art levels? Or something closer?
    - There are implications here for artist skill-building.
    - There are implications here for artist visioning.
    - Is there a stigma of the "cult of the amateur" that may be suppressing prices?
    - Is the practice of emulation too evocative of "knock-off" and "counterfeit" and so contributing to lower prices? Perhaps some works may evoke kitsch? Perhaps some works evoke works-for-hire, like graphic design illustrations?
    - Is there too close of a tie between the common art and the common clothing and household goods on which the imprints are made that are limiting the pricing? Are there ways to change up the reputation of common art?
    - Is there a tie to the locales where common art is sold—county fairs, flea markets, garage sales, and the like—that communicate too much of the "common" and too little of the actual talent and investment in some of the artworks?
    - Are there ways to use buyer competition in auctions to enable the bidding up of common art prices?
    - Are there links between online micropayment sites with access to mass swaths of humanity and the low artist compensation? There are implications here, too, for artist compensation and various paths for these. The model of micropayments may be negative.
- Or would changing the pricing of common art make such works less accessible, less of the practice of common folk? Less available to the general public as potential owners of art?

Perhaps the path of common artists selling to the general public (with the tastes of the general public) is a non-starter for achieving greater heights. Elite and public art have often been considered different things. Elite or high art includes high costs but validation from various experts. This art confers status, and in some cases, it carries with it various pretentions and challenges to value. Common or mass or public art has been a form of entertainment through human societies and histories (Bates & Ferri, Fall 2010, p. 1). These are art for the masses and often priced accessibly for that purpose.

(As a side note, many of the younger new artists who share their works on social videos go to glittery metallic paints as a way to add a dash of "magic." The "less is more" vision maybe comes later for many new artists. Certainly, finding a unique voice and original artist hand does seem to take some years at least. Artists have to control for their initial instincts, perhaps, in order to create a more sophisticated sense of style and voice).

Would it be helpful to set up professional critique of common art? Would it be helpful to have a database of sold artworks in order to raise the institutional memory of their provenance and ownership? What about encouraging collection of quality common art by museums and collectors? What about support by arts funding agencies? Perhaps there can be a page torn from the lessons of formal fine art to raise common art, for those who would like their common art to be more.

Professional artists have "arrived" when they achieve a particular level of recognition, in one sense. On another, they have arrived when they have achieved a particular level of "personal best" in their vision and execution. Still, if their works command certain prices, that may indicate arrival. Is there any such equivalent for non-professional or amateur artists?

Future Research

Future research that would benefit this space would include different approaches to exploring the monetizing of common art. Perhaps there can be research on additional art markets and mechanisms to empower the common art creatives. Some of the questions in the Discussions area may be empirically answered.

Conclusion

As people explore art and different materials and methods and their own senses of vision, they have to survive, and that means paying bills for necessities. A majority of common artists will stay in their respective niches. A few may proceed to higher achievements. If artist biographies are generalized out, each person may experience seminal events that affect their artistic vision. If the biographies are read as general truths, there are particular periods in life when a person is most productive (although a few are able to maintain high productivity well into their later years, with Picasso as an example).

Not all common art practitioners may be interested in additional monetization paths. However, some may, and society may benefit from creating some of these extra paths. There may be benefits for those intermediaries who can add value to the talent of common artists and to their respective works.

Acknowledgments

Thanks to the various common artists whose works I've enjoyed over the years. They shall go unnamed here, however, because I do not want people to read into my writing here and apply them to the respective artists on the Social Web.

References

Abe, A., & Fukushima, K. (2020). How will the information change the sense of values during art appreciation?. *Procedia Computer Science*, *176*, 3083-3092.

Alder, C., Chappell, D., & Polk, K. (2011). Frauds and fakes in the Australian aboriginal art market. Crime, law and social change, 56(2), 189-207.

Alexander, V. D., & Bowler, A. E. (2021). Contestation in aesthetic fields: Legitimation and legitimacy struggles in outsider art. *Poetics*, *84*, 101485.

Alluvatti, G. M., Capiluppi, A., De Ruvo, G., & Molfetta, M. (2011, September). User generated (web) content: trash or treasure. In *Proceedings of the 12th International Workshop on Principles of Software Evolution and the 7th annual ERCIM Workshop on Software Evolution* (pp. 81-90).

Assaf, A. (2018). Testing for bubbles in the art markets: An empirical investigation. *Economic Modelling,* 68, 340 – 355.

Assaf, A., Kristoufek, L., Demir, E., & Mitra, S. K. (2021). Market efficiency in the art markets using a combination of long memory, fractal dimension, and approximate entropy measures. *Journal of International Financial Markets, Institutions and Money*, *71*, 101312, 1-15.

Balietti, S., & Riedl, C. (2021). Incentives, competition, and inequality in markets for creative production. Research Policy, 50(4), 104212, 1-12.

Bates, S., & Ferri, A. J. (2010, Fall). What's entertainment? Notes toward a definition. *Studies in Popular Culture,* 33(1), 1 – 20.

Baumann, S. (2007). A general theory of artistic legitimization: How art worlds are like social movements. *Poetics,* 35, 47 – 65.

Bernales, A., Reus, L., & Valdenegro, V. (2020). Speculative bubbles under supply constraints, background risk and investment fraud in the art market. Journal of Corporate Finance, 101746, 1 - 25.

Bian, T. Y., Huang, J., Zhe, S., & Zhang, M. (2021). Anchoring effects in the Chinese art market. Finance Research Letters, 102050, 1 - 6.

Bianchi, M. (2015). Willingness to believe and betrayal aversion: The special role of trust in art exchanges. *Journal of Cultural Economics*, *39*(2), 133-151.

Bises, B. (1997). Economics and law of works of art in the single European market. *European Journal of Law and Economics*, *4*(4), 311-326.

Blume, J. (2017). Exploring the potentials and challenges of virtual distribution of contemporary art. In *Digital Environments* (pp. 97-116). Transcript-Verlag.

Bocart, F. Y.R.P., & Hafner, C.M. (2012). Econometric analysis of volatile art markets. *Computational Statistics and Data Analysis,* 56, 3091 – 3104.

Bocart, F., & Oosterlinck, K. (2011). Discoveries of fakes: Their impact on the art market. *Economics Letters,* 113, 124 – 126.

Bonus, H., & Ronte, D. (1997). Credibility and economic value in the visual arts. *Journal of cultural economics*, *21*(2), 103-118.

Botta, M., & Wiedemann, K. (2020). To discriminate or not to discriminate? Personalised pricing in online markets as exploitative abuse of dominance. *European Journal of Law and Economics,* 50, 381 – 404.

Buchholz, L., Fine, G.A., & Wohl, H. (2020). Art markets in crisis: How personal bonds and market subcultures mediate the effects of COVID-19. *American Journal of Cultural Sociology,* 8, 462 – 476.

Campbell, R. (2008). Art as a financial investment. *The Journal of Alternative Investments*, *10*(4), 119 - 150.

Canals-Cerdá, J. J. (2012). The value of a good reputation online: An application to art auctions. *Journal of cultural economics,* 36(1), 67-85.

Candela, G., Castellani, M., & Pattitoni, P. (2013). Reconsidering psychic return in art investments. *Economics Letters,* 118, 351 – 354.

Candela, G., & Scorcu, A.E. (1997). A price index for art market auctions. *Journal of Cultural Economics,* 21, 175 – 196.

Caserta, M., & Cuccia, T. (2001). The supply of arts labour: towards a dynamic approach. *Journal of Cultural Economics*, *25*(3), 185-201.

Charlin, V., & Cifuentes, A. (2020). An options-based approach to analyze auction guarantees in the art market. *North American Journal of Economics and Finance,* 51, 101094, 1 – 13.

Charlin, V., & Cifuentes, A. (2017). On the uncertainty of art market returns. *Finance Research Letters,* 21, 186 – 189.

Claassen, M. (2012). Artifacts.Net. *Leonardo.* 45(3), 278 – 279.

Collier, K. (2022, Jan. 10). NFT art sales are booming. Just without some artists' permission. NBCNews.

Coslor, E. (2016). Transparency in an opaque market: Evaluative frictions between 'thick' valuation and 'thin' price data in the art market. *Accounting, Organizations and Society,* 50, 13 – 26.

David, G., Oosterlinck, K., & Szafarz, A. (2013). Art market inefficiency. *Economics Letters,* 121, 23 – 25.

De Marchi, N., & Van Miegroet, H. J. (2006). The history of art markets. *Handbook of the Economics of Art and Culture*, *1*, 69-122.

De Silva, D. G., Pownall, R. A., & Wolk, L. (2012). Does the sun 'shine'on art prices?. *Journal of Economic Behavior & Organization*, *82*(1), 167-178.

Dolgin, A. (2009). The Economic Logic of Creative Reputations. In *The Economics of Symbolic Exchange* (pp. 145-250). Springer, Berlin, Heidelberg.

Ekelund, R. B., Ressler, R. W., & Watson, J. K. (2000). The "Death-Effect" in Art Prices: A Demand-Side Exploration. *Journal of Cultural Economics*, *24*(4), 283-300.

Epstein, Z., Levine, S., Rand, D. G., & Rahwan, I. (2020). Who gets credit for AI-generated art?. *Iscience,* 23(9), 101515, 1 - 16.

Etro, F., & Stepanova, E. (2018). Power-laws in art. *Physica A,* 506, 217 – 220.

Filipiak, D., & Filipowska, A. (2015, June). DBpedia in the art market. In *International Conference on Business Information Systems* (pp. 321-331). Springer, Cham.

Fine, G. A. (2003). Crafting authenticity: The validation of identity in self-taught art. *Theory and Society*, *32*(2), 153-180.

Fletcher, P., & Helmreich, A. (2019). Reframing the "International Art Market." *Studies in the History of Collecting & Art Markets,* 327 - 341.

Fraser, C. A., Dontcheva, M., Kim, J. O., & Klemmer, S. (2019). How live streaming does (and doesn't) change creative practices. *Interactions*, *27*(1), 46-51.

Garay, U. (2021). Determinants of art prices and performance by movements: Long-run evidence from an emerging market. *Journal of Business Research,* 127, 413 – 426.

Goetzmann, W. N. (1993). Accounting for taste: Art and the financial markets over three centuries. *The American Economic Review*, *83*(5), 1370-1376.

Grigoroudis, E., Noël, L., Galariotis, E., & Zopounidis, C. (2021). An ordinal regression approach for analyzing consumer preferences in the art market. *European Journal of Operational Research*, *290*(2), 718-733.

Guzman-Serrano, R. (2019, October). Where there are flies, media art you'll find: Digital (Im) materiality, artistic medium, and media art decay. In *Proceedings of the 9th International Conference on Digital and Interactive Arts* (pp. 1-7).

Hai-Jew, S. (2020). Abstracting Transnational Celebrity (and Sell) on a Social Video Sharing Platform: One 'Neutral' Exemplar. In S. Hai-Jew's *Maintaining Social Well-Being and Meaningful Work in a Highly Automated Job Market.* Hershey, Pennsylvania: IGI Global.

Hausmann, A., & Poellmann, L. (2013). Using social media for arts marketing: Theoretical analysis and empirical insights for performing arts organizations. *International Review of Public Nonprofit Marketing,* 10, 143 – 161.

Hodgson, D.J., & Seçkin, A. (2012) Dynamic price dependence of Canadian and international art markets: An empirical analysis. *Empirical Economics,* 43, 867 – 890.

Horvitz, J. E. (2009). An overview of the art market. *Collectible Investments for the High Net Worth Investor*, 85-117.

Hutter, M., Knebel, C., Pietzner, G., & Schäfer, M. (2007). Two games in town: A comparison of dealer and auction prices in contemporary visual arts markets. *Journal of Cultural Economics,* 31, 247 – 261.

Hutter, M., & Shusterman, R. (2006). Value and the valuation of art in economic and aesthetic theory. *Handbook of the Economics of Art and Culture*, *1*, 169-208.

Ippolito, J. (2002). Ten myths of Internet art. *Leonardo,* 35(5), 485 – 489, 489 – 498. The MIT Press.

Ishiguro, C., & Okada, T. (2021). How Does Art Viewing Inspires Creativity?. *The Journal of Creative Behavior,* 55(2), 489-500.

Ji, S. (2020). The true value of flowers and their effect on the Dutch economy. An interdisciplinary relationship between Art and Economics. *Research in Economics,* 74, 228 – 232.

Kaczynski, S., & Kominers, S.D. (2021, Nov. 10). How NFTs create value. *Harvard Business Review.*

Kharchenkova, S. (2018). The market metaphors: Making sense of the emerging market for contemporary art in China. *Poetics*, *71*, 71-82.

Kim, P., Deng, X., & Unnava, R. (2020). In the eye of the beholder: Cross-pollination between art-infused products and retail spaces. *Journal of Business Research*, *117*, 302-311.

Komarova, N. (2017). Ups and downs of art commerce: Narratives of "crisis" in the contemporary art markets of Russia and India. *Theory and Society*, *46*(4), 319-352.

Kräussl, R., Lehnert, T., & Martelin, N. (2016). Is there a bubble in the art market? *Journal of Empirical Finance,* 35, 99 – 109.

Kräussl, R., & Logher, R. (2010). Emerging art markets. *Emerging Markets Review,* 11, 301 – 318.

Kuznetsov, S., & Paulos, E. (2010, October). Rise of the expert amateur: DIY projects, communities, and cultures. In *Proceedings of the 6th Nordic conference on human-computer interaction: extending boundaries* (pp. 295-304).

La Nasa, J., Campanella, B., Sabatini, F., Rava, A., Shank, W., Lucero-Gomez, P., ... & Modugno, F. (2021). 60 years of street art: A comparative study of the artists' materials through spectroscopic and mass spectrometric approaches. *Journal of Cultural Heritage*, *48*, 129-140.

Lagier, J., & Godey, B. (2007). A scale for measuring aesthetic style in the field of luxury and art products. *International Journal of Arts Management*, 39-50.

Landes, W. M., & Levine, D. B. (2006). The economic analysis of art law. *Handbook of the economics of art and culture*, *1*, 211-251.

Lehman, K., Wickham, M., & Fillis, I. (2018). Exploring supply-side network interactions in the visual art production process. *Poetics*, *69*, 57-69.

Lucińska, A. (2015). The art market in the European Union. *International Advances in Economic Research*, *21*(1), 67-79.

Lind, R. (1992). The aesthetic essence of art. *The Journal of Aesthetics and Art Criticism*, *50*(2), 117-129.

Markowitz, S. J. (1994). The distinction between art and craft. *Journal of Aesthetic Education*, *28*(1), 55-70.

McCarthy, K. (2021, May 16). What are NFTs? Everything you need to know about non-fungible tokens: Explaining the unique digital assets. ABC News.

Molnár, V. (2018). The business of urban coolness: Emerging markets for street art. *Poetics*, *71*, 43-54.

Munteanu, A., & Pece, A. (2015). Investigating art market efficiency. Heritage as an Alternative Driver for Sustainable Development and Economic Recovery in South East Europe. *Procedia – Social and Behavioral Sciences,* 188, 82 – 88.

Nahm, J. (2010). Price determinants and genre effects in the Korean art market: a partial linear analysis of size effect. *Journal of cultural economics*, *34*(4), 281-297.

Newman, G. E., & Smith, R. K. (2018). Artworks are evaluated as extensions of their creators. *Advances in experimental philosophy of aesthetics*, 103-122.

Ollivier, M. (2008). Modes of openness to cultural diversity: Humanist, populist, practical, and indifferent. *Poetics*, *36*(2-3), 120-147.

O'Neil, K. M. (2008). Bringing art to market: The diversity of pricing styles in a local art market. *Poetics,* 36, 94–113.

Pace, T., O'Donnell, K., DeWitt, N., Bardzell, S., & Bardzell, J. (2013, February). From organizational to community creativity: Paragon leadership & creativity stories at Etsy. In *Proceedings of the 2013 conference on computer supported cooperative work* (pp. 1023-1034).

Pareschi, L., & Lusiani, M. (2020). What editors talk about when they talk about editors? A public discourse analysis of market and aesthetic logics. *Poetics*, *81*, 101444, 1-14.

Park, H., Ju, L., Liang, T., & Tu, Z. (2017). Horizon analysis of art investments: Evidence from the Chinese market. *Pacific-Basin Finance Journal*, *41*, 17-25.

Pénasse, J., Renneboog, L., & Spaenjers, C. (2014). Sentiment and art prices. *Economics Letters,* 432 – 434.

Prown, J. D. (1980). Style as evidence. *Winterthur Portfolio*, *15*(3), 197-210.

Rhodes, J. D. (2012). Belabored: Style as work. *Framework: The Journal of Cinema and Media*, *53*(1), 47-64.

Rubião, R. M. (2018). A Short but Deep Dive into the Economics of Arts: Art Entrepreneurs in a Peripheral Market. *Artivate*, *7*(2), 3-26.

Samdanis, M., & Lee, S.H. (2019). Uncertainty, strategic sensemaking and organizational failure in the art market: What went wrong with LVMH's investment in Phillips auctioneers? *Journal of Business Research,* 98, 475–488.

Santagata, W. (2010). The Market in Contemporary Art. In *The Culture Factory* (pp. 85-92). Springer, Berlin, Heidelberg.

Schönfeld, S., & Reinstaller, A. (2007). The effects of gallery and artist reputation on prices in the primary market for art: A note. *Journal of Cultural Economics*, *31*(2), 143-153.

Shusterman, R. (2003). Entertainment: A question for aesthetics. *The British Journal of Aesthetics*, *43*(3), 289-307.

Singer, L.P., & Lynch, G.A. (1997). Are multiple art markets rational? *Journal of Cultural Economics,* 21, 197–218.

Sooudi, O. K. (2010). Market memories. Collective memory and art market change in Mumbai. *Poetics*, *71*, 83-94.

Sung, M. (2022, Jan. 4). Creators turn to public shaming to seek compensation from brands they say don't credit them. NBCNews.

Taylor, J., Cardenas, M., & Edwards, S. (2019). Measuring Art Markets: The Colorado Art Market in 2017. *Artivate*, *8*(2), 5-19.

Thomas, K. (2019). When Disney came to Broadway: Assessing the impact of corporatization in an art world. *Poetics*, *77*, 101384.

Tschacher, W., & Tröndle, M. (2011). A dynamic systems perspective on fine art and its market. *Futures*, *43*(1), 67-75.

Wang, Q., Ogilvie, dt, & Richardson, L. (2021). Race/ethnicity, place, and art and culture entrepreneurship in underserved communities. *Cities,* 115, 103243, 1–10.

Worthington, A.C., & Higgs, H. (2003). Art as an investment: Short and long-term comovements in major painting markets. *Empirical Economics,* 28, 649–668.

Zeilinger, M. (2018). Digital art as 'monetised graphics': Enforcing intellectual property on the blockchain. *Philosophy & Technology,* 31(1), 15-41.

Zolberg, V. L. (2010). Marginality triumphant? On the asymmetry of conflict in the art world. *International Journal of Politics, Culture, and Society*, *23*(2-3), 99-112.

Chapter 12

Narrowbanding as a "Common Art" Artist Self-Branding Strategy Online

Shalin Hai-Jew*
Kansas State University, Manhattan, KS, USA

Abstract

On the Social Web, "common art" artists make their reputations by producing works with a particular style or look-and-feel. Their unique "hand" is sometimes bolstered by a recognizable name and a public persona. The various styles range from "starter" ones to more "established" ones, informed by informal to nonformal to formal training. The speed of the Web and Internet requires that artists' works are recognizable at a glance, based on a simplifying visual shorthand. Those who sell works may experience external motivations to cater to particular customers who prefer particular styles. These pressures, on the one hand, force artists into "narrowbanding" and going to a distinctive style or two. This narrowbanding militates against expanding talent range through various explorations, atypical styles, different media, multimedia, and other experimentations. On the other hand, artists need to continually grow or else stagnate and ossify into a particular practice. This work explores how general "style" is understood from common art shared on Web 2.0 through bottom-up coding, and this includes the exploration of the phenomenon of narrow bands (vs. wider ones).

Keywords: narrowbanding, common art, common artist, self-branding, widebanding, Social Web

Introduction

A popular image of an artist is one who works in a studio alone and creates works for a target audience of the wealthy collectors or a broad general public willing to engage online. In the current social moment, "common art" makers engage socially online. They hold web streams with other artists, with whom they co-create. They release works on their social image-sharing channels. They post works on web logs. They engage both patrons and followers on social video sharing sites. They find their smaller online communities on art social sites. They engage in peer-sharing of ideas and tips. Art, even when created in relative isolation in some cases,

* Corresponding Author's Email: haijes@gmail.com

In: Common Visual Art in a Social Digital Age
Editor: Shalin Hai-Jew
ISBN: 978-1-68507-664-1

does not emerge into an isolated world. In most cases, people make art that is viewed by and responded to by others. There is a communications element to the creation of art, where the artwork is the "message," even if the message is polysemous. One researcher writes: "...visual art is an instance of human communication, where the latter is understood in a biological sense, as coordinated behavior among organisms" (Straffon, 2016, p. 368). The larger society helps define what is seen as potentially artful, the materials and technologies that can be used to create art, the applied techniques, the historical context into which a current art emerges, and other dimensions.

"Common art" is generally referred to as amateur works by non-professionals. For some, such works may be private and used to help the individual artist work out issues. For others, they are creating works to a peer audience, to friends and family, to colleagues, and to a larger marketplace.

Those who are forming a social persona as an artist and who are perhaps creating a market for their works often work towards a particular style, a distinctive look-and-feel for their works. The high online competition, the speed of people's judgments, and the challenges of attaining sales online all force a "common artist" to converge on a style that "works" and to stick with that. After all, they have created a reputation and a niche for their work. They have found a formula that appeals to various individuals, such as patrons and shoppers. In such a context, how can common artists work towards personal growth, exploration, and evolving their unique artist "hand"?

Research Questions

This work explores three main interrelated research questions (RQs):

> RQ1: What are the common observable "common art" styles among "common art" practitioners on the Social Web? (Or: What is in the narrowbanding of art styles among common art artists on the Social Web?)
>
> RQ2: What are "common art" styles among "common art" practitioners on the Social Web that seem to be outside the apparent narrowbanding? What is in the widebanding or "long tail" of common art shared on the Social Web? What are some types of novel works?
>
> RQ3: What are ways to encourage wider artful experimentation among "common art" artists, to expand their "narrow" bands, even with the pressures to narrowband online?

The shared artworks must have something distinctive if they are to be remembered. In the public are forgettable works that do not observe "the first rule of artistic production" which is having a "*uniquely identifiable style*" (Bäcklund, 2016, p. 2). Getting to that point is no mean feat, given the thousands of hours needed to achieve expertise. While learners may engage in emulation along the way, they should not remain there. The more original their work, the more valuable it may be for others to engage with their efforts. One author writes:

> Yet the more complicated and elusive the style, the more does it stimulate exploration and reward success with illumination. An obvious style, easily identified by some superficial quirk,

> is properly decried as a mere mannerism. A complex and subtle style...resists reduction to a literal formula. (Goodman, 1975, p. 811)

Then, once that art style is displayed, there are risks of competitive infringements by others who try to emulate the style. Several research works debate how much of an artist's visual style and "trade dress" (of trademark law) might apply.

The research is focused around 1,068 social images seeded with the term "common art" from Google Images. Also, several well-known common art artists on YouTube, Instagram, and other sites were profiled based on their works.

Review of the Literature

In art, where does "visual style" reside? Is it in nature and evolution? Is it in the society from which a work or an artist or a school of art emerges? Is it in the person of the artist? The group of the artists? Is it in the work itself? Or does visual style reside in any number of areas simultaneously?

Visual Style Resides in Evolution and Human Biology View

According to some thinking, there is a competitive advantage for humanity to engage is aesthetic considerations, to enable cooperation. Charles Darwin postulated on aesthetic theory, with the following ideas:

> (1) the sense of beauty is a perceptual discrimination mechanism, internal and functional to the theoretical framework of sexual selection; (2) consequently, the sense of beauty is a powerful engine of change in structures and mental qualities of the species through a coevolutionary relationship with the bodily features of individuals; and (3) it is a crucial element in confirming the cognitive continuity between humans and other animals because its phylogeny reveals the origin of a sense of beauty in an evolutionary phase that precedes the development of human cognitive architecture. (Portera & Bartalesi, 2016, p. 380)

A core question is whether people are hard-wired to respond to aesthetics, or if they learn aesthetics culturally, in social contexts. The question is phrased as follows: "Are all aesthetic preferences in humans universal, innate, and therefore genetically encoded or do they emerge as a consequence of the mere exposure to cultural models?" (Portera & Bartalesi, 2016, p. 386) The general accepted understanding is that "nature and culture *really, factually* interact with each other, in forging and shaping humans and their preferences" (Portera & Bartalesi, 2016, p. 386).

There is the evolutionary angle, which is seen to affect the aesthetic sensibilities and preferences (Portera & Bartalesi, 2016, p. 375), with particular human needs met via art. It is thought that "human aesthetic sense originated during the so-called 'Upper Paleolithic Revolution' (also known as the 'Creative Explosion': 50,000 – 45,000 years B.C." (Portera & Bartalesi, 2016, p. 375).

Visual Style Resides in Society

"Visual art is one of the most characteristic human cultural traits" and is a "universal presence" extending over the past 100,000 years (Straffon, 2016, p. 357) and some say longer. Visual art meets human needs in various ways. Visual art serves as "a communication signal expressed in material media" (Straffon, 2016, p. 360). The shared understandings emerge from human cooperative behavior. This researcher writes about visual style:

> In colloquial terms, style means simply a way of doing things. But in archaeology, style generally refers to formal variability, or specific patterns of variation in the form of artifacts that are socially constrained (Chase 1991). Style as repeated patterning is not only a property of material culture, but it also pervades all human actions and institutions (e.g., diet, language, ritual, etc.), to the extent that they belong in a particular cultural context. Explaining how style itself comes into being need not invoke agency or intentionality. For instance, style can arise spontaneously as a side-effect of grouping; that is by simply living in a community, sharing a location, doing things together, and learning from each other, individuals can generate patterned behavior distinctive of their group (van der Post and Hogeweg 2008. And once certain patterns start being used in identical fashion in a group, they may become conventional and begin to serve for communication—they become a signal (Luria and Vygotsky 1992:57). Style in material culture can then be used as an active strategy to transmit information (Wobst 1977), so that differences in style can convey identity, affiliation or status. (Straffon, 2016, p. 365)

"Visual art style" is also a social signal, revealing intra-group and inter-group social markers. How people decorate themselves—through tattoos, through jewelry—authenticate their sense of belongingness. On a tangent, there is so much overlap in terms of the qualities of luxury and fine art that a common scale was created to assess the aesthetic style of such products (Lagier & Godey, 2007). Knowledge of both luxury and art, in particular of aesthetic styles, cognitively and emotionally, enables people to compare the art objects "with norms, with historical and social references" and better interpret the object and understand its financial value (Lagier & Godey, 2007, p. 44). There are emotional gains to be had as well. An appreciation of art through aesthetics may lead to a "search for sensations, for emotions, for pleasure" or evoke a "desire to escape, to relax, to forget" or spark a "need for discovery, adventure" and trigger an "expectation of variety" (Lagier & Godey, 2007, p. 44).

Understanding the particular historical moment, the socio-cultural context, and other elements is important in the understanding of art. Archaeological evidence may come into play in a time of artistic production.

Style is "a distinguishable ensemble of such characteristics" that make a definable pattern over "sufficiently extensive spans of time of geographical distance" (Ackerman, 1962, p. 227). In some cases, some artworks "lose all extrinsic evidence of their historical position, so no record survives of the artist(s), era, or locale which produced them" and leave works unmoored from time and space (Ackerman, 1962, p. 227). The historical record for art has large gaps for known artists much less lesser-known ones. Style is a way of "establishing relationships among individual works of art" (Ackerman, 1962, p. 228). In another sense, an art style is "a class of related solutions to a problem—or responses to a challenge" (Ackerman, 1962, p. 236), with practitioners influencing each other in a particular context. The idea that how people engage style in the larger society relates to their sense of alignment with the culture or whether they are taking a contested stance (Arnheim, 1981, p. 281), given that the arts are a method of "coping with the environment" (p. 288).

Visual Style Resides in the Artist and Their Unique Hand

Another view is that art style comes from the "exteriorizing" of the "interior" self to the world (Schapiro, as cited in Rhodes, Spring 2012, p. 49). Art is often analyzed through a biographical framework, through the "artists' personal knowledge and view" given that visual art was seen to reflect the creator's subjective sensibilities (Liu, Pu, & Xu, 2013, p. 1). This is one common understanding in an individualistic society, and perhaps beyond. Style in visual art is a "high-level semantic concept" requiring "human knowledge and experience" (Yang & Xu, 2011, p. 375). Art style is "labor" or what an "artist or artwork *does*" (Rhodes, Spring 2012, p. 48). Art style may stem from the internalization of social matter into the artist, who then expresses the ideas in their own work. In this process, they gain something of the group and perhaps lose something of themselves:

> If style is the signature of a group or an individual, then style is individuation-as-such, and individuation-as-subsumption (not quite disappearance, but certainly a form of deindividuation), which is also to say that style is signature *and* erasure. (Rhodes, Spring 2012, p. 48)

This is not to say that the individual artist does not bring something of their own motivation and will. One researcher writes: "Style is labor and the trace of labor (what labor leaves behind), an imposition of the will on the world, and in a manner that has not been prescribed. It is thus unlike other forms of labor in which the outcome is predicted and predictable" (Rhodes, Spring 2012, p. 59). There have been studies parsing out the various character traits of those who create art. One study suggests that those that create art are seen to have "complex" personalities, with greater ranges of variability in "responses to items measuring the same overall trait" (Haller & Courvoisier, 2010, p. 149). Visual art students were found to have "greater complexity in conscientiousness" than "psychology and music students" (Haller & Courvoisier, 2010, p. 149).

Visual Style Resides in Artwork View

A traditional approach suggests that visual style may be ascertained by analyzing the particular artwork, particular two general factors: form and style. In one seminal work, the author offered the idea that "subject is what is said, style is how" but then goes on to debunk this oversimplification of visual style. For example, "nonobjective painting" (non-representational painting) does not have a defined subject…and in some works, aspects of the subject inform on style (Goodman, 1975, p. 799). Conceptual or ideational art, abstract art, and other forms also do not aspire to representation. Another researcher writes:

> Form is restricted to the configuration of the object itself, while style refers to a distinctive manner or mode which, whether consciously intended or not, bears a relationship with other objects marked in their form by similar qualities. The argument... is that style is inescapably culturally expressive, that the formal data embodied in objects are therefore of value as cultural evidence, and that the analysis of style can be useful for other than purely art historical studies. (Prown, 1980, p. 197)

Various analytics are applied to authenticate or dis-authenticate works (Prown, 1980, p. 209).

Human Perception and Art

How different people view art depends on various factors. There is the biological angle, or the sense of physical sight, with various color and other perception. In representational art, the time course (or microgenesis) of art perception has been tested, with the finding that visual "content" is apprehended first [from 10 milliseconds (ms) onwards] and then style (at 50 milliseconds) (Augustin, Leder, Hutzler, & Carbon, 2008, p. 127). The research team explains:

> ...the development of the effect sizes of both effects over time suggests that a presentation time of only 10 ms seems to be sufficient for participants to extract information about similarity of content, and additional presentation time does not result in a general change of the relevance of content. Style, in contrast, steadily gains in relevance with increasing presentation time; the longer the time of exposure, the more stylistic information is extracted and drawn upon for judgment. In addition, the results of both experiments indicate that style is more relevant if content is kept constant... (Augustin, Leder, Hutzler, & Carbon, 2008, p. 135)

While they found processing saturation at 202 ms, style-based processing was ... "gaining in relevance throughout the timespan of 50 – 3000 ms" or up to about 3 seconds (Augustin, Leder, Hutzler, & Carbon, 2008, p. 136). A follow-on work about how visual art is perceived also found that art-specific content and art-specific style is visually perceived at different speeds. They write of the time course of art perception:

> Analyses of both measures support the notion that in the processing of art style follows content, with style-related information being available at around 224 ms or between 40 and 94 ms later than content-related information. (Augustin, Defranceschi, Fuchs, Carbon, & Hutzler, 2011, p. 2071)

The sequentiality of human perception in seeing art informs on yet another dimension of human visual systems that inform on the creation of art. Certainly, the appreciation of visual art goes well beyond sub-second views and involves longer-term viewing and re-viewing.

Formal Art Critique

Style is a key component of an artwork's meaning. The learning of visual style and the appreciation of aesthetics require cognitive art knowledge and emotional awareness. How art is received is also based in part on "the affective states of the viewers as well as their ability for cognitive mastery, measured by amount of expertise" (Belke, Leder, & Augustin, 2006, p. 115).

An art style is not considered generally inherent in a work because the viewer's sensibility is also important (as well as the intersubjectivities among viewers in the plural). One researcher has asked how to put aesthetics on more solid ground theoretically (Mezei, 1981), to move beyond the subjective to the more objective. There seems to be general agreement that visual style is in particular parts of a work and not "everywhere in a work of art" (Rhodes, Spring 2012, p. 47). Others have observed that how people think about style may be counterproductive:

> Now the phenomenon of style is not an object but a concept. We wrongly assign to style the constancy of an object in perception whenever we examine it diachronically. We have seen, however, that style depends on synchronous choices among synonymous possibilities, and that style itself is a phenomenon in perception without objective properties as to duration. (Kubler, 1979, 1987, p. 173)

Style is "extension in space rather than as duration" and the "purified residue would be an appreciably more useful tool of thought than when it is made to describe time as in conventional histories of the arts of expression…I have argued for the restriction of visual style to the description of nondurational, synchronous situations composed of related events" (Kubler, 1979, 1987, p. 173). The definition of art style is broadened and changing.

Various Computational Ways to Understand Visual Art Style

In the age of the Fourth Industrial Revolution (4IR), computational thinking and applications have been applied to art style. There are various of stylometry (style + metrics) in the visual art space. Deep neural network analysis has been applied to extract the main semantics of particular art styles. This work examined concepts such as "light, shape, pattern, line, and textures" (Kim, Liu, Elgammal, & Mazzone, Jan. 2018, p. 156). Another approach uses deep learning to identify art styles through the extraction of textual features (Chen & Yang, Oct. 2019). Several works involve the identifying of visual and other indicators to identify particular art styles from art imagesets, based on machine vision and machine learning (Lecoutre, Negrevergue, & Yger, 2017; Yang & Xu, 2011). These capabilities enable database managers to index large databases of artworks and to filter them by artistic style. Machine vision and machine learning algorithms have been applied to image datasets with aesthetic ratings to most effectively predict style and genre, with various curated art image datasets to advance the field (Karayev, Trentacoste, Han, Agarwala, Darrell, Hertzmann, & Winnemoeller, 2014, p. 1). Another program uses computational means to define periods of art styles based on Web data (De Boer, Van Someren, & Wielinga, June 2006). This work engages the following art styles and computationally identifies the start and end dates in history to capture periodicity: Abstract Expressionism, Art Deco, Art Nouveau, Baroque, Bauhaus, Counter-Reformation, Cubist, Dada, Expressionist, Impressionist, Mannerist, Neo-Impressionist, Post-Impressionism, Pre-Raphaelite, Reformation, Rococo, and Surrealist in the particular study (De Boer, Van Someren, & Wielinga, June 2006, p. 1620). Decades earlier, an art researcher observed: "Conventions of form and of symbolism yield the richest harvest of traits by which to distinguish style" where conventions are "an accepted vocabulary of elements" (Ackerman, 1962, p. 229). One work involves identifying style similarity between various vector clipart, based on variables such as "color, shading, texture, and stroke" (Garces, Agarwala, Gutierrez, & Hertzmann, 2014, p. 1).

Novel Machine-Generated Art in Defined Art Styles

Visual art may be identified by a set of defined rules learned by AI and then applied to generate novel art in particular styles. Computers have been used to generate artwork. One program that does this is part of a class called Creative Adversarial Networks (CANs). Here, the program creates art based on particular styles but deviates somewhat from the artworks used to train the algorithms for novelty ["by deviating from the learned styles" (Elgammal, Liu, Elhoseiny, & Mazzone, 2017, p. 1)]. The created artworks are then tested in the program to see if these works can "pass" as just another example in the art style set.

Computational Visual Art Style Transfer

There are also public commercially available software programs that transfer "visual styles" from one visual work to another. These include the transfer of color palettes, lines, and other aspects of visual style.

Research Methods

Art styles are broadly seen to develop from crude initial states to more refined (Ackerman, 1962), in both form and symbolism. Similarly, common artists may be understood to develop along a general trajectory. There is perhaps interest in art, some appreciation of it. Perhaps there is some light training, whether informal (incidental learning from normal life activities), nonformal (non-accredited learning), or formal (accredited learning). The "common art" artist experiments with various materials and techniques. The idea is to move beyond the rudimentary skills, typified by "school art" or homework styles. With sufficient investment, a sense of original vision and skill may be arrived at. In general, most stop short. Where most start broad and then converge on some favorite outputs, the idea is to start broad and stay broad while developing a variety of skills. The narrowing is a risk because it leads to lock-in, often premature. "Common art" artists are not assumed to all start with the same resources and opportunities.

This work then involves a review of the literature. This is augmented with visual analysis of social media data scraping of common artist works from across the Social Web. Included in the analysis is a set from Google Images Search with the seeding terms "common art." The tags to use for filtering were the following: "uncommon, creative, simple, greenham, mistakes, contemporary, rapper, renaissance, old, paint, life, anatomy, rene magritte, covid, portfolio, myrtle beach, art portfolio, portrait, boston ma, covid 19, contemporary art, lynn aldrich, acrylic painting, exhibition, media, drawing, facebook, flower." The 1,068 visuals were downloaded as thumbnails (Figure 1).

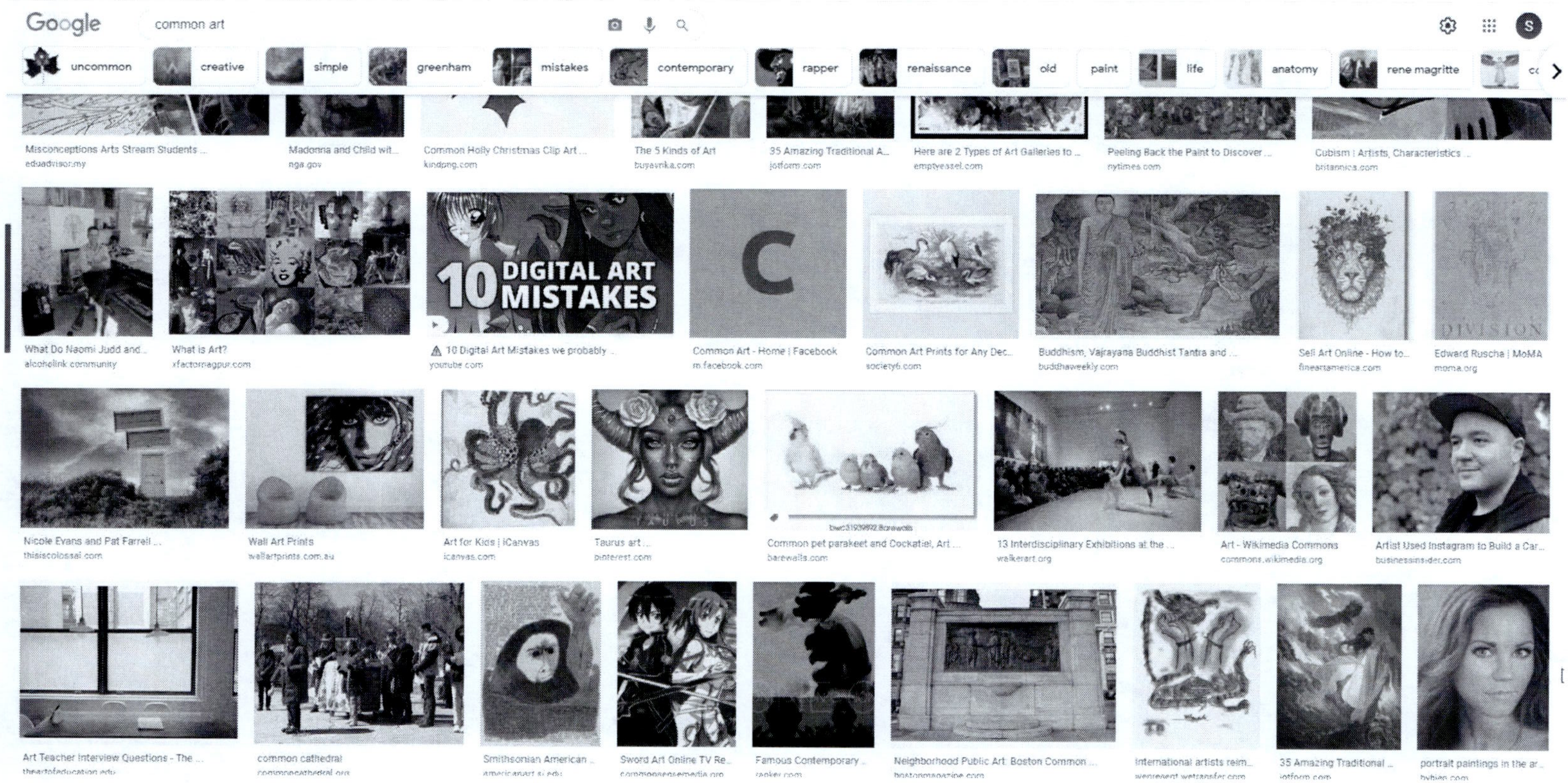

Figure 1. "Common Art" social image search (via Google Images Search).

Results

The "common art" social imageset was processed in various ways to provide a baseline understanding of the contents first.

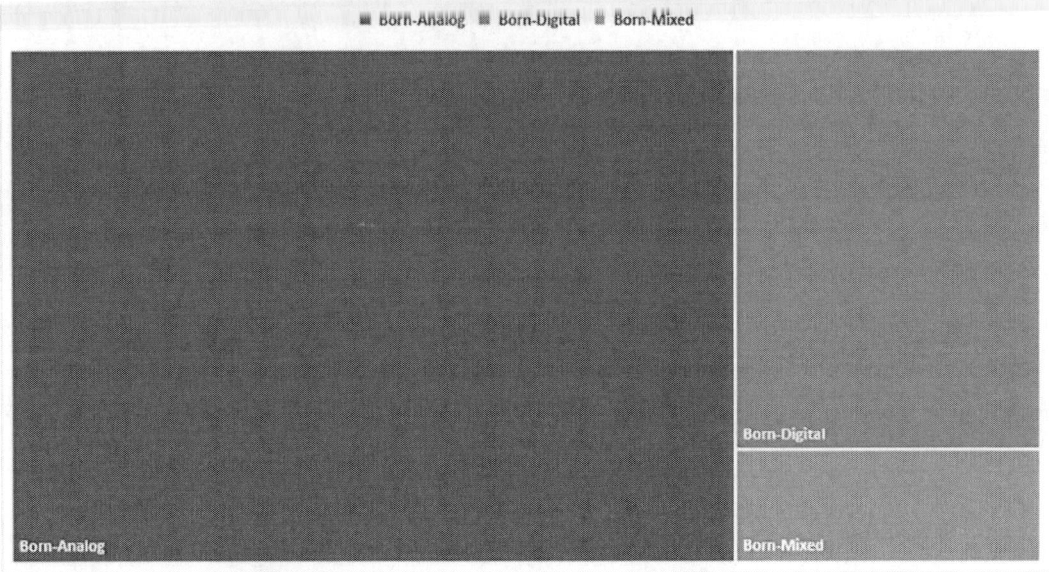

Figure 2. Born-Analog, Born-Digital, or Born-Mixed Works (area chart).

Born-Analog, Born-Digital, and Born-Mixed

First, an initial walk-through of these social images captured a sense of the origin of the visual. The "born-analog" would include physical paintings, physical drafts and drawings, physical sculptures, whiteboard drawings, murals, posters, dioramas, rocks, sculptured materials, hyperreal drawings on paper, book covers, collages, and real-world scenes. The original seeding image is considered from real-space. The "born-digital" visuals include images that were not seeded with a physical work but created apparently from scratch using digital drawing and diagraming software, drawing tablets, and so on. The ideas were originated in digital format. Some 3D scenes from machinima would be born-digital since the original scene was an online one. Then, the born-mixed category would be a work that combines elements that were clearly analog at one point and then elements that were included that were born-digital. (Table 1) Trying to understand the original "born" state of a visual work does involve some rough inference-making. The precision is not likely going to be as high as some other types of visual coding, say, by computer. It is not practical to engage endless recursion back to fully identify how a work originated. Fortunately, some artworks are highly recognizable, and their original states are clear. Digital artworks have a particular look and feel. The distribution is interesting because a large percentage of the works are born-analog (71%), then born-digital (23%), and then born-mixed (7%). [The percentages were rounded up.]

Table 1. Born-Analog, Born-Digital, or Born-Mixed Works

Born-Analog	Born-Digital	Born-Mixed (analog and digital)
949	311	87

Modalities of the "Common Art" Visuals

Then, the next walk-through of the social imagery involved identifying the type of modality in this "common art" social imageset. A modality is a form, not content per se (although there was some overlap here). A rough categorization of the file types was created after multiple iterated walk-throughs to saturation. These are listed in alphabetical order. (Table 2 and Figure 3) Again, the social imagery used was from the same imageset, but the different focus means different insights. Also, as noted before, some works may be cited in several categories. Some work may be multi-panel ones. So the numbers will not match up perfectly to the 1,068 collected social images.

The "cartoon" category included some manga characters, and some Disney ones (Mickey Mouse, Donald Duck, and Winnie the Pooh). The "drawing, sketching" category includes charcoal, pen and ink, and digital drawings and sketches; these include works from basic to highly sophisticated. The "icon, logo" included smaller digital objects. The "illustration" category includes analog and digital pictures such as those created to exemplify or describe particular visual phenomena in magazines and other publications. "Land art" involved depiction of artwork extended over a large expanse of land, with the artwork viewed aerially. "Machinima" refers to stills from machine + cinema, often from immersive virtual worlds and immersive game spaces. "Map" refers to anything represented land masses depicted in visual format. "Mixed media, collage" refers to sculptures, blow-up plastic visuals, and textured embroidery. "Mural" refers to various paintings on walls and arched ceilings and even a panel relief sculpture. Several works showed a blue-garbed healthcare working with colorful wings behind. (In the time of the SARS-CoV-2/COVID-19 pandemic, healthcare workers have taken on the brunt of the work at trying to save human lives through their profession and public messaging.) "Painting" refers to works using various pigmenting/coloring agents: watercolor, oil, acrylic, and digital. "Photo, scan" captures works captured using photography or flatbed (or camera) scanning. "Poster" refers to a digital visual of a paper poster or a digital version of a digital poster. The poster style has a particular look-and-feel. "Rough Sketch" refers to an undeveloped visual that has been manually created. This category can include doodles. "Screenshot" refers to a screen capture of a website or web application or graphical user interface. "Tattoo" refers to body art. These images include crossed tattooed forearms, a tree tattoo on an upper arm, an arm with an octopus tattoo sleeve, a horse tattoo, and a photo showing a tattoo being applied live. "Video Still" refers to a screengrab from a video, such as a television show or a movie. "Word(s)" refer to visuals in which words are the main focus. These include some advertisements flogging events and name brands.

Table 2. Social visual types by modality (from "Common Art" social imageset)

Social Visual Types (by Modality)	Frequency Counts
Cartoon	13
Drawing, Sketching	72
Icon, Logo	7
Illustration	234
Land Art	1
Machinima	5
Map	2
Mixed Media, Collage	80
Mural	28
Painting	496
Photo, Scan	285
Poster	10
Rough Sketch	11
Screenshot	11
Tattoo	8
Video Still	2
Word(s)	128

The same data may be seen in Figure 3. Here, the various modalities are the following, in descending order: paintings, photos/scans, illustrations, words, mixed media/collage, drawing/sketching, mural, cartoon, rough sketch, screenshot, poster, tattoo, icon/logo, machinima, map, video still, and land art. Note that the table is in alphabetical order but that the Pareto chart is in descending order.

These are rough codings, but they do show something of the frequency distribution of the various modality forms of the visual works. More coding follows, but those address some of the direct research questions. To review, the research questions are the following:

> RQ1: What are the common observable "common art" styles among "common art" practitioners on the Social Web? (Or: What is in the narrowbanding of art styles among common art artists on the Social Web?)

> RQ2: What are "common art" styles among "common art" practitioners on the Social Web that seem to be outside the apparent narrowbanding? What is in the widebanding or "long tail" of common art shared on the Social Web? What are some types of novel works?

> RQ3: What are ways to encourage wider artful experimentation among "common art" artists, to expand their "narrow" bands, even with the pressures to narrowband online?

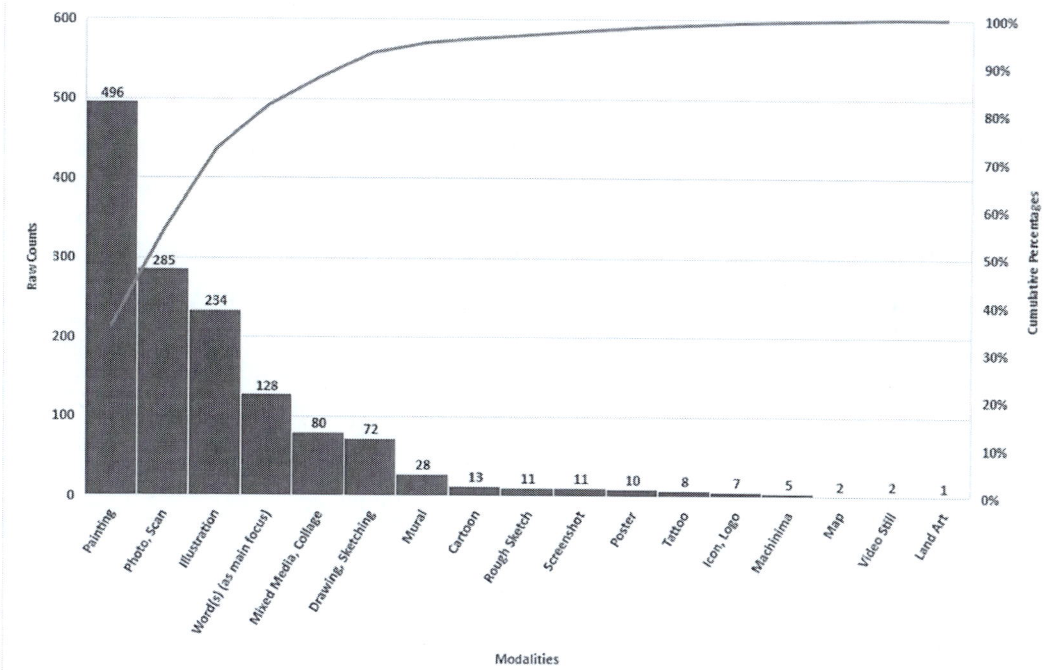

Figure 3. Social visual types by modality (from "Common Art" social imageset).

More in-depth insights follow, structured by the questions.

> RQ1: What are the common observable "common art" styles among "common art" practitioners on the Social Web? (Or: What is in the narrowbanding of art styles among common art artists on the Social Web?)

In terms of "common art" styles, based on bottom-up coding of the images, there are some recognizable patterns.

Coding imagery inherent involves some level of ambiguity. Imagery are multi-dimensional, and depending on the variables being observed in the coding table, a work may fit into several categories. While there were efforts to try to code an image with only one category, if several others applied, those were added. Some images were diptychs. Some had up to 15 – 16 sub-images. And one was a mosaic with hundreds of small images. The general idea was to keep an image as one. However, in compound visuals where there were clearly multiple images with discernible contents, those were coded as multiple images. Another source of ambiguity involves the fact that the images are mostly thumbnails with low spatial resolution. Even with the aid of zooming and of reverse image search through online tools, there are still limits to fully re-identifying some works. Also, inferring intention of the "common art" artist (Did they intend representation and figure but end up with abstraction?) can be challenging.

The iterated coding does enable seeing the social imageset with new eyes. As a case in point, there were two lewd images and one with a human body part that the author had not noticed in the first few rounds of coding, in part based on the art style, in part based on the nature of an illustration. The coding did focus on the centrality of visuals, the sizing, the foregrounding, and the uses of color. Even with one person coding over a number of days, there were some inconsistencies. Sequentiality was also seen to sometimes have an effect. For example, if one image looks clearly to be a mural, and the following one or two visuals also could be, there was a higher likelihood of the following images to be identified as such. As in qualitative research, the coding may vary somewhat day-to-day. What is seen as salient may change a little. The different coding frameworks for the different tables do affect what one sees.

The coding table may be viewed at Table 3. The coding table was set up based on bottom-up coding (from the image data) in general related clusters.

Table 3. Social visual types by subject matter (from "Common Art" social imageset)

Visual Types (by Subject Matter)	Frequency Counts (of Each Visual)
3D Work	73
Abstract Work	80
Doodle	5
Virtual World, Website	5
Group Human Figures	157
Individual Human Figures	300
Human Synecdoche (parts representing wholes)	33
Human Self-Portrait	6
Group Animal Figures	43
Individual Animal Figures	90
Humans and Animals Together	31
Melded Humanoid Animals, Animalistic Humans	5
Village View	5
City View	4
Landscape Painting, Nature Scenery	58
Night Scene	11
Food	2
Plants, Florals	102
Fruit Still-Life Work	16
Classic 17th - 20th Century Artwork (? Check the years of the artworks)	46
Contemporary Artwork, Some in Art Spaces	203
Artist Studio (and Art Supplies)	75
Building (Interiors and Exteriors)	53
Patterning	15
Futuristic Scenery	29
Mural	34
Logo, Brand	15
Digital Icon	2
Composite, Mashup	14
Photo Mosaic	1
Map	3
Messaging, Direct Conveyance of Information	107

"3D" includes sculptures, bas reliefs, jewelry, mannequins, outdoor sculptures, a giant gold vase, ceramic waves, foil embossing, art installations, fiber art, industrial machinery, and other materials. "Abstract Work" includes works of ink swirls, a looped line, a painting comprised of ellipses and dots, and many others. "Doodle" includes less detailed drawings, such as of simple flowers. "Virtual World, Website" includes screenshots of various online spaces. Human figures were very common in the imageset, whether in groups or as individuals. The groups showed couples, farmhands, children in a classroom, dancers, chess players, townspeople listening to a speaker, various configurations of families, stylish couples walking down a promenade, people reading a newspaper, and others. Individual human figures include political leaders, a music conductor (waving a baton), a man climbing down from a Trojan Horse, a hacker, a guitarist, a child sneezing into a handkerchief, nudes, closeups, and others. "Human Synecdoche" categories showed various parts of people to represent the whole: braided hair, eyes, arms, legs, skills, faces, a pregnant belly, hands, eyes, fingers, fingerprints, lungs, and so on. "Human Self-Portrait" included works that were self-reflective and evoked self-portraiture (by visual inference). Animals also figured in the works. Those visuals that had two or more animals in the image frame were labeled as "Group Animal Figures." These included mallard ducks, two pheasants, horses (such as in cave drawings), finches, tigers, dolphins, cows, schools of fish, and cats, among others. In terms of "Individual Animal Figures," these included a bird on a branch, a humanoid bird gesturing, a tiger, a crow, various octopuses, a raven, a snake, a lizard, an iguana, a dinosaur, butterflies, a pigeon, a squirrel, and others. A meshed category involved visuals that showed "Humans and Animals Together," such as a man on a horse, people working alongside cows, war scenes with people and horses, crows standing on branches with human skulls below, a man walking his dog, a woman with an eagle flying overhead, and others. A few images showed "Melded Humanoid Animals, Animalistic Humans," in drawings and sculptures. Some works showed locales, from "Village View" (more sparse village landscapes) to "City View" (skylines, urban landscapes). There were "Landscape Painting, Nature Scenery" visuals, including a homestead, water scenes, mountains, meadows, and others. In these, the landscape was the apparent subject. "Night Scene" was a small category, with a wolf howling at the moon, a cityscape at night, an island with a palm tree at night, and others. A few works fit into the "Food" category. Then, there were also "Plants, Florals" as a popular category, with various types of flora. There are illustrations of a dandelion with seeds floating into the air. There are bouquets of sunflowers. "Fruit Still-Life Work" was another category of works, showing various melons, an apple core, two shiny leaning pears, a peeled apple, and then some with skulls (which are included in the still life art category generally speaking). There were "Classic" artworks from the 17th to the 20th centuries. There was another category of more contemporary artworks. In the classic category were works by Van Gogh, Klimt, Kahlo, Munch, Dali, Seurat, Vermeer, Gauguin, and others. In the latter, there were works by Warhol, Johns, and some that evoked Banksy. "Artist Studio (and Art Supplies)" was another category. "Building" included both interiors and exteriors. "Patterning" included kaleidoscopic ones, inlaid designs, shapes in various colors, and others. "Futuristic Scenery" include social images with a sci-fi vibe, depictions of outer space, astronauts, and others. The "Mural" category showed various visuals: people, a dinosaur, a woman with closed eyes and objects floating in her hair, a flying duck, various celebrities, a fashionable woman wearing yellow-lensed sunglasses, a person wearing a facemask and holding a book (during a pandemic), various graffiti, and others. One was a clear political message related to George Floyd, an African American man who was killed by police while cuffed and lying on the ground (he had been arrested for supposedly passing a bad $20 bill). The "Logo, Brand" category involves smaller images, usually to convey a brand identity or commercial interest or event. The "Digital Icon" category involves small icons (up arrows, down arrows) used online. The "Composite, Mashup" involves works that evoke collages and paste papers. The "Photo Mosaic" category involves visuals comprised of many small visuals that are digitally stitched and create a larger composite image. A "Map" category involves works that refer to geographical land features and defined boundaries. The "Messaging" category shows works that directly convey information. For example, one cartoon shows a man looking at two diverging paths and puzzling over the decision: "Best for YOU" "Best for ALL." (This might be in reference to whether the person should take a vaccination against SARS-CoV-2/COVID-19 or not.)

A frequency analyses of the subject matter types in the social imageset shows that individual humans were the most popular, then contemporary artwork, then groups of people (in figurative art), and so on. (Figure 4 and Table 4)

Table 4. Descending frequency order of social visual types by subject matter (from "Common Art" social imageset)

Visual Types (by Subject Matter)	Frequency Counts (of Each Visual)
Individual Human Figures	300
Contemporary Artwork, Some in Art Spaces	203
Group Human Figures	157
Messaging, Direct Conveyance of Information	107
Plants, Florals	102
Individual Animal Figures	90
Abstract Work	80
Artist Studio (and Art Supplies)	75
3D Work	73
Landscape Painting, Nature Scenery	58
Building (Interiors and Exteriors)	53
Classic 17th - 20th Century Artwork (? Check the years of the artworks)	46
Group Animal Figures	43
Mural	34
Human Synecdoche (parts representing wholes)	33
Humans and Animals Together	31
Futuristic Scenery	29
Fruit Still-Life Work	16
Patterning	15
Logo, Brand	15
Composite, Mashup	14
Night Scene	11
Human Self-Portrait	6
Doodle	5
Virtual World, Website	5
Melded Humanoid Animals, Animalistic Humans	5
Village View	5
City View	4
Map	3
Food	2
Digital Icon	2
Photo Mosaic	1

A few of the works directly referenced the pandemic, which shows something of the sensitivity of the social image search on Google Images Search.

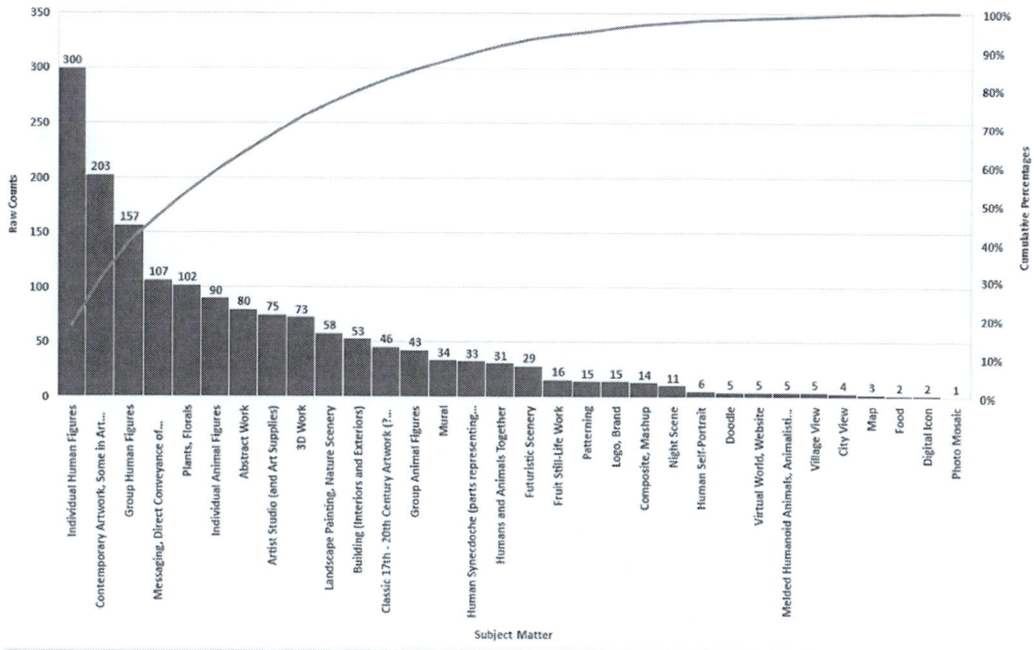

Figure 4. Social visual types by subject matter (from "Common Art" social imageset) (Pareto chart).

> RQ2: What are "common art" styles among "common art" practitioners on the Social Web that seem to be outside the apparent narrowbanding? What is in the widebanding or "long tail" of common art shared on the Social Web? What are some types of novel works?

If the above RQ1 shows the narrowbanding of "common art" artists on the Social Web, the "other" styles not commonly cited would be those that belong in the widebanding, inclusive of the long tail of niche art. To better understand the narrowbanding phenomena at the ego level, it helps to map several "common art" artist/creative "narrowbands" to see what they might look like. One common artist, DrawingWiffWaffles, is one that was studied earlier by the author. This is a young self-taught American artist who works in both analog sketchbooks (pencils, watercolors, markers, acrylics) and digital drawing tablets (Hai-Jew, 2020). She specializes in drawing people, with full personalities and facial expressions and characters. She shows clear affection for her characters, and she has some that she has created and made backstories for. She draws characters of different races with adeptness and non-stereotyping. She treats her characters with dignity and respect. She is drawn to fashion, mass media characters (such as Disney ones, Pokémon characters, and *Sesame Street* ones), and glamor. One of her activities on social videos involves unboxing various art boxes and trying out new art materials and supplies, often based on the prompt that comes with the art boxes. She goes out of her way to learn new skills: color theory, perspective, and more formal learning that she has not experienced based on her lack of formal schooling in terms of art. She takes on challenges, such as creating a neon look-and-feel in a digital drawing. She purposefully applied herself to drawing stronger hands, body poses, males, and animals, in various videos in which she is learning along with her followers. She is not "precious" or overly protective about her work, which makes the learning so much more rewarding and effective. She shares drawing from her own formative years, and she has done narrated sketchbook walk-throughs for her many global fans. She does comparisons and contrasts from her earlier art to her later more sophisticated works. She describes her work struggles: getting past creative blocks, dealing with "same-face syndrome," expanding range by going to Pinterest for a range of reference images, drawing hair, trying different art styles, using one hue to create an image from a particular inspiration, and others. She is expanding her particular narrowband in real time.

Another common artist is a Canadian one who goes by CeeCee (or ceecee in other contexts). Her social videos are calming. She speaks in a calm voice and sometimes is accompanied by instrumental music. She draws various flowers and nature scenes and "doodles," in a creative and original mix. She uses metallic paints as an accented touch. Her works seem ready for framing. They seem ready for appearance on decorative cards. In one funny series, she has a group of round ellipse birds with various personalities and styles. Some of her works show a charming whimsy. Some works show cityscapes, with a muted color palette. She also creates beautiful landscapes with rivers, trees, and hills. She calls some of her works "small art," and indeed, many of the papers she works with are cardstock size. Her works are subtle and interestingly recognizable. In various cases, she creates works as gifts for friends, information she includes in her narratives.

Both create works that have a particular unique look-and-feel. Both have used their talent to take them to stratospheric heights in terms of social media fandom. Both are engaging of their followers. The first uses humor and support; the latter shares some lightly personal information. Both are generous in sharing their learning about illustration.

This may beg the question of how to bridge to different styles from a narrowband. This depends on what the contents are of the particular narrowband for the particular artist. There may be bridging methods from one type of material to another, pigment sets to others, and so on. There may be emulation of other artists' works that the common artist admires. Perhaps there are other commercial works that may inform a new direction. What is "narrow" or "wide" depends in part on the particular artist. The idea is to move beyond the obsessionary range of the familiar and to break new ground, in whatever direction makes sense to the common artist.

If the experimentation is wholly different than a particular established brand identity, the common artist can swap out one identity for another. The creation of new accounts on the Social Web is of negligible difficulty. It is important to note that a "common art" artist can hold back on works until they feel ready to share. They can create multiple social media personas without penalty online. They can sell under different names. They can create multi-channels on various platforms, so the Social Web itself can be harnessed for their own growth.

> RQ3: What are ways to encourage wider artful experimentation among "common art" artists, to expand their "narrow" bands, even with the pressures to narrowband online?

This work suggests that "common artists" in the Social Web 2.0 space experience pressures online that force them into narrowbanding in terms of visual style. "Narrowbanding" here refers to an artist working within a recognizable style that is rewarding for them—whether the reward is attention or money or online talk or any of these and other incentives. There are various tensions from the pushes and pulls exerted on the artists. These are summarized in Table 5.

Table 5. Narrowband vs. wideband "Common Art" artistry

Narrowband (go with known and familiar)	**Wideband (go with unknown and unfamiliar)**
Online Competition	
Fast judgment online	Suspension of judgment online
Long memory online	Overwriting earlier memory with newer works
High competition online	Space to advance in private (offline) or pseudo-privacy
Focus on artwork as single pieces (vs. a body of artist work)	Focus on artist oeuvre over a lifespan of work (vs. single pieces, vs. particular periods or phases)
Social Followership	
Recognizable self-brand	Ability to develop without having to go public with particular new works
Social Web followers with familiarity expectations (constraints to growth); need to cater to followers	Social Web followers without familiarity expectations (no constraints to growth); need to cater to followers
Online and Offline Markets	
Rewards for kitsch (including markets)	Censure against emulation and kitsch; rewards for originality (including markets)
Going with what sells (monetary value proposition)	Not needing to sell (value proposition); going with the larger reward (and related costs) of self-expression
Cost counting	Ability to pay for investments in the art
Access to limited markets (online and offline)	Access to broader markets (online and offline)
Recognizable art style (comfort with); signature	Unrecognizable art style (comfort with); non-constrained signature
Narrowbanding, artistic depth, homogeneity	Widebanding, artistic range, heterogeneity
"Common Art" Artist Development	
Training (self, informal, nonformal, formal; continuing or not) (less)	Training (self, informal, nonformal, formal; continuing or not) (more)
Practice, skill development (going deep with skills and particular outputs)	Practice, skill development (going wide with skills and particular outputs... and deep)
Sense of constructive art critique (less)	Sense of constructive art critique (more)
No impetuses for experimentation, little space to experiment	Impetuses for experimentation Rewards for novel (rarer than for kitsch)
Sense of safety with public identity	Self-confidence without a public identity
Skill refinement (less)	Skill refinement (more)
Amount of time commitment (low)	Amount of time commitment (high)
High Art Acculturation	
Engagement with common art (and a limited range)	Engagement with high art (and a wide range)
Art show and openings attendance (low)	Art show and openings attendance (high)
Social engagement in high art circles (less)	Social engagement in high art circles (more)
Engagement with high art materials and styles (low)	Engagement with high art materials and styles (high)

As social beings, people need each other. Common art artists, however, given the reward structure of the various social media platforms, may be unduly swayed by the expectations of their followers. People experience "internet aesthetics and personal events" resulting in simulated nostalgia (Morrissey, 2021, p. 75), and they may want a public artist to continue to feed that sentimental feeling. They may not want an artist to go out of band. In this way, with their loud voices, they may dissuade an individual from experimenting broadly. An artist will have to have a clear sense of self and the ability to properly place other people's opinions aside as needed if they are to form their own unique "hand." They have to be comfortable in seeing themselves beyond their social personae. They have to experiment with the near-infinite variations possible.

People also tend towards patterning and the familiar. Categories of artworks tend to be "orderly and distinguishable because it is necessary to human beings not only to express themselves within established patterns, but to experience the world around them in accordance with such patterns" (Ackerman, 1962, p. 228). To create novel works, "common art" artists need to exercise the force of will and talent and perception to escape the inexorable pull of patterning.

Discussion

At a macro level, based on social imagery, the "narrowbanding" seems to be at work on the artworks shared, except for a few outlier images that show a more unique hand and/or visual sensibility. Many of the mainline artworks are images that are in the public domain and no longer under copyright protection. There are derivative visual works. If the "common art" show were "widebanded," there would be many more works that show a unique artist hand (and with much less visual derivation).

In terms of the "narrowbanding" vs. "widebanding" for two of the analyzed artists, there were patterns seen within the narrowband range for both, but both artists (DrawingWiffWaffles and CeeCee) are evolving and trying new things and expanding on their topics. They are both apparently pushing beyond any "narrowband," and in many ways, both have transcended their bands into something wider. From the outside, no one really has standing to suggest that an artist move in one direction or another because artwork is a product from the individual and their choices.

Future Research

At the macro level, are there particular subject matters that those in the narrowband engage in vs. those in the wideband? Are there differences in skillsets between the narrowband and the wideband?

What about at the micro level? In terms of the space between "narrowbanding" and "widebanding," where would the threshold be set to when a common art artist moves from one band to another? Is there a point of arrival, and is that visible to the artist? Is that point visible to outside observers?

The core thinking at this work may or may not hold depending on other factors. In terms of achieving the escape velocity from "common art" to fine art, do more common art artists make it from the narrowband position or the wideband one? (Is it better to create in-depth or in diversity? What approach leads faster to a sense of legitimacy?) Is it harder to achieve novel or original works from narrowbanding or widebanding?

Follow-on work would benefit from using computer image coding in order to remove some of the subjectivities of this work. That said, the object identification of AI by itself would not be sufficient. There would have to be more unique coding to enable this level of analysis.

Conclusion

This work involved the study of "common art" in a broad sense and then "common art" based on two popular online artists (DrawingWiffWaffles and CeeCee). The original idea was that artists are somewhat forced (or maybe nudged) into "narrowbanding" based on their art identities given some structures in the online social space (defined in this work). By the end of this work, though, there are extant open questions about both "narrowbanding" and "widebanding" and possible outcomes or effects from such self-definition by artists. A core assertion in this work is that artists are self-agents, and they can decide how to respond to external pressures and what they choose to internalize from the outer world (at least to some degree).

Acknowledgments

In every offering of art, the artists themselves reveal more of themselves than they realize. And yet the spirit of the artist is to give and to continue giving, regardless of self- and privacy-interests. Here is a toast to the artists of the world, at the end of 2021, with a hope of a much brighter 2022!

References

Ackerman, J. S. (1962). A theory of style. *The Journal of Aesthetics and Art Criticism, 20*(3), 227-237.

Arnheim, R. (1981). Style as a Gestalt problem. *The journal of Aesthetics and art criticism, 39*(3), 281-289.

Augustin, M. D., Defranceschi, B., Fuchs, H. K., Carbon, C. C., & Hutzler, F. (2011). The neural time course of art perception: An ERP study on the processing of style versus content in art. *Neuropsychologia, 49*(7), 2071-2081.

Augustin, M. D., Leder, H., Hutzler, F., & Carbon, C. C. (2008). Style follows content: On the microgenesis of art perception. *Acta psychologica, 128*(1), 127-138.

Bäcklund, J. (2016). The Paradox of Style as a Concept of Art. *The Aesthetics and Ethics of Copying*, 211-23.

Belke, B., Leder, H., & Augustin, D. (2006). Mastering style. Effects of explicit style-related information, art knowledge and affective state on appreciation of abstract paintings. *Psychology Science, 48*(2), 115 - 134.

Chen, L., & Yang, J. (2019, October). Recognizing the style of visual arts via adaptive cross-layer correlation. In *Proceedings of the 27th ACM international conference on multimedia* (pp. 2459-2467).

De Boer, V., Van Someren, M., & Wielinga, B. J. (2006, June). Extracting art style periods from the web. In *Proceedings of the ESWC 2006 Workshop on Mastering the Gap: From Information Extraction to Semantic Representation, Budva, Montenegro* (pp. 1613-1625).

Elgammal, A., Liu, B., Elhoseiny, M., & Mazzone, M. (2017). Can: Creative adversarial networks, generating" art" by learning about styles and deviating from style norms. *arXiv preprint arXiv:1706.07068*. 1 – 22.

Garces, E., Agarwala, A., Gutierrez, D., & Hertzmann, A. (2014). A similarity measure for illustration style. *ACM Transactions on Graphics (TOG), 33*(4), 1-9.

Goodman, N. (1975). The status of style. *Critical Inquiry, 1*(4), 799-811.

Hai-Jew, S. (2020). Abstracting Transnational Celebrity (and Sell) on a Social Video Sharing Platform: One 'Neutral' Exemplar. In S. Hai-Jew's *Maintaining Social Well-Being and Meaningful Work in a Highly Automated Job Market.* Hershey, Pennsylvania: IGI Global.

Haller, C. S., & Courvoisier, D. S. (2010). Personality and thinking style in different creative domains. Psychology of Aesthetics, Creativity, and the Arts, 4(3), 149-160.

Karayev, S., Trentacoste, M., Han, H., Agarwala, A., Darrell, T., Hertzmann, A., & Winnemoeller, H. (2013). Recognizing image style. *arXiv preprint arXiv:1311.3715.*

Kim, D. S., Liu, B., Elgammal, A., & Mazzone, M. (2018, January). Finding principal semantics of style in art. In *2018 IEEE 12th International Conference on Semantic Computing (ICSC)* (pp. 156-163). IEEE.

Kubler, G. (1979, 1987). *Toward a reductive theory of visual style.* In Berel Lang's *The Concept of Style.* Revised. Ithaca: Cornell University Press. 163 – 173.

Lagier, J., & Godey, B. (2007). A scale for measuring aesthetic style in the field of luxury and art products. *International Journal of Arts Management*, 39-50.

Lecoutre, A., Negrevergue, B., & Yger, F. (2017). Recognizing art style automatically in painting with deep learning. In the Proceedings of Machine Learning Research, *77, 327 – 342.*

Liu, Y., Pu, Y., & Xu, D. (2013). Computer analysis for visual art style. In *SIGGRAPH Asia 2013 Technical Briefs* (pp. 1-4).

Mezei, A. (1981). Toward improving the objective status of aesthetics: On style and content of figurative pictorial art. *Leonardo*, *14*(2), 118-121.

Morrissey, N. (2021). Metamodernism and vaporware: A study of Web 2.0 aesthetic culture. *Nota Bene: Canadian Undergraduate Journal of Musicology,* 14(1), 64 – 82.

Portera, M., & Bartalesi, L. (2016). Aesthetic preferences: An evolutionary approach. In *Understanding Cultural Traits* (pp. 375-388). Springer, Cham.

Prown, J. D. (1980). Style as evidence. *Winterthur Portfolio*, *15*(3), 197-210.

Rhodes, J. D. (2012). Belabored: Style as work. *Framework: The Journal of Cinema and Media*, *53*(1), 47-64.

Straffon, L. M. (2016). Signaling in style: On cooperation, identity and the origins of visual art. In *Understanding cultural traits* (pp. 357-373). Springer, Cham.

Yang, B., & Xu, D. (2011, September). Learning to recognize the art style of paintings using multi-cues. In *2011 International Conference of Information Technology, Computer Engineering and Management Sciences* (Vol. 1, pp. 375-379). IEEE.

Part 5: Common Visual Art and Sociality

Chapter 13

Visual Gists of Common Food Art on the Social Web

Shalin Hai-Jew[*]
Kansas State University, Manhattan, KS, USA

Abstract

"Food art" in the present moment has become a social media phenomenon. These are social image depictions of the following:

- food sculptures from the hospitality industry,
- children's lunches on plates and in lunch boxes,
- high art with requisite social commentary,
- decorated cakes as various *objet d'art,*

and other depictions. There are works by professionals (food designers, artists, digital artists, studio photographers) and amateurs (homemakers, and others). This work explores "food art" as a form of "common art" based on shared works on the Social Web. This work suggests that food does offer rich possibilities for both high- and low - art.

Keywords: food art, common art, Social Web, visual gists, social imagery, high-art, low-art

Introduction

Against all admonishments against playing with food, it turns out that many adults (and not just foodies) have become fairly adept at this, if social media images are any indication. Whether the images are "food art," though, is under debate.

If art is to be "timeless and lasting," then food may be excluded from being considered as art. In many senses, art and food inhabit "different universes" and "matter for different reasons" (Andina and Barbero, 2018, p. 353). Another research team arrives at the same observation about the different spaces each inhabits: "Is food art? There is no univocal answer to this question because food and art are both highly heterogeneous categories" (Liao and Meskin, 2018, p. 4). Still, food overlaps many aspects of people's lives: "…food stands at the crossroad of several main aspects of life: energy (what food is), creativity (the ways food can be prepared), and pleasure" (Andina and Barbero, 2018, p. 353).

---

[*] Corresponding Author's Email: haijes@gmail.com

In: Common Visual Art in a Social Digital Age
Editor: Shalin Hai-Jew
ISBN: 978-1-68507-664-1

One concern about how humans might assess food art is that they may be predisposed to being favorable towards food and perhaps not able to aesthetically evaluate food art for its aesthetic value in a disinterested way (Andina and Barbero, 2018, p. 354). Others have debated whether philosophically and practically food can be art (Quinet, 1981a). In the debate on whether food itself can be artful, various individuals weigh in on the issue differently. If emotions are critical to considering art, then "food art" does have both ties to human emotions and culture, argues another: "The fact that one can eat a meal and have associations with that food that cause aesthetic experiences, according to my definition make food art so long as that was the intent of the preparer" (Neely, 2007 p. 3). Art is something that is human and can be appreciated by all, not something at removal from people (Neely, 2007 p. 4).

What "food art" is is up for debate, with varying interpretations. In some cases, food has to be used, and the art has to be "aesthetically pleasing without altering the essence of the raw materials, leaving the function and value of food intact" (Milanesi, 2018, p. 426). Said another way, food has to be edible and nutritive: "True food-based art would thus have to centrally involve food functioning as food" (Liao and Meskin, 2018, p. 5). A counterpoint may be that not everything that is plated is meant to be eaten, such as in the case of inedible leaf garnishes (some of which are plated for symbolic and/or artful purposes based on different cuisine cultures) (Pemberton, 1999, p. 37). Another writes that "food art" is art that "uses food as its medium, instead of wood, metal, or stone" (Smith, 2014, p. 5), and it is not a requirement that such works be necessarily edible.

For others, food art is "high-brow" or "artified" food (Laio and Meskin, 2018, p. 6), in some cases "more recognizable as food than food-based artworks" (p. 6). Food art may be from everyday life but created with aesthetic concerns in mind (Liao and Meskin, 2018, p. 6). Multiple research works consider the sensory aesthetics of taste, smell, sound, and touch (texture), relevant to food art, in addition to sight, even though the visuals of food art may come to the fore in some cases.

For many, the sense of "culinary art" as an art is only in the sense of "craft" (Quinet, 1981b, p. 159). That "caloric and nutritive factors" are "not generally considered part of the aesthetic function of a thing" (Quinet, 1981b, p. 161). In terms of aesthetic valuation: "One might argue that the only food products deserving genuinely aesthetic recognition must be those with a complexity which can be appreciated only by *several senses*" ...or some combination (Quinet, 1981b, p. 168). This work explores the phenomenon of "food art" on the Social Web to capture a visual gist of what this phenomenon entails at the present moment. Abductive logic is applied to the collected social visuals.

Review of the Literature

The academic research literature on "food art" comes at the issue in some basic ways: art historic, human food, politics, tourism, IP, and research.

Historical Senses of Art and Food

Art involving food (its depiction) has been around for hundreds of years. "Food art" is a category of aesthetic works "that depicts food, drink or edible objects as the medium or subject matter of an artistic work to create an attractive visual display or provide social critique" ("Food art," July 14, 2021). "Food art" is conceptualized by some as dating back to "the earliest surviving expressions of artistic activity," to the Upper Paleolithic (c. 37,000 – 11,000 BC) with cave paintings of animals hunted for food and sculptures that have survived into the present (Rivera, 2004, p. 2). Others might consider those works "food art" prehistory. The depiction of food in high art is dated to the 15th century, such as Leonardo da Vinci in *The Last Supper* (1495 – 1498) ("Food art," July 14, 2021). "Food sculptures," not usually meant to be eaten, were a feature of state, regional, and international fairs in the late 19th and early 20th centuries; these were made of corn and butter and other ingredients. One object made of corn was a miniature model of a statehouse. Another was "a Liberty Bell of oranges and a larger-than-life equestrian knight covered in prunes" (Simpson, 2010, p. 23). At the fairs, the idea was to attract fair goers to agricultural products. Other works describe a "vernacular architecture" of structures: bean pagodas, wheat-broom corn castles, and street fronts covered in sorghum. In the modern era, "food art" is credited to Filippo Tommaso Marinetti (1909) (Butler, Jan. 13, 2017). As common art, food art shows up on social media as art made from food, some for pure decoration (a carved alligator from a watermelon to attract attention to a food table), some for eating (a sandwich pie surrounded by sliced vegetables to show a turtle for a child's lunch), some for social critique (a banana carved with the image of a white rhino on the day of its having gone extinct from the Earth; the likeness of various political leaders), and other applications.

Art and food have long been studied by food historians (Nygard, 2012, p. 170). Some common focuses have been on "sculpture, painting, and mosaics" that use food as a medium (Nygard, 2012, p. 171). Some artworks have included "food art" that includes textiles and other materials. Generally, food art has been analyzed using "art-historical theories and methodologies" (Nygard, 2012, p. 174). There are some less formal approaches, too. One researcher suggests that the term "food porn" can be used to describe some "food art" in a way to include the perspective of the food artist and his/her/their internal experiences (Tan, 2014, p. 4). The idea is to include the interiority of the experience.

Aspirational Food Depicted

The study of food-related paintings has been revelatory about just how "realistic" or "representational" such art can be. One study began with 750 food-related paintings; from these, 140 were extracted that were from Western Europe and the U.S. and which showed "small, family meals" (Wansink, Mukund, and Weislogel, 2016, p. 1). These were assessed to see how representational the depicted table was. One finding was that the most frequently eaten foods in the U.S. such as "chicken, eggs, and squash" were "least frequently depicted in paintings" (Wansink, Mukund, and Weislogel, 2016, p. 1). This might suggest that the artists were not trying to describe commonality but something else. The researchers found that food subjects tended perhaps to be something more aspirational. They write:

> In contrast, the most aspirational foods such as shellfish were commonly painted in countries with the smallest coastlines (Germany), and more than half (51.4%) of the paintings from the seafaring Netherlands contained non-indigenous tropical lemons. Moreover, although bread and apples have been commonly available over time, bread has been panted 74% less frequently and apples painted 302% more frequently. In general, paintings tend to feature meals with foods that were either aspirational to the commissioning family, aesthetically pleasing or technically difficult for the painter, or that encoded cultural, religious, or political information for informed viewers (Wansink, Mukund, and Weislogel, 2016, p. 1).

Rendering food in art form may suggest something eventful. This research team also observed that food depictions, as themes, change over time, and these are informed by various societal and other factors.

Emotional Comfort from Viewing Depictions of Food

People have been shown to find emotional comfort when engaging with depictions of food, even in the absence of directly consuming the food:

> Results show a consistent pattern: viewing/drawing comfort foods [food image (95% confidence interval): 2.72 – 4.85; food art (95% confidence interval): 2.65 – 4.62] and fruits [food image (95% confidence interval): 1.20 – 2.23; food art (95% confidence interval): 1.15 – 2.56] enhanced mood. For comfort foods, mood was augmented for those with clinical symptoms of depression [food image (95% confidence interval): 0.95 – 3.59; food art (95% confidence interval): 0.97 – 3.46] (Privitera, et al., 2018, p. 598).

There were even improved mood changes for those with depression.

Food Art and Politics

Food art plays an important role in cultural diplomacy (Schmitt, 2010). One work describes "current trends in contemporary public art to use food as an artistic medium that encourages intercultural exchange" and food serving as a form of "cultural diplomacy" (Schmitt, 2010, p. 1).

Another describes a more populist use of food for social commentary and political exchanges. Here, people use Russian salads with Russian words spelled out to communicate "patriotic ideology on the Russian internet" (Rann, 2016, p. 51). Such pictorial salads help Russians engage in social discourse "in the context of postmodernism in art, architecture and politics" (Rann, 2016, p. 51) on the Russophone Internet. Food art enables artful discussions in both high-art and low-art, and the role of food here continues the tradition of having people socialize around food.

Food Art and Tourism

Food art may contribute to the "food tourism" that is so central to people's travel (Garibaldi, Pozzi, and Viani, 2016, p 61). Gastronomic tourist products and other food experiences are attractions for many to particular sites. Tourists often share food photos from their travel adventures on their social media accounts. One study explored tourist motivations to share food photos as "a realization of the social life of tourists, promotion, food documentation, food art, relaxation, reference, and existence" (Wachyuni and Yusuf, 2021, p. 62). The sharing of social imagery is a central part of tourists' lifestyles.

User Preferences of Food Depictions in Visual Form

One study evaluated whether people preferred having visual food depictions as photos or as drawn art, in terms of modality. They found consumers had an increased sense of "food attractiveness" when presented with photos instead of drawings, and that photos had a positive influence on their "future purchase intention"(s) for cultural food (Wu, Liu, Huang, and Yu, 2021, p. 1).

Copyright Protection to Food Art

If artwork has authorship and originality, and the protections of intellectual property (copyright), what about for "food art"? Some researchers have explored the role of the legal rights of food artists such as "chefs and molecular gastronomists" who "do not possess the same legal rights as other artists, such as painters, sculptors, or composers" (Reebs, 2011, p. 41). In this work, the author reviews various case laws and their implications on "food art" and IP. One challenge is that "food art" often falls outside the legal definitions of "art" (Reebs, 2011, p. 50), and copyright protections do not "extend to ideas, procedures, or processes…" (Reebs, 2011, p. 52). A work published a few years later continued this exploration. This opened with cases of what some saw as copyright infringement between chefs, in a context of various sharing of ideas and practices in the cuisine industry. To consider whether food art, like sculptures made of food, is worthy of IP protection, one consideration is whether there are enough elements in the work to enable various unique combinations for achieving originality (Smith, 2014, p. 8). Another challenge is that "food art" is often not considered in a "fixed" form in a tangible sense.

While some consider the look of a dish as possibly able to be trademarked under so-called "trade dress" protection (appearance), there are complex considerations. Is the plating sufficiently distinctive? Part of the chef's repertoire and identity? When is a "foodist" an "author" as regards copyright? And others.

There have been considerations, too, of whether diners may post images of their food (by a chef) on social media without contravening others' copyright:

> As to the diners/amateur food photographers—practically speaking, it is unlikely that a chef would ever risk bad publicity to bring suit against a diner for photographing cuisine for personal use. Furthermore, because food presentation is not protectable under copyright law…, taking a photograph of uncopyrighted work is not creating an unauthorized derivative. Photographing

> food for the purpose of commentary or criticism is also fair use. Similarly, under trademark law, even if a chef can claim trade dress in his food plating, a diner's use of that food plating on social media to describe or refer to the chef's food would be considered nominative fair use. Finally, patent infringement occurs when a party, without authority, 'makes, uses, offers to sell, or sells' a patented product; patent infringement does not occur when a diner takes a photo of a patented design and posts it on Facebook. In conclusion, not 'taking intellectual property away from the restaurant,' and a diner would have valid defenses against most intellectual property claims against him. Nevertheless, a restaurant on private property could create a 'no photography' policy for any reason, and ask its diners to obey this policy (Smith, 2014, p. 23, with numbered source citations, which were not included in this block quote).

This means that most people who post food images on the Social Web are not practically at risk of a lawsuit for contravening others' copyright. [The cost of a lawsuit and negative publicity for the chef would be prohibitive.] In a time of foodies and extraordinary volumes of social sharing from the personal, the Social Web is replete with photos and other visuals of meals about to be consumed, meals fresh-made, meals presented at restaurants and hotels, and other variations. [Food tastes better with the social brag, the sense of taste (in every sense of that word), the acquired status, the expenditure, the physical and mental consumption of the food, the story, and other aspects].

Food Art for Advancing Science and Research

Various gastronomical art projects (food art) are used for research and learning, such as imagining "a future supper" and "new or overlooked sources of nutrition" (Fargione, 2019, p. 255). This work describes various approaches to amateur science and multimedia art to explore fresh ideas: How can humanity achieve nutritional needs while preserving the natural environment? How can technological innovations be used to solve the food challenge? (Fargione, 2019, p. 264) The questions are asked using various "meals," including shared ones from humans to animals, to address the issue of interspecies considerations.

In a time of the Fourth Industrial Revolution (4IR), there is work toward digitally enhanced food based on the concept of a "food replicator" (Schöning, Rogers, and Krüger, 2012, p. 4), ways to use laser intelligently to cook particular parts of bacon based on preferences, the use of 3D printing to print edible objects, cookies that interact with virtual reality through wearer headsets that enable people to see the cookies as cupcakes (Schöning, Rogers, and Krüger, 2012), and other creative examples.

Research Methods

To explore the current sense of "food art" on the Social Web, a set of "food art" images were extracted from the Google Image Search engine. The idea is to conduct a visual analysis of the respective thumbnails. The data scraping resulted in 1,089 items. The text-based tags for filtering the visuals include the following:

creative, easy, fruit, rice, beautiful, Instagram, vegetable, apple, anime, painting, dessert, amazing, drawing, pinterest, flower, cute, kawaii, fish, abstract, famous, banana, photography, egg, sandwich, edible, diy, watercolor, unique, plate, chocolate

Some observations follow.

[Side Note: "food art" was also used to search for visuals on an art site, and the visuals that were returned showed many human characters with outsized large and round stomachs. The themes were about over-consumption, with a focus on "deviance," the rejection of the normalization of over-weightedness.]

Results

From the social imagery, the respective images suggest that the works have to be recognizably food and recognizably art. It can be difficult enough to make food look appetizing in the normal course of things, but these have to look artful and theoretically stay edible. Any of a variety of treatments seemed acceptable: cooking knives, art knives, food coloring, syrups, fondant, toothpicks, 3D printing, and others.

The works were mostly from the American palate, with common foods at home and at hotels/convention centers. Many appealed to one's sense of humor.

One of the goals was to observe social norms from the collective imagery. Based on the visuals, what makes "food art"? The collection shows that there are works by professionals foodists (food sculptures from the hospitality industry) and non-professionals (homemakers with artful children's lunches on plates and in lunch boxes). Some works are high art by recognized artists making social commentary (with many involving drawings and carvings on bananas). There are decorated cakes with artful sugar creations working together as *objet d'art*. The foods are mostly 3D (because of the materiality of food), but the images are 2D (captured on a flat plane). Given the image downloads, the works are all visual-only, without any of the other human sensory perceptions brought into play (no smell, no taste, no touch, no hearing, etc.) The works all include food and perhaps some additional augmentation: plastic eyes for various creatures, a wooden treehouse in a broccoli tree, and so on.

A few of the collection involved sophisticated digitally edited images. One was a digital work apparently inspired by kiwi fruit. Some works were professionally lit and edited and framed, such as some emulations of food as art from the Renaissance period. Some works are meant to be viewed straight-on, and others are sufficiently designed to be viewed from any of 180-degrees and some at 360-degrees and in 3D.

There are actual limits to inferring how something was made just from an image of the finished product at the end. In some cases, food products are mentioned in the table where the food is salient. One image was so pixelated that it was unclear what materials went into it: this one was a face of a woman. Various themes were observed using bottom-up coding (Table 1).

Table 1. "Food Art" categorizations with examples from the social image set (Google Images)

Categories	**Examples**
Angels	Winged angels
Animals (fauna)	A mother panda and a baby one, a mother kangaroo with her joey (cut toast); a bird standing on a branch (apple halves and a large pretzel stick); a crab; an anteater; a rabbit; small fish swimming in a plate with onion oxygen bubbles floating up; fish swimming in a sea and breathing out round cereal air; a sea turtle; a reindeer; a lion; an octopus bread pudding with doughy legs coming out of a ramekin; a walking bird (a partially peeled orange); baby octopus (from frankfurter ends); a puppy (lettuce), moose (pancake); dragonfly (four hard-shelled tacos); a herd of sheep (rice and seaweed); goldfish (crackers); a peacock with an edible tail of finger foods; a caterpillar (banana); panda bears (rice bears in a curry sauce); a bear (made of rice and napping under an omelet blanket); a tiger, a barn owl (with a cantaloupe head and various greens for its body); a rooster; a dinosaur; elephants with trunks and large ears (made by frankfurters); goldfish (cakes); a koala bear holding on to a branch; rabbits (from marshmallows); alligator head (from an avocado); chicks (from hardboiled eggs); a fox on a toast bed under an egg, with an asparagus stalk next to it); a lizard (made from strawberry shortcake); a lizard (made from a melon); a bumble bee (made of cereal pieces and blueberries); a rhinoceros (watermelon); a ladybug (tomato slices); birds (made with meatballs in a pasta nest); a dinosaur (made with a waffle and berries all around); a hummingbird; rabbits (pancakes with coconut cream tails); horsehead (pancake); peacock (cheese, crackers, fruit, and meat platter); a bear (watermelon); baby rabbit (in a waffle basket); birds standing in a half-watermelon; spider (with McDonald's French fries and the box); a frog (watermelon); a duck (slices of apples); a bear (pancake) fishing off a banana boat and catching goldfish crackers]; hedgehogs (rice); a moose; a bird (made from a bagel and slices of turkey coldcuts); a giraffe wrapped around a banana; a piglet lying in a bed of rice; a butterfly (made from slices of avocado next to a kiwi flower); a fox eating a leg of lamb; flamingo; reindeer (with pretzel horns); a Dachschund (banana); a dragon (cucumber); a snail (pancake); poodle (cauliflower); poodle (broccoli); penguins (eggplants); an owl (radish), and others
Art-related Works	A painting palette with various chocolate candy balls as the daubs of paint (and decorative paintbrushes)
Artworks (recreated)	Edvard Munch's "The Scream"; Vincent Van Gogh's "Starry Night"; Leonardo da Vinci's "Mona Lisa"
As Itself (as an edible food)	Toast with blueberry eyes and noses and banana slice ears and some peanut butter; cookies with various facial expressions and personalities
Babies	A baby in a watermelon cradle
Bicycles	A bicycle with orange tires; a bicycle with parts made from vegetables
Celebration of Recognizable Characters	Characters: A Winnie the Pooh made from liquid egg yolks; Pinocchio; Spongebob Squarepants; Teenage Mutant Ninja Turtles (made of peas, cheese, and a red pepper grin); Grinch; Hermione from Harry Potter; minions (made from corn-on-the-cob, made from bread); movie characters; smiley faces (made with pizza toppings on pizzas); several Hello Kitty! cats; Fozzie Bear of Sesame Street; the main character in *Up!*; Angry Birds (salami slices); a snowman; Humpty Dumpty; Woody from *Toy Story;* Mickey Mouse (with a pie sandwich body and with celery stalks upholding strawberry hearts); characters from Addams Family; "Mike" in *Monsters, Inc.*; Mickey Mouse and Minnie Mouse together; a unicorn; Snoopy; Scooby Doo; Pikachu of Pokémon; Little Red Riding Hood and the Big Bad Wolf with its jaws open; penguins with eyes and beaks (chocolate-dipped strawberries); Chewbacca of *Star Wars*; Winnie the Pooh (tater casserole); The Simpson's family; Cookie Monster of Sesame Street (made from pineapple slices and strawberries), and others
Centerpieces (not usually meant for eating)	A block of flowers (either frozen ice or jellied for presentation); carved watermelons depicting an alligator, a horse's head

Categories	Examples
Children's Lunches	Various sandwich "pies" with arms and legs made of vegetables; a lunchbox with artful food; a rocket ship (thin-sliced carrots, bread, and crackers) A book cover advertising "healthy edible art for kids"
Cubed Foods	Cubed meat, fruit, vegetables, and sushi; a sushi meal out of a bento box with all the eatables in cubes/squares
Digital Games	Angry Birds; Pacman; Pokémon
Eating	A watermelon grill with various fruit skewers; various characters depicted eating
Famous Locations	An Eiffel Tower frosted cookie
Flora	Flowers (made by cheese bits on a pizza crust), a flower (meringue); a fern carved from a watermelon; a flower (pancake); sunflowers
Global Cities	A plate showing Rio de Janeiro in Brazil, with the iconic Christ the Redeemer statue depicted
Holidays	Easter Bunny hunting for eggs on a sunny day; a Christmas card scene; Halloween (ghost and jack-o'-lantern); A Christmas tree with a star on top (peas and carrots)
Horror	A human brain with dark hair on top (watermelon and some other materials); a skinned man rising from a watermelon half; a bread role baked as a face with a knife clenched in its teeth; a vegetable skeleton; a carved apple biting a person's thumb and drawing blood; a fondant-based sugar ice cream cone crash; a frightened watermelon face holding on to a water faucet extending from a tabletop (hydrophobia?); a scary clown with carrot hair; a woman lying face down in a casserole dish of cheesy macaroni
Hunting	An ice fishing scene portrayed on a banana
Literalist	Sushi rolls that spell out "sushi," raw steak pieces cut to spell out "STEAK"; a pizza slice that spells out "Pizza"; a "hello sunshine" message on a plate; a "Stay HOME" message (per pandemic) on a plate
Miniature Food (for a hamster)	A colorful fruit pie or tart
Motor Vehicles	A car driving along (with its body made by a pie on a road of cucumber strips and a broccoli tree); a watermelon boat floating on waves (idea of movement); a motorcycle (made from a lobster); a sailboat (from watermelon, banana, and coffee beans); an eggplant car with a character inside
Movie Scenes	The house floating away on balloons in *Up!*; another floating house where the balloons are jellybeans
Musical Instrument	A violin; a grand piano (made with a coconut and other materials)
Nature Scenes	Palm trees made with bananas, kiwi, lime, and tangelos among others; a beach scene made with cereal; nature drawn with persimmon seeds; a farm scene; a carrot round as the sun; floral scenes (vegetables along with ketchup and mustard sauces); rainbow pizza slices with colors from vegetables and cheese toppings; undersea with shrimp (cooked); undersea with small fish; a mountain (cheese, with quail eggs at the base); a broccoli head tree with a treehouse built into it; a grinning sun (pancake); a cream cheese cloud and an apple umbrella and blueberry raindrops; a house scene
Objects	A burning candle; a purse with handles made from asparagus; a clock (made with caramel)
Pandemic (SARS-CoV-2/COVID-19)	A plate that reads "STAY HOME" where the "o" is a small lunch pizza
People (commonfolk) (celebrities)	Commonfolk: A person holding up a glass of wine (depicted by root vegetables like carrots and others); a face made with Triscuits; two characters (with whole chickens each as bodies); two grinning rice people in a soup "bath"; a man pouring sugar on a sugar-coated pastry with a paint bucket (could be a "Photoshopped" man or a toy); a bespectacled older woman with hair made out of cauliflower Celebrities: Jerry Seinfeld; Roseanne Barr; Amy Winehouse; President Donald J. Trump; Frida Kahlo; Marilyn Monroe (in a remake of the scene of her skirt blowing up); others
Political Statement	Depictions of a president; rainbow pizza slices

Table 1. (Continued)

Categories	Examples
Risqué (naughty or "spicy" depictions)	A plate in which chicken wings stand in for women's legs (and the women are topless) (the tone is silly more than anything else); two sardines as legs of a lady in red high heels (cuttings from red peppers); some suggestively posed shapes (we'll leave it at that)
Rockets	Rockets (from skewered fruit)
Romance (love)	A couple (frankfurters) in a car (French bread) with tires (salami); two turtles turned towards each other; Mickey and Minnie coming in for a kiss; two chocolate ice cream bars wearing Mickey and Minnie Mouse hats with black ears and melting together as they make eyes at each other
School Project	Dried beans glued onto cardboard and sprayed with varnish; a tractor made out of dried beans
Stylish Women	Stylish women in various fashionable dress (made with breads, spinach leaves, and peppers); a carved avocado; a carved broccoli spear; bread for a face and pasta hair and seaweed for a body of a female person; flappers wearing skirts made of strawberries A series of stylish women with food skirts: pasta, tomatoes, and others
Symbology	The yin and yang symbol
Technologies	A little Windows computer with a mouse (cake); a smart phone (cake); a game controller (cake)
World Map	One carved from an apple with yellowing innards
Other	A charcuterie platter (with artful layout?); a platter of eats; a decorated popsicle with food coloring; two sundaes in cups with faces (and the ice cream as "hair" of the bear and the pig characters on the cups; cheese, fruit and meat towers; a hamburger representation made with paper and stuffing; healthy lunches with shaped bread, cheese, broccoli, and others; macarons, and others

Initially, there was a "visual wit" category, but later, it was clear that many of the works across the categories were visually witty. Part of this is from the visual dissonance between the food and the portrayal, give the multi-messaging. The sparkle also comes in part from the human visual system, which has some hard writing for faces, so it responds to the "eyes" of the various depicted characters using food and the general shape, and voila, the food evokes something of the person or the animal or the character.

If the sources of the various social images are to be inferred, most seem to be from professional works: the foodists themselves who created or co-created the pieces, diners who are appreciating various forms of "food art" at catered events, and such. Next seem to be works by homemakers who are sharing their handiwork. Some of the visuals seem to be from blogs and published works. A very few seem to be images from formal art (with a few "food art" practitioners).

The foods portrayed seemed to mostly be finger foods for adults (fruits, vegetables, meats, and cheeses) and then only lunch foods for children…and little about adult entrees, little around drinks (and nothing alcoholic). Perhaps certain foods lend themselves more to artful exploration than others. Trend-wise, perhaps "food art" is more about encouraging children to eat their lunches than other things.

Discussion

Among these works, there were very few that were "too beautiful to eat." Some appeared so delectable that just the visual of it sparked hunger and appetite. Many food art visuals were charming and visually witty. In the works, food and culture and visual art were celebrated. Most works were light on the symbolism but were mostly straight representational.

Future Research

Future research may focus on different types of "food art" over time. Perhaps there can be explorations of "food art" hosted on different social and art and other platforms, to enable the different gists of "food art" practices.

The creation of "smelly art" may have potential in the food art space as well although such pieces tend to involve artificial chemical-created scents (Shiner and Kriskovets, 2007). Technically, there are other ways of creating aromas as well.

Conclusion

If nothing else, "food art" shows that people enjoy playing with food, both the professionals and the non-professionals. Not only do they like to pose food with various visual depictions and even some messages (shoutouts to particular movie and game characters, representations of actual people, political messaging, and others), they often enjoy consuming artful food presented in delectably witty ways. This training for aesthetic eating begins early, with children's foods presented in storytelling scenes. Then, there is the pleasure of broad social sharing across the Web and Internet.

This work is comprised of a review of the literature around "food art," studied in various dimensions. Then, "food art" was used to seed the available visuals on the Social Web in this time period, through Google Images. The 1,000+ images were manually analyzed and coded to better understand the gist of "food art" as "common art," as shared by the general public.

Acknowledgment

In a recent project, I spent much time engaging with the work of *mukbangers*. In that time, I realize how much effort and thought goes into their work, even though it might seem simple enough to engage in performative eating for the cameras. The work of "food art," democratically understood, is broad. Thanks for the many insights, eaters of the world!

References

Andina T and Barbero C. (2018). Can food be art? *The Monist*, 101(3), 353-361.
Butler S. (2017, Jan. 13). A brief history of food as art. *Smithsonian Journeys Quarterly*.

Fargione D. (2019). *Utopian and Dystopian Meals: Food Art, Gastropolitics and the Anthropocene,* 255-270.

Food art. (2021, July 14). Wikipedia. Retrieved from https://en.wikipedia.org/wiki/Food_art.

Garibaldi R, Pozzi A and Viani E. (2016, September). Food, art and tourism as a boost for innovation: Successful experiences from Italy. In *ATLAS Annual Conference 2016*, (p. 61).

Liao SY and Meskin AR. (2018). Morality and aesthetics of food. In: Barnhill A, Doggett T and Budolfson M. eds. *The Oxford Handbook on Food Ethics.* Oxford University Press. 658-680.

Milanesi M. (2018). Exploring passion in hobby-related entrepreneurship. Evidence from Italian cases. *Journal of Business Research*, 92, 423-430.

Neely C. (2007). The significance of food in culture: Is taste an art form. *UW-L Journal of Undergraduate Research*, 5, 1-4.

Nygard T. (2013). Food and art. In *Routledge International Handbook of Food Studies* (pp. 185-192). Routledge.

Pemberton RW. (1999). Japanese food as art and symbol: Evidence from inedible leaf garnishes. *Petits Propos Culinaires*, 63, 37-49.

Privitera GJ, Welling D, Tejada G, Sweazy N, Cuifolo KN, King-Shepard QW and Doraiswamy PM. (2018). No calorie comfort: Viewing and drawing "comfort foods" similarly augment positive mood for those with depression. *Journal of Health Psychology*, 23(4), 598-607.

Quinet ML. (1981a). *Food as Art* (Doctoral dissertation, Duke University).

Quinet ML. (1981b). Food as Art: The problem of function. *British Journal of Aesthetics*, 21(2), 159-171.

Rann J. (2017). How to make a Russian salad: Food, art and patriotism on the internet in Russia. *Digital Icons: Studies in Russian, Eurasian and Central European New Media*, 16, 51-78.

Reebs CM. (2011). Sweet or sour: Extending copyright protection to food art. *DePaul J Art Tech and Intell Prop L, 22*, 41-74.

Rivera, I. (2004). Food and art: A Brief history. Master's thesis. Rochester Institute of Technology. 1-58.

Schmitt C. (2010). Food as an emerging diplomatic tool in contemporary public art.

Schöning J, Rogers Y and Krüger A. (2012). Digitally enhanced food. *IEEE Pervasive Computing,* 11(3), 4-6.

Shiner L and Kriskovets Y. (2007). The aesthetics of smelly art. *The Journal of Aesthetics and Art Criticism*, 65(3), 273-286.

Simpson PH. (2010). A Vernacular Recipe for Sculpture—Butter, Sugar, and Corn. *American Art*, 24(1), 23-26.

Smith CY. (2014). Food Art: Protecting Food Presentation Under US Intellectual Property Law. *J Marshall Rev Intell Prop L, 14*, 1.

Tan F. (2014). Food. Porn? Art!: In the Skin of a Food Artist. *Food Design on the Edge*, 4.

Wachyuni SS and Yusuf L. (2021). Camera eat first: Tourist motivation in sharing food photograph on Instagram. *International Journal of Tourism and Hospitality Review,* 8(1), 62-70.

Wansink B, Mukund A and Weislogel A. (2016). Food art does not reflect reality: A quantitative content analysis of meals in popular paintings. *SAGE Open*, 6(3), 2158244016654950.

Wu LL, Liu SQ, Huang H and Yu X. (2021). Photo vs. art? The design of consumption guidance in cultural food consumption. *International Journal of Hospitality Management*, 97, 103008, 1-13.

Chapter 14

"World Creating" in Contemporary Common Visual Art on the Social Web

Shalin Hai-Jew*
Kansas State University, Manhattan, KS, USA

Abstract

Common art has long been used for "world creating" to augment storytelling, gameplay, animations, fan expressions, and other endeavors. On the Social Web, four sets of still images created and tagged as "metaverse art," "alternate universe and art," "worldmaking and art," and "fantasy world amateur art" were collected in order to create a bottom-up coded instrument to understand what visual elements inform "worlding." This work also sheds light on the various types of worlds offered in the respective social imagesets and the affordances described in these fantasy worlds, based on the human imagination.

Keywords: world creating, common art, Social Web, social imagesets, metaverse art, alternative universe art, worldmaking art, fantasy worlds

Introduction

The ratio of nonfiction to fiction books in home libraries is said to be 1:25 or 1:30. This suggests a much larger appetite for various works of the imagination than for direct reality, for entertainment over non-entertainment, fantasy over the real. In terms of "common art," there is often depiction of the imaginary over the real, the abstract over the figurative, the symbolic over the actual. If world creating in the imagination is a common human pastime, through various arts and expressions, what does amateur visual art shared on the Social Web show about people's senses of alternate possibilities for the world?

Review of the Literature

In the real world, worldmaking involves healthy bureaucratic systems, rule of law, deft leadership, international diplomacy, and constant tending, to enable peace, development,

* Corresponding Author's Email: haijes@gmail.com

In: Common Visual Art in a Social Digital Age
Editor: Shalin Hai-Jew
ISBN: 978-1-68507-664-1

human rights, and human health, among others. It involves projecting out to various scenarios, with worldmaking itself used as "a framework for pluralistic, imagination scenario development" (Vervoort, Bendor, Kelliher, Strik, & Helfgott, 2015, p. 62); here, "scenario worldmaking" is enabled in part by "reordering, recombining, contrasting, challenging and inverting available present and future worlds" (p. 67). Worldmaking is achieved for various aims: using the imagination to describe what is possible, for better or for worse. Ideally, the human imagination expands what it means to be human. It forewarns against perceivable risks.

In written fiction, worldmaking involves the descriptions of ecosystems, world inhabitants, in-world physics, cultures, creatures, flora and fauna, and other elements. Plotlines may show various outcomes for various characters (egos) and groups (entities), based on their personalities and choices and serendipity. The various "tells" may come in particular details, snippets of conversations, nuanced descriptions, and other elements. Certain values (social justice, economics, or others) and other abstractions may be revealed in the story. An underlying tool is language, as natural and constructed symbol systems, which enable societies to form and collaborate and remember over time.

In art, in which various symbols are manipulated, artmaking is a form of worldmaking (Goodman, 1978, p. 1). Which are worlds that people want to live in? Those they would avoid? Why? If the various depictions are alternate universe, metaverses, fantasy worlds, what do they speak of possibilities? How do they critique the current real world? In terms of common art, what sorts of works are being shared on the Social Web? What sorts of larger-scale communications are being held through such artworks?

It is thought that the visuals involve both conscious and unconscious world creating ("worlding") albeit in a context of limited dimensionality (due to the physical 2D space and to culturally learned habits of art). It is assumed that there will be some degree of fidelity to the world and some degree of artificiality, for such images to "work," since the unknown is used to comment on the more known (current reality). This work may suggest something of eversion, or the flowing from the virtual to the real. Indeed, the human imagination is "our primary cognitive mechanism for anticipating and deliberating on the future" (Finn & Wylie, 2021, p. 1).

Research Methods

This work engages four research questions:

RQ 1: World creating at mass-scale and issues of interest: In terms of common art made by amateurs and shared on the Social Web, what do various still visuals suggest about a mass-scale "world creating" (with the images as stand-alone ones)? What are the apparent issues of interest?

RQ 2: Hopes and warnings for the future: What are anticipations of the future (especially hopes and warnings)? Are these for the near, middle, or far futures?

RQ 3: Components in still visuals to identify world creating in common art: What salient still visual elements (components) speak to this sense of "world creating"? What sort of a coding instrument may be created based on these identified visual elements?

RQ 4: Technical expertise and technologies: What level of technical expertise may be observed in the various social images? What technologies are apparently used?

To begin to answer the research questions, four social imagesets were captured from Google Images, based on the following seeding terms: "metaverse art" (851), "alternate universe and art" (1,121), "worldmaking and art" (810), and "fantasy world amateur art" (890) (Figure 1). These four social imagesets make for a total 3,672 images for this research work. The seeding search terms were based on a sense of inherency of world imagining and world creating.

The "metaverse art" set had the following tags on Google Images: persona 5, decetraland, yu gi oh, art fair, nft, game, virtual, roblox, virtual reality, wall art, ethereum, crypto, the metaverse, cryptocurrency, farm, virtual worlds, blockchain. The "alternate universe and art" social imageset had the following tags (used for filtering): backwards, diego brando, earth, modern art, going backwards, digital art, antarctica, jojo, deviantart, multiverse, fantasy, steel ball, draw, world, exist, multiple universes. The "worldmaking and art" imageset had the following tags: techno, mark david, malcolm baker, science, realism, participatory, critical essays, milne, diplomacy, andrew hemingway, american diplomacy, alex potts's, naturalism, teché participatory, architecture, participatory art. The "fantasy world amateur art" imageset had no available tags (perhaps because of the combination of search terms). The respective tags are kept in the lower case as is typical convention, and the spellings on the search engine site were kept. The tags do show that the respective imagesets have different focuses, and together, they do provide a range of different insights.

Results

The respective responses will depend in part on some level of inference, given what is viewed and coded manually (with several iterations over each set per question). There are limits to what is knowable from visual analysis alone, and there will be in-between spaces. The assumption here is that the respective communicators are working to educate and sensitize the senses to what is relevant. Each artist is assumed to have a unique point-of-view and sense-making. It is not assumed that all possible futures will necessarily be addressed but only selective ones of interest.

Per the focus on the four research questions, this section focuses on variant insights from the different imagesets.

RQ 1: World creating at mass-scale and issues of interest: In terms of common art made by amateurs and shared on the Social Web, what do various still visuals suggest about a mass-scale "world creating" (with the images as stand-alone ones)? What are the apparent issues of interest?

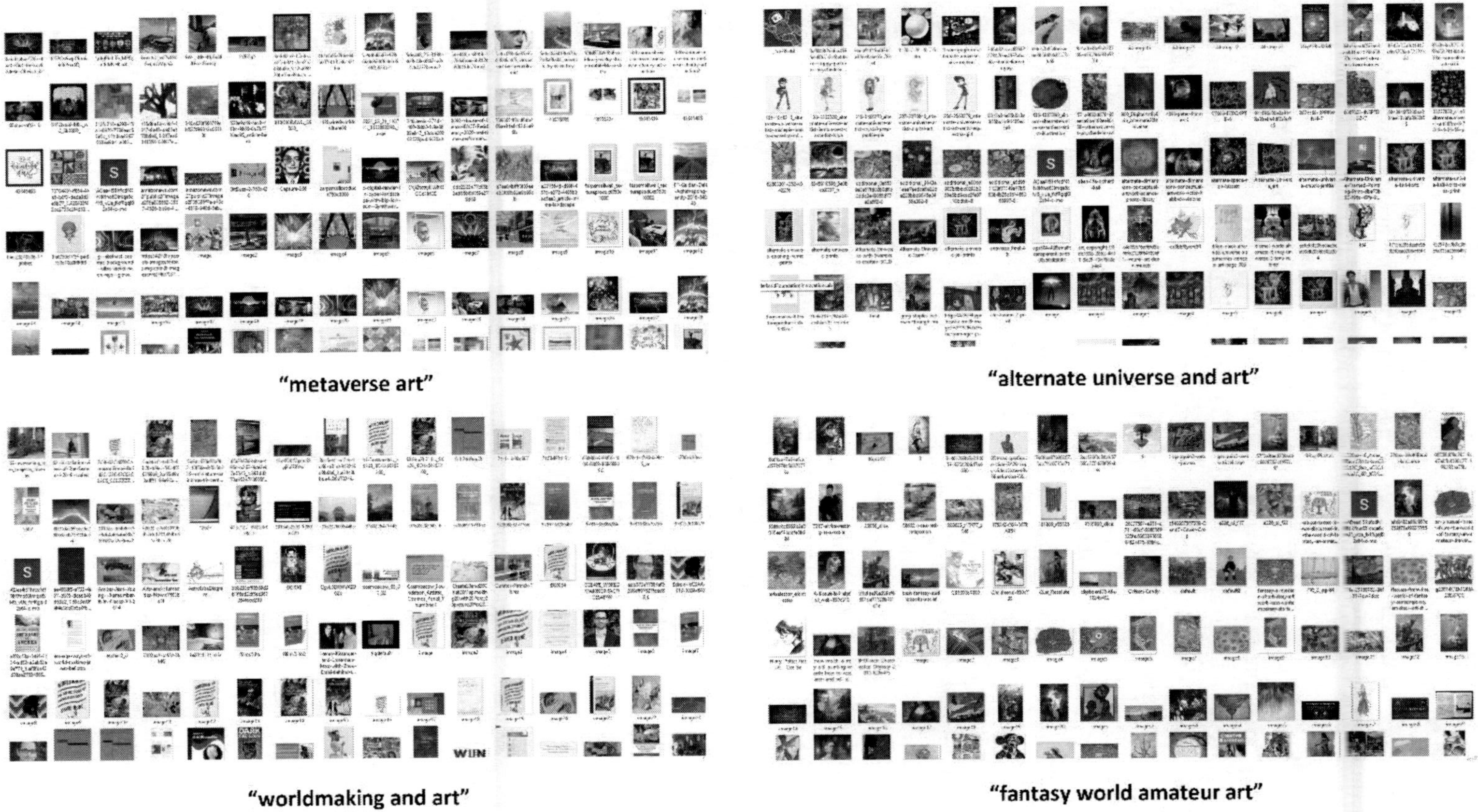

Figure 1. Four social imagesets around 'World Creating' and 'Common Art' (from Google Image Search).

Metaverse Art

A classic visual of "metaverse art" may be in a diagram of stacked and multiple universes with their own galaxies and stars and nebula, to show a 3D existence of multiple worlds in parallel. In the metaverse art imageset, a number of works show varied landscapes. Many describe planetary landscapes and a psychedelic planet with multiple rings around it in the sky, a red sun or moon (an orb) on a meshed landscape; various science fiction depictions; a space craft as a living structure, a neighborhood in Japan (Shibuya), blue abstract bubbles in a deep black background, and others. One photo shows a sculpture depicting a spaceship landing.

There are post-apocalyptic scenes of empty landscapes. There are railroad tracks, with a person walking into a darkly familiar future (and the words: "Why do they want to send us back to this place?"). Some landscape visuals seem positive: a night scene of a tree and many decorative whorls from the tree and in the atmosphere; a meadow with sunflowers, and others. There are architectural structures that defy gravity, such as one building depicted next to a snow-covered road in a remote snow-covered mountain locale. (The dramatic lines of the building are for effect more than for apparent architectural purpose.) In another, dump trucks are working on a 3D building (that actually already looks fully built). Naturalistic scenes are often covered in mist, which communicates mystery. There are stormy clouds, which communicate trouble. In another, two white-barked trees stand against varying backgrounds. Nature is presented in a way to show its preciousness. In another, there are rolling hills, with a giant planet with rings around it directly above, creating a nearness of outer space bodies in this metaverse. Several works show closer-in physical spaces, like bedrooms, and electronic overlays in physical spaces. Here the electronic and virtual are integrated in the analog physical real. Several works show virtual and real art galleries. One is a floating art gallery in the air, with various artworks on the walls. (This is suggestive of recursion.)

The characters portrayed in the "metaverse art" social imageset show some depictions of peoples from varied racial and ethnic and cultural backgrounds: women in head scarves, Chinese language neon signs, people strolling in recognizable global cities (like Paris), and others. Some of the characters are shown as warfighters and combatants, with hyper-muscular anatomy. Some visuals show outsized figures (with very long legs) on a podium. One composite image showed a naked man riding a brass bull, which was charging over rocks and water. Some of the characters are robots, others cyborgs, touching their faces with a plasticine hand. One montage shows a character made up of various elements from head to toe, in something of a "character board" of the person. Some depicted artifacts seem to be from the steampunk sci-fi aesthetics, such as a gas lamp and some clothing. A human figure, created using digital "mesh," touches hands with his doppelganger in another dimension. A man in pirate garb with a stitched mouth stands on a floating land mass, with other such masses in the background. In another work, a man is looking into a mirror and touching his other self in a different dimension. A fairy with wings is wearing diaphanous clothing, in a risqué work. A person walks down a path between two stands trees.

Animals also figure into the scenes. One work shows a collage of a tiger face, with various news clippings and headlines integrated. One shows a housecat with big eyes wearing a face mask against some sort of pathogen or particulate or gas; this cat is in a black background. A goat wears a flower crown. One shows a dove with a branch (not an olive one) in its mouth. Two flamingos stand together in another scene. One message board reads: "Your best friend doesn't always have to be human" and shows a horse with a flowing mane.

The action that the characters engage in include the following: fighting, exploring lunar landscapes, walking the red carpet, dancing, walking, romancing, and various forms of emoting. A common scene is of heroic caped male figures fighting monsters.

In some depictions, there is a literalist bent. Some of the imagery show people wearing virtual reality (VR) headsets and engaging in a space with virtual and physical elements floating around. In one, a masculine face and hand expressed in mesh is wearing a VR headset. One image referred to various "hives" and belongingness to various hives. The virtual world is described as its own metaverse, existing in parallel to real life (RL) and the real world. Some subsets of the images here were of art installations in art galleries and museums. Direct virtual immersive worlds were also depicted, with human-embodied avatars looking at contents on a large screen, various avatars interacting.

The metaverse metaphor is used for some conference advertisements. One shows a futuristic scene with words "crypto, artificial intelligence, blockchain, the metaverse," and other words written into the background. There is another ad for a "metaverse art" art exhibition.

Romance seems to be yet another theme. There are multiple watercolors of fashionable couples and individuals under black umbrellas walking on a reflective sidewalk. Some are walking down unknown streets. Others are in front of the Eiffel Tower. Some scenes show the stylish couples walking under red umbrellas. One work shows cartoon cactuses holding hands.

In this set, various visuals contained textual messages. Some were inspirational messages: "Welcome to the metaverse," "Live for today and make it so beautiful that it is worth remembering," "Family gathers here," and "give thanks." The cliché about "make lemonade" when live gives one lemons is repeated. Another message reads: "It's a beautiful day." One advises: "Be a pineapple: stand tall wear a crown and be sweet on the inside." Another touches lightly on faith: it reads: "believe," and there is a backdrop of butterflies and florals rendered in pastels. The verbal often helps focus the meaning and augment the visual, and vice versa.

Several of the works lauded farm life: "Life is good on the farm," "live love farm," "life is better in the country," "farm sweet farm," and "Have a very farmy (sic) Christmas," among others. Perhaps the farming lifestyle is its own universe, for those outside of that life. Some text exhorted: "Love" and "Calm." Some seem to be from marketing campaigns, one showing a footed bathtub and the words: "to beach." Another showed a deer with a full rack and the words: "elusive bull" (perhaps from a hunter's POV). One work was a stylized "buses and trains" sign, with different destinations listed. One was a "chalkboard" with a recipe for friendship, such as "endless shared secrets." Some signs indicate "coffee hour" and "wine hour." Another reads: "Love builds a happy home." Mood is evoked: "sandy toes and salty kisses." Videogame fighters are listed as "metaverse champions". There are some Bible verses quoted, especially from 1st Corinthians, about love. There are political statements, too. In one, Bitcoin is "inseminating" (their words) the Internet.

Alternate Universe and Art

The "alternate universe and art" collection seems to engage some senses of the impossible. There is the person in a space suit and helmet with stars in the face shield area. There is an illustration of Earth and then another further in the distance and surrounded by a milky cloud or mist. Creatures fight in foreign worlds. One, an ad for a photo studio, shows translucent balloons floating in air and drawing lighting.

A man lies in bed daydreaming about outer space, as the windows melt inwards. There is a set of city buildings on a city block and a liquid set below. There are artful "impossible" shapes, like a Möbius strip, a non-orientable surface. There is a claustrophobic view from the ground looking up through skyscrapers and rubble at a jetliner flying overhead. Some of the imagery is about discomfiture. Another shows either an anthropomorphic robot or a person in an exoskeleton rocketing around the skies.

Several visuals show portals into different worlds. In one, a little girl stands on a path leading into a bright sunny area. Along the path is a tree that looks like a weeping willow. Behind her is the doorway she passed through to enter the other world. The portal itself looks like an arch with sandstone blocks. Others show the Earth passing through a wormhole into a different reality. In another, a man is teleporting between dimensions, with his head already disappeared and his body soon to follow. Two separate visuals show a man touching hands with his own doppelganger in another reality. Perhaps this is about being aligned with the self. Another type of portal involves floating eggs, with humans being born into the present version of the world through these eggs (from which they hatch). Another work depicts a night landscape with a lot of wooden portals (door frames) through which different realities are possible.

Several of the works use "Starry Night" and its textured sky over various cityscapes or village scapes, to evoke something of a living outer space. Another visual posits that alternative reality is upside-down from the current reality. Another shows the inside of a cathedral; in the foreground a swirling hole that drops into a different cosmos. Multiple portals are depicted enabling people to achieve different states of being and reality. Reality is not singular but almost always multi-dimensional. A person stands on a rock face and looking at giant floating mushrooms in the sky. In this one, the viewer of the image may empathize with the individual in the scene.

One graffiti-inspired doodle shows floating equations and mathematical notations and drawn circles and angles. There are also Earth and planets represented. Another visual is suggestive of a potential microbial universe, at nano scale. In one visual, a person looks out from behind a three-ply surgical mask (which is timely to the pandemic). In another composite visual, there are high rises, smokestacks, rocket ships, and other technologies.

Reality is not simple, nor predictable. One visual shows a glowing deity with glowing eyes, but it is not clear about goodness or evil. There is a being with Mickey Mouse ears and a wolfen face. The script is flipped in another visual, where the dwarf is lying in a glass casket surround by seven Snow Whites. There are threatening outsized creatures in flowing garb. In another, creatures with very long legs stand in a foreign landscape. There is a horse morphing into a lizard that can take human riders. Creatures' morphology may indicate something of their functionality. In one visual, a young woman rides a turtle as it swims through the sky. There is a hand-drawn boy with green hair. Some scenes show creatures standing astride cities or floating in air, engaging in combat, with swords and shields. In terms of visual character development, some wear jewelry, body art, and decorations that may show something of character.

This set also has some creatures depicted from various sources: Totoro, My Little Pony, Green Goblin, the Teenage Mutant Ninja Turtles, and others. There are characters from an outlaw poster from the Old West. In some senses, there seems to be an inherited visual vocabulary from film.

Some visuals contain some direct messaging. One animal visual shows a giant frog experimenting on a pinned person to a table; lest people miss the point, there is a board with small pinned frogs for dissection nearby. (This reads as an anti-animal experimentation visual. Or it could just be a horror visual.) In another, two aliens with heads made of televisions with single eyes view Earth and humanity from a distance; this visual suggests that our broadcast television may be the way humanity is seen (as humans are "television-watching animals" given how much time of the day they spend watching). There are political statements. One visual reads: "Luke, I am your father" (in reference to Darth Vader and Luke Skywalker of *Star Wars*) and then the comment: "Taken away by Mandela effect." The political statement is about S. Africa and a political issue there, perhaps the calling out of others with a different point-of-view. One visual in this social imageset shows silhouettes of human faces facing each other with the Earth in between, suggesting something of power and responsibility. Another visual reads: "millennials are killing capitalism." Another work emphasizes the importance of "decolonizing" history; this points to some of the tensions between the developed and developing world. One visual shows a stenciled rat with a dollar sign on its necklace; it is holding up a sign reading: "We are all fakes," suggesting that people are falling short.

Worldmaking and Art

The "worldmaking and art" imageset brought to the fore the practice of realism (and hyper-realism) and naturalism in art, practices in which artists try to render the world as they saw it in the real, with high fidelity. One photo shows a man with an unpotted plant in the foreground working to design an interior space. A set of eight images on one visual show scenes of disaster and rubble, some from apparent weather events. A different painting showed a superhighway broken with rebar and other parts hanging off as a couple walk by underneath. One visual depicts a streaking comet with a long tail in a night sky over a house.

Another shows a soundstage with green screen on some walls, for chromakeying; here, people can create a sense of reality and input whatever backgrounds may seem justified. Another photo shows a glass installation that looks like streaks of light emerging from a center point, for something that is not quite 2D but is maybe 2.5D. Another was a "light art" installation, with intense white lights that look like a rift in the floor.

A large subset of the visuals shows a number of book covers on various topics: science and worldmaking, politics (a photo of Henry Kissinger and a Chinese leader, both worldmakers), war, world powers, diplomacy, and others. Art is seen as an important part of promoting human rights. In this set, there was Dutch artist M.C. Escher's famous "Drawing Hands" lithograph, in which a hand draws the other hand. This visually witty work evokes something about humans creating something of themselves, in real time. Another work shows two silhouettes of people's heads that also may be viewed as a geographical map. People can think the world into being, into change.

Several photos show adults and children looking at a skeleton on display in a museum or a formal space. This seems to read as people understanding themselves and something of what came before, their own histories.

Several of the works evoke a sense of a rules-based order. There was one image with a declared political stance: "power to all oppressed people gay liberation," "gay power," and "gay is natural." Several works involved "trans exploits". One work dealt with "insurgency" aesthetics. The activist space is a roiling one. Several works had the style of posters advocating workers' rights, including some with woodcut designs. Some of the works extolled feminism. Others pointed to transnational issues, with global reach and appealing idealisms across cultures. One work extolled "a world without borders." A core base assumption is that the *status quo* is not optimal, and human activism may help the world to be more socially just and socially hospitable. One work showed people putting money into computer terminals day and night. This set included several children's drawings on paper taped to a wall. One reference pointed to human performance (drama, dance, and others) as a form of worldmaking. One visual showed a sign in Chinese about COVID-19.

Several works showed visual representations of buildings and other large physical structures. These were supposedly futuristic depictions.

Fantasy World Amateur Art

The "fantasy world amateur art" seems to build on the fantasy genre, which involves worlds under threat and distressed populaces. Then, there are heroic warriors, who have emerged from a common person on a hero's journey. There are castles surrounded by high walls being scoped out by dragons. There are epic battles. Fantasy is about royalty, in their wealth and finer and power intrigues. Riders ride away from a castle that they have just attacked (the image is a side-by-side, with the line art on one side, and the fully rendered digital painting on the other). Here, there be dragons, and they are to be slayed. Another shows a lone fighter and his horse. In another, a person in a more modern military uniform carries a child to safety. Knights are up-armored and wield swords. They face off against fire-breathing dragons. In one visual, a half-conscious man is being consumed from legs up by a giant blobby creature.

The worlds are ones with their own different physics. A tree floats in a purple sky. The women are posed in scanty clothing and look passive and available. A magical world enables artists to get away with water reflecting only part of a physical scene on ground (but not the rest), or else perhaps this oversight is just about sloppiness. A young girl stands in a window looking on a watery scene while a goldfish swims next to her. In another scene, there is a lit building underwater with giant lotus-like flora floating at the surface. The details of the respective visual elements have to abide within the in-physics rules of the virtual world, but the rules are determined in part or in full by the common artist. In the first instance, the physics may be defined by some artistic convention, so the artist has only partial say.

Here, individuals wield various powers and magics. In one work, a young woman wields wisps of light as something suggesting magic and power and movement. A masked individual is shown riding a motorbike. A young blonde female wearing a skin-tight superhero suit has translucent circles emanating from her hands, symbolizing power. A young woman emerges out of a painting and comes to life, which is a depicted sense of "eversion," and the power of the imagination to make real. In another visual, two young people explore a cave while holding up a torch to light the way. Their lives are about exploration and adventure and risk. There are ships from the age of sailing discovery when new continents were yet to be found.

Humans, for all the depicted heroic moments, are sometimes also stylized as being very small creatures in a larger world. They dwell on rocky cliffsides. They live in stylized flora and fauna and are only a small part of the larger whole. Some of the flora is inspired from the real, such as an open ear of corn with open leaves.

There are animals in this social imageset, too: a rabbit in a coat and pants and professional pumps, storks standing together, cats sitting in a tree, a penguin, a kitten, a horse, some artful hyenas, and others. Some—lions, tigers, foxes—seem to be common "spirit animals" in the common parlance. There are imaginary creatures, too: unicorns, mermaids, dragons, and Pokémon (nee Pikachu). There are nymphs and dryads in a shared dance. Some are mythological animals. And some are people turning into animals (a woman into a panther), and others which are half-person, half-animal. One wood sculpture shows a standing male body with the head of a cat.

If fantasy is about a shift in time from the present into the future, it is also about the past. Some works evoke cave drawings, which date back to some 44,000 years ago. [Recent research suggests that the earliest human art may have been made by children some 169,000 to 226,000 years ago (Metcalfe, Sept. 15, 2021). These were discovered in the Tibetan region of China recently.] Some show faux works from myth, from ancient times, from antiquity. There are some reconstructions and re-enactments depicted of historical events. One painting shows workers laboring alongside a riverbank, in a romanticized view.

The architecture described here show modernist homes, some of which defy gravity. Others exist as undersea structures, which if they existed in the real, would be marvels of construction to defy the massive undersea pressures.

A few of the visuals are suggestive of "worldmaking" in the political sense. One work with text exhorts citizens: "Engage – reflect – act."

The fantasy future is filled with complex machines. The future is a physics-bending one, with changes to space, to time, and to light. A human face peeks out of the back of a man's head. The future is about impossibilities imagined. There are plants that do not have a real equivalent in the physical world. There are undersea scenes in which sea horses float by in a row. The fantasy landscapes feature an unnatural sheen; the light itself is different; the shadows sometimes have a life of their own. The scene is somewhat other-worldly. Light falls in ways that do not align with the natural world. The natural landscapes can be eerily empty of humanity, as if they were post-humanity landscapes.

A few works are visual illusions. One shows a row of sailing ships whose masts may also be viewed as cumulus clouds…and the row as a spanned bridge across water. Such illusions are not so common, perhaps because of the need for wit and high skills.

Some of the visuals also feature a horror tradition, of characters which look feral with evil and are dripping blood. A man walks by with a lamp held high but lighting the wrong areas; he is walking right by a giant monster, ready to attack him. Some of the works evoke a sense of general anxiety. A ladder emerges from an explosion, but there is no one climbing out. A man sitting on a horse shakes his club at a giant approaching winged monster that takes up most of the horizon. Even if not caught unawares, the human is caught up short.

Several of the visuals relate to commerce: "how to get fanart commissions," fantasy writing prompts, various books and trainings on how to create amateur fantasy art, and others. Some visuals show how-to techniques, such as how to use a dry brush. There are several artist magazine covers. There are various art sets depicted. One work shows a tablet and stylus, used for drawing and digital painting. There are books displayed on a table. One work describes "fantasy golf."

Some works involve political messaging, such as a "minstrel carnival" which reads as satire. There is a work about "afrofuturism." Some works follow Daliesque misshapen forms hanging off of trees. Some works draw from the *anime* and *manga* traditions from Japan. In a fantasy world, the world looks different, and the rules are different.

Several of the visuals are about books and courses for various types of art techniques, such as oil painting and water coloring and drawing. One referred to an art therapy coloring book. Several referred to sketchbooks.

Several works verge on erotica. One shows a woman holding on to a large dandelion flower that has its seeds blowing away…and she seems about to be blown up with it.

A chessboard shows pieces in the starting positions; a chessboard is often used to suggest strategy and opposing sides and perhaps zero sumness (one side's win is the other side's loss).

One work seems to depict a deity from Hinduism, so there is drawing from different religious traditions, albeit probably with plenty of distortion and perhaps usurpation. There are some works "after" particular artists. There is a variation on *The Last Supper* by Leonardo da Vinci. There are works emulating the old Dutch masters, with brilliant lighting to point human visual attention. There are multi-dimensional works per Pablo Picasso. Some works evoke Paul Gauguin's Tahiti period. There are evocations of Andy Warhol's face, if not his art. Some surrealist works emulate Salvador Dali and his flourishes. There are works emulating Vincent Van Gogh's distinctive brush strokes. There are the kitsch ethereal-lit cottages of faux Thomas Kinkade. In some cases, these are low-res pixelated copies of the digital works with edits. In others, they are actual paintings after the known artists' styles. There is not always an actual fit of the style to the content. Perhaps these are exercises in emulation.

The color palettes of the respective works vary. Where sinister scenes are depicted, the illustrators go with darker tones.

RQ 2: Hopes and warnings for the future: What are anticipations of the future (especially hopes and warnings)? Are these for the near, middle, or far futures?

The respective social images suggest both hopes and warnings for the future. In the "metaverse art" set, the hopes seem to be placed on technologies (humanoid robots), globalism (no xenophobia here, plenty of the allure of the foreign), cutting-edge architectures (much of which seems to defy physics), romance and sexuality (in various forms), nature (all variety of flora and fauna, including the imaginary), outer space exploration, magic, biotechnologies, traditions, culture, optimism, art, imagination, surrealism, virtual reality, warfighting, parallel universes, the farming life, human competition, heroics, crypto-currency, fame, and fashion. Threats include technologies, human surveillance, magic, and monsters. The monsters are especially posed as those surprising humanity, with the person depicted as walking oblivious to the threat in some cases.

In the "alternate universe and art" social imageset, hopes for the present-future seem to be placed in the following: space exploration (outer space and the cosmos), daydreaming and imagination, cities, machines, magic, new generations, biological solutions, spirituality and ceremony, math and physics, science writ large, electricity, the U.S. constitution, and alternate realities on the space-time continuum/discontinuity (reachable through wormholes), nature, and aliens of various kinds.

Threats stem from winged monsters and fire-breathing creatures, winged warring seahorses that can fly, and adversarial aliens. In the visuals, there are flying zeppelins that hover and rain down fire. Threats can emerge from wormholes and alternate realities, into a topsy-turvy world. Some visuals depict bio threats. One visual shows aliens on another planet with televisions where heads usually are and large bulging eyeballs; in the background is Earth. One interpretation can be that aliens are understanding humanity from a distance through television signals broadcast into the atmosphere: What do they understand of humans through human televised entertainment? Quite a few of the scenarios show destroyed cities and collapsing infrastructure, perhaps after or during mass-scale wars. (Combatants are not always depicted.) Another shows a streetscape in black, but overhead is a giant rotating orb spinning out of control and dominating the blue-black sky. The universe is off-its-trajectory, affected by dark matter and unseen forces. Then, too, the various works depict the spirit world, especially of devils.

In the "worldmaking and art" social imageset, there are hopes that stem from essential bringing of order to human societies. This begins with seeing the world with clarity and then engaging societies with policymaking and diplomacy, systems-building, and economic exchanges. This set contains many book covers, academic articles' first pages, and others, referring to political science, social activism, the arts and humanities, ethics, music, architecture, art, performing arts, modeling the world, science, warfare, peacemaking, and others. There are visuals about various conferences. Some direct political references point to feminism as a socio-political value. So much of human endeavor is about learning and collaboration and problem-solving. Some visuals include maps, the ordering of the world. The visuals here suggest a more rationalist approach to engaging the world and the issues for humanity. In some visuals, various depicted deities are a part of worldmaking. Perhaps these stand in various religions and worldviews. Some visuals depict the ever-presence of natural disasters and perhaps entropy as the natural state. Threats are all around, and the world is itself an inhospitable place.

In the "fantasy world amateur art" social imageset, hopes stem from the domestication of the oceans, with living structures built undersea. Warfighting is ever with humanity, both as hope and as threat. Technologies—biological, mechanical (machines), and other innovations—come to the fore as providing hope. People's provision of mutual aid is a boon, along with companionship. Some visuals point to fecundity as hope, since this represents health and the ability to fight effectively. There are visuals about travel, with the sense of anywhere-but-here possibilities. Some visuals point to nutrition. There is power also in wizarding. In terms of threats, the depicted ones include pollution, such as suffocating smoke in the environment. There are tattered flags, that show populations that lack the will to rally together, in shared endeavors, in shared defenses. Then, too, dragons are seen as threats against people.

RQ 3: Components in still visuals to identify world creating in common art: What salient still visual elements (components) speak to this sense of "world creating"? What sort of a coding instrument may be created based on these identified visual elements?

The core of this chapter was to emerge with an instrument that captures some components of the visual arts to analyze to better understand the sense of "world creating."

In a generic sense, these include the following elements:

Table 1. Macro themes around "World Creating" social imagery

Macro Themes	Visual Depictions
The world itself	The atmosphere (sky), the land, the water, and other aspects The portals into other dimensions (wormholes, black holes, and others)
The creatures in-world (and in parallel or external worlds)	Humans Animals Mixed human-animal creatures Wholly unique creatures
Adversaries	Other humans Microbial organisms Dragons and other creatures
Allies	Other humans Microbial organisms Dragons and other creatures
In-world/out-world technologies	Science: math, physics, and others Transport vehicles (balloons, planes, trains, cars, motorbikes, zeppelins, sailing ships, and others) Unmanned aerial vehicles (UAVs) Weaponry: guns, swords, magic, and others

Analyzing the respective visuals involves identifying the central areas of visual interest based on emotional focus, the uses of lines to drive human attention, the uses of color and lighting, and so on. The depictions of the various characters—their looks, their facial expressions, their clothing, their body positions, what is in their hands, and other elements--also inform on creature intentions, how they fit in the world, their relationships with others around them, and other factors. The portrayals show something about capabilities, based in part on form (morphology).

Table 1 focuses on the lowest common denominators. The decomposition of the respective visuals can certainly be taken further. How images are designed as a set or a sequence can be informative because those inform on recurring themes in a set…and occurrences over time in a sequence. Smaller levels of granularity may mean more important focuses.

RQ 4: Technical expertise and technologies: What level of technical expertise may be observed in the various social images? What technologies are apparently used?

The visuals in all four social imagesets show a variety from real physical spaces: art installations, building exteriors, historical street scenes, and others. In terms of artworks, there are various traditions: bas relief, sculpture; watercolor, oil painting, old-style wood cut posters, sumi-e, charcoal on paper, line art; sepia-tone photographs; coloring books; comics, cartoons; graffiti, murals; collages, mood boards; and others. And in terms of digital visual modalities, there are various traditions: 2D and 3D and 4D. There are several pieces of simple pixel art, one of a wizard wearing a coned hat. There are screenshots. There are rich types of digital painting.

A few recurring images appeared in more than one social imageset. The generics across all sets seem to be both landscapes and floral paintings (in oils, in watercolors). There were the cliched visual tropes of looking into the future by gazing at the sun on the horizon line or going down a path into the horizon.

In terms of the technical expertise shown in the visuals, these range from the low end of child's play, student artworks, and other amateur works. These include pencil drawings on notebook paper. These include screenshots of immersive virtual world imagery and perhaps also from *machinima.* At the high end, there are professional-level visuals suitable for the walls of galleries and book publication and distribution. These are rare, and these clearly require investments of trained knowledge, skills, and abilities (KSAs) and long immersion in the profession.

The color palettes vary. On the extreme ends are neon colors on black backgrounds…and mixes of 1960s psychedelic colors. Otherwise, the color palettes seem to be otherwise in the normal range.

Discussion

Imagining a better world is not just in the purview of leaders and policy experts. Common folk, with their varied street sensibilities, also engage in "worlding" and "world creating" in their imaginations. In a time of mass social sharing, their ideas may be seen in visuals, writing, and other creative forms. What do these suggest about world creating? World creating is seen as advancing on a number of tracks: social awareness, social activism, romance, technologies, and warfighting. The scenarios, the reimagining of time and space, are contested and not without tensions, in the same way that people and groups fight for their own sense of ideal futures.

Many of the visuals show individuals as singletons and in pairs and small groups. Perhaps the worlds being created depend on individual decisions, which lead to larger-scale emergent outcomes. There are implications of meso and macro-scale individuals, too, but in a zoomed-out government and planetary scale sort of way respectively.

The parallel universes come from other planets and universes. They come from micro or microbial worlds. They come from spiritual realms. They come from magic (indicated by floating crystals, indicated by light streaming from people's hands, and others) and hidden forces.

Some visuals suggest the need to adapt and change. One visual shows floating shapes of all unique and different variations, suggesting something of the complexity of the world and perhaps how history does not repeat directly.

Some of the works focus on the power of the human imagination, to solve and to foresee (anticipate). There is something here about humanity seeing themselves in different circumstances and making decisions accordingly. The self in different universes is recognizable, but only just. The ecosystem affects the person. In one comic, a man is looking at a mall map. Instead of reading, "You are here," it reads, "You are there." The man is looking at a version of himself standing down the hallway in front of another mall map.

In many senses, these works show humanity looking to technological means for pivots and world-changing effects. Technology is represented as robotics, as math and physics, as astronomy, and others.

Many of the works highlight the human capability for self-destruction and warring. They show destroyed and desolate landscapes. Perhaps an alternate universe is one between war and peace (but humanity cannot abide all conditions for the sake of peace). Humanity has always found reasons to go to war to settle accounts and make a world of their own choices and to select governments that they desire

There are threats from within and from without: from colliding planets to microbial life. Nothing less than survival is at stake. In some cases, defense means launching knights on horses against dragons. In many other cases, the defense is much more nuanced.

Future Research

Various approaches may be taken to enhance future research.

- *Coding instrument.* The coding instrument may be tested to see if the categories have achieved "saturation" or completeness for these purposes. Another question of interest involves how applicable the instrument is beyond the Western "common art" milieu and this present moment. Do visual languages differ for others? How so? What about symbology and representations? Varying belief systems? Fervency?
- *Social image sampling.* This work was based off an imageset of 3,672 images from the four imagesets seeded with the terms: metaverse art, "alternate universe and art," "worldmaking and art," and "fantasy world amateur art." There are different terms that may be used to seed social imagesets beyond what was used here, for a cross-section of what is available on the Social Web. Perhaps particular filtered visuals may be used to understand subsets. Perhaps visual "information retrieval" may be used instead of textual for different scraped social images.

Besides different seeding terms, there are ways to capture social imagery from art sites and other online venues. The different user bases from these respective sites will mean different sensibilities and visions of future or parallel worlds.

What about differing modalities used for world creating? What about stills from virtual reality/augmented reality/mixed reality ("VR," "AR," and "MR" in abbreviated formats)? Do the visuals used in immersive realities change from the still two-dimensional ones? Does the third dimension (z-axis) add some things and take away other aspects? What about with motion (video, animation)? What about changes over time and the 4th dimension? What about sequences? What about with audio soundscapes? Does multi-sensory immersion, with experiential depth, enhance the imaginaries and create a sense of what is possible beyond, say, words or images on a digital page?

- *Reaching out to "world creators."* It would be of interest to backtrack to find out who the respective world creators are and to conduct some interviews to ascertain their senses of their own visual creations and messaging, the original inspirations, and other aspects. How do their own personal concerns translate to larger-scale ones? Or, given polysemy, were they just pursuing pure entertainment? What was left out? What was misconstrued?
- *Genuine vs. spurious worlds.* Nelson Goodman posited that some made worlds are "genuine" and others "spurious." Perhaps future work may study which is which and how to differentiate these in the still imagery created by common artists. Nelson wrote

about the need for an imagined world to have some internal alignments and non-contradictions:

> To anyone but an arrant (sic) absolutist, alternative ostensibly conflicting versions often present good and equal claims to truth. We can hardly take conflicting statements as true in the same world without admitting all statements whatsoever (since all follow from any contradiction) as true in the same world, and that world itself as impossible. Thus we must either reject one of two ostensibly conflicting versions as false, or take them as true in different worlds, or find if we can another way of reconciling them. (Goodman, 1978, p. 110)

- *Motivating visions.* Another question involves what visions of an idealized (as-yet unreal) world motivate people to effort, to fighting, to sacrifice, and to even dying? What utopian scenarios are especially appealing? How do people weigh cost-benefit scenarios? What macro-level stories are being told that are compelling? At what level of belief and internalization? [Depictions of the real world are already highly contentious. Consider how sensitive mapping a country may be and its external and internal borders.] If reality is socially constructed, how can social imagery of common art be used to understand where there is agreement, disagreement, space for co-creation and co-action? What are friction points? Where is the human imagination most comfortable?
- *Practicalities.* Beyond world creating, there are also issues of "world building" and "world maintaining," both of which are critical, even if the starting of making a new world may be most glamorous and attention-getting. A practical sense asks who is creating and maintaining the world. It begs the question of how much agency humanity has. Or is humanity at the whim of so many external forces beyond which they have no or limited control?

If much of human endeavor first has to be conceptualized in the human imagination before it is made real, then certainly, there is benefit in understanding some of what is being conceptualized both in the massmind and on individual levels. One of the visuals here suggested that art is "everyday work" perhaps for the everyperson, which says something about people speaking into the future and having an effect on what comes to be.

Conclusion

This work is the first of its kind to capture a sense of world creating via "common art" shared on the Social Web. This work involved the answering of four research questions around four areas: world creating at mass-scale and issues of interest (RQ 1); hopes and warnings for the future (RQ 2); components in still visuals to identify world creating in common art (RQ 3), and technical expertise and technologies (RQ 4).

This work included the creating of a bottom-coding visual coding instrument for understanding such art through the framework of world creating. ["Worldmaking" came with too many other socio-political implications, the tensions between the "doves" and the "hawks."] This is apparently the first work of its kind and so can benefit from follow-on research.

In terms of the coded visuals, only a subset was directly relevant to the seeding terms, at least in the decontextualized senses of the respective visuals. Some were logos and icons. Some were hyper-abstract, like 3D spheres and triangles. The visuals themselves, even the detailed ones, are multi-meaninged and may be interpreted in different ways, as is so with some other symbolic systems like textual language. The visuals are not particularly creative, on the whole, but they are revelatory of some degree of thinking about a dissatisfactory world…and early considerations of various possible futures ahead, only a few of which might be desirable.

Acknowledgments

Thanks to those who have a strong hand in co-creating the world around me…with light and aesthetics.

References

Finn, E., & Wylie, R. (2021). Collaborative imagination: A methodological approach. *Futures,* 1 – 11).

Goodman, N. (1978). *Ways of worldmaking* (Vol. 51). Hackett Publishing.

Metcalfe, T. (2021, Sept. 15). Art or not? Ancient handprints spark debate. *NBC News.*

Vervoort, J. M., Bendor, R., Kelliher, A., Strik, O., & Helfgott, A. E. (2015). Scenarios and the art of worldmaking. *Futures*, *74*, 62-70.

Chapter 15

Event-Based Common Art: COVID-19 Visuals

Shalin Hai-Jew*
Kansas State University, Manhattan, KS, USA

Abstract

People experience time as a continuity but also as events (and perhaps periods of punctuated equilibrium). The events can be a series, or they can be one-offs, or they can manifest in other ways, through the lens of subjective human perception (and later of more formal histories). Regardless, people express their commemoration of various events through their common art. One exemplar case involves common art surrounding the SARS-CoV-2/COVID-19 pandemic, at this particular moment in Fall 2021, a year-and-a-half in. At this moment, the world has suffered some documented five million deaths from this dreaded disease, and many tens of millions are experiencing "long COVID" symptoms, which may or may not be lifelong. The global lived experience of going through a pandemic varies based on the governance and specific features of the locales (culture, economy, peoples, and others). Regardless, there have been very human universals and traumas: personal losses, fears, frustrations, interrupted ambitions, social strife, and other factors. This work explores two contemporaneous social imagesets: seeded with "common art and pandemic" and a "common art and COVID-19," for some senses of massmind in the present moment.

Keywords: event-based common art, COVID-19, SARS-CoV-2, modern pandemic, massmind, social imageset, social web

Introduction

In a time of a modern pandemic, the news coverage can be 24/7. The sense of threat is ever-pervasive. People approach the topic with different points-of-view. It can be that there is widespread fatigue of the topic already both because of the sense of global mortal threat, mass-scale human loss, the social tensions around the pandemic, and the pervasive news coverage. For many, there is hope that the end of the pandemic would arrive sooner rather than later, with some sort of regularity and coherence. The pandemic is projected to be suppressed more effectively once the vaccinations and infections (resulting in some natural immunity) result in

* Corresponding Author's Email: haijes@gmail.com.

In: Common Visual Art in a Social Digital Age
Editor: Shalin Hai-Jew
ISBN: 978-1-68507-664-1

a larger amount of the population with some protections against the virus. It is thought that once the pandemic is brought under some control, it will fade from the public mind even as professionals continue to work the issue: government officials, scientists, researchers, pharmaceutical companies, healthcare workers, and others.

One approach to understand the human massmind about an event is to capture a set of social imagery that can illuminate some potential thinking of the event.

1. What is seen as the focal high point(s) of the event? What is seen as peripheral to the event?
2. Who are the main personalities of the event? Why? What parts of the event do they represent? Why?
3. How are facts represented in the visuals? Do the visuals show more "mental models" or "conceptual models" (the latter being more of an expert view)?
4. What are the emotional tones of the event? What elements spark the emotional tones?
5. Are there visual patterns? Repeating color palettes? Certain repeating shapes and depictions? How are these patterns arrived at?
6. What are some of the various types of messaging in the collected visuals?
   (a) Are there missing messages, and if so, what? (How are such missing images identified?)
7. What do the social images show about meta-awareness of the event? What does it show about mass sentience? What does it show about mass coping? What does it show about where human attention is spent? Are there visual indicators of what makes the event human-salient? Are there symbols that typify the event?
8. Who are those sharing social imagery of the event? What are the sources of the social imagery? What are the apparent purposes of the shared social imagery?

It was assumed early on that the questions would not be fully addressed but addressed variously. There is value in brainstorming a broad set of questions for when the analytical methods and the available social imagery may broach a broader swath of the information.

This is a visual approach through the capture of social imagery on the Social Web. The high-dimensional possibilities of visuals may echo some of the high dimensionality of the event. Visuals may be used as stand-ins for expression where people may be inchoate, where words are insufficient or incomplete. The time sensitivity of image search may evoke something of the particular slice-in-time.

Delimitations

There are limits to this research. The social images are scraped from various platforms and captured in a decontextualized way. The tagging of the visuals is usually accomplished with folk labels, but computational tagging may have also informed the tagging of the images and what was surfaced.

Social images are necessarily ambiguous. The coding of images is somewhat interpretive. The scraped images are also mostly thumbnails, with low resolution. Manual coding is not necessarily reproducible in the way computational coding would be. The culture and the interpretive lens of the human coder will affect the outcomes.

Also, this research is being conducted in the midst of a pandemic, so there are the limitations of a lack of perspective, given the immersion in the event. Further, for "common art" artists, being in the current moment may be "too soon" to be processing the event with visuals. The immediacy of the scraped social images may be limited because of the time period.

Review of the Literature

The SARS-CoV-2/COVID-19 pandemic is thought to have started in late 2019. It continues through the present, in the Fall of 2021. In this particular moment, there are a half-dozen or more vaccines in the world to combat the pathogenic virus. The percentage of a country's population that is protected varies, from developing countries with only a few percent of their population protected to others with much higher rates (the UAE with 96% vaccinated with at least one dose). Globally, 3.64 billion people (47.5% of the world's population) has received at least one dose (Holder, Oct. 8, 2021). There are other mitigation measures in the meantime, including social distancing, testing, facemasking, hand hygiene, and other approaches. In the moment, the World Health Organization's dashboard shows 4,831,486 who have died and some 237 million confirmed cases globally ("WHO Coronavirus (COVID-19) Dashboard," Oct. 8, 2021). At present, investigators are trying to find out the original cause of the pandemic, in terms of Patient 0 and where the virus originated (either zoonotically or through lab leak or some other source).

The experience of living through a pandemic is not a simple one. The person-to-person transmission of a deadly pathogen traumatizes populations in very visceral ways, given the intimacy of viruses in the breath and the blood. It breaks trust between people. It disrupts industries. It damages economies. It constrains job markets. The pandemic manifests differently in different locations, and there are different fallouts based on different interventions. Even though the world's scientists have been generous in the sharing of SARS-CoV-2/COVID-19 information, not all have had the proper leadership or resources to respond optimally. This has been so even in wealthy Western countries.

Research Methods

For this work, two social imagesets were collected. One was seeded with "common art and pandemic" and the other with "common art and COVID-19". The first set was assumed to be more general, and the latter more specific. In this space, there is a value to comparisons across sets. (Figure 1 and Figure 2) The "pandemic" set is comprised of 235 social images, and the "COVID-19" set of 215 social images. Both were captured Sept. 26, 2021.

There were also explorations of "COVID-19" art on an art-sharing site on social media. This search resulted in a little over two dozen images at the top-level of the site. The works were of different visual styles and different visual contents. The small size of the imageset resulted in too little to analyze, even as anecdotal information.

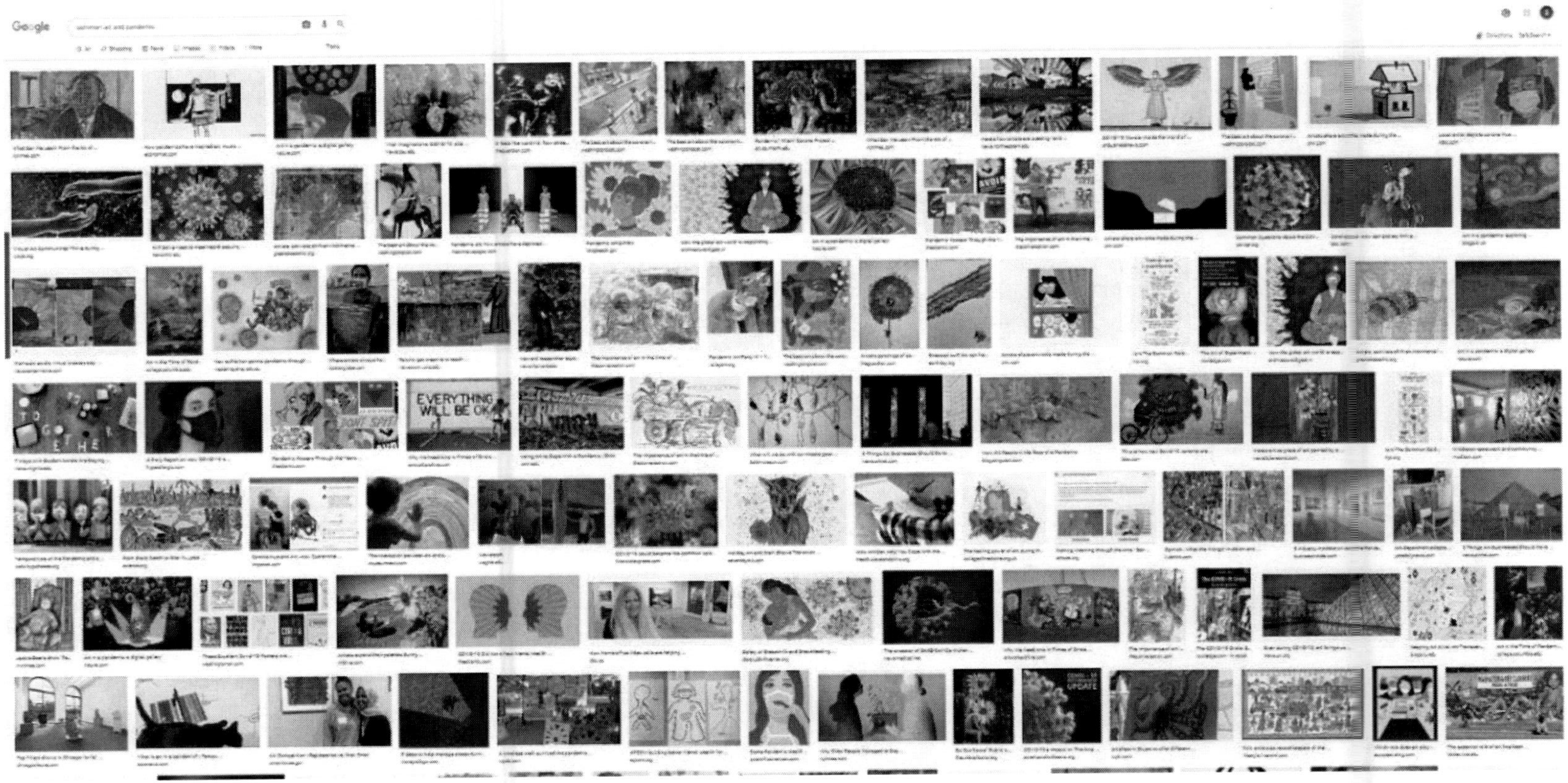

Figure 1. "Common Art and Pandemic" social imageset (from Google Images Search).

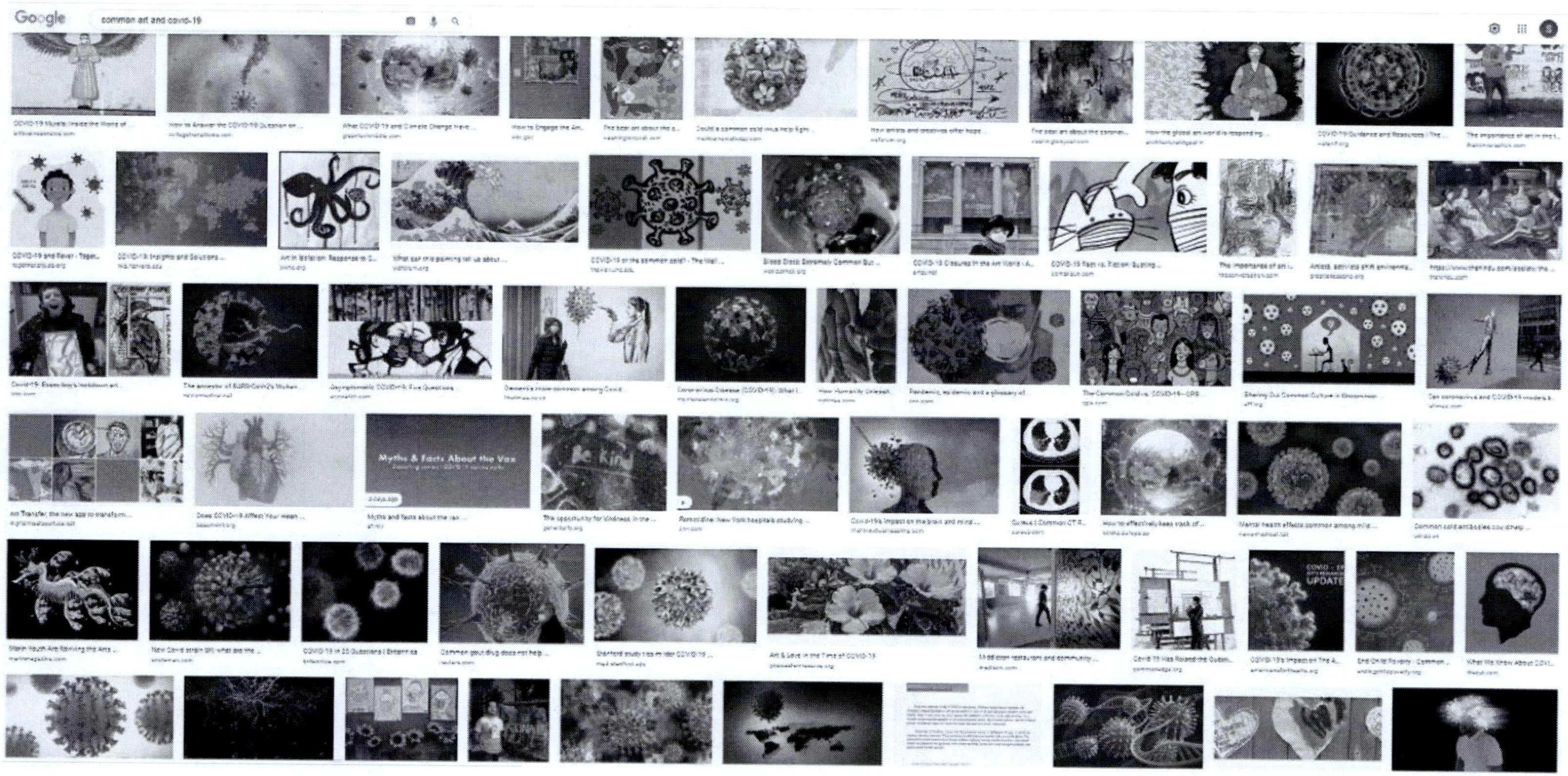

Figure 2. "Common Art and COVID-19" social imageset (from Google Images Search).

A number of focal questions were set up for a combination of top-down and bottom-up coding. The images were coded through multiple iterations.

1. What is seen as the focal high point(s) of the event? What is seen as peripheral to the event?
2. Who are the main personalities of the event? Why? What parts of the event do they represent? Why?
3. How are facts represented in the visuals? Do the visuals show more "mental models" or "conceptual models" (the latter being more of an expert view)?
4. What are the emotional tones of the event? What elements spark the emotional tones?
5. Are there visual patterns? Repeating color palettes? Certain repeating shapes and depictions? How are these patterns arrived at?
6. What are some of the various types of messaging in the collected visuals?
   (a) Are there missing messages, and if so, what? (How are such missing images identified?)
7. What do the social images show about meta-awareness of the event? What does it show about mass sentience? What does it show about mass coping? What does it show about where human attention is spent? Are there visual indicators of what makes the event human-salient? Are there symbols that typify the event?
8. Who are those sharing social imagery of the event? What are the sources of the social imagery? What are the apparent purposes of the shared social imagery?

Results

First, some rough notes were taken of the visuals in the respective social imagesets.

The Pandemic "Common Art" Social Imageset

The "pandemic" set showed various visuals. Some dealt with aspects of life under the pandemic directly: a woman painting lips on her facemask with a lipstick, a smart phone and facemask and viruses and particles in the air, and other such photos and illustrations. A mother holds a baby protectively while coronavirus particles float in the air around; the particles are bigger than her head. She represents humanity protecting and nurturing human life in at atmosphere of eminent threat. Other works show the importance of nurturance. One shows a duck with baby ducks sleeping on its back, with the message: "support those most vulnerable." The importance of human connectivity and touch is shown in one work, where a masked male and masked female dancer touch hands through a piece of cellophane. Another photo shows a stage scene. There are two young women who are in nurses' garb, and a woman sits in a chair between the two. [Without reverse image search and further research, the image itself does not signify much more.] One illustration shows hands being washed against a backdrop of paint splats and splashes, perhaps evoking a microbial universe (a la pseudo-Jackson Pollock-style). One work shows a weeping human eye, evoking something of the human condition in the present moment.

A few of the works go to cute, such as a little boy and a little girl hugging, as they look at artwork (of a sun). The message is made from quarantine on social media, but it is to give hope.

Information and Exhortation

Common art was used to inform. Various visual works shared information about colds and flus, hand hygiene, and vaccinations. One visual showed people interconnected with each other through a shared heart and lung (pulmonary) system. This suggested interdependencies between people. In another floral work, flowers were painted classically albeit with Clorox, Lysol wipes, and hand sanitizers, painted into the scene. Several of the visuals were book covers, with some touting anticipated "post-pandemic" realities.

Some works were posters in the style of health warnings of old (the 1900s): a poster exhorting people to avoid sharing drinking cups, a poster with the warning, "Don't spit!" one showing how to wear a mask, and so on. Another message reads: "breathe live." Another shows characters from the old Dutch masters albeit wearing facemasks. Another reads: "Wash your hands open your heart." There is a red and blue poster lauding Dr. Anthony Fauci for president. There is a poster comprised of a sentence: "IT'S CORONA VIRUS" and a stacked hidden message "It's on us." One poster shows a woman holding a lot of toilet paper, and there is the exhortation: "Leave plenty to go 'round." Another shows the world with the sign, "Sorry, we're closed." Another refers to social distancing: "Please stand away from me." One work refers to unemployment. There is a photo of a bright young woman in full graduation regalia and the notes: "need work" and "closed out of business." What is to happen to young people and their futures? There is the sense of the commentary reflecting and affecting the present but also something about remembering for the future, which might be different.

Heroes and Heroines

Besides people in isolation, including children, the people group included healthcare professionals as heroes. One visual showed two healthcare professionals in full personal protective equipment (PPE) embracing while each breathing only their own air. A gowned and masked and goggled healthcare professional is shown with rainbow-colored angel wings. Another visual shows two people each wearing surgical masks spraying to sanitize a space. One wears a backpack with toilet paper. One work depicts a healthcare worker with a facemask around her neck and flowers in her hair looking down at something off-canvas. Her back is bent, and she looks perhaps worn. These are representations of the heroes of the critical moment, among others. There are more literalist senses of superheroes, with the Hulk, Thor, Superman, and others in costume fighting the coronavirus. In this time, interestingly, the mundane seems heroic: A man wearing a facemask holds a painting advertising a community event. Meeting physically in community has its challenges. Another mundane visual: a woman sewing at a sewing machine and wearing a facemask is apparently making masks. All around her are coronavirus particles floating around, some with open-mouthed faces as they flee from her. One work depicts a singer (Billie Eilish) looking coolly at the camera. A healthcare worker is shown with many hands holding many tools to meet the needs of humanity. One of the tools, mysteriously, looks to be a pitchfork.

Life under Lockdown (with Time Passing)

Some of the visuals are wistful depicting life in a time of lockdowns and social distancing: One shows a person hiding in his house and looking out at a red flower; a woman holds up a pair of binoculars and looks out at the world from behind her window; a house stands with its roof open to the world, in a kind of airing out; a woman looks out at the world through her blinds. Several visuals show a very full human brain with a range of ideas crowding out the space. Another depicts a human brain with a whitish overlay, perhaps evoking the "brain fog" and "COVID-19 long hauler" syndrome. Another shows a human brain with red coronavirus particles and broken synapses.

Marking Time

Some of the social images show the marking of time: a black cat lazes in the foreground next to markers on white butcher paper, on which is written various months. Another play on time reads as symbolic: There is a side-by-side image. On the left, a young woman holds a drooping plant and hands it over to an older woman who has a flourishing and flowering one. One read is that the younger woman is giving a gift in youth to her future self. Or it could literally be about a younger generation giving the older generation the gift of a longer life (perhaps by living responsibly, where possible, in a time of a pandemic). Several photos show clocks being sold at a street fair. Several of the works show in plein air paintings, celebrating nature and landscapes. Others show a watercolor flower, a dead bird, a bumble bee, a palm leaf. Several drawings show people afflicting others with harm: one drawing shows people interacting violently with each other and many succumbing.

Global Children of All Faiths

One notable visual showed children all wearing facemasks with markings representing the religions of the world. This colorful work evokes something of the global nature of the pandemic. Some of the children are holding their hands in prayerful pose. Other depictions show children of various backgrounds in a classroom, in physical proximity. They are smiling at the viewer. The image strikes one as maybe something hopeful or something from a distant time, from years ago.

Several of the images seem to refer to an interesting side note in the journalistic coverage in the early days of the pandemic. This visual shows a llama with a flower in its mouth. This was reminiscent of an earlier story of llamas potentially having naturally generated antibodies which could be used to fight the novel coronavirus. [Without having read the extensive literature of the pandemic as it unfolded, the reference would have been elusive.]

Saving Art

In a kind of meta message, arts were shown as both meaning making and as salve. One visual shows a red and white first aid kit with a cross; it reads: "Art-based first aid. Mindfulness kit." A subset of the visuals shows artists at work: a person sketching in a paper sketchpad with a leaded pencil, a painting set up on a makeshift board leaning against a fireplace (home studio), and a woman in a baseball cap painting from under an umbrella in plein air. There are messages of hope in this set. One spells out in all caps: "EVERYTHING WILL BE OK." "We will get by" and "We will survive" are painted in red block letters on wood. People wearing masks walk by those messages. This photograph conveys something of human resilience. Some of the collages look to be table-top creations, perhaps from people's homes and places of safety. There are photos of graffiti, too, with people tagging messages of "unity." There are a number of photos of a famous art museum in Paris, some photos of artists in galleries with their works, and signs about art shows.

An oil or acrylic painting shows a young woman wearing a facemask and headset with flowers in background; on her face is a combination of anxiety and hope. A young woman wearing a surgical mask holds her head and has her eyes closed (in meditation?); a dove flies off to the right. There were multiple visuals of a person wearing a facemask and sitting in lotus position while many hands reach towards her. This evoked something of calm and equilibrium in a time of many demands. In another, a child is hand-painting a rainbow. One photo shows a medical laboratory. One visual shows a child wearing a facemask.

Some of the depictions show the coronavirus with a malicious personality, such as several works of chalk art on concrete. One shows strands of DNA as represented in the ribbon-like structures. In one mural, a healthcare professional is chastising an angry toothed coronavirus with red eyes, while a boy wearing a facemask and gloves rides by on a bicycle. In another depiction, the coronavirus is a purple sun shedding light on the world's peoples, standing in various geographical formations across the continents. Some illustrations show DNA strands coming out of the coronavirus shell. Visuals of the spiked (with s-protein) balls of virus floating in the air are a common motif. Another common motif is the recurring facemask. Interestingly, sunflowers appear a fair amount, too, perhaps as signs of hope. These are often depicted in positive light, drawn as faces on the bodies of people, and in backdrops of drawings by children. Some of the visuals showed "plague doctors," wearing beaks on their faces as a "protection" against infection by air (and who historically "treated" patients during the bubonic plague). ("Plague doctor," Oct. 5, 2021). These individuals were often drawn from non-medical ranks to take care of the afflicted, often without much effect, in the 17th century in Europe.

The COVID-19 Common Art Social Imageset

This second imageset shared many of the same images as the first.

There were images of coronavirus floating around the world. Another showed Planet Earth surrounded by red floating coronaviruses. [Earth is a repeating motif.] There is a message of overwhelmed humanity. Coronavirus particles make up a question mark. One visual showed people sharing hearts and lungs, in a collective pulmonary function. There are the images of mother-child and floating viruses in the air. Another showed an ear perhaps signifying listening; the ear is surrounded by coronavirus particles, and lightning bolts emanate from it perhaps suggesting a kind of focused energy towards the listening. In many depictions, the pathogenic virus is outside the body. In others, it is inside. One visual shows the virus mixed in with red blood cells. Another *in vivo* depiction shows infected lung tissue with dark spots and arrows pointing at them. Yet another shows side-by-side (vertical) lung scans. Perhaps this is a pre- and post-, showing progression of the colonizing of the human lungs.

There were the same heroic healthcare worker visuals. An artist is seen with agency, wearing a mask and painting a mural of a person who is masked. There are the repeating sunflowers and flowers in various of the works here, too. One work shows student paper hearts: "We support our nurses, docs + first responders" which looked to be decorated by children by written by an adult. Next are other hearts. One shows a cross-through "COVID-19," evoking the efforts of humanity to stamp out this dread virus. Another shows a red human heart speckled with coronaviruses, evoking something of the heart damage that many with the infection had experienced.

Of Human Struggle

COVID-19 is depicted as a ball and chain on a man's leg in one mural. A more gruesome version depicts the coronavirus as a ball on a chain swung up against the back of a person's head and breaking the head. There are visual stories of terrible loss: people carrying a casket. There are the weeping eyes in murals as the coronavirus floats in the air, pervasively.

One visual shows a boy with a high fever. A thermometer is depicted along one edge of the paper (100.4°F, 38°C. There are floating red (warning color) coronavirus particles. This depicts something of the mass anxiety of threats to children from the novel coronavirus.

Another drawing shows a male figure from torso up. All around his head are squiggles and shapes, which evoke free-floating anxieties and fears. A similar drawing shows a woman inundated with papers falling around her with syringes, coronavirus particles, bottles of medicine, and text, to show how overwhelming the current moment is with the flow of information.

There are a number of drawings of people who are masked but coughing and clearly not feeling well.

Unemployment

One data visualization shows falling employment for various individuals: those in construction, those in hospitality, those in cooking, and others. This visual reminds of the far reach of the pandemic's destructiveness.

Choropleth Maps

This imageset included a few choropleth maps, with the saturation of color in particular regions indicating the frequency of cases and infections and deaths during a large period of the pandemic and then the percentage of population inoculated in later choropleth maps. These have been a common visual motif in the latter set.

A few other maps are seen. One shows the continental U.S. and the U.S. flag in the background. The coronavirus icon is shown at the S.E. corner, near Florida (which has gone through massive devastating waves of infection due in part to poor state leadership at the top, including denialism of the risks of SARS-CoV-2).

Life-Saving Vaccines

Some of the newer themes in this set show the emergence of vaccines. One visual shows a smiling girl with a Band-Aid on her arm and a syringe next to her in a positive illustrative message about vaccines. One drawing shows a stick figure doctor holding up a syringe overhead.

Returning to Work in Face-to-Face Settings

Another one evokes returning to workplaces: one sign reads "COVID-19 Office Orientation" and shows a male and female colleague masked and keeping apart.

Of Faith for Strength

One mural showed a depiction of a Hindu deity, with people walking by in facemasks. This work evoked something of spirituality and faith. One work shows people wearing facemasks and holding their hands clasped in a prayerful position. A photo of sidewalk art shows a "demonic" face on a coronavirus with the recognizable crown of spikes.

Informational Offerings

Some of the social images in the "COVID-19" social imageset include posters, with informational purposes. One reads: "Worried you have been exposed to COVID-19?" Directions follow. There are posters about the health benefits of inoculating, handwashing, facemasking, social distancing, cleaning computer devices, and others. One describes a coronavirus app. Another poster describes COVID-19 symptoms. Another lists COVID-19 mitigation policies. Yet another shows a rubric of COVID-19 tests. One poster differentiates the symptoms of COVID-19 and the cold and flu and allergies. (There do seem to be some overlaps.)

One poster reads: "Do not inject or ingest Lysol. Live to fight another day!" This evokes the politically-led misinformation from the then-U.S. president on down who suggested various interventions to potentially fight SARS-CoV-2: bleach, light, hydroxychloroquine, and later ivermectin, and other substances, many toxic.

The visuals contain various exhortations:

- "Resilience means common sense."
- "Keep him safe."
- "Clean hands save lives."
- "Protect your elders."
- "Adapt. Respond. Thrive."
- "Be kind." (This is on a sidewalk chalk message.)

Some of the visuals include informational book covers.

Of Human Hope

One crayon drawing shows a yellow house, with a person standing in the doorway. The person is looking out at a green coronavirus lying flat on the grass with its protein spikes. It looks to be defeated. There is text, but the low resolution and the aliasing of the text make the words illegible. One images shows large words in a museum display: "We sit together in the dark to know how to love each other in the light." Quite a few of the photos show museum and art gallery displays. One photo shows a child drawing a chalk image of the Earth. One illustration shows a chart with a falling arrow and coronavirus in the background, perhaps signifying falling rates of infection.

As social beings, people strive to connect with others. One visual shows a couple kissing through a floral cloth mask, made of the same material. Theirs is a love connection.

A top-down drawing shows two children holding hands. Their connection evokes warmth and happiness.

Socio-Political Advocacy

Some of the images show more of a global awareness. One photo shows a plate with food on one side. There are two sets of hands accessing the plate. On the left side, the plate is empty, and there are nibbles from the plate itself (someone eating the plate). On the right side is some food (potatoes and green beans) and hands holding silverware (knife and fork) to start accessing the food. There is an evocation of perhaps the Global South and the Global North, the developing and the developed, the have-nots and the haves. This is a work that may have been designed to pierce apathy and provoke conscience. Another visual shows empty hands, often used to signify needful humanity. One shows a stylized human heart.

Some of the images evoke the global aspects of the pandemic. One shows people of all different backgrounds wearing masks.

One illustration shows a man and a cat both masked. The man is petting the cat, for its comfort and his own. This may show something of living in lockdown. A deeper meta reading may suggest the transmissibility of the virus from humans to animals, with documented cases in zoo big cats and between humans and pets. A different visual shows a man typing on a laptop with a cat sitting behind him while coronavirus floats outside. There is safety and productivity within the walls of a home.

Another aspect of advocacy involves fund-raising. With the shutdown of so many industries, people have had a difficult time making ends meet. One poster is about musicians holding a performance to raise money for themselves and other musicians.

A man in a t-shirt standing next to a mural that reads, "VACCINATE." One shows a crowd of people all wearing facemasks. Perhaps their actions model mutual care for others. One illustration shows a woman wearing a gas mask. A woman wearing a three-layered surgical mask bicycles by a mural with a woman wearing a facemask.

Both "Pandemic" and "COVID-19" Social Imagesets

The social visuals around "common art and pandemic" and "common art and COVID-19" do show some common themes as noted. Common visual motifs include the following: coronavirus particles, choropleth maps, facemasks, sunflowers, the Earth, people, and air made visible (perhaps as miasma or dirty air, thick with threats). These works require some observation and visual interpretation but are not that complex in terms of designed meanings. It makes sense though to not re-abstract the works or fall into platitudes because the works themselves are their own expression and maintain their own deep power. The works are by people for people, and they convey tips for survival, messages of resilience and hope. These are visual shoutouts to each other in an isolated time. There are glimmers of on-ground lived experiences.

In both image collections, there were images of octopuses, some holding paint palettes with various paints. Perhaps there was an art movement during this time using this animal.

In this section are the bottom-up coding observations. So, what did multiple iterated walk-throughs of the respective social imagesets show in terms of the top-down questions?

Discussion

This work uses as its target a complex and rolling event, lasting from late 2019 through the present (Fall 2021), and with some continuance into the near- and mid-term future. This event involves dynamic pieces: the mutating pathogenic virus, the public health researchers of the world, the political leaders of the world, intelligence agents, and others. The pandemic is lived at the individual ego-level but also at meso-group levels (families, friend groups, work groups, and others) and macro-group levels (societies, and others).

The research questions, created prior to the analysis of the social images, include the following:

1. What is seen as the focal high point(s) of the event? What is seen as peripheral to the event?
2. Who are the main personalities of the event? Why? What parts of the event do they represent? Why?
3. How are facts represented in the visuals? Do the visuals show more "mental models" or "conceptual models" (the latter being more of an expert view)?
4. What are the emotional tones of the event? What elements spark the emotional tones?
5. Are there visual patterns? Repeating color palettes? Certain repeating shapes and depictions? How are these patterns arrived at?
6. What are some of the various types of messaging in the collected visuals?
   (a) Are there missing messages, and if so, what? (How are such missing images identified?)
7. What do the social images show about meta-awareness of the event? What does it show about mass sentience? What does it show about mass coping? What does it show about where human attention is spent? Are there visual indicators of what makes the event human-salient? Are there symbols that typify the event?
8. Who are those sharing social imagery of the event? What are the sources of the social imagery? What are the apparent purposes of the shared social imagery?

1. What is seen as the focal high point(s) of the event? What is seen as peripheral to the event?
What is seen as focal to the COVID-19 pandemic is the sense of mortal threat to humanity, adults and children, and the importance of communal collaborative actions. The visuals share practical interventions (including health policy-supported ones), based on the science. There are visuals that provide encouragement and emotional salve, too, in the face of duress.

2. Who are the main personalities of the event? Why? What parts of the event do they represent? Why?
The main personality in these visuals is the coronavirus, depicted in various ways: personified as a malevolent force, shown as ribbon-like DNA, and shown as floating spiked balls as bioweapons. When humans are shown it is either cowering and hiding and hunkering down…or taking a stand by providing healthcare (for healthcare professionals) and masking (for common people).

3. How are facts represented in the visuals? Do the visuals show more "mental models" or "conceptual models" (the latter being more of an expert view)?
Where "mental models" evoke an amateur understanding and "conceptual models" evoke a professional understanding, the visuals—surprisingly—showed more of a leaning to the professionally provided information by public health professionals.

Some of the visual "common art" works pointed to religious beliefs but not in a way that directly displaced science and public health knowledge. There was not a sense of conflating spiritual practices—Hinduism, Judaism, Christianity, Islam, Sikhism, and others—with science-based practice. The spiritual beliefs are depicted as an emotional salve and perhaps an act of global inclusion.

4. What are the emotional tones of the event? What elements spark the emotional tones?
The visuals evoke emotional distress in many cases, given the showing of humans under threat and experiencing losses.

5. Are there visual patterns? Repeating color palettes? Certain repeating shapes and depictions? How are these patterns arrived at?
These works did show some recurring motifs. As noted earlier, they include coronavirus particles, choropleth maps, facemasks, sunflowers, the Earth, people, and air made visible (perhaps as miasma or dirty air, thick with threats).

6. What are some of the various types of messaging in the collected visuals?
(a) Are there Missing Messages, and if So, What? (How are Such Missing Images Identified?)

The visual messaging seemed to be two-fold. Foremost were ideas about how to try to protect the self and others against the SARS-CoV-2 pathogen. These seemed to be mostly based on public health messaging, simplified to particular behaviors. Second, there were outreaches to provide emotional salve through art. A communality exists alongside a sense of loneliness in the common art.

What was not seen was a direct calling out of those who chose not to vaccinate or chose not to mask (although there were plenty in the U.S. population who rejected both vaccinations and masks). There were some allusions to financial hardships, but these were fewer than other messaging. There were no racist messages per se related to the visuals even though racial strife did rise to the surface in many documented human interactions and crimes, stateside and elsewhere.

7. What do the social images show about meta-awareness of the event? What does it show about mass sentience? What does it show about mass coping? What does it show about where human attention is spent? Are there visual indicators of what makes the event human-salient? Are there symbols that typify the event?
It is not fair to assume that the small social imagesets necessary represent meta-awareness or mass-scale awareness. Those creating and sharing visuals may be assumed to be more engaged with the topic and more activist in their approaches. If these are suggestive, even lightly so,

perhaps the visuals show something of mass stress and mass fear and mass anxiety and struggles to cope.

Human attention was focused on the bio-threat and making do and getting by. It was focused on survival.

The human-salience of the issue was shown by the depiction of humans (adults and children) in contexts of bio-threat by air, by close contacts, by a lack of hygiene, and other messaging.

Symbolically, the SARS-CoV-2 pathogen was shown as a bioweapon (like a mace and ball, or a flail). The Earth symbolized the world's peoples. Hands symbolized care of people for each other. Sunflowers were used in a way to symbolize hope. Superheroes were used the symbolize "fight" and "altruism" and care for others.

8. Who are those sharing social imagery of the event? What are the sources of the social imagery? What are the apparent purposes of the shared social imagery?
Interestingly, it is not too difficult to infer where most of the visual information came from. Some are labeled by city government. Some are shared by commercial companies. Some of the works seem to be from healthcare professionals with professional health behavior messaging. Others were advertisements for art shows, museums, books, and other commercial products. Some works were shared by professional artists, others by common artists. Some works were shared by children. Some were shared by event organizers.

Future Research

The COVID-19 pandemic, which started in late 2019 and extends through the present, manifests differently in different geographical spaces. With the popularization of the vaccines in the West, there is hope perhaps that the actual pandemic may finish out by early 2022, with only a few hotspots in some locations. It would be of interest to conduct similar research in different locations of the world over different time slices…and at mass scale…with machine vision… It would be interesting to see how the visuals change over time in each location, through the different phases of the pandemic event (however those various phases are described). [Setting up phases for the COVID-19 pandemic: Perhaps there can be an early phase, then the respective waves, and then the gradual attaining of control, maybe with time periods broken out into monthly segments. Perhaps the pandemic may be divided into three stages, the exponential spread, the relative plateau, and the recovery. Or there can be political phases. Or there may be a bottom-up sense of phases by the types of social visuals depicted at each phase. Another may be mass-scale emotions, such as the handling of grief in Kübler-Ross's five stages of grief (1969): denial, anger, bargaining, depression, and acceptance.]

Another approach may be to collect the full set of available social images (N = all) from the event post-event, with the cast of a world's commemoration, in the flow of time. The emotions and the cast of the event may diminish with the lessening of actual life threat. Then, too, this set may be divided up into regions, to see if the retrospectives may be different.

Another approach may be to compare the social imagery from the current pandemic with the historical drawings from the 1918 – 1919 one.

Conclusion

A pandemic is experienced individually and also communally. People speak their own truths, but they also acquire truths from others. There is an interaction and a flow. The environment is echoic and changing. Some messages mask out others, and others amplify them. That may be seen in this social imagery collection both those seeded with "common art and pandemic" and "common art and COVID-19". Even as individuals and groups create messaging for target audiences, the same visuals may be seen by the broader public, and by researchers. Interestingly, the visuals shared in the social imagesets are mostly prosocial. They provide emotional catharsis; they provide reinforcement for proper health and social behaviors in a raging pandemic. In this, there is hope.

Acknowledgments

Here is to everyone who took efforts to protect the self and others from SARS-CoV-2/ COVID-19. How hard was it to mask up after all?

References

Holder, J. (2021, Oct. 8). Tracking coronavirus vaccinations around the world. *The New York Times.*

"Plague doctor." (2021, Oct. 5). *Wikipedia.* Retrieved Oct. 10, 2021, from https://en.wikipedia.org/wiki/Plague_doctor.

WHO Coronavirus (COVID-19) Dashboard. (2021, Oct. 8). World Health Organization. Retrieved Oct. 8, 2021, from https://covid19.who.int/.

Chapter 16

A Mass-Public Sense of Art from Select Social Media Platforms

Shalin Hai-Jew*

Kansas State University, Manhattan, Kansas, USA

Abstract

On the Social Web, various platforms enable the capturing of communications related to "art" and "common art." The platforms engaged in this work include the following: a text and data mining site, a social image sharing site, a microblogging site (accessed through both NCapture and Netlytic for different datasets), a news sharing site, and others. These capture sense of art that includes highbrow to lowbrow, formal to informal, and everything in between. This work samples some of the social media platforms to better understand some senses of common art on the Social Web, among the general masses.

Keywords: social media platforms, massmind, art, common art

Introduction

If the Social Web is a gathering place for the mass public, particularly in the time of the SARS-CoV-2/COVID-19 pandemic where interacting in person may be risky to health and well-being, then it may be an important place to explore some common interests, in this case: common art and art. Online is a wide diversity of spaces where those engaged in various aspects of art may gather and explore. The various sites have differing foci, art types and styles, and user bases. To understand common art will require different probes, and the differing sites stand to provide glimmers into the question. Certainly, many artists, art practitioners, art aficionados, and art professionals may not necessarily engage online; those who are findable online are a subset of the general population, with some demographics over-represented and others under-. This work serves as an exploratory chapter to see what may be learned about the general public's sense of common art based on the following sites: a text and data mining site, a social image sharing site, a microblogging site (accessed through both NCapture and Netlytic for different datasets), a news sharing site, and so on. This work does not aim to define "common art" in a definitive sense but only to capture whole or partial datasets and to offer some limited insights.

---

* Corresponding Author's Email: haijes@gmail.com.

In: Common Visual Art in a Social Digital Age
Editor: Shalin Hai-Jew
ISBN: 978-1-68507-664-1

Review of the Literature

A review of the literature does not show much direct research on social media and common art. There is some clear understanding that the Internet has affected the art world fundamentally, as it has most industries. Going to social media to understand large-scale insights is common practice, including the harnessing of big data analytics (Abkenar, Kashani, Mahdipour, & Jameii, 2021; Ghani, Hamid, Hashem, & Ahmed, 2019). Socially shared data may be analyzed to detect and predict social trends; one example involves the uses of non-photographic images on Twitter at mass scale (Yazdani & Manovich, 2015). The making of artworks by non-experts has been applied for therapeutic purposes for the common artists' health (Teoli, 2021; Hacmun, Regev, & Salomon, 2021). One work shares an important insight: that people "learn to see socially—as a significant factor in contemporary art making practice"; artists are informed by "contemporary art making practice and systems of representation" (Walker & Walker, 2004, p. 23). There is a social aspect to art-making. In a common art sense, people may be exposed broadly to art and aesthetics in the built environment, mass media, advertising, entertainment, and others; they may have some exposures in compulsory education.

Research Methods

This work aims to sample various platforms on the Social Web to better understand an electronic-mediated sense of "common art" and "art." The various platforms include the following: a text and data mining site, a social image sharing site, a microblogging site (accessed through both NCapture and Netlytic for different datasets), and a news sharing site.

Results

Each platform offered a glimmer or an angle of insight on a public sense of "common art."

A Text and Data Mining Site

The first site used was ProQuest's TDM Studio, or its Text and Data Mining Studio. This tool enables access to a shadow dataset of information based on queries of various ProQuest data holdings, in order to enable insights about various types of data (through topic modeling, through sentiment analysis, and through geographical analysis, among others). The available data is indirect; it is once removed from the actual data; it is a form of metadata. Various queries may be formulated using R and Python based on the pulled data.

In Figure 1, there is a map that shows a geographic analysis of "common art" articles in the *Los Angeles Times* over a multi-decade period. "Common art" is a global phenomenon, and the media coverage addresses such works from many regions of the world. (A more complex search was instigated across a range of sources, but the dataset never quite materialized and so was left off of this work).

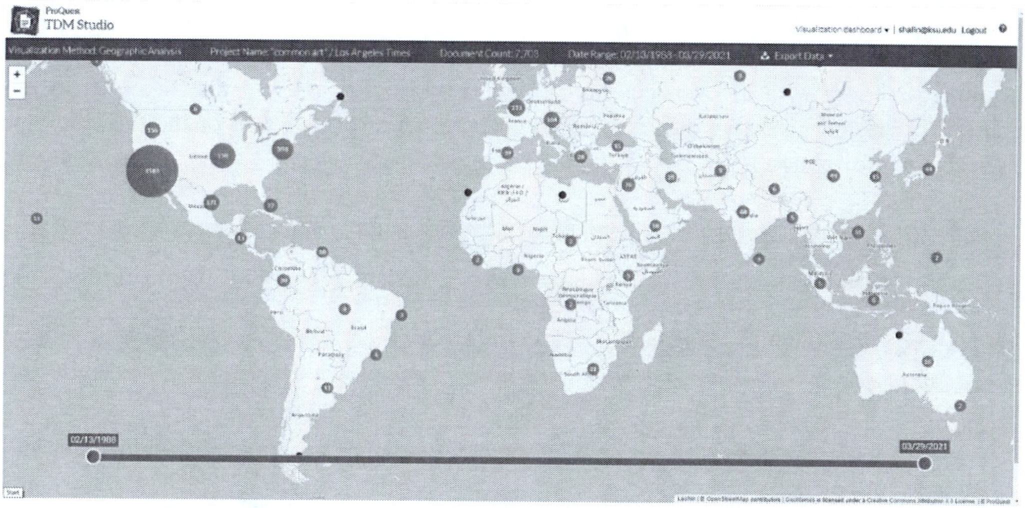

Figure 1. Geographic analysis of "common art" Articles in the *Los Angeles Times* (Feb. 13, 1998 – Mar. 29, 2021) Set of 7,703 Articles.

A Social Image Sharing Site

A related tags network was run with the seeding term "art" on the Flickr social image sharing platform. The "tags" used to label shared social visuals are a combination of "folk" (amateur) labels and computationally applied ones. Tags that are "related" are co-mentioned with other tags at a particular threshold. This network was pulled using a third-party tool built into NodeXL, and the parameter of the pull was for a 1.5-degree network. Interestingly, the graph was relatively small (62 vertices), with only two groups based on the Clauset-Newman-Moore clustering diagram (suggesting not much divergence given the lower number of groupings: two). (Table 1) Such related tags may show at a level of abstraction some co-occurring tags at a mass-scale level of sensibility.

Table 1. Graph metrics from the "Art" related tags network on Flickr (1.5 degrees)

Graph Metrics	Values
Graph Type	Directed
Vertices	62
Unique Edges	1487
Edges With Duplicates	0
Total Edges	1487
Self-Loops	0
Reciprocated Vertex Pair Ratio	0.331244405
Reciprocated Edge Ratio	0.497646268
Connected Components	1
Single-Vertex Connected Components	0
Maximum Vertices in a Connected Component	62
Maximum Edges in a Connected Component	1487
Maximum Geodesic Distance (Diameter)	2
Average Geodesic Distance	1.386576
Graph Density	0.393178213
Modularity	Not Applicable
NodeXL Version	1.0.1.336

In Figure 2, the first group to the left seems to focus on various types of common art and some descriptive dimensions. The one on the right seems to focus on more formal art features. The images shown with the vertices are provided by Flickr (and do not vary over different iterations of related tags network extractions). The level of abstraction of the tags may mean less specific information here.

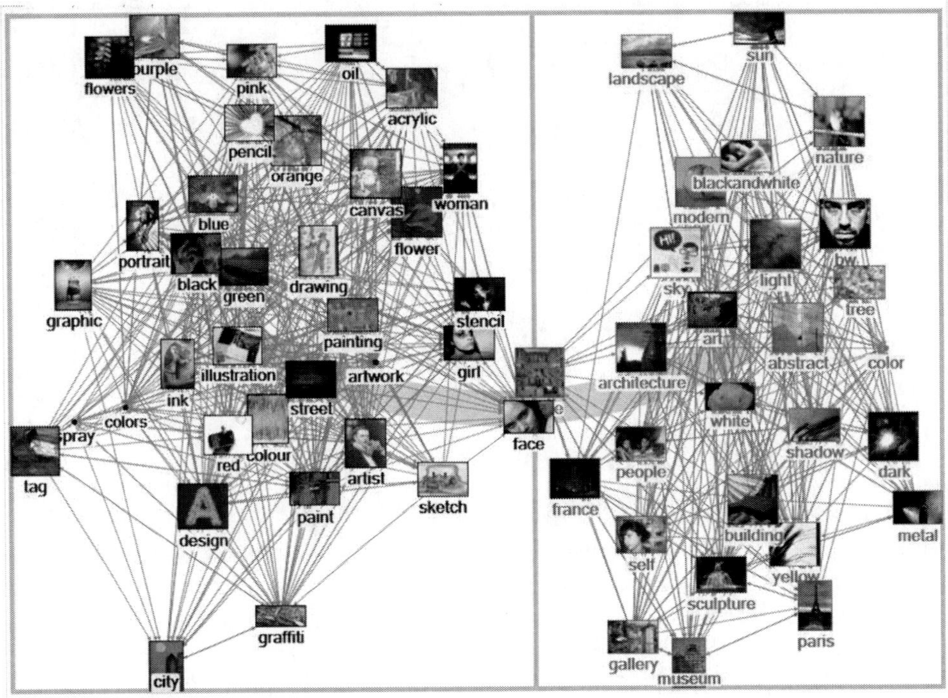

Figure 2. "Art" related tags network on Flickr (1.5 deg.).

A Microblogging Site (Accessed through Both NCapture and Netlytic for Different Datasets)

Twitter, the major microblogging site, was accessed using both NCapture (with NVivo) and also with Netlytic (a free online data query and social network visualization site).

NCapture and NVivo

A search for art-based social media accounts brought up the most popular ones based on the internal Twitter search. The search resulted in both those that are identified as scripted agents or robots…and others that represent arts organizations (museums, galleries, and the like). Individual accounts did not appear at the top several pages of the search. Some 17 social media accounts were identified, and their public data was captured on the same day in late 2021 using NCapture on the Chrome web browser. [The author attempted to capture imagery @pinterest, @etsy, @instagram, and some others on Twitter in order to capture a more common sense of "art," but those accounts were inaccessible for data scraping over a number of days.]

Word Frequency Counts

A frequency count was run, with "http" and "https" removed to the stopwords list. The word cloud shows the dominance of formal institutions in the arts space, with hashtags about collections and museums and art types and historical art references. #decorativearts suggests something of "common art" and "folk art" and "amateur art." A few @ accounts show again the focus on the so-called gatekeepers of formal art. This first set was run on the respective Twitter accounts treated separately as individual files (Figure 3).

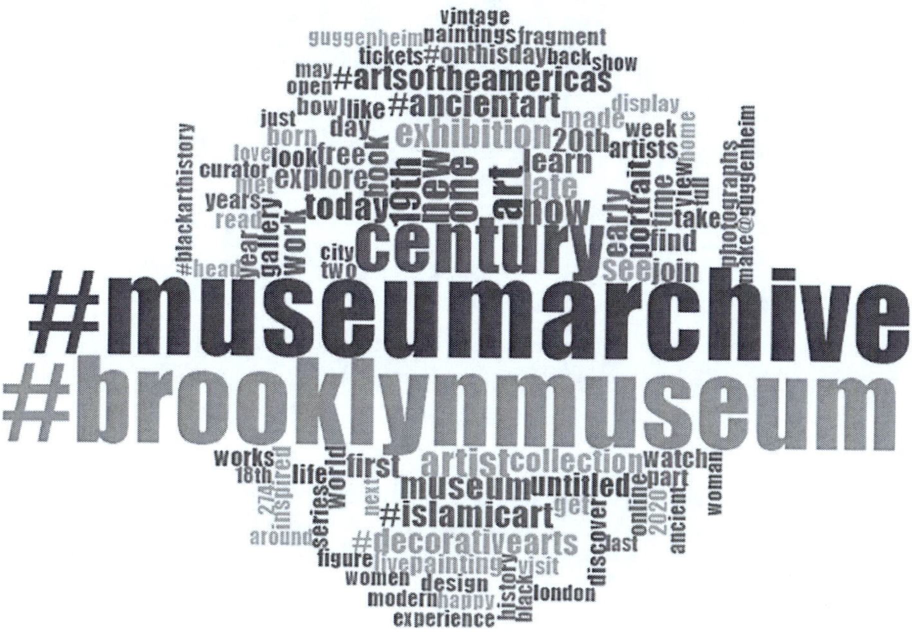

Figure 3. Word cloud from word frequency count of contents of 17 arts-related microblogging sites on Twitter (both 'Bot-Based' and 'Organization-Based') (single files in collection).

This next word cloud shows the same information albeit run on the files as combined ones. This prior conditional about how files are introduced into NVivo does have an effect on the extracted information. In this, the year 2021 comes to the forefront. Some social concerns come to the forefront, too, such as "artistsofcolor" and "black" and other foci. Some of the earlier details also show in this latter word cloud (Figure 4).

An "art" word tree was extracted from the 17 arts-related microblogging social account sites on Twitter. This snippet shows various discussions in the branches, and an outsized number of branches with "http" to reference websites (Figure 5).

A word associations cluster analysis may be seen in Figure 6. The hubs in the cluster diagrams are the respective formal museums.

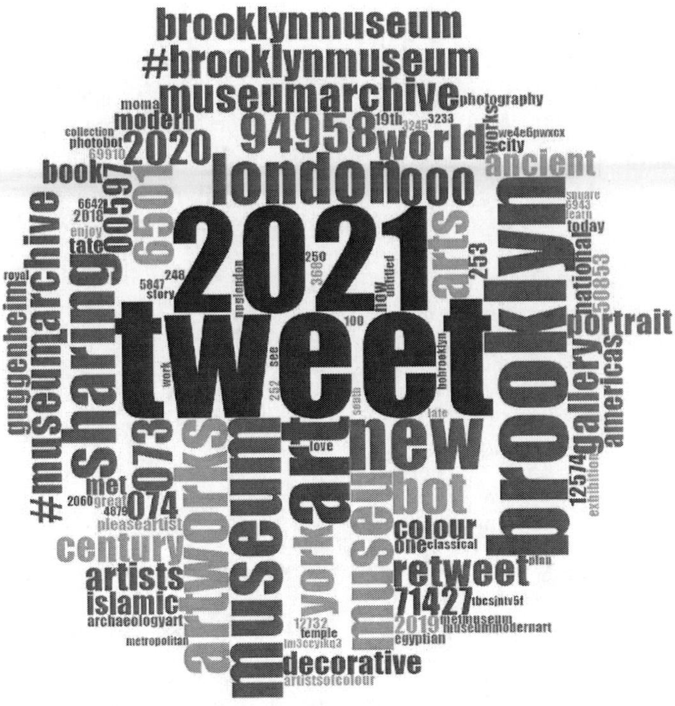

Figure 4. Word cloud from word frequency count of contents of 17 arts-related microblogging sites on Twitter (both 'Bot-Based' and 'Organization-Based') (combined files in collection).

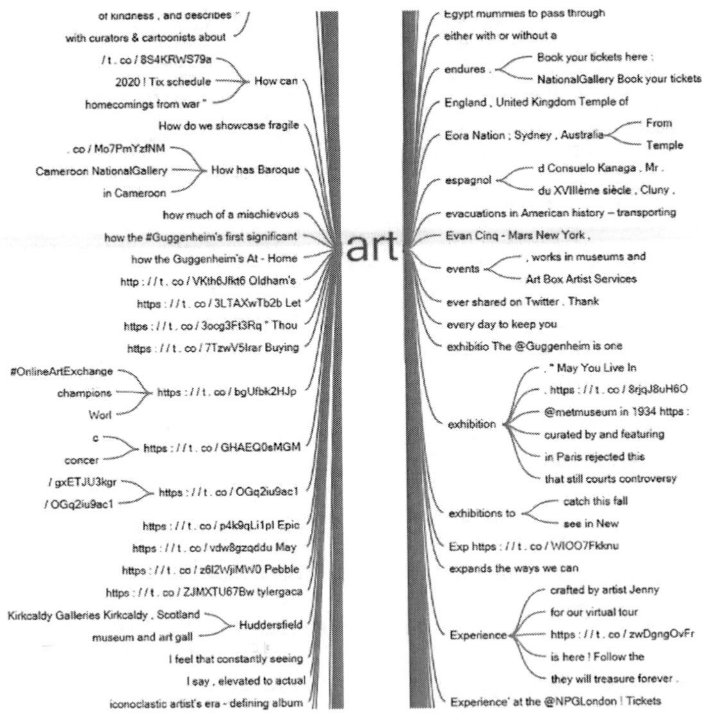

Figure 5. "Art" word tree snippet from 17 arts-related microblogging sites on Twitter (both 'Bot-Based' and 'Organization-Based').

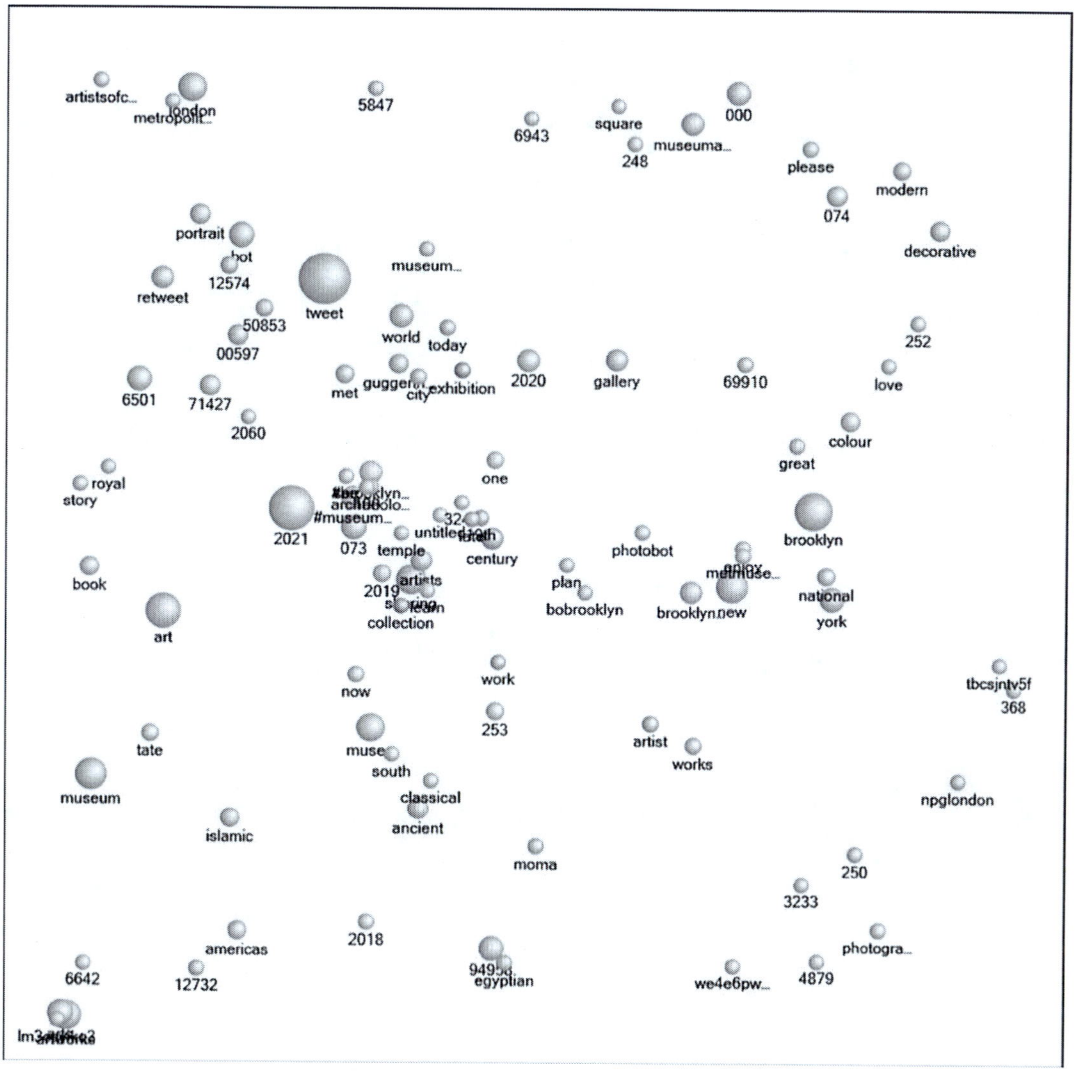

Figure 6. Word associations from word frequency count of contents of 17 arts-related microblogging sites on Twitter (both 'Bot-Based' and 'Organization-Based') (2d diagram).

Autocoded Topic Modeling

In the next figure, the machine-based coding of topics was applied to the 17 arts-based social accounts on Twitter (Figure 7). The top-level topics are the following: "https, art, artist, century, century https." In a zoomed-in sense, the related subtopics are more enriching and informative.

The autocoded topics with the 'bot accounts removed show a focus still of websites, art, and artists (Figure 8).

Then, an autocoding was run on the bot-based accounts only (Figure 9).

Finally, an excerpted topic and sub-topic table is offered for "art" and "artist" topics, which show the occluded topics. (Table 2) This is a partial table only. The codes or labels are represented verbatim as found by NVivo. These are kept in lower case as in common practice (for tags, for labels).

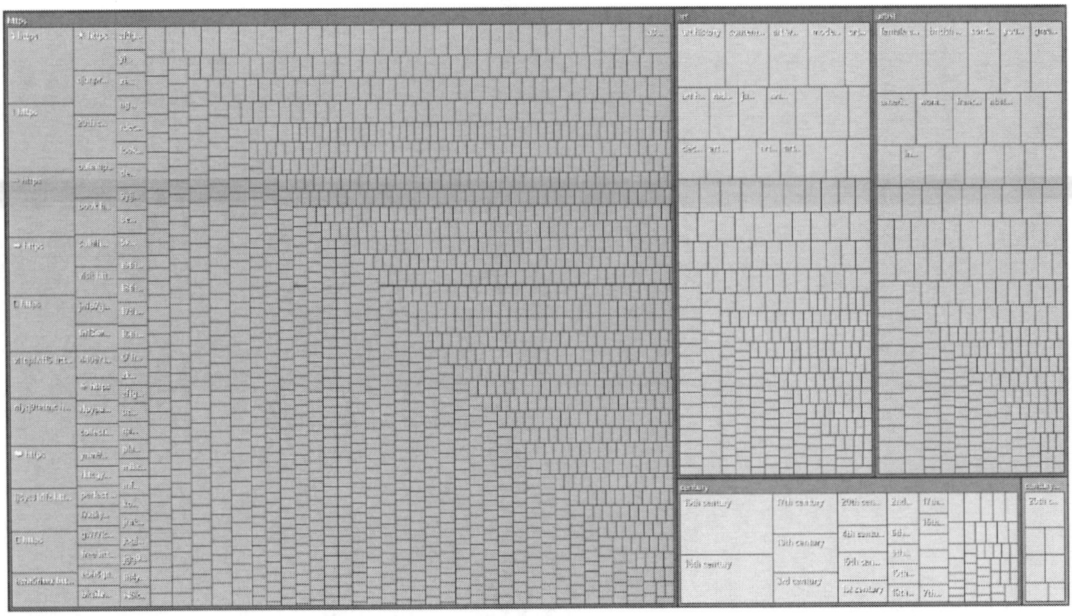

Figure 7. Autocoded topics in combined microblogging files of 17 arts-related microblogging sites on Twitter (both 'Bot-Based' and 'Organization-Based').

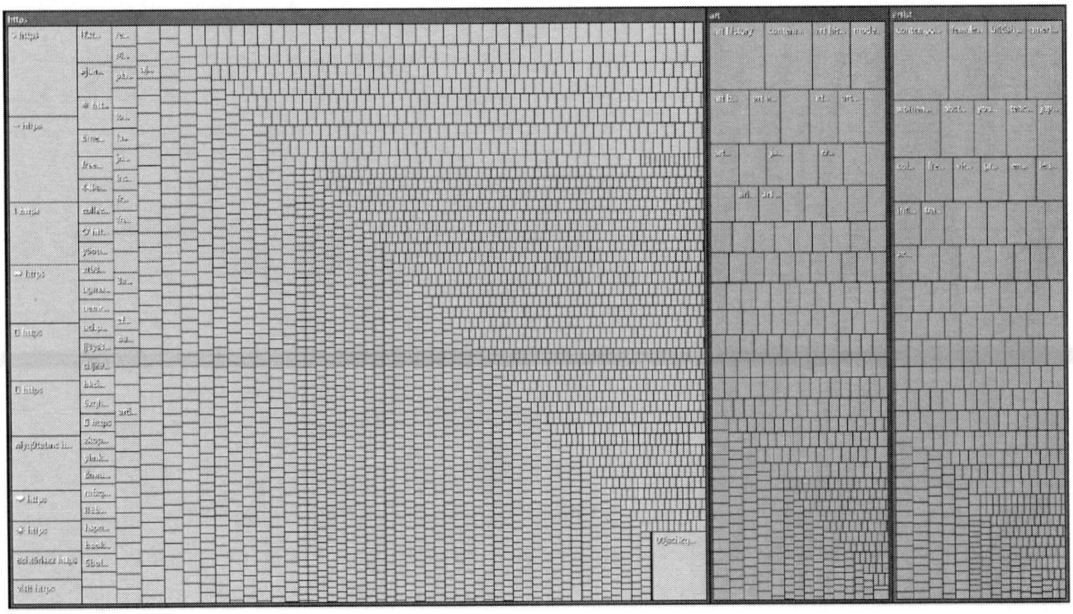

Figure 8. Autocoded topics from 17 arts-related microblogging sites on Twitter ('Organization-Based') ('Organization-Based' Only) (treemap diagram).

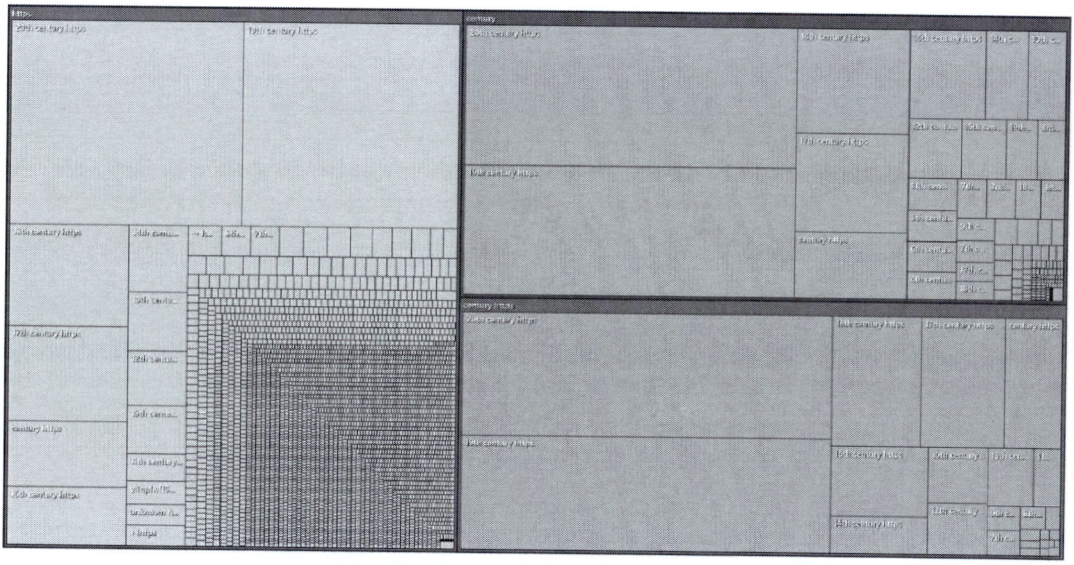

Figure 9. Autocoded topics in combined microblogging files of 17 arts-related microblogging sites on Twitter ('Bot-Based' only) (treemap diagram).

Table 2. Top-level "Art" and "Artist" topics (with subtopics) in the Autocoded Codebook (An excerpt)

art	
	18th century art
	1930 art critic
	1981 mail art project
	19th-century art
	19th-century art world
	20 art students
	20th cent art
	20th-century art
	20th-century art movements
	35 art exhibitions
	750 art kits
	abstract art
	accessible art
	accessible arts space
	activist art
	actual art
	adult art
	african art
	african rock art
	always art
	amazing art
	amazing art piece
	amazing art work
	amazing rock art
	american art
	american protest art

Table 2. (Continued)

art	
	andean art practice
	annual art calendar
	arab art
	art – love
	art ♥
	art ✍
	art activities
	art addict
	art adventure
	art books
	art books list
	art cart
	art challenge
	art change
	art circles
	art classes
	art collections
	art collector
	art critic
	art curator
	art dancing
	art dealer
	art display
	art dream
	art duo
	art education
	art endures
	art exhibitions
	art experience
	art expertise
	art experts
	art expression
	art extravaganza
	art facts
	art fans
	art form
	art fun
	art gallery
	art gallery visits
	art gifts
	art handlers
	art historian
	art history
	art history article
	art history class
	art history classic
	art history influence costume design
	art history knowledge
	art history lecture
	art history nerd

art	
	art history student
	art house films
	art https
	art identification technology
	art impresario
	art institutions
	art instutitions
	art intersect
	art journal
	art kits
	art knowledge
	art lover
	art lovers ♡
	art materials
	art movement
	art muscles
	art museum
	art object
	art outdoors
	art party
	art patronage
	art photographer
	art photography
	art piece
	art pilgrimage
	art presents
	art prevails
	art preview
	art print service
	art prints
	art process videos
	art products
	art professionals
	art project
	art publications
	art quiz
	art scene
	art school
	art shows
	art skills
	art space
	art spots
	art staycations
	art storage
	art student
	art students today
	art style
	art submissions
	art superstar
	art talk
	art theorist
	art trail
	art t-shirts

Table 2. (Continued)

art	
	art works
	art workshops
	art world
	art world colleagues
	art world prankster
	arts audiences
	arts events
	arts groups
	arts matter
	arts organisations
	arts organizations
	arts patron
	arts post-covid https
	arts programming
	arts sector
	arts subjects
	asian art
	at-home art classes
	augmented reality art gallery
	avant-garde art
	beautiful art
	became art https
	believed art
	bondage art
	boring art
	botanical art
	botched art restoration
	brazilian art
	breaking art
	breathtaking art
	bringing art
	bringing art outdoors
	british art
	british art history
	british pop art movement
	burgeoning art
	buy art
	canadian art group
	caribbean-british art
	ceramic art
	chinese art
	christian art
	cinematic art series
	civic-minded art
	classical art
	commercial art galleries
	complex art evacuations
	computer art
	computer-generated art
	concept art

art	
	conceptual art
	conceptual art exhibition
	concrete art
	contemporary art
	contemporary art collections
	contemporary art https
	contemporary art market today
	contemporary art scene
	contemporary art show
	contemporary art world
	cool art
	course arts
	creating art
	creative arts
	creative arts programme
	custom art print service
	daily art quiz
	danish art scene
	dead art
	deadly art
	decorative arts
	decorative wall art
	dedicated art history courses
	democratic art
	digital art experience
	digital art piece
	disability-led arts
	documentary art form
	dutch art history
	early concept art
	egyptian art
	egyptian art collection
	electronic art pioneer
	encountering art
	english art
	english art critic
	enjoying art
	era-defining album art
	european art
	european art history
	exceptional art experiences
	experimental studio art program
	exploring art
	exquisite art pieces
	extraordinary art
	famed arts institution
	fantastic fan art
	fascinating art
	favorite art joke
	favorite art museums
	favorite art spots
	favorite art teacher
	favourite art

Table 2. (Continued)

art	
	favourite art podcasts
	featuring art activities
	feline art
	female art historians
	feminist art
	feminist art historians
	fiber arts
	fibre arts
	finding art
	fine art
	fine art prints
	flagship art history course
	flagship arts
	folk art influences
	formal art practice
	formal art training
	fragile art works
	free art history
	free art kit
	free art materials
	free art trail
	free community art sessions
	free hands-on studio art courses
	french art
	fun art activities
	future art
	future arts scene
	global art contexts
	global art histories
	global arts orgs
	goth-inspired art
	graphic art
	great art
	great art ideas
	great art quiz
	great art stories
	groundbreaking art
	groundbreaking art world figure
	gutter art
	hands-on art challenges
	hands-on art history course
	happy art thread
	hidden art
	hidden art gem
	historical art
	home-made art
	imitating art 🔗 https
	immaterial art
	including art
	including art prints

art	
	incredible art
	independent art
	indian art
	indian cinema art
	industrial art exhibition
	influential art movements
	inside art
	in-situ rock art
	installation art
	installing art
	intense art experiences
	intensive art course
	internet art
	intimate art form
	intimate art weekends
	involving art
	iranian art
	islamic art
	italian art
	japanese art
	japanese metal art
	jewelled arts
	key art
	largest-scale art digitisation projects
	latinx art
	leading arts
	level art
	light change art
	little art
	little art tip
	live art
	live art returns
	live art workshop
	longtime art philanthropist
	magnificent art
	mail art
	mail art project
	major art
	major art discovery
	major art exhibition
	major art movements
	making art
	making art today
	martial arts
	media art collection online
	medieval art
	medieval art traditions
	mesmerizing art
	mesoamerican arts
	messy art
	mixing art
	modern art
	modern art collection

Table 2. (Continued)

art	
	modern art https
	modern art masters
	modern art movements
	modern art treasures
	modern art world
	modernist art
	monthly art boxes
	much art
	mughal art
	musical arts
	must-see art shows
	mystical art
	nail art
	necessary art
	needed art
	neoclassical art
	netherlandish art
	next art
	next art adventure
	non-objective art
	non-traditional art materials
	notable art events
	n't art
	online art
	online art history courses
	online art session
	online art tutorials
	online family art workshop
	optical art
	palestinian art
	part art project
	perfect art experiment
	performance art
	performance art pieces
	performing arts
	performing arts scene
	performing arts series
	personal art
	personal art history periods
	photographs art
	piccadilly art takeover
	pictorial art
	pioneered art photography
	pioneering arts education program
	polish art
	political art group
	pop art
	pop art superstar full tour
	postwar art
	potential art style concepts

art	
	pre-raphaelite art
	priceless art
	progressive arts
	public art
	public art gems
	public art initiatives
	public art projects
	public art trail
	pure art
	queer art history
	quick art fix
	radical art
	rainy art
	real art
	realise art
	renowned art dealer
	replicating art
	respectable art form
	room-sized art installations
	s art world
	saw art
	seeing art
	senior art
	sensuous art
	sharing art
	showcase art
	significant art award
	sometimes art
	specific art
	spectacular art
	staid art
	stained glass art
	striking art
	student art show
	studio art program
	surviving art
	syrian art
	taking art education online
	teaching art
	technically art
	textile arts
	thought art
	three-week art
	together art
	top art books
	top art shows
	town—art historian
	traditional arts
	tunisian art
	unique art experiences
	unique art museum
	upcoming art history course
	usable art glass

Table 2. (Continued)

art	
	used art commissions
	using art
	varying art
	vibrant art
	vibrant art prints
	victorian art
	victorian art critic
	video art
	video art conservation workshop
	video art survey
	virtual art adventure
	visitor experience art
	visual art
	visual art space
	visual arts category
	ways art history
	weekend course arts
	western art
	western art collection
	western art narrative
	whimsical art
	wild art
	world-class art
	world-renowned art history
	young art lovers
artist	
	♡ artist
	109 women artists
	13th artist
	16thc artists
	17th century artist
	18th-century artist
	19th-century artists
	2013 artist rooms
	2020 artist initiative
	20th-century artist
	25 year artist
	abstract artists
	acclaimed artist
	accomplished artist
	actionspace artists
	admired artists
	aesthetic artists
	african artist
	african-american artist
	afro-peruvian artist
	amateur artists
	amazing artists
	american artist
	american artist jules

artist	artist
	american-belgian artist
	anglo-netherlandish artist
	arabian artist
	arctic artists
	artist activations
	artist alphonse
	artist bodys
	artist bridges
	artist brief
	artist collaborations
	artist collectives
	artist commissions
	artist constantin
	artist duo
	artist figurines online
	artist friends
	artist group
	artist holiday cards
	artist howardena pindell
	artist https
	artist interventions
	artist jules
	artist kalup
	artist kerstin
	artist khadija
	artist laszlo
	artist lynette
	artist movies
	artist painting sets
	artist panel
	artist project
	artist project series
	artist refugees
	artist series
	artist takeovers
	artist talks
	artist zanele
	artists signature
	artists today
	artists works
	artists—talks
	aspiring artist
	associate artist
	aussie artist
	australian artist
	austrian artist
	award-winning artist
	awesome artist
	baroque artists
	belgian artist
	beloved artist
	beloved downtown artist
	black artist

Table 2. (Continued)

artist	
	blog—artist
	botanical artist
	brazilian artist
	brilliant artists
	british artist
	british-american artist
	british-canadian artist
	british-finnish artist
	british-gambian artist
	british-nigerian artist
	brooklyn-based artist
	budding artists
	buzzing artist
	cabaret artist
	canadian-british artist
	case artist
	celebrated artist
	celebrated woman artist
	central artists
	centuries artists
	ceramic artist
	chicago-based artist
	chilean artist
	chinese avant-garde artist
	clever artist
	collection artist
	comic artist
	commercial artist
	concept artist
	conceptual artist
	congolese artist bodys
	contemporary artists
	contrast artists
	controversial artists
	countless artists
	court artist
	creative artist
	cuban artists
	cuban-american artist
	dada artists
	dance artist
	danish artist
	daring artists
	deaf artists
	decorative artist
	digital artist duo
	digital artists
	disabled artists
	distinctive artists
	drove artists

artist	
	dutch artist
	electronic artists
	elusive artist
	embroidered artist figures
	emerging artists
	encouraging artists
	english artist
	european artists
	exceptional artist
	exciting artists
	exhibiting artists
	exhibition artist
	experience artist
	experimental artists
	expert artists
	exploring artists
	extraordinary artist
	fall artist
	famous artists
	fantastic female artists
	favorite artist collaborations
	favorite artists
	favourite artist
	favourite artist power couples
	favourite living artists
	favourite woman artist
	featuring artists
	featuring neurodiverse artist
	fellow artist
	fellow fauvist artists
	fellow graffiti artist
	female artists
	feminist artist
	final artist
	finnish artist
	first-ever artist
	follow artist
	food artists
	foremost women artists
	former artist
	french artist
	french poster artist jules
	future artists
	gave women artists
	gay artist
	german artist
	gifted artist
	glasgow-born artist
	glass artist
	good artists
	graffiti artist
	graphic artist
	great artist

Table 2. (Continued)

artist	
	great women artists
	groundbreaking artist
	ground-breaking artists
	guggenheimabudhabi collection artist
	guitar-smashing rock artist
	guyanese artist
	historical native artists
	host artist
	how-to guide artist
	human figure artist
	hungarian artist
	hungarian-british artist
	iconic artists
	iconoclastic artist
	illustration artists
	immigrant artists
	important artists
	important performance artists
	impressionist artist
	impressive artists
	inaugural artist
	including artist
	including collection artist
	incomparable artist
	incredible artists
	independent artist
	indian artist
	indian artist lancelot ribeiro
	indigenous artists
	influential artist
	influential living artists
	innovative artists
	inspired artist
	inspiring ways artists
	installation artist
	interdisciplinary artist yeesookyung
	intergenerational artists
	intergenerational hair artists
	international artist
	international travelling artist
	internationally-acclaimed artist
	inventive artist
	invited artists
	iranian artist
	iranian-american theater artist
	iranian-born artist
	irish artist
	issues women artists
	italian artist
	japanese artist

artist	
	japanese artist hokusai
	kenyan-born artist
	korean artist
	kuwaiti artist
	landscape artist
	last week artists
	late artist
	late artist agnès
	later artists
	latinx artist
	latvian-american artist
	leading artists
	leading women artists
	lebanese artists
	legendary artist
	light artist
	little artist
	liverpool-born artist
	living artist
	local artists
	london-based artist
	long-deceased artist
	main artists
	major artist
	makeup artist
	make-up artist
	male artists
	manga artist
	meeting artists
	metalwork artist
	mexican artist
	mexican artist truthfulness
	midcentury artists
	minimalist artist
	modern artists
	multi-disciplinary artist
	multidisciplinary artist duo
	multifaceted artists
	multimedia artist
	mystery artist
	nairobi-born artist layers
	neon artist
	net artists
	netherlandish artist
	network artists
	next artist
	nigerian-american artist
	nigerian-born artist
	nominated artist
	non-verbal artist
	normal artist
	norwegian artist
	notorious graffiti artist

Table 2. (Continued)

artist	
	official war artist
	optical artists
	pakistani artist
	papier-mâché artists
	participating artists
	past artist interventions
	performance artist
	performing artists
	photographic artist
	photorealist artist
	pioneering artist
	pioneering woman artist
	pivotal artists
	plinth artist
	polish artist
	political artists
	pop artists
	portrait artist
	postwar artists
	post-war artists
	preeminent artist
	prize-winning artist
	professional artist
	professional manga artist
	prolific artists
	proud artists
	provincial artist
	queer artists
	queer moving-image artists
	radical artists
	reading—artist
	reimagined artists
	remarkable artist
	renowned artist
	renowned court artist
	reportage artist
	resident artist
	revealing artist
	revered artists
	revolutionary artist
	rococo artist
	roll artist
	romantic artist
	russian artist
	russian artist yulia tsvetkova
	russian-born artist
	saving artists
	self-taught artist
	self-trained artist
	several artists
	shape-shifting artist

artist	
	shared artists works
	shortlisted artist
	singaporean-british artist
	skilled artist
	sought-after artists
	spanish artist
	special artist
	staff artist
	stained glass artist
	struggling artists
	student artist
	superstar artists
	surrealist artist
	swedish artist
	swiss artist
	swiss landscape artist
	swiss-american artist duo
	talented artists
	tattoo artist
	teaching artists
	textile artist
	theater artist
	together artists
	trailblazing artist
	true artist
	turkish artist
	turned artist
	turn-of-the-century artist
	ultimate artist
	unfashionable artist
	unidentified artist
	unknown artist
	unknown artist https
	unsung artist
	venetian artists
	victorian artist
	video artist
	vietnam-born artist
	visual artist
	ways artists
	welcomed artists
	well-known lacquer artists
	welsh artist
	western artists
	winning artist
	woman artist
	women artists
	wonderful artist
	word artist
	world-famous manga artists
	world-renowned artists
	young artists
	young artists summer

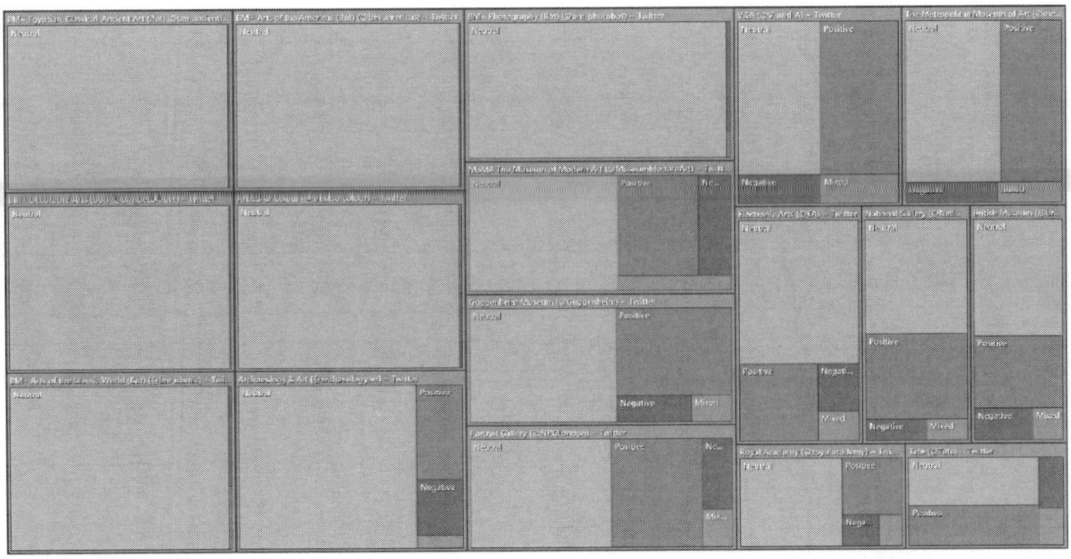

Figure 10. Autocoded sentiment analysis of 17 arts-related microblogging sites on Twitter (both 'Bot-Based' and 'Organization-Based') (treemap diagram).

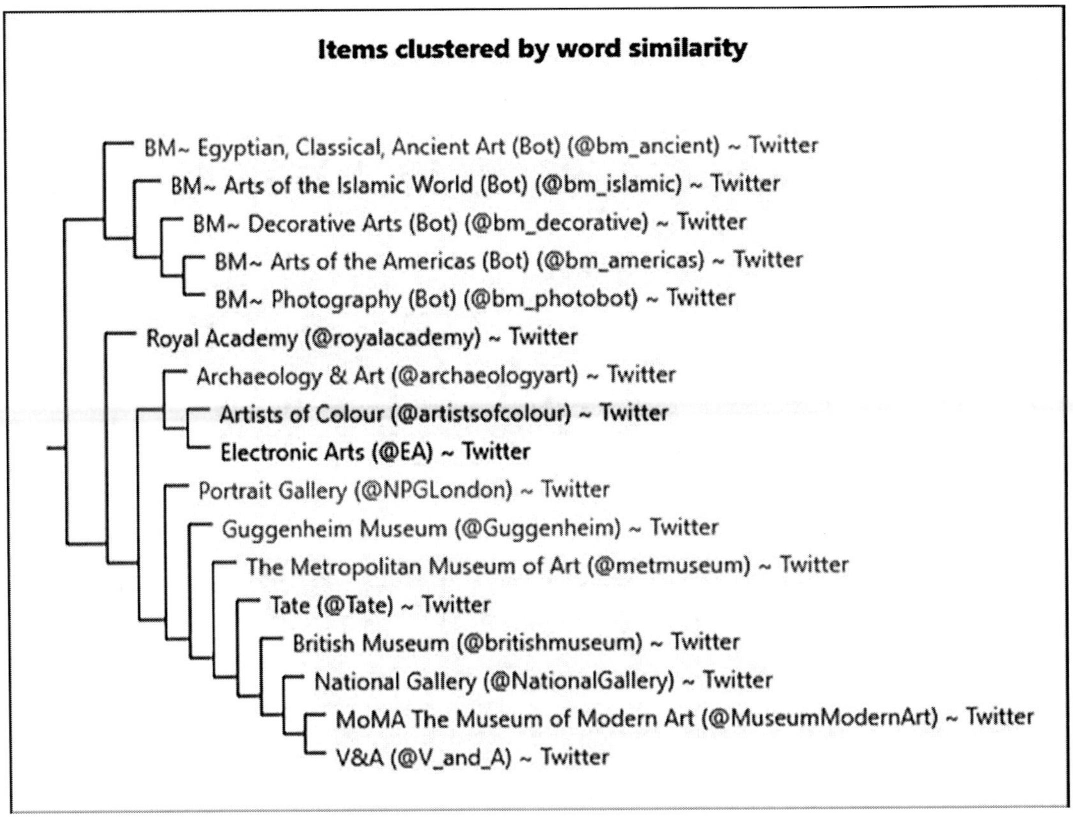

Figure 11. Arts-based social accounts clustered by account word similarity from 17 arts-related microblogging sites on Twitter (both 'Bot-Based' and 'Organization-Based') (horizontal dendrogram).

About Autocoded Sentiment

An autocoded sentiment analysis was run over the 17 arts-related social accounts on Twitter. The bot accounts tended to be highly neutral in language, without sentiment. The other accounts representing arts museums, galleries, and organizations had more sentiment (Figure 10).

About Social Relating Online (Based on Similarity Clustering and Analysis)

A word-similarity analysis between the accounts shows clustering of accounts in the horizontal dendrogram in Figure 11. This data extraction is suggestive of which organizations are interacting with which more often (or which accounts are interrelating on Twitter, which may be suggestive of in-world relating as well).

This social relating data may be seen in a 3d diagram (Figure 12). Here, the placement of the respective accounts and the color show proximity of social relating on Twitter (based on the slice-in-time extracted data in late 2021).

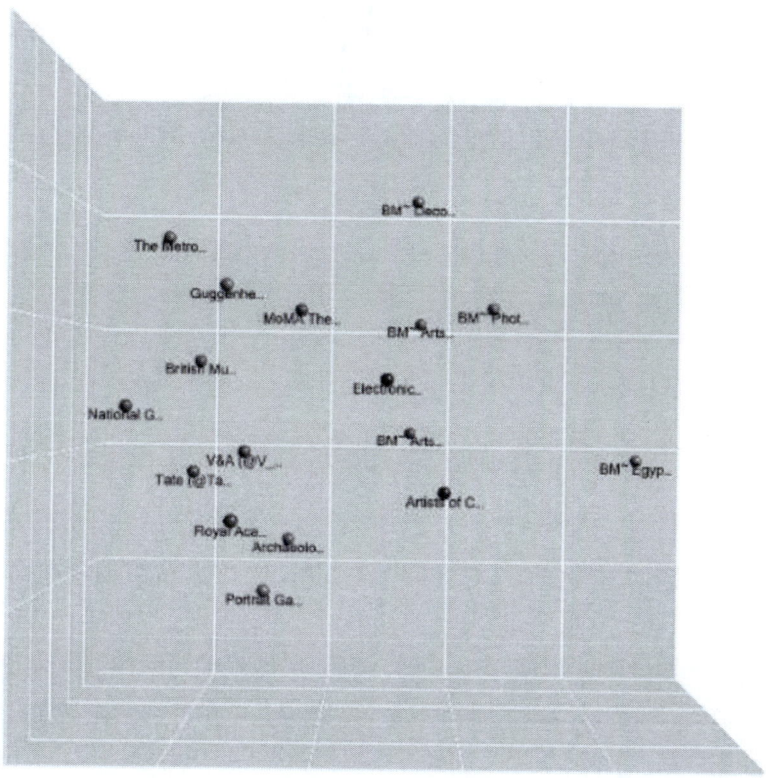

Figure 12. Social media accounts clustered by word similarity (3d diagram).

A re-visualization of the clustering of accounts in a ring lattice graph (or circle diagram) shows an engaging symmetric pattern in Figure 13. This shows the existence of interactivity, not the amount of interaction.

The autocoding of topics around just the ‘bot accounts show three high level topics: “https, century, century https,” so a focus around time.

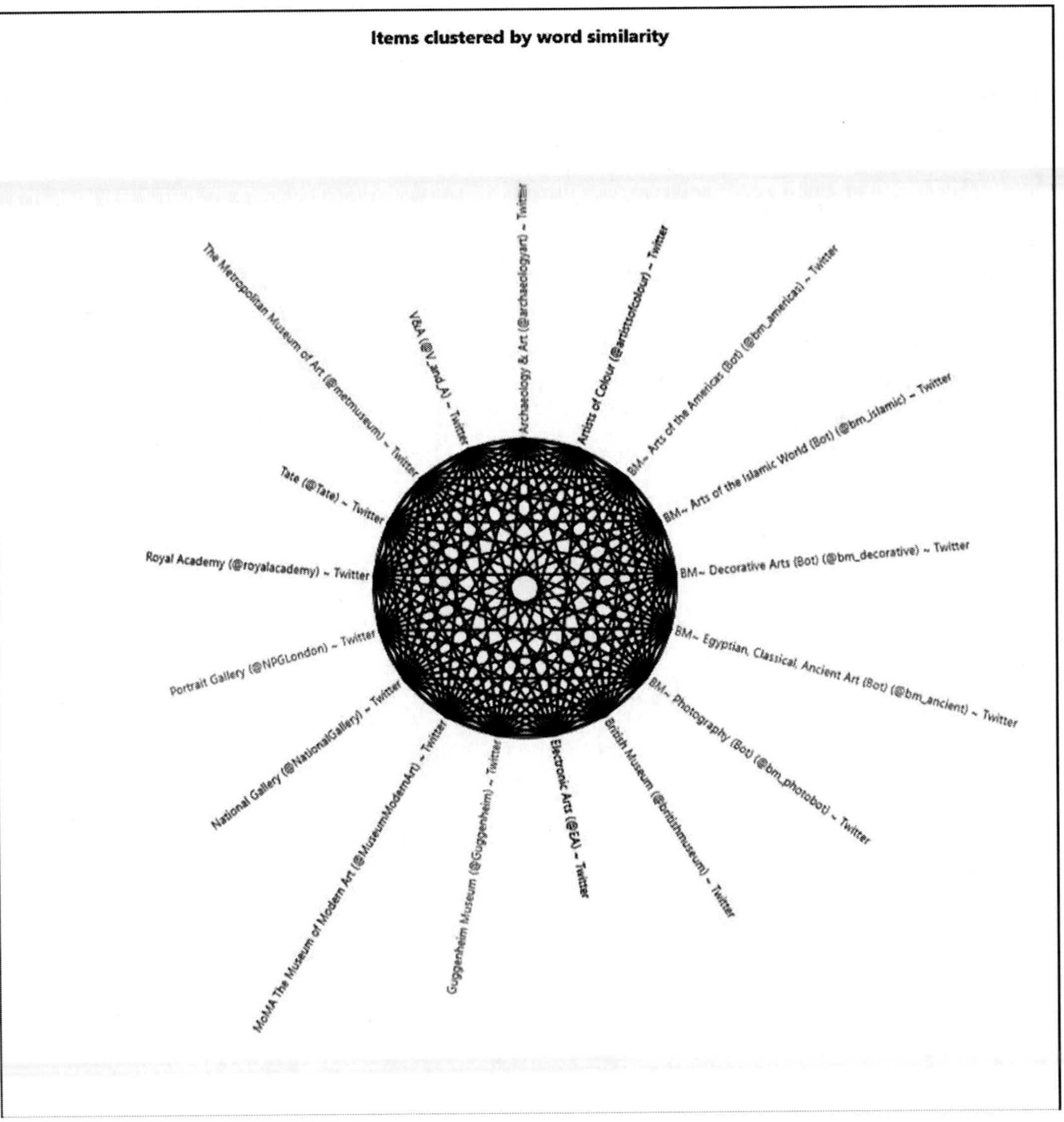

Figure 13. Arts-based Social accounts clustered by account word similarity from 17 arts-related microblogging sites on Twitter (both 'Bot-Based' and 'Organization-Based') (ring lattice graph or circle graph).

Distant Reading of the Tweets

A cluster analysis was run to see what sorts of conversations were being held via the exchanged microblogging Tweets. A horizontal dendrogram was created. The way to read this is to look at the "leaves" at the right, read the terms up the branches, and then all the way to the tree's trunk and roots to the left. When #islamicart is discussed, it is in connection with "vintage" and "photographs," for example, in the branch at the top (Figure 14).

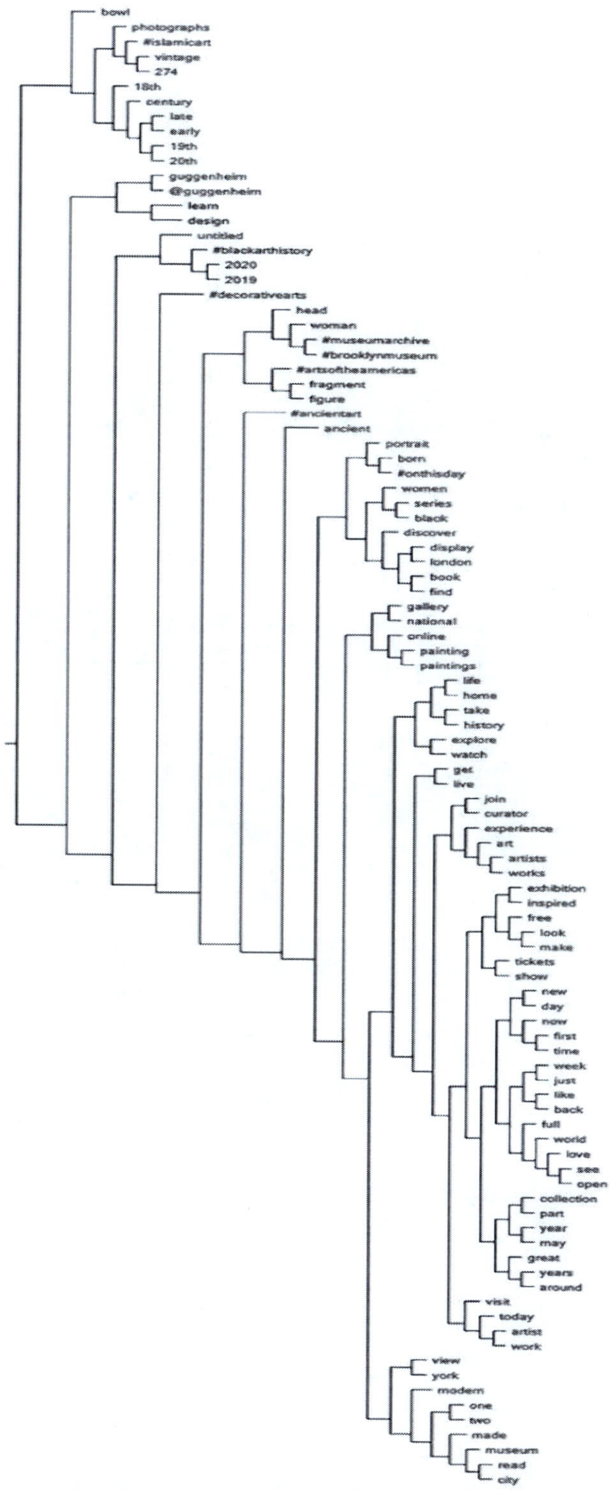

Figure 14. Word similarity clustering around words in microblogging messages from 17 arts-related microblogging sites on Twitter (both 'Bot-Based' and 'Organization-Based') (horizontal dendrogram).

The same word similarity clusters in the microblogging conversations may be seen in Figure 15. The messaging looks to be fairly dense (many links or edges), so perhaps the visual here is less powerful than it might be otherwise.

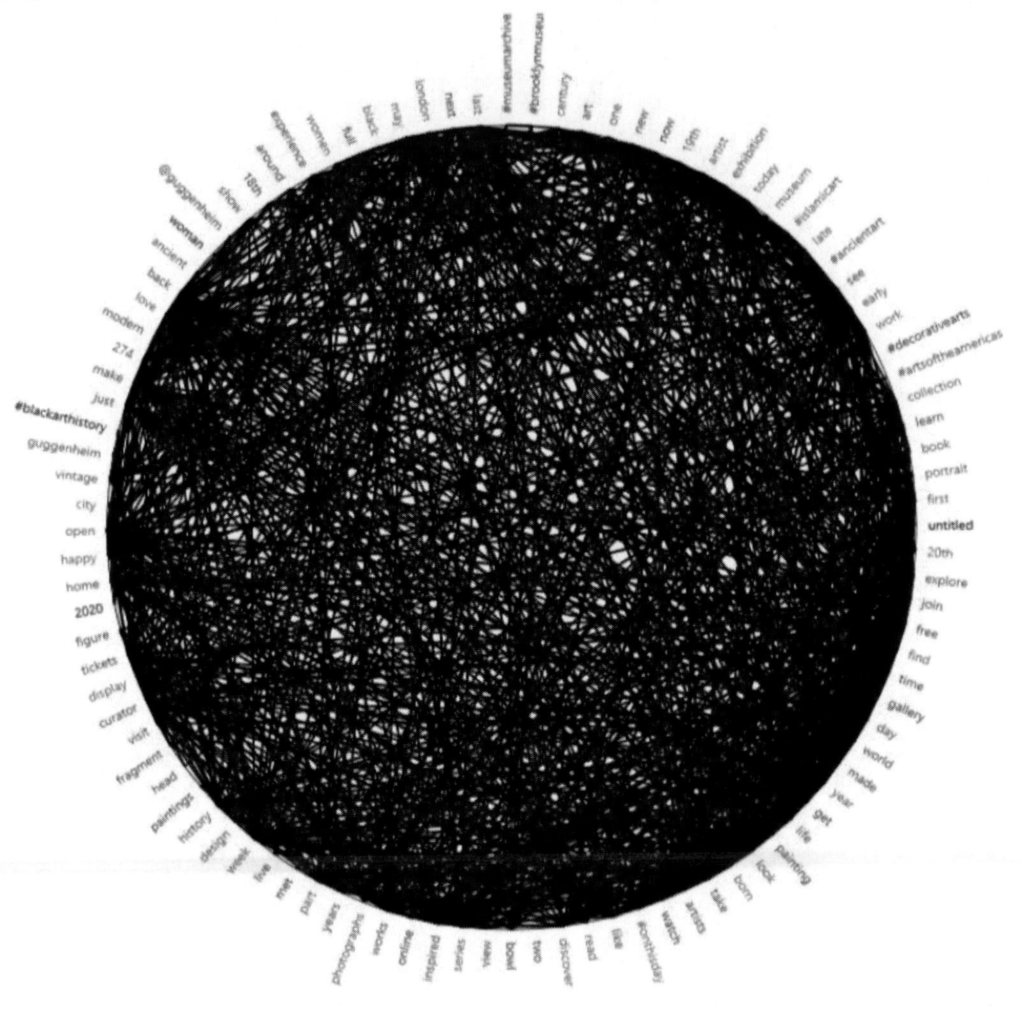

Figure 15. Word similarity clustering around words in microblogging messages from 17 arts-related microblogging sites on Twitter (both 'Bot-Based' and 'Organization-Based') (ring lattice graph).

Netlytic

To explore a hashtag network #art on Twitter, Netlytic (https://netlytic.org/index.php) was used to extract the 2,500 most recent messages based around #art. There is wide interest in non-fungible tokens (NFTs) in this space with ties to #cryptocurrencies. There are mentions of #animation and other types of art. There are particular subject foci, like #dragon and #fanart and #digital (Figure 16).

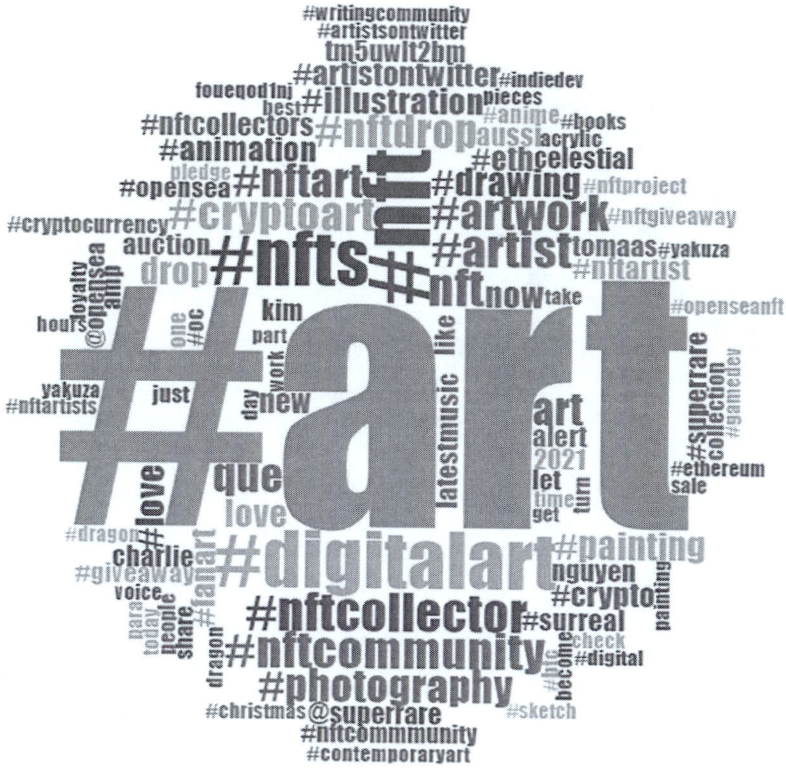

Figure 16. Word cloud from word frequency count of #Art hashtag network on Twitter (2,500 messages captured with Netlytic).

The most common topics from the #art hashtag network may be seen in Figure 17.

The most active social media accounts in this hashtag network are listed in Figure 18.

The #art hashtag network on Twitter shows some main clusters of interactants, some smaller subgraphs and motifs, and some isolate nodes (Figure 19).

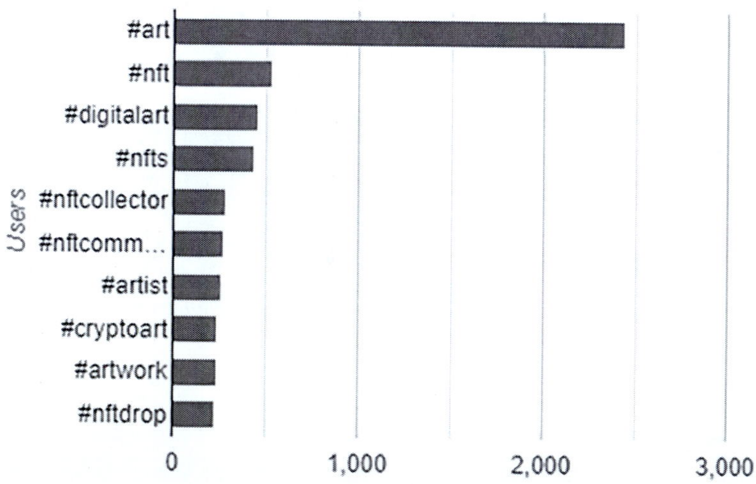

Figure 17. Most common topics from #Art hashtag network on Twitter (2,500 messages captured with Netlytic).

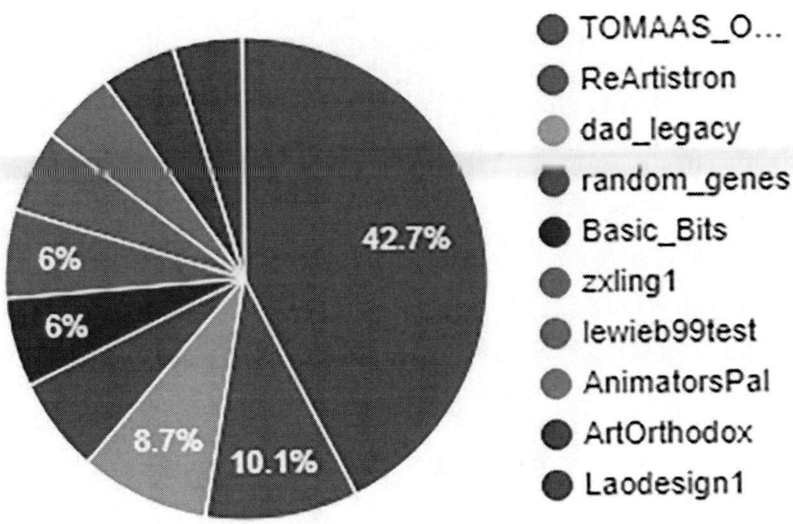

Figure 18. Top 10 social media account posters from #Art hashtag network on Twitter (2,500 messages captured with Netlytic).

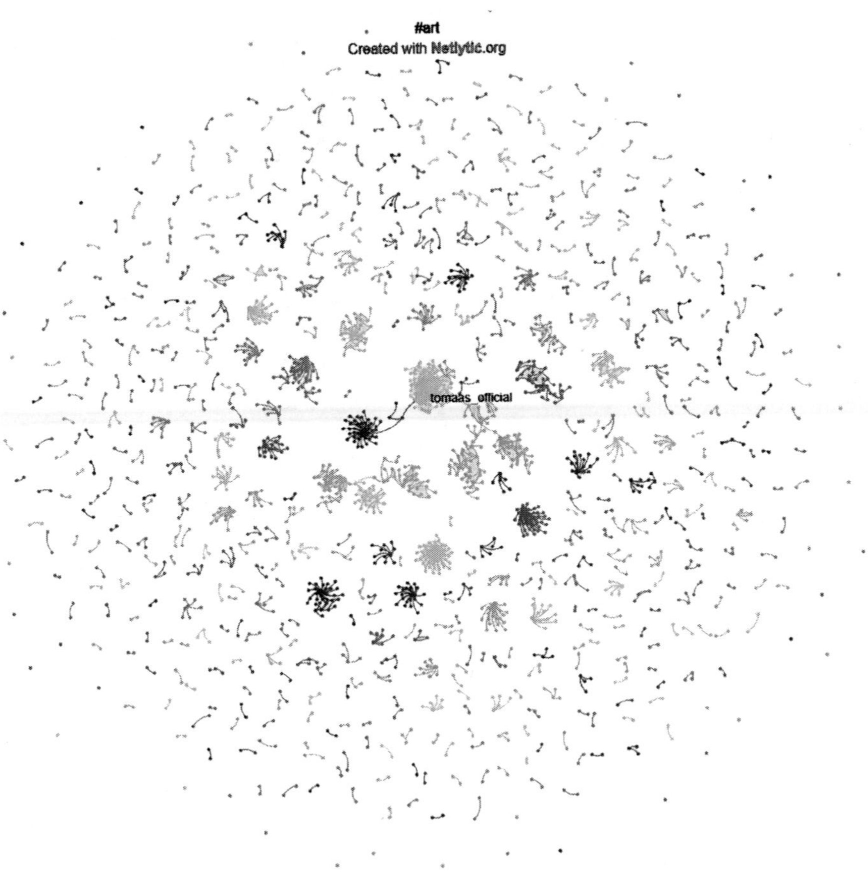

Figure 19. Social network from #Art hashtag network on Twitter (2,500 messages captured with Netlytic).

A News Sharing Site

Finally, the messages on a public "art" subreddit were captured on Reddit in the same time period. A word frequency count was run over the extracted data to try to capture a sense of what was being discussed. The word cloud evokes a sense of a temporal community where people go to share information and to engage lightly. There is not a sense of long-term interactions per se. A human reading of the subreddit gives the same impression. There seems to be a practical focus as well around artist work and ways to promote a person's work and to develop one's art (Figure 20).

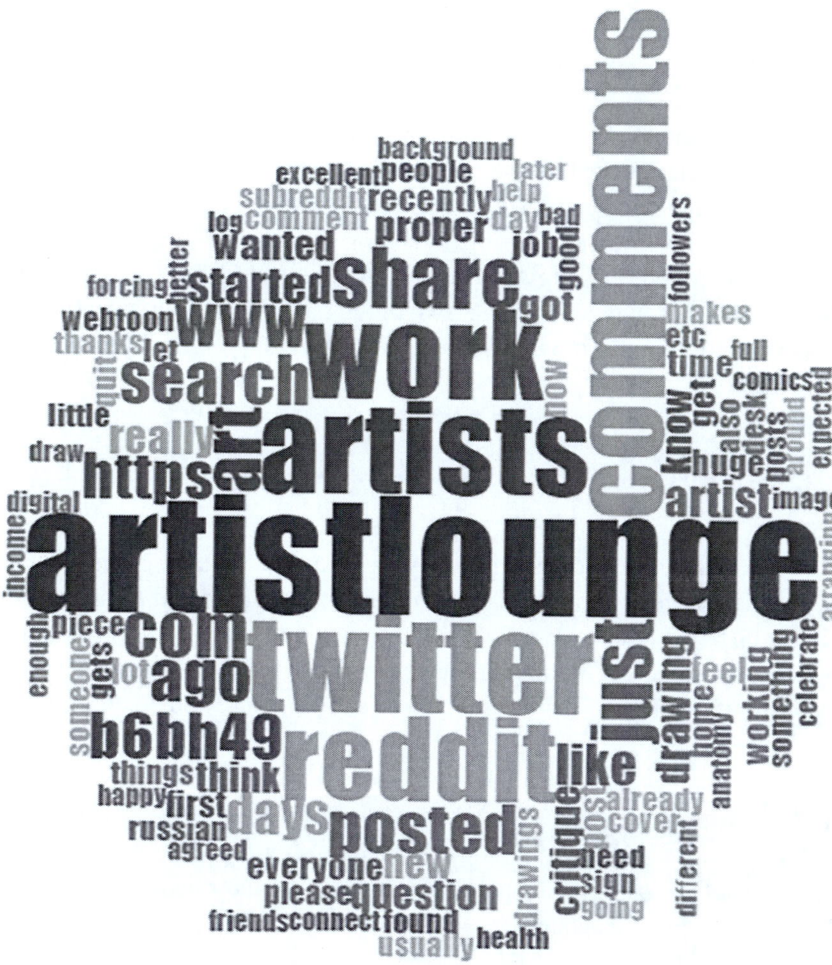

Figure 20. Word cloud from a word frequency count of an "Art" Subreddit on Reddit.

An autocoding of themes resulted in no themes. This happens if there is insufficient data. Other times, it happens if there is no apparent coalescence around particular themes (topics, subtopics).

Discussion

This chapter offers an exercise in sampling arts-related data from social media. This shows how people are harnessing various platforms for particular functional or instrumental ends in terms of their interests.

These data extractions do show a focus on formal art over informal. Perhaps these communications help read the general public into the professional sense of human art over generations, and this information may inform what the public sees as artful, and it may inform what they create as a result (given whatever their strengths and weaknesses at artful expression).

Future Research

There are many other social media platforms and types that may be explored. Some of these may be ones with proprietary data that may be shared by the respective companies.

Future work may involve datasets of n = all (instead of just contemporaneous information that is slice-in-time), for a more holistic understanding. Perhaps the analyses may be more web-scale and multimodal, including digital imagery and video. Machine vision may be brought into play. Subtler patterns may be extracted. With the harnessing of artificial intelligence and big data analytics, different questions may be asked. Different regionalisms around the world may be explored.

Conclusion

This work involved data extractions and analyses from the following sites: a text and data mining site, a social image sharing site, a microblogging site (accessed through both NCapture and Netlytic for different datasets), a news sharing site, and others. This work surfaced some insights about the sense of "art" in the public sphere via some locations on the Social Web. A fundamental insight is that there is promise in more study in these and other related approaches.

Acknowledgments

Thanks to the respective social media platforms for making their data available to the general public and to the occasional meandering researcher.

References

Abkenar, S. B., Kashani, M. H., Mahdipour, E., & Jameii, S. M. (2021). Big data analytics meets social media: A systematic review of techniques, open issues, and future directions. *Telematics and Informatics*, *57*, 101517.

Ghani, N. A., Hamid, S., Hashem, I. A. T., & Ahmed, E. (2019). Social media big data analytics: A survey. *Computers in Human Behavior*, *101*, 417-428.

Hacmun, I., Regev, D., & Salomon, R. (2021). Artistic creation in virtual reality for art therapy: A qualitative study with expert art therapists. *The Arts in Psychotherapy*, *72*, 101745.

Liu, C. Y., & Wu, C. J. (2021). STEM without art: A ship without a sail. Thinking Skills and Creativity, 100977, 1 - 12.

Teoli, L. A. (2021). Companioning artmaking: Creating art alongside clients in group art therapy. *The Arts in Psychotherapy*, *75*, 101806.

Walker, S., & Walker, S. (2004). Artmaking in an age of visual culture: Vision and visuality. *Visual Arts Research*, *30*(2), 23-37.

Yazdani, M., & Manovich, L. (2015, October). Predicting social trends from non-photographic images on Twitter. In *2015 IEEE international conference on big data (big data)* (pp. 1653-1660). IEEE.

Part 6: Common Visual Art in the Third and Fourth Dimensions

Chapter 17

Third Dimension in Digital Common Visual Art

Shalin Hai-Jew*
Kansas State University, Manhattan, Kansas, USA

Abstract

For years, much of common art was focused around two dimensions, the x- and y-axes, the flat planar surface. If the third dimension was addressed, it was done so isometrically, with the 3D object represented in the two dimensions. Then, as techniques and technologies evolved, the third dimension, the z-axis, emerged as an extension in space, enabling various types of visuals with heightened realism (life is lived in 3d and 4d), enriched senses of shape and form, intensified imaginaries, optical illusions, and complex information conveyance. In the present moment, on the Social Web, are depictions of metaverses colliding, virtual immersive scenes from games and virtual worlds, augmented reality overlays in the physical, and other expressions.

Keywords: 3D, common art, third dimension, x-axis, digital sculpture, machinima, virtual reality, augmented reality, isometric perspective

Introduction

A general definition of art is "an idea being expressed through materials and process" (Cronin, 2000, p. 41). For art that extends beyond two dimensions into the third one, the z-axis, there are enriched senses of shape and form and uses of space. The real is enhanced along with various senses of the fantastical. The third dimension has long been used in the industrial space, for the design of equipment, for flow visualizations, for simulations, and other applications. With the advent of various digital image editing tools, digital game design tools, virtual worlds, and other technologies, various 3d works have flowed to the Social Web, perhaps with some lag or latency from professional usages.

This work explores how the third dimension (3d) manifests in digital common visual art. What sorts of technologies and techniques are used in the works? What topics are depicted? Who seems to be creating the works and for whom and for what purposes?

* Corresponding Author's Email: haijes@gmail.com

In: Common Visual Art in a Social Digital Age
Editor: Shalin Hai-Jew
ISBN: 978-1-68507-664-1

Review of the Literature

The making of visual art "is one of the defining characteristics of the human species" (Morriss-Kay, 2010, p. 158) and various forms of art are practiced in virtually all human cultures (p. 158). Various disciplines require drawing skills among their practitioners for different purposes: notetaking, visual communication, description, and storytelling. Biological drawing requires "careful observation and description" (Dempsey & Betz, 2001, p. 271), including the ability to draw from memory. Rubbings are used to acquire textural features of some physical objects, like leaves (Dempsey & Betz, 2001, p. 272). Accurate drawing requires informational accuracy, from size to color to other elements (Dempsey & Betz, 2001, p. 278).

Human visual systems, where observing 3d shapes (as either elliptical or hyperbolic), tend to fall along patterns: "a preference for convex surfaces, a preference for surface contours aligned with the principal lines of curvature, and a preference for a surface orientation consistent with an object viewed from above" (Mamassian & Landy, 1998, p. 2817). A more recent study identified neural mechanisms of 3d processing. The topline finding is that "depth processing and object identification might be processed by separate pathways and at different latencies" (such as the requirement of longer time to process 3d objects than "planar graphics" and "perspective drawings") (Gao, Cao, Cao, Li, & Li, 2015, p. 65). Three-dimensional objects require more mental processing and time for capture.

Understanding how visual information is perceived, understood, and consumed, is important for 3d depictions. There are patterns, too, in where accuracy errors arise in drawing. The co-researchers write: "The difficulty adults find in drawing objects or scenes from real life is puzzling, assuming that there are few gross individual differences in the phenomenology of visual scenes and in fine motor control in the neurologically healthy population" (Chamberlain & Wageman, 2016, p. 195). Their research found that "domain-specific, flexible, top-down control of visual attention" is critical in developing skills in visual art (Chamberlain & Wageman, 2016, p. 195). Artists need to maintain knowledge of the object being drawn, the ability to wield visual attention in segmented ways, encoding the object and remembering it, the ability to maintain "perceptual consistency and illusion," and "perceptual grouping" (Chamberlain & Wageman, 2016, p. 205), according to their systematic review of the literature.

There is inherent ambiguity in object geometries, so these are defined for improved precision in the coding of object geometries and their decoding (Parzysz, Feb. 1988). Visual intercommunications require basic understandings of the assembling of visual elements and their interrelationships.

Generally, for those who would depict the world visually, the world is constructed of objects that are created from basic shapes: rectangles, ellipses, triangles, polygons, and others. In 3d, these are cubes, spheres, cylinders, pyramids, polygons, and other "primitives" or "prims" (as shapes). There are freeform shapes as well that can be drawn with hyper precision (down to the level of pixels or picture elements). They shapes are not flat, but they take up volumetric space. Drawing in 3d has long been considered an elusive and difficult skill, requiring the application of senses of "depth, perspective, and spatial orientation" in drawing solids on paper (Ibe, 1971, p. 180). Decades ago, in the age of "graphicacy," artists used commercial templates to convey the forms through tracing and emulation.

Developing Drawing Skill

In the U.S., a typical individual does not have formal training for drawing past age 9 or 10 (Chamberlain & Wageman, 2016), and their skills are not developed beyond this. One study explored the perceptual foundations for drawing ability and identified some key requisite capabilities: long-term memory, visual perception ["such as the identification and reproduction of geometric characteristics" (Chamberlain, Riley, McManus, Rankin, & Brunswick, Oct. 2011, p. 1) and "perception of angular relationships" (p. 19)], and "attitudes and abilities in education to drawing" (p. 1). The requisite skills are necessary, regardless of the "specialist medium" of the particular artist (Chamberlain, Riley, McManus, Rankin, & Brunswick, Oct. 2011, p. 1).

Another study conducted close-in observations of "stimulus fixation and subsequent motor activity in art drawing" using eye-tracking technologies to study artist drawing processes. The researchers were trying to better understand cognitive processes in artistic work and practice (Choi & DiPaola, Apr. 2015, p. 579). A different work found that user's spatial ability "affects the shape of the drawing, but not the line precision" (Barrera Machuca, Stuerzlinger, & Asente, 2019, p. 173), in 3d virtual environments. There is a "neurological relationship between visual creativity and language" (Morriss-Kay, 2010, p. 158).

The Decline of Drawing Skill in a Digital Age

In a digital age, with so many technological enablements for drawing diagrams and other visuals, it is thought that drawing skills have declined even further, even for professionals in fields that benefit from the discipline and thinking in drawing. One researcher writes:

> The study reveals that, in the UK, drawing skills are considered to be gradually declining, while traditional notions of skill are called into question. Drawing as a means of visual recording, representation and communication remains valued, although no longer essential as it once was; drawing to augment thought process is increasingly recognized as an integral skill which enables innovation… Increasing value is placed on drawing 'as process', as provision is moving towards individualized instruction requiring students to work independently. (Fava, 2020, p. 332)

Another work has made a similar argument: "the irruption of new computational technologies" has affected drawing as a tool for thinking and innovating (Butragueno, Salgado, & Raposo, 2019, p. 158). To preserve creative thinking, drawing is critical for experimentation in architecture (Butragueno, Salgado, & Raposo, 2019, p. 159). Traditional drawing is still relevant in the digital age to hone the artist and the work (Hawks, 2010).

A research study found that those who play 2d and 3d games at least an hour a week outperform non-gamers (those who play 2d and 3d games less than an hour a week) in terms of spatial cognition and drawing. The thinking is that such playing involves engaging spatial challenges and solving them during gameplay, which leads to increased visual attention capacity (Wyeld, Williams, & Barbuto, Nov. 2013, p. 221).

Visual artists are better at both perception and drawing than non-artists. One researcher explains that the "perceptual advantage seems to be closely linked to the activity of drawing" and relates to their "extensive experience in visual interaction with objects and images during drawing" (Kozbelt, 2001, p. 705). Artists also showed a greater proficiency in the visual analytic procedures applied (Kozbelt, 2001, p. 721), even though those procedures were similar to ones applied by novices (to lesser effect) (p. 705).

Computer Influences on Drawing

Computer graphics have been in use for some 50 years now. Various technologies have been developed to help people express themselves through visual depictions. Researchers have surfaced principles for 3d artists to learn from fine arts artists about 3d shapes and principles for their representation (Guo, 2001). One program was designed to assist people in drawing human faces from references (Dixon, Prasad, & Hammond, Apr. 2010). Another supports novices in drawing various subject matters from photos (Williford, Doke, Pahud, Hinckley, & Hammond, 2019). One is a nonvisual drawing system for blind users to draw (Bornschein & Weber, 2017). Another system helps artists find better reference imagery for their artistic objectives (Holinaty, Jacobson, & Chevalier, 2021). Many modern illustrators use reference imagery to broaden their creativity in compositing and digital painting.

Computer Assessment of Artist Skill, Artist Processes

A study of where artists draw lines to represent common three-dimensional objects as shapes shows high patterning, with 75% of lines within a millimeter of another line. Here, the artists' lines tended to adhere to "the occluding contours of the object" and "large gradients of the image intensity" by a majority of the study participants (Cole, et al., 2008, p. 88:1). This research finding suggests that people's vision and practice may inform how 3d shapes are depicted. [Some 14% of the lines could not be predicted however. This is explained as lines "based on local properties (e.g., lines from diffuse shading (Lee et al., 2007), or a new definition not yet described), or by clever combinations of current line definitions" (Cole, et al., 2008, p. 88:10). There are rational reasons for line emplacement by the participating artists, but these were not included in the algorithmic encoding for the research.]

Computational means have been used to assess how accurate or inaccurate visual drawings are. One study examined lifelike human portraiture vs. the reference photographs. The evaluation was achieved computationally based on three measures: "visual assessment, anthropometric measures, and geometric morphometric analysis" (Hayes & Milne, 2011, p. 149), with the finding that geometric morphometric analysis was the most accurate. What leads to distortions in the drawing involved cognitive mechanisms for perception of faces (often as a whole rather than in pieces and parts), leading to misperception of various facial landmarks of the sitter. The researchers write: "Clear patterns of shape distortion in how the sitters' external face shape, internal features, and their spatial configuration were depicted in *the portraits were able to be both subjectively assessed and objectively measured*" (Hayes & Milne, 2011, p. 149; boldfacing by the co-researchers).

Computer-Assisted Drawing

If cameras and scanning enable photorealistic capture and representation of an object or scene or person, non-photorealistic techniques enable the capture of more emulative of interpretive works as achieved by human hands. Indeed, such approaches have been around for decades and enable the creation of computer-assisted artwork creation.

Artificial intelligence (AI) machine-enhanced "co-creation" in drawing has been enabled in alignment with artist practices in the wild (Jansen & Sklar, 2021, p. 1). Such a bridging technology is thought to address issues of artists "drawing alone" and robotic systems "drawing alone" (Jansen & Sklar, 2021). Another enablement is to create "ink" drawings from 3d models (Sousa, Foster, Wyvill, & Samavati, Sept. 2003). Another technology offers computational means to create faces with exaggerated features for 3d caricatures (Han, Gao, & Yu, 2017). There are digital means to create a visual sense of compressed bas-relief from 3d scenes (Weyrich, Deng, Barnes, Rusinkiewicz, & Finkelstein, 2007). Users may directly annotate with vectorized strokes on 3d models as a form of non-photorealistic rendering through digital means to better express their personal art style (Kalnins, et al., 2002, p. 755). They can apply designs, textures, and shading. Another approach evokes 3d models with the drawing of only "a few good lines" (Sousa & Prusinkiewicz, Sept. 2003, p. 381), given the power of sparsity in line drawings in science and art. Yet another enables virtual embossing (Sourin, 2001), which emulates the visual look of using tools to press out forms in metals.

There are ways to capture the third dimension based on digital pen pressure, without "the need of multiple viewpoints or multiple lines to specify a 3D curve" (Lai & Zakaria, June 2010, p. 156). Indeed, there is a rich body of technologies that may be used to artistically render 3d objects (Geng, 2010). There are changes in terms of inputs to 3d drawing, such as in 3d space and not a constrained planar surface (Mealing, 2005, p. 244). What used to be in the purview of the engineering space, in terms of 3d modeling, has transitioned to artist and general public spaces (Cook & Agah, 2009). The visual grammars of 3d drawing are also changing with new approaches.

Another program enables human artists to direct viewer gaze and attention in their 3d drawings. Various effects such as "local variations in shading effects such as color saturation and contrast as well as the qualities such as texture and density" are applied to drive attention (Cole, DeCarlo, Finkelstein, Kin, Morley, & Santella, 2006, p. 377). Human users can define the digital camera position, focal area of interest, and "rendering style for the scene (Cole, DeCarlo, Finkelstein, Kin, Morley, & Santella, 2006, p. 377), and various tools like "fogginess" (p. 386) and vignetting are applied to drive viewer attention.

Whereas some are striving to disambiguate drawing, others see the inherent ambiguity in drawing as a net positive. Ambiguity in drawing "forms a strategy that enables and sustains drawing research" (Sawdon & Marshall, 2009, p. 1); ambiguity enables drawing to be "unbounded" (p. 1), without artificial constraints, given is ubiquitous role in many fields. In terms of research, non-photorealistic rendering techniques are thought to help researchers better understand art, its creation and its reception by viewers (Hertzmann, June 2010).

Computer technologies have also been harnessed to transcode *from* 3d visual depictions. One system enables the inferring of a 3d model object's or character's pose using a monocular 2d sketch version (Gouvatsos, Xiao, Marsden, & Zhang, 2017), for animation. Various computer technologies have been designed to simplify 3d models as 2d silhouettes (for lighter computational loads) (Rivers, Durand, & Igarashi, 2010). Based on contour drawings, one system infers 3d shapes computationally (Karpenko & Hughes, 2011). A more recent tool can take 3d objects and create hand drawing sketches as vector images to convey shapes (Ye, Zhou, & Fu, July 2019).

Research Methods

In late October, the author used "3d common art" as a seeding term to capture visuals from Google Images. The tags enabled for filtering include the following: three-dimensional, game, concept art, 3d street art, optical illusions, dolphin, art styles, octopus, bare walls, wall, wall art, flower, 3d modeling, naima, animation, (and) wall dècor. The extraction included 2,623 items, given that the visual extractions were achieved twice, with two different web scraping tools. The visuals were de-duplicated. Then, rough bottom-up coding was applied to see what the visuals portrayed.

Results

Some common themes include the following:

3d Methods

Some of the works evoked early types of optical illusion methods, achieved on paper, and triggering the human visual system. The human mind processes visual information from the human eyes (retinas) through the optic nerve and into the human brain in particular ways. Illusions play on those tendencies. The optical illusions are experienced by many as pleasure at the visual wit.

Classic Optical Illusion Play

In terms of classic optical illusions, some common ones include cubes with different color sides that may be seen as convex or concave depending on point-of-view. Several works evoke these. Some include cubes that are hollow but with depicted shadows below. There are staircases that go down under a sheet of paper. There are spiraling holes that go down into eternity through a paper portal. These works are isometric ones, with 3d visuals depicted as 2d, with depictions only at the top, left, and right planes, to simulate three dimensions.

One work shows red poppies in the foreground, and the background is rendered in gray; here, color is used to create the foreground to "pop" and the background to recede. Other works use the creating of perspective (horizon line, vanishing point or points, foreshortening, light effects, and other elements) and spatiality and light. One simple lineart shows a "daddy long legs" spider with form and embodiment in physical space.

Hyperrealism in Drawings

If Escher's famous hand-drawing-hands rising from a paper is a classic, many works follow on this vein. Various works evoke 3d hyperrealism in illustration: a glass cup, a green frog, a red lobster, a raised set of large plastic blocks (reminiscent of Legos), a Rubik's Cube, a 3d hand stirring liquid in a mug, a crow, a large old-style camera with an extended lens and filter, a mini-Eiffel Tower, a tarantula, and others. One conveys a visual joke. A man is walking along when he steps on the tines of a rake and is smacked in the face by the wooden handle. One shows tubes of acrylic paint with paint squeezed out on paper; these are not in the process of drying out but are hyper-real visuals in a self-reflexive pencil drawing. In one, a snake is held by a thin film of paper while a human hand holds the tip of its tail; the snake is caught in a hyperreal paper with its own power of capture. Similarly, an octopus is shown intertwined with the blinds where it has been caught and somewhat flattened. Next to these are posed the artists or hands holding drawing instruments. One ambiguous work shows a male hand holding a single gold ring in the center of the palm: Is the person giving back the ring? Has there been a change of heart? The point is to reveal the illusion, so viewers can marvel at the skill and gape at the work.

Hyperreal works require painstaking manual drawing efforts, often using colored pencils on paper alone, to create careful shading and details. These require hours of meticulous effort. Such works may become lost art because of the incurred costs on the human artist. Illusions may be created with digital editing in much less time (with digital image editing tools enabling pencil effects). In modern societies, with emphases on efficiencies and time saving, only a minority of peoples will develop the vision, the eye-hand coordination, and capabilities to evoke the hyperreal.

Mixed Realities, Crossovers between Metaverses, Analog and Digital

People live in mixed realities in various ways. They may have digital augmentations in physical space; they may immerse themselves in virtual immersive spaces through their senses (through sight, sound, touch, typically).

In the social imagery, there are various 3d works that evoke mixed realities. A child in a painting extends outside the two-dimensional frames. The child is sitting on railing outside the painting and petting a small cat. Another photo shows a bust of a person with a bird with open wings in front. A carved wooden box has two dolphins frolicking in water; this is a wood carved box, or it is a digital creation. In one, a dog looks to have been chiseled out of wood; it is hyper-realistic and has extension in space. Another visual shows a dolphin and a man in a moment of communion as they stand in shallow water; behind is a lit and light sky. Several works show humans riding dolphins. Another visual shows an aerial view of a cityscape, built with digital extrusions. In one visual, children are playing in a city street and jumping over water that reflects a very blue sky with white clouds (a surreal touch). In another, horses run out of a picture frame and into the foreground.

One clever work shows a man holding a giant red pencil to draw himself, and across from him is his image holding a modern camera taking a picture of himself. He is depicted in a photo while holding the giant red pencil, and he is depicted as a pencil drawing in the image where he is holding the camera. This visual is a play on Escher and visual wit.

Augmented Reality

There are photos of augmented reality creatures placed on paper as the surface: a flying hawk, a puppy sitting on cardboard with chewed edges, a hummingbird fluttering over a blank page, a large ladybug, a floating number "2" over a page, and others.

On the Web, there are applications that work with various devices to enable the creation of AR effects. Beyond cloud-based applications, AR may also be created with digital image editing apps. Beyond still images, video may also be delivered in an AR way.

Materialia

Some visuals look to be simple photos: one of the Sphinx in Egypt, ancient sculptures in bronze and some in stone, one of a rounded purse, a book cover of DIY nail art (and other book covers), a coil of neon yellow cord hanging on a wall, an octopus sculpture held by the artist, 3d wall stickers, a person holding various clay objects in her hands, and so on. One photo shows artful Gaudi-esque and organic shapes on a building, but the actual source is not specified. One photo shows Rodin's thinker in a museum. Some show regular clothing and shoes. Some works appeal to sentiment, such as a boy hugging a dog.

Other images showed various techniques, such as embroidery with cloth and string, origami paper folding with paper, visual depictions with food, plastic, glass or resin.

Embroidered Food Scenes

Then, there is a series of embroidery rings filled with depictions of food (some with spindles of thread on the cloth, to break the illusion): a large breakfast in one (toast, an egg over easy, a hash brown, a sausage, two strips of bacon, three mushrooms, and what looks to be a tomato soup); a hand holding a knife and fork and cutting into a sausage link on a plate with bacon; a part of a waffle; a cross-section of an orange (with the embroidery ring held up like a mirror in front of the illustrated orange); a single popped popcorn kernel; a sunny-side-up egg on toast, and others. These works not only use optical illusions to create the 3d effect but actual thread texturing and a recent approach called "felting."

Origami Art

Another art style used is the artful folding of paper. A few works showed origami. One example was of paper *baozi* or steamed buns.

Food Art

There are other types of food art. Strawberries are sliced and used to illustrate various 2d visuals of people and flowers. Similarly, food-dyed popcorn is used in others. There is a sugar-covered cat-shaped cookie with chocolate features being painted with edible digital red paint. One visual shows a fig and a half on a digital scale. Several show a frothy octopus marshmallow? Milk foam?) with its legs grasping the sides of a hot drink in a glass mug. One triptych shows a browning banana peel, a can of beans, and a box of McDonald's French fries; these evoke found or conceptual art.

Plastic Objects

One visual depicts a plastic pink computer with a monitor. Is it plastic, or is a digital rendering? Another shows plastic soccer players defending a goal on a field. Several visuals show human hands holding various creatures: a 3d bird, a 3d octopus, and so on. Some of them look clearly like they are 3d printed toys. One photo of a white lacy elephant head with tusks looks like it may be 3d printed. Others look to be immaterial and digital. Some of the dolls look to be handmade from various materials.

Playing with Transparencies (Plastic, Glass or Resin; Digital)

One work looks to be a depiction of a dandelion flower shedding seeds behind glass or resin. Another shows an octopus as part of a 3d painting on resin; its head is outside the resin, and its legs are in the transparent resin. Others show octopuses in serving bowls, soaking in resin "water." Another work plays with transparency in another way: the visual is of a shiny red apple with one green leaf (is it glass, plastic, digital, or hand-drawn)? Another apple is glassine, with flowers and other elements inside, and goldleaf on top. A green apple sculpture is shown in a time, next to an air vent. The inside of the apple is white and crystalline.

Other works involved mixed materials, multiple analog materials and digital.

Artful Forms of 3d (in Common Art)

The various 3d forms included bas reliefs, dioramas, wall murals, and various decorations and furniture.

Bas Reliefs and Dioramas

Several works evoke bas reliefs: a metallic octopus in a triptych sculpture, a person's face wearing a military hat, and others. One work shows a side view of a woman, and her hair is decorated in a steam punk artfulness. A few of the works read as dioramas, such as a scene of a monster under a bed.

On Wall Murals

One visual shows a basketball hoop in front of a peeling mural and a person in full color and form tossing a basketball at the hoop. Another mural shows a 10-speed bicycle leaned up against a wall. On the wall is a mural of a little girl learning to ride a bike while her father runs along beside her. Another mural painted on red doors shows a male riding a motorcycle; in the image, an actual motorcycle is parked next to the mural, as if the painted boy were riding an actual motorcycle. In one mural, a boy stands on a chair to reach up to a rectangular cutout in a wall with something in it. The photo shows an actual chair in the foreground as if a person had put it there to help the boy achieve his objective. There is play of convex and concave in the scene, and an interesting visual interplay.

Artful Decorations and Furniture

There are a few photos of 3d physical lamps, with various designs. Another shows some framing around electronic lightbulbs, in what looks to be an art space. One photo shows a mobile of dolphin-shaped forms. One is a floral wall hanging, as a decoration. Another shows a bird head mounted on a stick and placed in a rock base, evoking taxidermy. Some of the visuals are event-based, such as several based around Halloween. One diptych shows two desk sculptures of people in combat. One photo shows a variety of vases, which look to be 3d printed instead of baked in a kiln. There is a dramatic fruit bowl with holes in it.

Topical Inspirations

The inspirations for the 3d works were manifold. There were some humanoid characters, some composite works, mixed scenes, some political statements, and some fantasy scenes. Nature was a core inspiration, including threats from wildlife and from microorganisms (in a time of COVID-19). In terms of representations, there were symbols of good (dolphins), evil (malicious fictional characters), power, connection (human-animal bond, human-human bond), and other messages. Some works were decorative and celebrated aesthetics. A few works were informational.

Some Humanoid Characters

Some humanoid characters are shown. Several evoke 1950s pinups. One close-up shows what looks to be a humanoid robot without pores, and she triggers an uncanny valley response. One visual shows a humanoid avatar with arms out, reminiscent of *Second Life* avatars in a moment of being outfitted or updated.

Composites

Some of the visuals are illustrations of various knick-knacks: flowers, balls, metallic springs, floating bubbles, and other decoratives. Another shows a pile of various 3d objects as abstractions.

Recognizable Scenes with Unrecognizable Elements

Several of the depicted scenes show supernatural elements in otherwise normal scenes. A man rides a sled down ice in a "winter carnival" inside a store. A man looms over a virtual baseball field that has seating stands that come up to his knees. An imaginary green lizard walks down a sidewalk in a typical suburban neighborhood. A bed is surrounded by water, in which two dolphins play. In one thumbnail, among natural plants, there is a dinosaur with a ridged face and topaz-yellow eyes.

Political Statements

Some works apparently make political statements. One visual shows the Statue of Liberty with her hands on her face. Around her are depictions of malaise and dollar signs.

Fantasy (Imaginary) Scenes

There are fantasy scenes. Some painted illusions on concrete enable tourists to place themselves into a scene: in one, a human baby lies in a plate and is about to be devoured by a large lobster. In another, a person wearing a backpack is holding a giant pill and about to feed it into a giant open mouth. A man lies on the back of a giant turtle sculpture, apparently. Similarly, a young woman sits next to a giant snail sculpture. These evoke something of a physical immersive, or it may just be an illusion. In another, a boy in a sweatshirt pets a virtual tiger. Several displays show digital dolphins jumping out of a painting to jump through hoops held by people, in the interactive display. One visual depicts computer-generated imagery (CGI) and "fx" ("special effects"), with a human actor wearing various sensors; the human disappears and is replaced by a walking robot. One visual shows a robot made up entirely of polygons. [It is unclear why there are repeated visuals of lobsters and octopuses, but perhaps the complexity of forms makes them interesting for student assignments. Ostriches also seem to be a favorite. There are also repeating images of dandelion flowers with seeds blowing into the wind. One dandelion image shows them growing over the top of a multi-story building; these weeds are super-sized. Sunflowers—both mandala kinds and more natural ones—are another staple].

Some of the works evoke characters from the *Star Wars* universe (Yoda, Darth Vader). There are characters from video games. One visual shows a duck mesh, another as a buck with antlers also in digital mesh, so the depictions are in various stages of finish. One creature looks to be a combination of a squid and a sea turtle, with a defensive outer shell. In another, a contorted octopus fights a giant squid. Several visuals look to be screen grabs from movies, some in CGI and others in clay animation. One work looks to be a tribute to the late singer Michael Jackson. There are scenes from *The Little Mermaid* by Disney. Several pirates are depicted, some as human men, one as an octopus with a pirate hat. An old-style 15th to 17th century galleon is seen rising in one augmented reality visual. One visual shows a mouse which evokes Disney's Mickey Mouse but lacks many of the typical design elements.

Some visuals read like the beginning of stories. One shows a turtle with a literal mini house on its back, and the turtle looks like it has stopped to talk to a bird standing on a tree trunk.

Some scenes are based on a science fiction (sci-fi) tradition. In one, a spaceship approaches human civilization. One visual shows an island from a virtual immersive space. Several visuals show outer space. In some, there is a giant light show going on. In another, a black star is collapsing on itself. There are civilizations built in deep forests, a wizard's home in a large tree, a tiger meeting a robot in a forest, a winding road to a fantasy city at night, underwater cities, and others. A set of stairs leads up to something that looks like an altar. A sphere made of glowing triangles floats in space. One shows a human contortionist with exaggerated extra-human/super-human musculature and features. One shows a gleaming chrome-plated modern car. One character is running in a spaceship and looks to be trying to solve a problem.

Of Nature

In one visual, a bird has caught a fish that it is about to devour. One visual shows window panes that open into a field of sunflower plants, with a high depth of field and a far horizon line. There are some visual depictions of genetic sequences (expressed in what look to untrained eyes to be curly ribbons in a so-called "ribbon representation"). Several visuals show the artified version of the SARs-CoV-2/COVID-19 virus. Various animals are depicted as creatures with personalities (a surprised fish, a swaggering octopus), and some can be said to be personifications. A human skull is snagged insome branches. One image shows a cluster of mushrooms. A sea horse floats in a stylized undersea scene, in a forest of algae. A stork stands in silhouette.

A Pandemic Moment

Nearing the end of the second year of the COVID-19 pandemic, some of the scraped visuals directly reference the virus. One visual shows a green couch with giant outsized virus particles floating in a transparent rectangular box around the sofa. The visual evokes closed physical spaces and unmoving air.

Emerging Threats

Several works show emerging predators: an angry tiger with jaws wide open emerging from a page, a dinosaur breaking through a wall to chase a young man, sharks leaping out from paintings or holes in a wall, and other creatures crossing over from one space into the human one. An iguana comes out of frame to lick a lollipop held by a little girl, who is laughing. In one scene, a monster octopus has a formally dressed woman and man in its grip. A man faces down a papier-mâché (and other materials) dinosaur in his workshop. One visual shows a truck that has crashed off a road violently, evoking Hollywood crash scenes.

Danger?

A man is measuring distance with a tape as he appears to be standing next to a ladder with the ground far below him. This same visual is used showing two young men trying to stand on a ledge and not fall to their detriment. One sculpture shows a man trying to squeeze out from between two closing doors; his face is a swirl of shapes and colors. He may be trying to escape harm himself, or he may be trying to enter a denied space. In one work, a young girl is playing with something on the ground while in a window frame. Her posture does not suggest awareness that she is being watched, in her innocence, and the viewer can wonder if she is at risk in the modern world.

Illusory 3d vs. Actual 3d

In this "3d common art" social imageset, the majority of works are two-dimensional illusions; they are isometric images. The actual physical works (physical sculptures, furniture, room décor) and augmented reality works (immersive scenes, objects) are actual 3d with a z-axis, but these are limited as a percentage of the extracted social images. These objects and scenes may be seen from various angles and perspectives instead of being restricted to one 2d perspective.

What Was Not Seen?

Social visuals in the third dimension are not expected to be a comprehensive set given various factors: intellectual property (IP) protections of some works (such as from industry, such as from educational applications), the mass-scale public audience, and other factors.

What 3d images were not seen in this set? There were no apparent industrial 3d visuals. There were none that showed liquid flow modeling. A few were from museums and light educational applications. High-definition (high-def) 3d scanning of cultural heritage objects were only seen fleetingly. Such 3d modeling has been mentioned with high hopes among researchers to preserve heritage for future generations (Scopigno, Callieri, Cignoni, Corsini, Dellepiane, Ponchio, & Ranzuglia, 2011), but perhaps the expenses of such endeavors and legal IP protections may limit some sharing. Also, images shared on the Web tend to be lightweight and low-resolution given the expense of delivering high-res digital objects.

While many of the works implied action, most of the 3d did not extend to the fourth dimension (change over time, action). One work shows something that looks like fan blades, but these were in a depiction of stasis. There were depictions of the beginnings of animal "attacks" on people (to evoke a survival thrill). There were post-disaster depictions, such as a truck tumbling off a freeway. But the actual motion was not indicated with lines or blur.

Discussion

The bottom-up coding of the social imagery covered the following general (and loose) categories: 3d methods, materialia, forms of 3d, and topical inspirations. An additional section addressed what was not seen in the social imageset, such as industrial 3d visuals and motion (or 4d). Only a few images dealt with the insides of buildings, and none showed direct mapping with point clouds.

It is possible to make some inferences about those sharing the 3d visuals based on some of the works. The range of skills seems to extend from the amateur to the professional. The various works include student assignments. One study suggests that part-time artists spend about 10 minutes to an hour on each work, but professional practicing ones spend longer (Jansen & Sklar, 2021, p. 10). The most common ones seem to have been created by amateur artists, with a few by professional ones. This is not to say that many of the works did not require many hours of learning and training and education, given the complexity of the space. (Screenshots of *machinima* or of professional films do not count as professional works. The originality of those creations is credited to the actual creators, not those who took a screenshot).

Future Research

Future research may involve different social imagesets, perhaps captured with different seeding terms. There may be different works observed, changing technological sophistication of the 3d works, changes in topics, and different semiotics. Perhaps works from different countries and different cultures may shed light on different practices and foci.

Conclusion

This work involved the exploration of "3d common art" on the Social Web. This work found convergence to some basic techniques and depictions and topics, from a fairly large social imageset. The third dimension was used for visual wit and human amusement. The topics identified seemed to be fairly common visual fare: flora and fauna, people, characters, and worlds (from the real, the hyper real, and the imaginary), and mainstream culture.

References

Barrera Machuca, M. D., Stuerzlinger, W., & Asente, P. (2019). The effect of spatial ability on immersive 3d drawing. In *Proceedings of the 2019 on Creativity and Cognition* (pp. 173-186).

Bornschein, J., & Weber, G. (2017). Digital drawing tools for blind users: A state-of-the-art and requirement analysis. In PETRA '17. June 21 - 23, 2017. Island of Rhodes, Greece. 21 - 28.

Butragueno, B., Salgado, M., & Raposo, J. F. (2019, Fall). 3D Exquisite Corpse: Drawing as a thinking tool. Stanford Proceedings Book. 158 - 164.

Chamberlain, R., Riley, H., McManus, C., Rankin, Q., & Brunswick, N. (2011, October). The perceptual foundations of drawing ability. In *Proceedings of an interdisciplinary symposium on drawing, cognition and education* (pp. 1-19). Pre-print.

Chamberlain, R., & Wagemans, J. (2016). The genesis of errors in drawing. *Neuroscience & Biobehavioral Reviews*, *65*, 195-207.

Choi, S. K., & DiPaola, S. (2015, April). Touch of the eye: Does observation reflect haptic metaphors in art drawing? In *Proceedings of the 33rd Annual ACM Conference Extended Abstracts on Human Factors in Computing Systems* (pp. 579-588).

Cole, F., DeCarlo, D., Finkelstein, A., Kin, K., Morley, R. K., & Santella, A. (2006). Directing gaze in 3D models with stylized focus. *Rendering Techniques*, *2006*, 17th, 377 – 387.

Cole, F., Golovinskiy, A., Limpaecher, A., Barros, H. S., Finkelstein, A., Funkhouser, T., & Rusinkiewicz, S. (2008). Where do people draw lines?. In ACM SIGGRAPH 2008 papers (pp. 1-11).

Cook, M. T., & Agah, A. (2009). A survey of sketch-based 3-D modeling techniques. *Interacting with computers*, *21*(3), 201-211.

Cronin, R. (2000). Object: Drawing. *Espace Sculpture*, (54), 41-43.

Dempsey, B. C., & Betz, B. J. (2001). Biological drawing: A scientific tool for learning. *The American Biology Teacher*, 271-279.

Dixon, D., Prasad, M., & Hammond, T. (2010, April). icandraw: Using sketch recognition and corrective feedback to assist a user in drawing human faces. In *Proceedings of the SIGCHI Conference on Human Factors in Computing Systems* (pp. 897-906).

Fava, M. (2020). A decline in drawing ability? *International Journal of Art & Design Education*, *39*(2), 319-332.

Gao, F., Cao, B., Cao, Y., Li, F., & Li, H. (2015). Electrophysiological evidence of separate pathways for the perception of depth and 3D objects. *International Journal of Psychophysiology*, *96*(2), 65-73.

Geng, W. (2010). Artistic rendering for 3D object. In *The algorithms and principles of non-photorealistic graphics* (pp. 161-228). Springer, Berlin, Heidelberg.

Gouvatsos, A., Xiao, Z., Marsden, N., & Zhang, J. J. (2017). Posing 3D Models from Drawings. *Computers in Entertainment (CIE)*, *15*(2), 1-14.

Guo, X. (2001). Performing Leonardo's skill on computer: an in-depth study of connections and differences between computer 3D modeling/rendering and representational drawing/painting.

Han, X., Gao, C., & Yu, Y. (2017). Deepsketch2face: a deep learning based sketching system for 3d face and caricature modeling. *ACM Transactions on graphics (TOG)*, *36*(4), 1-12.

Hawks, P. (2010). The relevance of traditional drawing in the digital age. *Electronic Visualisation and the Arts (EVA 2010)*, 328-331.

Hayes, S., & Milne, N. (2011). What's wrong with this picture? An experiment in quantifying accuracy in 2D portrait drawing. *Visual Communication*, *10*(2), 149-174.

Hertzmann, A. (2010, June). Non-photorealistic rendering and the science of art. In *Proceedings of the 8th International Symposium on Non-Photorealistic Animation and Rendering* (pp. 147-157).

Holinaty, J., Jacobson, A., & Chevalier, F. (2021). Supporting reference imagery for digital drawing. In the proceedings of ICCV workshop. 2434 - 2442.

Ibe, M. D. (1971). Things you can try: Drawing 3-D figures from 2-D templates. *The Arithmetic Teacher*, *18*(3), 180-193.

Jansen, C., & Sklar, E. (2021). Exploring co-creative drawing workflows. *Frontiers in Robotics and AI*. 1 – 26.

Kalnins, R. D., Markosian, L., Meier, B. J., Kowalski, M. A., Lee, J. C., Davidson, P. L., ... & Finkelstein, A. (2002, July). WYSIWYG NPR: Drawing strokes directly on 3D models. In *Proceedings of the 29th annual conference on Computer graphics and interactive techniques* (pp. 755-762).

Karpenko, O., & Hughes, J. F. (2011). Inferring 3d free-form shapes from complex contour drawings. In *Sketch-based Interfaces and Modeling* (pp. 313-340). Springer, London.

Kozbelt, A. (2001). Artists as experts in visual cognition. *Visual cognition*, *8*(6), 705-723.

Lai, C. Y., & Zakaria, N. (2010, June). Pressure-based 3d curve drawing. In *International Symposium on Smart Graphics* (pp. 156-159). Springer, Berlin, Heidelberg.

Mamassian, P., & Landy, M. S. (1998). Observer biases in the 3D interpretation of line drawings. *Vision research*, *38*(18), 2817-2832.

Mealing, S. (2005, April). Drawing in three dimensions: a paradigm shift. In *Proceedings of the 5th conference on Creativity & cognition* (pp. 244-247).

Morriss-Kay, G. M. (2010). The evolution of human artistic creativity. *Journal of Anatomy,* 216, 158 – 176.

Parzysz, B. (1988). "Knowing" vs "seeing." Problems of the plane representation of space geometry figures. *Educational studies in mathematics*, *19*(1), 79-92.

Rivers, A., Durand, F., & Igarashi, T. (2010). 3d modeling with silhouettes. *ACM Transactions on Graphics:* 29(4), 109, 1 – 8.

Sawdon, P. & Marshall, R. (2009). Drawing: An ambiguous practice. *Intersections:* 35th Annual Conference of the Association of Art Historians, MIRIAD. Manchester Metropolitan University. 2 - 4 Apr. 2009. 1 - 10.

Scopigno, R., Callieri, M., Cignoni, P., Corsini, M., Dellepiane, M., Ponchio, F., & Ranzuglia, G. (2011). 3D models for cultural heritage: Beyond plain visualization. *Computer*, *44*(7), 48-55.

Sourin, A. (2001, March). Functionally based virtual computer art. In *Proceedings of the 2001 symposium on Interactive 3D graphics* (pp. 77-84).

Sousa, M. C., Foster, K., Wyvill, B., & Samavati, F. (2003, September). Precise ink drawing of 3D models. In *Computer Graphics Forum* (Vol. 22, No. 3, pp. 369-379). Oxford, UK: Blackwell Publishing, Inc.

Sousa, M. C., & Prusinkiewicz, P. (2003, September). A few good lines: Suggestive drawing of 3d models. In *Computer Graphics Forum* (Vol. 22, No. 3, pp. 381-390). Oxford, UK: Blackwell Publishing, Inc.

Weyrich, T., Deng, J., Barnes, C., Rusinkiewicz, S., & Finkelstein, A. (2007). Digital bas-relief from 3d scenes. *ACM Trans. Graph.,* 26(3), 32:1 - 32:7.

Williford, B., Doke, A., Pahud, M., Hinckley, K., & Hammond, T. (2019). DrawMyPhoto: assisting novices in drawing from photographs. In *Proceedings of the 2019 on Creativity and Cognition* (pp. 198-209).

Wyeld, T., Williams, B., & Barbuto, Z. (2013, November). How are gamers better at drawing teapots than non-gamers?. In *Proceedings of the 25th Australian Computer-Human Interaction Conference: Augmentation, Application, Innovation, Collaboration* (pp. 221-224).

Ye, M., Zhou, S., & Fu, H. (2019, July). DeepShapeSketch: Generating hand drawing sketches from 3D objects. In *2019 International Joint Conference on Neural Networks (IJCNN)* (pp. 1-8). IEEE.

Chapter 18

Mixed Motions: A Pre-Survey of Common Art Animations on the Social Web

Shalin Hai-Jew*
Kansas State University, Manhattan, KS, USA

Abstract

Some common artists create various animations on the Social Web for public consumption. These involve various experiences, scenes, characters, and stories. They involve various technologies, both analog and digital. Analog-digital tools involve clay animation, sand animation, and robotics. Digital tools are of two general types: those that enable keyframing (defining particular key poses and scenes, and then using computers to create the in-between frames) or those that enable procedural animation (using computer programs to autogenerate the animation). In the public space, programs in use for animation include a mix of both types: programs that can algorithmic art (with varying degrees of human inputs), still motion capture, immersive virtual worlds (for machinima), time-based data modeling, agent-based modeling, artificial life algorithms, and other applications. There is harnessing of singular and mixed methods of animation for the various segments. This work explores the research literature on digital animations, digital art, and some common art animations on the Social Web. A pre-survey coding list is created for future work towards understanding the foci of common artists in their shared animations on Web 2.0.

Keywords: animation, animation art, digital animation art, common art, Social Web

Introduction

A subset of "common art" on the Social Web includes art animations, the so-called 4th dimension that involves the illusion of movement or motion, or changes over time. To support the analysis of such common art, this work reviews the available literature and captures some common art animations, in order to propose a systematic coding approach as a pre-survey tool.

* Corresponding Author's Email: haijes@gmail.com

In: Common Visual Art in a Social Digital Age
Editor: Shalin Hai-Jew
ISBN: 978-1-68507-664-1

Review of the Literature

Imagine wind moving through trees. Imagine a river flowing in a canyon. Imagine a dancer performing on a stage. Imagine two people engaging each other in a judo match. Imagine a group of children smiling at the camera. Imagine a speaker addressing the camera in a web conference meeting. Imagine a flock of birds flying through the air, or a school of fish swimming through water. Each of the prompts here are common motions…and while these may have brought images to mind, in the world of animation, these are all hard problems with particular challenges to solve. This is so whether the animation is photorealistic (and referential to the real) or non-photorealistic. One way to consider the challenges is that every object in a screen or a virtual space has to have some visual representation, and all motions (simultaneous and sequential) have to be indicated to show in-world phenomena: weather systems, fluid dynamics, character motions, character interactions with each other and with the environment, facial expressions, character speech, flocking behaviors, and so on.

What Is Animation? Digital Animation?

A core factor of animation is movement (Luz, 2010, p. 564). How that movement is created is considered an important part of the definition of animation.

A traditional definition of animation is "a non-recorded (non-live action) illusion of motion and as a frame-by-frame production" (Martinez, 2015, p. 42). In traditional animation, manual "drawing" was an actual integral part of the work (Hosea, 2010, p. 353), but modern technologies have supplanted the direct need for that in some cases. An exclusionary definition of animation is as "a distinct type of moving image with solely illusory movement" (Martinez, 2015, p. 42). These require animators to actualize the respective illusions of movement. Traditional animations required human manual drawing, but this has been replaced in part by computer-aided drawing (Hosea, 2010) and even programmed algorithmic drawing.

The mode of production that is animation involves the illusion of movement, not actual recorded movement, in terms of the traditional definitions. Specifically: "*Its illusion of motion results from the creation or generation of a set of graphic positions with enough differences from each other to produce an intervallic illusion of motion*" (Martinez, 2015, p. 44). The intervallic (interval-based) illusion of motion is "the periodic and sequential display of a series of images that results in an illusion of movement for a viewer's perception, for which each image bears slight differences in the position of similar graphic elements" (Martinez, 2015, p. 44). Some other ways to categorize animation are by what directs the animations. One approach involves the role of an animator as agent in creating the illusion of motion. Another type, "causal animation," points to "animated illusions of motion whose arrangement of images is generated by chance series of images or by a systemic conversion of causal processes into a series of graphic positions" including both analog and digital media (and include auto-generated animations and machine programmed ones) (Martinez, 2015, p. 46) where the programmer can be considered an animator (p. 52). A variety of variables may be considered in assessing whether a modern work is an actual animation or a partial one.

Motion Capture Animation?

The modern use of "motion capture" involves video and sensors placed on a person to capture their actions. This action data is then used to apply to various characters and locations, with wider flexibility. One researcher describes motion capture this way:

> The basic process captures live movement as digital data instead of completed images, providing a three-dimensional rendering of the action. The rendering can then be easily inserted into any digital environment, freeing a performance from the constraints of a static setting. The downside, however, is that motion capture provides much less immediate detail than is available in a photograph or reel of film...The result, therefore, defies the usual definitions of recorded versus synthetic cinema. An image is being recorded, to be sure, but in practical terms, the data are impossible to view—let alone exhibit—until they have gone through multiple layers of digital modifications. (Freedman, 2012, p. 39)

Such animations require additional work to be sufficiently refined to function as animation. The motion capture footage—such as with interacting actors—requires animators to "interpret movements to design/animate upon images. The definition of a character outline is something that has to be created in each frame, so that the final result can give life to the character's movement and soul" (Luz, 2010, p. 567). Computer-generated images (CGI) and other effects have to be overlaid on the live action captured on video or on data from live action captures on video. The work of animators is redefined in the modern era given the new approaches. Various technologies and technical methods are used to connect the motion data to character skeletons (Holden, Saito, & Komura, 2015, p. 165). Such motion capture technologies are expensive (Freedman, 2012, p. 38) and used by larger media corporations. Some animation purists suggest that motion capture is a shortcut and not true animation; motion capture is seen as "reproduction of recorded movement" and something reconstituted as animation but not quite meeting the traditional standard (Martinez, 2015, p. 42). In the field, there are automated methods for creating digital illusions of motion, too, which many may also not consider to be pure animation, with various criteria related to "animation's illusion of motion" and "individual frame-by-frame production" (Martinez, 2015, p. 42).

Another type of animation involves maps. Cartographic animations are of two general types: those that depict changes over time, or those that are nontemporal based on change "caused by a variable other than time" (Peterson, 2020, p. 408). Some of these are interactive.

Various Technologies for Animation

Digital illustration and animation technologies have become much more available to the broad masses due to dropping costs. In the early 1980s, "high-end computer graphics" required "multiple refrigerator-size cabinets for computers costing more than $100,000 and film recorders at $100,000-$250,000" and software costs in addition (Csuri, 1991, p. 30). From the 1990s onwards, given the ability to create animations for "synthetic" realities (Csuri, 1991, p. 32), there were predictions of the emergence of "computer folk art" (Csuri, 1991, p. 34). The technologies are harnessed to increase the efficiency of animation design work (Liu & Zhang, 2021, p. 1). One technology, for example, supports animator/artist work by turning 2d poses into 3d renditions to enable character animation (Davis, Agrawala, Chuang, Popović, & Salesin, 2006).

Indeed, the animation industry is in different phases of development in different countries (Shamsuddin, Islam, & Islam, 2013, p. 818). Some practitioners in modern animation link it to older forms of art (like the Chinese papercut) in order to advance work in the field (Wang & Han, 2020, p. 256) and older forms of animation (BaiMao & ShaoGang, 2020, p. 17) and even ancient ink animation practices (Ruirui & Cheng, 2012, p. 1295). Countries are working through how to harness digital animation as an industry for developing countries (Yao, 2019; Yang, 2019; Wang, 2015; Ye, 2015; Ruirui & Di, 2012). One work involves an environmental scan of the "animation art ecology" to understand those involved in this community, the various works, the technologies, and other factors, in order to plan a development approach in a developing country (Zhou, 2020, p. 411).

Researchers describe various custom technologies and techniques to achieve particular animation ends. Some media companies build proprietary tools to enable feature animation production to meet the needs of the target audiences of the respective companies (Kim, Wild, Anes, Kim, & Kong, 2021, p. 1). One work described custom professional toolsets to "achieve the different artistic styles of various films" and enhance animations for modern films (Somasundaram, Gebru, Sokoloski, & Yellig, 2021, p. 1).

Various surfaces are broken out into "subdivision surfaces" to model animations with more flexibility (DeRose, Kass, & Truong, 1998, p. 85). One research work described the technological challenges of dealing with character joint collapse in "skeletal subspace deformation" (Merry, Marais, & Gain, 2006, p. 1400). Various discoveries and innovations inform the state of the sophisticated animation and digital image tools in use today.

In visual media, character design conveys the inner motivations and personality of the individual. Clothing movement adds "emotion and drama" in a scene (Kutt, 2018, p. 4). One example is a system that makes character hair move in appealing "shapes and silhouettes" "while maintaining the organic motion produced by physical simulation" (Kaur, Simmons, & Whited, 2018, p. 1). This system manages hair in chunks connected to the character's skull in different locations in a "grooming" process to enable its basic movements in an animation (Kaur, Simmons, & Whited, 2018, p. 1). Another work also addresses artful ways to express the movement of human hair in animations, with the right amount of "collisions" and "elasticity" while considering friction (Gornowicz & Borac, 2015, p. 41).

Another work describes artificial light design for animation-based storytelling, to direct human attention, communicate character, tell elements of story, convey moods, and so forth (Walvoord, 2019, p. 1). A separate work describes a technique involving enhanced ray tracing for lighting digital scenes more effectively (Moon, Reddy, & Tychonievich, 2021). One work reviewed how particulate matter was used in a mainstream motion picture movie which takes place mostly undersea. The particulate matters "convey fluid motion, camera speed, ambient water environments…" and amplified the "emotional impact of a shot" (Chang, Conover, & Gustafson, 2016, p. 1).

One work describes a technology that models the tensing and relaxing of muscles of humans and various creatures to simulate in-world actions (Neff & Fiume, 2022, p. 81). This system takes into account musculature and physiology, and how these may be seen in various shapes. Another system controls for the quality of sketchy animations by lowering visual noise (Noris, et al., 2011, p. 93). Another approach combines hybrid methods of both simulation and keyframing and extends the capabilities of both techniques to support the work of animators

(Bai, Kaufman, Liu, & Popović, 2016). A later work combines keyframe animation and procedural animation to enable heightened animator power in creating animation clips (Ahlström, Holmqvist, & Goswami, 2017).

Other technologies are designed to model ocean waves, in dynamic and patterned interactions. There are tools to help in the planning of behaviors of groups of humans and other characters, given that all have to be in plausible motion simultaneously. The animating of virtual characters in groups for realistic motion requires consideration for the need for "continuous streams of motions" (Lau & Kuffner, 2005, pp. 271-272).

One technology serves as a digital "clay animator" (Goto & Hoshino, 2002, p. 158). Another renders "3D animated geometry" into a watercolor style (Montesdeoca, Seah, & Rall, 2016, p. 51). Another innovation enabled ways to animate objects and sequences in a painterly style (Meier, 1996, p. 477), with convincing visual effects.

Closer towards characterization, various facial animation systems were developed for high-end films; these technologies were developed and/or evolved under the aegis of various animation companies (Modesto & Walsh, 2014, p. 1). Facial expressions have to be believable and communicate a wide range of emotions and thoughts. Facial animations support the actions of avatars in virtual environments as they interact with humans and human-embodied avatars (Molano, Díaz, & Sarmiento, 2019, p. 73). These, too, have to be plausible. Verbalizations, such as speech, are modeled in animations, too (Xie & Liu, 2007). Hilarious laughter and related facial and body motions are depicted, with inputs such as the "pseudo-phonemes of laughter," various acoustic features, and duration and the outputs as animations of characters (Ding, Prepin, Huang, Pelachaud, & Artières, 2014, p. 773).

Computer animations generate a variety of data requiring thoughtful data management (Liang, Sit, Chang, & Zhang, 2016). Some systems have built-in testing to control against collisions and mis-animations.

Various technologies are used to enable and enhance and make efficient the work of digital animations. In the academic literature, various advances are described that seem to have made their way into modern technologies, in many cases.

Enabling Bio-Physical Plausibility

Those who would experience the animations are trained on a sense of naïve in-world physics, where gravity affects everything on Earth, for example, and where physics rules affect how various material objects behave and interact. Human vision itself has high discernment of details. While there may be some suspension of disbelief in the viewing of animations, based on stylistic features and culturally trained viewing, the consumption of animations will be against the expectations of known physics and expected in-world behaviors. Anomalies will be noted.

One system helps model "plausible responses to physical disturbances and environmental variations" in a cartoon context (Levine & Popović, 2012, p. 221). Another system helps animators blend "animated-specified expressive motion with physics-based realism" (Kondo, Kanai, & Anjyo, 2005, p. 127). There are reusable libraries of animations, an idea proposed in the academic research literature back in 2006 (de Juan & Bodenheimer, 2006) and perhaps earlier.

Another offers variations on full-body human motions, like "walking, running, hopping, crawling, rolling, cartwheeling, and other motions" (Levine & Popović, 2012, p. 221). One technology enables a so-called "harmonic skeleton" for the realistic depiction of animals in various conditions and contexts, with full anatomical modeling including bones, joints, muscles, and skin, instead of just using geometrical shapes, textures, and topologies. One technology generates a skeleton underlying the animal's structure to enable a heightened sense of the real (Aujay, Hétroy, Lazarus, & Depraz, 2007, p. 151). A different system enables the depiction of human grasping motions with their hands around various shaped objects for animation based on observed kinematics (Rijpkema & Girard, 1991, p. 339). Yet another conveys the nuances of eye movement, including the "movement of the globes, the periorbital soft tissues and eyelids and also the formation of wrinkles in the tissues" (based on "monocular high speed video camera") to enable accurate animations of depicted gaze (Neog, Ranjan, Cardoso, & Pai, 2015, p. 198).

Another system enables the creation of "elastically deformable objects" (Kondo, Kanai, & Anjyo, 2005, p. 127) and more accurate shape contouring. A cartoon shading system for celluloid animation is described in another work (Hudon, Grogan, Pagés, Ondřej, & Smolić, 2019). Another work describes visual cueing using shadows to indicate movement, such as for celluloid (transparency-based) animations (Petrović, Fujito, Williams, & Finkelstein, 2000, p. 511).

There is a system to help human animators more effectively depict cartoon style animations, with special focuses on "squash-and-stretch deformations" (Chenney, Pingel, Iverson, & Szymanski, 2002, p. 133).

When certain bodily actions are activated in a character, various forms of editing may be applied: "Amplitude editing allows the animator to vary the joint ranges covered during a motion. Extend editing allows an animator to vary how fully a character occupies space during a movement—using space freely or keeping the movement close to his body" (Neff & Fiume, 2003, p. 239).

Some tools enable the setting of parameters and then running the programs to create motion, such as with agent-based modeling. There are also artificial life programs that model particular movement, such as flocking agents (Sasaki, 2016, p. 204). There are various other systems that enable the uses of pre-defined rules—expressed in algorithms (and computational programming)—to create art creations and animations vs. more "arbitrary" creative means (King, 1995, p. 113). Another system enables the application of particular behavior constraints on group behaviors for flocking behavior (such as maintaining group center mass) (Anderson, McDaniel, & Chenney, 2003, p. 286).

Enabling Facial Expressiveness

Facial expressions (animations) are "one of the subtlest parts in computer-generated virtual faces and characters" (Deng & Ma, 2008, p. 67). For avatars and other agents to engage with people, the nonverbals from facial expressions to body language are critical. There is a system that takes as input expressions on a human face and conveys that to a hand-drawn digital facial representation (Buck, et al., 2005, p. 101). The system maps the expression from the human face to the digitally rendered one. This transfer can be achieved through photos and through cameras, with facial tracking capabilities.

Another system uses a polygon mesh to communicate a creature's skeleton, musculature, and skin morphing simultaneously to convey natural animated movement (Simmons, Wilhelms, & Van Gelder, 2002). Such programs require understandings of anatomy and other dependencies for creature motion.

Animation in 3D

Various productions involve different challenges. Non-photorealistic animation in 3D provides various challenges, with animators balancing "the screen-space rules of a 2D visual style against 3D motion coherence, but also…stereo spatialization and interactive camera movement, at a rate of 90 frames per second" in a context of immersive storytelling (Curtis, Dart, Latzko, & Kahrs, 2020, p. 1). There are animation pipelines for virtual reality (VR) and augmented reality (AR) storytelling, as defined by professionals in animation studios (Berford, Diaz-Padron, Kaleas, Oz, & Penney, 2017).

Art-Based Animations

Work in the digital art space and the advent of the WWW and Internet resulted in foundational changes to contemporary art and the formal learning around fine art. Specifically, "3D modeling and animation software with game engines" have been harnessed for creative (Wands, 2019, p. 426).

Animations beyond Art

Animation practices in education, industry, and entertainment all require different animation approaches to meet the different needs of the respective target audiences (Banner & Ostherr, 2015). Animations are used in education, such as the conveyance of scientific information in cogent ways via "animation-based information communication" (Burns, Woodcock, Gaura, Newman, & Mount, 2006, p. 797). These animations may show various science-based phenomena: changes over time, interrelationships, systems functions, and other details. The sizes of the various entities have to be fairly accurate, and there needs to be explanatory depth. There are 3D animations used in geological museum exhibits (Zhe, Xiao, & GuiYuan, 2020, p. 219). "Animation cartography" refers to the making of animations from 3d point clouds. Animation supported science, and vice versa:

> The first decades of the twentieth century thus saw animation emerge as both a tool for producing scientific knowledge and a vehicle for explaining scientific concepts to the general public. At the same time, scientific experiments catalyzed the development of animation technologies and stylistic techniques. (Banner & Ostherr, 2015, p. 179)

Those who would create science-based animations had to meld the cultures and practices between science and animation practice (Banner & Ostherr, 2015, p. 192). The transience of multimedia, such as through motion and changes over time, poses perceptual and working memory and learning challenges (Kalyuga, 2011, p. 307), in the education context.

Animations are used as simulations in various industries, by offering a "digital twin" of modeled reality. There are cyber-physical production systems in which animations may be used for representation. There are physics simulations (Glatt, Sinnwell, Yi, Donohoe, Ravani, & Aurich, 2021, p. 231). One work describes animations used in the development and deployment of collaborative robotics to ensure more ergonomic workplaces (Maurice, Padois, Measson, & Bidaud, 2019, p. 771).

Another use case is cultural preservation, such as of valuable traditional arts and crafts (Xue, 2020, p. 680). The described cultural preservation sequence goes as follows: "create model, light rigs, texture mapping, making animation, (and) render output" for 3d modeling of crafts (Xue, 2020, p. 681). Digital animation has been harnessed to share research findings with those who have participated in the research and more of the general public (Vaughn, Jacoby, Williams, Guerra, Thomas, & Richmond, 2013). Some augmented-reality drawings with automatic animations are created to bolster design work (Lins, et al., 2014, p. 106). The practice of animation design is seen to enhance the richness of the human experience of immersive virtual reality (Liu, 2019).

Animation itself is a subject of study given that it is seen to contain cultural evocations. Animation is a "rhetorical tool" for the sharing of data (Leslie & McKim, 2017, p. 3); it is harnessed for social activism and communications in culture and politics (p. 1). Animation is a "trope for human action on/in the world" and enabling the drawing of "connections between social, technological, and psychic structures" (Silvio, 2010, p. 422). It is both a product of the surrounding culture and a form with impact on the surrounding culture. One researcher writes:

> Drawing on all of these approaches, let us provisionally define *animation* as broadly as possible, as the projection of qualities perceived as human—life, power, agency, will, personality, and so on—outside of the self, and into the sensory environment, through acts of creation, perception, and interaction. This projection, like any human expression, requires a medium, and we can take the comparative study of technes of animation—in art, in religion, in everyday life—as the goal of an anthropology of animation. Hopefully this definition not only covers a wide range of cultural practices, from animism to robotics, but also emphasizes the importance of analyzing such practices for the anthropological project of exploring differences in how the human and the nonhuman are defined and how the self and the world are experienced. (Silvio, 2010, p. 427)

There are "characteristics of animation that allow it to draw connections between social, technological, and psychic structures, and then examining some of the ways that the models of animation and performance interact in contemporary subcultural practices" including "animation, performance, remediation, media ideologies, techno-cultures" (Silvio, 2010, p. 422). The researcher describes "animation as a trope for human action on/in the world" (Silvio, 2010, p. 422); it evokes a sense of the capturing of "life" albeit in various ways and along various dimensions (Silvio, 2010, p. 425).

Animation Art as a Product of the Moment?

Creativity is a constant in humanity over time and generations. One study compared the Italian Renaissance with the current digital age in order to learn about human creativity. The researchers found some constants in their work. One observation is that creative work involves "a combinative activity, operating on motifs in culture, and bounded by their social acceptance" (Sapsed & Tschang, 2014, p. 127), so artworks are social and a product of their context. Also, creative work "involves techniques that expand the frontier of creative input" and involves experimentation and "much iteration, facilitated by the media, techniques and technologies" (Sapsed & Tschang, 2014, p. 127). These ideas are relevant to the study of "common art" artists, who may be informed by their respective cultures but also the available animation technologies of the present day. New art emerges from "revolutionary creative insights" but "once a genre or period of art is established, much 'new' art will tend to encompass changes in content, or stylistic approaches, often mixed with more familiar motifs or techniques" (Sapsed & Tschang, 2014, p. 131). If these general ideas apply to the present moment, perhaps it may be said that the emergence of animation technologies has sparked a "punctuated equilibrium" moment and is resulting in the making of new forms of common art.

Digital technologies enable "new aesthetics" in the storytelling in the animation space (Luz, 2010, p. 562) and rich digital enablements and room for the standing up of industries (Shuo, 2021). Some digital animation art is created using infrared trackers and VR technologies (Liu, 2019, p. 340), involving gestural inputs. Another involves "space canvases" for WYSIWYG ("what you see is what you get") 3D animation (Fei, Lee, Joslin, & Xin, 2008, p. 1).

In the modern era, for common artists and others, some of the animation-making technologies are virtually free. Some are free and open-source code bases that generate motion art; others are web-hosted tools. Some are creating custom software for their own types of animations, seeded with various data inputs, including human biometric data. The social sharing of methods and techniques on the Social Web has meant that motion design is not only in the purview of professionals and various production houses. The democratization of various digital illustration and animation technologies has enabled the broadscale advancement of common art animations, shared on the Social Web.

This is not to say that common art animations are necessarily easy to create, particularly those which are figurative (vs. abstract). A common artist working in animation does need to acquire and develop some complex skillsets: digital image editing tools, animation tools, and others. They need to understand color and shape and motion. Animation artists need a basic sense of in-world physics (Garcia, Carter, Granner, & Chai, 2009; Chai & Garcia, 2011), so their depictions make sense to the viewers. They require the regular discipline of regular production, in order to improve on skills. They need exposure to various styles, so that they can expand beyond their provincial sensibilities. Each skill is necessary, and there are many "hard problems" that such common artists need to solve along the way. If they have gone the self-taught route, this means effortful work; even if they go the formal learning route, that in itself can be expensive and effortful. There is a common sense of the need for inculcating computational thinking into art students, so that they can apply custom code to their studio art and other practices (Knochel & Patton, 2015, p. 21). Formal courses on animal art and technology, in some cases, does include motion capture (Duesing & Hodgins, 2004, p. 1). Today's common artists may be engaging in sequences of "combination and iteration" that has resulted in art throughout time (Sapsed & Tschang, 2014, p. 139). Digital animation as "a key aesthetic technique within contemporary art" (Leslie & McKim, 2017, p. 3); it is a technology in the present age that informs the creative *zeitgeist*. One fine art artist, who engages artful expressions using both still and moving images, has described the process of expressing abstract surrealism in the artworks (Weng, 2014, p. 82).

In the academic research literature about curriculum and pedagogy, there are various learning outcomes defined, including the ability to rig objects for animation and putting together a finished animation scenario. Still, the learning outcomes vary, and these are complex. In either course (formal or informal), or in a mixed learning course, there will be gaps in knowledge and practice. A complex skillset requires years to attain. There are learning paths that are formal (accredited courses and course sequences), nonformal (unaccredited courses), and informal (incidental learning based on experiences from life not focused on education).

Once the base skillset is acquired, the common artist also has to think in creative ways, in order to achieve novel outputs. One common animation sequence is to begin with editing digital imagery for proper color design to be used for animations (Ye, 2021, p. 1), so the work may begin with the creation of still characters and scenes that will later be animated. They have to find the self-inspirations in the world and in themselves. The animations have to be in the service of some expression of stories, of values, to enable some coherence and interpretation by viewers. The audience, particular targets and the general public, are trained on a diet of animation clips in entertainment, advertising, education, simulations, video games, and other communications fare, which may set a very high standard for expectations for visual appeal, timing, aesthetics, and other aspects of animation clips.

Those engaged in this work know that the work is effortful, but it is consumed quickly by viewers, and they move on to other animations, given the many commercial sources of such visualizations. Online, there are many who are on the path to trying to acquire the animation skillset in order to go professional (or to acquire side gigs), but there are few animation professionals dabbling for free in terms of sharing side works on the Social Web. Those who do animation for the big entertainment companies earn in the six figures. For common artists, there are opportunity costs in creating free work for broad general consumption. Said another way, people may better use their time in other pursuits when their professional days are already spent in this space. Another strategy involves working as part of large-scale collaboration animation projects, but these have not really emerged in the non-commercial space; these require a fair amount of leadership and commitment to actualize projects.

Besides the heavy time investment (Molano, Díaz, & Sarmiento, 2019, p. 74) and complex technologies involved, there are complex legal challenges with intellectual property, which is different in applied laws in different countries and regions. There are different cultural consumption patterns based on different cultures, so a more sophisticated understanding of multi-cultural communications is required. That said, animation is a common art medium for "contemporary artists" (Leslie & McKim, 2017, p. 3).

Research Methods

Based on a review of the literature, and a light review of some publicly available "common art" animations (with "animation art" and "animation art digital" as search phrases), a set of basic questions was generated to use as guides for a more thorough future analysis. Over a dozen-and-a-half spaces were identified which could surface amateur animations (including online art communities, social image sharing sites, social video sharing sites, the broad Social Web, discussion boards with focuses on animations, social networking sites, and others), but it became clear that tracking down such works might go well beyond the purview of the current work. The multi-sourcing itself was a challenge. There was not one location to capture a broad sampling of the available common art animations online. The various technologies and file extensions for animations also were challenging, given the diversity of file formats.

A Tool for a Pre-Survey of Common Art Animations

This chapter involves a review of the literature and then a light review of some of the available common art animations on the Social Web to provide a pre-survey coding approach for how such animations may be explored. This work lays the groundwork for more systematic future study of amateur animations shared on the Social Web. As such, the conceptualization is that there are three phases: pre-survey, survey, and post-survey. (Table 1) In each phase are three cross-cutting sub-phases: preparation, research work, and post-research analytics.

Table 1. Pre-survey, survey, and post-survey of common art animations

	(1) Pre-survey of common art animations	**(2) Survey of common art animations**	**(3) Post-survey of common art animations**
(1) Preparation	Review of the literature Exploration of common art animations on the Social Web Review of the publicly available digital animation and related technologies Target platforms and spaces and methods for acquiring common art animations Light cultural analysis	Review of the systematic coding approach (and codebook) Systematic cultural analysis	
(2) Research Work	Design of a systematic coding system for understanding common art animations on the Social Web	Collection of common art animations on the Social Web Data cleaning Coding of the common art animations	Communications of the research findings Construction of data visualizations

Table 1. (Continued)

	(1) Pre-survey of common art animations	**(2) Survey of common art animations**	**(3) Post-survey of common art animations**
(3) Post-Research Analytics	Review of the systematic coding system for comprehensiveness, relevance, and other standards	Consideration of early implications of the research findings Review of the systematic coding approach (and codebook)... post contact with information	Review of the research findings for implications (to platforms, to technologies, to practice, to culture, and other factors) Proposal of adjustments to the research instrument (and codebook) New hypothesizing New research methods in the space

This work involves the "pre-survey" phase with the creation of a plan for systematic coding of amateur animations and a proposed coding list for common art animations shared online. One work back in 2015 offered a survey of the technologies enabling the rendering of animations on the web. At that time, the team found that none of the available technologies "yet provide a coherent approach in terms of transmission, compression and handling of the animation data on the client side (browser)" (Ahire, Evans, & Blat, 2015, p. 249). Still, in technology, each year can be an eon, and advances can seem sudden based on accumulated work and surprise insights.

Results

The initial results suggest that the "common art" animations should be defined in an inclusive way, including motion capture (if those methods are used), including virtual worlds, including augmented reality, and so on. Perhaps animations based on particular non-art-based applications may be excluded.

A Light Review of "Common" and "Common Art" Animations

A light review of the available "common" animations showed mostly very short-form animations, such as sub-second clipart movement, sub-second emoji actions, and brief motion capture memetic captures to accentuate short messages (like microblogging messages and SMS messages). Some depictions were of characters, like recognizable actors in various iconic roles. The art was often simple lineart.

Oftentimes, the underlying art was something swiped from other sources, like snippets of television show scenes and movie scenes with screen capture technologies.

In terms of more artful shares of animations, the "common art" ones, these were often generative forms of common art animations. Here, various software programs were used to generate the animation. [Processing is a favorite in this space. Some include agent-based modeling animations, too.] Artists who are also programmers share their code with others, so generating the visual is often a matter of a simple opening of the program and running it and doing a screen capture.

A perusal of "animations" in one edgy art site showed screen after screen of various short-form animations: a black cat jumping into the frame and running past; blinking skeletons and blinking animals; a sneezing girl; a running female robot (or "fembot"); a surprised cow; a running fox; a reptilian eye opening; dancing individuals; two fighters engaging each other with swords and other manual weaponry; a creature swishing its tail; and others. A subset of the artful animations were risqué ones: various individuals and pairs in bondage; a bouncy walk; a blow-up sex doll being inflated; and so on. Many of these read as juvenile more than actual x-rated fare. Overall, these common art animations seemed to be about a fleeting message to provoke a thought or a jolt of emotion or perhaps amusement. There were no long-form sorts of animations in the animated art explored.

Further exploration was done in a space for online artists and illustrators. The animations here have a professional sheen, and many are advertisements. One advertises a sports broadcasting company by showing a hockey puck encased in ice as it moves from one space to another, with various evolutions in each. A personality-full droplet of water is used to convey a message of environmental protection. The artful animations here are accompanied by music and some with voiceovers. The presentation is lush, with some animations as videos in various sequences (with still slides interspersed in between). One work is a "comedy," with a lonely crocodile dancing with abandon and ultimately giving himself a self-hug. Works that are clustered on particular platforms seem to have a certain level of refinement, but then, there are mixes of the professional and the "common" and "amateur." Here, the animations are somewhat longer (one was 16 seconds, another went a minute and a half). Of the sampled "commercial" animations, those were the general min-max ranges.

The Four Facets Approach to Coding "Common Art" Animations

The questions that resulted were in four areas: the social media platforms hosting the "common art" animations, the "common art" animations themselves, the creators, and the consumers. The platforms provide a kind of ecosystem; the animations are the target content; and the creators and consumers engage in an informational exchange (with the animations as the message). The research questions are represented as RQs. The general order is to first understand the social media platforms on which the animations are found because different animation contents seem to cluster in different online locations. The "ecosystem" in which the art animations "live" inform the content. Next, there are the actual "common art" animations shared online. Then, there is a layer of analysis of who the creatives are behind the respective "common art" animations, with this information collected both through the self-reportage of the artists and other information streams. Finally, there is the analysis of the consumers of common art. Understanding the exchange between the creators and the consumers may be an enriching approach.

RQ1: WHAT: SOCIAL MEDIA PLATFORMS (FACET 2): What are the various social media platforms used to acquire the "common art" animations?

- Which of the social media platforms are generalist ones? Which of the social media platforms are niche ones? Why?
- What are the histories of the respective target platforms? How did the respective target platforms evolve?
- Who are the respective users (the user bases) of those respective platforms?
- What are the respective social media platforms' technological enablements and constraints?
- How much coverage of the Social Web do these platforms represent, and why?

RQ2: WHAT: "COMMON ART" ANIMATIONS (FACET 1): What sorts of "common art" animations exist on various Social Web 2.0 platforms?

- What stories are being told with the "common art" animations?
- What styles do these "common art" animations draw from?
- What artworks are used for the animations? Are these original or stock images?
- What is the duration of these animations (in one iteration)?
- What apparent technologies or combinations of technologies are used?
- What apparent techniques or combinations of techniques are used?
- How artful are the respective "common art" animations?
- What are the artful influences on these "common art" animations?
- What do the "common art" animations depict?
- What is being communicated with the "common art" animations?
- Based on the works: What are the apparent skillsets of those sharing the "common art" animations?
    - Where are the gaps in the skillsets (as compared to more expert animations)?
- What are the apparent purposes of such "common art" animations?
    - How effective are the respective "common art" animations based on the apparent purpose(s)?

RQ3: WHO: "COMMON ART" ANIMATION CREATIVES (FACET 3): Who is doing the sharing of the "common art" animations? How do they self-identify? How do they present? What do they say about their rationales for engaging in "common art" animations?

- Why are people creating and sharing "common art" animations (based on their posted self-reportage)?
- What are the most common reported reasons?
- What are the most uncommon reported reasons?
- Based on the professional and other biographies: What are the apparent skillsets of those sharing the "common art" animations?
    - Where are the gaps in the skillsets (as compared to more expert animations)?

RQ4: WHO: "COMMON ART" ANIMATION CONSUMERS (FACET 4): Who are the apparent target audience members? Who is actually using the "common art" animations?

- How long do these users engage?
- How are the respective "common art" animations used? For intended use? For non-intended use?
- What are surface uses? Sub-surface uses?

These questions are intended to lay the groundwork for future research, in the area of "common art" animations. These questions are fairly ambitious and demanding. This work will require focus, time, and perhaps, teamwork.

The higher-level approach may be seen in the "Four Facets Diamond…" (Figure 1). This diamond shows the exploration of common art animations (facet 1) on social media platforms (representing the Social Web) (facet 2) for sharing between creatives (facet 3) and animation consumers (facet 4).

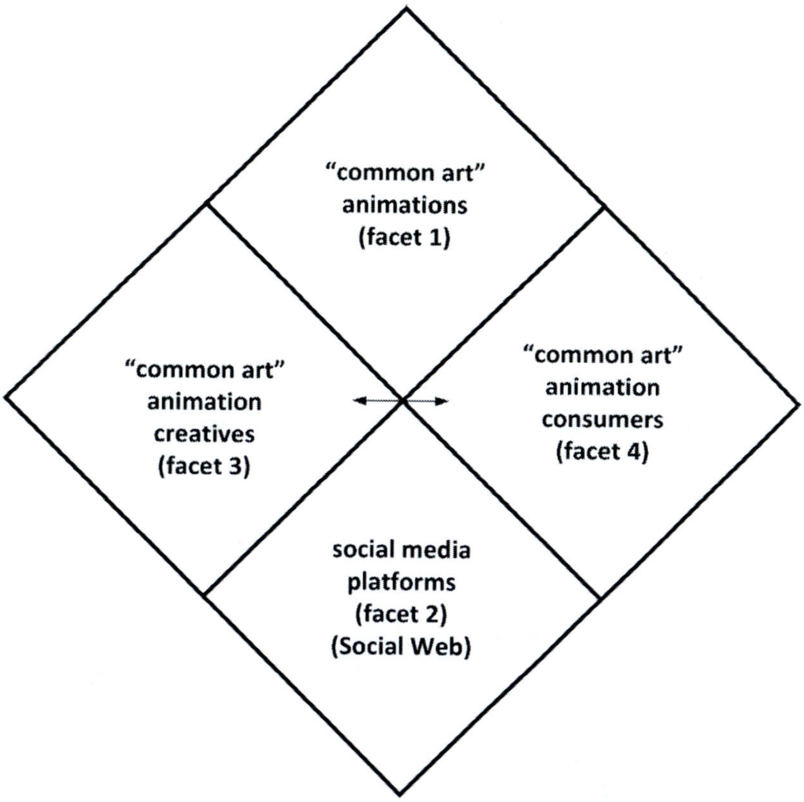

Figure 1. Four Facets Diamond for study of "Common Art" animations on the Social Web.

Note that the bottom facet (facet 2) uses a plural for the social media platforms. Oftentimes, artists have presences on a variety of platforms, and their followers and friends follow them across a range of platform types.

Discussion

The questions are not all equally answerable, but it is perhaps important to ask even if answers may be challenging to arrive at to a satisfactory level. There are limits to how much can be known from a finished refined animation, and some of the inferences about the inspiration; the pre-production, the production, and the post-production; the techniques; the technologies, and such, may be limited. The various inputs to an animation may only be back-tracked practically so far. Assessing across cultures will also have limits.

Future Research

The suggested future research of "common art" animations will involve defining how to collect an optimized set of such objects for analysis, and a refining of the set of questions RQ1 – RQ4 above.

Conclusion

Animations for common artists, as mentioned earlier, requires complex technologies and skillsets and artful visions. One fine artist conceptualizes "artist animation" as "time-based paintings" (Weng, 2011, p. 706), illuminated through rich explanatory depth.

Acknowledgments

Thanks to the common art animators who are so publicly generous with their works.

References

Ahire, A. L., Evans, A., & Blat, J. (2015, June). Animation on the web: a survey. In *Proceedings of the 20th International Conference on 3D Web Technology* (pp. 249-257).

Ahlström, E., Holmqvist, L., & Goswami, P. (2017, July). Comparing traditional key frame and hybrid animation. In *Proceedings of the ACM SIGGRAPH/Eurographics Symposium on Computer Animation* (pp. 1-2).

Anderson, M., McDaniel, E., & Chenney, S. (2003, July). Constrained animation of flocks. In *Proceedings of the 2003 ACM SIGGRAPH/Eurographics symposium on Computer animation* (pp. 286-297).

Aujay, G., Hétroy, F., Lazarus, F., & Depraz, C. (2007, August). Harmonic skeleton for realistic character animation. In *SCA 2007-ACM-SIGGRAPH/Eurographics Symposium on Computer Animation* (pp. 151-160). Eurographics Association.

Bai, Y., Kaufman, D., Liu, C., & Popović, J. (2016). Artist-directed dynamics for 2d animation. *ACM Trans. Graph,* 35(4), 145: 1 – 10.

BaiMao, G., & ShaoGang, W. (2020). The comparison of creative characteristics of Chinese traditional animation and digital animation and thinking on development. *IETI Transactions on Economics and Management,* 1(2), 17-25.

Banner, O., & Ostherr, K. (2015). Design in motion: Introducing science/animation. *Discourse*, 37(3), 175-192.

Berford, B., Diaz-Padron, C., Kaleas, T., Oz, I., & Penney, D. (2017). Building an animation pipeline for VR stories. In *ACM SIGGRAPH 2017 Talks* (pp. 1-2).

Buck, I., Finkelstein, A., Jacobs, C., Klein, A., Salesiny, D. H., Seims, J., ... & Toyama, K. (2006). Performance-driven hand-drawn animation. In *ACM SIGGRAPH 2006 Courses* (pp. 101 - 108).

Burns, J., Woodcock, A., Gaura, E., Newman, R. M., & Mount, S. (2006, July). Daisies on Mars: disseminating scientific information by use of developmental animation. In *Tenth International Conference on Information Visualisation (IV'06)* (pp. 797-803). IEEE.

Chai, D., & Garcia, A. L. (2011). Physics for animation artists. *The Physics Teacher*, *49*(8), 478-480.

Chang, D., Conover, A., & Gustafson, S. (2016). Finding particulate in *Finding Dory*. In *ACM SIGGRAPH 2016 Talks* (pp. 1-2).

Chenney, S., Pingel, M., Iverson, R., & Szymanski, M. (2002, June). Simulating cartoon style animation. In *Proceedings of the 2nd International Symposium on Non-photorealistic Animation and Rendering* (pp. 133-138).

Csuri, C. A. (1991). Art and animation. *IEEE Computer Graphics and Applications*, *11*(01), 30-35.

Curtis, C., Dart, K., Latzko, T., & Kahrs, J. (2020). Real-time non-photorealistic animation for immersive storytelling in "Age of Sail." *Graphics and Visual Computing*, 3, 100012, 1-12.

Davis, J., Agrawala, M., Chuang, E., Popović, Z., & Salesin, D. (2006). A sketching interface for articulated figure animation. In *Acm Siggraph* 2006 courses (pp. 320-328, 383).

de Juan, C. N., & Bodenheimer, B. (2006). Re-using traditional animation: Methods for semi-automatic segmentation and inbetweening. In *the proceedings of Eurographics/ACM SIGGRAPH Symposium on Computer Animation*. 223-232, 368.

Deng, Z., & Ma, X. (2008, July). Perceptually guided expressive facial animation. In *Proceedings of the 2008 ACM SIGGRAPH/Eurographics Symposium on Computer Animation* (pp. 67-76).

DeRose, T., Kass, M., & Truong, T. (1998, July). Subdivision surfaces in character animation. In *Proceedings of the 25th annual conference on Computer graphics and interactive techniques* (pp. 85-94).

Ding, Y., Prepin, K., Huang, J., Pelachaud, C., & Artières, T. (2014, May). Laughter animation synthesis. In *Proceedings of the 2014 international conference on Autonomous agents and multi-agent systems* (pp. 773-780).

Duesing, J., & Hodgins, J. K. (2004). Team teaching animation art and technology. In *ACM SIGGRAPH 2004 Educators program* (pp. 1-3).

Fei, G., Lee, W. S., Joslin, C., & Xin, Z. (2008, December). 3d animation creation using space canvases for free-hand drawing. In *Proceedings of The 7th ACM SIGGRAPH International Conference on Virtual-Reality Continuum and Its Applications in Industry* (pp. 1-6).

Freedman, Y. (2012). Is it real… or is it motion capture? The battle to redefine animation in the age of digital performance. *The Velvet Light Trap*, (69), 38-49.

Garcia, A. L., Carter, A. A., Granner, J. C., & Chai, D. (2009, February). Physics for animation artists. In *SIGGRAPH Posters*.

Glatt, M., Sinnwell, C., Yi, L., Donohoe, S., Ravani, B., & Aurich, J. C. (2021). Modeling and implementation of a digital twin of material flows based on physics simulation. *Journal of Manufacturing Systems*, *58*, 231-245.

Gornowicz, G., & Borac, S. (2015, August). Efficient and stable approach to elasticity and collisions for hair animation. In *Proceedings of the 2015 Symposium on Digital Production* (pp. 41-49).

Goto, D., & Hoshino, J. (2002, July). Computer generated clay animation. In *ACM SIGGRAPH 2002 conference abstracts and applications* (pp. 158-158).

Holden, D., Saito, J., & Komura, T. (2015). Learning an inverse rig mapping for character animation. In *the proceedings of SCA '15*. Aug. 7–9, 2015. Los Angeles, California. 165–173.

Hosea, B. (2010). Drawing animation. *Animation: An interdisciplinary journal*, 5(3), 353-367.

Hudon, M., Grogan, M., Pagés, R., Ondřej, J., & Smolić, A. (2019). 2DToonShade: A stroke based toon shading system. *Computers & Graphics: X*, *1*, 100003, 1 = 14.

Kalyuga, S. (2011). Effects of information transiency in multimedia learning. *Procedia-Social and Behavioral Sciences*, *30*, 307-311.

Kaur, A., Simmons, M., & Whited, B. (2018). Hierarchical controls for art-directed hair at Disney. In *ACM SIGGRAPH 2018 Talks* (pp. 1-2).

Kim, J., Wild, J., Anes, F., Kim, S., & Kong*, S. (2021, August). Artist-centered design for feature animation. In *Special Interest Group on Computer Graphics and Interactive Techniques Conference* (pp. 1-2).

King, M. (1995). Programmed graphics in computer art and animation. *Leonardo, 28*(2), 113-121.

Knochel, A. D., & Patton, R. M. (2015). If art education then critical digital making: Computational thinking and creative code. *Studies in Art Education, 57*(1), 21-38.

Kondo, R., Kanai, T., & Anjyo, K. (2005). Directable animation of elastic objects. In the proceedings of the Eurographics/ACM SIGGRAPH Symposium on Computer Animation. 127-134.

Kutt, A. (2018). Art-directed costumes at Pixar: design, tailoring, and simulation in production. In *SIGGRAPH Asia 2018 Courses* (pp. 1-102).

Lau, M., & Kuffner, J. J. (2005, July). Behavior planning for character animation. In *Proceedings of the 2005 ACM SIGGRAPH/Eurographics symposium on Computer animation* (pp. 271-280).

Leslie, E., & McKim, J. (2017). Life remade: critical animation in the digital age. Birbeck: University of London. 1-12.

Levine, S., & Popović, J. (2012). Physically plausible simulation for character animation. In the proceedings of the Eurographics' ACM SIGGRAPH Symposium on Computer Animation. 221 - 230.

Liang, H., Sit, J., Chang, J., & Zhang, J. J. (2016). Computer animation data management: Review of evolution phases and emerging issues. *International journal of information management, 36*(6), 1089-1100.

Lins, C., Arruda, W., Neto, E., Roberto, R., Teichrieb, V., Freitas, D., & Teixeira, J.M. "Animar: Augmenting the reality of storyboards and animations." In *2014 XVI Symposium on Virtual and Augmented Reality*, pp. 106-109. IEEE, 2014.

Liu, B. (2019). Research of digital media art based on virtual reality on animation design. *Advances in Social Science, Education and Humanities Research,* 325, 340–344.

Liu, Y., & Zhang, X. (2021). Research on the application of animation design based on digital media technology. *Journal of Physics: Conference Series,* 1873, 1–8.

Luz, F. C. (2010, August). Digital animation: Repercussions of new media on traditional animation concepts. In *International Conference on Technologies for E-Learning and Digital Entertainment* (pp. 562-569). Springer, Berlin, Heidelberg.

Martinez, O. O. L. (2015). Criteria for defining animation: A revision of the definition of animation in the advent of digital moving images. *Animation: An Interdisciplinary Journal,* 10(1), 42–57.

Maurice, P., Padois, V., Measson, Y., & Bidaud, P. (2019). Digital human modeling for collaborative robotics. In *DHM and Posturography* (pp. 771-779). Academic Press.

Meier, B. J. (1996, August). Painterly rendering for animation. In *Proceedings of the 23rd annual conference on Computer graphics and interactive techniques* (pp. 477-484).

Merry, B., Marais, P., & Gain, J. (2006). Animation space: A truly linear framework for character animation. *ACM Transactions on Graphics (TOG), 25*(4), 1400-1423.

Modesto, L., & Walsh, D. (2014). DreamWorks animation's face system, a historical perspective: from ANTZ and Shrek to Mr Peabody & Sherman. In *ACM SIGGRAPH 2014 Talks* (pp. 1-1).

Molano, J. S. V., Díaz, G. M., & Sarmiento, W. J. (2019). Parametric facial animation for affective interaction workflow for avatar retargeting. *Electronic Notes in Theoretical Computer Science, 343*, 73-88.

Montesdeoca, S. E., Seah, H. S., & Rall, H. M. (2016, May). Art-directed watercolor rendered animation. In *Expressive* (pp. 51-58).

Moon, N., Reddy, M., & Tychonievich, L. (2021). Non-photorealistic ray tracing with paint and toon shading. In *ACM SIGGRAPH 2021 Posters* (pp. 1-2).

Neff, M., & Fiume, E. (2003, July). Aesthetic edits for character animation. In *Proceedings of the 2003 ACM SIGGRAPH/Eurographics symposium on Computer animation* (pp. 239-244).

Neff, M., & Fiume, E. (2002, July). Modeling tension and relaxation for computer animation. In *Proceedings of the 2002 ACM SIGGRAPH/Eurographics symposium on Computer animation* (pp. 81-88).

Neog, D. R., Ranjan, A., Cardoso, J. L., & Pai, D. K. (2015, August). Gaze driven animation of eyes. In *Proceedings of the 14th ACM SIGGRAPH/Eurographics Symposium on Computer Animation* (pp. 198-198).

Noris, G., Sýkora, D., Coros, S., Whited, B., Simmons, M., Hornung, A., Gross, M., & Sumner, R. W. (2011). Temporal noise control for sketchy animation. *In the proceedings of NPAR 2011.* Vancouver, British Columbia, Canada. Aug. 5–7, 2011. 93–98.

Peterson, M.P. (2020). Cartographic animation. *International Encyclopedia of Human Geography,* 2nd ed. Vol. 2. Elsevier. 61–64.

Petrović, L., Fujito, B., Williams, L., & Finkelstein, A. (2000). Shadows for cel animation. In *SIGGRAPH* 2000. New Orleans, LA. 511–516.

Rijpkema, H., & Girard, M. (1991). Computer animation of knowledge-based human grasping. *ACM Siggraph Computer Graphics, 25*(4), 339-348.

Ruirui, Z. & Cheng, C. (2012). Ink animation art in the digital age. *Energy Procedia, 17,* 1295-1298.

Ruirui, Z., & Di, W. (2012). The analysis on current situation and development trend of experimental animation in our country. *Energy Procedia,* 17, 1314-1318.

Sapsed, J., & Tschang, F. T. (2014). Art is long, innovation is short: Lessons from the Renaissance and the digital age. *Technological Forecasting and Social Change, 83,* 127-141.

Sasaki, K. (2016, September). Changing movement pattern of artificial characters in isometric space. In *2016 International Conference on Cyberworlds (CW)* (pp. 204-210). IEEE.

Shamsuddin, A. K., Islam, M. B., & Islam, M. K. (2013). Evaluating content based animation through concept art. *International Journal of Trends in Computer Science, 2*(11), 818-830.

Shuo, S. (2021). The manifestation of animation and the reform of animation teaching in digital media era. *Advances in Vocational and Technical Education,* 92–97.

Silvio, T. (2010). Animation: The new performance? *Journal of Linguistic Anthropology,* 30(2), 422–438.

Simmons, M., Wilhelms, J., & Van Gelder, A. (2002, July). Model-based reconstruction for creature animation. In *Proceedings of the 2002 ACM SIGGRAPH/Eurographics symposium on Computer animation* (pp. 139-146).

Somasundaram, A., Gebru, F., Sokoloski, W., & Yellig, N. (2021). DreamWorks art-driven shot sculpting toolset. *In the proceedings of SIGGRAPH '21 Talks.* Aug. 9–13, 2021. Virtual Event, USA. 1 – 2.

Vaughn, N. A., Jacoby, S. F., Williams, T., Guerra, T., Thomas, N. A., & Richmond, T. S. (2013). Digital animation as a method to disseminate research findings to the community using a community-based participatory approach. *American Journal of Community Psychology, 51*(1-2), 30-42.

Walvoord, D., & Animation, D. (2019). Lighting design for stylized animation. In *ACM SIGGRAPH 2019 Courses* (pp. 1-42).

Wands, B. (2019). The education of a digital fine artist. In *Museums and Digital Culture* (pp. 417-434). Springer, Cham.

Wang, Y. (2015, May). Research on artistic characteristics of network animation short films in New Digital Media Era. In 1st International Conference on Arts, Design and Contemporary Education (ICADCE 2015). Atlantis Press. 352–356.

Wang, Y., & Han, Z. (2020, October). The enlightenment of the cultural elements of paper-cut to the creation of modern animation. In *2020 International Conference on Computers, Information Processing and Advanced Education (CIPAE)* (pp. 256-258). IEEE.

Weng, V. M. (2014). From 'Stillness Becoming' to 'Making Time': Digital surface within my new media-art practice. *Procedia-Social and Behavioral Sciences, 122,* 82-91.

Weng, V. M. (2011). Re-imagining painting in digital fiction time, colour, and space in recent experimental moving images. *Procedia Computer Science, 3,* 706-713.

Xie, L., & Liu, Z. Q. (2007). A coupled HMM approach to video-realistic speech animation. *Pattern Recognition, 40*(8), 2325-2340.

Xue, Y. (2020, November). Protection and development of traditional arts and crafts based on computer 3D animation modeling technology. In *2020 IEEE 3rd International Conference of Safe Production and Informatization (IICSPI)* (pp. 680-683). IEEE.

Yang, S. (2019). The basic theory and production process of digital animation. *In the proceedings of the 2019 7th International Education, Economics, Social Science, Arts, Sports and Management Engineering Conference (IEEESASM 2019).* 402-406.

Yao, S. (2019). The influence of digital media art on animation design. *In the 2019 3rd International Conference on Art Design, Language, and Humanities.* 130–135.

Ye, F. (2021). Application of Photoshop graphics and image processing in the field of animation. *Journal of Sensors,* 2021. 1-18.

Ye, Y. (2015). Research on television animation creation based on 3D digital technology. *In the proceedings of the 2nd International Conference on Electrical, Computer Engineering and Electronics.* 123–125.

Zhe, Y., Xiao, M., & Gui Yuan, G. (2020, April). The research and application of 3D animation in the smart guide design of geological museums. In *Proceedings of the 2020 2nd International Conference on Big Data and Artificial Intelligence* (pp. 219-225).

Zhou, Y. (2020, July). Interactive relationships in animation art ecology. In *International Conference on Human-Computer Interaction* (pp. 411-424). Springer, Cham.

Conclusion

Future Promise in Exploring Common Visual Art

Visual culture is all around, and visuals convey meaning in ways that other forms of communication cannot. In the same way that people acclimate into various societies through cultural attunement, people also feed back into that space with their own creations and artifacts. Common Visual Art in a Social Digital Age (2022) provides insights on a slice of the Social Web in a particular moment, through a particular lens. This collection includes 17 chapters from different angles.

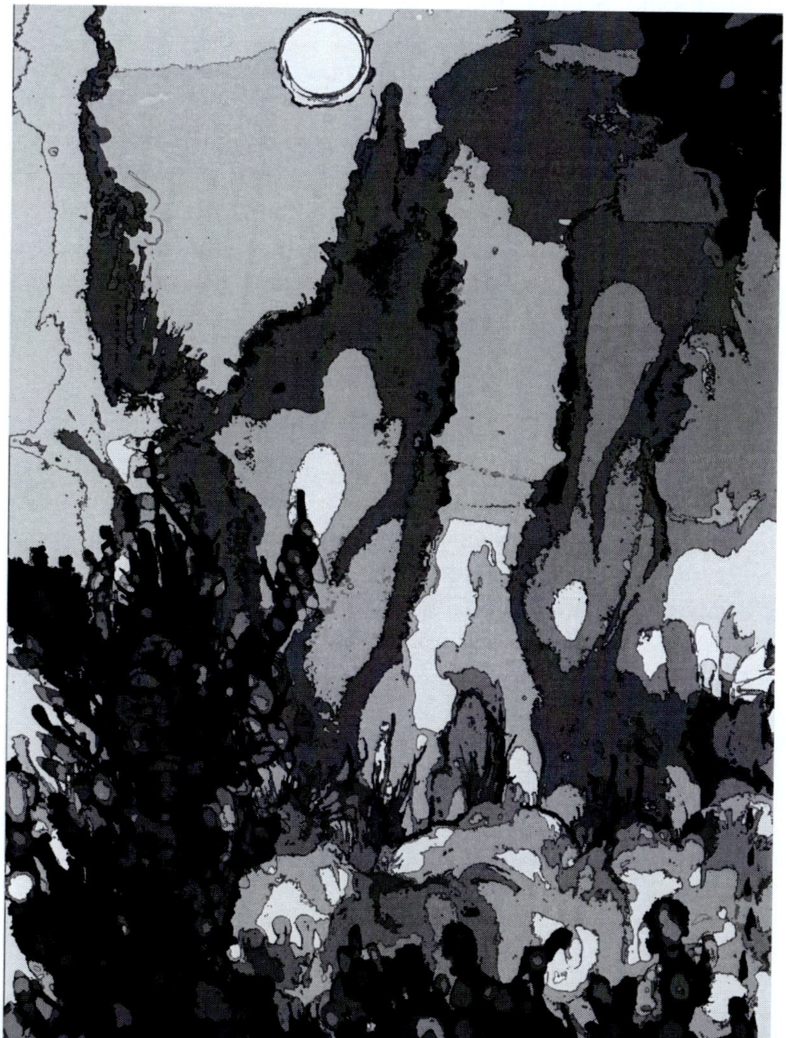

Figure 1. Lavender Air (alcohol ink on synthetic paper and digitally edited, by Shalin Hai-Jew)

Amateur or "common" art, entry-level fare, provides an interesting frame through which to understand the present moment, given how such art is influenced by the culture (think fanart) and the available technologies and techniques and also what is in people's minds, individually and collectively. In a working democracy, there is an openness which suspends excessive critical judgment. There is a valuing of voice as a unique representation of each person. There is an inclusiveness for humanity which is a core basis for nationhood. Such artworks, shared broadly on the Social Web, shows something of conscious and unconscious insights of the respective artists. There is something deeply social and generously sharing of such peer-created art. And then there is the hedonic pleasure of experiencing someone else's talent, whether rough or refined.

In a recent email conversation with a long-time friend, she mentioned that she had done a Google "stalk" just to see what I'd been up to in the intervening time since we'd talked last. We lived states apart, and even though our children were of the general same age, we were only in intermittent touch. She mentioned that many of the people she knew had turned to art-making. It may be that we all need creative outlets and emotional salves in this time. Among her social friends, I was probably among one of the least art-minded, at least in the stereotypical sense.

This work leaves me with the sense that the real modality of art, for now and into the near-future, is still digital (whether born-digital or born-analog or some combination). It is still digital whether the art is merely scanned analog or algorithmic art. The digital version has much broader reach. The digital version has powerful archival potential, even in the light of the "slow fires" that may render some digital file types inaccessible one day (if there is insufficient attention to the challenge).

"Common Art" as a Global or Universal Phenomena

One way to acquire a sense of "common art" at a macro level is to use the ProQuest TDM Studio, which enables access to big data and shadow datasets based on the data extractions. The "TDM" refers to "text and data mining." A dataset was set up for "common art" from a wide range of databases and archived publications: ProQuest Dissertations and Theses, New York Times, The Globe and Mail, Los Angeles Times, Chicago Tribune, The Washington Post, The Guardian, Sydney Morning Herald, The Times of India, Wall Street Journal, South China Morning Post.

The locations mentioned in the respective published works were geographically mapped within TDM Studio, in Figure 2.

A review of the articles using artificial intelligence (AI) results in topic modeling, with the listings in descending order (Table 1).

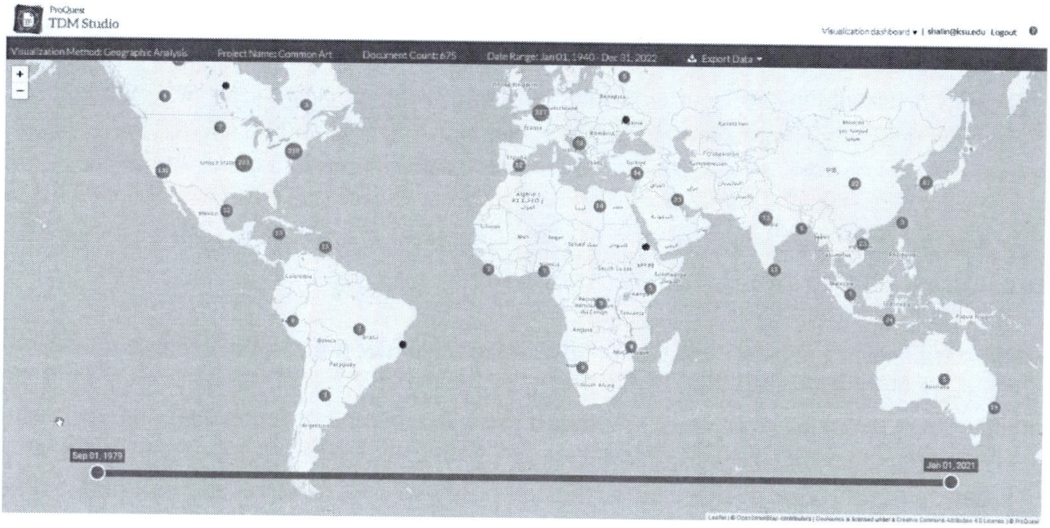

Figure 2. Geographical map of locations mentioned in "Common Art" Publications.

Table 1. Topic modeling of the articles in the "Common Art" articleset across databases and journalistic publications

	Related Subtopics in Respective Topic Categories
Topic 1	art, work, dissertation, century, new, study, historical, works, chapter, american...
Topic 2	art, study, education, students, research, teachers, data, school,
Topic 3	cultural, social, culture, american, political, public, identity, artists, art,
Topic 4	art, new, museum, work, like, years, says, paintings, artist, works...
Topic 5	women, century, social, study, images, dissertation, performance,
Topic 6	international, law, design, legal, war, people, thesis, rights, human, arts...
Topic 7	study, group, stress, studies, reproductive, expression, specific,
Topic 8	artists, art, new, said, york, los, angeles, materials, school, public...
Topic 9	ve, like, common, children, people, mr, old, year, time, draw...
Topic 10	music, van, chapter, dance, dissertation, research, sound, early, soul,

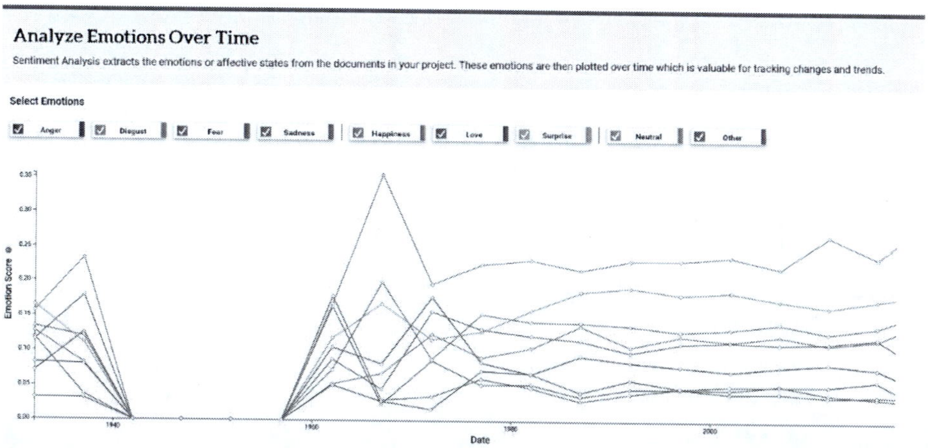

Figure 3. Autocoded emotion analysis of the "Common Art" articleset across databases and journalistic publications.

The platform also enables the auto-extraction of emotions from the respective collected text set. (Figure 3)

The sequence down the right side for the most recent articles shows the following (in descending popularity order): Neutral, surprise, happiness, disgust, other, anger, love, fear, and sadness.

Future Research in the Common Art Space

Certainly, whenever one starts a project, based on an ephemeral idea, it is because one thinks that the work will be possible and viable, that there is sufficient support in the world. After all, there is always the risk to excessive self-indulgence, the foisting of a personal obsession into the world. Pursuing impossible things can be a serious waste of time, with excessive opportunity costs. From a distance, an idea is all promise; close-up, it is all work (amidst the world's indifference).

Now, almost a year after, I am seeing this work in that practical light. Perhaps my enthusiasms were more reflective of my own excitement rather than what was possible in the wider world. Perhaps those that engage in common art are not lured by research and academic writing. I ended up with an edited text but with most works that were single-authored by me. Ideally, I would have preferred much more diversity in contributions. This of course did go through double-blind peer review and revisions.

I do know that if an obsession emerges, one has to fulfill it. The world moves so quickly that if one does not pursue the opportunity, it truly evaporates like a bubble in air, in wind. Opportunities have to be grasped iteratively, day over day over day.

An Early "Anticipated" Table of Contents (TOC)

This collection approaches the topic in various ways. It has surfaced fresh insights. It has laid the groundwork for future research, given the mixed methods approaches. Still, when I look at the anticipated Table of Contents from the call, I see so much has not been addressed:

- Turning ideas into visuals (and visuals into ideas)
- How to layer or engage visual complexity
- User-generated art on the Social Web
- Different art communities online
- Various art pipelines (analog, analog and digital, digital); mixes of modalities
- Digitized mixed media and analog materialia
- Human-machine art
- Born-digital artwork and methods
- Special effects and motion
- Digital doodling
- Digital drawing
- Digital painting
- Uses of user-generated art online and offline

- Aesthetics of computational art
- User-generated art across cultures
- Equipment and software programs used for common art shared online
- Self-portraiture in common art online
- Low art, high art in user-generated art online
- Utilitarian common art
- Common art as political commentary
- User-generated art shops online
- Representational vs. abstract
- Fidelity vs. artifice
- Unique artist "hand" of shared online works (art criticism)
- Online art events
- And others

Those who have interest in common art may take any number of approaches to study different subject matters. The public social media-based approach of dismissing non-professional artworks, holding them up to mockery, engaging in putdowns, is short-sighted and closes off learning possibilities. The vernacular has always contained information that may provide insights on various social and other issues. Perhaps researchers from the academic and other realms may explore common art to address their research questions and hypotheses.

Continuing Research

Based on *Common Visual Art in a Social Digital Age,* there are suggested additional future research. What of other common fine art challenges that bring the vaunted works into everyday lives? What of other art salves in a time of the SARS-CoV-2/COVID-19 pandemic? Explorations of communal common art spaces? More sophisticated digital doodling, perhaps with different technologies and techniques? Different types of high-touch and high-tech algorithmic art? Studies of various types of fanart? Explorations of data art? Contemporary line art? Other "isolate" art during the COVID-19 pandemic? Adult coloring books? Visual journaling? Various methods for monetizing common art? Various branding strategies for common artists and common artist groups and collectives? Common food art? Methods for world creating and world expanding? Event-based common art? The mass-public communications around formal and informal art on social media platforms? Other forms of massmind understandings of art in its various forms as seen on the Social Web? More 3D? More 4D? An actual structured survey of common art animations on the Social Web? Indeed, there are many ways to riff off of the work that has already been achieved.

A Hopeful Closing Note

Finally, the pressure of time looms large in a pandemic moment two years in, with new variants of the SARS-CoV-2 arising with heightened capabilities and increased threat. And even if this was not the current reality, time itself moves very quickly. Those who have ambitions but do not move on them will find the original impetus nullified, and many are left with nothing of the passion or the inspiration. They will find the original passion replaced by something more mundane, less thrilling. Every moment has to be seized and exploited fully, or else time just keeps flowing and accruing. We all would do well to get on with it.

I have enjoyed spending under a year on this project, from conception to completion. Multiple times, while accessing various repositories of research articles and conducting scholarly searches, I have been stopped by the various database systems based on "unusual traffic" from my IP (Internet Protocol) address. I have had to prove my humanity with a reverse Turing test. In other cases, I have been paused in the work until the system was sufficiently certain that I was human. In other words, I triggered security systems with a threshold of activity that perhaps emulated that of automated agents. The unusual traffic was me, trying to better understand common art, based on the available literature. My tendency is to scrape everything that might even be remotely relevant and then to use only a small percentage of the read articles in terms of citations. Based on subscription limits, though, I will not have access to everything. And there are limits to effort, with most of the work achieved on nights, vacations, and weekends. Thankfully, the various databases and research systems and search engines gave me a pass. And I was able to continue with the work, after some pauses. There are some downsides to ambition and drive, and that is that one has to take on the work to fulfill those hungers. Decades into my career, the hungers have never left me, and I understand them as the pure unalloyed blessings they are. (The trick is to take a breath and wait for the second wind.)

Many of the visuals I've encountered will stay with me, having elicited visceral responses and being encoded into memory. I am grateful to Nova Science Publishers for this opportunity.

I am hopeful that *Common Visual Art in a Social Digital Age* (2022) contributes some insights to this personal and social practice. There are few works that look at "common" or "folk" art broadly, particularly in this contemporaneous and creative moment.

About the Author

Dr. Shalin Hai-Jew works as an instructional designer and researcher at Kansas State University. Prior, she taught at college and university levels for many years and concluded that part of her life as a tenured professor at a college in Washington State. She has published research on various professional topics for years. She reviews for a number of publishers in the areas of education, AI, and other fields. She lived and worked in the People's Republic of China for four years as a college instructor (1988-1990, 1992-1994). She is a published poet. She earned BAs in English and psychology and an MA in English from the University of Washington in Seattle and an EdD in Educational Leadership from Seattle University. At the UW, she was a Hugh Paradise Scholarship recipient, and at Seattle University, she was a Morford Scholar fellow. She was born in Huntsville, Alabama, in the U.S. She dabbles in common art in her spare time.

Email: shalin@ksu.edu, haijes@gmail.com (preferred)

Contributors

Elizabeth Bull is a University of Southern Maine graduate ('17) with BA degrees from both the department of Communication and Media Studies and the department of Studio Art, with a concentration in Sculpture. Currently employed at the University of Southern Maine Libraries, she intends to pursue graduate study in an interdisciplinary arts program to explore the intersectionalities of communication processes and the social and communicative role of the arts as both an extension and instigation of human communication. She is also a practicing book-artist, with her work drawing inspiration from the inherent capacity of the visual arts to transcend space, time, language, gender, and culture. She lives, works, and creates in Lewiston, Maine.

ORCID ID: https://orcid.org/0000-0002-6768-6348.

Maureen Ebben is an Associate Professor in the Department of Communication and Media Studies at the University of Southern Maine, Portland. An awarding-winning teacher and scholar, her research uses critical intersectional approaches to explore the socio-technical aspects of digital technologies that shape the communication of everyday life. Her work has been published in the volumes, *Career Re-Invention in the Post Pandemic Era; Badass Feminist Politics: Exploring Radical Edges of Feminist Theory, Communication, and Activism; Post-Pandemic Pedagogy: Predicting the Change to Come; Maintaining Social Well-Being and Meaningful Work in a Highly Automated Job Market; Privacy Concerns Surrounding Personal Information Sharing on Health and Fitness Mobile Apps*, as well as journals such as *Learning, Media, and Technology* and *Women and Language* and others. She is a member of the National Communication Association, and the Organization for the Study of Communication, Language, and Gender. Dr. Ebben earned her PhD in communication from the University of Illinois at Champaign-Urbana, and her MA in sociology from Goldsmiths' College, University of London, England.

ORCID ID: https://orcid.org/0000-0001-8620-372X.

Index